ERRATA

Page 11

wo species of rheas (which resemble the African ostrich), the puma, (called *huemul* in Patagonia), did not cross the Strait of Magellan erra del Fuego. Those that did include the fox, several species of rodents and the guanaco.

The
the de
into Ti

EUROPEAN ENCOUNTERS WITH THE YAMANA PEOPLE OF CAPE HORN, BEFORE AND AFTER DARWIN

Cape Horn has been associated with its native inhabitants, the Yamana, as if the final furious expression of the continent were coupled with the most wretched people on earth. Even the great Darwin referred to them as "miserable degraded savages," "the most abject and miserable creatures I anywhere behold." This book is a documented (not fictional) narration of dramas played out from 1578 to 2000, in the Cape Horn area, by the Yamana, Charles Darwin, and Robert Fitz-Roy, among others. One objective of this work is to clarify why Darwin had such a negative impression of the "Fuegians," as he called them, and how his writing on them relates to that of others. Another objective, the second, is to challenge the concept of ethnohistory by incorporating an "ethnos" (the Yamana) into world history, by pointing out their role in the sequence of events of the last 400 years in the Cape Horn area and their contribution to our understanding of human society. The third objective is to treat the "events" that take place in Cape Horn – the discoveries and experiences of Francis Drake, James Cook, Herman Melville, Darwin, James Weddell, Charles Wilkes and James Ross – not only when they encountered the Yamana but how their discoveries and experiences affected the world at large.

The second chapter focuses on the whalers and sealers and the impact of their activity in the markets of the United States and Europe as well as on the Yamana. The last chapters concentrate mainly on the Anglican missionaries and the colonists – on the effects of their presence on the Yamana as a people. The epidemics that nearly extinguished them are another main theme. This book evokes the Europeans' motives for going to Tierra del Fuego and the Yamana's motives for staying there some 6,000 years, what the outsiders gained and what the Yamana lost. The narrations are based on geographical, historical and ethnographic sources and Anne Chapman's work with the last few descendants of the Yamana. The body of this book has been written for the public at large, while the notes are for students and specialists; therefore it is a general work as well as a source reference and textbook.

Anne Chapman is a Franco-American ethnologist. She has done extensive fieldwork in Honduras with the Tolupan (Jicaque) since 1955 and the Lenca since 1965. In Tierra del Fuego (Argentina and Chile), she has worked, as of 1964, with the last members of the Selk'nam (Onas) people as well as with four descendants of the Yamana, from 1985 into the 1990s, who were knowledgeable about their tradition and spoke the ancient language.

European Encounters with the Yamana People of Cape Horn, Before and After Darwin

ANNE CHAPMAN

CAMBRIDGE
UNIVERSITY PRESS

CAMBRIDGE UNIVERSITY PRESS
Cambridge, New York, Melbourne, Madrid, Cape Town, Singapore,
São Paulo, Delhi, Dubai, Tokyo

Cambridge University Press
32 Avenue of the Americas, New York, NY 10013-2473, USA

www.cambridge.org
Information on this title: www.cambridge.org/9780521513791

© Anne Chapman 2010

First published 2010

Printed in the United States of America

A catalog record for this publication is available from the British Library.

Library of Congress Cataloging in Publication data
Chapman, Anne MacKaye, 1922–
European encounters with the Yamana people of Cape Horn,
before and after Darwin / Anne Chapman.
p. cm.
Includes bibliographical references and index.
ISBN 978-0-521-51379-1 (hbk.)
1. Yahgan Indians – History.   2. Yahgan Indians – Social life and customs.   3. Indians of
South America – First contact with Europeans – Chile – Horn, Cape.   4. Horn, Cape
(Chile) – History.   5. Horn, Cape (Chile) – Ethnic relations.   6. Tierra del Fuego
(Chile) – History.   7. Tierra del Fuego (Chile) – Ethnic relations.   I. Title.
F2986.C453   2009
983′.64600498092309 – dc22   2009014173

ISBN   978-0-521-51379-1 Hardback

I DEDICATE THIS BOOK TO THE JEMMY BUTTONS OF THE WORLD AND THEIR FRIENDS.

Contents

List of Figures

Acknowledgements

It was, as I recall, in March 1991 in Buenos Aires that, quite suddenly, while going over Fitz-Roy's and Darwin's voyage, thinking about my four Yahgan friends and informants in Chile, it occurred to me to attempt to reconstruct the "story" of the Yahgans from their very first contacts with outsiders to the present. I was retired by then so I could not expect any institutional support. "Through the years," to quote some popular song, off and on, to the present, this text has been researched, written and rewritten, especially written during the '90s, when I was living part-time in Oakdale, Long Island. During those years my brother, Theodor Landon Chapman, encouraged me "to carry on," given his unbounded enthusiasm for Charles Darwin. He is the first person I wish to thank, in his memory. This was not an heroic enterprise, as he seemed to think, but it was time-consuming. While in Oakdale I took advantage of the Dowling College Library, whose librarians were always very helpful. About 1996, my friend of many years, Edith Courturier, suggested that I send the beginning chapters to the anthropologists Kristine Jones and James Saeger, which I did, and they both responded with helpful comments, as did June Nash, another anthropologist, whom I admired for her work in Bolivia and Mexico. Somewhat later I sent my first chapter on the missionaries to the Reverend Roy Mac Kaye Atwood, my late cousin, who was pleased to reply to me. Later, while still on Long Island, I was very encouraged by two brief letters from Stephen Jay Gould. In one he suggested that I read Keith Stewart Thompson on the *Beagle*'s voyage.

During one of my frequent visits to Buenos Aires, I consulted the archive of the Diocese of the Anglican Church, whose director and employees were extremely cooperative, enabling me to copy a great number of articles from the *South American Mission Magazine*, which is so essential for my subject. There, in Buenos Aires, I also consulted the library of the

Museo Etnográfico, where I was always welcomed. Later, having completed a first draft, I attempted to convince a number of editors to publish the text, but it was invariably considered far too long, with too many notes and illustrations – that is, too costly for a best-seller. Meanwhile, while I was visiting my friend Edith Courturier again, in Washington, DC, she arranged an interview with Sandra Herbert, a Darwin scholar and professor of the history of science at the University of Maryland. She very willingly read several chapters, made very pertinent comments on them that applied to the entire text and encouraged me to persist. Through her I met Janet Browne, in London, whose first volume of her biography on Darwin I had received as a gift from Colin McEwan. She was also extremely helpful and suggested improvements, especially on the two chapters concerning Darwin. Later, again in London, I contacted Stephen Hugh-Jones, whom I had met years before. He was very encouraging and made many very helpful comments, then and also quite recently. Betty Meggers at the Smithsonian made several pertinent suggestions concerning my "style" of writing. George Stocking Jr., by mail from the University of Chicago, convinced me to write in the first person and made other pertinent comments. In Punta Arenas, Chile, Mateo Martinic as well as other members of the Instituto de la Patagonia and the University of Magallanes, especially Flavia Morello and Alfredo Prieto, have given me unfailing support for this and other projects concerning the "Fuegians." I also wish to thank Gonzalo Sanchez, in Santiago, Chile, for his enthusiastic support of this work during these last years, as well as Jorge Mery García for sending me an article by the Chilean historian José Miguel Barros, in addition to many other articles and for contacts in Santiago. I am especially grateful to the late Eugenia Borgoño, Gabriela Christeller, Cecilia Hidalgo, Ana González Montes, Catalina Saugy and many others in Buenos Aires for their assistance and encouragement.

Adrian Matatia, librarian of the Musée de l'Homme, has been most helpful here in Paris, where I depended on the wealth of material for my subjects in this library as well as the photothèque which, years ago, gave me a nearly complete collection of the photographs of the Yamana taken in 1882 and 1883 by members of the Mission Scientifique au Cap Horn, which are among the best of this group. Now the president of the Musée de Quai Branly, Stéphane Martin, has graciously permitted me to use some of these photographs in Chapters 12 and 13. The facilities offered at the library of the Maison de Sciences de l'Homme in Paris were also essential for my work. I will always be grateful to the Centre National de la Recherche Scientifique for allowing me to choose my topics of research and financing my long periods of fieldwork in Tierra del Fuego, as well as Honduras, from 1964 until my retirement in 1987.

I am especially indebted to William H. Wilcox, in Washington, DC, who read the entire typescript several times, correcting many of the grammatical and context errors, as well as to Lewis Burgess in New York City and Claude F. Baudez in Paris, both of whom also read the entire text, and whose comments were extremely useful. Later, in Santiago, Chile, Mario Fonseca also read the entire text and encouraged me to persist, as did Peter Mason, who made many helpful suggestions. I am most especially grateful to Roberto Edwards, Director of Fundación América and the Taller Experimental Cuerpos Pintados, who supported my work on this text during several seasons, from 1999 to 2003, in Santiago, as well as his assistant Bárbara Astaburuaga. I especially want to thank Carolina Odone, Paula Honorato, Silvia Quiroga and Christian Báez for their assistance during that time. Soledad González Montes and her husband, Carlos Marichal, have constantly encouraged me through the years, especially for this text. Adriana Vescove and Andrea Daffunchio, in Buenos Aires, did excellent work on the two maps presented in the Introduction. I also wish to thank Natalia Crespi and Verónica del Valle in Buenos Aires, and Lotfi Bezzeghoud, the computer expert here in Paris, for their help with the illustrations, and very recently Veronica Strukelj and Ixel Quesada for help with the text.

I am above all grateful to Rosa Clemente, Cristina and Ursula Calderón, and Hermelinda Acuña, descendants of the Yahgans, for sharing their memories with me in Ukika, Navarino Island, Chile, during the mid-1980s and early 1990s. I cite them in the second and last chapters and hope, in the future, to publish more of their testimonies. I also wish to thank the Chilean Navy for the facilities they offered me to travel in little-known parts of the Cape Horn area and the Argentine Navy for my several trips to Staten Island, an uninhabited island of the southeastern tip of Tierra del Fuego, Argentina.

During these last few years, here in Paris, my good friend Viviana Manríquez has assisted me with her suggestions, her ability with the computer and her knowledge of the history and anthropology of her native Chile. Then in 2007, having reduced and re-formed my text to the utmost, she and her husband Hugo Moraga contacted their friend Frank Salomon, professor of anthropology at the University of Wisconsin. He very willingly read my chapters on the *Beagle* voyages and then most thoughtfully advised me to submit my revised text to Frank Smith, Executive Editor at Cambridge University Press in New York City. Thanks initially to Frank Smith and then especially to the two Cambridge readers and the Cambridge University Press Syndic, it was finally accepted. I also wish to thank Jeanie Lee at the Cambridge University Press office in New York for helping me secure permissions for the illustrations and Brigitte Coulton for being so patient while I made the final corrections to this long text. My rather special manner of writing involves a certain liberty with grammatical standards, for which I take entire responsibility. I was especially keen on publishing this text with Cambridge because it had been Darwin's university and became the depository of his archives and also because England is the homeland of most of the "outsiders" who encountered the Yamana through these last four centuries.

I owe a great deal to my friend Ixel Quesada who so carefully reviewed the entire text and made the final corrections the first week of December 2009.

Paris, December 2009

Glossary

Alakaluf (spelt in a variety of ways). Apparently the meaning of this term is unknown. It was first reported by Fitz-Roy. He undoubtedly heard it in 1829, during his first expedition, as the name of a small island or a group of islets called Alikhoolip, south of the large Londonderry Island and east of the twin Gilbert Islands (Chapter 3). However, though he became aware that the Alakaluf and the Yamana spoke different languages, he called both groups Fuegians, and the Yamana, also Tekeenica. The contemporary Alakaluf (see Kawésqar) do not recognise it as a term for their people. However, I use it because these people are known by this term in print.

Falkland Islands. These islands are referred to in English and on many maps as "[The] Falkland Islands" simply because the British government has owned them since 1833. In Argentina they are known as Islas Malvinas. The former name dates from an expedition led by John Strong in 1690, who named the islands after his patron, Anthony Cary, the 5th Viscount Falkland. "Malvinas" is derived from the French name "Îles Malouines," bestowed in 1764 by Louis Antoine de Bougainville, after the mariners and fishermen from the Breton port of Saint Malo. He became the island's first known human settler, though not for long (see Chapter 2).

Fuegian. Used here as a generic term for the four ethnic groups of Tierra del Fuego (Yamana, Alakaluf, Selk'nam and Haush), even though the term is usually employed as a synonym for the "canoe people," the Yamana and the Alakaluf.

Haush (spelt Haus, Aus). During the nineteenth century they were referred to as Eastern Onas. Maneken or Manekenku is apparently their genuine name but is rarely used. The Haush, like the Selk'nam, were a "foot people," mainly guanaco hunters. In historical times, the Haush occupied the southeastern portion (the Mitre Peninsula) of Isla Grande, from San Pablo Cape, where they mixed with the Selk'nam, to Sloggett Bay, where some intermarried with the Yamana. Formerly, prior to the arrival of the Selk'nam, at least several thousand years ago, the Haush occupied most of the Isla Grande. Some time before the arrival of Europeans, they had been "confined" to the southeastern portion of the island by the more aggressive and combative Selk'nam. When first encountered by Europeans (the

Nodal brothers from Spain) in 1619, they already were confined to the Mitre Peninsula. There they supplemented their diet of guanaco meat with the meat of seals (the sea lions and the fur seals), which were more abundant there than in the Selk'nam portion of the Isla Grande.

Islas Malvinas. See Falkland Islands, above.

Kawésqar. A term employed as their authentic name by the surviving Alakaluf living in Puerto Eden. It is also used as a generic term for all the Alakaluf by linguists and historians, such as the Chilean scholar Mateo Martinic. The Kawésqar or Alakaluf, the "canoe people," neighbours of the Yamana, also lived along the Strait of Magellan east to about Elizabeth Island and up the Chilean archipelago to the Gulf of Peñas. To the south they inhabited the region between Brecknock Peninsula and Devil's Island, where, although they were the majority, they sometimes married the Yamana, at least in the nineteenth century.

Native. A term designating any and everyone identified with a distinctive culture, locality, particular nation or country. It seems neutral and is used freely.

Ona. Derived from a Yahgan word referring to the north. Thomas Bridges defines it in his *Yamana–English Dictionary* (second edition 1987, p. 10) as "*ona* (*on'isin* the mainland of Fireland) [that is, the Isla Grande]. The Foot Indians *on'a-shagan* (*onaiiusha*) [later known as Selk'nam]. The N. coast of Beagle Channel." Here Bridges refers again to the Isla Grande, to its south coast, along Beagle Channel, which was Yamana territory. Thus there is a certain lack of clarity in his definition, as *on'a-shagan* appears as the term for both the Selk'nam and the Foot Indians and as a term for the south coast of Isla Grande. Recall that Bridges invariably used "Ona" as the name of the Selk'nam, which is a simplification of *on'a-shagan*. Gusinde (1982: vol. I: 240) pointed out that the Yamana called the Alakaluf *aóna yámana*, "people of the north." So apparently the word *aona* (or ona) signifies "north" in the Yahgan language. It was frequently used by Jemmy Button and written as "Oens-men" (Chapter 5). However, it was not employed by the Selk'nam themselves. Lola Kiepja, the last Selk'nam shaman, whom I knew, thought Ona was an English word, because the few tourists who came to see her were mostly English-speaking and they invariably called her or questioned her using this term. It is currently used instead of Selk'nam, the authentic name, mainly because it is easy to spell and pronounce (see below).

Pecheray (or Pecherais). A term first used by Bougainville, the eighteenth-century explorer, for the Alakaluf along the Strait of Magellan. It is apparently an Alakaluf form of greeting, which has been translated differently by various authors. Captain Cook used the term, in 1769, to refer to the Haush in Good Success Bay. Also see Gusinde (1926) in the Bibliography.

Selk'nam (also known as Onas and Oens-men). The authentic name of the largest group of guanaco hunters. The etymology of Selk'nam was not known by the last members of this group. It does not appear to be derived from any other word, and its meaning has been lost over the eons. The Selk'nam, like the Haush, were "foot people." They occupied most of the Isla Grande in historical times and probably long before. During the nineteenth century, they were neighbours of the Alakaluf along the shores of Useless Bay (across from Dawson Island) and of the Haush, as mentioned above. They mingled with the Yamana when they crossed the cordillera and descended along the north shore of Beagle Channel, as frequently mentioned in this text.

Tekeenica. A term used in the nineteenth century, mainly by Fitz-Roy, to refer to the Yahgans living in the area of Hoste Island (see below). According to Lucas Bridges (1987: 36), this term was not employed by the Yahgans simply because it was not a word. It is derived from the expression *teke uneka*. Lucas Bridges explained that Fitz-Roy probably began using this term (during his first expedition) when he pointed to a bay (see below) and a Yahgan replied, *teke uneka*, which signifies "I don't understand what you mean." He thought the expression was the word Tekeenica and used it to refer to the Yahgans living in that area. So the bay that Fitz-Roy pointed to appears on the Chilean maps as Tekenika Bay, located on Hoste Island, between Pasteur and Hardy peninsulas, bordering the much larger Nassau Bay. I use the latter term, to not confuse the reader with the name of the bay and Fitz-Roy's term.

Yacana-kunny. A term used by the Tehuelche for the Selk'nam, who were also called simply Yacana by Fitz-Roy.

Yahgan and Yamana. Terms used interchangeably in this book to refer to the same people. These "canoe people" inhabited the southern portion of Tierra del Fuego, both shores of Beagle Channel to Cape Horn, and to the west areas as far as the Brecknock Peninsula, where they mingled with the Alakaluf who were the main inhabitants there at least in the nineteenth century. The Yamana probably camped in Staten Island also (see, in the Bibliography, Chapman, A. (1983), available only in Spanish). Along the north shore of Beagle Channel, the eastern Yamana had frequent contact with the Selk'nam, at least during the nineteenth century. The Yamana were also neighbours of the Haush in the area of Sloggett Bay.

I use "Yamana" and "Yahgan" as synonyms because of a certain confusion concerning their definitions. The anthropologists, archaeologists, and other writers favour "Yamana," as did Father Martin Gusinde, author of the main study of Fuegian cultures, even though he was aware that it signifies humanity at large. T. Bridges (1987: 265) defined the term *hanna-iamalim* as "used by the natives specifically of themselves [as] My countrymen, My country people." I have never seen this term used in other publications nor heard it from the descendants. However, this is an expression, not a name. "Yahgan" seemed inappropriate to Bridges because it is a local name; nevertheless, he favoured it as a generic term and intended that it be used in the title of his dictionary because his informants were from that area or nearby. He (1987: 659) defined "Yaga" as "The name of the Murray Narrows, or rather the coasts on either side and the parts in the neighbourhood." In Spanish it is spelt Yagán; in English, Yahgan.

Long after Bridges' death but in agreement with his family, Gusinde, thanks to whom the dictionary was finally published, took the liberty of replacing the term "Yahgan" with "Yamana" in the title of Bridges' dictionary. Natalie Goodall pointed out in her preface to the second edition that "His [Thomas Bridges'] descendants feel that although Yamana is the form at present most generally used for these people, the language represented in this dictionary should be called Yahgan." In his dictionary, Bridges defined the word "Yamana" as follows: "By this term the Yahgan tribe distinguished themselves from all other natives who spoke a different language as well as from all foreign peoples; this term primarily means Humanity." There is an obvious ambiguity in this definition. In SAMM (1880: 74) Bridges stated that a term for the Yamana or Yahgan people as a whole does not exist. Also the last speakers of the language, Cristina Calderón and her sister Ursula, explained to me that the term "Yamana" does not apply to them (as a people) because it signifies all humanity; the human being of any nationality, ethnicity or race. They also insisted that "Yamana" signifies the male gender. For these reasons the Calderón sisters are opposed to the use of "Yamana" to designate their people and prefer to be called Yahgan. The linguist Christos Clairis (1985: 18) noted a similar statement made by the late Clara Alvarez, who was also Yahgan.

The ambiguity of the word "yamana" (humanity/male gender) is apparent in other languages, such as the English "man," the Spanish "*hombre*," the French "*homme*" and the German "*Mann*." This ambiguity is especially noted by feminists like myself, who refrain from using these words to apply to all of humanity. But in this text I try to accommodate the anthropologists as well as the descendants of this group and use both terms ("Yamana" and "Yahgan") interchangeably, hoping not to offend anyone or confuse the reader.

Yapoo. A term derived from the Yahgan *aiapux*, or otter. It became a derogatory term employed by the Alakaluf, especially by York Minster, for the Yahgan-Yamana (Chapters 3 to 5).

Introduction

This narration begins in 1578, with Francis Drake, and follows through, to the twentieth century, with other "outsiders" and with the native peoples, mainly the Yamana. I propose to travel with the reader, during these four centuries, through this desolate though often inspiring natural landscape: Tierra del Fuego, the islands south of the Magellan Strait to Cape Horn.[1]

Cape Horn has been associated with its native inhabitants, as if the final furious expression of the continent were coupled with the most wretched people on earth. Cape Horn, the southernmost part of the earth this side of Antarctica, is known principally for the tribulations of famous explorers and adventurous navigators. It has inspired and awed seamen for almost 400 years. Even in calm weather, a haunting silence shrouds the vast ocean beyond, disturbed only by the waves throbbing against the rocky coasts, where seals lounge and squalling petrels weave through the air. But now few animals remain there and fewer people. Now Horn Island is uninhabited except for men of the Chilean Navy and Coast Guard in the meteorological station. Despite the progress in navigation, "the Cape" still evokes the most dreaded seas on earth and from year to year draws tourists; but to the Yamana it was home.

The Yamana are among the most defiled people in the world. The early navigators either ignored them or treated them with disdain. Even the great Darwin referred to them as "stunted, miserable wretches," "miserable degraded savages," "the most abject and miserable creatures I anywhere behold" who "kill and devour their old women before they kill their dogs"; he added, "viewing such men, one can hardly make oneself believe that they are fellow-creature, and inhabitants of the same world." Although he also wrote of their progress under the aegis of the

FIGURE I.I. Cape Horn, viewed from the East.

missionaries, again, in *The Descent of Man*, he referred to them as he had forty years before.

They are mentioned by historians and anthropologists, although sometimes they are simply ignored.[2] In note 3, I comment on the relevant publications on the Yamana, when possible, those that are available in English.[3]

I treat them as fellow human beings, on a par with the well-known personages who encountered them. Far from being wretched, the Yamana lacked nothing in human terms. They experienced more than their share of problems owing to the exigencies of an often hostile environment and the threat of starvation. But the obduracy of nature apparently inspired their love of country, a country they found infinitely exciting and of great beauty, as can be appreciated by some of the documents cited in this text and by comments of the few descendants I came to know.

The archaeological literature is full of adaptation hyperboles as if these people, hunters of marine mammals and gatherers of shellfish, were constantly struggling to survive.[4] Even though they lived closer to nature and in a more hazardous natural environment than many of us do today, their daily quest for food and shelter did not overwhelm them except during periods of unusually harsh weather. They were not constantly striving to adapt to their environment, even though the search for food was almost constant. They were well acquainted with their territory and the seasons and knew where and when to find seals, shellfish, fish, certain birds and other food. Acutely aware of the danger of the sudden climatic changes they, as well as their neighbours the Alakaluf (Kaweskar), were accomplished navigators in their canoes of tree bark. The Yamana navigated the treacherous seas around Cape Horn and through the Strait of Le Maire; although moving from one campsite to another they travelled as close to the shores as possible. They were constantly alert to the subtle changes in their surroundings that might warn them of a coming storm, and they could see much farther into the horizon than the Europeans, as Darwin noted. Although they had good appetites, they often had other matters on their minds, such as when and where to hold their great ceremonies. However, canoe accidents were apparently quite frequent, and from time to time storms overwhelmed them and hunger struck. If a damaged canoe could not be repaired, a family might become isolated on a remote island and starve to death. When someone was assassinated, vengeance was taken on the real or assumed culprit. Unhappy marriages were not exceptional. These and other human frailties were part of their habitual routine. Nevertheless, they not only adapted and survived (for some 6,000 years), they often enjoyed life. They had a cheerful temperament until their lives were disrupted by outsiders.

Although the Yamana are among the best-documented native peoples in South America, they are not well known to the English reader because the main sources, those of the Anglican missionaries and the volumes on the Yamana by Father Martin Gusinde, are not widely read. The latter are not easily available in English. Therefore I allude to salient aspects of their culture. I also follow the lives of some twelve Yamana, all of whom died long before I first went to Tierra del Fuego in 1964. Thanks to the quality of the historical documents and to the years I spent concentrating on this text, their personalities have become so vivid that they have become my friends – some, my heroes.[5] I am sure that more information can be found concerning some of them, and hopefully documented biographies will be written about them. Even though the lives and achievements of the outsiders (European in the majority) are familiar to many readers, they here are treated in similar fashion. For instance, I follow the lives of Drake, Cook, Darwin, Fitz-Roy, Martial, Hyades and certain sealers after their visits to Tierra del Fuego, as well as the missionaries after their retirement.

Certainly, in the future, more people the world over will admire the Yamana for their physical stamina and ingenuity in dealing with an often unpredictable environment, their creative ceremonies, their talent for mimicry and ear for music, their caustic and often amusing oral literature, their geometrical, almost code-like paintings (on their faces and on slabs of wood), their dynamic society generated by a subtle combination of cooperation and competition, their amazingly rich language and their sociability. They usually welcomed the European navigators cheerfully even though the men did not always resist the temptation to "pocket" pieces of iron on the decks of the ships.

With respect to their simple technology, T. W. Deacon said very clearly: "Anthropologists in the early twentieth century quickly realised that the technological status of a society was no predictor of the complexity of its language or the symbolic richness of its traditions." Moreover a simple technology requires a complex knowledge of how to use it. Such knowledge was usually not transmitted in the publications concerning them.

In 2009, there is now only one person, Cristina Calderón, who speaks the Yamana language fluently. She appears in the final chapter, along with the other three women with whom I had the opportunity to work as an anthropologist from 1985 through part of the following decade.

This is not a historical novel; no part of this narration is fiction. I pay close attention to the sources. The events and personages are dramatic enough in themselves; nothing has been "fictionalised" in order to make them more appealing to the reader. Yet this approach had to be coherent. I could not simply choose the most dramatic episodes and proclaim that I was not "fictionalising." My insistence on providing a documented narration meant that certain episodes could not be eliminated simply because I feared that the reader might fall asleep, or skip pages. For instance, I follow the two *Beagle* expeditions in Tierra del Fuego (1827–30 and 1832–34) and describe all of its encounters with the Fuegians. No matter how uneventful they may appear, all are significant for one reason or another. Hopefully you will follow the unfolding of these histories. The text may be read without consulting the notes. Most simply identify the sources consulted; however, quite a few are rather long because they treat themes of interest for teachers, students and other scrupulous readers.

The main sources provide a great deal of detail on a variety of subjects. Were this wealth of data to be included, this book would comprise thousands of pages. Now I will appear to contradict myself, because I also insist that the details give the "living in" to the histories and the encounters. All depends on the objectives of the "work." I selected details from the sources concerning what appeared to me essential for an understanding of the theoretical questions Darwin first posed in terms of progress made since the primitive "savages" to the "civilised" Europeans of his day, particularly concerning the Yamana (whom he called Fuegians). My selection was also made in an effort to elucidate or reveal the conflicts, ambitions, illusions and the achievements of the "actors," natives as well as outsiders and their roles on different levels of significance: personal, home-country and international. I follow the lives of completely distinct people – as, for example, those of Captain Cook and Jemmy Button's eldest daughter. Despite this diversity, the entire text, covering four centuries, is a single narrative because most of the events and the personages are directly or indirectly linked, forming a worldview of those 400 years which were so vital for Europe, for the Fuegians and for Chile and Argentina.

Although I focus on the Yamana, I also include the other "Fuegians," their neighbours, when they enter the narration for one reason or another: especially the Alakaluf (Kaweskar), the Selk'nam (Ona) and the Haush as well as the Tehuelches (also called Aónikenk); even though the latter were not "Fuegians" they were neighbours.

As mentioned above, I focus almost equally on the "insiders" and the "outsiders": the former, the Yamana, who appear in the sources and the few I knew, and their neighbours. The outsiders include explorers, scientists, missionaries, whalers, sealers, and finally Argentine and Chilean government employees, historians, journalists in addition to anthropologists and three famous visitors in the final chapter. My intention is to fill a void – to situate the Yamana and the other Fuegians in universal history as relevant actors during these past four centuries, to bring them into the fold of written history from that outer rim of human experiences, from that separate category of savages, primitives, marginal survivors or exotic curiosities. This book opens another door to the past by joining the experiences of the insiders and outsiders, of the Fuegians and Europeans in a single narrative.

Immanuel Wallerstein advocated such an approach from a slightly different angle when he stated: "Instead of drawing a line between the modern and the premodern, the civilized and the barbaric, the advanced and the backward...historical social scientists have to...subject all zones, all groups, all strata to the same kind of critical analysis."[6]

The landscape in which they travelled – in canoes, sailing ships, whaleboats and steamships – is evoked almost constantly. The localities where the Yamana camped, the explorers anchored their ships and the missionaries settled are pictured in some detail. The difficulties the climate created for the Europeans and for the Yamana are also empathised. I

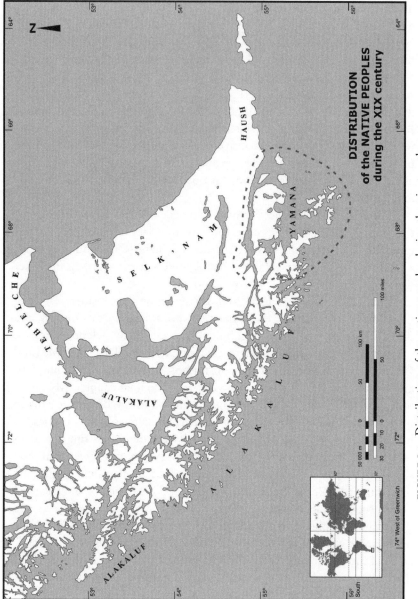

FIGURE 1.2. Distribution of the native peoples during the nineteenth century.

6

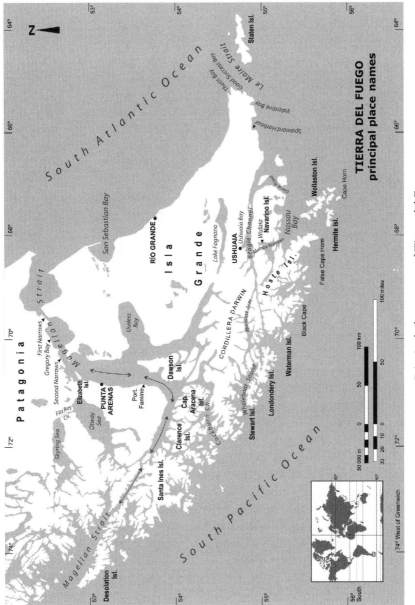

FIGURE I.3. Principal place names of Tierra del Fuego.

hope to convey vivid impressions of this fascinating area, of how it was dealt with by people of such different backgrounds and objectives for being there.

This book combines archaeological, historical, geographical, natural, cultural and biographical data from published sources with original information I obtained through the years from the few descendants of the Yamana (four women). It also alludes to my experience of living and travelling in the area. As the narration unfolds, my comments should be evident to the reader. Each of us has only one life, but we can experience the lives of others, without stretching our imagination, through our knowledge and sensitivity.

The Fuegians' basic economy of hunting, gathering and fishing, for short H/G/F, lasted at least for ninety percent of our existence as *Homo sapiens sapiens*, that is, nearly 90,000 years of our 100,000 or more years' existence as a species. Why did these Palaeolithic societies continue for so long? Why did they last as a universal phenomenon until about 13,000 years ago (10,000 or 11,000 BC), when agricultural–sedentary villages, the so-called Neolithic epoch, emerged? They lasted so long perhaps because, with the different emphases on H/G/F, these people had the know-how to live in a great variety of places (coast and inland, deserts and forests, etc.), and their economy and society were flexible enough to adjust to the formidable changes in climate that occurred during these many thousands of years. These societies were more or less egalitarian (more for the men and less for the women) and their populations were small. They were not subjected to the overwhelming stresses of hierarchy that eventually shortened "the lives" of many of the great civilisations that followed. However the former were not simple band societies as some anthropologists contended. I would guess that some were like the Fuegians among whom certain individuals had a great deal of prestige, notably the shamans, although few economic privileges. Also the great variety of such societies included those who engaged in armed combat among their "own people." For instance the Selk'nam fought among themselves often to extend (or defend) their hunting grounds and to kidnap women. The latter were always scarce because of polygamy. They attacked their neighbours (the Haush) many centuries before contact with Europeans, mainly for territory and probably also for women. Incursions of the Selk'nam against the Yamana, in the nineteenth century were often for pillage (also for goods left by the Europeans), at least until the final attack in 1859 (Chapter 9). The H/G/F way of living was usually ecologically adjusted. It did not destroy the fauna or the forests and plants, so it enabled people to remain settled in circumscribed areas for thousands of years, as did the Yamana and their neighbours. If these Fuegian cultures can be treated as prototypes of H/G/F communities (though by no means exclusively) it is because, as far as is known, they never had had contact with full or even part-time agriculturists (such as the Mapuches of central Chile). The Yamana and other Fuegians had always been H/G/F, though of course they had modified their infra and super structures at different times through the ages. Not only because ecological conditions changed but also because of the varying intensity and quality of their relations within their cultural sphere and beyond it, with their neighbours. At different times, certain subgroups (such as lineages or clans) became unusually powerful, having great extensions of territory, at the cost of those that were less well organised. This happened among the Selk'nam shortly before contact, with Lola Kiepja's maternal grandfather whose lineage was the largest in the area, extending as it did from Lake Fagnano to the Atlantic coast. The mythology also varied, not only from one generation to another, but also simultaneously (at the same time) as for instance when a myth was "used," interpreted, to enhance the prestige of a narrator (the relater of the myth), his lineage or clan. The Fuegian and probably the "Palaeolithic societies" as well, were dynamic despite their adherence to H/G /F economic patterns and lack of writing.

The further we go back in time through many millennia, we become aware of the quintessence of our human heritage in Africa, with the first *Homo sapiens*. When we began walking upright, our front legs and feet became arms and hands, giving more work to the brain and less to the muscles, until, perhaps some 100,000 years ago, we became, for better or for worse, twice "*Sapiens*," leaving our cousins, the *Homo sapiens neanderthalense*, to their fate. However, we were not destined, programmed or designed to become *Homo sapiens sapiens*. Natural selection (or "descent with modification," as Darwin sometimes calls his theory) is not predetermined. We have not been "selected" by Nature (or "anyone" else) to rule the biosphere. Nature has no axe to grind, no favourites. Near the end of *On the Origin of Species*, Darwin wrote, "natural selection works solely by and for the good of each individual, all corporeal and mental endowments will tend to progress towards perfection." It "works" in different ways in terms of the individuals of a specific species. Darwin closes his treatise with these memorable lines: "There is grandeur in this view of life, from so simple a beginning endless forms most beautiful and most wonderful have been and are being evolved."

The highly esteemed late biologist Ernst Mayr developed Darwin's statement concerning our species in this lucid passage:

When speech developed between 300,000 and 200,000 years ago in small groups of hunter–gatherers owing to a selective premium on improved communication, the situation was favourable for a further increase in brain size. However, around 100,000 years ago this increase came to a halt and from then to the present, the human brain growth has stayed the same size and [of] equal capacity.

So apparently our "mental endowment" has not progressed since some 100,000 years ago. Mayr seemed rather disappointed when he added:

One would have expected continued brain growth in the 100,000 years preceding the development of agriculture, which occurred around 10,000 years ago. A Great Leap forward in culture, as Diamond calls it, seems to come about very rapidly during this period, yet it was not correlated with an equivalent jump in brain size or changes in other physical characteristics. Just why this should be so has been speculated about, but no convincing answer has been found.[7]

So according to Mayr there is no biological reason for the "invention" of agriculture and sedentary life, nor for the "civilisations" that followed. We have the same brain capacity as our Palaeolithic hunting–gathering *Homo sapiens sapiens*, neither more nor less. Darwin also realised that the hunting–gathering Yamana he met in Tierra del Fuego had the same mental capacity as the British.[8] Also, in his conclusions of *The Expression of the Emotions in Man and Animals*, he noted that:

all the chief expressions exhibited by man are the same throughout the world. This fact is interesting, as it affords a new argument in favour of the several races being descended from a single parent-stock, which must have been almost completely human in structure, *and to a large extent in mind*, before the period at which the races diverged from each other.[9]

Lévi-Strauss adhered to the same thesis. "I see no reason why mankind should have waited until recent times to produce minds of the caliber of a Plato or an Einstein. Already over two or three hundred thousand years ago, there were probably men of similar capacity." And he added: "the human brain is the same everywhere . . . not the input and output."[10]

Although the Yamana's "inputs and outputs" are vastly different from those of Wall Street brokers and our famous scientists, the Yamana may have discussed and argued about their different interpretations of their oral tradition something like Wall Street brokers agree and disagree on the reasons for the rise and fall of the stock market or scientists their hypotheses. Writing and mathematics have not made the scientists more intelligent than the "scholars" of oral traditions, but it has enabled the scientists to obtain a much greater grasp of certain realities. The inputs and outputs vary greatly, but not the inquisitive minds.

"Prehistory" tells us that the ancestors of the first Americans migrated from Asia across the Bering Strait.[11] This statement is almost a fact; in any case it is accepted as a reality by scientists, although the time spans are not. Estimates of the dates of the first migrations into America vary with the archaeologists from fifty or more thousand years ago to twelve thousand years ago (see below).[12]

The Yamana foremothers and forefathers may have been among the earliest migrants, exiting from campsites somewhere in Asia. Whether the earliest or not, when they set out they probably did not constitute the distinct ethnic or language group they later became. The Chilean anthropologist Patricia Soto-Heim proposed that while the Selk'nam and the Tehuelches "relate more to the men of the Upper Palaeolithic of China and Russia, the Alakaluf and the Yamana appear to resemble the Paleo-Siberians."[13] It does seem reasonable that the former, the "foot people" (mainly guanaco hunters) and the latter, the "canoe people" (mainly seal hunters) had different origins in Asia so many thousand years ago.

Darwin was already aware of early migrations of extinct animals, as he wrote in his Beagle narrative:

It seem most probable that the North American elephants, mastodons, horse, and hollow-horned ruminants migrated on land since submerged near Behring's Straits, from Siberia into North America, and hence on land since submerged in the West Indies, [see below] into South America, where for a time they mingled with forms characteristic of that southern continent, and have since become extinct.[14]

Some of these animals reached Patagonia, among them the giant ground sloth and an ancestor of the modern horse; both became extinct only about 10,000 years ago and may have been pursued by the earliest hunters of that region.[15]

The ancestors of the animals that exist today in southern South America either migrated from the Old World or remained there after the continents split apart during the Cretaceous Period, 136 to 65 million years ago. The two species of rheas (which resemble the African ostrich), the puma, the deer (called *huemul* in Patagonia), all managed to cross the Strait of Magellan into Tierra del Fuego, including the fox, several species of rodents and the guanaco. However, certain ancestors of the latter returned to the Old World and became camels. When and how the seals, shellfish and birds came to Tierra del Fuego are open questions. The whales have probably been at home in the vast seas of the world ever since their ancestors became waterborne.

The humans had to use the ice-free passages through Canada: one was along the west coast and the other was an interior corridor because huge glaciers blocked the rest of Canada.[16] A possible obstacle for foot passage to South America would have been the Isthmus of Panama area, not the "submerged" West Indies, because apparently it was never submerged, as Darwin wrote above. The present-day Isthmus of Panama with its 200 miles of swampy tropical rain forest may have been a savannah at that time, owing to a shift in high pressure.[17]

Another route from Siberia to America would have been by sea: from the Kamchatka Peninsula (Siberia), stopping off on the Aleutian Islands and then paddling, rowing or sailing down the Pacific coast of North America while subsisting mainly on fish, seals and shellfish. This coastal route may have been preferable to the interior ice-free corridors despite its violent storms and thick fogs.

As the millennia were passing, the different migrations of the "Paleo-Indians" were spanning across North America while others continued down the Pacific coast. Many settled perhaps for thousands of years and then moved on or remained in chosen habitats until the Europeans disrupted their lives. The dog was certainly an important auxiliary for the hunt since earliest times, though rarely for transportation, as its carrying capacity is limited. The llama and alpaca were domesticated much later.[18] The lack of large domestic animals for transportation certainly slowed the pace of these peoples and may have encouraged a preference for watercraft.

As of 1997, many archaeologists agree with their colleague Tom Dilehay that people had arrived in central Chile at a site called Monte Verde, by some 16,000 years ago.[19]

They probably came down the coast of South America in various groups, their minds and their "knapsacks" full of cultural "goodies": customs, shamanistic lore, rituals, fire-making techniques, tools, weapons, ornaments, games – that is, an entire mode of living. The cultural process is always on a continuum. It creates and assimilates (from allies and even enemies). It adapts, adopts, invents and discards techniques for exploiting resources, oral traditions and whatever.

They were probably constantly rearranging and sorting out their cultural baggage. Some may have guarded "souvenirs" of the Old World. The Yamana (and the Selk'nam) apparently guarded their chants, which Alan Lomax, a musicologist, found resembled the primitive "bands" (peoples) of Siberia. Erich von Hornbolstel, another musicologist, traced the Fuegian chants to "the forerunners [the remote ancestors] of the real [the actual] Indians' immigration into the American continent."[20]

To make a long story short and avoid too many conjectures, let us join those who were in central Chile at least 16,000 years ago and possibly earlier, long millennia before the "seeds" of the great Andean civilizations were sown. They must have had powerful motives to move into unknown territory in family groups, with little carrying capacity. They probably sent advanced parties of scouts ahead to examine the terrain, something like what the families of Alakaluf and Selk'nam did in 1885 when they traversed an unknown area, seeking refuge in Ushuaia along Beagle Channel (Chapter 13).

In South America, the last Pleistocene glaciers did not cover the adjacent coasts above 39° south latitude (central Chile), so the migrants were unhampered by ice and snow as they slowly settled and penetrated along the Pacific coast of Colombia, Ecuador and the desert coasts of Peru and northern Chile. However, the glaciers covered much of the cordillera to the south and did not retreat from the Magellan Strait until 10,000 or 8,000 years ago.

Consider, for example, that the shore measures some 4,500 miles (some 800 miles in a straight line by air) from Puerto Montt, central-southern Chile (at 41° south latitude), to Cape Froward at the middle of Magellan Strait (almost 54° south latitude). In 1932–33 the archaeologist Junius Bird and his wife Peggy sailed and rowed in a small boat down the archipelago, from Puerto Montt to Punta Arenas on the Magellan Strait (from 41° to 53°10' south latitude). They found almost no place to walk along the shores. Bird explained:

The reason lies not only in the densely tangled forest but also in the rough nature of the country – mountains and hills that drop precipitously beneath the sea with little or no foreshore. Beaches are few and widely separated. Glaciers and swift-flowing rivers offer further obstacles. It is clear, then, that occupation of this territory must have depended on the development of an adequate boat or canoe.[21]

The serious obstacle, according to Bird, was the Taitao Peninsula, south of Puerto Montt. He calculated that further south, the Gulf of Peñas, could have been rather easily traversed by carrying the canoe across the Isthmus of Ofqui. Beyond the Gulf of Peñas, towards the Magellan Strait, Bird and his wife found nothing that might have discouraged a rather rapid occupation, except perhaps the excessive rain.[22]

If the Yamana did take such a route, they were already expert navigators, with well-equipped canoes, accustomed to paddling in the rain and snow, camping on inhospitable coasts and lighting a fire in a storm. Bird noted that, despite the almost constant rainfall, the coastal route offered two advantages: the tepu tree (*Tepualia stipularis*), which provides excellent firewood that can be cut even when green and in a heavy rain. He also observed that the shell of the giant mussel (*Mytilus chilensis*) is "almost as effective as a knife of iron."[23]

So there is reliable evidence that the ancestors of the Yamana–Yahgan could have navigated down along the Pacific coast, through the islands and islets of the archipelago from Puerto Montt to the shores of the Magellan Strait.[24] The archaeologist Samuel K. Lothrop, in his article on canoe navigation, commented: "Evidence of all kinds blends in agreement that the Yahgan and Alacaluf, the Canoe Indians, came down the west coast of South America, here the remains of their ancestors or relatives can be identified at least as far north as Peru."[25]

In any event, the early Yamana were penetrating terrain, not knowing whether or not they would come upon more habitable land beyond it. Eventually they did find a better habitat (better than the Pacific archipelago, which Bird and his wife had navigated).

It is difficult to imagine how many millennia it may have taken the Yamana to navigate from their "homeland" in the Old World (perhaps Siberia) to Tierra del Fuego. Along "the way," they may have slowly created a linguistic identity. Their language may be remotely related to Andean languages.[26] Gradually the Yamana culture acquired the characteristics of their tradition, which eventually became partially known to outsiders in the nineteenth and twentieth centuries.[27]

So far there is no evidence that any of the Fuegians had contact with people who practised agriculture.[28] Apparently they were the first and only people who lived in this the uttermost part of the inhabited earth, the Beagle Channel region to Cape Horn, until the arrival of the Europeans.[29]

The other "Fuegians" (the Alakaluf, Selk'nam and Haush) have their own stories to tell. They arrived south of the Magellan Strait at different periods and occupied other areas of Tierra del Fuego. The Alakaluf settled along the Pacific coast (now Chile), north of the Yamana. Although a "canoe people" like the Yamana, the Alakaluf never went to the very end of the inhabitable earth, to Cape Horn, probably because the Yamana were already there. The Haush and Selk'nam came on land, from continental Patagonia (now Argentina) bordering the Atlantic coast; they eventually settled in the largest island of Tierra del Fuego, called the Isla Grande.[30]

But why did the Yamana go so far? An idea or hypothesis that appealed to Darwin and other scholars is that the Yamana, being weak, primitive, nomadic hunters, were pushed and shoved to the very rim of the inhabitable land by "more advanced" settlers farther north, such as the pre-Incas, or by some unknown superior hunters. These "pushers" would have had no interest in giving the Yamana a final shove off the end of the earth in order to take over their land. Who, in their right mind, would choose to live in Tierra del Fuego, let alone on Horn Island? So the story goes that the Yamana–Yahgan must have been forced to take refuge in this dreary "uttermost part of the earth."

Junius Bird, who knew the area better than his colleagues, affirmed: "Contrary to what one might suppose, the most desirable part of the archipelago is in the extreme south, along the southern side of Tierra del Fuego [Yamana territory]."[31]

Younger archaeologists, such as Luis Abel Orquera and Ernesto Piana, agree with Bird that this area offered abundant resources, and they too challenged the still prevailing notion that the Yamana were cornered in a hostile environment because of their alleged cultural inferiority.[32] Though not a promised land, this area, Tierra del Fuego, was more hospitable than the rain-drenched archipelago facing the Pacific, where the Alakaluf settled (probably much later) and even a bit warmer than the coasts of Magellan Strait (see end of Chapter 2). Of course the Yamana did not know this beforehand, but once they had arrived there, they stayed – for some 6,000 years, according to studies made by the archaeologists mentioned above and Dominque Legoupil. These Yamana were the real pioneers in this part of the world. They settled down there, hopefully forever. Their "forever" lasted until the nineteenth century, when the Europeans devastated any projects for the future they might have cherished. Few Yamana survived the European occupation of their land, the capture of their souls and the epidemics (Chapters 11 to 15).

It is time to cease treating the Fuegians and other known hunter–gatherers–fishers the world over as primitives on the far edge of history, on the margins of conscience. The memory of the Yamana and the other Fuegians vibrates in the minds of their descendants and many of the neo-Fuegians as well. This memory will probably be honoured by more than a few "outsiders" for countless centuries to come.[33]

1578 to 1775: Drake Encounters the Fuegians; The First Massacres of Europeans and Fuegians; Captain Cook Inaugurates a New Era

Drake the Audacious

"All the world is a stage.... And one man in his time plays many parts."[1] Francis Drake played many parts, but here we are concerned with only two, both during 1578. The first when he and his crew "rode" a tempestuous sea further south than any European had ever gone, and the second when they became the first Europeans to meet the natives in that "uttermost part of the world," near Cape Horn. Years later Shakespeare met and talked "to the great navigators of the day, like Raleigh and Drake."[2] So the latter may have told Shakespeare about his adventures in Tierra del Fuego.

Drake not only flouted Spain's monopoly of the Magellan Strait, he traversed its 334 miles in sixteen days, including "calls to take on water and kill penguins," less than half the thirty-seven days that the great Ferdinand Magellan had taken in 1520. Luckily for Drake, no Spaniards were there at the time. If Drake and his shipmates were toasting one another for outsmarting Magellan and the Spaniards, they would soon be humbled by the great Pacific, or by God himself, according to Francis Fletcher, the chaplain and main chronicler of the expedition: "God by a contrary wind and intolerable tempest, seemed to set himself against us, forcing us not only to alter our course and determination, but with great trouble, long time, many dangers, hard escapes, and finally separating of our fleet, to yeeld ourselues into his will."[3]

Drake's *Golden Hind*, *Marigold* and *Elizabeth* were exiting Magellan Strait on 7 September 1578, to make their way north, up the Pacific, when they were hurled out to sea into that "intolerable tempest."[4] The fury of the sea persisted "so violent and of such continuance not seen since

Noah's flood." The *Marigold* sank with her entire crew on 30 September. The men on the other two ships heard the crew shouting desperately for help but were too far away to rescue them. The *Elizabeth* was luckier, she found shelter nearby, where the crew waited anxiously until 8 October for the flagship, the *Golden Hind*. Then the captain of the *Elizabeth*, thinking that the *Golden Hind* had also succumbed to the tempest, turned his ship eastward back through the Magellan Strait heading for home, where he arrived nine months later. Meanwhile the *Golden Hind* was tossed about in the southern latitudes during fifty-two days, from 7 September to 28 October.[5]

When Drake returned to London two years later, in 1580, Queen Elizabeth welcomed him profusely, though she was not aware, nor was almost anyone else, that the *Golden Hind* had been swept to what, according to the maps of that time, should have been the shores of the continent called *Terra Australis Incognita*.

Since 1520, when Magellan discovered the strait named for him, its southern coast (Tierra del Fuego) had been mapped as the boundary of *Terra Australis Incognita*. By the time of Drake, the boundary had been moved further south. This fascinating tale began with the ancient Greeks, but it was Ptolemy (90–168 AD) who convinced future generations that *Terra Australis Incognita* really existed. Ptolemy, an "encyclopaedic genius" living in Alexandria, made a comprehensive survey "of the whole scientific knowledge of an age." His manuscripts and maps – showing *Terra Australis Incognita* as "an enormous southern continent" encircling the earth – were considered valid in 1475, when they were first printed in Europe. And still, for exactly 300 more years, Ptolemy's *Terra Australis Incognita* was drawn on the maps at this southern latitude as an undisputed reality until Captain Cook surprised almost everyone with his astonishing discoveries (see the end of this chapter).

Drake and his *Golden Hind* were swept around by the gales for nearly the entire month of September 1578 and until 7 October when he and his crew found themselves at about 57° south latitude. Just where they were "is anyone's guess," according to the historian Samuel Eliot Morison. If they were at "about" 57° south latitude, they were well beyond Cape Horn (which is at 55°96′ south latitude). If so Drake had been further south than any European navigator. He probably imagined that he was near *Terra Australis Incognita*, though he saw only a few small islands and the vast seas mingling "in a most large and free scope." He knew then that Tierra del Fuego was not the *terra incognita*, "wherein many strange monsters lived." He probably thought it was still further south.[6] Because of this feat (though accidental), the stormy route leading to Antarctica is called the Drake Passage.

Drake Encounters the Fuegians

During the second week of October, the storms having somewhat subsided, Drake and his exhausted men stopped over on one of the islands along the Pacific (possibly in Desolate Bay at about 54°40' south latitude).[7] During this week, the Fuegian natives at this "uttermost end of the earth" emerged from the back of beyond, onto the stage of history. Thus Drake and his men became the first outsiders to meet the southernmost inhabitants of the world. They went ashore, perhaps in Desolate Bay, to fetch fresh water and rest their "weak and sickly bodies." During a three days' stay there they saw the native inhabitants "trauelling for their liuing from one island to another, in their canowes, both men, women, and young infants wrapt in skins, and hanging at their mothers' backs." They bartered with these Fuegians (Alakaluf or Yamana). "We had traffique for such things as they had, as chaines of certaine shells and such other trifles. Here the Lord gave us three dayes to breath ourselues and to provide such things as we wanted . . . "[8] This is all that Fletcher reported. Their curiosity was not aroused, probably because they were unaware that they were in the presence of the southernmost inhabitants of the entire globe.

The second encounter occurred a week or so later, very probably on Henderson Island, at 55°35' south latitude (about sixty miles northwest of Cape Horn). Henderson Island "had never yet been seen by a European," according again to the historian Morison.[9] Drake and his men tarried there from 24 October until 1 November. He named it and the few surrounding islands Elizabethides Isles. Having "taken possession" of them for his queen, he and Fletcher carved her name and the date on a stone at the southernmost point of the largest island (probably Henderson). Then Drake "threw himself on his belly . . . and stretched out his arms as far as he could toward the South Pole, boasting that he had been farther south than any man." Morison found this gesture "typical of Drake – always something of the big boy in him."[10] While Drake and Fletcher were wandering about the island, picking delicious currants, they noticed "some inhabitants . . . manners, apparel, houses, canowes and meanes of liuing." They resembled the Alakaluf they had seen, about seven weeks before, along the continental shore of Magellan Strait. A bit later, they saw "families of natives . . . passing in canoes from one to another [island];

the children wrapped in skins hanging at their mothers' backs."[11] Again they were not impressed. Be that as it may, these encounters mark the beginning of a future that the natives could not possibly have imagined, nor could anyone else. Neither Drake nor the public noticed that these were unique encounters.

Drake Sails on to Glory

When the weather finally calmed down, on 1 November, they turned the *Golden Hind* northward, and away they sailed up the Pacific coast, plundering Spanish colonies and attacking the ships they happened upon, even those in the busy port of Acapulco. They may have ventured as far north as Puget Sound (near the future border between the United States and Canada) while searching for a northwest passage back across the continent to the North Atlantic. Or Drake may have given up his search for such a passage near the great bay to be named San Francisco. Then or later, he headed the *Golden Hind* into the Pacific and arrived home in 1580. Glory greeted him as the first Englishman to have circumnavigated the entire globe; her majesty honoured him and he found himself wealthier by some 10,000 pounds sterling, his share of the plunder. Later, in 1594, he was knighted by his queen, as "one of England's greatest heroes," for his role in the battle that defeated the Spanish Armada.[12]

The greatest achievement of his voyage was the voyage itself: to make it back home the long way, and to flout Spain's monopoly of the strait. If this were not enough for such an intrepid navigator and illustrious rogue, later, in 1594, he achieved fame as a military genius. Again, he was the first European to encounter inhabitants beyond the Magellan Strait, though he was not aware of this feat.[13] And yet again, having sailed further south than any other navigator of his day, he would certainly be proud to know ("always something of the big boy in him") that all global maps still carry his name as the "Drake Passage," a span of rough sea some 600 miles (1,111 kilometres) long between Cape Horn and the outlying islands of Antarctica.

Spain Is Furious

Drake's passage through the Magellan Strait pleased his queen in the same measure that it enraged the Spanish Crown. A year later, 1579, Philip II equipped Pedro Sarmiento de Gamboa with two vessels and ordered him to solve the problem of how to keep those "English dogs...the enemy of our *Santa Fe* [our holy faith]" from invading his strait again. Following Sarmiento's first exploration, Philip II sent him back to the Strait of

Magellan with orders to fortify both shores of its Atlantic entrance and colonise it. Gamboa's second fleet was indeed formidable. He departed from Spain in September 1581 with twenty-three vessels and 4,600 volunteers (and some children) – according to the marine historian Jean-René Vanney. Two and a half years later, in February 1584, when they arrived at the Atlantic entrance to the strait 4,200 volunteers had deserted or died along the way; only about 400 volunteers remained in five of the original twenty-three vessels. A few months later, Sarmiento departed for Spain, assuring the surviving 400 that he would return to aid them, but he never did. Though not intentionally, he left them to perish on the shores of Magellan Strait. Three years passed when, in 1587, Thomas Cavendish, an English buccaneer, rescued a certain Tomé Hernández, one of the eighteen or twenty who were then still alive. The others refused to be rescued by Cavendish, an "English dog." Tomé's story of this disaster was published some thirty years afterwards.¹⁴ Sarmiento de Gamboa's monument of bad luck and mismanagement culminated with the suffering and death by starvation of all but one of the 400 survivors. I found no information concerning contacts these survivors probably had with the Alakaluf living there, though probably they were not friendly, because the 400 survivors had not learned from them how to avoid starvation.

A "Sinister Cliff"

Following Sarmiento's incredible fiasco, Isaac Le Maire, a wealthy merchant of the Netherlands, entered history. He was searching for a free passage to the Pacific, so that his ships might trade in the Far East with the Spice Islands (Indonesia) for their precious cloves, peppers and incense, which were in great demand in Europe. Issac was not like Drake; he only gambled his fortune. He stayed home. He felt certain that the Magellan Strait was not the only passage through America, that there was another water route to the Pacific. He may have seen a map suggesting its existence.

Issac equipped two ships, the *Eendracht* (Harmony) and the smaller *Hoorn*, named for one of the main ports of the Netherlands. He engaged his son Jacques and Admiral Willem C. Schouten, a navigator of great experience, to command his expedition.¹⁵ The *Hoorn* was destroyed by fire on 18 December 1615, in a bay in southern Patagonia (now Argentina). The crew survived, so on they sailed on the *Eendracht*. Five weeks later, on 24 January 1616, they passed the Atlantic entrance to the Magellan Strait, where Drake had dared to enter. They continued on where no European ship had ever ventured, along the Atlantic coast of the largest island of Tierra del Fuego (later known as the Isla Grande). That very day they sighted an opening beyond the Isla Grande and veered into what was to be named the Strait of Le Maire. On their right they saw the tip of the Isla Grande and on their left an island they called Statenland to honour the governing body, the States General of the Netherlands, which was supporting their expedition. They may have imagined that it was a island off the coast of *Terra Australis Incognita*, which they could not see.

As the little Dutch ship made its way through the Le Maire Strait, neither Schouten nor Le Maire knew for sure where they were heading. Could this be the passage to the Pacific Ocean they were seeking, or were they going straight into *Terra Australis Incognita*? The sailors may have feared that they were going right off the edge of the earth. As they navigated this strait, they saw no signs of human life but were amazed by the great flocks of penguins and the "thousands" of whales. On 29 January they reached a "sinister cliff," at the southernmost extremity of the earth then known. They must have rejoiced when they viewed the endless span of the great Pacific they were seeking. They had discovered a second water route from Europe through America to the Pacific, and Spain's monopoly of a water route to the Pacific was shattered forever. They named the sinister cliff *Cape Hoorn* to honour Schouten's birthplace, the port town Hoorn, whose citizens had helped finance the expedition.

The Magellan Strait and the Cape Horn route will prove to be the only viable water passages through the American continent, linking the two great oceans, until the Panama Canal was constructed three centuries later. Although Drake had navigated the Magellan Strait in only sixteen days, it was a hazardous route for sailing ships, especially its western section "the narrowest, most devious, most circuitous of all the straits connecting two great bodies of water."[16]

The Cape Horn route and other routes that skirt the cape further south, despite their terrifying reputation, were preferred for almost 250 years, until steamships made the Magellan Strait more navigable. The Cape Horn routes were favoured for so long because they offered much more "sea room" and normally required less time to traverse than the Magellan Strait. Schouten's lament of "much trouble, misery and disease" while sailing around the "sinister cliff" fell on deaf ears.

Having passed Cape Horn, in 1616, the *Endracht* entered the vast uncharted Pacific and eventually reached the Spice Islands, the later city of Batavia on the island of Java (near Jakarta, now the capital of Indonesia).

Other Dutchmen of the East India Company had established a port of trade called Batavia years before, coming from the other direction, skirting the Cape of Good Hope, the southern tip of Africa.

The Dutch governor-general of Batavia accused Le Maire and Schouten of trespassing on the Dutch East India Company's territory, probably because theirs was a private enterprise, not associated with the Netherlands' government. He even locked them in irons, confiscated their ship, and had the audacity to send them back to Holland as prisoners. Jacques Le Maire died on the way home, at the age of thirty-one, possibly of chagrin due to this outrageous treatment. Schouten did arrive back home, where Isaac Le Maire managed to free him and to compel the Dutch East India Company to return his ship and pay damages.[17]

The Le Maire family gained "everlasting" renown for the strait named in their honour, as did Port Hoorn in the Netherlands. Although the Dutch did not encounter the Yamana natives in 1616, this voyage marks the beginning of European traffic through their territory.

The "Good Success Indians"

Despite Sarmiento's human and political disasters, Spain planned to take possession of the Cape Horn route, again by fortifying the entrance to a strait, this time the Le Maire Strait. With hardly a second thought, in 1619, the Spanish Crown dispatched two caravels (small sailing vessels with two or three masts) manned by two brothers whose last name was Nodal. Early the following year, while passing through the still uncharted Le Maire Strait, the caravels pulled into "a very good bay" that the brothers named Good Success, in honour of one of their vessels, *Nuestra Señora de Buen Suceso* (Our Lady of Good Success). And good success it was for them, and for future navigators, that such a refuge exists midway through these dangerous waters. The Nodal brothers soon realised that it would be impossible to fortify the entrance to this strait. They were impressed by the abundance of fat sardines and seals in and along the strait.

While the Nodal crew was loading water from the river that flows into Good Success Bay "fifteen of the natives came down to the water place shouting *a a a...*," stretching their arms toward the strangers while tossing their headbands of white feathers in the air. European contact had begun with these natives, later known as the Haush. They seemed not to take offence at the strangers landing in their country. "Laying down their arms, they assisted them in wooding and watering, without betraying the least distrust." This welcome given by the Haush is truly amazing, because these Spaniards were the first outsiders they had ever seen. Surely they had never imagined the existence of such heavily bearded men, clad so strangely from head to foot, speaking such a curious lisping language. Nor had the Nodal brothers and their crew ever seen such hairless faces "covered with a whitish clay" and bodies painted red, such cloaks of "sheep" (guanaco) skin, such robust men sporting leather girdles, "pretty" shell bracelets, and crowns made of the down of feathers of sea birds. "They seemed to be of a docile disposition; for, in the short time the Spaniards stayed there, they had taught several of them to repeat the Lord's prayer.... Their arms were bows and arrows headed with sharp flints, and stone knives." They declined to taste the "European provisions" they were offered and preferred to eat their own herb, "which had a bitter taste" and a yellow flower, "which they find in abundance on the shore." Their camp was very large, if, as the Nodal brothers reported, it really consisted "of fifty huts, made up with stakes, and covered with reeds." Never since, through four centuries, has such a large number of huts been mentioned for any Fuegian settlement.[18] The Haush will continue to welcome strangers during the coming centuries, despite the great damage the British and Yankee fishermen will do to their resources of seals and whales (Chapter 2).

While inspecting the Spaniards' clothes, the Haush pointed to their red apparel, indicating that they wished to be given a piece or two of that attractive cloth, but they had to be satisfied with glass beads. The Spaniards noticed that the Haush were good runners. But the Haush apparently did not trust the Spaniards "much." In this they were perceptive because the Nodal brothers later wrote that they had considered capturing several of these "savages" but had given up the idea.

The Haush were land-bound, tireless hikers and perhaps too peaceful. They had been "masters of their destiny," inhabitants of most of the largest island in Tierra del Fuego, the Isla Grande, until they were confined to the "boot" of the island by the more aggressive Selk'nam, the so-called Onas. This is an assumption based mainly on the many place names of Haush origin in the territory occupied by the Selk'nam and on my own research.[19]

After the brothers departed from Good Success Bay, they discovered a group of rocky islets located sixty miles (111 kilometres) southwest of Cape Horn and named them for Diego Ramírez, their cartographer. Human beings have never inhabited these islets (at 56°30′ south latitude), but the seals favoured them until British and Yankee commercial fisheries almost exterminated them (Chapter 2).

The Nodal expedition then sailed up the Pacific coast and through the Magellan Strait to its Atlantic exit. When the brothers reported to home base, the Crown became convinced that it was impossible to fortify the entrance to Le Maire Strait and that the Cape Horn route would remain a challenge.

The Dutch Struggle for World Domination

This seventeenth century was an age of conquest no longer by Spain or Portugal and not yet by England but by the Netherlands. It was also an age of commerce. The free route via Cape Horn led to the Spice Islands, but more threatening to Spain, it led to the vast west coast of South America, to the great riches of the newly conquered Inca empire. When the truce between Spain and the Netherlands, which had lasted twelve years, terminated in 1621, the governing body of the United Provinces of the Netherlands consolidated the Dutch East India Company, its powerful commercial enterprise, which had so severely punished Le Maire and Schouten in 1616. The appropriation of the Spanish possession of Peru was only one of the Netherlands' great projects.

Another of their great projects was to consolidate and expand their presence in North America. By 1624, they had purchased an island from the native Indians – smaller than that which borders the Le Maire Strait, and also named it Statenland (Staten Island, which faces the Statue of Liberty across the Bay of New York, is joined to Brooklyn by a bridge). Two years later they purchased Manhattan Island (twelve and a half miles long and two and a half miles wide) from the natives for pockets full of trinkets valued at twenty-four dollars, according to legend. If true, the Indians were completely deceived, tricked. They certainly had not the slightest awareness that they could sell or were selling their island.

The Dutch merchants of the Netherlands had wild dreams, a grand strategy for world dominion: beat the English in the "race" to colonise America, take over their trade routes, monopolise the lucrative European commerce in spices, defeat Spain's armada in Peru, quite a "menu" for a tiny republic that had so recently won its freedom from Spain. Forty years and two wars later, in 1664, the British finally expelled the Dutch from Manhattan Island. In 1623, however, the Dutch prospects looked very promising.

The Dutch Encounter Natives

Meanwhile the Dutch were implementing another facet of their grand project; crush the Spanish armada stationed on the Peruvian coast, solicit the support of the Indians and the African slaves, and with their help reconquer Peru. They assembled an extraordinary fleet: eleven war vessels armed with nearly 300 cannons, manned by crews totalling 1,637 men. This expedition proved to be "the most important by far that ever was undertaken into those parts by the Dutch."[20] The squadron was named the Nassau Fleet to honour the Count of Nassau, Prince of Orange, the *stadholder* (chief of state) of the United Provinces of the Netherlands. He was the principal backer of the expedition. It was also financed by most of the provinces of the Republic (now known as Holland). Spain had to be defeated before "she" drained Peru of its riches.

The Nassau Fleet was put under the command Admiral Jacques L'Hermite in consideration of his long experience with the Dutch East India Company. Valentin Jansz served as the chief pilot because he had recently navigated the "Hoorn" area with the Nodal brothers.[21]

In April 1623, this enormous fleet sailed from Goree Bay (South Holland) and months later passed safely through the Le Maire Strait. Shortly thereafter, the fleet was battered by snow, hail and wind for an entire week. Finally, in February 1624, having flanked Cape Horn, the ships veered "inland" and sailed along an island later named Hermite. The commander was looking for a bay large enough to anchor his eleven vessels and supply his crews with drinking water and his ships with firewood in preparation for the long voyage up the coast of Chile to Peru. He located a spacious bay, afterwards named Nassau, and signalled to the officers of his other ships to cast anchors. Then he sighted a small bay on the coast of Nassau Bay, possibly on 18 February 1624 which was named Schapenham (for the vice-admiral, the second in command). It seemed to be the best place to refurbish the fleet. So a few days later, on 22 February, nineteen unarmed sailors from one of his ships, the *Arent* (Eagle), were sent ashore in shallops (light boats) to fetch water and firewood. The sailors were conversing amicably by signs with the "savages" (the Yamana) near the watering place, on the shore of the bay, when a storm broke and obliged them to remain there through the night.

The next day, when the bad weather cleared, the crew of the *Arent* saw no sign of their nineteen comrades. The captain of the *Arent*, probably worried, sent some of his crew to aid them. They must have been aghast when they landed and saw five dead bodies of their shipmates strewn on the shore. Of the nineteen who had been marooned, only two were alive, and not harmed. Perhaps they had hidden in the bushes; in any case, the natives had spared them. The two were probably still horror-stricken when they told their shipmates what had happened.

The Savages had come down upon them, as soon as it grew dark, and had knocked seventeen on the head, with their slings and wooden clubs; which yet was the more easy for them to do, since none of these poor men had any arms. Yet none of the seamen had offered the least injury or insult to these Savages.

The five corpses were identified, though not by name, as the pilot, two regular seamen and two boys. The two survivors and the rescuers suspected cannibalism, because the pilot's corpse was "strangely mangled" and the others cut into quarters. Five were dead on the shore and two were alive, but where were the other twelve? "It was supposed" that the "savages" had carried them off to eat them: no trace of them was ever reported.

This engraving should be looked at closely. Five ships of L'Hermite's squadron are shown in the background, in Nassau Bay; in front is a small boat (perhaps of the rescuers from the *Arent*). In the right foreground a Yamana family is depicted; at the left, natives are gathering shellfish while others are paddling in three canoes. Above left along the coast, the Yamana are massacring the Dutch sailors with spears and bows and arrows; two natives are twisting the corpse of a cadaver, as if beginning to tear it to pieces; and three others are dragging dead seamen as if taking them to the huts beyond to be eaten. On the shore three sailors attempt escape. Above, along the coast, a structure supports a canoe being made by the Yamana. Recall that this engraving, like the many others made in Bry's studio in the Netherlands, was inspired by the accounts of the expedition; therefore it shows the natives as cannibals.

As to their manners, they [the Yamana] are rather beasts than men; for they tear human bodies to pieces, and eat the flesh, raw and bloody as it is. There is not the least spark of religion or policy to be observed amongst them. On the contrary, they are, in every respect, brutal; in so much that, if any have occasion to make water, they let fly against any one that is near them, if he does not get out of their way.[22]

The last lines are surely meant to highlight their brutal nature. Thus the Yamana entered history as cannibals, a reputation that will last for almost two and a half centuries.

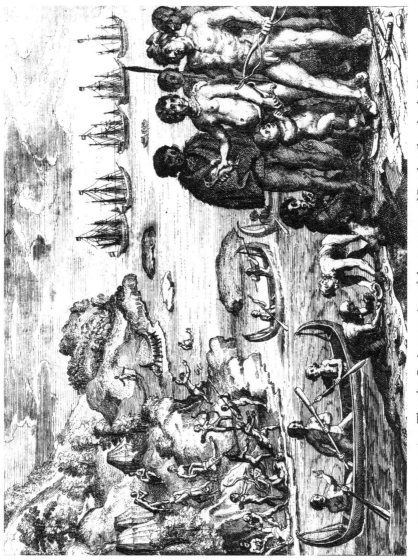

FIGURE 1.1. 1624: Theodor Bry's engraving of the massacre of Dutch sailors by the Yamana.

The Dutch Meet Other Yamanas

L'Hermite sent Vice-Admiral Schapenham, with twenty men in a tender (60 tones) called *Windhond* (Greyhound), to explore the area further north, up Nassau Bay, before the massacre, or a day or so after it occurred (22 or 25 February).[23] These were the first Europeans known to venture into that area of Navarino Island (called Navarine in English, though better known in Spanish as Navarino), whose original name was Wulla.[24] At first they sighted smoke, in a bay they called Windhond (now Grandi Sound), near the southwestern corner of Navarino Island, which is almost square.[25] The Dutchmen interpreted the fire as a welcome signal and went to meet the natives, communicating by gestures with their "hosts," who must have wondered from where such strange creatures had come or dropped down from.

These natives (also Yamanas) were said to be very strong, well proportioned, about the same height as the Europeans (who were shorter then) and "as fair as any in Europe." Their "very good" teeth were as sharp as "the edge of a knife" and their thick black hair was kept long "to make them more frightful." The men wore sealskins (*chien marin*) on their shoulders and the women wore similar skins around their waists, as well as shell necklaces. Some of the men were painted half red and half white; others were entirely red except for their waists, which were painted white. The Dutch were amazed that they were nearly naked in this cold climate. They noticed their tepee shaped huts (later called wigwams) made of tree trunks, the floors two or three feet under ground and the exteriors packed over with mud to afford greater protection from the wind and cold.[26]

The explorers inspected the natives' weapons: bows and arrows, long javelins with sharp bone points, "great wooden clubs," slings and very sharp stone knives, besides "stone hooks" for fishing.[27] "They are never without their arms in their hands, because they are always at war among themselves." Despite the herds of "cows" (guanacos) on the island, no meat was offered to the strangers. The Dutch thought they were "always at war" because of their weapons and the massacre of seventeen seamen that had occurred before this report was written. The natives' canoes commanded their special attention:

Their canoes are truly remarkable. They strip one of the largest trees of all its bark and bend it skilfully, sewing the strips in certain places, *giving it the shape of a Venetian gondola*. To construct them in this manner, they place the bark on special logs in a manner similar to that employed in the shipyards of Holland [as shown in Bry's engraving in Figure 1.1].... These canoes measure 10, 12, 14, 16 feet long and approximately two feet wide. Seven or eight men can sit comfortably in them and they can navigate as fast as a launch with oars.[28]

Never again would a Fuegian canoe be compared to a Venetian gondola. Note that the men paddled the canoes. Later, one or two women did the paddling except when speed was required or when the women tired.

The "Nonperfectible Canoe"

The Navarino canoes of 1624 were probably "nonperfectible," the very best ever made by the Yamana, which could be made with the materials available. The Fuegian canoes were nearly perfect, although, like the sophisticated machinery today, not infallible. Any invention may ultimately exhaust its possibilities for improvement and become nonperfectible though not perfect. The canoe-makers had achieved this relative state of perfection probably sometime after the Yamana reached the area (6,000 years ago), when countless minds struggled to solve the problems involved with their need for such a vehicle, the materials available, and the changing environment in which they lived.[29]

As late as 1891, the missionary John Lawrence commented on the superiority of the Yahgan (Yamana) canoe over the missionaries' sailboats for navigating in open waters during squalls.[30] In the nineteenth century, the construction of a canoe was a family affair, so not all were top quality. Some canoe makers had less ability than others, or the canoe was made in haste, or had to be made with the inferior material available. Archaeologists have deduced that a bark canoe (of the *Nothofagus* beech) was probably already used when the Yamana settled along Beagle Channel some 6,000 years ago.[31] But just when this canoe was perfected may never be known.

The Yamana canoes of 1624 were said to resemble the (Alakaluf) canoe, which Drake and Fletcher had so admired in August 1578 on the north shore of Magellan Strait. Fletcher reported that this canoe was fit "for the pleasure of some great and noble personage, yea, of some prince."[32]

The Alakaluf bark canoes were larger than those of the Yamana and may have been more sturdy because they were used to navigate along the dangerous outer islands. The Yamana were more confined to the inner channels, although they navigated the Cape Horn area and the equally dangerous Le Maire Strait.

The first and last time the Alakaluf canoe was thought to delight princes was in 1578, and only once, in 1624, was the Yahgan canoe compared to a Venetian gondola.

FIGURE 1.2. A Yamana family in their canoe: note the fire burning in the middle of the canoe. Painting by Eduardo Armstrong from Barros y Armstrong (1975). Courtesy of the Estate of Eduardo Armstrong, Santiago, Chile.

An Archaeologist Explores a Dutch Site

In 1991, a French archaeologist Dominique Legoupil and her team surveyed the bay where the Dutch first met the Navarino natives, now identified on the Chilean maps as Seno (Sound) Grandi, on the southwestern shore of Navarino Island. They located a total of forty-three sites there and further south in the area near Cape Horn. The earliest material they found was dated at about 4,000 BC.[33] This is very revealing though not unexpected, as the earliest finds along Beagle Channel, also Yamana territory, show approximately the same date.[34]

In 1987 Grandi Bay impressed me as the archaeologist's wonderland. There were (and hopefully still are) large shell mounds almost everywhere on the shores of the many forested islets inside the bay. Apparently the area is well protected from the prevailing winds. I spotted the Dutch "cows," the guanacos, which were still roaming along the shore.

The Nassau Fleet Sails On

I return now to February 1624. Following the encounter with the vigorous Yamana on the southwestern "corner" of Navarino Island, Schapenham and his crew continued along its southern coast. At its southeastern corner they crossed a stretch of sheltered water to a much smaller island, later called Lennox. They named this stretch of water Goree Road for the port town in Holland from which the Nassau expedition had sailed. It will become famous during later centuries as the best anchorage and resting place of the entire Cape Horn area. On Lennox Island, the Dutch sighted other "savages" who were painted all black, but they had little else to say about them and returned to their fleet that same day, apparently on 25 February.[35]

Once the fleet of eleven vessels was reunited in Nassau Bay, and supposedly the five corpses were buried with honours nearby, its departure was delayed by adverse weather until early March 1624. A month later, the fleet reached the two Juan Fernández Islands, opposite central Chile, where the crews peacefully replenished their supplies of water and firewood (no natives there). Then, like Drake, they plundered coastal settlements of Chile and Peru, attacking Spanish ships along the way. To begin to "reconquer" Peru, in early May they blockaded Callao, the port of Lima, where the Spanish Viceroy Diego Fernández de Córdoba had assembled the "whole force of Peru." After several months of sea battles near Callao, the Dutch decided to give up. The enemy was too strong. The viceroy had disarmed the Indians, whom he did not trust, but had organised a company of "free Negroes" to defend the Spanish Crown. They were said to have distinguished themselves by their attachment to their masters, to be proud of their liberty but afraid that they might become slaves again once they were no longer needed to defend the crown.

In June 1624, during the blockade of Callao, L'Hermite died of sickness. Once the battle was given up, Schapenham, the new commander, conducted the fleet up the coast of South America. The crews found easy victims in the port of Guayaquil, Ecuador. They burned most of their booty because they couldn't fit it in their ships; they also killed a hundred men for good measure. Later on they tarried for two months in Acapulco, attacking the Spaniards and plundering whatever was nearby. Having crossed the Pacific, they spent five months on an island near Java, probably storing up spices. Late in 1625 they sailed on to Batavia, the famous Dutch port of trade for spices where Schapenham died and the fleet was dismantled. In July 1626, some of the original vessels returned to the Netherlands; others were left in Batavia for the benefit of the Dutch East India Company. Thus the Netherlands squandered its military might on prolonged and useless battles in Peru. The wealth gained by plundering towns and ships must have been a pitiful compensation for this fleet, "the most important by far that ever was undertaken into those parts by the Dutch."[36] The English will repeat this beautiful fiasco in 1741, during their attempt to "reconquer" Peru (see below).

But Why Did the Yamana Kill the Dutch Sailors?

Were the natives terrified when they saw that mass of immense "canoes" nearby? Did they panic when confronted with such strangely clad, hairy-faced men, speaking sounds never heard before? Whether or not the Yamana ate twelve of the seventeen men they killed will probably never be documented, though it may have happened. L'Hermite's crews were convinced that the men had been eaten because they found no trace of them and because the five cadavers lying on the shore had been mutilated, as if cut up to serve as meat. Two and a half centuries later, the missionaries will strongly deny that the Yamana were cannibals, despite comments that convinced Fitz-Roy and Darwin that they "really" were (Chapters 4 and 5).

According to reliable evidence the Yamana were not cannibals, though they may have eaten those twelve Dutch seamen. Obviously there is a distinction to be made between isolated acts of cannibalism and characterising an entire people as such. If this distinction is not understood, virtually all the nations in the world today should be called cannibalistic simply because such acts have been committed by people in unusual circumstances, as among survivors of shipwrecks and plane crashes. When cannibalism (anthropophagy) becomes accepted behaviour, it almost invariably acquires symbolic meaning and is enacted as a ritual of some sort. Reports of any such symbolism or ritual are entirely lacking in the documents concerning the Yamana, nor has any other incident of possible cannibalism been documented, though hearsay abounded (Chapters 4 and 5).

The captain of the *Beagle*, Robert Fitz-Roy, thought that the massacre of the seventeen Dutch sailors in 1624 may have been revenge for the massacre, in 1599, of other Fuegians by another Dutch expedition, near the entrance to the Magellan Strait.[37]

The Dutch Kill Other Fuegians

"The Dutch were the first to shed the blood of the natives in Tierra del Fuego," according to the Chilean historian Mateo Martinic. Although the Selk'nam (Onas), who were killed, are not the main subject of this book, this episode is inserted here because of Fitz-Roy's suggestion mentioned above. The event began in 1599, when the Dutchman, Admiral Olivier Van Noort, and his men surprised a group of Selk'nam at the Atlantic entrance to Magellan Strait, on its south shore, on Penguin Island, near Cape Orange (now Punta Catalina). Van Noort anchored his ship nearby in order to kill penguins for food.

When the natives saw strangers embarking, they shot arrows at them, threw the dead penguins back into the sea from a cliff as shown in Figure 1.3, and fled into a cave nearby. The Dutch crew pursued them and several were wounded by the arrows, but the crew shot and killed twenty-five or forty Selk'nam. There was one adult survivor, a woman. A short while after the massacre, Van Noort captured six children and continued sailing down the Magellan Strait, toward the Pacific exit. All the children soon died on board his ship. He went ashore near Port Gallant (on the continent, about the middle of the strait), where he must have been astonished to meet fellow Dutch explorers, Captain Sebald De Weert and his crew, who pleaded that they were on the verge of starving. Despite the pleas, Van Noort refused to help his countrymen and sailed on. De Weert somehow managed to sail in the opposite direction, toward the Atlantic exit of the strait. He stopped over near Cape Orange, where Van Noort had recently killed the penguin hunters. There De Veert met the woman survivor who showed him her wounds, inflicted by Van Noort's crew.[38]

By 1624, "this news" may have travelled some 300 miles, from the one survivor of 1599, reached the Yamana in Nassau Bay and incited them to take vengeance against the strangers, as Fitz-Roy assumed. But this seems unlikely. The Yamana may well have been terror-stricken by the Dutch

FIGURE 1.3. 1599: Theodor Bry's engraving of the massacre of Selk'nam by the Dutch.

fleet: if so this may have motivated the massacre and possible cannibalism of the seamen.

Another Route to the Pacific

In 1643, a Dutch fleet of five vessels was about to enter the Le Maire Strait when a violent storm forced its commander, Hendrick Brouwer, to navigate around Staten Island instead of through the strait. As he saw no sign of the coast of *Terra Australis Incognita*, the European cartographers moved their fabled continent a bit further south. Thanks to Brouwer's mishap, the captains of other ships now knew that they could sail below Staten Island, and enter the Pacific south of Cape Horn, and thereby circumnavigate the two dangerous passes (Le Maire Strait and Cape Horn). However, this route was not ideal either, because it approached the turbulent waters of Drake Passage.[39]

By the end of the seventeenth century, the Dutch had given up most of their illusions of world dominion and Spain was having a hard time holding on to its colonies. Meanwhile, merchant ships from Europe were using these southernmost routes to trade in the ports from Chile to Mexico and in Indonesia's Spice Islands. The English buccaneers, filibusters (freebooters), and pirates were still roaming the world, attacking merchant ships and plundering colonies on both sides of America, clearing the path for British commercial expansion. The French were not far behind, though they were less aggressive. Until the advent of the steam engine about 1850, many navigators preferred the longer southern route below Cape Horn, while others still favoured the shorter, more dangerous, passages around Cape Horn and below Staten Island. During the eighteenth century, the sources describe occasional encounters with the Haush in Good Success Bay and the Yamana in the vicinity of Cape Horn. It is very likely that there were far more meetings than those recorded.

The French Arrive

A Jesuit in Good Success Bay

When the French Jesuit Père Labbe and his companions spent five days in Good Success Bay, early November 1711, a "savage" (a Haush) emerged from the nearby forest to see who had arrived. The French made welcoming signs to him, but he immediately positioned his bow and arrow aiming at them, then changed his mind and decided to taste their bread, wine and even their brandy. He spit them all out. The Jesuit was not discouraged and proceeded to show him how to make the sign of the cross, as he draped him with a rosary. When they were about to depart, the "lone savage" let out a loud, plaintive cry, whereupon a woman, curved over by her great age, appeared, leading thirty other "savages" to greet the newcomers. All were dressed in "sea wolf" (fur seal) skins and adorned with their usual seashell necklaces and bracelets. The good Jesuit ended the few lines of his report with this thought: "These people seem quite docile and I believe it would not be difficult to instruct them."[40]

The Yamana Snatch Anything Red

Sieur de Villemarin, from the French port Saint Malo in Brittany, appeared in Good Success Bay two years later.[41] A few canoe natives climbed on board his vessel to see what would be offered. No doubt these were Yamana, as the Haush were strictly a land people. They refused to taste the Sieur's food but were utterly fascinated by anything red. One Yamana was extraordinarily bold:

Spying a red cap on the head of an officer, who came to receive him, [he] snatched it off daringly, and put it on [under] his arm; another, seeing the red comb of a fowl, tore it off to carry away; they would have taken away an officer's red breeches... they appeared robust, better shaped than the Indians of Chili; and the women they had with them handsomer, and all of them great thieves.[42]

It is not surprising that these Yamana "thieves" were in the Strait of Le Maire. They probably paddled there to visit their Haush neighbours or to hunt seals along the coast of the strait.

After the 1624 Massacre

In 1715, Captain Joachin d'Arquisade, a French explorer, and his officers spent a peaceful day with the Yamana in the same bay (Nassau) near where the Dutch sailors had been massacred. Seated around a fire, the Frenchmen conversed by signs with these "savages" (who were painted red) while their children played in the trees. They gave their guests bows, arrows and shell necklaces. The visitors were about to depart when d'Arquisade pointed toward the sun to provoke their reaction. Then they repeated his gesture, a sure indication, the captain decided, that these "poor creatures adored the sun." This rather flimsy hypothesis will occur to the sealer Weddell over a hundred years later (Chapter 2). In 1715, the contact was friendly, perhaps because only one ship appeared in the bay or the Yamana realised by then that they had nothing to fear from such strangers.[43]

A Happy Passage Around the Cape

In 1747 Le Hen Brignon, the captain of another vessel from the French port Saint Malo, sailed through the Le Maire Strait and around Cape Horn during the same season as Anson six years later (see below). He reported: "In fact, few journals tell us of a more happy passage than ours was." His fleet sailed through the Le Maire Strait in only an hour and a half. They "saw vast numbers of sea wolves [fur seals] round our ship. These animals diverted us greatly by their leaping and playing in the water. We also saw many whales." The crew also noticed several huts and smoke along the shore, which they imagined to be either of "savages" or shipwrecked Europeans, but did not bother to inquire. A few days later, having passed the strait, "we had no violent storm, even while we doubled Cape Horn; so far from it, that March 22d... we had a dead calm.... This occasioned a general joy in all the ship's company. *Te Deum* was sung."[44] The Frenchman from Saint Malo proved that the seasons in this part of the world do not always determine the state of the weather. The explorers who were bold enough to come this way had to take the risk. The Yamana were less exposed: they kept close to the shores with an eye on just where they could find shelter if a storm should strike.

French merchants and especially fishermen from Saint Malo were very active in this part of the world, since the expedition of Beauchesne (1698–1701). But the French didn't take advantage of their economic priority in the region (see below).

The English Venture Where the Dutch Had Failed

Following Drake, the "sea hawks" (pirates and filibusters, mostly English) continued harassing and robbing the Spanish towns and ships along the Pacific coast. Finally, the British decided, in 1740, to reconquer Peru, to succeed where the Dutch had failed. Admiral George Anson was selected for the purpose. Like L'Hermite's squadron in 1624, Anson's consisted of eleven ships (six warships, armed with 236 cannons and five smaller supply ships). Anson's crew of 1,410 men was also nearly the same in number as L'Hermite's, though its quality was not. Anson had to accept some invalids over sixty years old from Chelsea Hospital, who had to be carried on board. On 18 September 1740, this "grand armada" departed. Seven months later, on an unusually calm day in March 1741, the eleven vessels were moving out of Le Maire Strait when violent winds and currents suddenly struck them with terrifying velocity. Unrelenting storms, gales and squalls continued for almost three months. This was certainly some of the most violent and prolonged tempestuous weather recorded in the history of the area though not the only one (Chapter 5). The fleet slowly made its way, circled widely below Cape Horn, and then turned north, up the Pacific coast of Chile. During these persistent storms, four of Anson's warships sank and another, the *Wager*, was wrecked. Lord Byron, the poet's grandfather, survived the wreck, and began his famous adventures among the Alakaluf.[45] When Anson's squadron reached the Juan Fernández Islands (opposite central Chile), over half the crew, more than 800 men had been swept into the sea or perished from scurvy and exhaustion.[46] This may have been one of the highest noncombat death tolls suffered by the British Navy during the eighteenth century, though Spain's record is higher (see below).

Anson's Spanish adversary was José Pizarro, who may have been a descendant of the conquerer of Peru. Although his squadron (five warships and one *patache*, a supply ship), was smaller than Anson's, his crew was twice the size (over 3,000 men). In 1740, Pizarro set out to confront his enemy. Following a series of mishaps, he eventually ran into the same fierce weather as Anson had. The latter reported that the overwhelming storms that struck Pizarro's fleet had "diminished the naval power of Spain by about 3,000 hands (the flower of the sailors) and by four considerable ships of war and a patache."[47]

If Anson's figure is reliable, a total of nearly 3,800 men (including Anson's 800) were sacrificed during these misadventures, without a shot being fired! The enemies never met. Pizarro and his survivors struggled back to home base in their remaining vessel, while Anson sailed on, also with just one main vessel but on to riches and glory. In the Philippines he plundered a Spanish galleon, the *Covadonga*, whose cargo sold for 400,000 pounds, a great fortune in any epoch.[48] Anson and his men were probably happy to be alive when they arrived back home, all the more so when they were rewarded with generous portions of their "ill-gotten gains."

The British public avidly read the reports of Anson's three months of terrifying storms, the frightful deaths and suffering of his crew and of Byron's six years of distress and adventure following his shipwreck. If the

Yamana were sitting on top of Cape Horn waiting for the next act, they did well to keep their seats.

Captain Cook: A New Era

Captain James Cook was the first navigator known to history who crossed the Antarctic Circle (which is at 66°32′ south latitude). He crossed it three times. These great achievements occurred during his second voyage, in the *Resolution*. He went farthest south off New Zealand on 30 January 1774, at 71°10′ south latitude. John C. Beaglehole (a name easy to remember), Cook's most complete and authoritative biographer, explained that at the moment of this crossing, Cook "had reached the highest of his own latitudes, far beyond that which any other sailor had ever attempted. . . . Here progress was stopped, finally and absolutely, by an immense field of ice, solid and forbidding."[49]

Cook took the risks of confronting immense fields of ice because his plan for this second voyage "was directed at solving the problem of the Great South Land [*Terra Australis Incognita*] at the southernmost possible latitude."[50] Beaglehole explained why this fable was so stubborn and why the European cartographers were still convinced that its existence was an undisputed fact.

Symmetry demanded it [the *Terra Australis Incognita*], the balance of the earth demanded it – for in the absence of this tremendous mass of land, what, asked Mercator [an eminent cartographer], was there to prevent the world from toppling over to destruction amidst the stars? [given the masses of land at a comparable latitude north] The great southern continent was to most thinkers of the time more than mere knowledge founded on discovery and experience – it was a feeling, a tradition, a logical and now even a theological necessity, a compelling and inescapable mathematical certitude. Its discovery must come.[51]

Cook proved that these astounding statements were false. No trace of such a "continent" existed. Even his contemporary, the famous cartographer Alexander Dalrymple (1737–1808), had insisted that this enormous southern continent had to exist. Daniel J. Boorstin, in his excellent history of discoveries, wrote that the aristocratic Dalrymple "considered himself the leading living authority on the uncharted continent," and had aspired to command the expedition that was finally given to "a little-known non-commissioned officer named James Cook."[52] Ironically, the latter shattered the former's tightly reasoned conviction. Cook's second voyage has tremendous significance, if only because he supplied the evidence that this age-old paradigm of a *Terra Australis Incognita* was false, thereby transforming the image of the earth and basing it on first-hand knowledge. Thus began a "new era" in geophysics. The real continent, the Antarctica, was yet to be discovered (Chapter 6).

The quotation from Edwin Mickleburg follows because it brilliantly depicts another new era inaugurated by Cook: "It was Cook who established the process whereby Europe would come to dominate the rest of the world, politically, economically and culturally. Apart from their intrinsic geographical and scientific achievements . . . it was the fate of Cook . . . to be the man who would open the way for the onslaught." He added that Cook "was one of the last to see the world in a state of natural balance."[53] His discoveries, and the European colonisation, imperialism and the religious missions that followed threw that "world" out of balance, the world of the natives of the Pacific islands, Australia, New Zealand, Tasmania, and Tierra del Fuego.

Cook's second ship, the *Adventure*, was separated from the *Resolution* during a storm off New Zealand in October 1774. Cook searched for the vessel but to no avail. So in November 1774, he departed from New Zealand into the Pacific, heading toward the entrance to the Magellan Strait. From there he planned to sail down the Pacific coast of Tierra del Fuego and round Cape Horn, pass through the Le Maire Strait, and finally home. He explained why he chose this route. "As the world has but a very imperfect knowledge of this Coast, I thought the Coasting it would be of more advantage to both Navigation and Geography than any thing I could expect to find in a higher latitude."[54]

During three dreary, calm, landless weeks he was on a route "never traversed by a ship before." Captain Cook crossed the Pacific and finally reached the tip of Desolation Island, at the entrance to Magellan Strait, on 17 December 1774.[55]

Captain Cook Meets the Fuegians Again

He had met the Fuegians (the Haush) at Good Success Bay, along the Le Maire Strait in January 1769, during his first voyage. Now, in December 1774, he turned south from the Pacific entrance (or exit) of Magellan Strait, sailing for two days along the Pacific rim of Tierra del Fuego. Passing an island, later named Basket (Chapter 3), he gave the locality the not very original name of Desolation Cape because "near it commenced the most desolate and barren Country I ever saw." Desolation Cape was not far from Desolate Bay, where Drake had probably first seen the Fuegians nearly 200 years earlier. These two "desolations" are not to be confused with Desolation Island mentioned above, at the Pacific entrance to the Magellan Strait. On he sailed. As he viewed the mountains beyond Desolate Bay (later called the Cordillera of Darwin), he wrote yet again that they were "the most desolate" of any he had ever seen.[56]

He continued along the outer islands. Soon the high cliff of Waterman Island came into view. It reminded him of the cathedral tower of York, his hometown, so he named it York Minster (Chapter 3). The crew relaxed for an entire week, secure in a pleasant harbour on the inner shore of Waterman Island, facing Christmas Sound, which Cook named for that day of 1774 summer in the southern latitudes. While Cook's crew were busy preparing the Christmas feast, natives appeared. But the crew's enthusiasm was elsewhere, greatly enhanced by the abundance of ducks, cormorants (called shags) and geese, to be served as pies; the excellent mussels gathered on the rocks; and the delicious wild celery nearby, all this to be accompanied by the bottles of Madeira wine waiting in the hold. Cook boasted, "our friends in England did not, perhaps, celebrate Christmas more cheerfully than we did."

While Cook was shooting geese on Goose Island (so named then), natives in nine canoes paddled up to the ship to take a look at the strangers. He didn't see them that day, but he was told that they seemed acquainted with Europeans. He did see them on Christmas Day, when "they made us another visit; I found them to be of the same Nation as I had formerly [in 1769] in Success Bay and the same which M. Bougainville distinguishes [along the Magellan Strait] by the name of Pecheras, a word which these had on every occasion in their mouths. They are a little, ugly, half-starved beardless Race. . . . " Here Cook was mistaken: the natives he had encountered in Good Success Bay were the Haush, not the Alakaluf, though he correctly referred to the Alakaluf as the Pecheras Indians, who inhabited the coasts of Magellan Strait.[57] The Christmas Sound natives were probably also Alakaluf. They may have been little and beardless, and Cook thought them ugly, but why "half-starved" amid such an abundance of fowl, mussels, fish, seals, and celery?

Most of them were "almost naked," clad in sealskins, which covered their shoulders, while others wore cloaks of two or three skins sewn together that reached to their knees. The women covered their "privates" with a flap of the same. Two young children were "as naked as they were born; thus they are inured from their infancy to Cold and hardships." While he was observing their bows, arrows and harpoons with boneheads, used to kill seals and fish, he wondered if they also killed

FIGURE 1.4. Seal hunting: note the scanty clothing. Painting by Eduardo Armstrong from Barros y Armstrong (1975). Courtesy of the Estate of Eduardo Armstrong, Santiago, Chile.

whales with the harpoons. He was the first to report on canoes having sails made of large seal hides.[58] But soon the festive dinner was on Cook's mind. The natives, having already left the ship, did "not wait to partake of our Christmas Cheer, indeed I believe no one invited them, and for good reasons, for their dirty persons and the stench they carried about them was enough to spoil any man's appetite."[59]

Cook was less disapproving when they returned after the feast. "It was a Cold evening and distressing to see them stand trembling and naked on the deck and I could do no less than give them some Baize and old Canvas to cover themselves." When he ordered that baize (biscuits) be given them, he commented: "I did not observe that they were so fond of it as I have heard said" and added in a note "but this might be owing to the badness of it. . . . " They did not accept his rotten biscuits, but old canvases pleased them, and later they gave sealskin cloaks in return. Cook wondered why they didn't dress more warmly, line their sealskin cloaks with skins and feathers of the aquatic birds and make them larger.[60] Such large, bulky cloaks would have been too cumbersome for the women while paddling and for the men while harpooning seals from a canoe or a coast as seen in this figure.

The anthropologist Robert Lowie's text, quoted here, concerns the Yahgan (Yamana) and applies equally well to the Alakaluf. "A Yahgan does not expect to be kept warm by his skin cape; for that end he relies upon his fire, which is truly indispensable, and on the grease he applies to his body in exceptionally cold weather."[61]

Captain Cook ended his comments with more unflattering remarks.

In short, of all the Nations I have seen the Pecheras [Alakaluf] are certainly the most wretched. They are doomed to live in one of the most inhospitable climates in the world, without having sagacity enough to provide themselves with such necessaries as may render life convenient. . . . in short one sees nothing about them that is not disgusting in the highest degree. . . . [62]

Beaglehole, despite his great admiration for Cook, contested this passage, by quoting Darwin in defence of the natives, to the effect that there was no reason to believe that the Fuegians had decreased in number; "therefore we must suppose that they enjoy a sufficient share of happiness . . . to render life worth living." Surprising as it may seem to some readers, this is not the only time Darwin is quoted in defence of the Fuegians (the Yamana and the Alakaluf).

Young Georg

The Admiralty had engaged the professional naturalist John Reinhold Forster who, despite his wide acclaim, was also known as "a pedantic German scholar. . . . " He was allowed to be accompanied by his twenty-year-old son, Georg.[63] Beaglehole considered this appointment to be "one of the Admiralty's vast mistakes . . . though he [the elder Forster] had the virtues of learning and acuteness . . . he was less fitted than no man was ever [to accompany Cook] by physical or mental constitution." This was to prove a rather trying "mistake" for the captain and his crew, given the long duration of this voyage (1772–75). Georg, though young, was said to be "brilliantly gifted, serious, intellectually alive, romantic."[64] He seemed to merit this flattery despite his less dignified qualities (see below).

The elder Forster treated his readers to twenty-five pages on the beauties of the civilised nations and their equally civilised citizens, whom he contrasted to the wretched, degenerate, miserable, and forlorn "outcasts" of Christmas Sound. However, his opinion of them proves to be less vehement than his son's. Papa Forster even praised these "wretched outcasts" for their workmanship, as for instance he stated that: " . . . the poles, to which they fix their bone shell-hooks, are ten or twelve feet long, perfectly strait, smooth and octangular, which, in my opinion, evidently proves their skill in shaping wood; the same observation may be applied in regard to their clothing...."[65]

In contrast to his father, Georg became an adamant critic of the natives even though, the day after Christmas, he was "glad" to see them at first, when four canoes approached the ship, each carrying five to eight persons, and the crew beckoned them to board the ship. But when they did climb on board, Georg changed his mind. He was put out because they failed to show any signs of being pleased. "The whole assemblage of their features formed the most loathsome picture of misery and wretchedness to which human nature can possibly be reduced." The women were as "uncouth and ugly" as the men. Besides the pieces of sealskin tied around their waists, they wore shell necklaces and "bonnets" of goosequill feathers that occasionally stood upright, reminding Georg of the French headdresses of the seventeenth century. (A rather elegant attire, I suggest, though Georg would not have agreed.) In return for glass beads, the natives gave the crew "very small, ill-shaped bows," a "wretched irregular" arrowhead of black slate, and "ragged sealskins." Apparently the Alakaluf gave them their wornout clothes and useless weapons. He decided that these natives demonstrated "the strangest compound of stupidity, indifference and inactivity." He was annoyed because they failed to comprehend the signs he made to communicate with them, signs that, as he wrote later, "the most wretched nation in the South Sea" had easily understood. What is more, they were "too stupid, too indolent or too wretchedly destitute of means to guard against the inclemency." His national pride was offended because they were "totally insensible of the superiority of our situation, and did not once, with a single gesture, express their admiration of the ship, and its many great and remarkable objects." Then he became really indignant: "If ever the pre-eminence of a civilised life over that of the savage could have been reasonably disputed, we might, from the bare contemplation of these miserable people, draw the most striking conclusions in favour of our superior happiness."

But then he turned inward, despairing that despite the great advantages that heaven bestowed on "our civilised communities ... [are] stained with vices and enormities...." But again he was disgusted by the natives' "filthy habit" of consuming the oily and "vile blubber" of seals, even though they offered to share them with the sailors. He was not impressed by this generous offer, though he did grant that these fatty morsels fortified them against the cold. Repelled as he was by their "insupportable rank stench," he found it had the advantage of refraining their "boldest and roughest sailors" from attempting to make "any intimate acquaintance with the women."

Following such expressions of contempt, he admitted, as Cook had noted, that the biscuits offered them were even more unwholesome than their "rotten seal's flesh." And I add: what strange behaviour of these civilised men to offer rotten bread to natives who were manifestly friendly and generous with gifts for them.

Nor did Georg refrain from demeaning the natives for a quality that others might have lauded. "I did not observe any kind of subordination among these people. . . . " Like his father, he concluded that these Fuegians were outcasts of some neighbouring tribe, that they had been forced to inhabit this "dreary inhospitable part of Tierra del Fuego. . . . "[66] These natives, probably Alakalufs, were not outcasts, although they inhabited an area far from the more populated region along the Magellan Strait. During that early southern summer of 1774 the weather was calm and the food plentiful, so there is no obvious explanation of why Georg wrote that it was "horrid country . . . dreary and inhospitable."

I had the impression when I was there, in 1988, of Christmas Sound (which parallels the west coast of Hoste Island) as a beautiful channel, sprinkled with islets and hemmed in by forested coasts, the distant mountains enhancing the perspective.

Georg called to mind the massacre of the seventeen L'Hermite's sailors, suggesting that these "cannibals [also] kill each other in order to regale themselves." This behaviour he attributed to hunger in these "barren extremities of the world." Such absurd remarks reveal the gratuitous animosity Georg felt for these people.

A Very British Christmas

As the natives silently paddled away when the Christmas festivities began, Georg (who had not yet seen them) commented: "Our sailors . . . had already begun their holiday the evening before [Christmas day], and continued to carouse during two days without intermission, till captain Cook ordered the greatest part of them to be packed into a boat, and put ashore, to recover from their drunkenness in the fresh air." What impression might these Alakalufs have had of these rowdy sailors, lounging on the shore in drunken stupor, especially since, like all the Fuegians, they had no experience with stimulants of any kind? Little could the natives realise what Christmas Day meant for the British sailors. Darwin remarked two days before he embarked on his *Beagle* voyage (late December 1831) that on Christmas Day, "Wherever they [the sailors] may be, they claim Christmas day for themselves, & this they exclusively give up to drunkenness – that sole & never failing pleasure to which a sailor always looks forward to."

Two days before the *Resolution* departed from Christmas Sound, on 27 December (1774), the natives came on board for their final visit. "The word *pesseray*, which they repeated from time to time was pronounced ... [with] that vacant stare which is the characteristic of the most consummate stupidity."[67] These are young Forster's final words concerning these Fuegians, devoid as they are of a spark of comprehension. Given the language and cultural barriers, we do not know what the Fuegians thought about these navigators. On the other hand, it seems too facile to explain away Cook's and young Forster's comments simply as notions prevalent among the English in the 1770s or as reasonable, given the brevity of their contact with the natives.

If their country was dreary and inhospitable, as Georg contended, all the more might the natives have inspired admiration for having solved the problems of survival, equipped only with tools made of wood, bone, shell, and stone. Because of their simplicity, these tools necessitated intelligence and ingenuity to render them effective. Were not Fuegians (Alakalufs as well as Yamana) as fearless navigators as Captain Cook? They defied those "horrid" seas in their family-made canoes. Their ability to survive for thousands of years in such an unpredictable environment is cause enough to admire them, even without considering their ceremonies and their vivid corpus of oral literature. And the Yamana language, documented by Thomas Bridges as having over 32,000 words, of a people who at the time only numbered about 3,000 souls, is evidence of their alert and creative minds. These comments are not intended as lessons to the eighteenth-century explorers. They are directed to those who hold such views today.

Father Martin Gusinde quoted an unidentified Yamana who would probably have replied to Captain Cook and young Georg as follows:

The whites are arrogant. But we know very well that they are incapable of fishing and hunting in our land, of manufacturing canoes, lighting a fire, of comprehending the abilities of the *yékamush* [shamans], of making the weapons we use. ... It is very painful for us when the whites speak of us and our customs with disdain.[68]

As mentioned, the Christmas Sound natives encountered by Cook were very probably Alakaluf. Why then, the reader may ask, are they included in this book, whose focus is on the Yamana? Answer: they were neighbours with similar modes of living, and their lives intermingled. A detailed history of the Alakaluf should be written soon, before misconceptions concerning them are cited so often that they acquire the semblance of undisputed truths.[69]

A Brighter Light

In support of my comment that Cook's and Georg's notions should not be explained, or excused, as those prevalent at their time, is the attitude of Lieutenant Charles Clerke, who, like Cook, was the son of a farmer. Cook so highly esteemed him that he engaged him for all of his three great voyages. Beaglehole praised him as "always cheerful, talkative, amusing – a generous spirit who made friends easily."[70] In contrast with Cook and Georg: Clerke exclaimed: "even the Poor Inhabitants (wretched as they seemingly are) contributed all they could to our enjoyment by their confidence and sociality." Then too, he found "the Indian Lasses industrious in exerting all their influence upon both parties to bring about reconciliations and introduce friendship."[71]

Captain Cook's "Fatal Impact"

Once the crew had sobered up, on 29 December, they weighed anchor and passed Cape Horn in calm weather. The next day while going through the Strait of Le Maire, hundreds of seals played about their ship. Some thirty whales lay on their backs flapping their long pectoral fins, "breaching," leaping into the air, and flopping down with a heavy thud, spraying the ship again and again, almost as if they were taunting the visitors. They were also "blowing" and their water had "a most detestable, rank and poisonous stench" on the deck. A decade or two later most of these whales will have "disappeared" (Chapter 2).

When Cook anchored his ship in Good Success Bay he sent Lieutenant Pickersgill ashore to search for signs that the crew of his second ship, the *Adventure*, might have left if they had entered the bay to obtain fresh water and wood or for some other reason. Pickersgill found no indication that the ship had been there, but he did meet a few natives (the Haush again). Georg, who accompanied Pickersgill to the shore, described them as "well dressed in guanacoe-skins, and large cloaks of seal-skins, with a much more chearful [sic] and happy countenance, than the poor tribe whom we had left at Christmas Sound." Cook reported: "They were the same sort of People as we had seen in Christmas Sound." Here again he confused them with the Alakaluf.[72] The seals and whales were still intact, but not for long.

The last day of the year they crossed the Le Maire Strait, sailed along the north coast of Staten Island, to the small offshore islands that he named New Year's Islands.[73] There were so many seals on the shores of these islands that "the noise they made one would have thought that the island was stocked with Cows and Calves." They were alive with "sea bears" (fur seals) and sea lion seals, ducks, geese, cormorants, thousands of penguins, and many other sea and land birds. Cook exclaimed: "It is wonderful to see how the defferent [sic] Animals which inhabited this little spot are reconciled to each other, they seem to have entered into a league not to disturb each others tranquility."[74] But soon their "tranquillity" would be disturbed. In 1982 I saw only three sea lions during a three-week camping trip on the north shore of Staten Island, near where Cook had been. No fur seals were spotted there, only a few ducks, geese, cormorants, and a solitary penguin. On the south shore we did sight fur seals, in Cape Canepa, and many penguins along the shore of Franklin Bay. The animals on the north shore had not recovered from the decades of relentless killing, during the nineteenth century, by Yankee, British, and Argentine commercial hunters.[75]

Cook discovered a group of bleak, barren, mountainous islands covered with snow some 1,600 miles (2,964 kilometres) due east of Staten Island. He took possession of them in honour of His Majesty, naming them George the Third.[76] Now they are known as the South Georgia Islands, and they are still British. Cook's comments on the numerous seals and whales there and along the north coast of Staten Island, in addition to the precision of his charts, sufficed to make them killing grounds for the commercial hunters. When his account was published in 1777, British sealers read it avidly, rushed to the South Georgia Islands (and beyond), and were soon followed by the Yankees.[77] The new Harrison chronometres, which indicated the longitude with heretofore unheard of accuracy, greatly facilitated navigation in these uncharted seas.

Alan Moorehead, in his book entitled *The Fatal Impact . . .* , made these revealing comments:

The extraordinary thing about these desolate places [the islands of this southern latitude] was that the cold sea supported such a wealth of marine and bird life. Even on the lushest tropical island Cook had not seen such teeming abundance: *whales spouting about the ship in every direction, seals inhabiting every frozen rock*, and always the myriad birds wheeling overhead. Until now no man had ever visited these islands, these were their last few years of peace.[78]

Massive extinctions of the marine fauna lay in the near future. There was no stopping these commercial hunters, bolstered by the profit system and the rising demands of industrial capitalism. There was no stopping this "new era" (Chapter 2).

Moorehead astutely remarked that here Cook had "stumbled upon what was probably the largest congregation of wildlife that existed in the world." He had "stumbled" upon it. His main objective was not to locate seals and whales for the British fisheries but to ascertain whether or not the "The Great Southern Continent" (*Terra Australis Incognita*) existed.

A Very Great Achievement

South Georgia bore not the slightest resemblance to the legendary *Terra Australis*. Cook was not disappointed, because he knew better. But Clerke lamented: "Alas these pleasing dreams are reduced to a small isle, and that a very poor one, too." Georg and his father were equally disheartened. Instead of the luxurious growth of *Terra Australis Incognita*, they saw only tussock grass, wild burnet, moss, and rocks. There was no sign of human life either, not even the "bent little people stinking of seal oil like the Fuegians."[79] Georg seemed to miss them: no one to inspire his lofty indignation about the miseries of humankind.

On the last day of January 1775, Cook sighted the most southerly islands of the entire voyage which he called Thule because Thule "denotes the most distant goal of human endeavour or a land remote beyond all reckoning." These are now known as the South Sandwich Islands (not to be confused with the Hawaiian Islands, which Cook had named Sandwich). Thule Islands are even more desolate than South Georgia.[80] He insisted yet again, on 21 February, that the "continent" *Tierra Australis Incognita* was nowhere to be found.

I had now made the circuit of the Southern Ocean in a high Latitude and traversed it in such a manner as to leave not the least room for the Possibility of their being a continent [*Terra Australis Incognita*], unless near the Pole and out of the reach of Navigation.... Thus I flatter myself that the intention of the Voyage has in every respect been fully answered.[81]

Captain James Cook had now definitely shattered, for all time, the tenacious belief in the existence of a *Terra Australis Incognita*. Although he had dispelled this beautiful paradigm, he was sure that there was land beyond, further south, which was the source of "most of the ice which is spread over the vast Southern Ocean...." He surmised the existence of the Antarctica continent fifty years before it was discovered (Chapter 6). However, the risks he had taken while sailing through these high latitudes, avoiding floating icebergs that could trap his vessel, in freezing weather beyond the reach of rescue of any sort, convinced him that, that no one would ever "venture farther than I have done and that the lands which may lie to the South will never be explored...." Beaglehole felt that this rather arrogant affirmation was "so different from the modest understatements habitually practised by him."[82] However, above all, Beaglehole lauded Cook's great achievement: "After Cook's second voyage, no knowledgeable person could entertain this age-old illusion of a *Terra Australis Incognita*, which until then hardly anyone had doubted." Beaglehole explained: "The Antarctic is the fact which has survived; and Antarctica is not the provincia aurea [not *Terra Australis Incognita*], the golden and spicy province, the land of dye-woods and parrots and castles, the jumble of fable and misinterpretation that was piled on Greek reasoning and Marco Polo."[83]

The geography of the earth would never again be the same. Cook initiated the scientific era of discovery in the southern latitudes, by rendering this paradigm obsolete. But the first to grasp its significance were not the cartographers, the philosophers, or other members of the European intelligentsia but rather the sealers and then whalers of both old England and New England (Chapter 2). The historical "process" was in action: it probably would have happened sooner or later without Cook, but it did not.

Cook, confident that he had completed his "mission," turned the *Resolution* homeward and reached Cape Town on 21 March 1775. There he was given the letter the commander of the *Adventure* had left for him, twelve months earlier, on his way back to England. The letter revealed that in December 1773, ten crew members of the *Adventure* had been killed and eaten by the native Maoris near Queen Charlotte Sound, New Zealand. Cook was incredulous when he learned of the atrocity, though he seemed to excuse the Maoris for feasting on his crew: "I shall make no reflections on this Melancholy affair until I hear more about it. I must however observe in favour of the New Zealanders [the Maoris] that I have always found them of a Brave, Noble, Open and benevolent disposition." The crew deeply resented Cook's failure to avenge the massacre of their shipmates.[84]

On 30 July 1775 the *Resolution* anchored off Spithead (between the Isle of Wight and Portsmouth), three years and eighteen days after departure, having sailed upward of 70,000 miles (nearly 130,000 kilometres), thus completing what Beaglehole praised "as the greatest voyage of exploration in history." And Moorehead: " If there had been any doubt before, this voyage established him as one of greatest navigators of all times."

Among Cook's extraordinary achievements was that, during this long voyage, he was one of the first navigators to protect his crew from scurvy, the most calamitous seamen's disease.[85]

In the next chapter we turn to the other consequence of Cook's second voyage, mentioned above: the totally unexpected discovery that there existed great quantities of marine animals in the South Atlantic.

2

1780 to 1825: Moby Dicks in Tierra del Fuego; The Whalers and Sealers Arrive

The Whale – The Great Gift of Nature

The descendants of the Yahgans who lived in Ukika, Navarino Island, Chile never lost their predilection for whale meat and blubber. Even in the middle of the twentieth century, news of a beached whale would summon those nearby who, like their grandfathers, would call their neighbours to join the feast. Rosa Yagan, one of the very last who had vivid memories of her childhood, spoke of whales with great enthusiasm. She died in 1984. Thanks to Patricia Stambuk, we have a record of episodes of her life, which include the following.

For my race nothing was better than finding a whale. The Yahgans searched the coasts from the hill-tops for a beached whale.... Once we found one on Wollastone [near Cape Horn].... Such beautiful oil came out of it!... We made a fire and put the chucks of meat on the hot stones, roasting the meat like in an oven, until it was well-cooked.... We were all very happy with the whale-meals and we stayed there quite a long time.[1]

Rosa Clemente, who also had vivid memories of the past and lived until 1992, was equally enthusiastic. She told me when two stranded whales were found near her home (on the shore of Beagle Channel), she and the others ate "steakes from their backs and fried the fat like sausages." They got seven big cans (*tambores*) of oil from them that they sold in Ushuaia.[2]

Thomas Bridges, the head missionary during the years 1870 to 1886, remarked that whale-blubber was the most highly esteemed dish and that they "hoard up the blubber for months, by burying it in mud under a run of fresh water."[3]

Ursula Calderón, whose parents were also Yahgan (she passed away in January 2003), commented that those who lived near Cape Horn "spent the winter wherever there was a whale. They never felt cold, because they covered their bodies with seal oil; even the rain didn't bother them. And they didn't get sick. There were thousands of Indians everywhere, like them – naked."[4] Whale and seal oils were favourite beverages and were carried around in bladders and sipped any time of day.

Certain bones of the whale were made into harpoon points, which were preferred to seal bones because they were longer. Whales, like the right whale that feed on the tiny krill fish have baleens, long fringes of bone along the upper jaw, which serve as a sieve. These were used to brace the interiors of the canoes.[5] The sperm whale was another great favourite. It has teeth (on its lower jaw, instead of baleens) and feeds on large fish and octopus.

The Yoalox brothers were the "culture heroes" of the Yamana; in the myths published by the German ethnologist Father Martin Gusinde, the older Yoalox "was particularly fond of sea lion fat and whale oil." They tasted so good to him, especially the latter, that he wanted to turn the water in the channels of Tierra del Fuego into whale oil, so "the people would always have fresh whale oil on hand . . . and life would be a good deal more pleasant." But the younger Yoalox did not allow him to do so. He insisted: "People must be obliged to work always. . . . People must not be granted pleasure without work." The younger prevailed. His advice became "law" (my term), always applied. Finally it was he, not his elder brother, who seduced the beautiful Maku-kipa and fathered the first human beings.[6]

The Orcas Work for the Yahgans

They hardly ever attempted to kill healthy whales. Lucas Bridges recalled: "My father heard of only one occasion when the Yahgans actually did a whale to death. A whole fleet of canoes was used, and the attack lasted over twenty-four hours."[7]

The waterways south of the Magellan Strait are very deep and whales had often been reported particularly for Beagle Channel, the Cape Horn area, the Le Maire Strait, and the coasts of Staten Island.

The Yahgans I knew called the orca *pez-espada* (swordfish) probably because of its sword-like fin, which protrudes when it swims near the surface. Thomas Bridges also noted: "When these natives get a good whale (always killed by swordfish, which they consequently esteem sacred) they are very happy." The Yahgans held the orcas in such high esteem because they hunted the whales for them. The orcas are known as "killer whales." They usually surround the whale in a group of three or more, bite into its lips and tongue, which they eat, and leave the whale to die – a miserable

FIGURE 2.1. The Whale Feast.

death. When the Yahgans spotted such a wounded whale, they rushed in their canoes and finished him (or her) off with their spears and harpoons. At times a whale would escape from the orcas and swim into a bay where the water was too shallow, become stranded and die. Then also the Yahgans would profit from this gift of nature.

The woman in this sketch is carrying the blubber of a stranded whale (in the background) to be eaten by her people. Whales sometimes become stranded on their own because they are sick or disoriented. In the 1870s, the Yamana paddled their canoes with great excitement to feast on several packs of whales that had suddenly appeared stranded near Beagle Channel (Chapter 11). Natalie Goodall reported that in 1965, thirteen whales were stranded on the coast of Beagle Channel (Harberton farm) and that a sperm whale was beached on the shore of Cabo Maria (Atlantic coast) in 1973.[8] A few years before that, I saw many whale bones on the shore of San Sebastian Bay (also Atlantic coast), which have since disappeared.

Rosa Clemente, Ursula Calderón and Hermelinda Acuña had vivid memories of the "old times," as does Cristina Calderón who is still alive (in 2009). One of their favourite subjects was the orcas. Their accounts of them are published here for the first time. Rosa Clemente said that the orcas wounded seals and whales for her people to eat and that it was forbidden to even attempt to kill them. When the orcas came swimming

FIGURE 2.2. 1969: I am posing on whale bones, perhaps those of sperm whale, in San Sebastian Bay, Isla Grande, Argentina.

along Beagle Channel, only the old people were allowed to look at them. Rosa told me about what happened once.

> In Molinari [Hoste Island] I heard old Mary shouting to them [the orcas]. I was not outside on the beach . . . we [the children] had to stay hidden, inside [the hut]. They didn't allow us to look at them. I heard her because she shouted so loud. On the beach there were a lot of old people. My grandfather was there and my papa was there. There were not many orcas, only two or three. The orcas stayed above, nearly on top of the water, listening to old Mary. She talked to them for quite a while and the orcas stayed there listening to her. Afterward they said good-bye to her, by moving their fins and went nearby to the Island of the Seals [Isla de Lobos]. Then they [the old people] went right away to the coast of that little island and found a lot of dead seals . . . [the orcas had killed for them].[9]

The orcas listened to the old people. Rosa Clemente said that the spirits or souls, *kashpi*, of the "witches" (*brujos*, meaning shamans) who had died were lonely in that other world, so they often returned to their home area inside an orca in order to lure someone of their family to join them in at the other world.[10] But Cristina insisted that the orca is like a boat that brings the spirit (of the dead shaman) from the other world. If children approached, or even looked at, the orcas when they brought a dead shaman's *kashpi* back to earth, their own *kashpi* would be in danger of being taken to the world beyond, that is, of dying right there on the beach.[11]

Lola Kiepja, the last Selk'nam shaman, recorded a chant for me (number 29 of her shaman chants) to induce a whale to come to shore, during which she imitates its voice and calls to it as "my father." The Yahgan shamans also had privileged relations with the whales as well as the orcas. Ursula said that they, "the *yekamush*, had dreams and told the people just where a stranded whale could be found." They usually took the shamans' advice, got in their canoes, and went to the place the shamans had described and apparently found the stranded whale.

Julia, one of the last Yamana shamans, also spoke and sang to the orcas, although "she was scared of them." Three of my Yahgan friends knew why Julia was so afraid. Her husband, Alfredo, a famous *yekamush*, had been dead nine or ten years when several orcas appeared in a bay on the coast of Navarino Island. Julia knew that he (his *kashpi*) had finally come, riding on or inside one those orcas, to take her away with him to the other world. She realised that she was in danger of dying right there, that he was seeking her to take her to that "beyond" where the *kashpis* reside. She did not want to die. She shouted to him (in Yahgan): "You abandoned me [by dying], You left me a long time ago. Don't bother me anymore." She struggled against the power of his *kasphi* by chanting for three days and nights, didn't eat and drank only sips of water. Hermelinda, who was present in Julia's hut, said that Julia didn't allow her or the other children to leave the hut during those three days.[12]

When a Yahgan man sighted a stranded whale from his canoe, he shouted or motioned to his companions, indicating just where he had seen it, and the first to arrive at the site made four smoke signals to notify the nearby families. The news got around quickly because the smoke signals were easily seen from the canoes. The party might settle for a month or more to enjoy the bounty, while the meat and blubber were still edible, and to perform their ceremonies. Ursula insisted: "When the people saw the smoke [signals], all the canoes gathered there and they built the house [the hut] for the Chexaus [ceremony] and stayed there in the Chexaus [hut] until they finished eating all the whale."[13]

The Orcas Work "Overtime"

The orcas not only "worked" for the Yahgans. They also assisted modern whalers (of English descent) in Twofold Bay, a town south of Sydney (Australia), as reported in 1928. These whalers named individual orcas of a specific pack that came every season to attack the whales. They were grateful, because with the orcas' help, a whale could be killed in an hour instead of twelve hours in their boats without the orcas' assistance. "They were fond of their pack of killers [orcas] and, when the last of them, Old Tom, died…his skeleton was put on show at the nearby town of Eden."[14] Note this extraordinary example of adoration of the "killer whales" among people of such different origins.

The Yahgans also Depend on Seals

Ursula spoke about their seal preferences: "The fur seal is not so good to eat, the sea lion is tastier but we ate the fur seal also when there weren't any sea lions. The otter was never eaten because it smells so terrible." Seals as well as whales were plentiful in the area before the British and Yankees began killing them in the late eighteenth century (see below).

The Yamanas killed seals on the shore by beating their nasal area with a club or throwing rocks or spears at them. A hunter, in his canoe, would use a harpoon. First the hunter would wound the seal, then jump out of his canoe onto the nearby shore and draw the wounded seal to shore with the thong that was tied around his waist and attached to the harpoon, retrieve his harpoon from the wounded seal and finish it off with the same harpoon. The fur seal had the bad habit of following vessels, any boat, leaping up and down probably enjoying the surf and swell of the wake of the vessel. The hunter might take advantage of its proximity to aim his harpoon at one of those playful seals. But normally harpooning a seal, especially a big male sea lion, from the canoe was much more difficult than simply clubbing it and was probably done when there were no seals on the rockeries.[15]

The Yamana needed the South American fur seal, the *Arctocephalus australis* (also called a bear seal because of its warm fur), for capes and bedding. The South American sea lion seal, the *Otaria flavescens*, was sought principally for its meat and blubber; its hide was suitable for ropes of different sizes, hut covers, and occasionally for sails. The Yamana needed both of these seals year-round. I found little data on the sea elephant seal *Mirounga leonine*, although its blubber and meat were also eaten.[16] The Yahgans I knew probably never tasted one. In 1587, Thomas Cavendish and his crew very much appreciated the meat of young elephant seals in Port Desire (southern Patagonia), as quoted by the historian Morison: "Here the men marveled at the multitude of big 'seals' (elephant seals) 'of a wonderful great big nose…and monstrous of shape,' and killed many of the young, which they found to be marvelous good meate [sic], and being boiled or roasted, are hardly to be knowen from lamb or mutton."[17]

Seal meat and fat (blubber) was sometimes offered to visiting navigators as a special treat, as Georg Forster noted in 1774 (Chapter 1). It was invariably refused, sometimes politely. The Yahgans also relished serving berries sprinkled with seal oil. Seal blubber, like that of the whales, was heated and eaten or reduced to oil as a favourite beverage. They also smeared these oils on their bodies for protection against the cold. These ointments produced an odour that was exceedingly repulsive to strangers. Captain Cook and Georg Forster found it disgusting, as did Weddell and Webster (see below). But the Yamanas were immune to its odour and unaware that it could offend anyone. The Yamana eventually learned to hide their fur capes from the sealers, knowing that they might steal them.

The Commercial Fishermen Arrive

The whalers had arrived in the Cape Horn area by 1788. Herman Melville noted the first voyage of the whalers around Cape Horn, although he dated it ten years earlier. He knew that they preferred the sperm whale and the right whale above all others. The Yankee whalers called the latter "right" because it was the "right" kind of prey, easy to kill: swam slowly, often floated when killed, and was a rich source of oil.[18]

When the whales and seals were being depleted by overkilling in the North Atlantic (namely northeastern United States, Canada and Greenland), the accounts of Cook's second voyage and the Forsters' books were being avidly studied (Chapter 1). Thus the big fishing companies learned that Le Maire Strait, Staten Island and the South Georgia Islands were densely populated by seals and whales. Given the fierce competition among whalers and sealers, they usually refrained from publishing the locality of their killing sites, at least until they retired. The famous Yankee sealer Edmund Fanning was an exception (see below).

More than a few of them had surely seen and met the Yamana at one time or another, especially the "rank and file" of the sealing vessels, whose captains would leave them on the rockeries (rocky coasts, temporary "home" of the seals) for weeks at a time or even stranded there, like whales (Chapters 11 and 13).

Whaling and Sealing
Many whales have specific breeding areas, often in deepwater bays or estuaries. The mating partners usually locate each other by sonic signals.

Alan Moorehead, in his superb book *The Fatal Impact*, pointed out that the first whalers in the South Pacific,

> simply set up a shore factory in some estuary where the animals were known to breed and then attacked them from small boats. The whales never seemed to learn from their experiences; the survivors came back again and again, even those which had escaped from earlier encounters and now had harpoons and broken lances sticking in their backs. It is true later on...that the animals began to recognize men as their mortal enemies.[19]

After mating takes place, the males of most of the whale species separate from the pod (the pack) until the following year.[20] However, the sperm whales (also called cachalots) mate in any season. Whales are among the greatest travellers in the world, so the whalers also pursued them in the open sea whenever they spotted them. Except for the grey and the sperm whales, which at times did attack their aggressors, their usual defence against the hunters was flight. "The actual pursuit and capture of the whales was accomplished from rowing boats carrying about six men. Once the boat had managed to approach within a few metres of a whale, a harpoon was thrown into its body, and when the whale was finally exhausted, it was killed with hand lances."[21]

Once harpooned, the whales often went into a "death flurry," dragging the whaleboat for miles, and the whalers often fell out of their boats while pursuing and attacking them. According to Roger Payne, an experienced whale expert, the whales were blamed anyway, and such stories "were used to fuel the myth of whales as savage and dangerous monsters."[22]

Usually male sperm whales fought back, and this may explain Herman Melville's initial fascination with them (see below). Moorehead reported: "If a male [sperm whale] was attacked, the cows and calves took off, but if a cow or a calf was struck, the whole pack turned back to try to render help, and all would be destroyed. In this the sperm whales resemble the elephants, which were soon to be shot in tens of thousands in central Africa."[23]

Recall that whales are mammals and have to surface to breathe; this is when the hunters usually attacked them. The sperm whale can "store" sufficient oxygen to remain below water for an hour or even longer.

Seals (Pinnipedia), in contrast to whales, are land-bound, though of course not entirely. They mate and reproduce, and the females tend their young on rockeries, usually during the summer season. They return there at some time during the year to moult. Therefore they might well spend several months on land. The orcas are known to sweep up to the shore of a rockery, grab a distracted pup, and toss it into the air before devouring it. Land (the rockery) is a more dangerous place for seals than water. But they are "luckier" than the whales because they never become stranded in shallow water and can hide from human hunters in water-flooded caves or settle in new rookeries. The seal's usual defence is hiding as well as flight, although an infuriated male might try to defend himself and his harem by attacking a hunter. The male elephant seal was sometimes shot as he reared and opened his huge mouth in a gesture of defence. James Weddell, the famous sealer, observed: "It is curious to remark that the sea-elephant, when lying on the shore and threatened with death, will often make no effort to escape into the water but lie still and shed tears, merely raising the head to look at the assailant; and, though very timid, will wait with composure for the club or the lance which takes its life."[24]

The professional sealers usually clubbed the seals to death on land as they tried to escape to the sea, using a long staff having a head studded with nails, the cruellest method for killing them. The main danger for the commercial sealers was approaching the rookeries in stormy weather or high tides in their small whaleboats. Except for an infuriated male, the seal was an incredibly docile prey. Hundreds of thousands were killed on the rookeries in one or two seasons in the South Atlantic during the late eighteenth and early nineteenth centuries, when sealing was such a highly profitable business. Alan Moorhead noted: "No one will ever know how many whales and seals were killed in the southern ocean in the ensuing fifty years [to about 1830]. Was it ten million or fifty million? Figures become meaningless, the killing went on and on until there was virtually nothing left to kill, nothing at any rate that could be easily and profitably killed."[25]

Sealers were not idolised like the whalers, certainly because sealing was a more prosaic occupation than whaling.

Moby Dick

Commercial whaling in the great Pacific began with the sperm whale when the *Emilia* (or *Amelia*), sailed around Cape Horn in 1788. Her crew members were the first Europeans to harpoon a whale, a sperm whale, in the Pacific.[26] Melville, by mistake, dated the event ten years earlier.

In 1778, a fine ship, the *Amelia*... boldly rounded Cape Horn, and was the first among the nations to lower a whale boat of any sort in the great South Sea. The voyage was a skilful and lucky one; and returning to her berth with her hold full of the precious sperm, the *Amelia*'s example was soon followed by other ships, English and American, and *thus the vast sperm whale grounds of the Pacific were thrown open.*[27]

That year (1788), "the great chapter in the history of the whaling industry began – rounding Cape Horn!"

Edouard A. Stackpole, the author of *Whales & Destiny*, proclaimed: "No tiny whaling ship had ever dared to 'round the Horn' before, [where] winds roared a hundred miles an hour and waves towered fifty feet into the sky." The *Emilia*, after being tossed about in a gale for twenty-one days, finally rounded the Horn into "a whaleman's paradise." Captain Shields of the *Emilia* exclaimed "I never saw so many large sperm whales...." The news spread incredibly fast. Hundreds of whale ships were already working in the area by 1790, when the *Emilia* returned from her first trip to London."[28] The presence of sperm whales in the Pacific was welcome news for the European and Yankee fisheries. But whalers were not welcome news for the Yamana Indians.

In 1777 and 1788 there is an amazing near coincidence of events: the publication of Cook's and Forster's accounts of the abundance of whales and seals in the south Atlantic (in 1777) and the passage of the *Emilia* beyond Cape Horn and the discovery of sperm whales in the nearby Pacific (in 1788).These two events sufficed to inaugurate the "Whaling Revolution" (my term). Life would never be the same again for the whales who "helped" inaugurate the Industrial Revolution (see below).

With Melville's *Moby Dick or, the Whale* (first published in 1851), the sperm whale becomes the ultimate challenge to whalers, personified by Captain Ahab, who, before the opening of the novel, was already "fired with revenge." He had lost half of a leg when attacked by Moby Dick and his stomp was made of the jaw of sperm whale. Denham Sutcliffe, an admirer of the great novel, considered Captain Ahab "a grand figure, not less so perhaps than Shakespeare's Lear or Milton's Satan...."[29] While Captain Ahab may be "a grand figure," Melville's admiration for the sperm whale (the species) is evident throughout his novel. Moby Dick (a white sperm whale) emerges as the prototype of the species. The novel is concluding when Starbuck cries, "Oh! Ahab"... "not too late is it, even now the third day, to desist. See! Moby Dick seeks thee not. It is thou, thou, that madly seekest him." Captain Ahab is again "fired with revenge," but this time he drowns while attempting to slaughter his enemy. He drowns with all but one of his crew, who survives to tell the story. Moby Dick swims away and the novel terminates as, "all collapsed and the great shroud of the sea rolled on as it rolled five thousand years ago."

Melville's morality tale might be stated as follows: revenge destroys him who refuses to free himself from it, while the true hero frees himself from that "fire for revenge." If so, Moby Dick, not Ahab, becomes the "grand figure" of "one of the greatest sea stories – and morality tales – ever written."

There were at least four and perhaps more real sperm whales named and recognised from year to year by the whalers.[30] One of them was Mocha Dick, from whom Melville derived the name Moby Dick, though he did not exactly say so. Mocha is the name of an island at 38°20′ south latitude, some 38 miles off the shore of central Chile. A. B. C. Whipple, in his excellent book *The Whaler*, explained that Mocha Dick passed into popular mythology, although he "was a real-life, flesh, blood and blubber bull sperm whale named not for his colour [white] . . . but because his first reported attack was against a whaleboat near Mocha Island, off [the coast of] Chile, around 1810."

Nathaniel Philbrick dedicated his book *In the Heart of the Sea* to "the tragedy of the whale ship *Essex* . . . the event that inspired the climactic scene of Herman Melville's *Moby Dick*. . . . Never before, in the entire history of the Nantucket whale fishery, had a whale been known to attack [and sink] a ship." The culprit was an eighty-five-foot bull sperm whale, the ship weighed 238 tones – approximately three times more than the whale, the place was 1,500 nautical miles west of the Galapagos, and the day 23 February 1821. The crew and the whale survived. Owen Chase, the first mate, wrote in his book (published that same year), that when the *Essex* struck three of the sperm's companions, the sperm whale became "as if fired with revenge for their sufferings" – an expression often used by Melville. This male sperm whale had been possessed, Philbrick related, "by what Chase finally took to be a very human concern for the other whales."[31]

Mocha Dick's attacks on whalers' boats (from 1810 to 1859) are dramatically presented by Whipple, who also stated: "By every account, Mocha Dick was endowed not only with prodigious strength but with a malign intelligence as well: he feigned death; he stood vigil after a fellow whale was killed."[32]

Jane Billinghurst, in her fascinating book *The Spirit of the Whale*, also proposed that Mocha Dick had "inspired" *Moby Dick or, the Whale*. I quote her: "In creating the rogue whale Moby Dick, Melville also included characteristics ascribed to Mocha Dick, a huge white bull sperm whale who from 1810 to 1859 terrorized whalers in the Pacific, killing at least thirty men in the process."[33] So we can assume that Mocha Dick became Melville's Moby Dick.[34]

Let us pause and bid farewell to the real Mocha Dick, finally killed by a Swedish whaler in 1859. According to Melville: "He was blind in one eye and evidently too tired to struggle as the lance punctured his lungs. Mocha Dick carried 19 irons [harpoons] in his scarred hide – mementos of more than 100 battles in which at least 30 men had been killed and scores of whaleboats destroyed."[35]

Sperm whales were not only famous as the "ultimate challenge" to whalers, as "Moby Dicks," but also as the most valuable of all the whales in the marketplace partly "because of the reservoir of pure oil in their great square heads."[36] This "pure oil," also called spermaceti, is sometimes confused with the male genital organ (fluid). Once the male whale is killed, the oil, exposed to air, becomes a waxy substance, and then becomes liquefied again, as an oil. It proved to be an excellent ingredient for ointments, lubricants, candles, polishes and even cosmetics. Melville's description of the sperm liquid is lucid:

Though in life it remains perfectly fluid, yet, upon exposure to the air, after death, it soon begins to concrete; sending forth beautiful crystalline shoots, as when the first thin delicate ice is just forming in water. A large whale's case [its head] generally yields about five hundred gallons of sperm, though from unavoidable circumstances, considerable of it is spilled, leaks, and dribbles away.

This great quantity of sperm oil was only one item. The male and female whale's blubber and fat were boiled and melted down into another type of oil. Melville explained: "Assuming the blubber to be the skin of the whale; then . . . this skin, as in the case of a very large sperm whale, will yield the bulk of one hundred barrels of oil."[37]

In addition to the sperm oil and blubber oil, a third substance was found to be a very attractive commodity. It prolonged the scent of perfumes and was even "considered to be a powerful aphrodisiac."[38] Called ambergris, it protects the whale's intestines from irritating objects. Thus the sperm whale had an extraordinary commercial value: for its oils and its ambergris besides its meat and teeth.

The male sperm whale was called the king of the whales as the most valuable and one of the most dangerous (with the grey whale) and heroic until technology defeated him in 1864, five years after the real Mocha Dick was finally killed.

The Dynamic Markets for Whales and Seals

"Whale oil lighted the lamps of the world and lubricated the gears of the dawning Industrial Age." Whipple began his book with these words. The oil derived from whale blubber brought tremendous profits to European and United States fisheries. Although whales were more difficult to hunt and kill than seals, the profits were proportionally greater.

As mentioned, by the late eighteenth and early nineteenth centuries, most of the fisheries and fishermen rushed from the North Atlantic, having almost exterminated their prey there, to the southern regions of the planet. Note that they rushed south precisely when the markets had "skyrocketed." Europe and the United States were industrialising, commercialising these profitable items at an incredible rate.

The gamut of whale products was enormous. The oil was required for lighting streets, shops, homes, and factories, for tanning leather, as an ingredient for polishes, fertilisers, soap, paint, medicines, and later for greasing steam engines. Casks of whale oil were used as currency in the "Yankee capital," New Bedford, when the capital moved there (in 1839) from Nantucket. Whipple insisted that New Bedford was one of the wealthiest "cities" in the world at the time (with only 20,000 inhabitants).[39] Whale meat was sold as food for humans and pets. While a few whales have teeth, such as the sperm whale (though only on the bottom jaw), most have baleen (in lieu of teeth), among them the right, grey and blue whales. As mentioned in Chapter 1, baleen is a sort of curtain of horny bone, which hangs from the whale's upper jaw and filters the water for krill and small fish. The baleen, tough and flexible as it is, became a very marketable item for corset stays, skirt hoops, chair springs, hairbrush bristles, buggy whips, tennis rackets and the like. As noted, the Yamana employed it to line the interiors of their canoes.

The whaling capitalists were either the owners of the big fishing companies or the captains of the ships. Few ships did both whaling and sealing because they required different technologies and had different killing sites.

The whalers as well as the sealers worked with astounding rapidity. The profits were huge, thanks to the expanding market, the cheap labour of the "ordinary" seamen, and the free prey. The whales and seals in the seas did not cost a cent, nor did those along the shores of no man's lands, often lonely coasts of the continents on the rim of the Pacific and its islands. These incentives motivated enormous profits and equally enormous kills in just one season. "Kill as many as the ship will hold before someone else gets here," was certainly the order of the day. Britone Cooper Busch, in *The War against the Seals*, gave an example of the particular nature of such competition and its consequences for the seals.

If fur seals managed to survive the slaughter, which followed, it was due to their love of crashing surf and windward rocks. Try as sealers would to exterminate every last adult and pup for its skin on the assumption – accurate enough – that otherwise another sealer would perform the act, some of each survived, though only barely enough in some cases.[40]

His last remark explains how some seals survived in Tierra del Fuego. I am thinking especially of the fur seals, which are very rare in Tierra del Fuego but some have survived in Bay Captain Cánepa, on the south coast of Staten Island. I saw them there in 1982.

"The Rivalry..."

The following was inspired by Edouard Stackpole's excellent book entitled *Whales & Destiny. The Rivalry Between America, France, and Britain for the Control of the Southern Whale Fishery, 1785–1825.*

France Still but Not for Long

The French historian Jean-René Vanney explained that the rivalry between the French and the British, which was already taking place in 1772, reveals a really surprising difference in the scope of their respective programs. Vanney pointed out that the French often improvised and rushed the preparation of their voyages, sometimes looking for the *bon coup* in terms of attacking a problem rather than committing to a long-term campaign. In contrast, the British methodically planned their projects, which had already been conceived in terms of scientific progress – and, it may be added, in terms of their geopolitical and economic interests as well.[41]

The first shipment of whale oil and sealskins from the Malvinas (later Falkland) Islands was made in 1764 by the explorer Louis Antoine Bougainville. But the French fishermen in Brittany were not able to take advantage of this initiative, probably for the reasons evoked by Vanney.

In 1785 Louis XVI, despite his worries at home, commissioned an expedition under the command of J. F. de Galaup, known as La Pérouse, among whose objectives was "the hunting of whales in the southern seas." In his log for 25 January 1786, he wrote that while passing through the Strait of Le Maire, the "savages" lit large fires inviting them to shore. He ignored the savages but not the whales that were swimming "majestically within fire of our frigates: they will continue to be sovereign in these seas until the moment when the whalers declare war against them as they have in Spitzberg and in Greenland. I doubt that there be a better place in the world than here for whaling."

This was eleven years after Captain Cook, when the Strait of Le Maire was still thickly populated by whales, but not for long.

By the early nineteenth century, the experienced French fishermen, living in a country still disorganized by a revolution and by Napoleon's defeat at the battle of Trafalgar, had "lowered their flag" as the British became the masters of the seas, according to Colnett (see below).

Great Britain – Everywhere

Stackpole noted that the government, the state of Great Britain, as a maritime nation, supported its merchant whalers and that "any efforts by a rival power to interfere with her Southern Whale Fishery was interpreted by Britain as a threat." Even before the *Emilia* had returned to London from her first voyage around Cape Horn (in 1790), "both sides of the South American continent were under consideration by the [British] merchants."[42]

Following Cook's second voyage, Great Britain increasingly attributed great economic and political importance to whaling and sealing, as exemplified by the declarations, in 1793, of Captain James Colnett. Having been nominated by the Admiralty and supported by south sea fisheries of London, he was assigned to discover localities for whale fishers who voyaged round Cape Horn, in order to "afford them the necessary advantages of refreshment and security to refit their ships."[43] Colnett insisted that Staten Island was well situated for rendezvous for warships and merchant ships. He added significantly: "If the navigation round Cape Horn should ever become common, such a place we must possess; and agreeable to the last convention with Spain, we are entitled to keep possession of it [Staten Island], and apply it to any purpose of peace or war."

Colnett had no compunctions about revealing Britain's needs and projects. In 1793, he foresaw that: "Commercial search after furs, seals and whales will lead adventurers to traverse the Coasts of Tierra del Fuego and Patagonia for them. While whales and seals were becoming scarce and shy in other parts where they have hitherto taken, so that new haunts must be resorted to, in order to keep up the spirit of our fisheries."[44]

By the 1790s, British whaling ships by the hundreds were taking the route around Cape Horn, entering the Pacific along the Chilean coast. Soon they were harpooning off Australia, Tasmania, New Zealand, later

near Japan, and many unknown islands in the vast Pacific. From the
very onset of whaling, from 1788, and somewhat later sealing ships,
passed through the Cape Horn area. The Yamana were certainly aware
of the boatloads of whalers harpooning in their bays and channels, of
sealers busy killing on their rockeries, and of the vessels wrecked in their
dangerous waters.

The Yankees – Catching Up

The Yankee whalers were heralded as more than mere moneymakers; they
were "The Great American Adventure." Many were Quakers, acting in
God's name. Whipple explained: "In a time when fundamentalist beliefs
were wide spread, the huge mammal was perceived as the incarnation
of evil."[45] Moby Dick was "the gliding great demon of the seas life,"
according to Captain Ahab.

The pulse of the young nation was beating to the rhythm of its newly
won independence. It was an exciting time to live unless you were an
Indian or an African. The Yankees were not bolstered by an imperial
navy nor generously subsidised by an attentive government, as were their
British cousins, so for the Yankees it was a matter of pure capitalistic
competition at home and with their greatest competitor, the British. Soon
the Yankee fisheries became the greatest beneficiaries in the world, even
for fur seals in Chinese markets.[46]

The Yankee ship *Minerva*, in 1803, passed Cape Horn. Her log is cited
here with its idiosyncratic spelling: "It is Singular that Such a Fridgid
& Dreary Coast [Cape Horn] Should Abount with Sea anamels. Such
Olavertrases Pinguins, Seals, Sea Eliphants & Co. all Skiping and Playing
as if overjoyd and thankful for the Particular Plenty Bistowd on them by
the Creator." Britone C. Busch, who cited this log, clarified that: "Despite
such admiration, the fur seals were soon gone from the more accessible
islands."[47]

Edmund Fanning, a native of Connecticut and an active sealer, became
one of the most prominent Yankee entrepreneurs of the entire industry.
He was the catalyst of the sealing trade, according to Robert Albion who
emphasised that Fanning's seamen clubbed "the hopeless seals to death by
the thousands; it was pitiless, brutal and bloddy – but highly profitable."

When Fanning arrived on the South Georgia Islands in the season, late
1800 to early 1801, he found, as he might have expected, that his British
competitors had been there first. Nonetheless he harvested 57,000 sealskins. In September 1817, while heading for the South Seas, he stopped
over in the vicinity of Cape Horn, where his crew found fur seals, highly

coveted for "their thick coat and fine cast of a reddish hue." It was not said if any remained. Near Cape Horn, in Nassau Bay, he also came upon vast numbers of the prized right whales.[48] There, soon afterwards, Fanning's other ships and those of his competitors continued "harvesting" those top-quality seals and whales until only a few survivors remained.

Fanning's major publication (1833) supported the US claim that the American sealer Nathaniel Palmer had the priority over the British sealer George Powell for claiming the outlying Antarctic islands for their respective countries (Chapter 6). About this time (1838) Edgar Allan Poe published his famous and only novel.[49]

The Pivot for the Fisheries

Massive killing of whales, wherever it took place, diminished the number that passed along or penetrated the channels of Tierra del Fuego. The nomadic feature of the whales justifies the attention paid to whaling beyond Yamana territory.

Human beings had never inhabited the Falkland Islands until Europeans settled there. They were first sighted in 1690 by an English expedition led by John Strong, who named the islands after his patron, Anthony Cary, the Fifth Viscount Falkland. Intensive whale and seal commerce began there before Captain Cook published (in 1777) and before the *Emilia* initiated the whale hunts in the South Pacific (in 1788). The French explorer Louis Antoine Bougainville first exported whale and seal oil from the "Falkland Islands" to Saint Malo in 1766 and later many fishermen–merchants from Saint Malo went there for the same purpose, whence the name "Islas Malvinas," adopted by the Argentines. But the islands belonged to Spain, though as of 1816, they came under the rule of the newly independent republic of Argentina. In 1833, the British took over the islands and renamed them the Falklands (Chapter 5).

A sealing vessel from Boston, appeared there in 1775 (two years before Cook published), according to the historian Nigel Bonner.[50] That same year Yankee whalers in Brazil "would rendezvous in the Falkland Island...[and] complete their cargoes with oil from elephant seals." A big male elephant seal "produced" 210 gallons of oil. Whale and elephant seal oils were better graded than ordinary seal oil.

Thanks to the reports of Cook's second expedition, the big fishing companies, Fanning's among others, had become alerted to the importance of the South Georgia Islands, so the Falklands became a base from which to extend their activities there and elsewhere. By 1825, South Georgia yielded "not fewer than 1,200,000" pelts, probably of the fur seal.

V. F. Boyson, in his excellent book *The Falkland Islands*, related that from 1807 to 1820 the Malvinas had become "infested with whalers, the crews of which destroyed all [the] birds and beasts and fishes without mercy."[51] From the Malvinas it was no great leap to Tierra del Fuego, where British sealers had been active since the late 1770s.[52]

Staten Island

About 1790 Spain installed the headquarters of a large whaling and sealing company in Patagonia, at Port Desire, near the Atlantic entrance to the Magellan Strait. British and Yankee vessels clashed with the Spanish patrol ships along the coasts of Patagonia and Staten Island. Even so, before the end of the eighteenth century, the Yankee sealers who dared confront Staten Island's treacherous undercurrents started harvesting "substantial" pods of seals there and continued to do so into the late nineteenth century, when the Argentine sealer Luis Piedra Buena and others competed with them.[53] There is no report of the Yamana or of any Indians living on Staten Island. However, as I discovered in 1982, they had camped there many centuries before. They may have gone there from time to time after the island was first sighted in 1616.[54] If so, when the boisterous sealers arrived, they would probably have fled, never to return.

Sealers to Antarctica: Whalers – Elsewhere

From 1788 on the Yankee whalers were scouting far and wide – as wide as the Indian Ocean and as far as the Bering Strait with greater efficiency as their technology improved until 1860 and with a reduced market afterwards (see below). By the 1820s the sealers, who had probably almost extinguished the seals in the Cape Horn area, began concentrating on the Antarctic. Near the tip of the Antarctic Peninsula, along the South Shetland Islands (beyond the turbulent Drake Passage) in just two years, 1821 and 1822, some 320,000 seals were killed and three- or four-day-old pups ("at the lowest calculation" 100,000) died soon afterwards, having lost their mothers. Yankee and British sealers were active there including James Weddell. But unlike the others, the latter was aware that the sealers were practising a "system of extermination." Weddell reported that at the end of 1822, the seals on the South Shetland Islands were already "nearly extinct."[55]

"By 1829, it was said, there was not a fur seal to be seen in the South Shetlands.... The attention of sealers became diverted from the fur seal to the elephant seal, which yielded a good quality oil, but was less profitable and the elephant was less abundant. They are pathetically easy to kill . . . "

This quote is from the book by G. E. Fogg.[56] The profitable market for the Yankee fisheries (the big whale and seal companies) increased steadily until about 1860. Even before then the "Great American Adventure" had lost its vital force. Quaker whalers had given up their pious vocation; some were writing their memoirs about their heroic hand-harpooning from rowboats.[57] The innovative technology of the 1850s was not in their future.

The Yamana Territory

The slaughter of marine animals in the Cape Horn area during this first period of Yankee whaling and sealing (from 1790 to about 1829) was so devastating that the animals never recovered to anything like their original numbers. The "destiny" of the fur seals is a good example. For instance, in 1823 and 1824, James Weddell, who was employed to secure fur seal pelts, stopped over in three bays near Cape Horn to obtain drinking water and firewood where he just happened to encounter the Yamana, but he had to go to the South Shetland Islands and to the rockeries on Diego Ramirez and Idelfonso Islets for the fur seals he was after (see below). This explains why Darwin, in 1833 and 1834, observed that the Yahgans were living almost entirely on shellfish and fish (Chapter 5).

The Argentine archaeologists José Luis Orquera and Ernesto Piana were aware that "between 1790 and 1822 this source [the seals] was almost at the limit of extinction. . . . Being deprived of their major source of food, the canoe people of extreme southern America had to make out with other resources whose energy value was much less."[58]

Sixty years later, 1882–83, L. F. Martial, the commander of the French expedition to Cape Horn, declared: "Finally, isn't it possible that the fierce war against the seals, by the fisheries, that diminished to a great degree one of most important sources of food for the Yahgans, was one of the principal causes of their depopulation?"[59] Lucas Bridges commented that the Yahgans he knew about the beginning of the twentieth century "lived almost entirely on fish and limpets; they had very few skins with which to clothe themselves." Gusinde also pointed out that European whalers had almost exterminated the whales in the Cape Horn region by the early 1900s.[60] Today whales are sometimes seen spouting in the Cape Horn area, and quite recently pods appeared stranded in Tierra del Fuego. There are also a few seal rockeries along Beagle Channel, Staten Island and elsewhere. But the great populations of whales and seals prior to the 1780s have "disappeared" in Tierra del Fuego.

A Glance at the Whaling Industry from the Mid-Nineteenth Century to the Present

By 1850 the United States had acquired its present territory by a revolution from Britain, by purchase from France, by military defeats of Mexico. Only the American Indians continued to defy the sovereignty that the United States had proclaimed. With great expectations of promised lands, the most restless new Americans were pushing the "frontier" westward, urged on by the 1849 gold rush.

About 1850, when steamships were supplanting the sailing ships, they not only greatly facilitated whaling but also increased the market for oil. However, this greater demand for oil also stimulated the search for petroleum, which culminated in Pennsylvania in 1860 when natural petroleum was first exploited for industry. This was bad news for the whalers and good for the whales, but not for long. The fishing vessel converted to steam power greatly increased their size, velocity and efficiency. The invention of the explosive harpoon, in use in 1856, accelerated the actual killing and made it almost impossible for the whales to escape, much less fight back.

Roger Payne, one of the world's leading experts on whales, explained how the invention of steam-power increased the efficiency of the explosive harpoon.

It was the Norwegian Svend Foyn who made in 1854 "a most wonderful invention" – a cannon mounted on the bow of a high-speed, steam-powered "catcher boat" that could fire a harpoon into a whale...the invention of the exploding harpoon – basically a grenade mounted on the tip of a harpoon that exploded a few seconds after impact to blow steel shrapnel through the whale's body, hopefully killing it swiftly. The advantage...was that the harpoon not only attached the whale to the boat but also killed it.[61]

Cannon-directed explosive harpoons on the fast-moving steamships might have wiped the remaining whales off the face of the earth if the third event had not interfered, in 1860, with the first producing oil well in Old Creek, Pennsylvania, mentioned above.

Shortly after these three events (steamships, explosive harpoons and petroleum) happened, a fourth event – the American Civil War of 1861 to 1866 – almost brought the economy to a halt.

Soon thereafter kerosene (a petroleum product) supplied the huge market for industry. Barbara Freese, in her remarkable book *Coal*, observed that "Kerosene was the first petroleum product to find a wide market [after the Civil War].... These fossil light sources helped put an end to the use of sperm whale oil. Coal and oil [petroleum] thus helped save the whales, just as coal had for centuries helped save the remaining forests."[62]

However, the newly equipped sperm whalers and sealers as well had kept their markets for soap, paint tanning and fur. Later they acquired larger ones for cosmetics, fertilizers, pet food and human food.[63] Let me skip now to the next event (the fifth), the so far final innovation that transformed the whaling industry – the factory ship – "on which whales killed by diesel-powered boats could be processed in an hour." Inaugurated in 1923, it introduced the modern epoch of whaling. Billinghurst remarked: "By the 1970s it was apparent that whales really were in danger of disappearing forever."[64]

The fisheries were partly curtailed in 1986 by a worldwide ban on whaling. But the loophole in the ban permits whales to be taken for "research" and by the thousands. In 1988, the whale expert James Darling reported: "No longer must we kill whales to study them." But the "researchers" do kill them, and whales' corpses do appear in the marketplace and then on the plates of Japanese diners.[65]

As for the seals, Busch concluded his 1985 book *War against the Seals* as follows: "Mankind's predilection to despoil the earth's lands and seas with dangerous pollutant has reached no end...it cannot be said that we have seen the final episode of 'the war against the seals.'" The war continues today (2009); the market for baby seal pelts in Canada, Russia, Ukraine and Poland has prompted the Canadian government to lift the quota for baby seal hunting, so on it goes at a rate of 23,000 baby seals killed during just one season despite public protests against it. "Here on ice patches of the Gulf of St. Lawrence, the hunt looks nearly as brutal as ever...[a hunter explained]. 'We do it for the money...but it's also a tradition in our blood.'"[66] So here we are, money in the pocket and tradition in the blood join forces to wipe out the seals, just as money in the bank and "research" may wipe out the whales.

The Sealer James Weddell

The narration continues with James Weddell, the most outstanding British sealer to frequent the Cape Horn area. He was a "natural scientist," gifted with a fervent curiosity about nature and strange people. He also possessed an unusual talent to pen his observations and experiences. Son of a Scotch upholsterer living in London, a poor family, he was orphaned at an early age and later drafted into the Royal Navy for the duration of a war against France (perhaps the Napoleonic wars of 1805–6). At the age of thirty-two, he found a job with the famous British whaling and sealing firm S. Enderby & Sons. From 1819 to 1821, he was employed as the captain of two small vessels sealing along the coasts of the Antarctic Peninsula. During his second voyage, September 1822 to May 1824, he encountered the Yamana in the vicinity of Cape Horn.

Weddell is famous in the annals of navigation on several accounts. He broke Captain Cook's record in the southern latitude in February 1823, when he entered a very wide bay, now called the Weddell Sea, on the coast of the Antarctic below Cape Horn. There he reached 74°15' south latitude, three degrees (214 kilometres) further south than Cook had reached in 1774 sailing from New Zealand. Later, in February 1841, Captain James Clark Ross surpassed Weddell's record by almost four degrees (Chapter 6).

An ocean current is also named in Weddell's memory and a seal as well. The complete sealskin he donated to the Edinburgh Museum, when he returned to his native Scotland in 1824, proved to be an unknown species, so it was named *Leptynochtes weddelli*, since called the Weddell seal.[67]

Breaking Captain Cook's record, having a sea, an ocean current and a seal named for oneself are more than enough to guarantee anyone's immortality. But perhaps Weddell's greatest claim for recognition will become his exceptional regard for the Yamana. With Weddell, they cease to be the "thick-coming fancies" of Cook and young Forster and assume an honourable place as actors in the theatre of history.

Weddell wrote about his encounters with the Yamana (whom he called Fuegians) while sailing through virtually unknown waters. He also recorded the conditions of the sea and climate and the characteristics of the fauna, flora and landscape, although he never forgot that his job was to return to home port loaded with fur seal pelts, which were fetching high prices in the European and Chinese markets. Though committed to his job, he attempted to alert the world to the consequences of the uncontrolled killing of these defenceless fur seals. Foreseeing their extermination, he cited an example to be followed: the reserve for seals on the Isla Lobos at the mouth of the La Plata estuary, Uruguay. This first protective legislation for seals is dated at 1820, although by this time, as Busch pointed out, the seals on the Isla de Lobos "had been cleaned off."[68] Since then the seals have returned, so today this island is again a refuge for them and can be visited from the beach of the resort town Punta del Este, Uruguay. The problem was that in the South Atlantic and elsewhere there were no authorities, no coast guard, to enforce such restrictions. Had one sealer refrained from killing a suckling cow, another would certainly have taken her. Weddell realised this and was probably aware that he too hastened the elimination of the fur seals.[69] No individual could prevent the extermination of the seals and whales; only national and international regulations backed by enforcement could, but these are ineffectual for whales, given the "loophole" in the 1986 ban mentioned above.

Two encounters, though not with the Fuegians, serve to situate Weddell in his time and widen the horizon of our "links." First, he met Captain Jewitt in 1820 off the shore of the Malvinas Islands, which were to be renamed the Falkland Islands thirteen years later, in 1833, when the British "reconquered" them (Chapter 5). Jewitt, a North American, had the command of the *Heroina*, a frigate (a fast-moving naval vessel, usually heavily armed), with instructions from his superiors in Buenos Aires, officials of the new Argentine republic, to assure her possession of the islands. Boyson remarked: "The solemnity of the occasion was somewhat marred by the dilapidated appearance of his [Jewitt's] frigate, [and] the loss of 80 men (out of 200) sick or dead." It was about then that Weddell "kindly" piloted Jewitt's *Heroina* to the nearest anchorage. Later, in the Malvinas, he also "linked" to the French captain, Louis de Freycinet, whose vessel, the *Uranie*, had been wrecked on the coast. Captain Freycinet introduced Weddell to his young wife, Rose Marie, one of the first women, perhaps the first, to circumnavigate the globe.[70]

Weddell arrived near Cape Horn during his second voyage (1822–24) in late November 1823 in the *Jane* (160 tones). A week later Matthew Brisbane, his mate, joined him in the *Beaufoy*, a single-mast cutter of sixty-five tones. The two crews totalled only thirty-five men. Weddell found that the long summer days (the three months beginning on 21 December) in the Cape Horn area had "an enlivening effect; and, when the weather is fine and the water smooth, the wildness of the scenery is quite romantic." He made a very pertinent climatic observation, the key phrase being "much depends on the direction of the wind." Strong southern winds from Antarctica are frequent in the middle of summer and can bring the thermometre down below zero. In contrast, a north wind will often bring weather "almost as fine as that of summer in England." The temperature is determined more by the source and direction of the wind than by the seasons. Moreover, the climate is not as severe as is often imagined. (See the end of this chapter.)

Although Weddell was more sympathetic to the Fuegians (the Yahgans/Yamana) than his predecessors, he was not shy about expressing his convictions concerning the superiority of his "civilisation" and of the

FIGURE 2.3. "A Man and a Woman of Tierra del Fuego." Drawing by Weddell.

Fuegians as "the lowest of mankind." He was aghast at their "miserable" appearance and punished them for petty thievery on board his ship. Despite the punishments and disparaging remarks, Weddell often had friendly and amusing encounters with them. He found them "to be not only tractable and inoffensive, but also, in many of their employments, active and ingenious."[71]

He met the Yamana in three bays or coves during nearly six weeks in the area, from late November 1823 to January of the next year. Previously the sealers and whalers who had been there may have encountered Fuegians in these bays, but no such accounts have as yet been found as far as I know.

Weddell First Meets the Yamana

On 23 November 1823, Weddell anchored the *Jane* in a small bay already named Saint Martin's Cove on the east coast of Hermite Island, near Cape Horn. He was probably correct when he affirmed that he and his crew were the first visitors in this cove "at least of the present generation." Probably the Yankees or British sealers had preceded him there (see below).

Saint Martin's Cove would soon acquire fame as the best anchorage near Cape Horn, much closer to the cape than Goree Road though it had much less anchorage space (Chapter 1). I assume that this cove had also been a chosen haunt of the Yamana, because they were almost always there when navigators arrived. Five years after Weddell, the Yamana greeted the English navigator Captain Henry Foster. In 1830 they met the commander of the *Beagle*, Captain Robert Fitz-Roy, three years later Fitz-Roy again and Charles Darwin and in 1842 they met Sir James Clark Ross, the famous British explorer (Chapters 3 to 6). In 1823, Weddell remained there for ten days securing wood and water while repairing the *Jane*, which had been damaged by ice in the Antarctic.

The entrance to Saint Martin's Cove, a beautiful little bay, is far wider than its base, which is lined with a rather narrow pebble beach backed by an upward sweep of land covered by a thick growth of stunted beech trees and brush. A small stream traverses its pebbled beach. The entire island is shrouded in a dense forest, interspersed by swamps, bogs, and narrow dips in the land between the hills. Originally there were no land mammals on the island. In 1988, when my assistants and I filmed the cove, we saw a few rats from ships. They had probably been there since Weddell's visit if not before. No seals were seen, only a few species of shellfish, although plenty of ducks.

Three days after Weddell arrived, on 26 November (1823), the Yamana came paddling toward his ship in two canoes, singing and gesturing. They refused to come on board despite his motions of welcome. They seemed astonished, not so much by him or his men but by the *Jane*. For a full quarter of an hour they paddled around the *Jane* "gabbling." Weddell reported that "At length their wonder at our persons having in some degree subsided, they paddled fore and after about the ship, and were to all appearance undecided whether the vessel was dead or alive; for never having seen a ship before, it would not be expected that they should at once reason from the analogy which their canoes afforded." Therefore these Yamana had never seen a ship before, so they were probably not in the cove if and when the commercial fishermen had been there.

This is not the only time the Yamana wondered if a ship might be alive, as will be related later (Chapter 13). Finally two men climbed on board. The crew was struck by their "very miserable appearance," and they seemed "astoneished at all they saw." Anything made of iron attracted their attention. To their great delight Weddell gave each a piece of a metal hoop that had been wrapped around an empty barrel. But they were afraid to approach the large cast iron pot on the deck. Weddell offered them beef, bread and "good Madeira wine." They tasted the beef but declined the rest.

Much later, by the end of the nineteenth century, the Fuegians will develop a taste for alcoholic drinks. With the arrival of numerous often rowdy seamen in the 1880s, alcoholism became a sort of epidemic (Chapter 13).

Weddell, like Georg Forster in 1774, was not sorry that the women remained in the canoes, thinking it advisable that the crew avoid temptations. But unlike young Forster, he politely offered the ladies a little wine in a japanned cup. The wine spilt out while they were examining this marvellous container, which they "cunningly retained." Weddell was resigned to its loss, thinking that it would be useful to them. He was amused the following day when he saw strips of his metal cup worn as necklaces.

At sunrise that next morning the party returned in their two canoes. Shouting loudly again, they expressed their wish to come on board. A third canoe arrived, and all the twenty-two men, women and children climbed on board. Weddell escorted them around his ship, noting how pleased they were by the bright stove and the mirror. "The monkey trick of looking behind the mirror for the reflected object was frequently practised; and though they had no doubt often seen themselves reflected in the water, yet having never before observed so sudden and distinct an appearance, their intuitive judgement was not sufficiently acute to satisfy them of the similarity."

Despite the guided tour and the watch kept over them, one visitor stole an iron belaying pin. Weddell lost no time impressing upon him that such conduct was a grave offence. He tied the "criminal" in the rigging ropes. A "smart lash with a cat-o-nine-tails" made him comprehend. "This gentle chastisement had the desired effect, for they were ever after afraid even to lift a piece of iron without permission." Note that the objects that attracted them most were made of iron.

The following morning, the same Fuegians returned "in a different dress, or rather colouring." The women had changed their face paint from red to black while the men were decorated with red and white streaks across their faces. If the designs and colours of the paints were intended to please their hosts, the message was lost on Weddell, who found their appearance "utterly grotesque." During the first meeting, two days earlier, the Fuegians had given Weddell any small article they had with them in which he had shown an interest, "but by now they had acquired an idea of barter." From then on they signalled to barter for pieces of iron hoops and other small objects on the deck that appealed to them in exchange for their bows, arrows and shell necklaces. The Yamana did not possess any "surplus": all they bartered had to be made again.

Like other navigators and Darwin, Weddell was impressed by the contrast between the labour the women performed and the idleness of the men. He saw the women paddling the canoes, gathering shellfish and tending to the children. He thought they also built the wigwams. All this labour while "the men sit at their ease." However, he found redeeming qualities in the men such as the affection they showed for their wives and children. He perceived that the women, despite the drudgery, were "better featured than the men: many of their faces are interesting, and in my opinion, they have a more lively sense of what passes." Once he noticed the women on board looking intently at one of his crew, a youth with "engaging features." As the young man was busily working on the ship, Weddell imagined that they had confused the handsome sailor for one of their own sex.[72] But it seems more likely that they appreciated his "engaging features" as a man.

His guests appeared to be so fond of their dogs (who resembled small foxes) that he wondered if they attributed supernatural power to them. A century later a Yamana declared to Gusinde: "The dog may really have a soul (*kashpi*) of its own, but only he, other animals do not." Lucas Bridges commented that the dogs helped them very much and that they were never abandoned, never left stranded in an isolated place.[73] Dogs were a great asset for hunting otters, certain birds, and guanacos. They accompanied the families in the canoes and slept with them as bed warmers.

The *Beaufoy* pulled into Saint Martin's Cove about a week after Weddell had arrived in the *Jane*. The sailors of the *Beaufoy* were delighted to meet the natives. One of the sailors offered coffee in a tin pot to a Fuegian who had come on board. Having drunk the coffee, he "was using all his art to steal the pot." When the sailor asked to him to return it, the Fuegian returned (mimicked) his words (in English) but not the pot. Finally the sailor lost patience, and shouted: "You copper-coloured rascal, where is my tin pot?" The "rascal" again repeated his words with such perfection that the onlooking sailors burst out laughing. The only one who did not laugh proceeded to search the ungrateful visitor, located the pot under his arm and seized it. Master Brisbane promptly sent the culprit to his canoe, forbidding him by gestures to return on board. But there was no whipping: Brisbane was proving to be more indulgent than his captain.

Ten days after Weddell had anchored in Saint Martin's Cove, when he was about to leave, he noticed the Indians paddling rapidly away. He ordered a boat to be lowered, jumped into it, and caught up with them. Thinking they were fearful of being searched for stolen goods, he reassured them by giving each man a piece of an iron hoop and each woman a bright half penny with a hole in it to suspend from the neck. He bade the Saint Martin natives farewell with this thought: "At this age of the world, it appears almost incredible, and certainly disgraceful, that there should still exist such a tractable people in almost pristine ignorance." The "almost pristine ignorance" was mutual. Weddell was as ignorant of the Fuegians' world as they were of his.

Shortly thereafter the two vessels headed up the Pacific coast to islets known as Idelfonso. Three or four days sufficed to "harvest" a large quantity of fur sealskins.[74] Thomas Bridges asserted that the Yahgans (as he called them) had visited Idelfonso Islets (at 55°44′ south latitude) thirteen and a half miles from Black Point (Punta Negra), the southern extremity of Hoste Island.[75]

Weddell's Second Encounter

The two ships sailed back to the inhabited area, and on 7 December 1823, the crews found good anchorage on one of the smaller Morton Islands, in a bay Weddell named Clear Bottom (not on the Chilean maps). Here they were in the vicinity of Henderson Island, where Drake had seen Fuegians 250 years earlier. During the first full day there the crew spotted four canoes approaching their ships. Soon they heard the occupants shouting and making "ludicrous attitudes expressive of joy." Weddell surmised that this was their first contact with Europeans, because they seemed so amazed and also because they possessed no foreign articles, as he noticed later. When the four canoes were near the *Jane*, Weddell ordered a whaleboat to be lowered. He and several of the crew, holding up pieces of iron hoops, rowed towards the four canoes. When the boats were about to meet, the women in two of the canoes scrambled into the other two, while the men paddled the four canoes following the whaleboat back to the *Jane*, keeping pace in a heavy "head sea." Several men quickly came on board and barter ensued. Weddell enticed them with what they most desired: pieces of the iron hoops. He explained: "We gave in exchange some things almost useless to us, but very interesting to them."[76] This comment succinctly expresses the beauty of barter: you offer that which you do not need or seems worthless in exchange for something you desire or that appears more valuable.[77]

Weddell and Brisbane spent some time admiring the sling that they had received in the barter transaction – its symmetrical stone, its pouch made of sealskin, and its string, about three feet long, made of animal gut "handsomely plaited," terminated by knots "of ingenious workmanship." One of the young men demonstrated to the crew how to use the sling. He and his companions were "a good deal astonished" when Brisbane demonstrated that he too was dextrous with the sling. He had learned this art at home, in faraway England.[78] Despite its simplicity, a well-aimed stone thrown forcefully from a sling is a formidable weapon, as Captain Fitz-Roy was to learn several years later (Chapter 3). Weddell was also intrigued by two finely pointed "spear heads" made of hard bone, about seven inches (18 centimetres) long. One had a single large barb while the other had many small barbs down its side. Thin ropes of hide were attached to the heads so they could be retrieved if they missed their mark. Again one of the Yamana demonstrated their use. He grasped the spear with the longest pole, which was ten feet (3 metres) long, held the pole firmly near the middle at the height of his right eye, and threw it with "great precision." This time Brisbane did not offer to demonstrate his ability.

When the *Beaufoy* sailed on to Antarctica (South Shetland Islands) on 9 December, the *Jane* was left with only two small boats so Weddell decided to purchase one of the canoes. While pointing to the canoe he had chosen, he made signs to the owners offering two barrel hoops. He commented that his offer may have seemed excessive and explained that he made it because he realised that the canoe had "cost them much labour." The family who owned it shouted for joy and rapidly shifted to another canoe, taking their belongings with them. While Weddell was hoisting the canoe onto the *Jane*, he wondered why it was so heavy. He soon found out: a six-inch (15-centimetre) layer of clay was spread over its entire base. As ballast, it served to steady the canoe, which was made of the usual three wide strips of beech bark sewn together. He noted that most of the beech trees (*betuloides*, the evergreen species) in the area were crooked, though a straight trunk of ten or twelve feet could be found in the interior of the island. His canoe was of about average size: twelve feet four inches (3.75 metres) long and two feet, two inches (66 centimetres) wide. It proved to be strong, "capable of going against the wind at a quick rate." It was so strong, Weddell thought, mainly because of the semicircular ribs, that overlaid its interior. Secured with clay cement, they formed a lining of the entire interior of the canoe and gave solidity to the frame. These ribs were preferably made of whale baleen, although strips of wood were also used.

Weddell noted that his canoe had seven sections. The fishing gear protruded from the first section, the front or the prow. A woman, usually the wife, sat in the next section with the foremost paddle. The fire was set in the third division, where children and dogs huddled to keep warm and a meal could be cooked. In the fourth section the bailing container (made of bark) was placed. A man, normally the husband, occupied the fifth section. The next was a place for a companion woman with the aft paddle. The stern served as a "locker" for the rest of the equipment, including the long spear poles and personal items. However, not all the canoes were divided into such clearly defined sections. At times the husband or older son stood in the prow spearing fish or a seal, while gesturing to the women rowers to guide the canoe.

Weddell was pleased with his canoe and also to see that its previous owners were "quite merry, and seemingly happy in the possession of the hoops with which I had paid them." But his mood changed when he noticed his guests on board ravenously gobbling up the mucilaginous substances, dirty rancid seal fat, which had been lying about the deck for several days. He interrupted their meal by offering them chunks of young seal meat and bread, which they accepted, probably pleased, as they stored them away in their canoes. They sipped a little wine, which they seemed not to like.[79]

A wrestling match between a young sailor and an equally young Fuegian took place after dinner, when the crew sought a little distraction. Weddell was amused at the beginning of the match, when the merry seaman,

commenced singing and dancing, at which the Fuegians formed a circle round him, and imitated his song and dance most minutely. The circular movement, however, presently turned into a sort of play, in which a sailor and Fuegian were endeavouring to throw each other. I at first fully expected to see the Fuegian fall, but I was mistaken: he stood so firm, that it appeared more probable that our sailor, who was a stout athletic young man of twenty-three, would ultimately be thrown.

The sailor was thrown and the Fuegians enjoyed their triumph. Weddell was mortified, fearing that they might get the idea that they possessed greater strength than his crew. "I could not avoid being angry with our sailor for his inactivity, and desired him in future never to contend with them in that way."[80] Ten years later Captain Fitz-Roy, having read this passage, prudently prohibited his men from engaging in such competitive wrestling bouts (Chapter 4). The match between the young Fuegian and Weddell's sailor was polite compared to the one Colonel Charles Wellington Furlong will witness between two Yahgans in 1907 (Chapter 15).

Yamana youths were trained to wrestle in earnest (though to avoid fatal outcomes), so it is not surprising that one of them overwhelmed the strongest English youth in Weddell's crew.

Weddell decided to discover whether or not the Fuegians had any awareness of "The Divine." Very like the French captain in 1715 (Chapter 1), he beckoned them to his side and read passages from the Bible, perhaps assuming that the magic of the sacred words, though in English, would have the desired effect. While reading and making gestures in an attempt to convey such notions as resurrection and supplication, he observed their reactions. He interpreted their attentive attitude, looking steadfastly at his face as they repeated his words, as indications of their "astonishment." He apparently forgot, at the moment, that the Fuegians were great mimics, though he did realise that they surmised that the book was talking (or whispering) to him and that he was simply repeating what the book was telling him, which in a sense was true. "One of them held his ear down to the book believing that it spoke, and another wished to put it into his canoe: in short, they were all interested in the book, and could they have made proper use of it I would willingly have given it to them."

Weddell gave his guests a variety of used garments. They were willing to taste exotic foods, were attracted to anything red, and were keen on obtaining pieces of iron, but they did not ask for clothes. The clothes that were later distributed among the Fuegians hastened their demise (Chapters 11 to 14). But in 1823 no one could have foreseen the effects that the giveaway clothes were to have on the Fuegians' health. The crew and the Fuegians as well, enjoyed scenes during which, Weddell remarked, they "were all so clothed in patches that they made a most amusing appearance."

While in Clear Bottom Bay, Weddell noticed that the Indians lacked a chief and seemed to have no need for one. Here he had greater insight than Captain Cook, young Forster and even Darwin. Weddell expressed admiration for the generosity and affection they showed toward one another.

The philanthropic principle which these people exhibit towards one another, and their inoffensive behaviour to strangers, surely entitles them to this observation in their favour, that though they are the most distant from civilised life, owing principally to local circumstances, they are the most docile and tractable of any savages we are acquainted with, and no doubt might, therefore, be instructed in those arts which raise man above the brute.

His perception goes far but is strangely contradictory. If he could have freed himself from his "civilised identity," he might have realised that the Yamana's "philanthropic principle" was such that they did not need to be raised "above the brute." But perhaps my comment is unfair, given the "all too human" propensity to overvalue one's own ethnicity.

In Clear Bottom Bay, Weddell had seen the Fuegians during only four days (8, 9, 17 and 18 December). In the interim he had returned to outer

FIGURE 2.4. "The brig *Jane* in need of repair and the cutter *Beaufoy*," in Indian Cove. Drawing by Weddell.

islets, Diego Ramirez, to kill fur seals for their pelts. On 19 December he bade farewell to the Clear Bottom Bay natives and sailed away. He passed another week sealing in Idelfonso. On Christmas Day he was joined by the *Beaufoy*, which had returned from the South Shetland Islands, where Brisbane had not been able to put to shore because of ice sheets. To give an idea of the enormous size of such ice sheets, which sometimes break off from the shore and float in the Weddell Sea, a mass of ice of 3,250 square miles (8,417 square kilometres), calculated as weighing 720 million tones, was reported in a Chilean newspaper at the beginning of 2002.

His Last Encounter
Both ships left Idelfonso the day after Christmas and found good anchorage in a small bay that Weddell called Indian Cove at the west entrance to New Year's Sound (Seno Año Nuevo on the Chilean maps). Weddell stated that he gave the sound this name because he was there on the first day of 1824. By a curious coincidence, Captain Cook had been there on the same day of 1775.

Weddell stayed in Indian Cove, off and on, from 26 December to 4 January, when repairs were made on the *Jane*, whose bows had been damaged by running against masses of ice near Idelfonso.

The base of Indian Cove is wide, but the beach there is very narrow, and wet bog lands cover the sloping hills surrounding most of the cove. It did not seem very inviting as a campsite in 1988, when I was there with a film crew. This may explain why, during Weddell's stay, the Yamana were not camping on the shore of the cove but rather on the island at its entrance.

Again Weddell received an enthusiastic welcome there. The natives paddled toward the *Jane* "shouting as usual, and spreading out their arms, apparently impressed with a sensation of fear and joy." They were motioned to come on board, and once they were on the deck, Weddell realised that they had had contact with Spaniards. He heard two words in Spanish, *canoa* and *perro*, and noticed that the features of several Fuegians were different from the others. He wondered if their high noses and somewhat tall height indicated traces of Spanish ancestry dating back almost 250 years to the Spanish presence in Magellan Strait. He was thinking of Sarmiento de Gamboa's disastrous attempt to colonise the Magellan Strait in the 1580s, mentioned in Chapter 1. Weddell imagined that during the long ordeal, from 1584 to 1587, when the 400 survivors who had reached Famine Bay were starving to death, some of the desperate men might have procreated with the Indian women (Alakaluf), and that their descendants, through the centuries, had passed part of their genes on to the Yamana of Indian Cove. Weddell's hypothesis seems rather farfetched. If the latter had any Spanish ancestry, it seems more plausible that it would have been derived from recent navigators, sealers or castaways whose stories have never been told in print.

About forty Fuegians climbed on board the *Jane*: some completely naked though painted with red ochre, while others wore otter-skin capes. Weddell purchased the skins "off their backs" in exchange for used clothes. One of them slipped on a white flannel shirt "in great ecstasy." His ecstasy was short-lived. The shirt, held "in high estimation," was passed around and worn for eight or ten minutes by each visitor; then it was torn apart, divided, and the pieces were shared by all. This, Weddell observed "was an instance of their holding property in common." It is also another example of the Yamanas' "philanthropic principle," which most foreign visitors were not prone to recognise.

As the men willingly helped the crew fill the casks with water "with as much expedition as our own people," Weddell quickly hired them to pull and haul all sorts of equipment around the deck, which they did with ease. He was pleased despite the deafening noise they made as they roared in unison with each pull, imitating the sailors. Meanwhile the women and children in the canoes received small presents and were entertained by the sailors singing, accompanied by a fiddle and a German flute. "The women, indeed, were in ecstasy at hearing a song given by a young man who had a fine voice." Weddell began powdering the heads of the women with flour, which also greatly pleased them, but soon he found the amusement too costly and the fun came to an end. Then it occurred to him to acquaint them with firearms. When he fired a large gun "the women shrieked and the men were appalled, and looked at the engine with a vacant gaze." Weddell was adversely impressed by their reactions, so he took precautions. He immediately armed his eight crew members with cutlasses (knives), muskets and pistols. His caution seemed justified when, three days later, on 30 December at about 4 AM, forty or fifty Fuegians jumped on board without notice. The second mate rushed down to the captain's room shouting "the natives intend to take possession of the vessel!" Pistols in hand, Weddell rushed up the stairs and almost ran into some of the intruders rushing down. The instant they saw him and his pistols they jerked around and flew up ahead of him. But when he stepped on deck he realised that the second mate's fears were groundless and ordered the crew not to fire on the natives. A possible tragedy was avoided by Weddell's cool head.

Some hours later he assembled the pacified visitors for a Bible reading, just as he had done in Clear Bottom Bay. This time he seemed disappointed as he observed them, "looking each other in the face, with a countenance expressive of extreme wonder, and speaking to one another in a low tone of voice; but notwithstanding these appearances of a religious principle, I could discern nothing like a form of worship among them."

Perhaps to console himself Weddell began admiring a stranded necklace of small, beautifully coloured shells they had just given him. He wondered "how they can perform the plaiting by the hand." In return for some "small presents," they also gave him several skilfully made baskets, small bows about three feet, eight inches (1.07 metres) long, twenty-five-inch (64 centimetre) arrow shafts, topped by sharp, triangular, detachable flint heads, and another arrowhead inserted in a nine-inch (23-centimetre) handle, which he thought was used as a stiletto. Obviously Weddell was pleased with all these gifts.

It was not long before the Fuegians began "pilfering" from the *Jane*. Apparently they did not regard it as such, because they offered *Jane's* booty to the crew of the *Beaufoy* (which had just returned), and vice versa, trading between the cutter and the brig.

Weddell seemed resigned: "Their knowledge of barter had evidently increased their spirit for thieving."[81] The Yamana may have been playing a game simply to confuse or amuse the crews. The French novelist Jules Verne offered a different analysis: the Fuegians were in "a complete state of stupidity," while Weddell and his crew were so stingy with their pieces of iron bands and so much wealth, that the Fuegians felt free to take anything that pleased them.[82] Weddell may have been somewhat stingy, but just why Jules Verne assumed that the Fuegians were stupid is not so clear.

The last day of the year Brisbane showed that he was not stingy. When the *Beaufoy* arrived, loaded with the skins of fur seals, the Fuegians climbed on board, anticipating a feast of seal meat or fat. "They were not disappointed, for Mr Brisbane had brought them a quantity, and it was shared out among them."

Weddell thought them very clever at cutting the blubber from sealskin until he noticed an old man who was much too clever. While slicing the blubber, the old gentleman "hauled a skin, bit by bit, under his arm in a most dextrous manner." When he was forced to give it up, he laughed most heartily, but not Weddell. This incident substantiates Jules Verne's comment: Weddell was somewhat stingy with his piles of sealskins, not one of which was offered to his Yamana guests.

Despite this awkward incident, this same day Weddell and Brisbane were guided ashore to visit the natives at home (on the island at the entrance to Indian Cove). Upon arrival, about sixty men greeted them and escorted them around their "town" (a few wigwams). As neither women nor children were seen, the visitors imagined that they had been sent into the nearby woods. Meanwhile several fires were lit to show their "joy at our visit, but the fires also seemed to be an invitation to other Fuegians." Sure enough, soon two canoes arrived with guests from the upper part of New Year's Sound. Entering a wigwam, Weddell noticed "a sea-gull, perfectly tame, and jumping about, which conveys an idea of their affection for the lower animals." The seagull was a common pet (for a similar example, see Chapter 15).

Meanwhile the Yamana had prepared a serving of mussels for their guests and "vied with each other in bringing me the best." Despite the friendly welcome, Weddell and his men, who were armed, kept their boat close on hand. Meanwhile the "too clever old man" appeared, and Weddell gave him to understand that he had been forgiven. He and the others gazed with awe as Weddell shot two (untamed) sea gulls with just one discharge of his fowling piece. He explained to his readers that he did not allow his hosts to see him load his gun, and that after firing it he always put the muzzle in his mouth. This gesture gave the impression that he loaded his gun "by speaking into it." Weddell was doing his best to mystify them. No wonder they also thought that the Bible spoke to him.

One of the crew and a Yamana began singing and dancing together, but the fun suddenly came to a halt because two other seamen started for the woods. The natives were uneasy, apparently because their wives were hiding just where the two men were headed. Weddell promptly ordered them to solve their urge some other place. Later a young seaman fled to the waiting boat, escaping from a Yamana man who had mistaken him for a woman. So the "boat close on hand" had served a purpose.

The women and children finally emerged from their hiding place. They and the men numbered almost eighty (a large number for one camp, though it probably included the neighbours). The oldest were three men fifty to sixty years old. Weddell saw no case of sickness among them except one man with palsy. That day or the next, the *Jane* departed for three days, again to the Diego Ramírez islets to finish the sealing business. When the *Jane* returned to Indian Cove on 4 January, eleven canoes came paddling so rapidly to greet Weddell that he feared some would capsize, but all arrived safely and the natives came on board. Shortly afterwards Weddell and his men bade a fond farewell to their numerous hosts, who returned to their canoes "reluctantly."

Then Weddell sailed on to Patagonia. The visits had been a success for all concerned. The *Beaufoy* remained in the area for another two weeks to continue the seal harvest. Brisbane reported later that the natives had "behaved in a quiet, friendly manner." He did more sealing off the Malvinas Islands and the South Georgia Islands and joined Weddell in March in Patagonia. Somewhat later they both sailed for England, arriving in May 1824.[83]

Brisbane Returns

A year and a half later (October 1825) Brisbane returned to the area. This time he used Maxwell Cove (Hermite Island) as a base for his sealing excursions. Some of the natives who came on board remembered having seen him nearby in Saint Martin's Cove. They bartered for iron hoops and were peaceful as usual, although they had not lost their pilfering habit. But now it was done in a gentlemanly fashion and the few who succumbed to the temptation were treated with consideration. Nevertheless, Brisbane became rather offended by one "pilferer" who, while having a wound on his leg bandaged by a seaman, attempted to steal a tumbler and a pivoted piece of a lock. Brisbane found consolation with the women. They never tried to steal anything when they brought their children on board for medical assistance (there is no report of women ever pilfering on the visiting ships). Finally, Brisbane was probably gratified that, with very few exceptions, they all had behaved in a most British manner. Like Weddell, he frequently employed them to work on his ship, to his complete satisfaction. Despite their preference for seal fat and other "gross substances," they enjoyed the ship's fare they were offered, all except the "spirituous liquors."

Brisbane noted an object not yet mentioned: the leg bone of an albatross used as a straw to sip water from a pail made of bark, which is a more elegant way to drink than stooping down to drink out of the river, as the Yamana are shown in photos.

In early December 1825, Brisbane sailed on to Indian Cove and found the same natives he and Weddell had met two years earlier. A 200-gallon iron pot they had given them had been dented by stones thrown at it, in an attempt to break it (probably in order to give everyone a piece or to make tools). They agreed to sell Brisbane otter skins, but at such a "comparatively exorbitant" price that he had the impression that, during his absence, their knowledge of trade had much improved, if so by other sealers during the interlude.

In mid-December 1825, Brisbane returned to Maxwell Cove and was about to depart when some forty Fuegians gathered to bid him and his crew a heartfelt farewell.[84] Brisbane was easygoing and had an excellent rapport with all the Yahgans.

The *Chanticleer* Arrives in Saint Martin's Cove

By 1826, British interests in South America had become immense. That year the Admiralty sent the *Adventure* and the *Beagle* to Tierra del Fuego and in 1828 the *Chanticleer* to the South Shetland Islands off the Antarctic Peninsula. The age of the great discoveries was over. Both of these expeditions were concerned with problems of geophysics, navigation and the economic potentials of regions already discovered.

The *Chanticleer* sailed into Saint Martin's Cove in 1829, five years after Weddell had departed. The *Chanticleer*, a sloop (a three-mast, fast vessel) was named for a rooster of medieval fables, perhaps an important person's herald. The expedition (1828–30), under the command of Captain Henry Foster (not to be confused with the Forsters, the father and son of Captain Cook's expedition), had not come to harvest seals or quarry whales but to tackle an ambitious research project. The science historian Sandra Herbert pointed out that the Admiralty (as advised by the Royal Society) assigned this expedition to ascertain "the true figure of the earth, and the law of variation of gravity in different points of its surface." The *Beagle* project, in comparison "was a very modest affair indeed," she added. Dr W. H. B. Webster fulfilled the traditional role of surgeons and was assigned to the scientific endeavours not directly concerned with the expedition's objectives. The contrast between Webster and Darwin, which Herbert analyzed, will become evident in Chapter 5.[85]

I venture to say that Webster, though a physician, was more like Weddell than Darwin. His vivid style and diverse interests coupled with a remarkable faculty for observation, make his testimonies about the Yamana, the fauna, and the climate particularly instructive.

The crew of *Chanticleer*, having spent almost two months exploring Staten Island in late 1828, sailed on to the South Shetland Islands and the Palmer Peninsula, the "handle" of the Antarctic continent. Nearing Saint Martin's Cove on 25 March, Webster exclaimed: "Here all the beauties of the wildest Alpine scenery burst upon our view." He would soon think otherwise.

Foster and his crew remained there for three weeks in 1829, although they contacted the Fuegians only during the first week, late March to 3 April, for a reason to be explained. The expedition was delayed there because of adverse weather and to make measurements, called "pendulum experiments," for calculating the longitude. While entering the cove, the crew noticed smoke curling up among the trees from the tip of a wigwam. Soon the natives paddled out to greet them, but they were not invited on board because the officers thought they would prove "troublesome" on deck while the crew was bringing the ship to anchor. So they paddled home, perhaps a little disheartened. A few days later Webster and some of his shipmates were welcomed in their huts and returned several times during the week. The glass beads and gilded buttons, among the gifts the Fuegians received from the crew, pleased them, but the hatchets failed to interest them. (No mention is made of iron hoops or red cloth.) Despite their good will and pleasant manners, Webster thought they were indolent. "A very little labour seemed to exhaust them; and instead of doing it themselves, they were continually applying to our men to cut wood for their fire. They would even ask them to launch their canoes . . . they seemed to be weak and incapable of undergoing labour."

Perhaps their recollection how they had laboured for Weddell and Brisbane was still fresh and they had decided to take it easy with the next visitors. Webster was also appalled at the sight of their huts, "the most wretched of this kind of structure." But he admired the women's necklaces, made of small bones and red snail shells. Both sexes wore the sealskin capes, though some of the men were naked. In addition to their capes, the women wore "aprons." As a medical doctor, Webster noticed that all of them had sore eyes, owing to smoke from the fires in their huts, which they huddled around "in listless apathy." They shared their beds with heat suppliers, their "very ferocious dogs," which resembled foxes or Eskimo huskies. He remarked that everyone possessed a dog, a canoe, and fishing tackle. But "their riches," as Webster called them, were far more than these three possessions. He found them good-natured, smiling, docile, with no symptoms of fear or cowardice and, despite their indolence, "fully capable of receiving instruction... their habits simple and inoffensive; their general demeanour modest and becoming." Webster, like Weddell, recognized their moral qualities.

Webster was amused by the women's fishing ability, which fifty years later intrigued Dr Hyades, the French physician (Chapter 13). First they fastened a limpet on a line without a hook of any kind, and when a fish swallowed the bait, they would slowly draw the fish to the surface and then quickly lift it out of the water with one hand while holding on to the line with the other.[86]

For the first time, the women were seen as "chubby," more so than the men, and (despite their sore eyes) most were "generally well conditioned." Webster noticed the women's slender wrists, small hands, and handsome tapering fingers, "which they use with a gracefulness not to be found elsewhere among their class in the scale of the creation." He inspected the Yamanas' slings, their bows, and their "neatly made" arrows with points of obsidian used for hunting birds. He affirmed that "warfare appears not to trouble these people." He was also aware of the vital importance of their knowledge of how to ignite fire with two pieces of pyrite. Webster was a keen observer. He offered a different image of these people than that of Captain Cook and young Forster, although Webster, like them, found "the vicinity of their persons by no means desirable."[87]

The Seals Learn...

Webster is to be credited, again along with Weddell, for calling attention to the effect commercial fishing was having on the colonies of fur seals. He was aware that the occasional killing of seals by the Indians could not have produced a drastic change in the seals' behaviour. The following text is quoted almost entirely because here Webster offers a truly exceptional image of the strategies the seals were adopting in their efforts to offset the danger of the massive slaughter by the commercial sealers.

When these animals are for the first time visited by man they evince no more apprehension of danger from their new guests than did the natives of San Salvador when first visited by the Spaniards.... But they soon... acquire habits of distrust and caution, and devise ways and means for counteracting human stratagem and treachery. They select more solitary retreats, on the tops of rocks, beneath high projecting cliffs, from which they can precipitate themselves into the water the moment they perceive the approach of their arch enemy. While encamped in their rockeries, three or four sentinels are always posted to keep a lookout while the others sleep; and the moment a boat makes its appearance, though it be a mile from the shore, these faithful watchmen promptly give the alarm, when in an instant the whole rockery is in motion. Everyone makes for the surf with all possible expedition; so that by the time the boat reaches the shore, they will nearly all be in the water, with the exception of a few females that have pups or young ones to take care of. These will remain to defend and protect their charge until the last moment; when, if hard pushed, they will seize their pups by the back of the neck with their teeth, and dive into the surf, where they are obliged to hold the heads of the pups above water to prevent their suffocation. The males, many of them, will also stand their ground, and fight very hard for the young seals; often till they perish in the noble cause.[88]

The decline in the seal population was playing havoc with the Yamana's principal resource, as already mentioned, and the surviving seals were more difficult to locate.

And the Climate?
While Webster's weather analysis is common knowledge to meteorologists and archaeologists, it may not be so to the rest of us. He clearly explained that, in the comparable northern latitudes where the sun's rays fall on land (Alaska, northern Canada and Greenland), the heat is not absorbed nearly as much as in the Cape Horn area, where the radiation falls on immense expanses of water that retains heat, and the water is very deep, so that both factors result in a greater degree of mildness, even during winter, than in the northern latitudes. The sea preserves a nearly uniform medium temperature of about 44°F (20.9°C) and the air above it can never remain far below that temperature for any length of time. Consequently the temperature remains relatively stable throughout the year.[89] However, like Weddell, Webster insisted that the beneficial effects of the climate were offset by the direction and force of the wind

and the humidity. "Situated at the southern extremity of South America, it is exposed, to the rudest violence of the wind. Here everything is dripping with rain, and bending under the violence of the wind, the effects of which a few short intervals of calm are not sufficient to compensate."[90]

The quantity of rain that fell during one month of that year (1829) from 21 April to 21 May, was eight inches, which is more than a third of the quantity that falls annually in England. The wind could strike as gales and squalls, and change course with uncanny rapidity. Again Webster explained:

Southwest gales are exceeding violent at Cape Horn, and are accompanied by the most terrific squalls that I have ever witnessed; these squalls may be considered hurricanes for the short time they last. They rush down the hills in the ravines with the most awful violence, threatening destruction to all before them, carrying the sea up in spray over the sides of the cove some hundred feet.[91]

Webster was the first chronicler to have published (in 1837) an analysis of the climate in the Cape Horn area, according to the marine historian Vanney.[92] He reported the thermometre readings for May 1829, a month before the onset of southern winter (June to September), a mean of 40°F (18.7°C), maximum 48°F (23.1°C) and minimum 30°F (−1.11°C). The bays or ports in the Cape Horn area are never frozen over, nor does the snow lie on the ground for more than two or three days. However, he overstated when he wrote: "The Fuegian Indians are perfectly naked; they care for no dress and seldom use it." As mentioned above, he observed them mostly on board his ship, when by this time they had learned to leave their capes at home (see also Fitz-Roy's comments near the end of Chapter 3).

Then Webster added these revealing remarks: "Again, vegetation, that unerring index of climate in all parts of the world, proclaims the winter of these southern regions to be mild and temperate."[93] "Revealing" because the vegetation responds more to the mild temperature than to the force of wind: an observation that Captain King explained below.

Farewell Natives

Webster may have been distressed by the farewell the *Chanticleer* crew unwittingly gave this hospitable people. The night of 3 April the crew fired rockets while experimenting with their pendulum clock, mentioned above. This display so startled the natives that they fled from the ship and never returned, "imagining that we were in possession of an evil spirit which we could always let loose among them at pleasure."

The Yamana Deal with the Climate

In their family-made bark canoes and scant clothing, they were at home in this maritime environment that most of the Europeans found devastating. They had the advantage of an accumulated knowledge of the climate, especially the winds and the currents, thanks to their long experience in the area. They could predict the weather of the near future, though not infallibly. For instance the French navigator, Louis Ferdinand Martial, reported that the Fuegians (the Yamana), "like all savages are gifted with highly developed senses, they carefully observe the natural phenomena and direct their behaviour accordingly: the form of the clouds, the direction and force of the wind, the apparition of a rainbow are all sources of information which they pay great attention to before engaging in any activity."[94]

Darwin also insisted that the Fuegians had much keener eyesight than the Europeans. The acuteness certainly aided them as they scanned the sky for signs of a coming storm. When possible they kept to the more protected inland waterways. They were familiar with the details of the topography; the location of the best camping sites, where and when their different foods were available, the dangerous passes, and the accessible coasts in case of an emergency. On the other hand, there were unexpected changes in the weather, miscalculations concerning tides, underwater obstacles they had not noticed, load capacities of the canoes they had not correctly estimated, and so forth. Navigation problems certainly existed with the bark canoes though they were very different from those of the large sailing vessels.

In the course of thousands of years the Fuegians became genetically adapted to this climate. Moreover, at birth the newborn was bathed in seawater and the infant was often exposed to rain and even to falling snow, balanced on the mother's lap while she was paddling a canoe. Not only did Yamana anoint themselves and their children with seal and whale oil (when available) as often mentioned, they kept as close as possible to a fire that they transported everywhere in their canoes. And, as Webster observed, the temperature was not as severe as might be expected.

But Why Were They Shivering?
The Fuegians were seen shivering on board the ships and in their canoes and not so much because of the temperature but because, following Weddell's and Webster's analyses, they were exposed to the violent winds that often brought rain, hail and sometimes snow. They were very

probably not shivering while they were navigating along the shores or in their huts with a fire close by. But they shivered when they were exposed to the wind, standing on the decks of the vessels nearly naked or while waiting or paddling in their canoes on the side of a ship in the middle of a channel or a bay where they would also be exposed to the wind. Even when the Yamana did not fear being obliged to trade their seal capes, these were quite heavy and would have proved cumbersome while climbing up and down the ships' cord ladders. These may be sufficient reasons to explain their shivering in the presence of strangers. Briefly, they were far less sensitive to the cold than the Europeans because they were genetically resistant, because they were rarely if ever without a fire nearby and because they anointed their bodies with seal or whale fat.

The native Yamana had "survived" there during 6,000 years (according to the archaeologists), even cheerfully, to judge from their happy mood when greeting most of the early navigators.

Why So Often Hungry?

By 1830, if not a few years before, their diet consisted of a variety of shellfish, fish, birds and eggs besides berries, mushrooms and by then, exceptionally, of seal and whale fat and meat. They had to keep on the move to obtain sufficient sustenance except when a stranded whale was available. They stored whale and seal meat at times in the beds of fresh water rivers and preserved fungi by drying them over the fire but not sufficient food to carry them through days of scarcity. Moreover, since their food was shared, there was not always enough to satisfy the appetites and preferences of everyone in the group so relative scarcity could occur at any moment. Here is my answer to the above question: they took advantage of the navigators' bounty as they did of the whale's bounty. They had no mealtime schedules, so they ate when the eating was good, on board the ships as "on board" a whale.

Later one of the missionaries' helpers and Gusinde remarked that they managed to survive more adequately than large sectors of Europe's poor.[95]

Captain King Arrives

Webster and his crew must have been overjoyed when, on 17 April 1829 the *Adventure* "broke in upon our solitude; for our friends the Fuegian Indians had left us."[96] One of His Majesty's Ships, the *Adventure*, under the command of Captain Phillip Parker King, had dropped anchor near the entrance to Saint Martin's Cove, loaded with provisions for the *Chanticleer*. Eight months earlier, in Montevideo, Captain Foster had asked Captain King to bring him supplies at this time and place, in order to save him the voyage back to Montevideo and enable him to sail directly to the Cape of Good Hope on the way back to England. The *Adventure* remained in the Cape Horn region an entire month (mid-April–mid-May 1829) while her crew surveyed the islands nearby and made observations of the climate. No Fuegians were sighted. They failed to appear, Captain King was told, because they were wary of the rockets fired on 3 April.

Comparing Climates

Webster commented that Port Famine (near Punta Arenas, about the middle of the continental shore of the Magellan Strait) is two degrees nearer the equator than the Hermite area (near Cape Horn); nevertheless at Port Famine the winter "appears to be colder, as the thermometre falls lower" than in the Hermite area,[97] precisely because of the greater expanse of land that surrounds Port Famine, as Webster noted.

However, Captain King had been surprised to see the tropical fuchsia and veronica plants in that central part of the Magellan Strait, near Port Famine, on the continent. He was surprised because the winter temperatures are low and the wind blows constantly, bringing constant rain. The existence of such tropical plants in that unlikely environment greatly impressed King. "There must be, therefore, some peculiar quality to the atmosphere of this otherwise rigorous climate that favours [such] vegetation; for if not, these comparatively delicate plants could not live and flourish through the long and severe winters of this region."

In this area of the Strait of Magellan, King also noticed parrots eating seeds of the tree called winter's bark, and hummingbirds feeding on the fuchsia flowers even "after two or three days of constant rain, snow and sleet, during which the thermometre had been at the freezing point." He attributed the prevalence of these warm-country birds and plants to the mildness of the climate, despite the low temperatures. This observation seemed contradictory. In an attempt to explain it he referred to his personal experience of not feeling at all cold when the internal and external temperatures were at freezing point or several degrees below, even though he was not "particularly warmly clad." This he attributed to "the peculiar stillness of the air" at that level, even though the overhead wind was high.[98]

Varieties of both the parrot (the Austral parakeet) and hummingbird (the green-backed fire crown), cited by King, also thrive in Tierra del Fuego. Darwin identified two species of hummingbirds he had observed there: the *Trochilus forficatus*, which covers 2,500 miles (4,630 kilometres) from Lima to Tierra del Fuego and the *Trochilus gigas*. Darwin also noted the presence of evergreen trees flourishing "luxuriantly" there, as well as parrots and hummingbirds feeding on the seeds of the winter's bark trees. He was also aware that the "equable climate" there was due to the large area of sea as compared with the land.[99]

Webster's, King's, as well as Darwin's observations contradict the commonsense notion that further south, the closer to the Antarctic one moves, the colder the climate becomes. It does, of course, become colder as the Antarctic Conversion is approached. However, King and Darwin did not explain the absence of tropical birds and mild-climate flora in the Cape Horn area, which is even "warmer" than the Magellan Strait area. The reasons again may be the wind, the gales and squalls, and the humidity of the latter area.

Farwell Captain Foster

King was aware that Foster was suffering from a deep depression and later thought that his death later by drowning may not have been accidental.

This was my last meeting with Captain Foster who, the night before we sailed, communicated to me a presentiment, which he could not shake off, that he should not survive the voyage. . . . In the premature death of this young and accomplished officer, the Society has to deplore the loss of a zealous and active votary to science. . . . Captain Foster was unfortunately drowned, near the close of this voyage [in 1831], while descending River Chagres [Panama] in a canoe.[100]

Just why Foster took the voyage home via Panama is not explained here.

In June 1829, having aided Foster to his utmost, King took the *Adventure* up the Pacific to Valparaíso. From there he rode on horseback to Santiago to reassure the Chilean authorities that His Majesty had no intention of annexing the island of Chiloé, the *Adventure*'s next port. But we are ahead of our story and will revert in the next chapter to three years earlier, when the *Adventure* and the *Beagle* departed from Plymouth Sound.

3

1826 to 1830: The First Voyage of His Majesty's Ships to Tierra del Fuego; Four Fuegians Taken to England

The Expedition Weighs Anchor

His Majesty's ships the *Adventure* (330 tones), the flagship, and the *Beagle* (235 tones) sailed from Plymouth Sound bound for Tierra del Fuego on 22 May 1826.[1] By way of comparison, in 1998 the Royal Caribbean Line boasted that *Majesty of the Seas*, its pleasure ship, weighed almost 74,000 tones.

Captain Philip Parker King, thirty-five years of age, a highly esteemed seaman, was the commander of the expedition and captain of the *Adventure*, the flagship. Captain Pringle Stokes, somewhat younger, was the second in command and responsible for the *Beagle*. The Admiralty had instructed Captain King to survey the southern coasts of Uruguay, Argentina, and Chile: the estuary of the Río La de la Plata, the Atlantic coast of Patagonia, the Magellan Strait, the intricate maze of islands as far as Cape Horn, as well as the labyrinth of channels along the Pacific coast of Chile to Chiloé Island, at the northern extremity of the archipelago. He should also avail himself of "every opportunity of collecting and preserving, specimens of such objects of Natural History as may be new, rare, or interesting." The explorer Eric Shipton remarked that this was "certainly a formidable task for two small, square-rigged vessels operating in one of the most tempestuous regions of the world."[2]

The British Meet the Tehuelches

The two ships entered the Magellan Strait on 26 December 1826, seven months after their departure from England. Six days later, natives were sighted "on horseback riding to and fro upon the beach" beyond the First Narrows, in Gregory Bay, on the north shore of the strait. These natives were Patagonians; though recently labelled Aónikenk, they are better known as Tehuelches. The explorers visited them several days, and were impressed by their horses and their long fur capes made of guanaco skins, puma hides and even skunk fur. Captain King took particular notice of Maria, "the tribal chief," and one of her children, "a principal person," mounted "upon a very fine horse, well groomed, and equipped with a bridle and saddle that would have done credit to a respectable horseman of Buenos Aires or Montevideo." Maria spoke to King freely, a bit in Spanish and a bit less in English. King thought that the principal person was Maria's daughter, one of her five children. But he soon realised that he was mistaken. He explained:

The absence of whiskers and beard gives all the younger men a very effeminate look, and many cannot be distinguished, in appearance, from the women, but by the mode in which they wrap their mantles around them, and by their hair, which is turned up and confined by a fillet of worsted yarn. The women . . . wear their hair divided, and gathered into long tresses or tails, which hang one before each ear.

Three young male natives boarded the *Adventure* and sailed beyond the Second Narrows to a place called Black Cape (Cabo Negro), where Maria and the rest of her tribe rode on horseback after killing several guanacos to supply the ships with meat.[3] Some seven years later, in March 1834, Darwin will also be pleased to meet Maria (Chapter 5).

The Patagonians seemed "to take a particular liking to Parker King," Keith Thomson suggested "because they [he and the other British] were less stingy with the trading [less than the Spaniards]."[4]

At Black Cape Maria supplied King and the crews with guanaco meat in exchange for "useful presents." Here he noted that "the country assumed a very different character; instead of a low coast and open treeless shore, we saw steep hills, covered with lofty trees, and thick underwood."[5] This sudden change in the landscape corresponded to different habitats. The flat, treeless country to the east was a Tehuelche camping ground, while the Alakaluf lived in the forest country to the west.

The two ships met again further down the coast at a place called Freshwater (Agua Fresca), beyond Sandy Point, the site of the future port of Punta Arenas. Here they saw the Fuegians (Alakalufs) for the first time. That summer of 1827, the temperatures were unusually high, ranging from 67°F (33.7°C) to 87°F (44.8°C); therefore it is not surprising that the native men were clothed in short sealskin capes. The women must have been too warm, wrapped in their large guanaco mantles. King thought

FIGURE 3.1. The *Beagle* in the Magellan Strait.

that these canoe-paddling Alakaluf were, "a most miserable, squalid race, very inferior, in every respect, to the Patagonians." Later he decided that the former were not "usually" deficient in intellect.

The two ships sailed on and found a better anchorage a few days later in a bay, at about the middle of Magellan Strait, known as Port Famine because of the many Spaniards who had died of hunger there in the late sixteenth century (Chapter 1). Captain King found it to be an excellent harbour and chose it as the base for the entire expedition.

Captain Stokes Explores

As commander of the expedition, King ordered Stokes to survey "the least known, and the most dangerous part of the Strait," from Port Famine to its exit at the Pacific Ocean. This assignment proved to be formidable and had to be accomplished between mid-January and early March. The risks of navigating the western half of the Magellan Strait have always been daunting and above all in sailing vessels and when it was mostly uncharted. Stokes often had to take a small boat (a cutter) to explore the coasts for days on end and leave the ship in the charge of Lieutenant Skyring, his mate. A surveying ship always carried several small boats (cutters and whaleboats) to penetrate narrow channels and shallow waters that the mother ship was too large and cumbersome to handle.

During these excursions in the boats, Stokes and his men had to proceed with great care to avoid capsizing. They were often cold and soaked but unable to go ashore to light a fire because there were few places to moor along these tightly forested coasts, covered with rocks and swept by strong currents. Also the water along the shores was often too deep to secure an anchor. Rescue would be difficult, as they had no contact with their ship.

A month after weighing anchor from Port Famine, the *Beagle* was still unable to reach the exit. Stokes was forced back three times by violent squalls as he attempted to leave Tamar Island, near the exit.[6]

He Meets the Alakaluf

Finally Stokes located another anchorage nearer the exit in Mercy Harbour (Bahía Misericordia), on the large island Captain Cook had named Desolation. A canoe loaded with Alakalufs paddled up to greet the newcomers and remained nearby for five days in early February 1827. Stokes discovered that these natives hunted seals, sea otters and even porpoises besides gathering mussels, limpets and "sea eggs" and occasionally located the carcass of a beached whale, thanks to the flocks of gulls pecking at it and its fetid odour. Despite such abundant resources, they came aboard the *Beagle* and "greedily" consumed all the food they were offered. And like "Weddell's Fuegians" (Chapter 2), they preferred the seal fat they were given, which "was scrupulously divided, and placed in the little baskets formed of rushes, to be reserved for eating last, as the richest treat." As soon as they boarded the *Beagle*, they began shivering, again like the Yamana. Stokes was amazed at these "wretched creatures shivering at every breeze." They were not the hardy savages he had imagined: "I have never met people so sensible of cold as these Fuegian Indians." However, unlike Weddell's Fuegians, they willingly drank the wine and brandy they were served.

Stokes remarked on the Alakalufs' "wonderful aptitude for imitating the sounds of a strange language." He was "amazed" when he visited them on the shore and observed the affection the parents lavished on their children. "I often witnessed the tenderness with which they tried to quiet the alarms our presence at first occasioned, and the pleasure, which they showed when we bestowed upon the little ones any trifling trinket."

Stokes was also impressed by the respect the mother showed for her young son. It all started when one of the seamen thought the bargain for a dog made by Stokes had been agreed upon by the mother, whom they assumed to be its owner. When the seaman seized the dog, the woman screamed so dismally that Stokes told him to desist. Then Stokes increased his offer, but she still refused while pointing to two other dogs to replace the chosen one. When Stokes' offer became irresistible, she called to someone nearby in the "thick jungle." Out came her young son, the real owner of the dog, so the goods offered were shown to him. His people urged him to sell his pet, "but the little urchin would not consent. He offered to let me have his necklace, and what he received in exchange was put away in his own little basket." The child kept his darling pet.

Stokes was curious to find out if they preferred any colour among the strings of glass beads he was offering them, but they clutched all of them indiscriminately.[7] They were not crazy about red, as the Yamanas were farther south.

Another Difficult Assignment

Huge breakers thundered in from the great ocean, striking the *Beagle* almost continually during the five-day stay in Mercy Harbour. Then began what Keith Thomson described as, "the most difficult of all their tasks: the survey of the western opening of Magellan Strait."[8] The crew managed to manoeuvre the ship to the entrance of the strait, opposite Desolation Island, near a group of four towering rocks 800 feet (244 metres) high, named Evangelistas by Magellan when he passed through this exit in 1520. The English called them the Islands of the Directions, because they are lead markers for the entrance to the strait.

In 1953 Annette Laming, the French archaeologist, was able to reach the Evangelista Islet where the Chilean Navy had built a lighthouse. She described it as "perhaps the lighthouse of most difficult access in the world. . . . There are no beaches on any of the Evangelistas, no places to pull up to shore, and everywhere the high pointed rocks are covered with slippery algae against which the waves break endlessly."[9]

Captain Stokes anchored the *Beagle* near one of the Evangelistas. The ship remained there several days while he departed in a small boat with two days' provisions to survey the surroundings. As he and his men rowed through this labyrinth of islets, vast numbers of right whales were swimming about and fur seals reclining on the rocky shores.[10] The British and Yankees had missed these whales and seals, perhaps because the area is so dangerous (Chapter 2).

Stokes Rescues Castaways

Stokes was baffled on his way back to Port Famine, early March, when he sighted a rowboat with six men gesturing from a distance, seeking help. He was amazed when they came on board and informed him that their ship had been wrecked almost four months earlier in a violent storm and that the other survivors were waiting to be rescued on Fury Island, near Brecknock Peninsula, on the Pacific front. The exhausted men explained that their wrecked schooner belonged to the sealer James Weddell, who had returned to England several years before, and that it was manned by Matthew Brisbane (Chapter 2). Then the castaways told their story. Their ship, the *Prince of Saxee Cobourg*, was sinking fast in a storm early last December (1826). The crew of twenty-two men got safely on shore in their whaleboats, with most of their provisions and their cargo of sealskins. There, on Fury Island, they built shelters and waited, hoping that a vessel would come by. The weeks dragged on but none appeared on the horizon. One of the crew was badly burned by an exploding keg of gunpowder and another died of some sickness. Brisbane punished three men for attempting mutiny when they tried to escape in one of the whaleboats. Each man was taken (in a whaleboat) to a different island with only a week's provision of food and left there alone. No news of them was ever reported. Then the remaining crew began losing hope of ever being rescued, so Brisbane allowed seven men to leave in the largest whaleboat. They would try for Carmen de Patagones at the mouth of Río Negro on the Atlantic coast, the nearest point of civilised habitation about a thousand miles (1,852 kilometres) away. Port Lewis on the Malvinas Islands (renamed Falkland Islands in 1833) was nearer than Carmen de Patagones, but it was too difficult to navigate there in a whaleboat. Later it became known that the seven men had reached their destination and eventually had volunteered to serve in the army of the Argentine Republic in a war against Brazil.

About a week before Stokes rescued the others, Brisbane had sent them, the second mate and five seamen, in the last whaleboat to the Magellan Strait, hoping to find help. The men who had stayed on Fury Island feared that Indians might attack them, make off with their few belongings, and leave them more destitute than ever.[11]

After Captain Stokes heard the details of the disaster, he selected a dozen or so men to accompany the castaways back to Fury Island. They went in two boats, each equipped with ten oars. After two days of rowing some eighty miles (148 kilometres), they sighted Fury Island. The two weary survivors on watch could barely distinguish the boats approaching from a distance. They seized their guns, shouting to alert their companions, "the Indians, the Indians!" When the boats came nearer, they recognised their rescuers and were overcome with joy. Later they told their rescuers that a party of Fuegians (Alakalufs) had recently visited them but had "conducted themselves very peacefully."[12] The Alakaluf came to Fury Island and neighbouring Skyring Island from time to time, despite the often furious sea, for the fowl, the fish in the kelp, the seals, and possibly to collect pyrite on Skyring.

Early April the *Beagle* reached Port Famine, with the eleven Fury Island castaways, where the *Adventure* was waiting. When both ships sailed to Río de Janeiro, Brisbane and the other survivors stayed in Tierra del Fuego. Brisbane will reappear six years from now (Chapter 5).

To Río de Janeiro and Back

April 1827 to January 1828 the two ships left Tierra del Fuego to be refitted and the stores replenished in Río de Janeiro. On the return trip, in Montevideo, King purchased a schooner as an auxiliary, which he named *Adelaide* in honour of the queen to be (wife of the future William IV). The three ships were detained on the return route surveying sections of the Patagonian coast (Argentina) and returned to Port Famine in January 1828.

A Whaleboat – Stolen

Several Alakalufs stole a whaleboat from the *Adelaide* a few months later, along the coast of Magellan Strait. The culprits had swum through the icy water, severed the rope that secured the boat to the schooner, and tugged it away in the silence of the night. The crew's brief search came to naught and the episode ended there.[13] Another whaleboat will be stolen, this time from the *Beagle*, about two years later, but the episode will not end so nicely (see below).

Stokes' Last Exploration

In mid-March 1828, Commander King assigned Stokes to a more difficult mission than the previous one. First he should complete the survey he had begun the year before, explore the exit of the strait (52°23' south latitude) again, and from there proceed north, surveying the archipelago, to the large, turbulent Gulf of Peñas (47°20' south latitude). Five degrees of latitude had to be surveyed in four months, between late March and the end of July 1828, in an area known for its squalls of hurricane force and incessant rain and hail. If Stokes' first expedition demanded all the stamina that he and his crew could summon, this assignment will drain them, particularly Stokes, who carried the "burden of command." The wisdom or folly of his decisions and actions will determine the health, morale and very lives of his crew as well as the outcome of his mission.[14]

By late March, autumn was under way, as were the long winter nights. Moreover, to conduct the surveys, Stokes and his men had to make their way through the channels in one or two boats and often wait out the storms in rock-strewn coves, or huddled against a shore. As during his first assignment, their boats risked being cracked open by submerged reefs, hurled against the rocks, or tipped over in wind-swept inlets. And again, often they had no bottom to secure the anchors because of the great depth of the water in the channels. Rowing in these conditions, the crew was usually soaked, exhausted and tensed while trying to remain alert and complete their assignments as fast as possible during daylight. The region, from the western exit of the Magellan Strait up north to the Gulf of Peñas, was and is more foreboding than the Tierra del Fuego islands south of the strait. The temperature may be only slightly colder (see end of Chapter 2) than further south, but the rains are constant. Stokes wrote on 12 April that "The effect of this wet and miserable weather, of which we had had so much since leaving Port Famine, was too manifest by the state of the sick list, of which were now many patients with catarrhal, pulmonary and rheumatic complaints."

However, all was not gloom and doom. Along the inner channels in the protected bays and coves north of the exit to the strait there were and still are some veritable paradises of wooded groves and sandy beaches. A month after departure, on 27 April, Stokes encountered a beautiful cape at the extreme northern shore of the Gulf of Peñas that they named Port Otway for the commander in chief of the British vessels assigned to South America. The stormy weather obliged them to remain there nearly a fortnight, from late April into May. They returned there as often as possible: ten days later and again in mid-June, when many of the crew were ill and sorely needed a rest.[15] By then they had surveyed the northern shore and the islands in the Gulf of Peñas, but winter was closing in. Despite the weather, they surveyed an island called San Javier, or Xavier, where John Byron, the grandfather of the poet, had been wrecked in the *Wager*, almost a hundred years earlier, in 1741 (Chapter 1). Stokes got no sounding there with a line at nine fathoms (54 feet, or 16.4 metres). However, he managed to secure three anchors nearby at twenty fathoms (120 feet, or 37 metres) during the worst weather he was ever to experience. He wrote poignantly:

Nothing could be more dreary than the scene around us. The lofty, bleak, and barren heights that surround the inhospitable shores of this inlet [of San Javier] were covered . . . with dense clouds, upon which the fierce squalls that assailed us beat . . . as if to complete the dreariness and utter desolation of the scene, even birds seemed to shun its neighbourhood. The weather was that in which . . . "the soul of man dies in him."[16]

Stokes' soul was dying. The dismal landscape, the ever-present dangers while navigating, the deteriorating health of his men, the necessity of directing each in his various tasks while manipulating the instruments to effect the surveys – all weighed heavily upon him. "Showers of rain and hail, which beat with such violence against a man's face, that he can hardly withstand it." The only traces of human settlement along the coasts of the Gulf of Peñas were the forsaken remains of wigwams near San Javier Island.

While they were still in the Gulf of Peñas, Stokes evoked a longing for human contact. "The place being destitute of inhabitants, is without that source of recreation, which intercourse with any people, however uncivilised, would afford a ship's company after a laborious and disagreeable cruise in these dreary solitudes."[17]

Commander King wrote later: "Captain Stokes began to show symptoms of a malady, that had evidently been brought on by the dreadful state of anxiety he had gone through during the survey of the Gulf of Peñas."[18]

Before the voyage was over, Stokes had plunged into a bottomless depression. Three days after reaching Port Famine, on 1 August 1828, he shot himself. But even then he had not freed his soul. His delirium lasted four more days, "his mind wandered to many of the circumstances and hair-breadth escapes of the Beagle's cruise." And he still lingered on "in most intense pain" until 12 August.

King was shocked and deeply troubled by this tragedy. He passed the command of the *Beagle* on to Lieutenant Skyring, who "deserved the highest praise and consideration" for so courageously assisting Stokes during both expeditions. However, King's appointment of Skyring had to be approved by Admiral Robert Otway, his superior, whom they were scheduled to meet soon in Río de Janeiro.[19]

To Río de Janeiro Again

The men, deeply affected by Stokes' agony and death, were anxious to leave Port Famine. Also, many were sick with scurvy, rheumatic afflictions, and lung pains. The three vessels weighed anchor after he was buried on the shore of Port Famine. Having stopped over in Montevideo for the men to be treated, they arrived in Río de Janeiro in mid-October 1828, just in time for the rendezvous with Admiral Otway.

King's Disappointment

The admiral countered King's proposal of Skyring as commander of the *Beagle* in favour of the "flag lieutenant" of his own ship, the *Ganges*. King was dismayed: "[It] seemed hard that Lieutenant Skyring, who had in every way so well earned his promotion, should be deprived of an appointment to which he very naturally considered himself entitled."[20]

The new commander of the *Beagle*, Robert Fitz-Roy, had been promoted to the rank of captain, though he was only twenty-three years old. He had been sailing on the *Ganges* with Admiral Otway and had previously completed four years as a junior lieutenant on another British ship, the *Thetis*. Even so, he was less experienced than Skyring and had never navigated the Strait of Magellan or the Fuegian channels. Did Fitz-Roy's ancestry, as a direct descendant of King Charles the Second and the nephew of the Duke of Grafton, determine his appointment?[21] Perhaps not: King's judgement that Fitz-Roy had fine qualities as a seaman is convincing, given his disillusion that Skyring had not been chosen. King truly admired Skyring. He insisted that despite Skyring's "shattering disappointment . . . [Skyring] acted with characteristic equanimity, never displayed the slightest rancour, and became and remained on excellent terms with his new superior."[22] While still in Río, Admiral Otway appointed Skyring to take charge of the *Adelaide* schooner, which King had purchased in Montevideo the previous year. Fitz-Roy may not have been aware as yet of Skyring's exceptional moral fortitude, though he already sensed the challenge of taking on the *Beagle*, "a battered ship and a demoralised set of men and leading them straight back to the same desolate region where their previous captain had been driven to suicide."[23]

As yet Fitz-Roy was not troubled by the mental disturbances that would haunt him later. In addition to his ability as a seaman, he was "blessed" with a curiosity that encompassed native inhabitants as well as the natural sciences. Very soon he expressed regret that there was no naturalist on board the *Beagle*, and he himself will write extensively about the Fuegians and the Patagonians, though without native informants (Chapter 5).

Fitz-Roy Sights the Alakaluf

Coming from Río de Janeiro, the *Beagle* turned into the Atlantic entrance of Magellan Strait. Beyond the Second Narrows, near Black Cape mentioned above, Fitz-Roy noticed natives in a canoe near the shore, especially a young woman, who would not have been "ill-looking, had she been well scrubbed." This is not the first time he is enthusiastic about a native young woman, but he found the others, an old woman, a few men and children, far less appealing. Their heads were very (too) small at the top and the backs of their heads had "very few bumps," which Fitz-Roy "knew" was evidence of their mental inferiority (Chapter 4). More realistically, he noticed that their bodies were smeared with clay and oil as a protection against the cold, and that one of their canoes measured twenty-two feet (7 metres).[24] The canoe Weddell purchased from the Yamana in Clear Bottom Bay was only twelve feet (4 metres) long. This difference is not surprising, because normally the Alakaluf canoes were larger than those of the Yamana. He did not express much interest in these Alakalufs despite his appreciation of the un-scrubbed young woman. The expedition continued on to Port Famine.

Following an absence of over nine months, the *Adelaide* and the *Beagle* returned to the Port Famine base in mid-April 1829. King continued down to Cape Horn in the *Adventure* to keep his promise to Captain Foster, as related at the end of the last chapter.

Fitz-Roy and Skyring – Crammed Schedules

Fitz-Roy and Skyring had to complete the surveys during these months. King gave Fitz-Roy three assignments: first to survey, with Skyring, the main channels that lead from the Magellan Strait to the south (the Magdalena, Cockburn and Barbara channels). For the second assignment, Fitz-Roy should explore the two waterways on the continent, north of the strait. And third, he was to complete Stokes' survey of the western section of the strait.[25] Fitz-Roy and Skyring were probably told then to meet King in Chile, on Chiloé Island, the northern extreme of the Pacific archipelago, sometime during July or August.

A few days after arriving in Port Famine, mid-April, the two ships pulled out and, working together, almost completed the first survey as planned. No natives were encountered during these surveys, but the men were struck by the beauty of the mountain range covered with "dazzling snow." Fitz-Roy finished his part of the assignment in two weeks and then anchored the *Beagle* in Port Gallant near the centre of the Magellan Strait (below Port Famine), while Skyring continued the survey.

Fitz-Roy Encounters Other Alakalufs

For the second assignment, exploration of the two waterways north of the strait, Fitz-Roy selected twelve men to accompany him in two boats

supplied with provisions for twenty-eight days. He took the best whaleboat and assigned the cutter to a young midshipman, who by an odd
coincidence had the surname Stokes, though he was not related to the
late captain. The *Beagle* was to remain in Port Gallant in charge of Lieutenant Kempe.

Starting out on 7 May, the crews confronted violent southwestern
winds and torrential rains that dampened them and their initial enthusiasm. One objective was to discover if there was a water route parallel to
the Magellan Strait toward the west, the Pacific Ocean. Fitz-Roy failed to
locate one because he had to turn back too soon (from Skyring lagoon,
see below). Such a route exists, but it is roundabout and difficult, nearly
impossible to navigate in a ship.[26]

Fitz-Roy was off to a good start; despite the torrential rains, he penetrated the continent via Jerome Channel, which he described as "so very
pretty; the whole shore was like a shrubbery . . . every sheltered spot is
covered with vegetation, and large trees seem to grow almost upon the
bare rock."[27] The Alakaluf would probably have agreed with him. Much
later the French archaeologist Joseph Emperaire located traces of their
camps there.[28]

During this trip Fitz-Roy reported on five encounters with the Alakalufs
and on four localities that were not on the charts and were barely
known to outsiders. They appear on the Chilean maps in English, as
Fitz-Roy named them. Beyond Jerome Channel they "discovered" the
first locality, Otway Water (a saltwater lagoon), some fifty miles (93 kilometres) long, that he named in honour of the commander in chief. This
"water" is connected, by a very narrow channel, named for Fitz-Roy, to
a smaller "saltwater," thirty-four miles (63 kilometres) long, which he
called Skyring, who should have had his job. These were the second and
third localities. The fourth was a small cluster of hills north of Fitz-Roy
Channel. He climbed one and called it Beagle Hill.[29]

Suddenly, about mid-May, four canoes and several wigwams came
into view, rowing along the shore of Otway Water. The native men
approached the shore hallooing and jumping to greet the strangers. They
were a colourful lot: one was painted entirely red, another entirely bluish,
and a third completely black. Several others were decorated with black
paint on the lower halves of their faces. Some wore skins over their
shoulders and the rest were naked except for the paint. Fitz-Roy thought
that this "tribe was very rich in Fuegian wealth" with their skins of
guanaco, otter, seal and deer (*huemul*), their arrows and lances. They
appeared "stronger, stouter, livelier and more active" than the Alakaluf

Fitz-Roy had seen along Magellan Strait, though their language, huts, weapons and canoes were similar. As Otway is salty, they showed the strangers where to dig for drinking water. Fitz-Roy was pleased that "they seemed inquisitive, and cunning, and shewed [sic] great surprise at a sextant and artificial horizon." When he put a watch to the ear of one of the men, the others came close to hear it tick, shaking their heads with astonishment. Fitz-Roy "felt certain" by their gestures that "they had an idea of a Superior Being." On safer ground, he deduced that they previously had contact with Europeans because they possessed knives, were fond of tobacco and were eager to barter. He or one of his companions noticed that they had hidden their pelts and other valuables in the woods. Although they were friendly, Fitz-Roy thought they seemed "apprehensive."[30] Past experience had evidently taught them to be wary of strangers and above all not to don their valuable pelts when greeting them, which probably explains why some of the men were naked.

Fitz-Roy became indignant when he noticed that one of his tinderboxes was missing and assumed that these natives had "artfully hid [it] under the sand," in order to make off with it later. It was soon found in the sand, where it had simply fallen and been trampled on by someone.[31] He was more relaxed about his tinder during the second encounter. A few days later, a man and boy approached the crew and simply requested some tinder to light a fire in their wigwam. The captain complied willingly and they went their way without more ado.

They continued through Fitz-Roy Channel and briefly surveyed the northern shore of Skyring Water. Fitz-Roy decided to turn back from here, as time was short, and to forgo surveying the entire salt lake in search of the other water route. On the return trip, toward the end of May, along "his" channel, he went ashore and entered a wigwam while greeting its three inhabitants, a woman and her two children. He was welcomed and soon began sketching a portrait of her. While showing it to her, he understood by her facial expression that it did not please her. Clearly she found the drawing too white, because she quickly painted her own cheeks red. Fitz-Roy got the message and added red to his drawing of her cheeks. Then she was "quite satisfied." In return, she daubed Fitz-Roy's and his companions' cheeks with red paint.[32] This was a truly beautiful gesture: she not only discreetly "told" Fitz-Roy how to improve his portrait of her, she also painted him and her other uninvited guests. Red was the favourite colour of the Alakalufs and of the Yamanas. Actually it was the only bright colour made into paints, as the others were shades of black and white.

Back in Magellan Strait they met the fourth group on the rather large Charles Island (Isla Carlos) on 5 June. Here was a family of five with their young dogs "seemingly more miserable than their owners." The husband agreed to barter one of the puppies for a bit of tobacco. But shortly the husband motioned that he wanted that puppy back because his wife had not consented to the sale. Fitz-Roy refused until "they began to abuse in right earnest, the woman alternately crying and scolding, and the man apparently calling on the wind and water to destroy us." Fitz-Roy was astonished, "to see so much feeling for a wretched little half-starved puppy, and made them happy by returning him, without requesting the tobacco." This incident recalls Stokes' encounter with the little boy so attached to his pet dog, that he refused to sell it despite the generous offers. Obviously dogs were more important to some of the Fuegians than just for hunting otters and as bed warmers.

The last (the fifth) group they met was also a family, on a very small island then called Prince, near Port Gallant. The man was wearing what had been a sailor's trousers he had obtained from the *Beagle* or the *Adelaide*. Somehow he had managed to tie the rags around his legs in six places. They wondered how the family resisted the cold, with hardly any clothes in their half covered wigwam. One minute they were sitting close to the fire, "and the next perhaps up to the waist in water, getting mussels and sea eggs. The woman and girls were diving for sea eggs, even in the middle of winter, though the water was never very cold ($42°$ to $44°$F)."[33] Recall that Webster had noted the same water temperature in the Cape Horn area (end of the last chapter).

Fitz-Roy and his men reached Port Gallant and the *Beagle* the night of 8 June. He was glad to climb into his comfortable bed. "Not even a frost-bitten foot could prevent me from sleeping soundly for the first time during many nights." He was also relieved when Skyring showed up soon afterwards in the *Adelaide*, with all the crew in good health and to hear that he had completed King's first assignment. The three channels, that had now been surveyed (Magdalena, Cockburn and Barbara) formed a triangle with some of the points previously fixed along the Magellan Strait by Stokes.

During Fitz-Roy's absence, two Yankee sealing vessels had stopped over in Port Gallant and greeted the crew that had remained in the *Beagle*. One of the vessels had been to Staten Island and the other had come from the Chilean Pacific coast. Fitz-Roy and Darwin would meet several such sealing ships during the second *Beagle* voyage. Many small-time commercial seal hunters remained in the area into the twentieth century (Chapter 15).

From Magellan Strait to Chiloé Island and Back

The two crews were busy surveying the western section of the strait during the last weeks of June, their third assignment, while preparing for the next long voyage. On 29 June, the two vessels headed for Chiloé, the large island at the northern extremity of the Chilean archipelago. Fitz-Roy took the outer Pacific Ocean route and did not come across the native inhabitants. He may have run into stormy weather, as it took him twenty days to cover some 760 miles (1,408 kilometres) and only a week on the return trip, or perhaps the directions of wind determined the difference. The *Beagle* sailed into San Carlos, the main port of Chiloé, about 20 July, when the *Adventure*, arrived from the opposite direction, from Valparaíso. There King had ridden on horseback to Santiago to reassure the Chilean authorities that His Majesty had no plan whatsoever concerning Chiloé. Back in Valparaíso, he sailed down the coast and joined the *Beagle* in San Carlos. By then, 1828 or 1829, the new Republic of Chile (since 1810) had finally taken over Chiloé Island from the Spanish Royalists and General Aldunate, its first governor, was extremely hospitable to his English visitors.

Skyring, in the *Adelaide*, was detained by bad weather for two more months while surveying channels of the archipelago. When he arrived late September, King praised him for his accomplishments. He and his crew had suffered no losses or illness, though their ship had been somewhat damaged and later repaired there, in San Carlos. The *Adelaide* weighed anchor from Chiloé, over two months later, in early December 1829. During the following five months, Skyring finished surveying the Pacific archipelago. His ship arrived safely in Port Famine, in early May 1830, where the *Adventure* was waiting.[34] I no longer refer in detail to the voyages of these two ships, though they are mentioned later on, in order to focus on the *Beagle*.

Fitz-Roy Begins Surveying the South of Magellan Strait

The *Beagle* departed from Chiloé, before the *Adelaide*, in mid-November 1829, taking the direct ocean route again and arriving a week later at the entrance to Magellan Strait, at Desolation Island, near where Stokes had been in 1827. During the first weeks of December, Fitz-Roy and his crew worked, surveying the outer coast of Desolation, seventy-one miles long, and that of the neighbouring Santa Inés Island, fifty-three miles long.[35] They were also searching for safe harbours for ships coming from or heading for Cape Horn.

The *Beagle* pulled into a bay of a small island off Desolation Island called Landfall (Recalada on the Chilean maps), where one or more Alakaluf families were camping. Soon sixteen people came in one canoe (a heavy load for a canoe only eight to twelve feet long) to greet the strangers while eating the petrel eggs and the raw chicks they had brought along. Fitz-Roy noticed that "in every respect" they resembled those he had met along the Magellan Strait. They refused to exchange their seal furs for beads and trinkets and requested useful articles, such as knives. Their manner of bartering convinced Fitz-Roy that they had had dealings with other Europeans, probably sealers.

Two days later, 21 December, he assigned several men to take the best whaleboat to survey the ocean front of Landfall Island. The headman of the group was Master Matthew Murray, who had been with Fitz-Roy on the *Ganges* and was transferred with him to the *Beagle* in Río de Janeiro. Fitz-Roy felt confident that Murray could be depended upon for this difficult task. Several sailors and Dr Wilson, the surgeon, were chosen to accompany Murray. Fitz-Roy told them "to get some angles and bearings necessary for continuing the survey." Having completed their work on the ocean side of Landfall, they attempted to return to the *Beagle* during several days, but powerful gusts of wind threatened to upset their whaleboat or drive it out to sea, where they would have no hope of rescue. Their provisions gave out the day before Christmas and continual rain had soaked their ammunition and tinder, so they had no fire, nor could they find shellfish or fowl. Given this desperate situation, the next day Murray told Wilson and the coxswain (the sailor in charge of the whaleboat, whose name was cited later as Elsmore), to hike across the island and signal for help from the *Beagle*. Soon after they started they felt weak and tired from climbing and the lack of food, but they continued on until they finally sighted the *Beagle* on the inland coast of Landfall Island far below. Their signals were perceived and a boat was dispatched to fetch them. Coming down to the coast to meet the boat, Wilson and Elsmore ran into about twenty Fuegians (undoubtedly also Alakalufs, as this area was their territory), mostly men and a few women and children, near their wigwams. The men attacked Elsmore by trying to pull off his clothes. He managed to free himself and the two reached the *Beagle* exhausted but alive. Murray and his companions were rescued soon afterwards and recuperated rapidly. This was Murray's first *Beagle* adventure; his next will happen soon, and his most famous one a few months from now, in April 1830. Elsmore will play his role in the very near future.

Once the men were safe, Fitz-Roy and some of the others hiked back to the group of wigwams where Elsmore had been attacked. The would-be robbers, families and all, had vanished, so Fitz-Roy entered one of their wigwams. Looking around inside at the assortment of tools, he noticed swords made from iron hoops and old cutlasses worn thin and realised right away that they had been obtained from sealing vessels. He deduced that the Fuegians there had imagined that Wilson and Elsmore were sealers, hence the rough treatment of the latter.

Fitz-Roy then commented on the Alakalufs he had met so far: on their main food of seals and penguins, and their ingenious method of trapping petrels. They tied a string around the leg of a live chick, inserted it in an empty petrels' nest (a hole in the ground), and then hid nearby holding on to the other end of the string. When the petrels returned to their nest, they attacked the young intruder, clutching it so fiercely that one or both petrels could be pulled out of the nest along with the chick, and that was that, the "hunters" enjoyed a light meal. Fitz-Roy also noted that wild fowl and shellfish were very scarce on the inner coast, "probably because the Fuegians had scared or consumed them."

Later William Low, a sealer, told Fitz-Roy that he had seen Fuegians on Landfall Island, surrounding a number of "(apparently) tame seals." Though vague, this extraordinary comment is the only reference I found to "tame seals" in Tierra del Fuego.[36] Low, a Scottish sealer with long experience in the area will join Fitz-Roy during his second voyage (Chapter 5).

Fitz-Roy climbed a mountain and, with the aid of his "glass," he encompassed a great distance towards Cape Horn and distinguished several hundred islets, huge rocks and breakers. He thought that the natives probably found their way easily through this "very broken land." But as he saw very few seals, he added, "where the natives go with their canoes, seals are never found in any numbers." His reason for the scarcity of seals in this area is undoubtedly mistaken. The commercial sealers, who normally slaughtered many thousand seals in just one assault, were certainly responsible for the scarcity there, and they were still in this area. Recall that the Alakalufs on Landfall Island had been in contact with sealers. A few days later, Fitz-Roy saw a sealing vessel that had been on one of the islands of the group he named for his grandfather, the Duke of Grafton. He mentioned another nearby site, Hope Harbour, also used by sealers.[37]

Fitz-Roy Buries a Memorial on One of the Grafton Islands

The *Beagle* dropped anchor below the promontory that juts into the sea at Cape Gloucester on the largest island of the Grafton group (named Carlos on the Chilean maps), which fronts the large island named Santa Inés. This promontory is so steep that it appeared "like a mountain rising out of the sea." A day or so later, early January (1830), Fitz-Roy decided that Cape Gloucester was too exposed and its bed too unreliable for anchorage so he moved the *Beagle* to a more sheltered cove nearby. Then he and twelve of his crew hiked back to Cape Gloucester to survey the area. Having camped along the shore, the next day they climbed to the summit of the promontory, where there was barely enough room to set up their theodolite, the instrument that measures horizontal and vertical angles. However, they found sufficient ground there to bury two memorials, one in a tin and the other in a bottle, probably the usual Union Jacks, buttons, and coins. Then they hurried back to their camp with their pockets full of rock specimens.[38] Hopefully a patriotic Chilean, a reliable historian, or an honest eco-tourist will recover these memorials as a public treasure before someone else does.

During their absence, several Fuegians (Alakalufs), had come to their camp in two canoes made of "boards sewed together." Fitz-Roy noted that these canoes were similar to the wooden pirogues he had seen near Chiloé Island.[39] The new arrivals were quiet and inoffensive, though distrustful. Fitz-Roy was amazed when he learned that they too had climbed the steep Gloucester promontory, and in just half the time that he and his men had taken. This is one of the very few references to the Alakaluf as expert climbers. Fitz-Roy does not explain why they had hiked up this steep promontory; perhaps to view the *Beagle* and the movements of the crew. However, he was curious to know how they managed to bring their canoes into such an exposed cove as Gloucester and thought that perhaps they had carried them overland from a more sheltered part of the island. The Alakaluf as well as the Yamana had many portage trails, where they lugged their canoes across stretches of land from one body of water to another (see below). Later Fitz-Roy noticed a canoe with a sealskin sail near one of the smaller Grafton islands. Captain Cook had seen such a sail in December 1774 in Christmas Sound, also Alakaluf territory. Apparently the Yamana did not make them, perhaps because they preferred to stay within the channels, while the Alakaluf often hunted along the more turbulent Pacific front.

Before they sailed on, Fitz-Roy offered some pertinent advice: "Should any future voyager feel inclined to make similar excursion towards Cape Gloucester, he had better not think too lightly of his task."[40]

Firestone (Pyrite) on Skyring Island

Continuing their voyage down the Pacific coast, they arrived in the vicinity of the famous Brecknock Peninsula, the "tail end" of Isla Grande, at the entrance to Cockburn Channel. Fitz-Roy climbed a mountain – about 2,700 feet (823 metres) high – on a small island opposite the peninsula and named the mountain and the island Skyring, just as he had one of the salt lagoons north of the Magellan Strait. He may have admired Skyring's magnanimity with regard to his appointment as commander of the *Beagle* and thought to show his gratitude in this manner.

He noticed pyrite in the rocks on Skyring Island and on another nearby (probably Fury Island). When such rocks are broken, they produce a strong odour of sulphur. Once extracted from the enveloping rock, pyrite can produce a spark when struck against a very hard substance: rock, flint (silex) or iron. This was the only method known in Tierra del Fuego to ignite a fire (see Chapter 4, near the end). If the pyrite on Skyring could easily be extracted from the rocks, it is very likely that the Alakaluf went to these islands to obtain it. Again Fitz-Roy regretted that there was no naturalist on board to analyse the mineral.[41] He will make sure that there will be one if and when he returns here.

He found a sheltered anchorage, in late January 1830, on Fury Island, where Brisbane had been shipwrecked, a "wild exposed place to be avoided if possible."[42] Natives arrived there to greet or visit the strangers, but they were not allowed on board because they were "dextrous thieves." Thieves or not, Fitz-Roy bartered "some of their very valuable property," probably for trinkets.[43]

Was Brecknock Peninsula Treacherous?

The area of Brecknock Peninsula is often cited as being so treacherous to navigate in bark canoes that the Alakaluf are believed not to have risked passing beyond it toward the east (see the two maps at the beginning of the book). It was thought to be a natural border separating them and the Yamana. However, it is evident that Brecknock Peninsula was neither a border area nor a terrifying obstacle for the Alakaluf, even though strong currents from the Pacific Ocean thrash on its rocky shores and at high tide clash with currents coming from the Cockburn Channel. During the nineteenth century if not before, the Alakaluf passed overland on a portage trail, in back of Brecknock, apparently without too much risk. They camped far to the east, at Point Divide, near Devil's Island, at the entrance to Beagle Channel. They were known to frequent Christmas Sound, where Captain Cook met them. There was intermarriage between Alakalauf and Yamana in this area (between Brecknock and Point Divide); just how much is difficult to determine. The fact that some (or many) natives in this area were bilingual connotes intermarriage. As we will soon see, Fuegia Basket's mother was Yahgan and her father Alakaluf. At least during the nineteenth century this entire region should be considered Alakaluf because they were certainly the majority there although the area was partially inhabited and visited by the Yamana.

There were, in effect, few strict boundaries fencing in the four Tierra del Fuego groups, – despite what has been published rather recently.[44] I found only two natural obstacles that the bark canoes could not overcome: Black Cape, at the extreme south of Hoste Island, and Cape San Diego, at the Atlantic entrance to the Le Maire Strait.

The Four "Fuegian" Groups

Quite a few natives were bilingual. This indicates that there were and had been considerable contacts among the four "Fuegian" groups, south of Magellan Strait, mainly through intermarriage (women were often captured during combats). But not all the contacts were violent. The groups shared important "peaceful traits" such as the technique for lighting a fire, certain myths, at least one ceremony (the Hain of the Selk'nam and Haush and the Kina of the Yamana and a somewhat similar ceremony of the Alakaluf). To view these cultures as four isolated entities is a mistake, even though they spoke different languages, and had customs of their own, distinguishing physical traits and a history (prehistory) of their separate arrival in Tierra del Fuego. The "canoe people," the Yamana and Alakaluf, had virtually the same mode of existence, as did the "foot people," the Selk'nam and Haush, the guanaco hunters. However, none of these four groups acted as a unit, as a "nation" or as a confederation of tribes. Each was composed of a number of lineages that claimed certain territories and had a great deal of autonomy. For example, the Selk'nam as a group were not enemies of the Yamana, despite Jemmy Button's fear of the Oens-men (the Selk'nam). Certain lineages of the Selk'nam attacked certain lineages of the Yamana, but these same Selk'nam had other Yamana allies. The Selk'nam lineages also attacked one another, often to avenge a real or assumed offence. Nor were the Yamana lineages always friendly to each other, as Jemmy Button also knew only too well (Chapters 4, 5, 8 and 9).

Maps in the Head and Maps on Paper

It is essential to recognise that the canoe people had very different maps of Tierra del Fuego than those that were published. Their maps were "in their heads" (oral tradition plus personal experiences). The narrow channels and fjords were not problems for them in their bark canoes, nor were the deep waters and rocky bottoms, although they were troublesome for the sailing vessels. The native navigators did not require good anchorages because the women either tied their canoes to kelp or, with the help of the men, dragged them onto the shore. Moreover, their mental maps had many portage trails, as just mentioned – shortcuts, where they carried their canoes over land from one body of water to another. Some of these short land-cuts are well known (see Chapter 14).[45] Sooner or later many more will certainly be discovered, perhaps by an experienced kayak sportsman or sportswoman who has read extensively about them. The canoe people had lived in their tangled landscape for thousands of years, so differently from the Europeans and the more recently arrived Chileans and Argentines, who introduce new techniques, animals and plants and import many of their daily needs. They use paper maps. Each type of map had a specific function, but the mental maps of the canoe people were far more detailed and embraced the entire area.

The Voyage Continues

Toward the end of January 1830 the *Beagle* sailed to the outlying Noir Island and remained there for several days, amid crowds of penguins and sea lions. According to a *Derrotero* (the Chilean Sailing Directions cited in the Bibliography), Noir Island is located fifteen miles (28 kilometres) southwest of Brecknock Peninsula. Fitz-Roy noted: "Strange to say, traces of the Fuegians (a wigwam, &c.) were found, that shows how far they will at times venture in their canoes." Archaeological work should be done there.

Fitz-Roy apparently looked forward to his next assignment. He was preparing to explore the little-known area, from Brecknock all the way to Cape Horn.[46] Sailing beyond Brecknock, he found anchorage along

Pratt Passage at the southeast extremity of a rather large island, which he named London. This was territory of the Alakaluf, whom Fitz-Roy still called Fuegian. Later he did distinguish the Alakaluf and the Yamana.

The next day, 29 January, he sent Master Murray with five men to explore a nearby area. They were to land on the south shore of an island (soon to be named Basket) near Cape Desolation, located by Captain Cook. Despite the "thick" weather, Fitz-Roy had full confidence in Murray's navigating skills; besides, he and his men were going only about fifteen miles from the Pratt base in the best whaleboat and would never be very far from the surrounding islands, where they could haul up if need be. Delays were common in this part of the world, but when an entire week passed without sight or sign of them, Fitz-Roy began wondering what might have happened.

February 1830: A Drama Having Multiple Consequences

Eight days (5 February) after the departure of Murray and his five men,[47] Fitz-Roy was awakened before dawn because Elsmore, the coxswain and one other had just been hauled on board from a basket! The three had paddled from the island – to be named Basket for this "basket canoe." Exhausted and hungry, they informed their incredulous captain and the amazed crew that natives had stolen their whaleboat and most of their provisions and that Murray and the other two were anxiously waiting on Basket Island, in a cove (later named for Murray, in memory of this singular event). They explained that the day before, shortly after 4 AM, one of the men noticed that their whaleboat had vanished, stolen, while all the men were sleeping. Fortunately the chronometre, theodolite and other instruments were safe. They immediately realised that they were stranded and quickly made the basket canoe of wicker, secured the surface with pieces of canvas from their tent, and lined the bottom with clay; but even so their basket proved to be very leaky. Elsmore and his two companions paddled all that day until early dawn with just one biscuit each. They located the *Beagle* in the darkness thanks to the barking of the ship's dogs.

Not a moment was to be lost. The thieves might return to plunder or even kill Murray and the two others. But hours passed while the *Beagle* crew prepared the other whaleboat, equipped it with oars and a mast, and stocked it with a two-week supply of food, two tents, and extra clothing. Fitz-Roy selected four men to accompany him. The five men and the three basket paddlers embarked, soon reached Murray Cove (on Basket

Island), and were overjoyed to find the three castaways safe and sound. They told Fitz-Roy and the others that the thieves had camped only a mile or so from where they had robbed the whaleboat. Their wigwams were so well concealed that Murray and his men had not seen them until later.[48]

The First Clue

The eleven men (six of Murray's crew and five of Fitz-Roy's) quickly embarked to catch the thieves and retrieve the whaleboat. About two miles (3.7 kilometres) out, on a small island, they found the mast in a recently abandoned wigwam. This was encouraging. Fitz-Roy declared "to chase the thieves I was determined." They turned northeast, penetrating Desolate Bay. This bay is quite wide and more than twelve miles (22 kilometres) deep. Its name is justified by its confusion of islets, rocks, violent winds, and stormy weather. From there they pushed beyond Desolate Bay into Courtenay Sound, although it looks like a bay on the map. As late as 1973 the Chilean Navy's sailing directions described Courtenay as not adequately surveyed or sufficiently explored. That evening, still 5 February, they came across a couple paddling a canoe. The wife impressed Fitz-Roy as the best-looking Fuegian so far. "Really well-featured: her voice was pleasing and her manner neither so suspicious nor timid as that of the rest. Though young she was uncommonly fat. Both she and her husband were perfectly naked."

The couple made gestures meaning that they had passed several canoes going north, further into Courtenay Sound.[49] Following the couple's advice, the pursuers continued searching the coves and fjords of the sound until the next day. They reached the foot "of a great chain of snowy mountains" (the prolongation of the Andes, later named Cordillera of Darwin). Some "rather doubtful traces of the thieves" were located, nothing more.

A Reliable Second Clue and the First Guide

They exited Courtnay Sound and Desolate Bay, turned into Whaleboat Sound (Canal Ballenero), thirty-two miles long (52 kilometres), and pulled up to a small island later called Leadline (in English on the Chilean maps), so named because there they "fell in with a native family, and on searching their two canoes found our boat's leadline." Fitz-Roy was overjoyed. "This was a prize indeed." He persuaded the old man of the family to join them to run down the guilty party from whom, the old man assured them, he had obtained a piece of the leadline.

The Third Clue

The old man guided them back to a nearby larger island (named Burnt, for a reason that will become clear). They spotted two canoes occupied by six women, several children, a one-eyed man and a lad seventeen or eighteen years old. They all dashed away, paddling both canoes, though they soon returned, landed and sat huddled together while Fitz-Roy and his men searched their canoes. Here they found a much larger "prize": part of the whaleboat's sail, an axe, the tool bag, and an oar. The handle of the oar had been made into a club to kill seals. The old man had proved reliable as a guide. Fitz-Roy reasoned that since no men were there, the six women must be the wives of the thieves who were off "in our boat, on a sealing expedition."

Another Volunteer Guide

The lad on Burnt Island agreed to help the search party, with the old man. Both were given clothes and red caps. They and the Fitz-Roy and Murray contingents rowed the two boats during four hours, until dark, in wind and rain, reconnoitring the coasts. The guides seemed to enjoy this odd experience, despite the weather. They all camped that night "a great distance" from Burnt Island.[50] It was cold, so Murray covered the two sleeping guides with his two tarpaulin (waterproof cover with tar) coats. The "lookout" (one of the sailors) woke up during the night and saw that the guides had vanished, probably into the dark thick woods, but they all felt too tired to search for them. Fitz-Roy lamented that instead of being grateful for having been so well clothed and even protected from the cold night, they had escaped with the outfits, the caps, and even the tarpaulin coats.

The next day, 8 February, the eleven pursuers examined several islands nearby without finding a trace of the ungrateful guides. Fitz-Roy was bitter, remembering how he had, "behaved kindly to the Fuegians but had not known how to treat them as they deserved." He was especially bitter thinking of the thieves who had robbed him of the "great treasure [his best whaleboat], upon the recovery or loss of which much of the success of our voyage depended."

Smoke Island and Footprints

On the way back to Burnt Island, Fitz-Roy sighted smoke rising on a small island to be named Smoke. They landed to inspect it. Near the source of the smoke, a smouldering fire, they saw footprints that were certainly those of the two ex- guides.[51] How these two could have managed to get to Smoke Island was not explained.

Back to Burnt Island, on to Basket Island and Again to Burnt

The pursuers rowed hurriedly back to Burnt Island, hoping to arrive in time "to prevent these people [the six women, the assumed wives of the thieves, the children and the one-eyed man] from escaping far, and spreading any intelligence likely to impede the return of our boat." When they arrived no natives were in sight, but their two canoes were there, so they burnt them and part of another being constructed. All this burning inspired the name of the island. They camped there that night. During the night or the following dawn, Fitz-Roy surmised that the thieves might have imagined that Murray and his companions were still on Basket Island; if so, they might have returned there to plunder Murray again; if so, they could be caught there, on Basket Island. Rowing fast, they reached Basket in the evening, but no one was there either.

The following day, 10 February, Fitz-Roy had another idea: go where the two escaped guides had motioned that the thieves had gone. So they "steered back to Courtenay Sound." During two days of arduous rowing, they covered much ground, but "without the smallest success."[52] It seems odd to me that they returned to Courtenay Sound, because they had already explored it when they began the pursuit (5–7 February).

The weather having improved on 12 February, the pursuers headed back to Burnt Island (for the third time) "to visit the boat stealers' family" – the six wives, the children, plus the one-eyed man. Then, finally, they spotted natives in a cove of Burnt Island, gathered around a recently constructed wigwam. A plan was devised: surprise them and take them as hostages to exchange for the whaleboat. The tactic and the strategy being understood, the next day each man was armed with a pistol or a larger gun, a cutlass and pieces of rope to tie up the eventual hostages. Having landed out of sight of them, two men remained in the boats. The others crept through the bushes, a long distance around, and quietly encircled the back of the wigwam. No one had heard them until their dogs started barking loudly, then the attackers rushed them. Some ran away, while others squatted against the banks of a nearby stream.

The Battle on Burnt Island

Fitz-Roy reported: "The foremost of our party, Elsmore by name, while jumping across the stream, slipped and fell just where two men and a woman were concealed. They instantly attacked him, trying to hold him down and beat out his brains with stones." Before his companions could assist him [Elsmore] "received several severe blows, and one eye was almost destroyed." At that moment, Murray fired and hit the man grasping Elsmore. He staggered and Elsmore escaped. The wounded native hurled stones from each hand with such "astonishing force and precision" that he broke a powder horn hung round Murray's neck, which knocked Murray backwards. Meanwhile the two other Fuegians (Alakalufs) threw stones but missed their targets. The wounded Fuegian hurled one more stone, then collapsed against the bank of the stream and died bleeding. He was probably the "lad," one of the two ungrateful ex-guides who had escaped with the two tarpaulin coats. This is my assumption, based on the fact that he, the young ex-guide, was never mentioned later, while the other ex-guide, the old man, often was. The dead youth, whoever he was, had died courageously defending his people, therefore he should be considered the Fuegian hero of this historical battle on Burnt Island.

The struggle continued though no more shots were fired. Three or four unidentified Fuegians got away, running down the beach. Meanwhile Fitz-Roy and Elsmore, who had almost recovered, began beating up the other native who had been attacking them from the embankment. Suddenly Fitz-Roy realised they were fighting with a woman, the oldest of her "tribe," and so powerful "that two of the strongest men of our party could scarcely pull her from the bank of the stream."

Somehow they managed to round up two men, three women and six children: eleven in all, the future hostages. The one-eyed man, who had been very active in the fight, had escaped with the three other women. Fitz-Roy expressed regret that a life had been lost but felt that it had been necessary to save Elsmore. When it was all over, the prisoners, "seemed very anxious to tell us where our boat was but pointed in a direction quite opposite to that which they had previously shown us." Their word was definitely not to be trusted. They were carefully guarded that night.[53] Burnt Island may someday be remembered because of the "Fuegian hero" and because, among the eleven Alakaluf captured, one of the six children, a girl, will become very famous.

The First Hostages

The next day the eleven victors with their eleven hostages set out to return to the *Beagle* waiting along Pratt Passage, off London Island. On the way, Fitz-Roy spotted natives in several canoes near a small island. He and his men searched the canoes to no avail and proceeded to the shore of the small island where they also searched their wigwams. Finding no evidence in recompense for the bothersome inspections, Fitz-Roy gave the natives several gifts. This pleased them no end, but not the eleven hostages who "were as discontented as the others were cheerful." Perhaps the hostages relaxed soon afterwards, on board the *Beagle*, where they were served shellfish and pork and clothed with old blankets.[54] After everyone rested a few days in Pratt Passage, the ship was moved down the line of the ocean-front islands to a better anchorage on Stewart Island at Cape Castlereagh, both of which Fitz-Roy named for his famous uncle, the Viscount Robert Stewart Castlereagh.[55]

The Fourth Clue

The chase resumed the next day, 17 February. Fitz-Roy boarded the remaining whaleboat with several seamen, taking the younger of the two adult male hostages as a guide. Murray and a few sailors were assigned to the cutter with two of the three women hostages as guides. Each party took a week's provisions. The other hostages, six children, a woman, and a man, remained on the *Beagle*. Fitz-Roy's and Murray's boats departed together, advanced two miles along the ocean front, the south shore, of Stewart Island, entered a cove, and discovered another piece of the leadline in a deserted wigwam. The three guides reassured Fitz-Roy and Murray by their gestures that they were on the right track and that the thieves were rather close, on the opposite side of the island. With this "information" in mind, they encircled the island to the north shore [inland shore] of Stewart Island, along Whaleboat Sound.

Three More Ungrateful Guides

That night they camped along Whaleboat Sound in a small bay later called Escape (Bahía Escape), for a reason that the reader may already have guessed. Upon arrival, the three hostage-guides were untied, generously fed, allowed to sleep close to the fire, and this time covered with Fitz-Roy's poncho and old blankets. It was his turn to keep watch. About midnight, while standing, keeping an eye on the two boats, with his back to the fire, he heard rustling. Turning around quickly he verified that the heap of blankets and his poncho were unmoved and was reassured. Then he stooped down close to the fire to glance at his watch when his dog woke up and began barking. Upon inspection, "the blankets looked the same, for they were artfully propped up by bushes." The three guides had escaped. This time Fitz-Roy and his men searched in the dark night, in the thick woods, in vain.

The morning after, Fitz-Roy and Murray assessed the situation: their three would-be guides (two women and a man) had probably walked across the narrow part of the island to the south shore, on the ocean side, and warned their accomplices that they were being trailed. Fitz-Roy took his boat along the coast looking for a short cut, a water route, to the other side of the island, which he did not find. When he returned that afternoon, Murray informed him that he had found the spot where the ex-guides had hidden after escaping, a mere dozen yards from the campfire. Then Fitz-Roy calculated that by now the thieves had somehow returned to their families on Burnt Island, the site of the recent battle. He sent Murray there, across Whaleboat Sound. Meanwhile, he changed his mind and thought that the husbands, the thieves, were more likely to be on the ocean front, the south shore of Stewart, hunting seals, as his three ex-hostages (ex-guides), had sort of indicated.

On to Gilbert Islands and "Barked Trees"

That evening, Fitz-Roy reached the two small Gilbert Islands, beyond Stewart. The following day, along a rather large bay (later named in his honour), he came upon wigwams on one of the Gilbert Islands, which showed traces of having recently been inhabited. He reasoned that the thieves had slept there while they were seal hunting in his whaleboat. "Here is cause for hope." He felt almost sure of success, because in places where the natives camped, the trees were usually "barked" (the bark removed) to repair or to make a canoe, but near these wigwams none of the trees showed traces of having been barked, simply because, logically, the thieves would not bark them to repair a whaleboat. This "non-evidence" reassured him that he was on the right track, so that day he and his men inspected all the coves around both of the Gilbert Islands, in vain.[56]

The next day, 20 February, they spotted three small canoes and their male occupants on the same island (one of the Gilberts), in a cove named Doris. This cove was not named for some faraway lady friend but for the Doris sea slug, mentioned by Darwin (Chapter 5).[57] All but two of the men ran away. Fitz-Roy had time to count them and realised that their number corresponded to the capacity of the three small canoes. He calculated that if the thieves had been among them (and had hidden the whaleboat someplace nearby), more men would have been there, as the capacity of his whaleboat was superior to that of three small canoes. Moreover, no whaleboat or equipment was found anywhere near there. Obviously these men were not the guilty party. A momentary fatigue overcame him. "I began to give up all hope of finding our boat in this direction. Having no clue to guide me farther, and much time having been lost, I reluctantly decided to return to the Beagle. Our only remaining hope, that the master [Murray] might have met with the [stolen] boat, was but very feeble."

The next day he rowed back to the north shore of Stewart Island, along Whaleboat Sound, hoping to find Murray in Escape Bay. Murray was there, having returned from Burnt Island with another clue.

Burnt Island Again and a Fifth Sure Clue
Murray told his story. When he reached Burnt Island, he sighted three or four of those who had run away after the 12 February battle. He waited nearby in his boat while several of his men rushed them, got very close to them, but not close enough. A bit later Murray found a sleeve of one of his tarpaulin coats in a "wretched" patched-up canoe. This was proof that one of the first escaped guides had returned there. But Murray could tarry no longer, as he had to keep his date with Fitz-Roy in Escape Bay.

The entire team left Escape Bay to return early the next day to the *Beagle* on the south shore of Stewart Island. As they were rowing along Whaleboat Sound Fitz-Roy noticed smoke on the opposite shore, on Smoke Island at the entrance to Thieves Sound, where on 8 February, smoke and footprints of the first ex-guides had been seen. They hurriedly crossed Whaleboat Sound but again only found a simmering fire. "We were then just as much at a loss as ever," Fitz-Roy commented wearily, as they prepared to camp there, on Smoke Island, that night.[58]

More Hostages Escape
They searched the shores of nearby Thieves Sound (for the second or third time) the next day, still no results. The disheartened searchers finally returned to the *Beagle* at Cape Castlereagh, on the tip of Stewart facing the Pacific. They were greeted with unwelcome news: five of the Burnt Island captives – the man, the woman, and three of the children – had escaped, swum ashore. Only three children of the original eleven hostages were still on board. Fitz-Roy was really distressed when he wrote: "Thus, after much trouble and anxiety, much valuable time lost, and as fine a boat of her kind as ever was seen being stolen from us by these savages, I found myself with three young children to take care of, and no prospects whatever of recovering the boat."

Tales of Woe
Fitz-Roy, Murray and their companions told the other shipmates about their chagrins and discomforts during the past week. Pulling in and out

of the coves and climbing the hills had been extremely fatiguing. The weather was miserable, so rainy that they were soaked day and night, "for although a large fire (when made in the rain) might dry one side [of a person], the other as quickly became wet." Everything was saturated. Hours on end, the men were shivering after having been cramped in the small boats all day. They also told how the three hostage-guides had escaped.

A bright light pierced these tales of woe. Young Stokes had been hard at work on the *Beagle*, making plans of the harbours and noting observations. Fitz-Roy also found some comfort with the thought that, "this cruise had also given me more insight into the real character of the Fuegians." Then it occurred to him, "that so long as we were ignorant of the Fuegian language, and the natives were equally ignorant of ours, we should never know much about them."[59]

Back to Gilbert Islands

The entire crew reunited, plus the three young hostages, the *Beagle* weighed anchor, heading for Doris Cove, where Fitz-Roy had been four days earlier. The ship moored there on 24 February for several days while the crew rested from the tribulations of the past three weeks. Fitz-Roy, still alert, observed that because of the many islands in this area, boats could go a long distance in safety. During these rest days, they examined "greenstones" and discovered that they also contained many veins of "firestones" – that is, pyrites. Although I found no report that the Alakaluf came here to obtain them, they probably did if the pyrites were visible.

Having pursued the culprits for eighteen days (5 to 23 February) Fitz-Roy had acquired three Alakaluf children and souvenirs (pieces) of his whaleboat. However loath he was to admit defeat, he probably thought he had better get on with his job. The remaining three boats were inadequate: too many men were required to handle the two cutters and the second whaleboat was only fit for harbour duty. A larger whaleboat, to replace the stolen one, was a must. So despite the frustrations, he ordered the men to begin assembling material to build one.[60]

The Pursuit Is (Almost) Given Up

The last day of February the *Beagle* headed out of Doris Cove, moved along the oceanfront, passing a long indented island that Fitz-Roy named Londonderry, again for his famous uncle Castlereagh, who became the first Marquess of Londonderry several years before his death (Chapter 5).

Two islands and a cape named for this one relative, however famous, may seem excessive. Perhaps Fitz-Roy was already thinking or fearing he might have inherited this uncle's propensity for depressions.

Having crossed Cook Bay, the ship sailed down along Waterman Island to the promontory that Captain Cook had named York Minster. This high cliff on the southern tip of Waterman, facing the sea, had reminded Cook of the lofty twin towers of the cathedral in York, his home city. Fitz-Roy surmised that the highest part of the promontory had crumbled during the past fifty odd years, since Cook was there, because it no longer resembled the towers of a cathedral. They moored the *Beagle* in Christmas Sound, where Cook had been that Christmas of 1774 (Chapter 1).

Soon they found a better anchorage in a sheltered cove later called March Harbour (Puerto March) on Waterman Island, because the *Beagle* was to remain there this entire month. Here a large whaleboat could be built in all tranquillity: water and wood were available and the *Beagle* could be kept in security from the gales, the high tides, and hopefully from the Fuegians.

Alikhoolip Becomes Alakaluf

Early March (1830), Fitz-Roy decided to return two of the child hostages to their territory. So Murray and several men were assigned to the large cutter for the job. Fitz-Roy was confident that they would come across some Fuegians (Alakalufs) with whom to leave the children. Murray and his men were given two weeks' provisions and ordered to survey the coasts from the Alikhoolip Islets to the northwest.[61] Fitz-Roy or Murray may have heard this name from one of the children; in any event Fitz-Roy was the first to publish the name of this island. Later it was spelled Alakaluf and applied to the entire group of the Fuegian-Alakalufs. Just why is not clear as it is only the name of a small island in their immense territory.

A Plan: "Fuegia" the First Sure Hostage

Fitz-Roy decided to keep the other child, a girl about nine years old. "She seemed so happy and healthy, that I determined to detain her as a hostage for the stolen boat, and try to teach her English." She was soon named Fuegia Basket in memory of the basket canoe Murray and his men had made in order to return to the *Beagle* following the theft of the elusive whaleboat. In any event she was invariably called Fuegia, though her real name was known (see below). She had charmed the crew, including Fitz-Roy, who spoke of her affectionately as "the pet on the lower deck."[62]

"York" the Second Hostage

A canoe full of Fuegians appeared on 3 March, just as Fitz-Roy and his companions were settling down. The latter had "no wish for their company." He was annoyed, thinking that they would board the ship "and steal every thing left within their reach." He ordered Wilson to shoot over their heads to scare them away. Glancing at the intruders, while Wilson about to obey, Fitz-Roy had second thoughts. Why not take another hostage for the stolen whaleboat? Why not try for the youngest man among them, who would have fewer ties with his family than the older ones? Persuaded that these were bright ideas, he lowered a boat, approached the canoe and signalled to the youngest man to join him. The youth, about twenty-four years old, climbed into his boat and sat down, apparently at ease. He was taken near the York Minster promontory (Catedral de York on the Chilean maps), so he was named for it: York for short. His "hosts" rarely used his real name, El'leparu (or Elleparu).[63] Neither did Fuegia's captors use her name, Yokcushlu (or Yorkicushlu). However I question the authenticity of this latter name simply because it looks like York plus *cushlu*, perhaps the wife of York, which she later became. But we are getting ahead of the story. York boarded the *Beagle* willingly but soon became sullen, despite his healthy appetite and the leftovers that he stored in a corner of the deck. Once he had bathed and was "adequately" dressed, he was free to move about the ship. His humour brightened when he met Fuegia. She too was happy to have someone to converse with in her own language, Alakaluf.[64]

Fitz-Roy concluded that the large area they had covered, from Stewart Island to Waterman Island, was not suitable for agriculture, and that only goats and dogs could thrive there. The commercial killing of seals was still so intense that "in a few years the shores will be destitute of seals." The only possible future he saw for "civilised man" there was mining copper, iron or other metals that might be found in these barren mountains. In effect, mining would be attempted in a nearby area in the early twentieth century.[65]

Unwelcomed Visitors

Several quiet days passed until 8 March, when Fitz-Roy sighted two canoes at the entrance to March Harbour. He immediately had the remaining whaleboat lowered and went to meet the "visitors," intent on searching them, for the usual reason. The two canoes had pulled up close to the sailors on land, who were busy making the new whaleboat.

Fitz-Roy counted the occupants of the two canoes: fourteen in all, twelve men and two women paddlers.

Suddenly the twelve men climbed on shore and began breaking off boughs from the trees, perhaps for the fires in the canoes, while the two women waited in the canoes, at the base of a large rock. The men motioned to Fitz-Roy to join them on land, but he refused and stayed in his boat, holding up pieces of iron barrel straps and knives to induce them to approach him in their canoes. He felt safer on the water. Apparently his refusal offended them. Their gestures became so threatening that Fitz-Roy looked over his shoulder and was reassured to see Lieutenant Kempe coming towards him with six seamen in the small cutter. Then the natives climbed on a big rock near the coast and began throwing stones at them while making aggressive motions with their slings and spears. Fitz-Roy and his men were unarmed, so they hurried back to the *Beagle* in the cutter to secure weapons. Meanwhile, the Alakaluf men ran down the rock and joined the two women in the canoes. Fitz-Roy resolved to drive the intruders out of the harbour, even without attempting to search the canoes. "Already they, or their countrymen, had robbed us of a boat, and endangered the lives of several persons." He suspected that they might rob parts of the boat being constructed and whatever else lying about. He imagined that they came "prepared for war," that it would be easy for them to attack the *Beagle*. They had certainly noticed Murray leaving in the large cutter full of men and were probably reassured that there were not many men on board the *Beagle*. Yet another indication of their warlike intentions occurred to Fitz-Roy: "They came prepared for war, being much painted, wearing white bands on their heads, carrying their slings and spears, and having left all their children and dogs, with most of their women, in some other place."

His mind was made up: chase them away before they attack. But by then they had already paddled away. He set out pursuing them in the old whaleboat with a small crew. Wilson, Kempe and his men followed in the cutter. Now all were well armed. They were about to overtake the canoes when the twelve men jumped on land and dashed to the top of another rock, leaving the two women paddlers in the canoes. The *Beagle* contingent slowed down, "leisurely," closing in on the two canoes. Fitz-Roy ordered his bowman to haul one of them alongside his boat and search it. But when his boat hook touched the canoe, the men on the rock hurdled all sizes of stones at them. One of Fitz-Roy's men was knocked down (but only stunned). Fitz-Roy and his warriors were firing at the attackers, without hitting anyone, when Kempe's cutter caught up with them.

More Clues

While they were somehow seizing the two canoes, their male enemies were behind the big rock, out of sight. Fitz-Roy did not reveal how the two women in the canoes reacted to the assault. As they were not captured they had probably joined their men behind the big rock. Fitz-Roy and the others began seizing the two canoes to search them. He was rewarded: he recovered Murray's beer bottles, several other "spirit" bottles, and a small part of the whaleboat's gear. Note that a great deal of the stolen whale boat's equipment had been dispersed rapidly among many Alakalufs over a considerable distance, which means that there was frequent contact among them.

The search completed, the two canoes were destroyed, burnt. Then Fitz-Roy thought best not to risk further injury to his men, despite his numerical superiority and firearms. He had (almost) made up his mind not to take more captives, more than Fuegia and York, because "the savages knew of no alternative but escape or death." He sent the stunned man back to the *Beagle* with Wilson and joined Kempe in the cutter "to watch the motions on or behind the rock." The twelve men and two women, seeing that no more battle was being proposed and that their canoes were destroyed, dispersed, running through the bushes and over the barren hills of Waterman Island, quickly out of sight. Fitz-Roy fired a few farewell shots towards them. A moment or two later he discerned smoke on Whittlebury Island, in the middle of Christmas Sound, but it was already late afternoon, so they all returned to the *Beagle*.[66]

At dawn, when the *Beagle* crew emerged on the deck and saw smoke still rising from wigwams on Whittlebury Island, Fitz-Roy motioned to the crew to lower the cutter. They rapidly navigated Christmas Sound, arrived near the source of the smoke, when the smoke suddenly vanished. "The natives had probably seen us, and put out their fire directly." Smoke or no smoke, they landed on Whittlebury Island and soon located the wigwams. Though no enemies were seen there, they found another clue, the "King's white line" (a spare line). This evidence was conclusive: those who had fled were "at least some" of the whaleboat thieves. The searchers were again hopeful: perhaps they could capture the whaleboat thieves, after all.

"Boat Memory" the Third Hostage

Suddenly they sighted two canoes paddling in a rather tempestuous sea on the far side of Whittlebury Island, facing Hoste Island. Fitz-Roy boarded the cutter, chased the canoes and seized one. At that moment, a young man and a girl jumped into the water, leaving an old woman and a child in the canoe. Still in his cutter, Fitz-Roy shouted orders to pursue the young man, who was swimming faster than the girl. During a quarter of an hour, they tagged him and finally nabbed him. Meanwhile the girl swam ashore, climbed into the brush, and joined the old woman and the child who were waiting there. Then the captain returned with his men to home base and with one more captive, whom he named Boat Memory, as a reminder of his futile pursuits. His real name was never revealed. Fitz-Roy calculated his age as twenty. I found no indication that Boat Memory was involved in the whaleboat theft or in the confrontation on Waterman Island. He and his family may simply have been camping in the vicinity.

The Alakaluf "Braves"
Fitz-Roy admired the fighting power, agility, and courage of these "savages," recalling how his five guides had vanished despite their vigilance, how the others had fought on Burnt Island, how five of his hostages had escaped from the *Beagle*, and now how these twelve men had defied them with such insolence and melted into the landscape.

The bodily strength of these savages is very great (York Minster is as strong as any two of our stoutest men), which with their agility, both on shore and in the water, and their quickness in attack and defence with stones and sticks, makes them difficult to deal with when out of their canoes. They are a brave, hardy race, and fight to the last struggle; though in the manner of a wild beast, it must be owned, else they would not, when excited, defy a whole boat's crew, and, single-handed, try to kill the men, as I have witnessed. That kindness toward these beings, and good treatment of them, is as yet useless, I almost think, both from my own experience and from much that I have heard of their conduct from sealing vessels.

Despite the eloquent phrases of the Alakaluf, his resentment was more profound than ever. Apparently he was making up his mind to apply more offensive tactics, convinced that a mutual understanding could be established only by "moral fear." Nevertheless, he never again applied a tactic of "moral fear," nor did he ever attack the Fuegians again, nor did they ever provoke him again. He returned to March Cove with his latest captive. Now he had definitely given up: his whaleboat was a memory (or a nightmare).

At Least – Three Captives
Boat Memory seemed frightened at first, but once on the deck he ate "enormously" and soon fell asleep. After he had bathed and was dressed

in a sailor outfit, he was enjoying the company of his two country people. Fuegia, too, was glad and laughed while chatting with him and York. The presence of three happy captives consoled the captain for his loss. He was especially impressed by Boat Memory.

"Boat" was the best-featured Fuegian I had seen, and being young and well made, was a very favourable specimen of the race; "York" was one of the stoutest men I had observed among them, but little "Fuegia" was almost as broad as she was high; she seemed to be so merry and happy, that I do not think she would willingly have quitted us. Three natives of Tierra del Fuego, better suited for the purpose of instruction, and for giving, as well as receiving information, could not, I think, have been found.

Was Fitz-Roy already entertaining the idea of taking them to England?

Some Good News

Master Murray arrived with good news though complaining of the weather and the Fuegians. He had encountered many people; in one place forty to fifty men, in addition to women and children. Most of the men were well armed with the usual slings and spears, and some had pieces of iron hoops fastened to sticks. They had proven to be "very troublesome" and not impressed with his musket unless it was pointed directly at them. Despite the annoyances, he managed to barter trifles for fish.[67] He had gone far beyond the Alikhoolip islets, traversed Whaleboat Sound, entered Desolate Bay, then Courtenay Sound, from where he was "nearly to the base" of the snow-covered cordillera (to be named for Darwin). On his way there or back, near Burnt Island, where the battle had occurred, he left the two children with an old woman in a canoe. She seemed to know them well "and to be very much pleased at having them placed in her care." This was the good news.

Rounding the Treacherous Black Cape

After Murray returned, Fitz-Roy announced that he was going to explore nearby New Year's Sound and would return by the end of March, when the whaleboat should be finished. In mid-March he departed, with Wilson, a small crew, and two weeks' provisions, in the large cutter heading towards the nearby extremity of Hoste Island. Two days later, they rounded Black Cape (Punta Negra), so named because craggy black rocks project from the cape (at the southwestern tip of Hoste Island). Fitz-Roy noted that this part of the coast is treacherous for vessels navigating close to shore because of the submerged rocky islets scattered all about.[68]

Apparently, there was no place nearby that could be used as a portage trail. Moreover, as Black Cape is entirely exposed to the Pacific, it receives the fierce shocks of the tempests, the prevailing winds from the west, and the strong pull of tidal currents that crash against its crags. These perils constituted the only natural barrier between the Alakaluf and the Yamana.

During this exploration, the cutter ploughed through strong gales and unrelenting rain and passed Morton Islands by 20 March, where Weddell had purchased the heavy Yamana canoe. Fitz-Roy climbed a hill on nearby Henderson Island, where Drake had probably seen Fuegians 252 years earlier. After entering New Year's Sound, two days later, he climbed the hilltops again, hoping to sight a shorter passage leading back to March Harbour and avoid Black Cape. He saw that there was no water passage back to Christmas Sound, so he had to return to March Harbour the same way.

Leaving New Year's Sound, they stopped over in Indian Cove, where Weddell had bid farewell to the Yahgans six years before, in 1824. Now there were only empty wigwams and traces of sealers. Then Fitz-Roy hurried back to March Harbour. But struck by a strong gale and contrary tides, it took them five days just to reach Black Cape. Despite the weather, Fitz-Roy observed mother seals teaching their pups to swim. "It was curious to see the old seal supporting the pup by its flipper, as if to let it breathe and rest, and then pushing it away into deep water to shift for itself." They passed Black Cape, struggling for six hours against a strong wind and a tide race. Fitz-Roy cautioned future navigators: "The outer coast is a wild one for a boat at any period of the year – and this was the month of March, about the worst time."[69] No doubt they rejoiced when they reached the calm waters of Christmas Sound. Back in March Harbour, they were certainly glad to learn that there had been no visits during their absence and that the new whaleboat was ready.

Fitz-Roy Meets the Yamana

The *Beagle* weighed anchor the last day of March, having spent the entire month in March Harbour, and headed for the Ildefonso Islets, some fifteen miles from the southernmost point of Hoste Island, where the Yahgans and Weddell had also been, as noted in last chapter.[70] Fitz-Roy surveyed the islets and noticed the seals the sealers had missed, scrambling up the summits. The next day, the first of April, they steered back toward Hoste Island, resisting a strong gale in a thick fog. Entering Nassau Bay, they took refuge in the bay called Schapenham (by the Dutch) on the east coast of Hoste Island. Fitz-Roy recalled having read about the 1624 massacre of seventeen Dutch seamen by the Yamana, in this very bay and thought it had been in revenge for the 1599 massacre of the Selk'nam by the Dutch (Chapter 1).

Sailing up Nassau Bay, searching for a better anchorage, they found, "a fine-looking clear bay well sheltered, and with regular sounding, from twelve to twenty fathoms (72 to 120 feet)." This was Orange Bay, one of the Yamana's favourite camping grounds, where, in 1715, Captain Joachin D'Arquisade spent a day socialising with the natives (also Chapter 1). The *Beagle* remained there for two weeks, until 16 April, while two broken anchors were being repaired. Fitz-Roy was glad to have the time, with a "safe anchorage," to restore his crew's health. Many of the men had become sick during their stay in March Harbour and others during the trip around Black Cape and back. "Colds and rheumatisms, owing to bleak winds and much wet, were the chief complaints."

He was truly enthusiastic about Orange Bay: large and deep enough for a squadron of battleships, easy access to the large bay of Nassau, abundant water, forests close by, and flocks of birds. Shellfish were scarce, but there were plenty of small fish in the kelp.[71] No mention of seals.

The weather was fine during the first days. Fitz-Roy was reassured: "Our [three] Fuegians were very cheerful, and apparently contented." Soon the crew met a people they had never seen before, known later as the Yamana or Yahgan (see Glossary). York and Boat called them Yapoo, the Yamana word for otter (*yapoo* or *iapooh*), a derogatory, mocking term.[72] Apparently the word did not offend them; in any event, they often paddled up to the ship offering fish to barter. Fitz-Roy soon realised that these people spoke a language that his captives did not understand. He was "sadly grieved" that they were not the same "tribe" and that "much enmity appeared to exist between them. "At first, 'York' and 'Boat' would not go near them; but afterwards took delight in trying to cheat them out of the things they offered to barter; and mocked their way of speaking and laughing; pointing at them and calling them 'Yahoo, yapoo.'"

Fuegia was hardly more welcoming. She came on deck, glanced at them and screamed. When a seaman jokingly told her by gestures to join them in their canoe and go live with them, she burst into tears and ran below to hide. Later York showed the scars of wounds he had received from fights with this "tribe."[73]

Fitz-Roy observed the women fishing simply, with a line tied to a small bait, no hook. When the fish swallowed the bait, "the hand holding the line jerks the prize out of the water, and the other catches it." The women then bite out a large piece of its belly, empty the insides, and hang the rest on a stick by the fire in the canoe. They either roasted their catch in the canoe-fire and ate it right away or took it back to camp.

Fitz-Roy also observed that these Fuegians built their dwelling, "in a manner differing from that of the western tribes [the Alakaluf]."[74] While the latter constructed wigwams of tall tree trunks, the Fuegians in Orange bay and further south, where tall trees were scarce, just placed a number of thin trunks or long branches around a small space, meeting at the top, and covered them with smaller branches or sealskins as best they could. Darwin called this hut a bee-hive (Chapter 4). These Fuegians, the Yamana, also built wigwams on Navarino Island, where tall trees were available.

Murray Makes a Great Discovery

On 6 April, Fitz-Roy sent Master Murray with a small crew and one of his best chronometres to explore the head, the north of Nassau Bay, where the Dutch had been in 1624. About the same time Midshipman Stokes was sent on another mission. Eight days later, Murray returned with the astounding news that he had gone beyond Nassau Bay, "through a narrow passage, about one-third of a mile wide, which led him into a straight channel, averaging about two miles or more in width, and extending east and west as far as the eye could reach."

Murray had "discovered" Beagle Channel, which is 120 miles long and three miles wide except for the Mackinlay Pass, where it narrows down to about one mile.[75] I wrote "discovered" for two reasons. First: it had been "discovered" by the Yahgans' ancestors some 6,000 years ago, according the archaeologists cited in the Introduction. The second reason: this channel may well have been "discovered" about 1556 by the French navigator Le Testu, coming from Dieppe, in Bretagne, according to a document cited and analysed by the Chilean historian José Miguel Barros.[76] However, as these discoveries were not made public to the outside world, were they discoveries? Such historic-ethnic-semantic problems are too complicated to treat briefly and must be left for others more competent than I.

Murray had sailed or rowed north from Orange Bay, through Nassau Bay, then through a "narrow passage" eight miles (15 kilometres) long, soon to be called Murray Narrows in his honour. There he turned east (to the right), into the great channel to be named Beagle by Fitz-Roy. Murray sailed on to about the middle of the channel, to the clay cliffs of Gable

Island, later given this name by the missionaries. (These names are on the Chilean and Argentine maps.) As his provisions were nearly exhausted, he hastened back to the *Beagle* with his startling news.

Until then, the European cartographers imagined that south of the Magellan Strait there was one very large island, a small one at its extremity, Staten Island, other islands in the vicinity of Cape Horn and along the Pacific coast up to Magellan Strait. After the 1839 publication of the three volumes of the *Narrative*, so often cited here, this area gradually became known as having a very complex pattern of several thousand islands and islets.[77]

Murray vividly evoked the busy traffic of canoes and other salient features of this area, the intersection of the Murray Narrows and the great Beagle Channel, which was Yamana's heartland (my term). Fitz-Roy was justifiably amazed by Murray's news (italics added).

Mr Murray saw great numbers of natives *near the narrow passage [Murray Narrows] and upwards of a hundred canoes were seen in one day*, each containing from two to six people. These Fuegians [Yahgans] had much guanaco skin, and many of the bones of that animal made into spearheads but very little sealskin.... Every canoe gave chase to our [Murray's] boat, eager to see the strangers, and exchange small fish, spearheads, or arrows, for buttons, beads, and other trifles. No arms or offensive weapons were seen among them, excepting fish spears, bows, arrows, and slings: they had not even clubs, nor such lances as are used by the western tribes [Alakaluf]. They seemed to be much more tractable, and less disposed to quarrel than those of the west. Wherever the boat went, she was followed by a train of canoes, each full of people, and having a fire smoking in the middle.[78]

Note that Murray noticed that the Fuegians, the Yahgan-Yamana, seemed more peacefully inclined than the western tribes, the Alakaluf.

When Midshipman Stokes returned to Orange Bay a day later, on 15 April, and heard about Murray's astounding discovery, one can imagine that he was disheartened by his uneventful exploration. He had gone "a long way to the north and west without finding a passage to New Year's Sound."

The very next day the *Beagle* crew departed from Orange Bay, not for Beagle Channel but rather for Cape Horn, and anchored near the cape in deep water off the coast of Hermite Island.[79]

The Cape Horn Memorial

The following morning, 17 April (1830), Fitz-Roy and his men located the cove called Saint Martin, on Hermite Island, where Foster had passed several weeks the year before and Weddell had been in 1823 (Chapter 2). As the *Beagle* had a good anchorage there, Fitz-Roy took his new whaleboat to inspect nearby Horn Island, where he saw many places to haul ashore. He returned to the *Beagle* on the morning of 19 April and prepared a memorial "securely enclosed in a stone jar." He set out again with Lieutenant Kempe, seven seamen, five days' provisions, several instruments, and the precious jar. Having landed on the north shore of Horn, they camped that night nearby and at daybreak hiked towards its cape. Having reached the highest point of the cape, facing the great ocean, they dug a pit, laid their offering in it, refilled it, and piled stones and heavy rocks eight feet high on top of it. Then they inserted a pole in the ground, from which the Union Jack fluttered in the wind. The eight men solemnly gathered around the monument, toasted to the health of His Majesty George IV, and gave three hearty cheers.[80] Almost 160 years later, in 1990, Captain Christian de Bonafos, a high-ranking officer of the Chilean Navy and several of his comrades, read Fitz-Roy's text and retrieved the memorial jar. It contained a buckle, officers' bronzes (military awards), a dozen or so bronze buttons, a wooden seal that was almost destroyed by the humidity, remains of a Union Jack, forty-one coins, silver and bronze medals, a penknife with a tortoiseshell handle, and an iron dagger. According to an Internet message: "The Chilean Navy determined that this testimony be conserved in the Navy Museum of Valparaiso, for which reason it was turned over to the Admiral don José Toribio Merino Castro during his most recent official visit to the Naval Beagle District, in a handsome case made of the regional evergreen beech wood."[81]

The *Beagle* stayed in Saint Martin's Cove a week, until 24 April, because of adverse weather. No natives came to welcome her. The crew kept busy inspecting the wooden roads and constructions at the head of the cove built by Captain Foster.[82] A few days later the crew surveyed the south coast of Hermite Island and then visited Diego Ramírez islets, sixty miles (111 kilometres) southwest of Cape Horn, well known for its seals. However, Fitz-Roy did not mention them. Most had probably been exterminated by sealers, and the survivors had fled to other rockeries as Webster suggested (end of Chapter 2). There is no indication that the Yamana had been to these islets, which were probably too far away for their bark canoes, though they had certainly sighted them from Cape Horn or nearby hilltops, as Fitz-Roy had.

The *Beagle* returned to Hermite Island despite the violent squalls. The last day of April brought beautiful weather "more like the climate of

Madeira than that of fifty-nine south." They turned again towards "the famous cape" to complete the survey. The following night they bore northward and at sunset, on 1 May, entered a sheltered harbour of a rather large island the Yamana called Imiani (or Imian). For some reason Fitz-Roy named it Lennox in memory of Matthew Stuart, the fourth count of Lennox (Scotland).[83]

Murray was now assigned to survey the southeastern coast of the Isla Grande (what I call the boot of Isla Grande) beyond Beagle Channel. He set out in the new whaleboat with six men, instruments, three weeks' provisions, and firearms. Young Stokes was sent to the nearby Nassau Bay and New Island (Isla Nueva). The latter is almost as large as Lennox but seldom mentioned by the Europeans. Kempe remained on the *Beagle* to refit her with wood and water.

Fitz-Roy Explores the Yamana Heartland

That same day, 3 May, Fitz-Roy and a small crew departed from Lennox in the large cutter to explore and survey Murray's discoveries: the Narrows and Beagle Channel. The Yamana called the latter Ona-shagan, which very likely signifies North Channel (see Glossary). While sailing through Nassau Bay the first night, they pulled up to a long beach on the south coast of Navarino, where Fitz-Roy noticed that the guanacos were larger than those he had seen in Patagonia, on the continent, and that their tails were longer and bushier. His observation has been amply confirmed. South of Magellan Strait the guanacos inhabited Navarino Island and Isla Grande. Now they are a protected species on both of these islands.

The following day, they turned into Ponsonby Sound (between Navarino and Hoste islands). Heading north, towards Murray Narrows, they passed several canoes full of natives but did not stop, "time was too precious." After dark, 6 May, while camping near the entrance to the narrows, they concealed their fire to avoid being "disturbed by visits from the Fuegians."[84]

However, the next day, fast-paddling canoes chased them while they were sailing (or rowing) through the narrows. Fitz-Roy kept ahead, shunning "their endeavours to barter with us, or to gratify their curiosity." Having navigated the narrows they landed, probably on the northwest "corner" of Navarino Island, at the intersection of Murray Narrows and Beagle Channel, one of the busiest and most populated areas in Yamana territory, which I call the Yamana heartland. Canoes descended on them from all directions, bringing fish to barter while they were preparing dinner. Like Murray, Fitz-Roy saw that the natives were not armed and thought they seemed "less disposed to be mischievous, than the western race [the Alakaluf]." He was probably recalling the whaleboat thieves. Their language "sounded similar" to that which they had heard in Orange Bay.[85] True, it was the same language, Yamana.

The captain noticed a wigwam large enough for twenty men to stand in, and could shelter thirty or forty in cold weather. While his companions were preparing the meal, he strolled around and felt the pleasant sensation underfoot of firm, solid ground, in contrast to the soggy, marshy soil farther south (on the shores of Orange Bay and Hermite Island).[86] His hosts offered him "an estimable dainty . . . excrescences which grow on birch [beech] trees," a fungus later classed as *Cyttaria darwinii* and known as Indian bread. He and the others declined to taste this "dainty," although they appreciated the rockfish, smelt and yellow mullet they were offered. Fitz-Roy observed that the shellfish were scarce and small, and that there were not enough to depend on for daily subsistence. While visiting this "village" he surprised the residents in their wigwams and penned these revealing remarks: "Perhaps they did not willingly approach strangers with their usual skin dress about them, their first impulse, on seeing us, being to hide it. Several, whom I surprised at their wigwams, had large skins round their bodies, which they concealed directly they saw me." And he wrote later: "They always leave the most valuable skins hidden in the bushes. This hasty concealment of seal or otter skins is the result of visits from sealers, who frequently robbed Fuegian families of every skin in their possession."[87]

Note that before Murray's discovery of Beagle Channel, the Yamana had met sealers, probably Yankee and British and perhaps French from Saint Malo. Recall that the Alakalufs Fitz-Roy had seen on the continent also hid their valuable skins from strangers because the sealers had robbed them. Therefore it is not surprising that these Fuegians (the Yamana), were often naked or only clothed in scanty capes when meeting strangers.

He Enters Beagle Channel

That same day, 7 May 1830, the party turned into the great channel, sailing west, to the left, in the opposite direction taken by Murray. Fitz-Roy reported impassively on this event, perhaps because he was wary of the natives. Their canoes did arrive while he and his men were setting up their tent. Then they debated whether to drive the "intruders away . . . or be plagued with them all night." Neither idea pleased them, so they packed up and found a refuge farther down the coast.[88] This scene will be repeated almost three years later (Chapter 5).

Fitz-Roy failed to comment on Beagle Channel, on the beauty of this broad generous waterway, fed by small rivers and framed by the stark granite heights of its protective mountains, its sprawling coasts lined with dense forests of beech trees and an occasional pebble or sandy beach, its rocky islets that host reclining seals, nesting cormorants and strutting geese. The channel is still breathtaking and must have been more so when Murray and Fitz-Roy first saw it.

Having slept peacefully the night of 7 May, they embarked at sunrise, a fine breeze from the east pushing them along until squalls from the northwest slowed their pace. They moored the cutter that evening on a small island, later referred to as Point Divide because it divides Beagle Channel into its northwest and southwest "arms." This small island received the name Devil (Isla del Diablo), because one of Fitz-Roy's men noticed two large eyes staring at him out of a thick bush and screamed, or perhaps whispered, to his shipmates that the Devil was peering at him. Fitz-Roy commented: "A hearty laugh at his expense was followed by a shot at the bush, which brought to the ground a magnificent horned owl." The island might better have been named in memory of this magnificent denizen instead of the Devil.

An unusually large wigwam caught Fitz-Roy's attention when he went ashore on nearby Isla Grande. He imagined that it had been a "Meeting House" and that the location might be a neutral ground between the two tribes (Alakaluf and Yamana).[89] His comments seem justified: the "wigwam" may well have been a ceremonial hut and the area a sort of boundary between the two groups (see the maps).

Down Glacier Lane, the Northwest Arm

Having inspected the "Meeting House," Fitz-Roy and his companions continued a short way into the channel, the Northwest Arm, admiring the "lofty cliffs" of the cordillera, later named after Darwin. Fitz-Roy was impressed by the immense glaciers that descended to the shore of this "arm" in "a death-like stillness... which crashed, and reverberated around like eruptions of a distant volcano." He and young Darwin will witness another tremendous crash from one of these glaciers (Chapter 5). The cordillera's average height is 5,000 feet (1,524 metres), while its highest mountain, the Sarmiento, reaches to about 7,450 feet (2,271 metres). Apparently the north coast of this "arm" was never inhabited, though native campsites have been noticed on its south shore, on Gordon Island.[90]

FIGURE 3.2. The Yamana greet the *Beagle* at the intersection of Beagle Channel and Murray Narrows.

Back in Beagle Channel on 11 May, the explorers went ashore again on Navarino Island near the entrance to Murray Narrows. Fitz-Roy and his crew were seated quietly around a fire near a wigwam whose occupants had fled but soon returned and began bartering beads and buttons for fish. Fitz-Roy exceptionally offered a knife for a very fine dog, which the natives were "extremely reluctant to part with."

"Jemmy Button" the Fourth Hostage

Soon afterwards, as they were approaching Murray Narrows, three canoes pulled up to their cutter with more natives anxious to barter. And sure enough this time they offered a button for "Jemmy Button, as the boat's crew called him, on account of his price, seemed to be pleased at his change, and fancied he was going to kill guanaco, or wana-kaye, as he called them – as they were to be found near that place."[91]

Fitz-Roy could not have imagined then that he had witnessed an event that will forever be highlighted in the annals of the native people of these last parts of the inhabited earth.

Near this intersection (Beagle Channel and Murray Narrows), the thirteen- or fourteen-year-old lad, Orundelico, entered history as Jemmy

Button.[92] Fitz-Roy explained the moment of this great event of 11 May 1830 (italics added):

I told one of the boys in a canoe to come into our boat *and gave the man who was with him a large shining mother-of-pearl button.* The boy got into my boat directly and sat down. Seeing him and his friends seem quite contented, I pulled onwards, and, a light breeze springing up, made sail. Thinking that this accidental occurrence might prove useful to the natives, as well as to ourselves, I determined to take advantage of it.

This quotation is almost invariably interpreted as if "Jemmy" had been purchased for a button, hence his "surname." However, in reality, when he boarded the cutter, Fitz-Roy gave a button to the man who was with him, perhaps his father or an uncle, who apparently (see below) had no idea of selling him. Perhaps at the moment Fitz-Roy did think he was purchasing the boy, however, some months later, he acknowledged to Parker King that he did not know if Jemmy Button's friends in the canoe "intended that he should remain with us permanently." So, according to Fitz-Roy's own words, Jemmy was not purchased, he was captured, however peacefully.[93] Jemmy himself apparently thought he would be left off nearby to hunt guanacos, although there is no indication that he tried to escape from the cutter. After he departed, his mother searched for him everywhere also thinking that he had been let off on Navarino Island to hunt guanacos (Chapter 5).

Lucas Bridges, who knew the Yahgan as his playmates and throughout his youth, affirmed in his famous book that it was ridiculous to imagine that Jemmy Button had been purchased for a button, "as no native would have sold his child in exchange for HMS Beagle with all it had on board."[94]

Fitz-Roy Returns to the *Beagle*

That same day, 13 May 1830, the cutter headed back to Lennox Island, where the *Beagle* was waiting. On the way, sailing along the south coast of Navarino, they sighted a "crow's nest" in which several Yamanas were seated, hoping to spear a guanaco if it came close enough. Later Hyades stated that the Yamana hunted the guanaco with harpoons, not their bows and arrows, as the Selk'nam, because theirs were too small and were used mainly for killing birds.[95]

When they boarded the *Beagle* that evening on Lennox Island with Jemmy, the three Alakalufs, who were in "high spirits," laughed at him, calling him a Yapoo (otter), and told Fitz-Roy to put more clothes on him.

Kempe, who had remained on the ship during these three weeks studying the harbour, told of buying large quantities of fish from "extremely quiet and inoffensive" natives who had come there from time to time, once in ten canoes.⁹⁶

Murray Contacts the Haush

Murray returned a few days later, reporting that his trip to the southeast coast of Isla Grande, beyond Beagle Channel, had been uneventful. He had seen herds of guanacos along the coast. On the shore of Valentine Bay, he met eight men (undoubtedly the Haush), clothed in guanaco skins that hung down to their heels, the woolly side turned out (as usual). They willingly exchanged bows and arrows for a knife, which they called *cuchillo* in Spanish, but they refused to part with their "fine dogs, one being much like a young lion." Murray found Valentine Bay "unfit for vessels, being exposed to a heavy swell, and affording but bad anchorage [too shallow]."⁹⁷ It was a favourite camping ground for the Haush, who were not navigators, so the "bad anchorage" was of no concern to them. It is still uninhabited today except for occasional archaeologists. I was impressed, in 1970, by its beautiful sandy beach scattered with monumental rocks, resembling Henry Moore's sculptures, where some seals reclined while a few herds of guanacos wandered nearby through the forest and flocks of birds found plenty to eat.

Further down the coast, Murray climbed the summit of Cape Good Success (not to be confused with the bay of the same name) from where he saw Staten Island on the far horizon. He returned to Lennox Cove by the same route, having confronted many "difficulties and risks" which he failed to specify.⁹⁸

Young Stokes had departed in the small whaleboat on 3 May and returned to the *Beagle* on the seventeenth, the same day as Murray. He had examined all the shores in the vicinity of eastern Beagle Channel, probably near Cambaceres Bay and the future Harberton farm. He met many Indians there without experiencing "any collision or trouble with them." Stokes seems to have been invariably involved in uneventful explorations or perhaps he simply failed to report details of what he saw.

The Long Voyage Back to England

The entire crew was now reunited on the *Beagle* in Lennox Cove with the four Fuegians. The crew was busy during ten days, from 13 to 23 May, surveying and sounding the cove and preparing for the long voyage home.

The local Yamana were still fishing in the kelp nearby and occasionally paddled up to the *Beagle* to barter, as they had with Kempe. Fitz-Roy, aware that York and Boat Memory did not understand their language, was amused to observe them "going about the decks collecting broken crockery-ware, or any trash, to exchange for fish brought alongside by the 'Yapoos' as they called them."⁹⁹ The Yamana wanted broken glass to make tiny arrowheads, which they used to hunt birds. Many have been found in the area by the archaeologists.

The day after departure from Lennox Cove, 24 May 1830, they entered Le Maire Strait in thick snow squalls. A gale also threatened from the south, the Antarctic, so they took refuge in Good Success Bay. The gale increased, sending huge, jerking swells into the bay and pulling with great force at the cables, already damaged by the intense frost. Fitz-Roy was awakened late the first night by shouts that a cable had split. When he rushed to the deck, he saw and felt the ship "turning her broadside to the swell, and dropping down upon her lee anchor." He and the crew finally secured her. The waves and currents had subsided the next morning, but soon another furious gale struck, and lasted three days. When the weather calmed down, the officers relaxed, took bearings and soundings while the rest of the crew hauled wood and water from the shore. They noticed several wigwams and hoof-prints of guanacos but saw no one. No natives appeared during the two weeks the *Beagle* remained there.

The four "captives" also went on land several times, rowing a boat to and from the shore "without appearing to harbour a thought of escape." As they did not attempt escape, is it unfair to Fitz-Roy to call them captives? Fitz-Roy was convinced that they understood (despite the language barrier) "why they were taken, and look forward with pleasure to seeing our country, as well as to returning to their own." Even though they could not have had the slightest notion of where they were being taken, the question of whether or not all four can, or should be, considered captives remains largely unanswered so far. When the weather calmed down at the end of May, Fitz-Roy and a small crew set out, probably in the new whaleboat, to determine the position of San Diego Cape, at the Atlantic entrance to the Le Maire Strait, and measure the tides along its rocky shores and the latitudes.¹⁰⁰

During the week ending 5 June, Fitz-Roy rounded San Diego Cape and sailed up the Atlantic coast of Isla Grande to a wide and beautiful bay, later called Policarpo, which proved too shallow for anchorage for the *Beagle*. Back in Good Success Bay, most of the crew were still storing water and wood for the long voyage home. In his Sailing Directions,

Fitz-Roy cautioned future navigators that the race of tides that batter Cape San Diego is so violent that it should be skirted by at least by three miles.[101] The Yamana did visit Good Success Bay, although it was in Haush territory, but they seldom if ever ventured beyond Cape San Diego. This was the other "natural limit," with Black Cape, for the canoe-cruising Yamana, and it is still dangerous today, despite the great advances in navigation.

Were the Four Fuegians Captured?

Finally the *Beagle* weighed anchor, on 8 June 1830, from Good Success Bay, homeward bound. Jemmy Button and his three companions could not have imagined just where they were being taken or that they would not return home for so long (two years and six months). Half of this time would be spent on the water and in the ports on the way to England and back, the other half in England, learning the language and some of the customs of their strange hosts.

Recall that, in early March, Fitz-Roy had kept Fuegia Basket when he could easily have sent her with Murray and the other two children, who were well received by a friendly old woman. At that time, it was unlikely that he could have traded Fuegia for the stolen boat, because the real thieves had not been found, after being pursued for three weeks. While in March Harbour (Waterman Island), Fitz-Roy had "invited" York Minster on board his ship, thinking that he also could be used as a hostage, although another whaleboat was already being constructed. He may still have been confused as to just what he could or should do with his two hostages. When he captured the third, Boat Memory, his stolen whaleboat had become a "memory," or a nightmare. By the time he peacefully kept Jemmy on board, he had already decided to take the three to England, including Jemmy.

In no case had the hostages' families or friends been notified of their departures. The friendly disposition of the four indicates that they trusted Fitz-Roy despite the language barrier and somehow understood that he would return them to their homeland. Nonetheless, it seems obvious to me, without over-interpreting the texts, that however willingly the four consented to face an unknown future, they were captives.

As he sailed up the coast of Patagonia on 10 June, Fitz-Roy asked himself how he had become involved in such an adventure. By then he was convinced that he should take the Fuegians to England out of "common humanity" rather than leave them in enemy territory, as he did not have time to return them to their homeland. However, as just noted, he could easily have left them in their homeland. Then he explained: "I began to think of the various advantages which might result to them and their countrymen, as well as to us, by taking them to England, educating them there as far as might be practical, and then bringing them back to Tierra del Fuego."

Note that Fitz-Roy made no allusion to Christianising them, yet this was probably one of the "advantages" he already had in mind. One "advantage" certainly was, as he stated above, the convenience of having friendly English-speaking natives in the Tierra del Fuego area. Why? If you guess you are probably right: for the geopolitical interests of Great Britain. On the way back to England he was disappointed that they were much slower in learning English than he had anticipated, given their extraordinary ability to mimic. Later he convinced himself that it would be to their "advantage" to return to their homeland with a supply of tools and clothes as well as knowledge from which their countrymen might well benefit.[102] Approaching Plymouth in September 1830, he recalled their "estimated ages": Fuegia, nine years old; Jemmy, fourteen; Boat Memory, twenty; and York Minster, twenty-six.

Fitz-Roy is certainly to be honoured for having kept his word to return them to their home, despite the very real problems he had to face (Chapter 4). During the long voyage from June to September 1830, they helped the crew, "were tractable and good-humoured." Unfortunately there is no testimony directly from them during these months. In later years Fuegia Basket invariably spoke well, to passing navigators, of her experiences in England, and Jemmy frequently and fondly remembered his British friends, often naming each and sending them special presents. Even twenty-five years later, he named his thirteen British friends (Chapter 8). Nor did he ever entirely forget his English, and even tried to teach it to his family. There is no report on comments York may have made during later years, but once he returned to Tierra del Fuego, he was obviously gratified by the presents he was able to load in his canoe and take home. Even so it seems to me that Boat Memory and the other three were captives.

Résumé of This First Voyage: 1826 to 1830

Captains Stokes, Fitz-Roy and Lieutenant Skyring achieved a great deal with the *Beagle* during this first voyage. Some of the surveys and measurements had been carried out by the *Adventure*, aided by the *Adelaide*, and other tasks only by the *Beagle*. Thomson pointed out that "the *Beagle* was marginally easier to work in these close and dangerous waters than the

unwieldy *Adventure*." The *Beagle* crew had been more active and more
exposed to perils of tempests than the crew of the *Adventure*. However,
both crews had made the surveys and soundings from Uruguay down
much of the Atlantic coast of Argentina, with particular attention to the
Patagonian coast from Río Negro to the Magellan Strait.

Stokes, in the *Beagle*, had partially surveyed the western (most difficult)
portion of the Magellan Strait, and an alternative route from Tomar Bay
on the north shore of the main strait, via the Nelson Strait to the Pacific,
as well as part of the archipelago north of the Magellan Strait, including the Gulf of Peñas. In 1829 and 1830, Skyring in the *Adelaide* had
completed Stokes' surveys to the vicinity of Chiloé Island. The following
year, the *Beagle*'s and *Adelaide*'s crews surveyed the main routes from the
Magellan Strait through the Magdalena, Cockburn and Barbara channels
to the Pacific. On the continent, Jerome Channel and two salt "waters,"
Otway and Skyring, were partially charted by Fitz-Roy. With the aide of
Master Murray, he made surveys of the islands along the Pacific front
from Magellan Strait to Cape Horn, of Orange Bay (Hoste Island), and
of the Le Maire Strait, especially Cape San Diego and sections of the
north Atlantic shore of the Isla Grande. The outer islets – Noire, Diego
Ramírez and Ildefonso – were precisely located and partially surveyed.
The crowning achievement was Murray's discovery of Beagle Channel,
because it signalled an immense advance of the cartography, the geography and the hydrography at this "end of the world." Fitz-Roy had
demonstrated his ability during this voyage by "no less than 82 coastal
sheets and 80 plans and 40 views of harbours." But "there was still an
enormous amount of work to be done in that region."[103] Memorials had
been buried, specimens of fauna, flora and rocks collected.

The achievements of this expedition would not have been realised
without Stokes' dedication, for which he paid the "ultimate price";
without Skyring's support of Stokes during his most trying moments and
his noble attitude towards Fitz-Roy; and without the latter's passionate
fixation on exploring and documenting this virtually unknown area for
future navigation.

Fitz-Roy's treatment of the four Fuegians was double-edged: he captured them and then kept them on board, even though he could have
left them in their homeland. He also ignored the feelings of their parents;
but once on board he treated them kindly. He apparently thought that
the four Fuegians, as friendly English-speaking allies, would be useful for
future British interests in the area, although the Admiralty did not seem
to agree with him (Chapter 4).

The four Fuegians demonstrated great courage, as proven by their willingness to risk their lives on their interpretations of the gestures and manners of complete strangers. Their heroic attitude, together with Fitz-Roy's sincere commitment to care for them in England and to return them to their home country, gives this expedition a quality that the previous expeditions to Tierra del Fuego lacked. Three cheers for this expedition, as Jemmy Button might have shouted.

4

1830 to 1832: Fuegians in England; Fitz-Roy and Darwin Meet; The *Beagle* Returns to Tierra del Fuego with Darwin and Three Fuegians

The Long Voyage Home

The *Beagle* departed from Tierra del Fuego on 5 June 1830, arrived in Montevideo on the 27th and remained there almost two weeks. There Fitz-Roy had his four protégés vaccinated, but "the virus did not take any effect on them."

In Montevideo Fuegia was the guest of an English family "who were extremely kind to her," while Fitz-Roy went sightseeing with the other three. They were "so very like the Indians of the neighbourhood" that no one noticed them.[1]

When they entered the great bay of Río de Janeiro on 2 August, they met the crew of the *Adventure* and the Commander, Philip Parker King. Four days later the two ships sailed together homeward bound.

Stupid or Sensible? Savage or Civilised?

Fitz-Roy wrote surprisingly little about his Fuegian shipmates during this four-month voyage. He did notice that their attention was fixed on the animals, ships and boats far more than the people and houses when the *Beagle* passed within view of them along the coasts or in the ports. During the voyage he thought they were "almost stupid and unobservant." However, on the very first pages of his volume two (mainly about the second *Beagle* voyage), he changed his mind about three of them.

I attained a further acquaintance with their abilities and natural inclinations. Far, very far indeed, were three of the number from deserving to be called savage ... though the other, named York Minster, was certainly a displeasing specimen of uncivilised human nature. ... but that they were not so [stupid and unobservant] in reality was shown by their eager chattering to one another ... and by the sensible remarks made by them a long time afterwards, when we fancied they had altogether forgotten unimportant occurrences.

The Fuegians saw a steam vessel for the first time when the *Beagle* pulled into Falmouth Harbour, near Plymouth, on 14 October 1830. They could not decide what sort of an extraordinary monster it was: a huge fish, a land animal or the devil, nor did the sailors' explanations convince them. Fitz-Roy imagined that the reaction of someone seeing a train for the first time might have evoked similar comments to those of "these ignorant, though rather intelligent barbarians." If York did not appeal to him, Boat Memory did. "He had a good disposition, very good abilities, and though born a savage, had a pleasant, intelligent appearance. He was quite an exception to the general character of the Fuegians, having good features and a well-proportioned frame."

Fitz-Roy's Worries

Fitz-Roy, a key person in this unfolding drama, although a devout Christian of strict morals, made some extremely derogatory remarks concerning the Yamana (see below). In a long letter to Captain King dated 12 September 1830, he related details of the whaleboat theft and explained the circumstances that occasioned his decision to bring the four Fuegians to England (Chapter 3). He clarified that during these months he had maintained them at his own expense and requested "some public advantage" to help him with further costs. He committed himself to procure a suitable education for them and, after two or three years, to send or take them back to their country with a large stock of useful articles.

Upon arrival Captain King forwarded Fitz-Roy's letter to the Lords, the Commissioners of the Admiralty. Fitz-Roy must have been exceedingly gratified five days later, when he received a reply that the Lords approved of his "benevolent intentions towards these four people" and assured him that they would provide "any facilities towards maintaining and educating them in England" and would give them a passage home.

Boat Memory Dies

Shortly after arrival, early October, Fitz-Roy took his four friends to a comfortable lodging in Falmouth, where they were vaccinated a second time. Recall that the vaccine had not taken effect in Montevideo this year, in June or early July. A few days later, on 17 October, they were driven a few miles from Falmouth to a farmhouse, where they incurred less risk of contagion than in the populous port. Despite these precautions, two weeks later, Boat Memory showed the symptoms of smallpox. Fearing contagion of the others, their special friend James Bennett accompanied the four to the Royal Naval Hospital in Plymouth, where they were vaccinated again, for the last time.[2] But these vaccines were too late for Boat Memory. He succumbed in the hospital about 10 November. Fitz-Roy was distraught. "This poor fellow was a very great favourite with all who knew him, as well as with myself. . . . [His death] was a severe blow to me, for I was deeply sensible of the responsibility which had been incurred; and, however unintentionally, could not but feel how much I was implicated in shortening his existence."[3]

The others remained in the hospital until December while arrangements were being made for their stay.

The Three Fuegians in Boarding School

Early December 1830, the three remaining protégés, accompanied by Master Murray and James Bennett, their special friends, went on a long stagecoach ride from Plymouth to Walthamstow, a small town northeast of London. While passing through London, beyond Charing Cross, York suddenly shouted "Look!" staring at the statue of the lion in front of Northumberland House, "which he certainly thought alive, and walking there." Along the way, the three were struck and probably amused by the repeated changing of horses. Meanwhile, Fitz-Roy had contacted a certain Reverend Joseph Wigram through the Church Missionary Society. Wigram had introduced him to Reverend William Wilson, the pastor in Walthamstow, who had agreed to receive the Fuegians in his parish and to engage the master of the local school to receive them in his home as boarders and pupils. Both reverends promised to keep a watchful eye on them. Wigram also lived in Walthamstow. The schoolmaster and his wife, Mr and Mrs Jenkens, were pleased to find their three pupils so well disposed, quiet, and cleanly, not at all the fierce, dirty savages they had imagined. If the Jenkens were still alive many years later, they would have been pleased to learn that Jemmy recalled their name in 1858 and that Fuegia Basket, in 1873, spoke gratefully of her stay in England (Chapters 8 and 11).

The new pupils were pleased with the rooms prepared for them. Through the coming months the schoolmaster endeavoured to teach them English, the "plainer truths of Christianity," and techniques of farming. Jemmy and Fuegia were the favourite pupils and showed progress; York less, although he took an interest in smith's work, carpentry and animals. "By degrees, a good many words of their own languages were collected." Recall that Jemmy spoke Yamana while Fuegia and York spoke Alakaluf, though they understood enough of the other language to converse among themselves. The three adapted well to their strange environment, and remained healthy during their ten-month stay. Visitors flocked to see them: the neighbours, members of missionary societies, philanthropic ladies, Fitz-Roy, his sister and their aristocratic friends. Most or all came bearing useful and not-so-useful gifts, including "equipment" for a mission station, which was to be established in Tierra del Fuego. Fitz-Roy's sister was especially kind to them. Jemmy spoke of her long afterwards as "Cappen Sisser" (Chapter 9).

A Visit to the Majesties
During the summer of 1831, King William IV expressed a wish to meet the three Fuegians. Fitz-Roy escorted them, of course in a stagecoach, to Saint James' Palace and was very pleased by the reception they were accorded, especially by His Majesty's attentions. "No person ever asked me so many sensible and thoroughly pertinent questions about their country, as well as themselves." Queen Adelaide was so charmed by Fuegia that she placed one of her bonnets on Fuegia's head and slipped one of her rings on Fuegia's middle finger. Fuegia often wore both, even on the voyage back to Tierra del Fuego. Her Majesty also gave Fuegia money to buy an outfit of clothes, although undoubtedly she was well dressed for the occasion.[4]

A Visit to a Head Reader
Fitz-Roy also escorted his Fuegians to a phrenologist "to have their heads read." Apparently the phrenologist's diagnosis consisted mainly of determining the size and location of the "bumps" on the head of a client in order to determine the quality and/or quantity of the client's intellectual capacity. Janet Browne, author of an extremely well-documented book on Darwin's voyage, explained: "All three, the phrenologist concluded, possessed several marked 'animal' traits that would be difficult to eradicate, even through education. Their intellectual bumps – those associated with civilised mankind – were found to be small, whereas their 'propensities' – the parts of the brain believed most characteristic of a barbarian – were large and full."[5]

Some thirty years later, in 1864, other Fuegians, including one of Jemmy Button's sons, will have their "heads read," also in England, with different results (Chapter 10).

Meanwhile Fitz-Roy Is Busy

The Admiralty Changes "Its Mind"

Fitz-Roy completed his official duties six months after returning to England, in March 1831, to the utmost satisfaction of his commanding officer. By then he was already making plans to continue the survey in Tierra del Fuego and take the Fuegians back to their homeland, under the auspices of the Admiralty. But the Lords had second thoughts: they decided not to allocate the promised funds and had "no intention to prosecute the survey." Fitz-Roy was deeply disappointed on both accounts. He became, "anxious about the Fuegians . . . to trust them in any other kind of vessel – because of the risk that would attend their being landed anywhere, excepting on the territories of their own tribes." So he decided to shorten their visit in England and to proceed on his own. He obtained permission for a twelve months' leave of absence from the navy and made up his mind to pay the expenses and to take them back to Tierra del Fuego himself. In June he chartered a small merchant vessel with a crew of five and purchased a dozen or so goats to give to the Fuegians upon arrival. His sincere commitment to their well-being cannot be questioned. He also showed unusual concern for the Maori natives when he was governor in New Zealand from 1843 to 1845. The *Encyclopaedia Britannica* notes that he "was recalled in 1845 largely because he contended that the natives', the Maoris', land claims were as valid as those of the British settlers."[6]

The Admiralty Changes Its Mind Again

Fitz-Roy's "kind uncle," the influential Duke of Grafton, heard of the Admiralty's refusal and prevailed upon the Lords to reconsider and approve of his nephew's plan.[7] Francis Beaufort, director of the Hydrographer's Office of the Admiralty, "lavished proprietorial care on it [a second *Beagle* expedition]. . . . The survey he anticipated would be a showpiece for the Hydrographer's Office."[8] Fitz-Roy had proven his ability during the first voyage, which was more than enough for Beaufort. Janet Browne clarified that Fitz-Roy's surveys and mapping acquired great economic and political significance for Great Britain because "the southern parts of Patagonia and Chile were potentially significant in commercial and naval terms. It was important too . . . to forestall French and North American interests in the area."[9]

Fitz-Roy was overjoyed by the Admiralty's final approval of his proposal and that his "well-tried little vessel" would be assigned to him. His enthusiasm led him to envision registering "a chain of meridian distances" around the world, across the Pacific and back to England via the Cape of Good Hope. He was allotted the twenty-four chronometres deemed indispensable for recording the exact time (the Greenwich Mean Time) and determining longitudes with accuracy. Janet Browne called attention to the great importance of this second voyage because it was to be "the first full-scale attempt made by the British to plot the course of an entire circumnavigation by marine chronometres."[10]

He Finds a Missionary

Fitz-Roy accepted Reverend Wilson's suggestion that a certain Richard Matthews initiate teaching the Fuegians "the plainer truths of Christianity" in their homeland. Although Matthews was rather too young and inexperienced to assume such a challenge, the recommendations concerning his character and his conduct assured Fitz-Roy that he would be capable of meeting it; besides, he was the only volunteer.[11]

And a Naturalist

Fitz-Roy was still searching for a naturalist four months before the *Beagle* finally departed on the second voyage. It was standard practice at the time for the British Navy to assign the expedition's surgeon to make observations and collections as a naturalist. During this second voyage the surgeon, Robert Mac-Cormick (or McKormick), expected to perform this duty in his spare time. But Fitz-Roy went beyond the normal procedure: he requested that a full-time naturalist be assigned to his expedition. Moreover, he felt the need for a companion of his own social class to share his meals and to converse with as an equal during the long voyage. Would Charles Darwin have been the scientist he became without his voyage on the *Beagle*? Fitz-Roy's initiative of contracting young Darwin may well lie at the origin of all that followed in the scientific world and should guarantee that Fitz-Roy be remembered as Stephen J. Gould insisted.[12]

Darwin had no claim to nobility, but his family's prestige, respectability, and wealth sufficed as equivalent to Fitz-Roy's aristocratic heritage. Erasmus Darwin, Charles' paternal grandfather, a well-known physician and poet of his day, is still cited for having applied evolutionary principles in his study of "laws of organic life." Darwin's father was also a distinguished physician. His maternal uncle (and future father-in-law), Josiah Wedgwood, was the owner of an immensely successful pottery factory. Although Darwin had not been brought up in a strict biblical milieu, he was raised as a Unitarian and his father had urged him to become a country parson. Moreover, Darwin's two professors at Cambridge University – Adam Sedgwick and especially John Stevens Henslow – highly

FIGURE 4.1. 1840: Charles Darwin when he was 31 years old. Apparently there is no portrait or sketch of Darwin during the voyage. Watercolour on paper by George Richmond (1809–96). Down House, Kent, UK. The Bridgeman Art Library.

recommended him to Fitz-Roy as a student of the natural sciences. Henslow will become Darwin's monitor and his main contact and scientific support during the long *Beagle* voyage. His constant and unfailing loyalty was essential to Darwin's accomplishments during the voyage and afterwards. He wrote many encouraging letters to Darwin and received his numerous envoys of boxes and crates containing a great variety of specimens. Darwin became known among British scientists even before the voyage ended, thanks to Henslow. He remained Darwin's loyal friend and supporter through difficult times after the voyage, even though he did not accept Darwin's theory concerning the origin of life on earth.

At the onset, the Darwin–Fitz-Roy relation might not appear to augur well: Darwin the liberal Whig and Fitz-Roy the conservative Tory.[13] Although Fitz-Roy was an ardent Christian, at the time he was not inclined to interpret the Bible as the source of geological and biological knowledge. It was only after he returned from the second *Beagle* voyage (after 1836) that he became firmly convinced that the Bible related the truth concerning subjects that now, in 1831, he wanted a naturalist to investigate. During this second voyage, he and Darwin met in the middle of the road, though they were headed in opposite directions.[14] Neither philosophical beliefs nor religion were bones of contention during the long voyage. They agreed on a wide range of subjects, particularly on the possibility that the human being, no matter how savage or barbarian, could progress to the level of civilised Britains. Both were convinced that the missionaries could serve an indispensable role, "as front-line agents," for implementing the transition to cultural progress epitomised by the Christian nations, such as Great Britain.[15] However, a serious dispute will arise, given their Whig/Tory discrepancy, as will become clear.

Fitz-Roy and Darwin met on 5 September 1831 in London and the following week sailed together to Plymouth to inspect the *Beagle*. On that very day, Darwin wrote to his sister Susan that he refrained from praising Fitz-Roy "as I feel inclined to do, for you would not believe me. One thing I am certain of [,] nothing could be more open & kind than he was to me." He also expressed his enthusiasm in a letter to his teacher, Henslow:

Cap. Fitzroy is every thing that is delightful, if I was to praise half so much as I feel inclined, you would say it was absurd, only once seeing him. I think he really wishes to have me. He offers me to mess with him & he will take care I have such room as is possible.... You cannot imagine anything more pleasant, kind & open than Cap. Fitzroy's manners were to me. – I am sure it will be my fault, if we do not suit.[16]

Fitz-Roy had a different impression when Darwin walked into the room. He "took a dislike to him, particularly his nose; it was not the nose of a man who could endure the rigours of a voyage around the world." Years later Darwin recalled that he had "run a very narrow risk of being rejected, on account of the shape of my nose!" If the size, location and number of bumps on the head could reveal intelligence, the shape of a nose might reveal a person's character. Why not? But that very day, 5 September or soon afterwards, Fitz-Roy overlooked or tried to ignore the nose and praised Darwin "as a young man of promising ability, extremely fond of geology, and indeed all branches of natural history." Fitz-Roy had made up his mind; he wanted Darwin as his naturalist. He wrote to Francis Beaufort (the head hydrographer of the Admiralty): "I like what I see and hear of him, much, and I now request that you will apply for him to accompany me as a Naturalist."[17]

Two of Darwin's Strongly Held Convictions

According to one of Darwin's sons, "The two subjects which moved my Father perhaps more strongly than any others were cruelty to animals

& slavery. His detestation of both was intense, and his indignation was overpowering in case of any levity or want of feeling on these matters."[18]

Throughout his life Darwin's love and admiration for animals, though focused on his pet dogs, included all animals from monkeys to worms. Janet Browne commented that "he gave human attributes to almost every species he met, including flatworms and beetles.... He felt himself part of a single world united by the same kind of mental responses." He contributed regularly to the Royal Society for the Prevention of Cruelty to Animals and "was troubled throughout his life by the problems raised by vivisection."[19]

Although Darwin's love for animals never ceased, in his later years he supported experiments on living animals as a necessity for physiological research.[20]

Not vivisection but slavery provoked a critical conflict during the voyage. Darwin was a passionate abolitionist. "Those who look tenderly at the slave-owner, and with a cold heart at the slave, never seem to put themselves into the position of the latter – what a cheerless prospect.... picture to yourself the chance, ever hanging over you, of your wife and your little children ... being torn from you and sold like beasts to the first bidder!"[21]

He was appalled by the treatment of slaves he witnessed on plantations in Bahía, Brazil, apparently on 12 March 1832. Fitz-Roy became so infuriated over his criticism of a Brazilian slave owner that he announced that they could no longer share the same quarters. Darwin thought he might be compelled to leave the ship. His objection to slavery was unfailing. After a while Fitz-Roy apologised to him. The subject was rarely mentioned again.[22]

Slavery existed where they were headed, in Uruguay and Argentina, though it was far less prevalent than in Brazil, partly because the large sugar, cotton and rice plantations that employed slaves were lacking in these countries. Slavery had been abolished in Chile in 1823.

Darwin's Appraisal of the Fuegians[23]

Janet Browne suggested that "Darwin had no foundation for believing that Negro slaves or native Fuegians were in some way closer to animals than he was.... and the barrier between a state of savagery and one of civilisation was remarkably small."[24]

But if the barrier between savagery and civilisation was so small, why did Darwin write about the Fuegians (the Yamanas) with such contempt? I propose that his often repeated conviction that they (the

Fuegian–Yamana) were cannibals (of the worst sort, because they ate the grandmothers) was decisive. I have the impression that it distorted his entire image of them – that had he known that they were not cannibals, that they did not eat the grandmothers or anyone else, he would not have represented them as the "lowest most savage state." Desmond and Moore paraphrased his thoughts on this subject (somewhat like Browne), as disclosed in his B notebook: "Even races of people were spreading laterally *into their peculiar niches*, Jemmy Button's Fuegians into a desolate, windswept wilderness, civilised Englishmen into their factory cities."[25] Darwin put himself in the niche of the African slave but not in the Fuegians' niche. He was far more sympathetic to the former than to the latter, certainly because the Africans had been torn from their homeland and enslaved and again probably because it never occurred to him that they could be savage cannibals. Neither Darwin nor Fitz-Roy presumed to be students of the Fuegian cultures, although the latter wrote quite extensively about them and the Tehuelches of Patagonia.[26] Darwin was repelled by the Fuegians, the Yamana–Yahgan, whom he placed "in a lower state of improvement than any other part of the world"[27] (with the exception of Jemmy Button and other Yamanas he met). The Tehuelche Indians, called "Patagonians," who were not accused of cannibalism, impressed him favourably (Chapter 5). Although he ridiculed the Haush Indians in Good Success Bay, his indignation was not aroused. It was, however, when he heard stories about Yamana cannibalism (see below). Darwin certainly cannot be accused of being a racist. However, the anthropologist Marvin Harris did accuse him of racism mainly because of his attitude toward the Yamana. On the contrary, Carl Sagan, a highly esteemed authority on astronomy and space sciences, found "some justification for the manner in which Darwin derided" the Fuegians.[28]

Darwin's comments fit nicely into the notion, still prevalent today, that human beings as a whole have evolved from the savage simplicity of rude primitives, such as the Fuegians, to the sophisticated complexity of civilised ladies and gentlemen. To be more precise: why does this paradigm of mankind "evolving" from simple primitives to the great ancient civilizations, culminating with our industrial societies, have such a long life? Many years ago J. W. Burrow proposed that the reason stems from the idea of progress. He referred to Victorian England, but his analyses are valid today. In his own words, "The Victorians . . . do much to explain why nineteenth-century social theory should have taken the idea of social evolution as its key concept. They also help to explain the persistence of evolutionary positivism long after alternative theories had arisen on the continent."

In terms of Thomas Kuhn's paradigms, Burrow's added: "Theories do not automatically disappear because more sophisticated theories are put forward, at least in fields . . . most heavily charged hopes and beliefs of mankind."[29]

Darwin's contradictions lay deep in his mind. He was convinced that all people are intellectually equivalent. He strongly opposed slavery and recognised that the African slave and the three Fuegians he met were as intelligent as anyone else.[30] He did not express any animosity toward the Yamana he met in Wulaia, nor did he allude to them as cannibals (see below). Yet at the same time he seems convinced that the native "Fuegians" (as he called the Yamana) were the most degraded people on earth.

Despite Darwin's cultural ranking from the lowest (the Fuegians, aboriginal Australians and the like) to the highest (the civilised Europeans), he proposed that the gap could be closed, even in one generation, obviously because he believed that innate intelligence is the same in all human beings.

Outstanding examples were Fuegia Basket and Jemmy Button, who had been "savages of the lowest type imaginable" and had become "Anglicised Fuegians," nearly civilised, within a very short time (while on the *Beagle* and in England, that is from June 1830 to January 1833). His attitude was similar in this respect to that of the Anglican missionaries, who worked on the premise that the Fuegians were savages yet capable of being "saved": civilised and converted to Christianity.

Janet Browne evoked Darwin's "strong commitment to the idea of progress, the theme of the age [in which he lived]." He, like many of his contemporaries, firmly believed in this sort of progress despite, as Browne insisted, "the brutal working conditions, the exploitation of women and children" in England and elsewhere. Improvement was thought to be an "inbuilt tendency" in virtually all aspects of life.[31]

The late Stephen J. Gould, an outstanding palaeontologist and brilliant "populariser" of biological evolution, recalled that Darwin was opposed to the concept of progress as applied to all animal (including the human) species. Gould even advocated that Darwin's term "descent with modification" be used by biologists instead of "evolution," insofar as progress is implied in the latter term.[32] Gould's suggestion has been largely ignored except by a few scientists. Biological "evolution" appears to be here to stay, not "descent with modification."

John C. Greene, a well-known Darwin scholar, commented on other possible contradictions: "It is not surprising, then, that readers of *The Descent of Man* have drawn different conclusions about Darwin's views on social evolution. Darwin seems to contradict himself, leaving scholars free to draw whatever conclusions fit best with their preconceived ideas about Darwin and his role in Western thought."

If Darwin did contradict himself in Tierra del Fuego and in *The Descent of Man*, this may be, I suggest, because somehow he could not resolve an enigma: if "progress" could not explain the moral and social differences that he assumed existed between the customs of savages and those of the civilised, what did? Perhaps Christianity? As an agnostic, he was not personally convinced, but in *Descent* he wondered about its and other moral principles that developed what he calls conscience. The question is answered in *Descent*, but not entirely to his satisfaction, given his ambiguity that at times took the form of contradictions. I will add here a conclusion from my unpublished text on *The Descent of Man*: "Despite his flexible method [his treatment of 'instinct' and 'habit'] and his failure to demonstrate that his theory of natural selection applied to behaviour [defined as 'habit' and, under certain conditions, as 'instinct'] there is much to learn from *Descent*."

Now We Return to that Memorable Voyage.

Preparations for Departure of the Second *Beagle* Voyage

The week after Fitz-Roy and Darwin first met, on 5 September in London, they sailed to Plymouth to inspect the *Beagle*, although departure was to be delayed more than they had anticipated.

The three protégés, having spent ten months in Walthamstow, bade farewell to their friends in October 1831 and rode in a stagecoach back to London for the last time, accompanied by the schoolmaster Jenkens. From there, they boarded a steam packet to Davenport near Plymouth with the heavy cargo of gifts that the well-meaning churchgoers had inundated them. The seamen joked when they tried to fit it all into the small hold of the *Beagle*, especially the complete sets of crockery.[33] Darwin was appalled, later, when he inspected the heaps of gifts: "The choice of articles showed the most culpable folly & negligence. Wine-glasses, butter-bolts, tea-trays, soup turins, mahogany dressing case, fine white linen, beaver hats & an endless variety of similar things. The means absolutely wasted on such things would have purchased an immense stock of really useful articles."[34]

However inappropriate the gifts were, Jemmy, Fuegia and York highly valued each and every one. They well knew or imagined that things of this sort could be put to multiple uses. Jared Diamond in his brilliant book *Guns, Germs, and Steel* mentioned a somewhat similar situation he witnessed while leaving a group of native New Guineans. They played with his discarded objects "to figure out whether they might be useful." Some things, such as discarded tin cans, posed no problem, while others were "tested for purposes very different from the one for which they were manufactured."[35]

Darwin arrived in Devonport, the navy yard of Plymouth, on 24 October, and remained there and in Plymouth over two months until the *Beagle* weighed anchor on 27 December. Besides the "many & unexpected delays," his reiterated complaint was the lack of space on the *Beagle*. He would have to squeeze himself into his "private corner," hang his hammock over his table, and so forth. However, the thought of seasickness may have worried him even more. On 13 November, he made "a casual entry in his diary" that the Fuegians had arrived, accompanied by their schoolmaster, Jenkins, and that the missionary, Matthews, had arrived at the same time.[36]

The date for departure was finally respected. On 27 December 1831, the *Beagle* sailed away with Fitz-Roy as commander and surveyor of the second expedition of "The *Beagle*'s Circumnavigation of the Globe." Darwin did not realise until later that the voyage was to last nearly five years.

The *Beagle* Crew and Its "Supernumeraries"

Captain King came to see them off with his son, Philip Gidley King, who embarked on the *Beagle* as a midshipman. King the elder retired in 1834 and settled in Australia, where Darwin paid him a visit toward the end of the voyage, in January 1836.[37] The entire group sailing on the *Beagle* totalled seventy-four; the crew of sixty-five plus nine passengers, who were called supernumeraries. Besides the captain, the crew was composed of the eleven officers and petty officers, a surgeon, his assistant, three midshipmen, eight marines, thirty-four seamen and six boys. Only those who will become familiar as the narration continues are mentioned here. Jemmy's close friend during both voyages, Benjamin Bynoe, was the assistant surgeon and later the "acting surgeon." Fitz-Roy was aware of Bynoe's fine qualities: his "affectionate kindness . . . his skill and attention . . . [that] will never be forgotten by any of his shipmates."

Darwin also recalled Bynoe's "very kind attention to me when I was ill at Valparaíso" in September 1834.[38] Another midshipman, besides Philip Gidley King, was Robert Nicholas Hamond, Fitz-Roy's shipmate on the *Thetis* during the voyage that had lasted from 1824 to 1828. Hamond joined the *Beagle* in Montevideo and was known as "a very nice gentlemanlike person." Lieutenant John Clements Wickham, Fitz-Roy's special friend, had been on the first *Beagle* voyage and was now the second in command. He proved to be a great help to Fitz-Roy in his moments of profound crises. Darwin also esteemed him as "a glorious fellow" and "far the most conversible person on board." At thirty-three, he was the oldest officer. Lieutenant Bartholomew James Sulivan was Fitz-Roy's oldest friend on board. They had been together on the *Thetis*. Fitz-Roy had requested that Sulivan be transferred to the *Beagle* when he assumed command of her in October 1828 (Chapter 3). Sulivan, who later became governor of the Falklands, was promoted to Admiral in 1877 and through the years remained a staunch supporter of the missionaries in Tierra del Fuego. Young John Lort Stokes, the assistant surveyor, was no relation to the first commander of the *Beagle*, whose tragic suicide had not been forgotten (Chapter 3). Young Stokes had also been on the first voyage, although he was rarely mentioned then. He became Darwin's cabin mate and the officer whose company Darwin seemed to prefer. James Bennett, Jemmy's other special friend, was not mentioned by Fitz-Roy initially, though he was later. Bennett had also been on the first *Beagle* voyage and had accompanied the Fuegians in England.[39] However, it is curious that Master Murray remained in England. He had assisted Fitz-Roy as no other on Landfall Island, chasing the whaleboat thieves, and had discovered Beagle Channel. Fitz-Roy seemed to have esteemed him highly.

Syms Covington, Darwin's servant, was one of the nine "supernumeraries." He often accompanied Darwin on excursions on horseback in Uruguay, Argentina and Chile. After the voyage, Covington became Darwin's secretary and servant until 1839, when he migrated to Australia. Fitz-Roy's servant, seldom mentioned by name, was another supernumerary. George James Stebbing, the "instrument maker," though responsible for the twenty-four chronometres, was listed as a supernumerary, as was Augustus Earle. Earle, already a well-known artist, resigned from his post on the *Beagle* in August 1832 in Montevideo owing to ill health. Like Darwin, he abhorred slavery. But Darwin, and Fitz-Roy became "quite indignant" on reading Earle's book, published in 1832, in which he severely criticized the missionaries he had met in New Zealand.[40]

Conrad Martens replaced Earle in Montevideo in 1832. Darwin referred to Martens as having "rather too much of the drawing-master about him; he is very unlike to Earle's eccentric character." Earle was perhaps a more inspired creator than Martens, although the latter proved to be an extremely gifted landscape artist. He left the *Beagle* in Valparaíso late September 1834 and settled in Sydney, where he continued drawing and remained in contact with Fitz-Roy.[41]

Philos, the Flycatcher

Attention should be called to the other five supernumeraries: Matthews, the trainee missionary; the newly civilised Fuegia; her jealous suitor, York; and the fifteen- or sixteen-year-old Jemmy, who was rarely seasick on the long voyages, though often homesick. The fifth, who would be seasick almost as frequently as homesick, was the twenty-two-year-old Charles Darwin, affectionately called Philos by Fitz-Roy and Flycatcher by the crew. During the long voyage, he never ceased collecting flies as well as vast varieties of fish, birds, plants, rocks, shells, bones of contemporary quadrupeds and fossils of long extinct "bony giants." At least two of these fossils' "grandchildren" roam the arid steppes of Patagonia today: the humble armadillo and a huge rodent, the capybara (waterhog). Darwin's eagerness to observe, inspect and collect seems insatiable. Although he sent Henslow numerous boxes of natural science specimens, he did not collect artefacts, much less human skeletons.[42] His collections, experiences, observations and discoveries during this voyage would provide inspiration and evidence to construct his seminal work *On the Origin of Species*, in which he proposed that all living forms gradually "evolved," through descent with modification, mainly by natural selection, from simple cell-like progenitors.

Janet Browne explained:

Ever since returning from the *Beagle* voyage in 1836...he had believed that living beings were not created by divine fiat.... He would become one of the most famous scientists of his day...not least for the manner in which he changed the way human beings thought about themselves and their own place in nature.... At his most determined, he questioned everything his contemporaries believed about living nature, calling forth a picture shorn of the Garden of Eden.... The natural world has no moral validity or purpose, he argued. Animals and plants are not the product of special design or special creation.... No one could afterwards regard organic beings and their natural setting with anything like the same eyes as before.... As well as rewriting the story of life, he was telling the tale of the rise of science in Victorian Britain.[43]

People the world over, perhaps since the beginning of human time, believed, believe, that we were "created" by a divinity or by the forces of nature out of a primordial chaos, or were the first-born of an original supernatural couple. According the Yamana, the beautiful Maku-kipa gave birth to the first humans, fathered by Yoalox the younger.

Be that as it may, we are part of a natural process of great antiquity whose secrets are being unveiled by science. Science and Creation respond to a search for the meaning of life. They may not go hand in hand, but they are with us to stay for an unknown future. Recall that Darwin became an agnostic: the door of his mind was open. Although he expressed no doubts about the validity of science, he emphasized the significance of religion in his later work, *The Descent of Man*. However, Darwin warned Sulivan (a fervent Christian): "I shall... publish another book partly on man [*The Descent of Man*], which I dare say many will decry as very wicked."[44]

Fitz-Roy not only offered Darwin the voyage, although Darwin's father paid his personal expenses, he also gave him the first volume of *Principles of Geology* by Charles Lyell, who proved to be Darwin's greatest teacher. Most or perhaps all Darwin scholars recognise that Lyell's *Geology* was Darwin's initial inspiration in the vast field of natural science, that he applied Lyell's methods of investigating and reasoning in geology, to his own interest in biology. Darwin also went beyond his teacher, as all "good" disciples do.[45] It is difficult to imagine a more carefully documented book than Sandra Herbert's *Charles Darwin, Geologist*, in which she explained in detail Lyell's impact on Darwin's thinking.

December 1831 to December 1832: Destination Tierra del Fuego

The voyage to Tierra del Fuego took nearly a year, to 17 December 1832, mainly because of many stopovers: among others: Tenerife (one of the Canary islands), Cape Verde Islands, Bahía, Río de Janeiro, Montevideo, Buenos Aires, Bahía Blanca and the mouth of Rio Negro (northern Patagonia, Argentina).[46]

Darwin's "Portraits" of the Three Fuegians
During the long voyage to Tierra del Fuego, he had ample time to become acquainted with his three Fuegian shipmates. However, he wrote so briefly about them during the voyage that Sandra Herbert suggested that he was not yet aware of "the extent of his own interest" in them.[47] He mentioned them frequently after the arrival in Tierra del Fuego. His only "portraits"

FIGURE 4.2. 1832: York Minster. Drawing by Fitz-Roy.

of them, entirely quoted below, were apparently written after the voyage, as they were not recorded in his diary.

York Minster was a full-grown, short, thick, powerful man: his disposition was reserved, taciturn, morose, and when excited violently passionate; his affections were very strong towards a few friends on board; his intellect good.

Fuegia Basket was a nice, modest, reserved young girl with a rather pleasing but sometimes sullen expression and very quick in learning anything, especially languages. This she showed in picking up some Portuguese and Spanish when left on shore for only a short time at Río de Janeiro and Monte Video, and in her knowledge of English. York Minster was very jealous of any attention paid to her; for it was clear he determined to marry her as soon as they were settled on shore.

Jemmy Button was a universal favourite, but likewise passionate; the expression of his face at once showed his nice disposition. He was merry, and often laughed and was remarkably sympathetic with anyone in pain: when the water was rough, I was often a little sea-sick, and he used to come to me and say in a plaintive voice, "Poor, poor fellow!" But the notion, after his aquatic life, of a man being sea-sick, was too ludicrous, and he was generally obliged to turn on one side to hide a smile or laugh, and then he would repeat his "Poor, poor fellow!" He was of a patriotic disposition and he liked to praise his own tribe and country, in which he truly said there were "plenty of trees," and he abused all the other tribes: he stoutly declared that there was no Devil in his land. Jemmy was short, thick and fat, but vain of his personal appearance; he used to wear gloves, his hair was neatly cut, and he was distressed if his well-polished shoes were dirtied. He was fond of admiring himself in a looking-glass."

FIGURE 4.3. 1832: Fuegia Basket. Drawing by Fitz-Roy.

And Darwin concluded: "It seems yet wonderful to me, when I think over all his many good qualities, that he should have been of the same race, and doubtless partaken of the same character, with the miserable, degraded savages whom we first met here."[48] Here Darwin attempted to explain how or why he considered Jemmy an exception to what he thought were "miserable degraded savages."

FIGURE 4.4. 1832: Jemmy Button. Drawing by Fitz-Roy.

The "Oens-Men"

I should clarify right away that the "Oens-men" was Jemmy Button's term for the Selk'nam, and that his term is a derivation of the Yahgan word *on'a-shagan*. "Ona" is often used in print for the Selk'nam (see Glossary). Darwin's first view of the Selk'nam occurred in mid-December 1832, when the *Beagle* was sailing beyond the Atlantic entrance to Magellan Strait, down the coast of Tierra del Fuego, along the shore of Isla Grande. "A group of Indians" standing on a high cliff hailed the ship with smoke from a fire ignited for the purpose. From the distance, the crew could distinguish tall men, nearly naked, with large dogs. York and Jemmy were leaning over the deck rail peering at them when they suddenly shouted: "Oens-men very bad men," telling the captain to fire on them. Fitz-Roy refused to comply. From now on Jemmy will often evoke the enmity between his "tribe" and these Oens-men, later spelt Onas, the Selk'nam as I mention above. These were "foot people" (not navigators) – guanaco hunters who inhabited most of Isla Grande.[49] Darwin will see them again from a distance in February 1834 (Chapter 5).

Darwin's First Encounters with the "Fuegians" at Home

About noon on 17 December (1832), the *Beagle* turned, at Cape San Diego, into the Le Maire Strait, pushed on by a northerly wind amidst high breakers. As the ship veered into nearby Good Success Bay, the crew sighted "a group of Fuegians" on a summit at the entrance to the bay, eagerly shouting and waving skins, beckoning them to come ashore. Fitz-Roy ignored their greetings, so they quickly lit a fire despite the downpour and welcomed them again. He admired their ability to light a fire so rapidly in such a heavy rain, recalling the times he spent more than two hours struggling to do likewise.[50]

An astonished Darwin gazed at them; "partly concealed by the entangled forest... as we passed by, they sprang up and waving their tattered cloaks sent forth a loud and sonorous shout. The savages followed the ship, and just before dark we saw their fire, and again heard their wild cry."

A gale and heavy squalls whipped across the bay from the surrounding mountains, so no one went ashore that evening. As the sea was even more tempestuous in the strait, outside the bay, Darwin thought the name "Good Success Bay" appropriate. Appropriate though it was, in reality the bay was named for *Nuestra Señora del Buen Suceso* (*Our Lady of Good Success*), the ship of the Nodal expedition, the first European vessel to anchor there, in 1619 (Chapter 1).

The next day (18 December) Fitz-Roy, Darwin, Matthews, Lieutenant Hamond and other officers "went to meet the Fuegians in their own land."[51] These natives, later known as Haush, were not navigators; they were "foot people," mainly guanaco hunters, like their neighbours the Oens-men (the Selk'nam). One of them "began to shout most vehemently," directing the strangers just where to pull ashore. When Fitz-Roy and the others landed, the four men (the Haush) "looked rather alarmed, but continued talking and making gestures with great rapidity."[52] Apparently the visitors did not see the women and children, because Darwin commented that they "had been sent away."

Darwin appeared to be fascinated at first. "It was without exception the most curious and interesting spectacle I ever beheld: I could not have believed how wide was the difference between savage and civilised man: it is greater than between a wild and domesticated animal, inasmuch as in man there is a greater power of improvement."

The long mantles of guanaco skin (fur) the men wore were thrown over one shoulder, leaving the right arm free to grasp their bows quickly. Darwin commented, "for any exercise they must be absolutely naked." He knew that they had to be able to throw off their mantles when they spied a guanaco in the distance. "Their skin is of dirty coppery red colour." Three were "powerful young men," about six feet tall, whose faces were painted with streaks of black powdered charcoal. The fourth, the oldest, was their spokesman and appeared to be their chief. His face was painted with a bright red line from ear to ear, and white lines above the eyelids. He wore a headband of white feathers (an attribute of a shaman rather than a chief). Fitz-Roy, like Darwin, remarked that they resembled the Patagonians, the Tehuelches. In effect, the Haush as well as the Selk'nam, were remotely related to the Patagonian Indians and were taller than the Yamana and more symmetrically built, perhaps partly because the former exercised their entire bodies by hunting while the latter spent long hours sitting in their canoes. Darwin described the Yamana he saw later, near Cape Horn, as "stunted, miserable wretches" (Chapter 5).

The Haush and the Selk'nam had a common origin – the Patagonian mainland (now mostly Argentina) and inhabited the same island (Isla Grande). Although both groups were guanaco hunters, the Haush had become more dependent on seals because these were abundant at the southeastern tip of the island, where they were living in 1618 when first seen by Europeans in Good Success Bay. The Selk'nam had forced the Haush to this extremity of the island. The Selk'nam were warriors, men of action. The Haush were peaceful and more contemplative. The Selk'nam recognised the greater wisdom of the Haush, who were known as the "fathers of the word." There seems to have been a great difference in the temperament of these two groups despite their common origin and culture.[53]

As Darwin glanced at the four men he had just met in Good Success Bay, he recalled a play he had seen in Edinburgh in 1824. "The party altogether closely resembled the devils which come on the stage in plays like *Der Freischütz*." Darwin didn't believe in devils so this comment probably refers to the excited gestures of the Haush.

Young Matthews, the would-be missionary, thought that these Fuegians were "no worse than he had supposed them to be." In contrast to this dry comment, Lieutenant Hamond exclaimed: "What a pity such fine fellows should be left in such a barbarous state!"[54]

Darwin thought they appeared to be "distrustful, surprised and startled" and their attitudes "abject." However, after receiving pieces of red cloth, which they tied around their necks, "they became good friends." The "old man" welcomed each of his four guests by patting their breasts and making a "chuckling kind of noise, as people do when feeding chickens." Then Darwin strolled down the beach with him, "who demonstrated his good humor several times" by patting Darwin's breast again. He further reassured Darwin by three more hard slaps simultaneously on his breast and back, "then bared his bosom for me to return the compliment, which being done, he seemed highly pleased." Following all these cosy greetings, the linguistic barrier was erected. The Haush may have chatted with their guests, hoping that some meaning would seep through the barrier. If so, their efforts came to naught. Darwin remarked that their language (which he called Fuegian) "scarcely deserves to be called articulate," with its many "hoarse, guttural and clicking sounds."

The salutations over, the Haush attempted to amuse or impress their guests by mimicking their coughing and yawning and repeating, "with perfect correctness each word in any sentence we addressed them, and they remembered such words for some time." Darwin commented (or at least wrote): "Which of us, for instance, could follow an American Indian through a sentence of more than three words?" This phrase would have pleased the Haush, had they understood him.

Darwin surmised that their talent for mimicry was common to all savages, such as the "Caffirs" (now a derogatory term) of South Africa and the native Australians. He wondered if this could be explained by the greater practice of perception and the keener senses of people in "a savage state as compared with those long civilised."[55]

That evening (still daylight), after dinner on the ship, they returned to the beach with York and Jemmy, who apparently went ashore there for the first time. Soon after landing, several of the officers squinted and made monkey faces to amuse their hosts. Thereupon one of the young Haush, his face painted black with white bands over the eyes, joined the game of monkey faces by "making still more hideous grimaces." About then a sailor began singing and dancing a waltz and the others, including Darwin, joined in the fun. "When a song was struck up, I thought they would have fallen down with astonishment; & with equal delight they viewed our dancing and immediately began themselves to waltz with one of the officers." After waltzing around, one of the young natives motioned to a "chosen opponent," the tallest of the *Beagle* crew, to compare his height (and good looks) with him. The two men stood back to back, as the former tried to find higher ground and stand on tiptoe. Darwin was observing him closely: "He opened his mouth to show his teeth, and turned his face for a side view; and all this was done with such alacrity, that I dare say he thought himself the handsomest man in Tierra del Fuego. After our first feeling of grave astonishment was over, nothing could be more ludicrous than the odd mixture of surprise and imitation which these savages every moment exhibited."

Even though Fitz-Roy also found them good-humoured, he objected when they offered to test their strength by wrestling with some of the crew. He refused to allow competition of this sort between his men and the Haush, nor did he permit wrestling later with the "puny" Yamana men. He had learned, from reading Weddell's account, published in 1827, about one of his sailors who lost a wrestling match with a young Yamana (Chapter 2).

Skin colour was another matter. The Haush compared theirs with that of several of the sailors, expressing "the liveliest surprise and admiration at its whiteness, just in the same way in which I have seen the orang-utan do at the Zoological Gardens." Darwin was very fond of animals, so this comment was not an insult.

In a more serious vein, Darwin noticed: "They knew what guns were & much dreaded them, & nothing would tempt them to take one in their hands." They asked for knives, using the Spanish word as *cuchilla* (*cuchillo*). To make sure they were understood, the men pretended to hold a piece of meat in their mouths while making gestures of slicing it.

The old man "addressed a long harangue to Jemmy, which it seems was to invite him to stay with them." Darwin clarified that "Jemmy understood very little of their language, and was, moreover, thoroughly ashamed of his countrymen." Fitz-Roy thought that "It was amusing and interesting to see their meeting with York and Jemmy, who would not acknowledge them as countrymen, but laughed at and mocked them." He observed that even though York didn't understand their language, he suddenly burst out laughing at something the old man had said to him. York couldn't resist telling Fitz-Roy what the old man had said about him, that "he was dirty and to pull out his beard." Darwin again noticed that the natives realised immediately that York and Jemmy were from Tierra del Fuego but that they understood very little of their language. He wondered why the old man had admonished York to pull out the twenty hairs of his "beard" while the "untrimmed" beards of the crew failed to incite any comment. I might add here that York's people, and Jemmy's as well as the Haush, all considered eyebrows and any face hair repulsive, of course except eyelashes.[56] The strangers' beards didn't concern them perhaps because everything about them was strange.

For Fitz-Roy it was "painful" to contemplate such savages as "even remotely descended from human beings." It was painful because he could not help thinking of his own ancestors, the Britons, whom Caesar had seen "painted and clothed in skins, like these Fuegians." They reminded him of children, like his ancestors, although the latter had gradually grown into civilised Englishmen.

Darwin Recalls These First Encounters
In the last pages of his *Voyage of the Beagle*, he wrote (probably in 1838):

One's mind hurries back over past centuries, and then asks, could our progenitors have been men like these? – men, whose very signs and expressions are less intelligible to us than those of the domesticated animals; men, who do not possess the instinct of those animals, nor yet appear to boast of human reason, or at least of arts consequent on that reason. I do not believe it is possible to describe or paint the difference between savage and civilised man. It is the difference between a wild and tame animal.[57]

A short while after leaving Good Success Bay he wrote to his mentor, Professor Henslow:

The Fuegians [the Haush] are in a more miserable state of barbarism than I had expected ever to have seen a human being. . . . I do not think any spectacle can be more interesting, than the first sight of Man in his primitive wildness. . . . I shall never forget, when entering Good Success Bay, the yell with which a party received us. They were seated on a rocky point, surrounded by the dark forest of beech; as they threw their arms wildly round their heads & their long hair streaming they seemed the troubled spirits of another world.[58]

And to his sister Caroline, more than a year later, in April 1833: "No drawing or description will at all explain the extreme interest which is created by the first sight of savages. It is an interest which almost repays one for a cruize in these latitudes: & this I assure you is saying a good deal."[59]

Again, the following month (May 1833), in a letter to his cousin William Darwin Fox, he referred to these Haush: "In Tierra del Fuego I saw bona fide savages; & they are as savage as the most curious person would desire. A wild man is indeed a miserable animal, but one well worth seeing."[60]

Yet again, well over a year later (early 1835), he was thinking of the Good Success natives:

...I have seen nothing which more completely astonished me, than the first sight of a Savage; It was a naked Fuegian his long hair blowing about, his face besmeared with paint. There is in their countenances, an expression, which I believe to those who have not seen it, must be inconceivably wild. Standing on a rock he uttered tones & made gesticulations than which, the crys of domestic animals are far more intelligible.[61]

And in 1876, when his life's work had taken form, he wrote with nostalgia:

I remember when in Good Success Bay, in Tierra del Fuego, thinking (and I believe that I wrote home to the effect) that I could not employ my life better than in adding a little to natural science. This I have done to the best of my abilities, and critics may say what they like, but they cannot destroy this conviction.[62]

Obviously he was impressed by the Haush, however he did not use the strong language, nor did he accuse them of cannibalism, as he did the Yamana.[63]

Imagine for a Moment

One of the Haush men might have told his wife (or wives) and children about these encounters in Good Success Bay: "I was surprised when I first spotted . . . their enormous canoe with three huge sails coming towards us into the bay. The men came ashore the next day, all rather young. I was surprised but I wasn't amazed because we've seen such canoes [ships] and men like them before, with disgusting hair all over their faces, no paint at all, and such colourless skin. They were all wrapped up, even their heads and wore the largest, longest sandals [boots] I've ever seen, as if they couldn't resist a little cold, so much clothes they couldn't run if they tried. But they were friendly and droll, laughing at our mimicry, and singing and dancing to please us. It was jolly. We all had fun, especially when I think of those not-so-funny sealers roaming around the strait destroying our food supply."

Darwin's "Good Success Excursions"

The next day, 19 December, Darwin and several companions penetrated inland, pushing and crawling through the thick forest, climbing over decaying trees and "putrefying vegetable matter," and treading lightly over the swampy peat bogs. They hiked up the hills along the rocky banks of the streams and down steep valleys. It was easier climbing the mountainside, "where a great slip had cleared a straight space." (Such cleared spaces are still to be seen there.) Arriving at a summit, Darwin felt "amply repaid by the grandeur of the scene," although it depressed him. "Death, instead of Life, seemed the predominate spirit."[64]

On the third and last full day in Good Success Bay, 20 December, Darwin and others ventured a bit farther inland. On the way, they recalled the misadventure of Captain Cook's first voyage in 1769, when Sir Joseph Banks, the aristocratic botanist, explored the same hinterland with two servants, who died there of exposure during a snowstorm in the midsummer of January. Darwin and his party, who were there in the same season, were more fortunate or more cautious. They reached the summit of the highest mountain flanking the bay, Mount Banks, which Darwin did not mention by name, though Fitz-Roy did. Towards the south (probably Montes Negros) they came upon "a scene of savage magnificence, well becoming Tierra del Fuego. There was a degree of mysterious grandeur in the mountain behind mountain, with the deep intervening valleys, all covered by one thick, dusky mass of forest. The atmosphere, likewise, in this climate, where gale succeeds gale, with rain, hail, and sleet, seems blacker than anywhere else."[65]

While he was collecting plants he noticed several woolly guanacos in the distance, shot at them, but missed and paid them this homage: "These beautiful animals are truly alpine in their habits, & in their wildness well come the surrounding landscape. I cannot imagine anything more graceful than their action: they start on a canter & when passing through rough ground they dash like a thorough bred hunter."[66]

On to Cape Horn

The next day, 21 December 1832, when Fitz-Roy headed the *Beagle* towards Cape Horn, Darwin noted in his diary that the sea and atmosphere were so calm that it would surprise those, "who think that in this region winds & waters never cease fighting." But the very next night Cape Horn "demanded its tribute and sent us a gale right in our teeth."[67]

A Merry Christmas

Christmas Eve was passed in a high sea: squalls and hail descended with such violence that the *Beagle* took refuge in Saint Martin's Cove (Caleta Saint Martin on the Chilean maps), which Darwin invariably called Wigwam Cove, Hermite Island. Weddell had been there eleven years earlier and Fitz-Roy just two years previously. Saint Martin's Cove will continue to be the favourite refuge nearest Cape Horn for the English-speaking navigators (Chapter 6).

Despite the heavy gale and rough seas, Christmas Day was merry in this "snug little harbour." After breakfast, Darwin, Sulivan and Hamond climbed Kater's Peak (1,700 feet or 518.16 metres), which overlooks the bay. They were rewarded with a magnificent view of the islands formed of mountaintops, where the Cordillera of the Andes sinks into the sea at Cape Horn. "Whilst looking round on this inhospitable region, we could scarcely credit that man existed on it." Sulivan rolled huge rocks down from the summit while Darwin hammered others with his geological tools (for specimens). The three made a riot of noise, screaming to hear their echoes and firing guns at the birds in caverns nearby.

When they returned to the *Beagle*, they were told that they had been seen from the ship, crawling over the rocks. They were puzzled when they realised that it would have been impossible to see them because the *Beagle* was anchored under a hill that blocked the view of Kater's peak. Darwin surmised that the men they saw crawling over the rocks were Fuegians (Yamanas). The racket of shouts, tumbling rocks, and gunfire had probably kept them away from the *Beagle*. "They must have thought us the powers of darkness; or whatever else, fear has kept them concealed." This is one of the rare mentions of the Yamana as mountain climbers. The navigators almost invariably noticed the men's spindly legs and might have thought such a feat impossible.

That midnight, violent squalls funnelled down through the surrounding hills, striking the water in the cove. Snow, hail and rain followed, all this in early summer. The ship was steadied there during six long days and nights by "three anchors down and plenty of chain cable out." Neither Fitz-Roy nor Darwin account for these days except for lamenting the "wretched climate" and briefly mentioning visits to nearby bays and islands from 27 to 29 December. They did not see any natives during this last week of 1832.[68]

Darwin's "Ethnological Meditations"

His "ethnological meditations" (my term) on the Fuegians read, in chapter 10 of his *Voyage*, as if he had penned most of them when he and the others were obliged to remain in and near "Wigwam Cove" (Saint Martin's Cove), the last week of 1832, owing to the "very bad weather." Actually many of his chapter 10 texts refer to the future: to February 1833, when they spent a week in Wulaia, Jemmy's territory, and the following year, late February 1834, when they went ashore on Wollaston Island, near Cape Horn. Darwin was certainly aware of this lack of correspondence of the dates. After his return to England, he obviously decided, while organizing his text for the publication, to place most of his data on Tierra del Fuego in one chapter (in chapter 10) for greater clarity and to forgo his usual chronological method of his narration (see note 23).[69]

Although the following texts have often been cited to characterise the Fuegians, keep in mind that, at the time, Darwin probably had no idea he would be quoted as an authority (and criticised) for his impressions of the Yamana.

He began what I call his meditations by explaining that every bay in the neighbourhood of Wigwam Cove (as he called Saint Martin's Cove) might be called Wigwam "with equal propriety," in the sense that in nearly all the bays they visited there was evidence that the Indians had inhabited them.[70]

The Wollaston Islanders (Yamanas)

Follows a rather long quote from his chapter 10 in order to comment on it. Actually he didn't visit Wollaston Islands until 25–26 February 1834 as I point out in my next chapter.

While going one day on shore near Wollaston Island, we pulled along side a canoe with six Fuegians. *These were the most abject and miserable creatures I anywhere beheld.* . . . [They] were quite naked, and even one full-grown woman was absolutely so. It was raining heavily, and the fresh water, together with the spray, trickled down her body. In another harbour not far distant a woman who was suckling a recently-born child came one day alongside the vessel, and remained there out of mere curiosity, whilst the sleet fell and thawed on her naked bosom and on the skin of her naked baby! These poor wretches were stunted in their growth, they're hideous faces bedaubed with white paint, *their skins filthy and greasy*, their hair entangled, *their voices discordant and their gestures violent.* Viewing such men, one can hardly make oneself believe that they are fellow creatures and inhabitants of the same world. It is a common subject of conjecture what pleasure in life some of the lower animals can enjoy: how much more reasonably the same question may be asked with respect to these barbarians! At night five or six human beings, naked and scarcely protected from the wind and rain of this tempestuous climate *sleep on the wet ground coiled up like animals.*[71]

He painted this devastating picture of these Wollaston Islanders (Yamanas). Recall that five years earlier, Dr Webster, in 1829, had a very different impression of those nearby, on Hermite Island. He thought that they were "fully capable of receiving instruction... their habits simple and inoffensive; their general demeanour modest and becoming" (end of Chapter 2). Captain Wilke also had a favourable impression of the Wollaston natives he encountered in 1839 (see Chapter 6). Darwin obviously lacked compassion for the Yamana he happened to encounter near Wollaston Island. I question his impressions of them when he failed to describe several scenes he apparently witnessed. If their voices were "discordant" and their gestures "violent," were they trying to communicate something urgent to the strangers? Did he actually see them sleeping "on wet ground coiled up like animals"? Or did someone tell him they did? Nor did he ask himself why they had such "filthy and greasy" skins. George Stocking Jr. referred to these comments as "a kind of hurried, unanalysed ethnographic gestalt, in which paint and grease and body structure blended into a single perception of physical type."[72]

Their Huts "Resembled a Haycock"

"It merely consists of a few broken branches stuck in the ground, and very imperfectly thatched on one side with a few tufts of grass and rushes. The whole cannot be the work of an hour and it is only used for a few days."[73] Carlos Spegazzini referred to other Yamana "haycock" huts: "Their hemispheric form [has] such perfect curves, that one wonders how they were able to obtain them with such coarse materials."[74] This quotation is not meant to counter Darwin but only to point out that the Yamanas constructed similar huts in a more perfected form. Darwin was aware that, as they were to be inhabited for only a few days, they were built rapidly and often "imperfectly."

Fire Was Essential Day and Night

Darwin stated in *The Descent of Man* that the "discovery" of fire, was "probably the greatest ever made by man, except for language, and dates from before the dawn of history."[75] Although he does not mention fire in his "meditations," his awareness of its essential importance justifies its inclusion here. Fitz-Roy insisted on the importance of keeping the fire alive at all times, although "they are at no loss to rekindle it.... With two stones (iron and pyrites) they procure a spark."[76] Iron pyrite (called fool's gold and fire-stone) was also used and not difficult to obtain, but it was less effective.[77]

Most effective was pyrite, which must be struck against a hard stone, such as flint (a variety of quartz) or silex (in Spanish *pedernal*), later a nail, an axe head, or almost any iron or steel object. Even two pieces of flint can produce a spark, but this method is more difficult and time-consuming.[78] But why is pyrite so effective? The brief answer is because of the sulfuric gases it contains.[79]

The Yamana referred to these two stones (pyrite and silex or flint) as a couple, a *matuku*: the wife, *kipa*, was the flint, and the husband, *wa*, was the piece of pyrite. This couple was carried by the men wherever they went, often wrapped in a small leather bag hung from the neck.[80] The other Fuegians – the Alakaluf, Selk'nam and Haush – did likewise.

The only published report on pyrite I found refers to Mercury Sound (Seno Mercurio) on Captain Aracena Island, along the Cockburn Channel in Alakaluf territory. Lucas Bridges is the source. He visited the site and wrote the following: "In a snug harbour a well-worn trail led to a large deposit of refuse, evidence that the natives had worked there for centuries. The heaps of chippings were huge, and to this day there are to be seen the rounded masses of iron pyrites from which, with great labour, both Yahgan and Alacaloof obtained their supplies."[81]

Although Mercury Sound was deep into Alakaluf territory, the Yamana had access to it – according to Lucas Bridges, noted above – and probably to other sites of pyrite mentioned in this note.[82] They may also have bartered for pyrite with the Alakaluf.

The tinder, of course, had to be any very dry, flammable material. Duvet (baby bird feathers), ground fungus or scraps of dry wood were the usual materials, as well as dry insects' nests, dry grass and the like.

All the reports remark on how the Fuegians kept the fire alive, day and night, while camping on land and always burning in the centre of the canoe. There was very little danger that the canoe would be damaged because the fire was placed on a support of mud and sand, constantly supervised, and the canoe itself was damp.

"Miserable Food"

Darwin surmised that the Fuegians lived,

chiefly upon shell-fish, [and] are obliged constantly to change their place of residence: but they return at intervals to the same spots, as is evident from the piles of old shells, which must often amount to many tons in weight. These heaps can be distinguished at a long distance by the bright green colour of certain plants, which invariably grow on them.[83]

He had the erroneous impression that the Fuegians were "living chiefly upon shellfish." He also observed or was told that the women dove to collect "sea eggs," that while sitting in their canoes they jerked out little fish. "If a seal is killed or the floating carcass of putrid whale discovered, it is a feast and such miserable food is assisted by a few tasteless berries and fungi."[84] He had no way of knowing by then (1833–34) that their primary food had been seriously reduced by the English and Yankee sealers and whalers (Chapter 2). Even though whales had not been a reliable source of food because stranding was eventual – however, they were often stranded and their meat and blubber had been important supplements for all the Fuegians.

Fitz-Roy was less disparaging than Darwin about fishing and noted that his crew learned from the Indian women how to fish and could catch several dozen in a few hours. Darwin was mistaken when he stated that the natives did not use wild celery and scurvy grass.[85] In reality, celery was eaten, although it was not a favourite food, and tough grass served as bedding, as lining for sandals, and the like. Although Darwin did not presume to be making "scientific" or ethnographic statements concerning the Fuegians' diet much less their mode of living, he often debased them by his manner of describing them.

Besides the whales the Yamana had another gift of nature: "vast schools or shoals" of small fish called sprats that appeared in certain known places and seasons. Lucas Bridges explained that these great quantities of sprats also attracted "seals, penguins, mollymauks and other sea-birds, and deep-water fish, which came in the autumn in pursuit of the vast schools or shoals of sprats. A time of superabundance for the natives. The arrival . . . was as welcome as a harvest festival and might last two months."[86]

But Were They Cannibals?

Darwin was utterly indignant when he heard about the horrible fate of the old women. Follows his often quoted text:

From the concurrent but quite independent evidence of the boy [Bob] taken by Mr. Low, and of Jemmy Button, *it is certainly true*, that when pressed in winter by hunger, *they kill and devour their old women before they kill their dogs*: the boy, being asked by Mr. Low why they did this, answered, "Doggies catch otters, old women no." The boy described the manner in which they are killed by being held over smoke and thus choked; he imitated their screams *as a joke*, and described the parts of their bodies, which are considered best to eat. Horrid as such a death by the hands of their friends and relatives must be, the fears of the old women, when hunger begins to press, are more painful to think of; we were told that they then often run away into the mountains, *but that they are pursued by the men and brought back to the slaughter house at their own fire-sides!*[87]

Darwin himself noted that Bob, one of the informants for these cannibalistic stores, was "called a liar, which in truth he was." It is also strange that Darwin cited Jemmy as a reliable source for cannibalism, when a few pages before he stated "it was generally impossible to find out, by cross-questioning, whether one had rightly understood anything which they [Jemmy and York] had asserted." He also remarked that Jemmy would not eat land birds because they "eat dead men." Therefore he had ample reasons for doubting these stories.

In Montevideo (July 1830), on the way to England, Jemmy and York communicated (mostly by gestures) to Fitz-Roy that their people "made a practice of eating their enemies taken in war." The women ate the arms and the men the legs while the trunk and head were thrown into the sea.[88] "A still more revolting account was given...respecting the horrible fate of the eldest women of their own tribes, when there is an unusual scarcity of food." Jemmy and York repeated these stories so often, as they learned to express themselves more fluently in English, that finally Fitz-Roy no longer hesitated "to state my firm belief in the most debasing trait of their character which will be found in these pages." Mr Low, the Scottish sealer whom Fitz-Roy met later (Chapter 5), mentioned above, was also convinced that the Fuegians were indeed cannibals.[89]

Darwin never heard the stories himself but had learned of them from Fitz-Roy and Low, but he never doubted their words. Cannibalism was expected among a people at such a "low level" of humanity, and this may also explain why he was so credulous.

In a long letter to his sister Caroline in March 1833, he expressed himself forcefully. "These Fuegians are Cannibals; but we have good reason to suppose it carried on to an extent which hitherto has been unheard of in the world." This is a truly amazing statement coming from someone who was usually so meticulous in his writings, although the letter was not intended to be published. In another brief passage from this letter, he wrote: "Was ever anything so atrocious heard of, to work them [the women] like slaves to procure food in the summer & occasionally in winter [then] to eat them – I feel quite a disgust at the very sound of the voices of these miserable savages."[90]

In his great work of 1859, he recalled the Yamana: "We see the value set on animals even by the barbarians of Tierra del Fuego, by their killing and devouring their old women, in times of dearth, as of less value than their dogs."[91]

Definitive refutation of cannibalism among the Yamana came from Thomas Bridges' son Lucas, who knew the Yahgan since his birth. He explained how Fitz-Roy and Darwin had been misled:

We [Lucas and his siblings] who later passed many years of our lives in daily contact with these people can find only one explanation for this shocking mistake [Darwin's and Fitz-Roy's conviction that the Yamana were cannibals]. We suppose that, when questioned, York Minster, or Jemmy Button, would not trouble in the least to answer truthfully, but would merely give the reply that he felt was expected or desired. In the early days their limited knowledge of English would not allow them to explain at any length, and, as we know, it is much easier to answer "yes" than "no." So the statements with which these young men and little Fuegia Basket have been credited were, in fact, no more than agreement with suggestions made by their questioners.[92]

Leonard Engel, the editor of the 1962 edition of *The Voyage of the Beagle*, also clarified in a footnote:

Unfortunately, both Darwin and Fitz-Roy were misled on the point, for the Fuegians were not cannibals and honoured rather than ate their old women. Old women were in demand as second and third wives . . . because of their experience in the management of canoes and many duties performed by the Fuegian wife. A form of euthanasia by strangulation was practiced but this was confined to the incurably sick and disabled.[93]

The Yamana may have eaten the twelve Dutch sailors in 1624, but if so, this does not make them cannibals forever, before and after. Cannibalism has occurred in certain circumstances, probably from "time immemorial." Well-known examples are marooned, starving survivors of shipwrecks and airplane crashes who consume their dead companions, or, in desperate circumstances, draw chances to select who is to be killed for the purpose. These improvised cannibals would probably have been appalled at the idea at home. When cannibalism is an integral part of a culture, as presumably it was among the Aztecs, it is almost invariably ritualised. When warriors are the aggressors, it is usually to avenge the enemy and acquire his strength. But is cannibalism a cardinal sin? Were all societies to be judged or classified in terms of the enormity and quantity of the atrocities they committed against humanity, cannibalism might not be the worst.

I believe that this error, that the Yamana were cannibals, distorted Darwin's view of them more than any other impression he had of them.

Were They "A Fierce People"?[94]

Darwin affirmed: "The different tribes when at war are cannibals" and that each tribe, "Is surrounded by other hostile tribes speaking different dialects, and separated from each other only by a deserted border or neutral territory: the cause of their warfare appears to be the means of subsistence."[95]

Darwin let his imagination fly high. In reality, as far as is known, only two "tribes" were separated by a neutral territory, a zone along Beagle Channel and the cause of their "warfare" was not "the means of subsistence." Fitz-Roy was much less emphatic: "Warfare, though nearly continual, is so desultory, and on so small a scale among them, that the restraint and direction of their elders, advised as they are by the doctors [shamans], is sufficient."[96]

Darwin's assumption about their "warfare" did convince two top-ranking sociobiologists at Harvard University: Charles J. Lumsden and Edward O. Wilson.

Some extraordinary set of circumstances – the prime movers of the origin of mind – must have existed to bring the early hominids across the Rubicon and into the irreversible march of cultural evolution.... *One of the most intriguing explanations, suggested by Charles Darwin himself, is warfare.* There is plenty of evidence of violent aggression among recent bands of hunter-gatherers, [the Fuegians, among others] whose social organization most closely resembles that of primitive man.

However, these professors had second thoughts. Three pages later they affirmed: "The driving force then propelling the human species from the *Homo habilis* to the *Homo sapiens* level [was] not war, sex, climate or hunting on the savanna but 'gene-culture coevolution.'"[97] What a relief, neither we nor the Yamanas can be held responsible for our "gene-culture coevolution."

"War" and "warfare" are too loaded as terms to apply to the Yamana or even the Selk'nam. Among the latter when combats and fights occurred one or several of the male participants were often killed and women kidnapped. The occasional combats among the Yamana were often motivated by plunder, at least in the nineteenth century (Chapter 5). Other motives were vengeance for a murder, a death attributed to a shaman's "magic," mistreatment of a woman by her husband, and the like. Enemies were taken prisoner, usually not for long, but a woman who was kidnapped could be forced to become a wife, or one of the wives, of an enemy. At times she managed to escape and return to her family. When the Yamana fought on the water: the women paddlers closed in on their enemy's canoe while the men attacked one another with spears. To avoid a combat or following one, an avenging party might accept "gifts" as a compensation for the motive. Hyades insisted that there were never expeditions for war among the Yahgans but that they were very "touchy" (*susceptibles*) and inclined to quarrel or fight (Chapter 13). Hyades cited Thomas Bridges' data on murders among the Yamana as being surprisingly few: only two a year during the thirteen years from 1871 to 1884.[98] After the 1624 massacre, attacks are reported against "Jemmy's tribe" in 1833 and 1834 and, much later, in 1858 and especially in early November 1859 (Chapters 8 and 9). Although some of the Yamana lineages were more prone to combat than others, it may be said that in general the Yamana and the Haush were much more peaceful than the Selk'nam.

Their Language, Another Mistake

Darwin's accusation of cannibalism reminded Lucas Bridges of another serious error Darwin made.

The belief that the Fuegians were cannibals was not the only mistake Charles Darwin made about them. . . . We who learned as children to speak Yahgan knew that, within its own limitation, it is infinitely richer and more expressive than English or Spanish. My father's Yahgan (or Yamana) English Dictionary . . . contains no fewer than 32,000 words and inflections, the number of which might have been greatly increased without departing from correct speech.[99]

Lucas' statement seems to me conclusive.

Burials and Mourning

Darwin thought that the Fuegians (Yahgans) buried their dead in caves "and sometimes in the mountain forests," which was true. It had also been customary to burn the corpse on a pile of wood or thick bushes and to bury the ashes later, until the missionaries objected (Chapter 10). These natives had no cemeteries, nor did they worship their ancestors. The property of the deceased, except the dogs, was usually destroyed by fire or buried with the corpse. They avoided approaching the place where a family member had died, nor did they name the deceased, as will become clear when Jemmy learned of his father's death (Chapter 5). Such disregard is only apparent. A mourning ceremony might last off and on for months. On such occasions they carefully painted a variety of designs on their faces with carbon from the campfires, fasted and inflicted serious wounds on themselves while chanting hour upon hour, day after day.

Gusinde repeatedly described the Yamana expressing fury against their "supreme deity," Watawineiwa, by shouting, cursing him with vehemence, especially for taking the life of a child.

When a person had really been assassinated, the relatives would normally take revenge against the murderer sooner or later, as mentioned above. In such small local groups, the murderer was often discovered. A mock battle was usually performed to honour someone who had been murdered or even had died "normally," in quotations because a shaman might easily be accused of inflicting a normal death. When a murder was committed two groups would be formed, one among the men with clubs, another of women with especially painted long sticks or simply their canoe paddles. Each group would simulate, by gestures, of beating others of the same sex, although some might get really hurt. One group would be relatives and friends of the murdered victim, while the opposing group would include a suspect or the proven murderer. In the latter case, invariably a man, he would finally be beaten, though apparently not killed. If the person had simply died of old age or an accident and his or her death was recognised as no one's fault, two relatives of the deceased would defy and blame each other for not having taken better care of the deceased, while praising his or her qualities. The other participants, the "audience," would urge them on, chanting the laments.[100] Later (in 1907), when alcohol was ruining their lives, there is a vivid account of such mock battles that had become veritable brawls (Chapter 15).

No Religion, or Hardly Any

Darwin thought that they did not "perform any sort of religious worship," although he did not advocate converting them to Christianity. The nearest approach to "a religious feeling" that he had heard about was the manner in which York reacted to Bynoe during the voyage to England (in 1830).While shooting at young ducklings – for specimens, not food – York warned Bynoe that "much rain, snow, blow much" would come as punishment for wasting the ducklings, human food, in this manner. York's comments suggested to Darwin that elements of nature were considered avenging agents and that "in a race a little more advanced in culture, the elements would become personified."[101] In *The Descent of Man*, he repeated the above incident, adding that they could never discover that the Fuegians believed "in what we should call a God or practiced any religious rites." He added: "The highest form of religion – the grand idea of God hating sin and loving righteousness – was unknown during primeval times. . . . man has risen, though by slow and interrupted steps, from a lowly condition to the highest standard as yet attained by him in knowledge, morals and religion."[102]

Gusinde didn't agree with Darwin, at all. He was convinced that the Fuegians worshipped a universal God, though in different ways than the Christians. He seemed determined to present evidence that these "stone-age primitives" considered Watawineiwa an "All Mighty." Today Gusinde's hypothesis is subject to doubt by yours truly and among others, by Orquera and Piana mentioned above.

Having found no signs of religious worship, Darwin made this sarcastic remark: "perhaps the muttering of the old man before he distributed the putrid blubber to his famished party, may be of this nature."

Both he and Fitz-Roy affirmed that the Fuegians (the Yamana) had no "distinct belief in a future life." According to Gusinde, they believed that the soul (*keshpi* or *keshpix*) of the deceased "outlives the existence of the body." However, Nelly Lawrence, one of Gusinde's favourite informants, was convinced that they, her people, knew "nothing about the *keshpix* after death."[103] I think my informants would have agreed with Gusinde's notion of the *kashpi* (see beginning of Chapter 2).

Darwin knew that "Jemmy believed in dreams" because he told his friend Bynoe that he dreamt his father had died in 1832, during the return voyage of the *Beagle*. Therefore Jemmy was not surprised when he arrived home months later and learned that his father had passed away (Chapter 5). The shamans had dreams and visions during a trance, of that "outer world," that mystic universe from which they derived their power and inspiration.

Darwin evoked the subject of Yamana shamanism in one sentence: "Each family or tribe has a wizard or conjuring doctor, whose office we could never clearly ascertain." Shamanism is a religious phenomenon in the measure that it entails beliefs in the existence of supernatural powers that determine or influence human behaviour. Thanks to Gusinde, many of the attributes of the Yamana's particular brand of shamanism have become known to the outside world.[104]

Darwin stated that Jemmy "with justifiable pride, stoutly maintained that there was no devil in his land." Darwin found this remarkable because he was persuaded that the savage's belief in bad spirits was far more common than belief in good ones. Such a simplistic notion is again derived from the cultural evolution paradigm: the "savage" is at the antipodes of the "civilised," although Darwin conceded that the "barbarians" do or can independently raise themselves "a few steps in the scale of civilisation."[105]

Darwin also suggested that Fuegians were not much more superstitious than some of the sailors on the *Beagle* and gave the example of the old quartermaster who affirmed that the heavy gales off Cape Horn were caused by the presence of the Fuegians on board. Here Darwin seemed to equate Yahgan beliefs with superstitious notions of the British labouring class. The Yahgans were not superstitious; they had a coherent system of beliefs, which fortunately is partially known as it existed in its plentitude. Perhaps it should be clarified that Darwin is not being criticised for what he did not know about the Yamana but rather for what he wrote about them.

Perfect Equality: No Chiefs, No Government

In his diary for 6 February 1833, Darwin explained in more detail what he only mentioned in his tenth chapter of his *Beagle* voyage to which I have often referred. "The perfect equality of all the inhabitants will for many years prevent their civilisation. . . . Until some chief rises, who by his power might be able to keep to himself such presents as animals &c, there must be an end to all hopes of bettering their condition."[106]

Here he expressed his conviction that the emergence of civilisation could only take place in a society that had a chief. He insisted: "The different tribes have no government or chief; yet each is surrounded by other hostile tribes." Recall that Darwin was a Whig, not a socialist. He didn't laud the egalitarian aspects of the Fuegian societies as a socialist or communist might have done. However, Darwin was mistaken when he wrote about the Fuegians' "perfect equality." Their society was only partially egalitarian, mainly because of the subordination of women, as Darwin was aware.

The Yamana did not need chiefs. Their society did not generate a hierarchy of vying political or economic sectors, which in many societies require a chief, a king, a president, or even a benevolent dictator (if such is or was possible) to avoid, mitigate, or control conflicts within the social body. Although the shamans enjoyed prestige, they were neither headmen nor chiefs. On this level, the Yamana society was far more egalitarian than structured societies. A tolerable order was maintained, thanks to the network of egalitarian kin relations, and by their oral tradition, the advice of the elders, which defined right and wrong. These rules of conduct were taught to the young during months at a time during the ceremony called Chiexaus (Chapter 15).

No Home, No Domestic Affection

Darwin: "They cannot know the feeling of having a home, and still less that of domestic affection; for the husband is to the wife a brutal master to a laborious slave."[107] Here he implied that the Fuegian society was not one of such "perfect equality." He equated the lack of a home and the lack of domestic affection with the brutality of the husband. They can be treated separately.

First, the Yamana's "haycock" was only a temporary shelter, not a home. Hyades pointed out that they also found shelter under a protruding rock or in cave. Hyades emphasised that protecting the fire was the essential reason for building such a hut or shelter. Besides the principal fire, if the structure was large enough, they might have three or four smaller fires burning so that everyone could find a place near one of them.[108] Their wigwam was more like a home, even though it was also abandoned for months on end.

These people were "outdoors" far more than the sedentary British. They were as familiar with a gamut from excellent to less attractive camping sites over many miles, through the winding channels, as we are with the rooms of our house or apartment and our neighbourhood. Home could be a pebble beach, a pleasant stretch of sand, familiar rocks and islets, some during the winter months, others through the long summer days. Home was also the canoe, where the family spent about half its time – the canoe with its fireplace, potable water, a dog or two, domestic and hunting equipment, almost everything essential except a place to sleep and a bathroom. Whatever food or material they needed was in the water or along the shore. Occasionally they went inland to manufacture their canoes, for logs and firewood or to view the landscape from a hilltop. They also obtained a few essential items through barter, such as pyrite for igniting a fire. They often camped along the shore overnight or for a few days or for weeks during winter and even longer when they found a recently beached whale or the "vast shoals of sprats" mentioned above by Lucas Bridges. They did have a "feeling of home," a strong attachment to their homeland, their territory, as will be shown when Jemmy decided which of two worlds he preferred, his home or England (Chapter 5).

Second, the Yamana were a family people; the parents adored, spoiled and respected their children, according to comments of most of the outsiders through the centuries. The husband and his wife or wives often did not remain together "until death do us part," but the children were cared for by their families or other kin. There were no orphans until the missionaries came. Their family life had a generous amount of "domestic affection."

Third and finally, what was the quality of the man–woman relationship? Darwin saw the women paddling their "wretched canoes," patiently fishing in the tangled kelp, gathering shellfish on forlorn rocky coasts, nursing their babies while being dripped on by snow: all this work and hardship, while the men sprang on board, hands stretched out for whatever was offered or for seizing loose objects on deck without asking. He may also have noticed the males standing in the prow, directing the female paddlers, who struggled to decipher their husbands' gestures and shouts. Darwin usually saw the men as opportunists, domineering and exploitative. He did not see them hunting seals on a rocky coast, grasping cormorants while clinging to a windswept cliff, peeling bark off a tree to construct a canoe. He only saw fleeting moments in their lives, though he did notice them hard at work in Wulaia (Chapter 5).

Both sexes contributed to the essential labour (the shamans worked like everyone else), as Gusinde insisted. Be that as it may, it is essential to note that the women performed the unforgiving day-to-day labours, while the men's work allowed for leisure, free time even before the commercial fisheries exterminated most of the seals and whales in their area. The men, with some exceptions, held the positions of prestige as shamans and directors of the ceremonies. Nor did the husbands always treat their wives kindly. If a wife was abused, she could find support with her original family or kin group, but returning to them might prove too complicated or dangerous for her.

Weddell, Darwin, and others who followed saw that the women were overworked, but they were not so overworked when the seals were abundant and dead whales were often found stranded on the shores. However, gender inequality probably existed then but even so the Yamana women were held in higher esteem than they were among the Selk'nam.

A Horror Story

Darwin punctuated his belittling thoughts about the male Fuegians with a reference to John Byron's report of his 1741 experience as a castaway in the Gulf of Peñas area, Alakaluf territory. Byron saw "a wretched mother pick up her bleeding dying infant-boy, whom her husband had mercilessly dashed on the stones for dropping a basket of sea-eggs!" This horror story may be true. It made Darwin shudder: "How little can the higher powers of the mind be brought into play . . . to knock a limpet from the rock does not require even cunning, that lowest power of the mind." These remarks led Darwin to comment, "Their skill in some respects may be compared to the instinct of animals . . . the canoe, their most ingenious work, poor as it is, has remained the same, as we know from Drake, for the last two hundred and fifty years."[109]

The Yamana did not partake in the ingenuity of classical times, the inventiveness of the Renaissance, or the incipient Industrial Revolution. Modern science was in their future, if future they were to have. Darwin was aware of this, but even so he didn't attempt to understand their mode of living, or acknowledge their mastery of a difficult environment, despite the inferior status of the women. Brian Street, a literary historian, made this point: "Primitive peoples are considered to be slaves of custom and thus to be unable to break with the despotism of their own 'collective conscience.'"[110]

But Why Did They Settle in This End of Nowhere?
Darwin wondered:

Whilst beholding these savages, one asks, whence have they come? What could have tempted [them] . . . to leave the fine regions of the north, to travel down the Cordillera or backbone of America, to invent and build canoes, which are not used by the tribes of Chile, Peru and Brazil, and then to enter on one of the most inhospitable countries within the limits of the globe?

This question is still being asked today. The archaeologists Orquera, Piana and Legoupil, among others, have found some valid answers (see Introduction).

Despite Their Miseries
Darwin: "There is no reason to believe that the Fuegians decrease in number: therefore we must suppose that they enjoy a sufficient share of happiness, of whatever kind it may be, to render life worth having."

This is an amazing comment coming from Darwin, who expressed little empathy for these "savages." But in the next sentence he took the romance out of this thought: "Nature by making habit omnipotent, and its effects hereditary, has fitted the Fuegian to the climate and the productions of his miserable country."

Was "a miserable people fit a miserable country" Darwin's legacy? No, because it would overshadow his recognition that after all they were mentally on a par with the rest of humanity. Repelled as he was by some of the Fuegians "at home," he acknowledged that the three (or at least two, Fuegia Basket and Jemmy Button) with whom he was acquainted were his equals. Years later, in *The Descent of Man*, he affirmed: "The Fuegians rank among the lowest barbarians; but I was continually struck with surprise how closely the three natives on board H.M.S. 'Beagle' who had lived some years in England, and could talk a little English, resembled us in disposition and in most of our mental faculties."[111]

And again: "I was incessantly struck while living with the Fuegians on board the 'Beagle' with the many little traits of character showing *how similar their minds were to ours*; and so it was with the full-blooded Negro with whom I happened once to be intimate."[112]

Even though he considered the Fuegians he knew, mentioned above, his equals, he never altered his original impression of their people as "the lowest barbarians." Rather than explain that, after all, Darwin's attitude toward them was an expression of the prevailing mind-set of his epoch, it is revealing to recall that his British contemporaries Weddell and Brisbane (sealers), and Webster (the medical doctor in Foster's expedition) were more open-minded than he was and more inclined to recognise the Yamana as fellow human beings.

Ernst Mayr, one of the most outstanding biologists of the "New Synthesis," made a somewhat similar comment with reference to the immediate success of *On the Origin of Species*. "Curiously at that time the concept appealed particularly to laymen. Those who were best informed about biology, and especially about classification and morphology, upheld most strongly the dogma of creation and the constancy of species." Those who were "best informed" opposed Darwin. Mayr insisted: "It is Darwin, and Darwin alone, who deserves the credit for having changed this situation overnight."[113] However, with respect to the Fuegians, though he implicitly recognised they were "our" equals mentally, he never questioned his conviction that they were cannibals, as I noted above. Nor did see them in their own context but rather on a "scale," which began with the primitive and culminated with the civilised. In his own words: "If the state in which the Fuegians live should be fixed on a zero in the scale of governments, I am afraid the New Zealand [the native Maoris] would rank but a few degrees higher, while Tahiti, even as when first discovered, would occupy a respectable position."[114]

5

1833 to 1834: The Three Fuegians with Darwin and Fitz-Roy in Tierra del Fuego; Darwin and Fitz-Roy Visit the Falkland Islands; Adios Fuegians

The Worst Storm Ever

Darwin and the others were "tired and impatient by the delay caused by bad weather" when the *Beagle* finally departed from the Saint Martin's Cove on the last day of 1832. Fitz-Roy intended to land York and Fuegia among their own people, the Alakaluf, on Waterman Island along Christmas Sound, as he had promised them. Heading in that direction, the *Beagle* was suddenly thrown out to sea, swept into a relentless storm, a succession of gales, strong winds and high seas.

Three days later the *Beagle* had drifted southwest to 57°23′ south latitude (Cape Horn is at 55°59′ south latitude). Fitz-Roy remained undaunted. "Our good little ship weathered them cleverly, going from seven and a half to eight knots an hour, under close-reefed topsails and double-reefed courses, the top-gallant masts being on deck."[1] But the *Beagle* was still "heavily pitching" seven days later. Darwin was really upset. "I have scarcely for an hour been quite free from sea-sickness... my spirits, temper & stomach, I am well assured, will not hold out much longer."

On 11 January (twelve days after they left Saint Martin) a more violent squall struck as they were nearing the coast of the wild-looking York Minster cliff, Waterman Island: York's territory. The spray was rising over the cliff about 200 feet (61 metres) high as the crew struggled to shorten the sails. The rampaging squall did not let up. Darwin noted: "On the 12th the gale was very heavy, and we did not know exactly where we were, it was a most unpleasant sound to hear constantly repeated. 'Keep a good look-out to leeward.'" Prone to sea-sickness even in calm weather, he was yearning for the "warm serene air & the beautiful forms of the Tropics."[2]

The storm kept raging all the next morning, "with its full fury," as the ship lurched deeply. At noon, the sea "broke over us . . . the poor Beagle trembled at the shock, but soon, like a good ship that she was, she righted and came up to the wind again." Soon after 1 PM the sea rose to greater heights. Even Fitz-Roy became alarmed. "I was anxiously watching the successive waves, when three huge rollers approached, whose size and steepness at once told me that our sea-boat, good as she was, would be sorely tried." The third huge roller plunged the *Beagle* two or three feet under water, from the head to the stern, and one of the "beautiful whale-boats" had to be cut away. This was the worst gale Fitz-Roy had ever experienced. Darwin thought that this moment might be his last. "Had another sea followed the first, our fate would have been decided soon, and for ever." The sea did strike again, but the crisis was passing.[3]

The sea calmed down about 4 PM that day, but the *Beagle* was off her course. Darwin exclaimed: "We had now been twenty-four days [since 18 December when they left Good Success Bay] trying in vain to get westward; the men were worn out with fatigue. . . . Captain FitzRoy gave up the attempt to get westward by the outside coast. In the evening we ran in behind False Cape Horn [the southern extremity of Hoste Island]."

The next day Darwin lamented: "I have suffered an irreparable loss from yesterday's disaster, in my drying paper & plants being wetted with salt-water. Nothing resists the force of a heavy sea; it forces open doors & sky lights, & spread universal damage. None but those who have tried it, know the miseries of a really heavy gale of wind. May Providence keep the Beagle out of them."[4] His collections, in the poop and forecastle cabins on deck, were "much injured." The *Beagle* had nearly gone under on that 13 January 1833.

As they pulled in along the False Cape, Darwin exclaimed: "How delightful was that still night, after having been so long involved in the din of the warring elements!"[5]

Five months later he recalled these moments in a letter to his cousin William Darwin Fox: "We had plenty of very severe gales of wind: one beating match of three weeks off the Horn; when it often blew so hard, you could scarcely look at it. We shipped a sea – which spoiled all my paper for drying plants: oh the miseries of a real gale of wind!"[6]

Fitz-Roy informed Captain Beaufort that this storm convinced him that Anson (in 1741) had not exaggerated when he described the fury of the sea while rounding Cape Horn, and that a disaster had been avoided thanks to the good condition of the *Beagle*. "None of my Shipmates saw so much furious wind during the previous five years in the *Beagle*. Five vessels have been wrecked on 'Terra del' [Fuego] and at the Falklands."[7]

York Changes His Mind

Fitz-Roy had decided to leave off Fuegia and York on Waterman Island sometime later, so he rounded False Cape Horn and sailed up Nassau Bay in search of a harbour near Beagle Channel to take Jemmy home first. On 15 January, he located Goree Road, off the southeastern corner of Navarino Island, the haven discovered by the Dutch in 1624 (Chapter 1). He praised it as "one of the most spacious, accessible and safe anchorages in these regions." Everyone rested during the next four days from those three weeks of rugged sea, though they took turns preparing the ship for her next destination.

At this time York told Fitz-Roy that he and Fuegia had decided to stay with Jemmy, in his home territory, a campsite called Woollya (now spelt Wulaia) on the west coast of Navarino Island. Fitz-Roy was immensely relieved not to have to return to York Minster cliff (Waterman Island). Except for the death of Boat Memory (Chapter 4), he was keeping his promise of returning the Fuegians to their homeland, in good health and with plenty of gifts. The three appeared content to have put their trust in him.

On to Wulaia: Jemmy's Country

For this happy occasion Fitz-Roy decided to escort the three to Wulaia with thirty-two members of the crew, plus Darwin and Matthews. Of his officers he chose Benjamin Bynoe (Jemmy's special friend, the principal surgeon), lieutenants Hamond, Stewart and Johnson, plus the twenty-eight seamen. Jemmy's other special friend, James Bennett, was also one of the party. They were to be taken in three whaleboats and a yawl (a sailing boat, equipped with two masts), a veritable caravan. A deck had to be installed on the yawl for the heavy cargo of gifts. It could be pulled along by the whaleboats when the wind turned adverse. The *Beagle* with the rest of the crew were to await their return in Goree Road.[8]

The caravan set out from Goree Road up the east coast of Navarino on 19 January 1833. It was not long before the overloaded yawl had to be towed by the three whaleboats rowing against the wind and current. Beagle Channel came into full view when they rounded the northeastern corner of Navarino. Fitz-Roy was impressed as he looked down the channel to the left. "To the westward we saw an immense canal, looking like a work of gigantic art, extending between parallel ranges of mountains, of which the summits were capped with snow, though their sides were covered by endless forests. This singular canal-like passage is almost straight and of nearly uniform width (overlooking minute details) for one hundred and twenty miles."[9] Darwin was more laconic: "This channel...is a most remarkable feature in the geography of this, or indeed of any other country." It reminded him of Lochness valley, in Scotland, which he had probably visited.[10]

Big ships had not sailed in Beagle Channel since Fitz-Roy's trip in May 1830, though sealers and whalers had penetrated it long before 1833 (Chapter 2). The party went ashore in a "snug little cove," pitched their tents and relaxed. That evening of 19 January, Darwin was pleased. "Nothing could look more comfortable than this scene. The glassy water of the little harbour, with the branches of the trees hanging over the rocky beach, the boats at anchors, the tents supported by the crossed oars, and the smoke curling up the wooded valley, formed a picture of quiet retirement."[11]

As they sailed and rowed west along Beagle Channel, they passed MacKinlay Pass, where the channel narrows down from some three miles (4.8 kilometres) to about one mile (1.6 kilometres) because a rather large island, later named Gable, obstructs it. When Master Murray discovered the channel in April 1830, coming from the opposite direction, he turned back here, from the clay cliffs of Gable Island (Chapter 3).

Beagle Channel: Darwin Meets the Yamana at Home

The channel broadens out, beyond MacKinlay Pass, again to about three miles. Darwin observed: "We began to enter today the part of the country which is thickly inhabited." From there on, "the constant succession of fresh objects quite takes away the fatigue of sitting so many hours in one position." The natives built fires along the shore to greet the "little fleet."[12] The fires reminded Darwin of the meaning of Tierra del Fuego, so named because in 1520, when Magellan discovered the strait, the natives lit fires to spread the news of the arrival of his huge "canoe." Now they looked so astonished that Darwin thought that most of them had never seen white men before, much less such a caravan of boats. They ran for miles along the shore, hailing them. Darwin was amazed.

I shall never forget how wild and savage one group appeared: suddenly four or five men came to the edge of an overhanging cliff [of Gable Island]; they were absolutely naked, and their long hair streamed about their faces; they held rugged staffs in their hands, and, springing from the ground, they waved their arms around their heads, and sent forth the most hideous yells.[13]

Their appearance was "so strange, that is was scarcely like that of earthly inhabitants." Those along the south shore (Navarino Island), further down the channel, were clutching their slings and seemed "not inclined to be friendly." But once the crew landed, they became delighted by the "trifling presents," especially the biscuits and the red cloths that they immediately tied around their heads. While Darwin was having lunch, "one of the savages touched with his finger some of the meat preserved in tin cases which I was eating, and feeling it soft and cold, showed as much disgust at it, as I should have done at putrid blubber." Everyone laughed at the expression of disgust on the native's face, except Jemmy, who "was thoroughly ashamed."

The "Bad Neighbours"
Here Jemmy was among people of his own culture and language for the first time since he had departed two and a half years earlier. However, he clarified that these were not friends, not his "tribe," and that they often made war on his people. York laughed at them, shouting "large monkeys" and, as usual, "Yapoos." Fuegia hid and refused to look at them a second time. Jemmy insisted that they were "not at all like my people, who are very good and clean." Fitz-Roy had a different opinion. "Jemmy's own tribe was as inferior in every way as the worst of those whom he and York called 'monkeys – dirty – fools – not men.'" Darwin became visibly annoyed at their insistent demands for presents, even the buttons on his jacket, and their annoying shouts of *yammerschooner*, which he thought meant "give me." According to the missionary Thomas Bridges, this expression signified "be kind to us."[14] In this situation *yammerschooner*, may have meant "give us" as well as "be kind to us."

The following morning, 21 January, other canoes landed near where the crew was camping on Navarino Island. The natives jumped out of their canoes and began picking up stones on the shore, while the women and children rushed into the forest. Darwin was "much afraid" a skirmish might result. He was relieved when it did not: "it would have been shocking to have fired on such naked miserable creatures.... Like wild beasts, they do not appear to compare numbers; for each individual, if attacked, instead of retiring, will endeavour to dash your brains out with a stone, as certainly as a tiger under similar circumstances would tear you."

Fitz-Roy also became anxious as the tension mounted, especially when the Yahgans laughed at him as he flourished a cutlass at them. Then he fired his pistol twice, close to one native, who looked astounded and rubbed his head. Darwin surmised that a person who is ignorant of firearms might not realise their killing power. Even when he sees the wound caused by a bullet, "it may be some time before he is able at all to understand how it is effected; for the fact of a body [the bullet] being invisible from its velocity would perhaps be to him an idea totally inconceivable."[15]

Jemmy remained on the *Beagle*; he refused to go ashore to greet these bad neighbours. By morning, Fitz-Roy became really irritated with the unfriendly gestures of this "hostile tribe" and ordered his men to shake them off, return to the ship, and cross over to the north side of the channel (to the Isla Grande). Darwin agreed. "They are such thieves & so bold Cannibals that one naturally prefers separate quarters." But the hostile natives pursued them, paddling their canoes at full speed, which annoyed Fitz-Roy all the more. The caravan kept ahead, struggling against a strong breeze and tide.

Finally free of their pursuers, the crew landed the caravan on the north shore near a forest that had been burning over many leagues. This fire was so extensive that it had been mistaken for a volcanic eruption by a ship passing Cape Horn.[16]

The next day, 22 January, they were favoured by beautiful weather. Darwin was impressed. "The mountains were here [of Isla Grande] about three thousand feet high, and terminated in sharp and jagged points. They rose in one unbroken sweep from the water's edge, and were covered to the height of fourteen or fifteen hundred feet by the dusky-coloured forest."[17] Here it is obvious that he referred to the mountains behind the Bay of Ushuaia, the location of Yahgan campsites and the future city of the same name.

No-Man's Land

No natives were seen when the *Beagle* passed back to the opposite shore, Navarino Island. Jemmy explained to Fitz-Roy that this was the "land between bad people and his friends." Darwin also reported that it appeared to be neutral (uninhabited) ground.

After an unmolested night in what would appear to be neutral ground, between Jemmy's tribe and the people we saw yesterday, we sailed pleasantly along. I do not know anything which shows more clearly the hostile state of the different tribes, than these wide border or neutral tracts.... Although Jemmy Button well knew the force of our party, he was, at first, unwilling to land amidst the hostile tribe nearest to his own.[18]

This unoccupied territory lies between the hostile Yahgans and Jemmy's group, farther west.

Among Friends

That evening the *Beagle* arrived farther down the coast, near the entrance to Murray Narrows, probably in Lewaia Cove, very near where Jemmy had been abducted nearly two and a half years earlier, in May 1830 (Chapter 3). Here they were only a few hours pull to Wulaia, located just south of the narrows, along Ponsonby Sound.[19]

When the crew went ashore, they noticed three men and two women running to hide. When two sailors approached them quietly, the men were reassured and returned, seemingly at ease. Jemmy was now among friends. Fitz-Roy found them much better disposed than the "bad men," though "as abject and degraded in outward appearance as any Fuegians I had ever seen." He was surprised, perhaps amused, that Jemmy seemed to have almost forgotten his native tongue, whereas York appeared to understand what the friends were saying.[20]

Jemmy Learns That His Father Has Died

Jemmy had not forgotten his native language, as became apparent when one of the three local men told him that his mother and siblings were well but that his father had died during his absence. Fitz-Roy commented: "Poor Jemmy looked very grave and mysterious at the news, but showed no other symptom of sorrow." He had told his friends Bennett and Bynoe, on the return voyage, that a man had come to the side of his hammock and whispered to him that his father had died. He had first told this dream to Bynoe, who had tried to laugh him out of the idea. Fitz-Roy commented: "He fully believed that such was the case, and maintained his opinion up to the time of finding that his father had died."

After hearing the confirmation of the sad news, Jemmy gathered some branches, made a fire, and solemnly watched them burn. After this brief meditation, he talked and laughed as usual. He never mentioned his father's death again.[21] Neither Fitz-Roy or Darwin knew that, as a sign of respect, the Yamana never spoke of their deceased by their names in public; when they did speak of them, they used circumlocution, often a kin term.

York the Jealous Suitor

The weather was "so warm" (53°F, 11.6°C) that several of the crew bathed in Beagle Channel. That evening the seamen kidded York so incessantly about his "intended wife" that he became angry with one of his best friends, who was among the teasers. Fitz-Roy also noticed that York was excessively jealous of Fuegia. "If any one spoke to her, he watched every word; if he was not sitting by her side, he grumbled sulkily; but if he was accidentally separated and obliged to go in a different boat, his behaviour became sullen and morose."[22]

Darwin remarked that the three local men were "quiet and inoffensive." As evening set in, they gathered near the blazing campfire while the two women retired to their wigwam, near the tents the crew had set up. The seamen, though well clothed and sitting beside the fire were "far from too warm; yet these naked savages, though further off, were . . . steaming with perspiration at undergoing such a roasting." Despite the roasting, they joined in the singing but invariably a little behind, which Darwin found "quite ludicrous."

The Oens-Men Again

During the previous evening and now again, on 22 January, while everyone was gathered around the campfire, Jemmy told long stories about the Oens-men (better known as Onas). Darwin noted that:

He often told us how the savage Oens-men "when the leaf red" [autumn, September to December] they crossed the mountains from the eastern coast of Tierra del Fuego, and made inroads on the natives of this part of the country. . . . It was most curious to watch him when thus talking, and see his eyes gleaming and his whole face assume a new and wild expression.[23]

Darwin clarified that those who attacked were "the tall men, the foot Patagonians of the east coast." He called these Oens-men or Ohens-men as well as Patagonians. The real name of the Oens-men is Selk'nam, but was unknown at that time, and the term Patagonian has since referred to the Tehuelches. Many of these men were over six feet tall, while the Yamana men were rarely more than five and a half feet. The Selk'nam had large frames and were more evenly developed, being great hikers and runners, never sitting all day in a canoe, as the Yamana often did. The Selk'nam were superb hunters; when not hunting, they wore long cloaks made of guanaco skins and sometimes donned a matching triangular headpiece, which enhanced their figures.

FIGURE 5.1. A Selk'nam hunter: note his long bow, used for hunting as well as combat. Courtesy of Dr J. Piepke, Director of the Anthropos Institute, Sankt Augustin, Germany. Archive # GU 20.84.

Their main weapon, for both hunting and combat, was the bow and arrow, which was very finely crafted. Given their dexterity with this weapon and their physical strength, they were a formidable enemy for the Yamana.[24] Although not all the Selk'nam were enemies of the Yamana, some were their allies, as I noted in Chapter 3.

Darwin called the north coast of the Isla Grande the east coast, which seems logical because it lies along the Atlantic coast, though actually its direction is north.

Fitz-Roy added that Jemmy had said that almost every year these Oens-men "make desperate inroads upon the Tekeenica [Yamana] tribe, carrying off women and children, dogs, arrows, spears, and canoes; and killing the men whom they succeed in making prisoners." Jemmy insisted that these Oens-men made annual excursions at the time of the "red leaf." Fitz-Roy explained that during the autumn, the mountains (the border between the Selk'nam and the Yamana on the Isla Grande) were least difficult to pass. These Oens-men sometimes came "in parties from fifty to a hundred," over the mountains down to the shore of Beagle Channel. There they seized canoes belonging to the "Yapoos" (here Jemmy referred to the Yamana who were not allies of the Oens-men). Then they crossed Beagle Channel, paddling the canoes they had seized, which they tied together to avoid being separated. Once they landed, they drove "the smaller and much inferior Tekeenica [Yamana] people before them in every direction." Jemmy insisted that "there are hard battles sometimes and the Oens tribe lose men . . ." Fitz-Roy added that the latter seemed to be the strongest because they always managed to carry away their dead. He explained: "These periodical invasions of a tribe [again the Oens-men] whose abode is in the north-eastern quarter of Tierra del Fuego are not to be confounded with the frequent disputes and skirmishes which take place between the Tekeenica tribes." Recall that Jemmy's enemies were not only the Oens-men but also certain "tribes" of his own people. His stories are so often repeated in different contexts that they ring true, as the reader will appreciate below and in Chapters 8 and 9.[25]

An Advance Party Arrives

The next morning, 23 January 1833, Fitz-Roy and Darwin noticed several natives running towards them from the nearby hills, just as the caravan was about to embark for Wulaia. They were "breathless with haste, perspiring violently, and bleeding at the nose. Startled by their appearance, we thought they had been fighting."[26] The image of devils came to Darwin's mind (as it had in Good Success Bay). "Several of them had run so fast that their noses were bleeding, and their mouths frothed from the rapidity with which they talked; and with their naked bodies all bedaubed with black, white and red, they looked like so many demoniacs who had been fighting."[27]

Fitz-Roy and Darwin soon learned that the new arrivals had come from Wulaia, Jemmy's home territory. News of the caravan in the channel had gotten around fast. Fitz-Roy remained vigilant, despite their friendly disposition, while Jemmy, now speaking his own language, calmly told them about his trip and explained the motives of the visiting strangers.

Down Murray Narrows

The caravan's departure was delayed again when twelve canoes suddenly appeared, coming from every direction. Darwin counted four to five men in each canoe. Their deep voices rang out as they approached, welcoming the caravan, while the runners from Wulaia echoed their greetings. In the midst of all this joyous shouting, Fitz-Roy urged his men to speed up the preparations, lest the ever-increasing traffic obstruct their departure. The twelve canoes escorted the caravan as it pulled off the shore. Fitz-Roy was not worried about the commotion, because all the natives were friendly. The beauty of the surroundings also impressed him: the "cheerful sunny woodland, sloping gradually down to the Murray Narrow," flanked by the deep blue water of Beagle Channel and the snow-covered mountains (of Hoste Island).

Thirty or forty more canoes, "each full of natives, each with a column of blue smoke rising from the fire amidships, and almost all the men in them shouting at the full power of their deep sonorous voices." All were paddling towards the caravan as it glided through the narrows, while their voices resounded off the nearby cliffs, creating echoes of continual cheer. After the caravan passed through the narrows, it reached the wooded islets of Ponsonby Sound and a large Island (later called Button) where even more canoes joined in. The sailors were pulling hard in the four boats, advancing well ahead of their enthusiastic cortege. Fitz-Roy mused: "the day being very fine, without a breeze to ruffle the water, it was a scene which carried one's thoughts to the South Sea Islands but in Tierra del Fuego almost appeared like a dream."[28]

Wulaia: Jemmy – Home at Last

The Busy First Day

Darwin was pleased. "Jemmy was now in a district well known to him, and guided the boats to a quiet pretty cove named Woollya [now spelt Wulaia], surrounded by islets, every one of which and every point had its proper native name."[29]

Fitz-Roy and his men "were much pleased by the situation of Woollya and Jemmy was very proud of the praises bestowed upon his land." Fitz-Roy continued:

Rising gently from the water-side, there are considerable spaces of clear pasture land, well watered by brooks, and backed by hills of modourate height, where we afterwards found wood of the finest timber trees in the country. Rich grass and some beautiful flowers, which none of us had ever seen, pleased us when we landed, and augured well for the growth of our garden seeds.

FIGURE 5.2. View of the Wulaia coast. Photograph by the author.

Wulaia as I saw it in February 1987 merited Fitz-Roy's praises. Wooded offshore islets enhanced the view across Ponsonby Sound, where the snow-capped mountains of Hoste Island rise on the far horizon. However, empty cement buildings almost spoiled the illusion. They had been constructed as a radio station by the Chilean Navy, probably in the 1930s and since my visit have been torn down. It was not inhabited in 1987, nor were any guanacos grazing on the hillsides.

Fitz-Roy's No-Trespassing Zone

A few local men came to greet the caravan, while the women and children scattered. Darwin clarified that they were "a family of Jemmy's tribe, but not his relations." Fitz-Roy selected a clear space to install the tents, facing the shore near where the boats were moored in case they might be urgently needed. As an added precaution he then ordered his men to trace a line on the ground with spades, between the area where the tents were to be installed and the grassland beyond. Meanwhile, more natives had come and were informed (by gestures) not to pass over the line. Fitz-Roy placed some of his men as sentries, seated or standing along the line, and ordered them to guard it. He was very concerned about his numerical inferiority: about thirty in contrast to "some hundred natives." Having designated the no-trespassing zone, he prepared to receive his hosts, the local men, who were reticent. Soon the natives in the canoes that had followed the caravan "began to pour in." The men joined the crowd around the no-trespassing zone, while their women and children sat at a distance near their canoes. More canoes kept arriving and soon there were well over a hundred visitors. These men also sent their women and children to the abandoned wigwams further inland while they also thronged along the no-trespassing line, where they were signalled to halt. The *Beagle* crew continued handing out presents. Finally, thanks to their good temper and, Fitz-Roy added, "the broken Fuegian explanations of our dark-coloured shipmates [York and Jemmy], we succeeded in getting the natives squatted on their hams around the line."[30] A no-trespassing line, in their own land guarded by strangers, must have puzzled them. This was the first hint of the invasions to come, but they had no way of imagining such a future.

While Fitz-Roy was inspecting the setup, Jemmy was becoming increasingly out of sorts by the quizzing of his countrymen, though he kept on giving them nails and tools. But he soon joined York and the sailors, chopping wood, clearing the ground for a garden that was to be planted and constructing three wigwams: the largest for Matthews, another for York and Fuegia, and a third for himself. Darwin noticed that the "women took much notice of and were very kind to Fuegia."[31]

The first evening in Wulaia, Fitz-Roy and his men were aware that they were even more outnumbered than after they had landed. But at sunset, all the visiting natives departed in their canoes. Fitz-Roy wondered if they were planning some mischief. On second thought, he realised that they were probably not planning to attack, given the friendly way in which they had accepted the no-trespassing line. Come evening, a canoe was sent to the newly "baptized" Button Island, where Jemmy's family was said to be residing. This name was first used then and since appears on all the detailed maps.

The Second Day: Jemmy Reunites with His Family

Early the next morning, a deep voice was heard repeatedly coming from a small canoe, over a mile away.[32] Jemmy exclaimed "my brother!" shouting to Fitz-Roy that it was the voice of his oldest brother (later called Tom). Jemmy climbed a rock on the shore, watching the canoe slowly approaching. Darwin remarked on the great distance at which Jemmy identified the voice, adding: "To be sure their voices are wonderfully powerful. . . . All the organs of sense are highly perfected." Then he recalled: "When Jemmy quarrelled with any of the officers [on the *Beagle* during return trip], he would say 'me see ship, me no tell.' Both he & York have invariably been in the right, even when objects have been examined with a glass [binoculars]."³³

As the canoe pushed onto the shore, Jemmy advanced to greet his mother, two sisters, and three brothers (all of his siblings). He didn't learn any details about his father's death "as his relations would not speak about it." His mother glanced at him, then hastened to secure her canoe and hide the basket she was carrying. Later Fitz-Roy learned that her basket contained "all she possessed: tinder, fire-stone, paint, etc, and a bundle of fish." Jemmy's two sisters ran to catch up with her without looking back at him, while his brothers, an adult (Tom) and two grown boys, stared at him for a moment, then walked around him in complete silence. Fitz-Roy was amazed. "Animals when they meet show far more animation and anxiety than were displayed at this meeting." Darwin was more emphatic: "The meeting was less interesting than that between a horse, turned out into a field, when he joins an old companion."³⁴ Because there was no demonstration of affection, the strangers surmised there was none, but for the Yamana, this behaviour was custom; one should not show emotions on such occasions.

When Jemmy's elder brother talked to him, he didn't reply at first, though he did finally – in English. Darwin deduced "that Jemmy had almost forgotten his own language," and commented that "his English was very imperfect. It was laughable, but almost pitiable, to hear him speak to his wild brother in English, and then ask him in Spanish (*no sabe?*) whether he did not understand him."³⁵ Jemmy had probably picked up some Spanish from sealers before Fitz-Roy abducted him, in May 1830, and was now showing off his English to his big brother.

"The Button Boys"

None of the Button boys, Tom, Harry, Billy and Jemmy, fit the missionaries' model of the ideal native. Jemmy remained loyal to Fitz-Roy, Darwin and his other British friends, while his relations with the missionaries were very friendly, though he never became a convert (Chapters 8 and 9). Tom will disappoint the missionaries, despite his loving personality. Harry, younger than Tom and Jemmy, will remain in the background, while the youngest, Billy, will reappear during the traumatic events of November 1859 (Chapter 9). Jemmy's two sisters will also reappear: the youngest will be mistaken for his third wife and the other will become the mother of a great favourite of the missionary Thomas Bridges. No illustrations of them were found except two of Jemmy (Chapters 4 and 8). A photograph of Tom's son is reproduced in Chapter 13.

Startling News

York's comments to Darwin may surprise the reader. "We heard, however, that the mother had been inconsolable for the loss of Jemmy, and had searched everywhere for him, thinking that he might have been left [somewhere on the island] after having been taken in the boat."[36] Darwin did not grasp their significance. York was referring to 13 May 1830, the day Jemmy climbed onto Fitz-Roy's cutter. York's comments indicate that Jemmy was taken to England without his mother's knowledge or consent and presumably without his father's. In other words Fitz-Roy had kidnapped him, though not forcefully. That day in May, when Jemmy was on board Fitz-Roy's cutter, pulling into Murray Narrows, he may have thought that in a short while he would be let off somewhere nearby. Or perhaps, being a child of thirteen or fourteen, he may simply have thought it was fun, a new adventure.

The Third Day: Wigwams and Visitors Return

Some of the neighbours returned in their canoes on the next day and rapidly pitched in, helping the crew build the three wigwams and plant cabbage, potatoes, peas, turnips and the like. Such vegetables were unknown to the Yahgans, who, moreover, were fonder of fish and meat than any root or plant except certain mushrooms, which they did relish. Fitz-Roy probably imagined that they would learn to like the vegetables and that the gardens would encourage them to adopt a more sedentary and civilised routine of living. But why? He had brought along Matthews, so obviously he was hoping that the Yamana would begin to be proselytised and therefore should be trained and persuaded to forgo their nomadic way of living.

Meanwhile other canoes returned or arrived for the first time. These neighbours also joined in the labour, bringing wood and bundles of grass to thatch the wigwams.[37] With all this help, the three wigwams were nearly habitable by evening. York was very pleased with his wigwam, with Wulaia and with all the activity. He assured Fitz-Roy that Jemmy's eldest brother, Tom, was "very much friend" and the country a "very good land"; he repeated his intention to settle there.

Jemmy gave his brothers nails, tools, and his sisters and mother, English clothes. Fitz-Roy presented Jemmy's mother with a garment, for which she reciprocated with a large quantity of fish. Later Jemmy escorted her, dressed in her new outfit, to visit Fitz-Roy. He was informed that Tom or Tommy was a "doctor" (a *yekamush*, a shaman) who, despite his young age (early twenties) "was held in high estimation among his own tribe." Fitz-Roy explained that the "doctor's" (Tom's) occupation involved pretending to identify and to cure illnesses.

On that third day, several seamen and probably Darwin went hunting in the nearby hills, but the guanacos, the only prey, were so wild that they couldn't be killed even with firearms. That day Fitz-Roy met an important person, the older "Doctor Button," Jemmy's uncle (his father's brother). Also other "strangers" arrived.

The Eventful Fourth Day

These strangers were the "bad people – no friends," according to Jemmy. Fitz-Roy called them the "Yapoo Tekeenica tribe," meaning that they were bad Yahgans.[38] Jemmy had adopted the derogatory term "Yapoo" (otter) from York, who used it for all the Yamanas, while Jemmy applied it only to his Beagle Channel enemies, beyond "no man's land." But "Tekeenica" is not a word at all; it is a phrase in the Yahgan language, which Fitz-Roy mistook for their name.[39] Recall that I use "Yahgan" and "Yamana" interchangeably, although the former word applies especially to those who camped long Murray Narrows and the vicinity. They had no term for the entire group, although Yamana is generally accepted as such (see Glossary).

Darwin calculated that "at one time" there were 120 strangers present in Wulaia, while Fitz-Roy wrote on 26 January that more than 300 were there. As the strangers came on 25 or 26 June, Fitz-Roy and Darwin may have judged their numbers at different times. Also, these numbers were guesses, as there is no indication that they were ever counted. Fitz-Roy noticed that many who arrived this day were "strangers to Jemmy's family, that his brothers and mother had no influence over them" and that the strangers "cared for them as little as they did for us, and were intent only upon plunder."[40] These strangers were not Oens-men, for had they been, Jemmy would have been much more alarmed; they were his enemy neighbours, Yahgans.

Only Fitz-Roy recorded this episode in some detail, though he was not present. Quite a few of the seamen, including Darwin, were bathing in a nearby stream, while several natives sat by peacefully looking on, much amused by their white skin and "the act of washing." While this admiring was going on, some of the admirers absconded with the bathers' handkerchiefs, shoes, and whatever else lying about. Darwin noted: "They asked for every thing they saw & stole what they could." Fitz-Roy put an end to these "ablutions" somehow without offending anyone.

Darwin noted that while "the poor women [were] working like slaves for their subsistence," the men lounged about all day long, although he had previously observed the latter building the three wigwams and planting gardens. Fitz-Roy specified that strangers as well as the native men cooperated doing these tasks.[41]

York and Fuegia retired to their new home. Matthews slept in one of the boats and Jemmy in the latter's roomy wigwam, in which the crew had just constructed a solid floor of boards taken from the yawl. Matthews decided to safeguard his most valuable belongings under the floor.

Practice Shooting before Dark

That evening (daylight lasted until past midnight), the crew practiced firing at a target, ostensibly to keep their weapons in condition and to exercise the men "without frightening the natives." Fitz-Roy was still worried about his numerical inferiority: his crew of thirty-two compared to perhaps 300 strangers. He assumed that about two-thirds of them had never seen a gun. The strangers, sat watching, talking to each other, "as successful shots were made at the target, which was intentionally placed so that they could appreciate the effect of the shots. At sunset they went away as usual, but looking very grave and talking earnestly." Then, when the practice was over, Fitz-Roy wondered if "our exercise might have frightened them more than I wished." However, he hoped that it may "have induced them to leave the place." He reassured himself: "It is not improbable that, without some such a demonstration, they might have obliged us to fire on them instead of the target."[42] He was really worried about these strangers and his numerical inferiority.

The Furious Old Men

About an hour after dark, 25 or 26 January, the sentry on duty noticed a moving body. Thinking it was a wild animal, he was about to shoot at it when he realised it was a man. The suspect immediately dashed away and Fitz-Roy, who apparently was awakened, wondered whether the intruder might have been planning "to surprise us, if asleep, [or] perhaps only to steal." Later he and Darwin were informed that two or three old men had attempted to force their way into a tent when they were halted by the sentry and motioned to keep away. One of the aggressors spit in the sentry's face and went off in a violent passion, muttering to himself, turning around several times while making faces and angry gestures at the sentry. Darwin, who had not witnessed the incident either, added details, which he learned the following day.

The old man being told not to come so close, spat in the seaman's face & then retreating behind the trench, made motions, which it was said, could mean nothing but skinning & cutting up a man. He acted it over a Fuegian, who was asleep & eyed at the same time our man, as much to say, this is the way I should like to serve you.[43]

If Darwin's account is more true than imagined, it shows a degree of hostility towards Fitz-Roy and company, far beyond what they might have expected.

An Anxious Day before Departure

While the crew was finishing the last wigwam and planting the last vegetables, Fitz-Roy was surprised to see all the canoes departing. Of the 300 or so, less than a half dozen remained. While Darwin and some of the officers were taking a long walk and watching the natives from a nearby hill: "Suddenly, however, on the 27th, every woman & child disappeared. We were all uneasy at this, as neither York nor Jemmy could make out the cause." Darwin noted in his diary that "nearly all the men" had disappeared also. Jemmy was even more perplexed, because his family had left at about the same time without notifying him. Fitz-Roy wondered if the strangers had gone to prepare an attack and for this reason had taken their women and children along. He and Darwin probably asked each other whether or not they had been impressed by the display of firearms the day before and had feared that they would be shot at. Some of the sailors also suspected that the local natives intended to make a secret attack to steal the expedition's property because they were furious that the sentry had offended the old man, who then spit on him.

A planned attack by the "bad" Yahgans would explain why Jemmy's family had also departed so rapidly: they left fearing that they might be attacked as well. But if this were the case, why didn't Jemmy's family tell him their reason for leaving? Jemmy told Fitz-Roy that his family had simply said they were going fishing and would return that night, but they had not yet returned. By late morning, Fitz-Roy was convinced that no attack would occur. York and Jemmy were also sure that they incurred no risk from the "bad" Yapoos. Finally, everyone agreed that they had probably left in such a hurry fearing that they would be attacked by the firearms.

Matthews said he would pass his first night, 27 January, on shore alone among the Fuegians. Fitz-Roy thought he seemed steady "in his honest intention to do good." But Darwin wondered: "Matthews, with his usual quiet fortitude (remarkable in a man apparently possessing little energy of character), determined to stay with the Fuegians, who evinced no alarm for themselves; and so we left them to pass their first awful night." Darwin doubted that Matthews was, "qualified for so arduous an undertaking [as a missionary in Wulaia]." As Matthews was determined to spend his first night in Wulaia, Fitz-Roy and the others rowed away, as usual, to sleep in the caravan boats, about a mile from the shore.[44]

The Last Morning in Wulaia, for Now

They were relieved to find quiet upon their return on the morning of 28 January. The resident natives were behaving in a most friendly manner; some were spearing fish from their canoes. Matthews' resolve had not dampened. Jemmy informed the captain that friends had arrived at dawn, that his family would return soon, and that the "bad men," the Yapoos, had gone back to their own country. The work in the gardens continued and there were no more disturbing incidents. Fitz-Roy was also relieved that, during this week, nothing of any real consequence had been stolen, even though so many natives had been around the last two or three days. Jemmy had a knife picked out of his pocket by one native while another was talking to him, and wary York had been robbed too. Fuegia had not lost a thing. Fitz-Roy observed that the "kindness to her was remarkable, and among the women she was quite a pet."[45]

Down Glacier Lane and Back to Wulaia

On 28 January (1833) Fitz-Roy sent the yawl and a whaleboat, with most of the crew, back to the *Beagle* waiting in Goree Road, because he had decided to take the other two whaleboats to complete his survey of the Northwest Arm, begun in May 1830. Darwin commented that Fitz-Roy had "most kindly allowed me to accompany him." One whaleboat would be under Fitz-Roy's command and the other was assigned to Lieutenant Hamond. Matthews was still determined to stay on in Wulaia with his three Fuegian friends, so he was no worry. Ten days should suffice for him to make up his mind whether or not he wanted to remain there as a missionary.

About midday, they set out. Passing through Murray Narrows, they veered west, to the left, into Beagle Channel, carried along by a fresh easterly wind. Darwin was pleased. "The day to our astonishment was over-poweringly hot, so that our skins were scorched: with this beautiful weather, the view in the middle of the Beagle Channel was very remarkable." They moved up the channel among huge whales swimming about the ship, spouting in different directions. He saw "two of these monsters, probably male and female, slowly swimming one after the other, within less than a stone's throw of the shore." These whales reminded Darwin of spermaceti (sperm) whales, leaping as they did almost entirely out of the water.[46] So there were still some whales in the channel that the commercial fishers had missed.

That night, as they were setting up their two tents on the shore of the Isla Grande, several "unwelcome canoes" approached them. Fitz-Roy was very annoyed and gave orders to embark immediately. They folded up the tents, picked up their half-cooked supper, and off they went. "Twelve armed men, therefore, gave way to six unarmed, naked savages, and went on to another cove, where these annoying, because ignorant natives could not see us." Darwin was also uneasy. These "barbarians," who despite being inferior in number might "dash your brains out with a stone" with the courage of a wild beast.[47] Before midnight they located a quiet, hopefully secluded, spot nearby. While Fitz-Roy and the crew were preparing to sleep in the tents, Darwin extended his blanket-bag on the nearby shore of pebbles, as it was his turn to serve as the sentry. Alone in the silent night, he meditated.

It was my watch till one oclock [sic]; there is something very solemn in such scenes, the consciousness rushes on the mind in how remote a corner of the globe you are then in; all tends to this end, the quiet of the night is interrupted only by the heavy breathing of the men, and the cry of night-birds – the occasional bark of a dog reminds one that the Fuegians may be prowling, close to the tents, ready for a fatal rush.[48]

However, none of the Fuegians were prowling about nor did they rush on them. The next day they stopped over near Devil's Island, so named by Fitz-Roy's crew in 1830 (Chapter 3). While camping on a shore of the Isla Grande Fitz-Roy noticed the same large wigwam he had seen three years earlier and had named the "Parliament or Meeting House." As he had never seen remains of wigwams destroyed, he thought the Indians purposely allowed them to decay.[49] In effect, they usually returned to the same site and repaired the wigwam, which was easier than building a new one.

They entered the Northwest Arm (Brazo Noroeste on Chilean Maps), where five large glaciers (they are smaller now) descend to the north shore of the mile-wide channel, directly into the water. Darwin was enthralled.

The scenery here becomes even grander than before. The lofty mountains on the north side compose the granite axis, or backbone of the country, and boldly rise to a height of between three and four thousand feet, with one peak above six thousand feet. They are covered by a wide mantle of perpetual snow, and numerous cascades pour their waters, through the woods, into the narrow channel below. In many parts, magnificent glaciers extend from the mountain side to the water's edge. It is scarcely possible to imagine anything more beautiful than the beryl-like blue of these glaciers, and especially as contrasted with the dead white of the upper expanse of snow.[50]

Fitz-Roy later named these "lofty mountains" after Darwin. He observed that they appear higher than they really are because they rise so abruptly from the shore. This enormous range extends along this entire "arm" for thirty miles (48 kilometres) from the large bay on Beagle Channel, called Yendegaia – beyond a sound and an island, both also named Darwin (for a reason to be explained), to the tip of the Isla Grande at Brecknock Peninsula.[51]

Fitz-Roy was also fascinated by the glaciers.

Wherever these enormous glaciers were seen, we remarked the most beautiful light blue or sea green tints in portions of solid ice, caused by varied transmission, or reflection of light. Blue was the prevailing colour, and the contrast which its extremely delicate hue, with the dazzling white of other ice, afforded to the dark green foliage, the almost black precipices, and the deep, indigo blue water, was very remarkable.[52]

Darwin anticipated a coming event. "The fragments which had fallen from the glacier into the water, were floating away, and the channel with its icebergs presented, for the space of a mile, a miniature likeness of the Polar Sea."[53]

The Hero of the Day

Following these expressions of wonder, the two boats were hauled on shore about 200 yards (183 metres) from a glacier (called Romanche). The men were seated quietly around a fire preparing a hasty meal when a thundering noise shook them. They looked up as a thick slice of the glacier came crashing into the water and huge waves surged. The sound echoed in every direction as the great waves rolled towards them, threatening to sweep away their two boats or dash them to pieces. An instant later the two boats were lifted high and tossed back and forth near the shore. Several men dashed to retrieve them. Darwin noted: "One of the seamen just caught hold of the bows, as the curling breaker reached it [the boats]: he was knocked over and over, but not hurt and had saved the boats." Had the force of the tidal waves destroyed the boats, they would have been stranded a hundred miles from nowhere, without provisions in this lonely channel where boats hardly ever ventured except an occasional canoe.

Following this near catastrophe, they quickly pulled the boats back into the channel and set out to search for another shore where they could finish lunch "very far from any glacier." Later Fitz-Roy clarified that the "one seaman" who saved the boats was Darwin himself, the hero of the day.

Darwin Sound and Back through the Southwest Arm

The next day, 30 January, they emerged from the Northwest Arm into a sound beyond Gordon Island, which divides the flow of the water and forms the north and south "arms." Fitz-Roy named this sound, a rather large expanse of water, after Darwin, because he had "so willingly encountered the discomfort and risk of a long cruise in a small loaded boat." Darwin was not very pleased about his namesake, among "many unknown desolate islands." Besides, the weather that day was "wretchedly bad," but he was consoled because "It was a great comfort finding all the natives absent." They finally found a "miserable" place, on a large round boulder, to pitch the two tents. They tried to sleep surrounded by putrefying seaweed, "and when the tide rose, we had to get up and move our blanket-bags." An island in the middle of the sound also bears the name of the budding naturalist. He is honoured by four names in this area: a cordillera, a sound, an island and small mountain west of the cordillera. All are on the official Chilean maps today. If Fitz-Roy could have seen into the future, when *On the Origin of Species* was published in 1859, he might have thought four times before putting these four "Darwins" on the map for eternity.

Proceeding westward, along the large indented island that Fitz-Roy called Londonderry, they entered Whale Boat Sound, named in memory of his elusive whaleboat whose ghost may have been haunting him as he glanced from one coast to the other. By early February, they had surveyed this sound as far as Stewart (also spelt Stuart) Island, where, just three years earlier, Fitz-Roy's two ungrateful prisoner-guides had escaped (Chapter 3). Fitz-Roy ordered his men to turn the two boats back from there and return to Wulaia.

On 3 February, they entered the Southwest Arm, which extends for thirty-three miles (59.2 kilometres) between Gordon and Hoste islands. This "arm" excited little interest, perhaps because it lacks the breathtaking glaciers of its counterpart. The surveys here were done in a hasty manner. Fitz-Roy explained that "these shores, at present [are] almost useless to civilised man." To this day the Northwest Arm is preferred for its scenic beauty and as the shortest route between Beagle Channel and the Magellan Strait. Darwin checked off the Southwest Arm in a few sentences, noting that they had gone as far west as Stewart Island, about 150 miles (241 kilometres) from where the *Beagle* was waiting, "with no adventure, back to Ponsonby Sound."[54]

A Not-Too-Friendly Encounter

Darwin was mistaken; an "adventure" was waiting two days after they emerged from the Southwest Arm. The crew and their captain were not happy when they recognised the party of Yahgans, in the three "unwelcome canoes," whom they had managed to avoid the week before. These bothersome natives had crossed Beagle Channel. There they were in full view, on the shore of Hoste Island, painted red and white and adorned with goose feathers and down. Suddenly Fitz-Roy's dark mood brightened. "One of their women was noticed by several among us as being far from ill-looking; her features were regular, and, excepting a deficiency of hair on the eyebrow and rather thick lips, the contour of her face was sufficiently good to have been mistaken for that of a handsome Gypsy."[55]

Although at this moment he lauded this "handsome Gypsy," his impressions of other "Tekeenicas" (Yamanas) in the vicinity of Cape Horn were not pleasant. Eighty pages before he characterised them as "low in stature, ill-looking, and badly proportioned." The women's bodies were "largely out of proportion to their height; their features, especially those of the old, are scarcely less disagreeable than the repulsive ones of the men." He insisted: "About four feet and some inches is the stature of these she-Fuegians – by courtesy called women. They never walk upright: a stooping posture, and awkward movement, is their natural gait. They may be fit mates for such uncouth men; but to civilised people their appearance is disgusting. Very few exceptions were noticed." Nor were the "uncouth" Tekeenica men spared: "Sometimes these satires upon mankind wear a part of the skin of a guanaco or a seal-skin upon their backs."[56] This is strange verbal behaviour for a gentleman of his Christian convictions and pride. Darwin never sank to this level of contempt.

On that 5 February 1833, Fitz-Roy's and the crew's attention became glued on that woman not because she was "far from ill-looking" but because she was wearing a loose linen garment that had been given to Fuegia Basket. Tension mounted when they also noticed her companions sporting bits of ribbon and scraps of red cloth that must also have belonged to Fuegia, Jemmy, or perhaps York. Moreover, the natives' air of "almost defiance" prompted Fitz-Roy to suspect that his protégés and Matthews had been harmed. Enough was enough: they hurried on, back as quickly as possible to Wulaia.

When darkness set in, they camped along the coast. At daybreak, while hastening through Murray Narrows, they sighted several natives wearing strips of tartan cloth and white linen, "which we well knew were obtained from our poor friends." This was beginning to sound like the whaleboat chase of Chapter 3. Without stopping to inquire, they pulled along in greater haste. Soon they would discover what had or had not happened during their ten days' absence.

Back in Wulaia

Closing in on Wulaia at noon, 6 February, they sighted natives painted profusely and adorned with rags of English clothing. Fitz-Roy wondered if these rags might be the last remnants of "our friends' stock." As their two boats touched shore, the same natives who had been there ten days earlier greeted them "hallooing and jumping about as usual." Matthews appeared, also as usual, much to Fitz-Roy's "extreme relief." Presently Jemmy and York came, looking well, and Fuegia was safe in her wigwam. The worst fears, suspicions, and secret accusations were swallowed whole, as the anguish was expelled with sighs of relief.

Fitz-Roy took Matthews on board his whaleboat and moved it a short distance from the shore "to be free from interruption." Jemmy was on board the other whaleboat, while York waited on the beach. The local men were "squatted down on their hams to watch our proceedings, reminding me [Fitz-Roy] of a pack of hounds waiting for a fox to be unearthed." Matthews told Fitz-Roy his story.

He did not think himself safe, among such a set of utter savages as he found them to be, notwithstanding Jemmy's assurances to the contrary. No violence had been committed beyond holding down his head by force, as if in contempt of his strength; but he had been harshly threatened by several men, and from the signs used by them, he felt convinced they would take his life.[57]

The "Bad Men" Had Come

Matthews explained to Fitz-Roy that at first there were only a few quiet, inoffensive natives about, but three days later, "several canoes full of strangers to Jemmy's family arrived, and from that time on Matthews had had no peace by day and very little rest at night." These strangers tried to tire Matthews by making an incessant noise close to his head. An old man had threatened to kill him with a large stone if he did not give him what was demanded. Once, "a whole party came armed with stones and stakes and if he had nothing to give them, teased him by pulling the hair on his face." Darwin was told that "some of the younger men and Jemmy's brother were crying" but couldn't stop the intruders. Matthews had managed to quiet them with presents. Darwin concluded: "I think we arrived just in time to save his life." It was probably then that Matthews informed Fitz-Roy that he had decided not to remain in Tierra del Fuego.

Matthews also told Fitz-Roy that "his only partisans" were the women, who had always received him kindly, made room for him by the fire, and shared their food with him without asking for anything. The women will be singled out again for their kind treatment of another lone Englishman (Chapter 9). Jemmy had guarded Matthews' wigwam when he went visiting. But these visits ceased after the first three days, when the "strangers" appeared. From that time on, the attention of the strangers, and even some of the local men, was "engrossed by the tools, clothes and crockery ware" in Matthews' wigwam. His most valuable possessions had not been discovered, hidden as they were under the floor, and in the apex of his wigwam. Darwin reported that the articles that these natives did steal were torn up and divided among them, as was customary among the Yamana. York and Fuegia had not lost a thing, "but Jemmy was sadly plundered, even by his own family." The gardens had been "trampled over repeatedly" despite Jemmy's efforts to shield them. Fitz-Roy remarked that he looked very sorrowful as he slowly shook his head saying: "My people very bad; great fool[s]; know nothing at all very great fool[s]." When Jemmy related that his even own brother (not named) had stolen many things from him, he exclaimed "what fashion call that [no question mark]." Darwin continued: "He abused his countrymen, 'all bad men, no sabe (know) nothing,' and though I never hear him swear before [Jemmy added] 'dammed fools.'" He looked so disconsolate that Darwin was sure that at that time he would "have been glad to have returned [to England] with us."[58] It is evident that strangers were the "bad men" neighbours, the same who had suddenly left Wulaia on the twenty-sixth or twenty-seventh of January after the practice shooting. Once they knew that Fitz-Roy and his crew had departed on 28 January, they returned to Wulaia to rob Matthews. Some of the local men took advantage of their presence to do likewise.

First Departure from Wulaia

Fitz-Roy told his crew that they were all to proceed the following day, 7 February, back to the *Beagle*, which was waiting in Goree Road. But how to get Matthews' property out from beneath the floor and from the "attic" of his wigwam into the boats "in the face of a hundred Fuegians?"

Despite Fitz-Roy's worries, the task was accomplished expeditiously. By the time the last bundles were being carried to the boats, no disturbing incident had occurred, so he distributed axes, saws, gimlets, knives and nails to the helpers. He said good-bye to his three protégés and to the "wondering throng assembled on the beach," promising to return several days later.[59]

Darwin and most of the crew bade farewell to their three friends. He was really sorry to leave them, although he probably knew he would see them again. He wondered about their future.

It was quite melancholy leaving our Fuegians amongst their barbarous country-men: there was one comfort; they appeared to have no personal fears.... But in contradiction of what has often been stated, *3 years has been sufficient to change savages, into, as far as habits go, complete & voluntary Europeans.* York, who was a full grown man & with a strong violent mind, will I am certain in every respect live as far as his means go, like an Englishman. Poor Jemmy, looked rather disconsolate, & certainly would have liked to have returned with us. I am afraid whatever other ends their excursion to England produces, it will not be conducive to their happiness. They have far too much sense not to see the vast superiority of civilised over uncivilised habits; & yet I am afraid to the latter they must return.[60]

The above text is quoted from his diary. Some five years later, while compiling the text of volume 3 of the *Narration of the Surveying Voyages...* (published later as *The Voyage...*), he recognised that three years had not been sufficient to "change the savages..." and that York would never live "like an Englishman." Also, in *The Voyage...*, he ended the account of his trip in Tierra del Fuego much more emphatically than he had in his diary: "I fear it is more than doubtful, whether their visit [to England] will have been of any use to them."[61]

On 7 February (1833) everyone went directly back to Goree Road via the southern route through Nassau Bay. They reached the *Beagle* before dark, despite the rough sea. During the twenty days from 19 January to 7 February, they had covered 300 miles in open boats. Meanwhile, the *Beagle* had been refitted and was ready for her next assignment. The entire crew was reunited in Goree Road for three days, and on 10 February the *Beagle*, with all the men and boats, sailed back across Nassau Bay to Packsaddle Bay near Orange Bay, Hoste Island.

Fitz-Roy Returns to Wulaia

Fitz-Roy and a few men left the *Beagle* in Packsaddle Bay to return, in a whaleboat or the yawl, to Wulaia, up the coast along Ponsonby Sound. During these three days they explored the east coast of Hoste; they sighted natives but "had little intercourse with them." Approaching Wulaia on the morning of 14 February, Fitz-Roy was pleased to see the women fishing quietly from their canoes, a scene that augured well for peace. Soon his premonition seemed to be confirmed. When they reached Wulaia, they found York busy building a canoe out of the planks left for him by the caravan. Jemmy was also making a canoe, hollowing out the trunk of a large tree as he had seen done in Río de Janeiro on the return voyage. Fuegia was neatly dressed. She and York still had their possessions: only Jemmy had been robbed again. His mother came to greet Fitz-Roy, also "decently clothed." And vegetables were sprouting in the gardens.[62]

Meanwhile, the Bad Neighbours

The distressing news was that so-called "strangers" had returned on 8 February (1833), the day after Fitz-Roy and all the others had departed. This time Jemmy and his people had "very much jaw" with them and fought them using stone missiles. The enemy kidnapped ("stole") two women and Jemmy's party captured one woman. On 14 February, Jemmy assured Fitz-Roy that after a few days they had been driven away and that now he was getting along just fine. Fitz-Roy departed the next day, still hoping that his protégés would effect some positive changes among their countrymen and that upon his return (a year later) even Matthews might be persuaded to remain among them.[63] Just who the strangers had been was not stated. It seems obvious (to me) that they were the same Beagle Channel "bad" Yahgan neighbours who had attacked Matthews two weeks before. Had they been Oens-men, Jemmy would have been much more alarmed. Besides the Oens-men would not have brought along any of their women. However, they will attack Wulaia later (at the end of this chapter).

First Departure from Tierra del Fuego

On 15 February, Fitz-Roy joined the rest of the crew waiting in Packsaddle Bay. Darwin briefly mentioned two excursions on foot, made during Fitz-Roy's absence, across southern Hoste Island to survey its west coast, and remarked on the views from the hilltops and the beautiful weather.[64]

During the following days the crew surveyed the northern section of Wollaston Island but saw no natives. On 20 February, the *Beagle* returned with the entire crew to the "old quiet place in Goree Road" and weighed anchor the next day, heading towards Le Maire Strait and Good Success Bay. Fitz-Roy reported that "the night of the 22nd was one of the most stormy I ever witnessed." In the not-so-snug bay of Good Success, the

Beagle resisted the onslaught of the wind during five days. Even when the wind calmed down, they had difficulty securing the boats near the shore of the bay. The local natives (the Haush) did not appear during their entire stay. Darwin and others climbed Bank's Hill, as they had in December 1832, but confronted such strong winds and cold that they beat a hasty retreat back to the ship. Darwin was surprised to see that their footprints (boot prints) had not been effaced during the nine weeks since they had been there (in December 1832). They could even identify them, like the Haush and Selk'nam could identify their sandal prints. The crew spent most of the five days on board fishing for skate and codfish, which were delicious. They "put to sea" from Good Success on 26 February, sailing through a "most disagreeable swell off Cape San Diego," and then ran before another gale, hoping to make the Falkland safely and soon.

The Malvinas – Falkland Islands

The *Beagle*'s two trips to these islands are included here because they are part of our story, even though the Fuegians were not involved. These islands had never been inhabited by human beings. They may have been first sighted in 1522 by Esteban Gomez of the Magellan expedition or perhaps not until 1592 by the English navigator John Davis. These two claims are debated, as neither is well documented. However, it is certain that a century later John Strong landed on one of the islands and that ships from the French port of Saint Malo often visited them as of the mid-eighteenth century, although the French never claimed them. They remained under the auspices of the viceroyalty of La Plata as Islas Malvinas until the Revolution of Independence and the creation of the Argentine republic in 1810 (Chapter 2).

These islands changed their name before the first trip when the *Beagle* remained a month, early March to early April in 1833, when British took possession of the islands in January 1833 (see below) two months before – the first *Beagle* visit. These two visits are presented together here, just as Darwin presented his visits in Tierra del Fuego in one chapter of his *Voyage* . . . , treating different dates of the same subject on a continuum.

1 March to 6 April 1833: The *Beagle*'s First Visit to the Falklands

Two Tragedies and Tales of Wrecks
As they approached the Falklands, a tragedy intervened as the *Beagle* slowed down to take soundings: the high sea of short waves threw one of the crew, Nicholas White, overboard; despite his struggles, he drowned.

Fitz-Roy paid him a rather brief homage: "My own feelings at seeing him disappear may be imagined: it was some time before we sounded again." The very next week, when they arrived at the Falklands, the clerk Edward Hellyer, another crew member, became so entangled in the kelp while swimming to grasp a bird he had shot that he too drowned. The following day he was buried "on a lonely & dreary headland."[65] Recall how often the Yahgan women had to swim in the dangerous kelp while mooring and fetching their canoes.

After three or four nights on the rough sea, on 1 March 1833, they sighted the coast of West Falkland Island, some 250 miles (463 kilometres) from the Le Maire Strait. Gazing at the shore, Fitz-Roy seemed to miss Tierra del Fuego. Before him rose barren hills that traversed extensive tracts of somber treeless moor and bog lands. Moving along the low rocky coast smitten by a raging surf, his impressions darkened even more as he thought of these "unfortunate islands – scenes of feud and assassination, and cause of angry discussion among nations." As they sailed by one wreck after another, he and the crew must have felt relieved that they had arrived at all. Darwin observed: "It is quite lamentable to see so many casks & pieces of wreck in every cove & corner: we know of four large ships in this one harbour." One of these was the *Uranie*, a French discovery ship. The famous French navigator Louis de Freycinet, the captain, had been wrecked there in 1820 while trying to complete his voyage around the world. It was then that Weddell had aided him (Chapter 2).

A while later a boat hailed the *Beagle* and the crew learned of another wreck, again a French vessel, a whaling boat that had gone under during that "tremendous storm of 12–13 January." Fitz-Roy and his crew recalled that unforgettable storm off Cape Horn and Waterman Island just two months earlier, when the *Beagle* almost capsized. Following these melancholy scenes, they were relieved to hear that the French crew was camping under large tents made from the sails the men had salvaged from their ship. As the castaways were extremely impatient to be rescued, Fitz-Roy invited the entire crew of twenty-two on board and let them off at Port Louis, on East Falkland from whence they probably took the first boat available back home.[66]

Brisbane and His Wrecks

The *Beagle* was approaching Port Louis when Captain Brisbane, Weddell's trustworthy mate, on a merchant schooner, hailed the *Beagle*. After greeting Fitz-Roy and the crew, he was surprised and delighted to find that one of the crew had been an officer with ill-fated Stokes who had saved his life in March 1827, after his sealing vessel sank in Fury Bay (Chapter 3). Brisbane's adventures are evoked here because he is a member of this "cast" and his experiences shed more light on this epoch.

In 1829 Brisbane had departed in a sealing vessel, from East Malvinas Island with a crew of well-armed men. Towards the end of that year, he and his twenty men were "harvesting" seals in Haush territory, along the South Atlantic coast of the Isla Grande, not far from the entrance to the Le Maire Strait. Early 1830, his ship was wrecked there, although the entire crew survived. During three months, little by little, Brisbane and his companions constructed a small boat from the wreckage. Family groups of the Haush had been visiting them peacefully when, unexpectedly the men threatened them with bows and arrows and slings. Pressed by hunger and "much troubled" by these natives, they finally returned to Port Louis. No explanation was given concerning why the Haush became so aggressive. As they were known to be peaceful and to welcome European navigators, some incidents probably occurred to excite their anger.

Brisbane was wrecked a third time a year or so later on the desolate coast of South Georgia, which Captain Cook had discovered in January 1775 (Chapter 1). As before, Brisbane and his crew built a boat out of their wrecked sealing vessel. Instead of heading for the Malvinas, they "escaped" all the way to Montevideo. Fitz-Roy did not explain from whom they had "escaped" and why they took this incredibly long route instead of going directly to the Malvinas.[67]

That year (1831), Brisbane again returned to the Malvinas. Perhaps despairing of sealing, he may have looked around for a less risky job. Whatever his motive, he found work in the only store on the islands, in Port Louis, where he was employed by Lewis Vernet, a well-known sealer. At that time Vernet had the official job of representing Argentine sovereignty in the Malvinas. For the past several years Vernet had attempted to prevent the abusive intrusions of numerous foreign sealers, mainly English and American (Yankee), who were slaughtering seals all around the islands as well as slaughtering the wild cattle that roamed in the hinterlands (Chapter 2). During the previous twenty or so years, the seals, sea elephants, and whales had been so drastically reduced by the commercial fishermen that the Malvinas were now mainly used as a base by the sealers and whalers working elsewhere, in the nearby area. Later Fitz-Roy reported: "If means are not taken to prevent indiscriminate slaughter, one of the most profitable sources of revenue at the Falklands will be destroyed."[68]

In February 1832, a year or so before Fitz-Roy arrived, Captain Silas Duncan, commander of the *Lexington*, a United States warship, decided to strike against Vernet. Duncan was determined to punish him for having arrested three crews (or captains) of an American sealing ship. He couldn't locate Vernet, who happened to be away at the time (probably in Buenos Aires), so without waiting to receive orders from his superior officers, he assaulted Port Louis. After destroying every building and garden in sight, he took some of the local inhabitants prisoner, including Brisbane, whom he delivered to the government in Buenos Aires. Later Brisbane was freed and returned to the Malvinas. The British saw the advantage of Duncan's intervention and stepped in to complete the job for their own benefit.

The British Take Over; the Malvinas Become the Falklands

On 2 January 1833, two British warships sailed into Port Louis, hoisted the Union Jack, and forced the remaining solders in the Argentine garrison to evacuate the islands, renaming them Falkland Islands (see Glossary). Writing in 1980, the historian John A. Crow pointed out that after repeated Argentine protests, Great Britain occupied the islands by force and "has not relinquished them to this day."[69] Desmond and Moore comment on the motives that impelled this high-handed takeover. "It seemed ludicrous, the more so because only one Englishman actually lived on the islands, a storekeeper named Dickson [Dixon], who kept the flag."[70]

In effect, Dixon, an Irish Englishman, had been appointed to represent His Majesty's government. He had also been Vernet's storekeeper, just like Brisbane.[71] These two men will share the same destiny (see below).

When Fitz-Roy met Brisbane, early March 1833, he already had (at least) three wrecks to tell his grandchildren about, if descendants he was to have. But Brisbane was not thinking about grandchildren; he was furious at Captain Duncan for treating him "more like a wild beast than a human being [until he was sent to Argentina]."

Fitz-Roy was favourably impressed by Brisbane, whom he took on board. Before hearing Brisbane's story of Duncan's attack and the British take-over of the islands, Fitz-Roy had imagined Port Louis as a thriving, happy town. Gazing on it now (1 March 1833), he saw "a few half-ruined stone cottages; some straggling huts built of turf . . . here and there a miserable looking human being." Such was Port Louis just two months after England captured the islands from Argentina.[72]

These "Miserable Islands"

Darwin related in his diary that when they arrived at Port Louis, East Falkland, "The first news we received was, to our astonishment, that England had taken possession of the Falkland Islands." These "miserable islands" had a "desolate and wretched aspect," everywhere covered with peat and brown wiry grass, where wheat seldom ripened. Moreover, "rather more than half" of the population was "runaway rebels and murderers."[73] He wrote to his sister Caroline:

We found to our great surprise the English flag hoisted. I suppose the occupation of this place, has only just been noticed in the English paper; but we hear all the Southern part of America is in a ferment about [it]. By the awful language of Buenos Ayres one would suppose this great republic meant to declare war against England! These islands have a miserable appearance; they do not possess a tree; yet from their local situation will be of great importance to shipping; from this Cause the Captain intends making an accurate survey.[74]

Darwin saw the strategic importance of the Falkland Islands for trade and understood that this was why Fitz-Roy intended to make an accurate survey of them. While the latter was surveying, Darwin kept busy "wandering about the country, breaking rocks, & picking up the few living productions which this island [the eastern] has to boast of." One day he was delighted to find a rock full of fossil shells of the "most interesting geological era." However, he soon became bored "with so little for the Journal" in such a forlorn human and natural landscape.

William Low and His Tales of Wrecks

"Capt. Lowe," William Low, a Scottish sealing master, broke the monotony on 24 March 1833. Darwin was delighted and found him to be "a notorious & singular man, who has frequented these seas for many years & been the terror to all small vessels. It is commonly said that a Sealer, Slaver & Pirate are all of a trade: they all certainly require bold energetic men; & amongst Sealers there are frequently engagements for the best rookerys, & in these affrays Capt. Lowe has gained his celebrity."

Captain Low arrived in the *Unicorn*, his remaining schooner, with survivors of a Yankee sealing vessel wrecked during the devastating gales of 12–13 January, not far from where the *Beagle* nearly went under. Amid the stories of all these wrecks, Darwin thought fondly of their "little diving duck" (the *Beagle*) and was consoled, even proud "to have felt the very worst weather in one of the most notorious places in the world, & that in a class of vessel which is generally thought unfit to double the Horn."[75]

Low informed Fitz-Roy and Darwin of three other wrecks during that storm, which had lasted sixty-seven days, December 1832 to March 1833, and that the wreck of his two other vessels had ruined him during "the worst season he had known during twenty years' experiences." This prolonged storm recalls that of Anson in 1741, which also lasted some three months (Chapter 1).

The "Falkland Crowd"

Fitz-Roy was not too pleased with the crowd he met on East Falkland during this first visit, in March 1833. While Darwin was trying to keep busy during the month, Fitz-Roy and his men remained in Port Louis. He was having "much trouble" with the crews of whaling and small sealing vessels, "of which there were some thirty." The few settlers were also causing problems. Because the British had taken over the islands, they all seemed to think that "Mr. Vernet's private property" and the wild cattle and horses were their rightful possessions. Note that Mr Vernet, though frequently absent, was still the owner of the only store on the east island, besides considerable herds of tame cattle. Among the "crowd" of settlers, Fitz-Roy favoured Brisbane and conversed with him at length. He was also friendly with twelve "cut-throat looking gauchos" who were anxious to return home to Argentina. He thought they should stay on the island, on East Falkland, because they were "the only useful labourers" there, the only men who could supply the fresh beef of the wild cattle. He finally persuaded seven to remain and he was very impressed by one, Jean Simon, a really professional "head gaucho." He saw him in full action on horseback, dominating and finally slaughtering a "monstrous bull" with only lassos and "balls," called *bolas*.[76]

The Falkland crowd included five Indian prisoners "who had been taken by the Buenos Ayrean troops and allowed to leave prison [in Argentina] on the condition of going with Mr. Vernet to the Falklands."[77] They were probably the so-called Pampa Indians who were being exterminated by General Rosas' troops. Fitz-Roy's admiration for the gauchos will be sorely tried the next year, during his second visit.

Fitz-Roy Purchases Low's Schooner

As Low was wrecked economically, he offered to sell his share of the *Unicorn* to Fitz-Roy if his part owners would agree, which they soon did. On 26 March 1833, Fitz-Roy probably made a down payment to Low.

In any event, he paid the entire cost for the vessel later in Montevideo out of his own "pocket," trusting that the lords of the Admiralty would reimburse him, which they did not. The *Unicorn*, "a fine vessel of 170 tons" (the *Beagle* weighed 235 tons), was renamed *Adventure*, probably to please Parker King, whom Darwin would visit later in Australia. Fitz-Roy felt he needed a well-equipped second vessel to replace the two small boats he had hired the year before. The *Beagle* could not be used for the tedious tasks of surveying and at the same time carry a "chain of meridian distances around the globe." Although the additional vessel would increase the work to be done, Darwin hoped it would somehow shorten their cruise. But even if not, "it is always pleasant to be sailing in company . . . to break the monotonous horizon of the ocean."

On 6 April 1833 the *Beagle* left the Falklands heading for Rio Negro, Patagonia, and arrived there a week later. Another week later the *Adventure* showed up, and the two ships continued on to Maldonado, Uruguay. By July, the *Adventure* had been refitted, by members of Fitz-Roy's crew, from a sealing vessel to one fit for surveying. Once the sale was completed with the other owners in Uruguay, Fitz-Roy appointed Wickham as the *Adventure*'s commander.

10 March to 7 April 1834: The Second Trip to the Falklands

Some Very Bad News

A year later, the *Beagle* set out for the last time to the Falklands. When they arrived Darwin was shocked to hear what had happened.

Arriving in the middle of the day [10 March] at Berkeley Sound . . . Mr Smith, who is acting as Governor, came on board, & has related such complicated scenes of cold-blooded murder, robbery, plunder, suffering. . . . With poor Brisbane, four others were butchered; the principal murderer, Antuco, has given himself up; he says he knows he shall be hanged but he wishes some of the Englishmen, who were implicated, to suffer with him; pure thirst for blood seems to have incited him to this latter act.[78]

Brisbane had been assassinated on 26 August 1833, six months before Fitz-Roy and Darwin arrived in the Falklands the second time. He had been living in Vernet's general store, where he worked and was part owner. Vernet was still or again absent. Dixon, the British representative mentioned above, was killed with Brisbane and several others, including the head gaucho Jean Simon, who was murdered by his own "country-men." Fitz-Roy had greatly admired Simon and hoped that he would settle on the Falklands. He learned that these murders had been committed by four of the seven gauchos he had insisted remain there. The ringleader was Antonio Rivero, nicknamed Antuco. His cohorts were the three other gauchos and the five Indians, ex-prisoners. These nine men stormed the store, demanding hidden money, destroying everything in sight and shooting everyone except Brisbane, who was knifed by Antuco. He may have vaunted the fact that he had killed the British governor, Dixon, although he also killed his own *paisano*, the head gaucho Jean Simon.

Shortly before the *Beagle* arrived, the H.M.S. *Challenger* had left Lieutenant Smith, the new governor, there with six marines. Darwin was flabbergasted. "A Governor with no subjects except some desperate gauchos who were living in the middle of the island. Of course they have taken all the half wild cattle & horses; in my opinion the Falkland islands are ruined. . . . no Spanish Gauchos will come there, & without them to catch the wild cattle, the island is worth nothing."[79]

Darwin disagreed with his country's policy. In a letter to his sister, Catherine, he complained: "All the economy at home make the foreign movements of England most contemptible: how different from old Spain: here we, dog-in-the-manger fashion, seize an island and leave to protect it a Union Jack; the possessor has been of course murdered; we now send a Lieutenant [Smith], with four [or six] sailors, without authority or instructions." Then he recognised, as he had a year before, the strategic importance of the islands.

This island must some day become a very important halting place in the most turbulent sea in the world – it is mid-way between Australia & South sea to England, Between Chile & R. Plata & R. de Janeiro. There are fine harbors, plenty of fresh water & good beef; it would doubtlessly produce the coarser vegetables. In other respects it is a wretched place.[80]

Fitz-Roy learned that while the crew of the *Challenger* were attempting to capture the nine murderers, they had escaped, taking fifty or sixty stolen horses into the peat bogs. Finally the six marines, with local gauchos, caught all except one of them, and they were taken into custody in Argentina.

Fitz-Roy experienced the aftermath of Brisbane's murder in the most gruesome fashion. Having just arrived in Port Louis, he almost stumbled over feet protruding from a shallow grave. He was doubly startled when he recognised that the corpse, which had been mauled by dogs, was Brisbane's. Fitz-Roy was deeply chagrined when he was told that Brisbane had not been able to defend himself, that he was stabbed in the back while trying to defend his property and that of his friend, that the attackers had tied his corpse to a lasso, pulled it along by a horse about 200 yards from the store and left it there barely covered to be devoured by dogs. "This was the fate of an honest, industrious, and most faithful man: of a man who feared no danger, and despised no hardships."[81] Thus ends the story of the sealer Matthew Brisbane, who had won the admiration of the Yahgans near Cape Horn for his dexterity with a sling and for treating them like fellow human beings. At least three times, he had saved his shipmates when they were stranded for months on remote islands.

Meanwhile Fitz-Roy Had Hired William Low

A happy coincidence had occurred on 26 August 1833, a very short while before Brisbane and the others were murdered. Low, who at the time was still living on East Falkland, was unemployed, had no sealing vessel, and was tired of inaction, so he had left the islands in search of work the morning after Brisbane had been murdered. Low had not returned because he was convinced that his life was endangered by those "murderous gauchos," more so because he had been a good friend of Brisbane. Early in February 1834, a month before Fitz-Roy's second visit to the islands, "when in great distress, he [Low] fell in with our tender, the *Adventure*, and immediately offered his services as a pilot." This was a happy coincidence for Low because he was in even greater distress than the year before. Wickham, the commander of the *Adventure*, hired him provisionally and afterwards Fitz-Roy confirmed the engagement. Thus William Low had become the pilot of the new *Adventure*, his former schooner the *Unicorn*. Fitz-Roy was delighted to hire such a highly respected, experienced, and knowledgeable seaman. Low became Fitz-Roy's friend and informant concerning the Yamana and the Tehuelche.

Darwin Explores the Falkland Hinterland

During this second visit, Darwin made a four-day excursion (16 to 20 March), with two gaucho guides and six horses. The guides were "the only two Spaniards who were not directly concerned with the murder[s], but I am afraid my friends had a very good idea of what was going to take place. However they had no temptation to murder me & turned out to be most excellent Gauchos." They were amazingly dexterous on horseback rounding up and killing wild cattle with lassos and bolas. As firewood was scarce, they used the cattle bones as a substitute and were clever about igniting a fire with soaking-wet twigs or grass in a downpour.

Darwin also admired the bulls, whose massive necks and heads reminded him of Greek marble sculptures. The French had introduced cattle and horses into the islands in 1764. Darwin was curious to know why the wild horses were weak and small and had not increased in number, while the wild cattle had flourished. He was surprised that one of the rare if not the only native quadruped on the islands was a large wolflike fox (*Canis antarcticus*) that was not found in any part of South America. He wondered if it would perish – be exterminated like the dodo birds. Janet Browne noted that Fitz-Roy gave the British Museum "its only representative of the Falkland Islands fox." So the last one was sacrificed for science and the Falkland Islands fox species exterminated though not like the dodo birds.

Darwin studied the fossils contained in clay–slate and sandstone and observed the geological structure of the island, particularly the hills of quartz rock, whose fragments formed "streams of stones" as if they were flowing down to the bottom of the valleys. He was convinced that earthquakes had formed these hills. He was amused by a "brave bird," a penguin that fought and drove him back "erect and determined" as he approached it. He commented: "Thus we find in South America three birds which use their wings for other purposes besides flight: the penguin as fins, the steamer [duck] as paddles and the ostrich as sails." He was truly amazed when he calculated that 600,000 eggs were hatched by a large white sea slug called Doris. As he had only seen seven slugs of this species, he deduced: "No fallacy is more common with naturalists, than that the numbers of an individual species depend on its powers of propagation." Remember this while reading *On the Origin of Species*. He also intensely observed the "zoophyte corallines" and asked: "What can be more remarkable than to see a plant-like body producing an egg capable of swimming about and of choosing a proper place to adhere to, which then sprouts into branches?" His curiosity was aroused constantly, as was his admiration for the marvels of nature.

But the excursion was not all pleasant. His horse fell "at least a dozen times" trying to leap over the streams, bordered as they were by soft peat. Besides the falls, he endured the boisterous cold, heavy hailstorms, and sleepless nights on the soggy ground. "To finish our misery, we crossed an arm of the sea, which was up to the top of the horses backs, & the little waves from the violent winds broke over us. So that even the Gauchos were not sorry to reach the houses."

Most of the rest of this month he was hammering rocks, pulling up roots of the kelp to examine the tiny corallines attached to them and other such favourite pastimes.[82] Thus ends this brief account of their two trips to the Falklands.

Following the First Trip to the Falklands: April 1833 to Late January 1834

During these nine months, the *Beagle* made port several times in Uruguay and Argentina. Fitz-Roy and the crew continued the surveys along the coasts, and Darwin made important excursions on horseback. He was observing, taking notes, and collecting specimens as never before and sending them all to Professor Henslow, mainly from Montevideo. He was often exuberant, ill only once and wrote many letters home.

Late April and May 1833 and again in July, he rode on horseback for days on end through the back-country of Maldonado, Uruguay. In Argentina, mid-August, he rode from the delta of Rio Negro, near a fort called Carmen de Patagones, northern Patagonia, to a garrison along the Colorado River, the headquarters of General Juan Manuel Rosas, then the country's most powerful military and political figure, who was subduing and exterminating the Pampa Indians, among others.

Then, from 8 to 20 September 1833, again on horseback, he traversed the recently pacified region from the Colorado River to Buenos Aires, with a military escort given to him by General Rosas. He continued on to Santa Fe in early October. There he became ill with a fever, so he took a boat down the Parana River back to Buenos Aires. From there, he crossed the La Plata Estuary to Montevideo and in November, while waiting to meet the *Beagle*, he rode far into the countryside, beyond the inland town of Mercedes, Uruguay. He remained in the area for several weeks and found other important fossils (in addition to those he had discovered in September and October of 1832 near Bahia Blanca in Argentina).

During the last week of December 1833, Fitz-Roy began surveying the Atlantic coast of Patagonia. In late January 1834, he turned the *Beagle* into the Magellan Strait.[83]

Darwin Enters the Magellan Strait and Meets the Tehuelche Indians
A few days later, when the *Beagle* was beyond the First Narrows, sailing against strong westerly gales, Darwin was reminded of his illustrious predecessors, Ferdinand Magellan and Francis Drake. With tides rising forty to fifty feet and running five and six miles per hour: "Who can wonder at the dread of the early navigators of these Straits?"

Darwin was introduced to a tribe of "Patagonians," the Tehuelche, near their *toldos* (large shelters of guanaco or horse skins) in Gregory Bay on the continental shore of the strait. Among them was María, whom Darwin called Santa María. Captain King had met her when he entered the strait in September 1827 and Fitz-Roy in 1829 (Chapter 3). She and her companions had frequent contacts with traders and sealers, so they spoke some English as well as some Spanish. Darwin thought they were "half civilised and proportionally demoralized," also "rather wild." About six feet tall, they wore long mantles of guanaco hides. These large, heavily clothed men, their long black hair streaming about their faces, were astride small horses that seemed "ill fitted for their work." He thought they resembled the Indians who were "with [General] Rosas but are much more painted; many with their whole faces red, & brought to a point on the chin, others black. One man was ringed & dotted with white like a Fuegian." He was right; the Tehuelche did resemble the Indians who were with Rosas, the Pampa Indians. Both groups, among others including the Selk'nam and the Haush, had populated the vast area east of the Andes, from Uruguay and most of Argentina to the far tip of Tierra del Fuego. Most were hunters and gatherers; some were still "foot people" while others, like the Tehuelches, had become "horse people."

The Patagonians (Tehuelches) along the Magellan Strait seemed to like the Europeans. When Fitz-Roy invited three to come on board, "everyone seemed determined to be one of them." Darwin added: "At tea they [the privileged three] behaved quite like gentlemen used a knife & fork & helped themselves with a spoon. Nothing was so much relished as Sugar." But they were eager to return to land as soon as they felt the ship tipping back and forth.

The next day the "whole population of the Toldos" promptly lined up on the bank, anxious to barter their guanaco skins and ostrich (rhea) feathers for firearms. Being denied the latter, they were offered knives, axes and tobacco, but they only accepted the latter. Darwin found it impossible not to like "these mis-named giants, they were so thoroughly good-humoured and unsuspecting."[84] Fitz-Roy had a somewhat different impression. "They received us kindly, but . . . two men standing up in the midst of them, who . . . looked immoveably grave and stupidly dignified."

Maria greeted one of the *Beagle* crew she had met a year and a half earlier at Rio Negro. She and her tribe had ridden on horseback from the shore of the Magellan Strait to Rio Negro, some 800 miles, to trade their guanaco skins and rhea feathers, probably for firearms, other necessities and tobacco.[85] This was quite a trek for families with their babies and heavy tents, fording deep rivers and riding through the long stretches of dry, windswept plains of Patagonia, though they had spare horses to ride and eat. Darwin was aware of the vital importance of the horse, which so radically transformed the lives of the Patagonians (Tehuelche) and particularly of their neighbours, the famous Mapuches (Araucanos) who resisted the Spanish conquerors and their descendants for the longest time in all America, until 1859. Without the horses and their ability to tame the wild ones, the Mapuches could probably not have resisted so long. Thinking of the Tehuelches' horses, Darwin noted: "This is a very curious fact, showing the extraordinarily rapid multiplication of horses in South America. The horse was first landed at Buenos Aires in 1537, and the colony being then for a long time deserted, the horse ran wild and in 1580, only forty-three years afterwards, we hear of them at the Strait of Magellan!"[86]

Darwin's "Adventure" near Port Famine

The *Beagle* anchored in Port Famine, the base used during the first *Beagle* voyage. That day, 2 February (1834), they sighted, at a distance of ninety miles (145 kilometres), the highest mountain in Tierra del Fuego, Mount Sarmiento (6,800 feet or 2,073 metres) shrouded in a mantle of snow. A few days later, 6 February, Darwin ventured to climb a nearer, smaller, snowless mountain, the Tarn (some 2,600 feet or 792 metres). He and his companions crawled up the gloomy, cold, wet terrain of decaying, mouldering trunks, sinking knee-deep into the boggy, rotten terrain. During a pause, Darwin glanced down at the deep ravines, a "death-like scene of desolation." They had almost given up hope or desire of reaching the summit. They did reach a bare ridge from which Darwin scanned the landscape again through the piercing cold wind and fog. "Here was a true Tierra del [Fuego]; irregular chains of hills, mottled with patches of snow, deep yellowish-green valleys, & arms of the sea running in all directions." He felt somewhat rewarded by the view and by the fossil shells he collected on or near the ridge.

The next day Port Famine had become "splendidly clear." He longed for more of the same. "If Tierra del [Fuego] could boast one such day a week, she would not be so thoroughly detested as she is by all who know her.[87] Darwin failed to appreciate Fuegian weather.

Darwin Sights the Selk'nam

Fitz-Roy and the entire crew boarded the *Beagle* to make a rapid survey of the Atlantic coast of the Isla Grande. On the way, 13 February, while still in Magellan Strait, Darwin sighted the "Ohens men" (Selk'nam) on Elizabeth Island (Isabel in Spanish).

During the day we passed close to Elizabeth Island, on the North end of which there was a party of Fuegians with their canoe &c. They were tall men & clothed in mantles; & belong probably to the East Coast [of the Isla Grande]; the same set of men we saw in Good Success Bay; they are clearly different from the Fuegians, & ought to be called foot Patagonians. Jemmy Button had a great horror of these men, under the name of Ohens men.

Here Darwin's confusion of canoe Fuegians with the "Ohens men" may be explained as follows: he sighted two groups – Alakaluf with their canoe and a few "foot Patagonians," the tall men with mantles, that is the Selk'nam, the "foot Patagonians," who were not navigators. Darwin recognised that these "Ohens men" were similar to the Haush he had met in Good Success Bay in December 1832 (Chapter 4). The Alakaluf inhabited the central and western sections of the shore of the strait (on the continent), while the Oens-men (the Selk'nam) lived along the opposite shore of the strait, in Tierra del Fuego. They had probably gotten a canoe ride to Elizabeth Island with the Alakaluf.[88]

They Exit Magellan Strait

The crew went ashore in nearby Gregory Bay, as they had in January, to obtain guanaco meat from the Tehuelches. Darwin greeted "our friends the Indians [who] anxiously seemed to desire our Presence." The chief Maria was not present but "two boat Indians" were, two Alakalufs who he noticed, spoke a different language. He praised the facility with which the Indians learned languages; most of them spoke some Spanish and English. He commented that the mixture of the Indians with foreigners "will greatly contribute to their civilisation or demoralisation; as these two steps seem to go hand in hand."[89]

During the following week, Fitz-Roy completed his survey of the Atlantic coast of the Isla Grande to San Sebastian Bay. There Darwin admired the large numbers of spermaceti (sperm) whales. In 1969 I posed there for a photograph (in Chapter 2).

The Haush and the Yamana in Wollaston

Continuing down the coast of Isla Grande, they stopped over in Thetis Bay near the entrance to Le Maire Strait. There they met other "foot Patagonians, fine tall men with Guanaco mantles." These undoubted were the Haush, as Thetis Bay was part of their territory; the same group, though not the same men, they had met in Good Success Bay in December 1832. This time Darwin did not call them monkeys but rather "fine tall men . . . with nothing more than their slight arrows, manage to kill such strong wary animals [guanacos]."[90]

Having navigated the "uncomfortable Strait," the Le Maire, they crossed Nassau Bay and circled down to Wollaston Island, not far from Cape Horn. On the evening of 24 February (1834), the *Beagle* anchored "under Wollaston." The next day as they were going ashore in a boat, they pulled up to a canoe with six "Fuegians" aboard. Darwin noticed that they were all quite naked and was impressed by a woman with her naked newborn baby, both being soaked by the sleet. On Wollaston Island he "crawled" to the top of a nearby hill where he inspected the soil and viewed the surroundings. The last full day in the area, 26 February, everyone stayed on board because of the stormy weather. Darwin's impressions of these Yamana during this stopover are essential for understanding his derogatory opinions about the Fuegians in general, as I related in Darwin's "meditations" (end of Chapter 4).

Farewell Wulaia

Sailing from Wollaston, the *Beagle* crossed Nassau Bay again and passed along Goree Road, heading north towards Beagle Channel. They found a "beautiful little cove" near the northeast corner of Navarino Island, probably close to where they had been in January 1833 with their caravan. Now, the first day of March (1834), they met three canoes full of Yamanas, "Yapoo Tekeenica who were very quiet & civil & more amusing than any Monkeys." Darwin handed a large nail to one of the men and was pleased when he was served two fish on the point of a spear. He noticed again that when a present landed in the wrong canoe, the recipients passed it on to the canoe to which it was intended.

Darwin related that the next day they were "beating against the Westerly winds" along Beagle Channel, and two uneventful days later reached the "Northern part of Ponsonby sound," meaning the entrance to Murray Narrows, probably Lewaia. It was here or near here, the year before, that Jemmy had told his stories about the Oens-men. Now, on 4 March, ten or twelve canoes paddled up to the *Beagle*, full of natives anxious to barter fish and crabs "for bits of cloth & rags." A handsome young woman, whose face was painted black, smiled with satisfaction as she tied bits of the newly acquired "gay rags" round her head. Her husband "enjoyed the very universal privilege in this country of possessing two wives." Obviously jealous of the attention paid to his smiling wife, he ordered "his naked beauties" to paddle away.[91]

Having camped there, the next morning they headed down Murray Narrows. Darwin was delighted as the *Beagle* zigzagged through the narrows, tacking to take advantage of the changing wind; the men in the canoes paddled with all their might to keep up with her.

The natives did not at all understand the reason of our tacking, and, instead of meeting us at each tack, vainly strove to follow us in our zig-zag course. The more Fuegians the merrier; and very merry work it was. Both parties laughing, wondering, gaping at each other; we pitying them, for giving us good fish and crabs for rags, &c; they grasping at the chance of finding people so foolish as to exchange such splendid ornaments [and rags] for a good supper.[92]

Darwin was amused by the difference it made "being quite superior in force" on the *Beagle* instead of on a whaleboat, as the previous year. He recalled how annoyed he had been then by sound of the voices incessantly hollering *yammerschooner*. Now he was in a good mood. Here he experienced the advantage of barter for both parties: an exchange of objects to which one party assigns little value but that are highly valued by the other.[93]

He was flabbergasted, like young Forster in 1774, that these Fuegians showed so little interest in the many marvels of the *Beagle*, that their admiration was excited far more by scarlet cloth and blue beads. But the absence of women on the *Beagle* must have struck them as very odd. Despite Darwin's formidable powers of observation, he was not attentive to what the natives probably thought of the crew of lone men. Some twenty years later, in 1855, they were overjoyed when they met a captain's wife, Mrs Snow, perhaps the first white woman the Yahgans "at home" had ever seen (Chapter 8).[94]

The Last Reunion with the Yahgans

Seven canoes trailed the *Beagle* while passing through the narrows, "this being a populous part of the country." Then the crew, on 5 March, disembarked in Wulaia, anxious to learn how the three protégés had been making out during the year's absence, but not a soul was in sight. The wigwams built last year were deserted and the gardens trampled on. The sailors dug up a few turnips and potatoes, which were served at the captain's table. After the meal, Fitz-Roy and others wandered about, still without seeing anyone.[95] An hour or two later, they sighted three canoes paddling towards Wulaia from Button Island. In one of them they saw the Union Jack flying and a man standing as if washing the paint off his face. Darwin recognized him.

This man was poor Jemmy, now a thin haggard savage, with long disordered hair, and naked, except a bit of a blanket round his waist. We did not recognise him till he was close to us, for he was ashamed of himself, and turned his back to the ship. We had left him plump, fat, clean and well dressed; I never saw so complete and grievous a change.[96]

He also recalled how Jemmy had been "so particular about his clothes, that he was always afraid of even dirtying his shoes; scarcely ever without gloves & his hair neatly cut." Meanwhile, Fitz-Roy, using binoculars, distinguished the two natives washing their faces and recognised Tommy. When the other gave the sailor's greeting, Fitz-Roy knew he could only be Jemmy, "but, how altered! I could hardly restrain my feelings.... He was naked, like his companions, except a bit of skin about his loins; his hair was long and matted, just like theirs; he was wretchedly thin, and his eyes were affected by smoke."

Once on board, Fitz-Roy hurried him below to clothe him. Soon he was dining at the captain's table, "using his knife and fork properly, and in every way behaving as correctly as if he had never left us." Nor had he forgotten his English. To the astonishment of the crew, some members of Jemmy's family spoke to Fitz-Roy in "Jemmy's English." And Jemmy himself "recollected every one by name, and was very glad to see them all, especially Mr. Bynoe and James Bennett." He gave Bynoe "a fine otter skin which he had dressed and kept purposely" and another to Bennett. Darwin noted in his diary: "Poor Jemmy with his usual good feeling brought two beautiful otter skins for his two old friends & some spear heads & arrows of his own making for the Captain." When asked if he had been ill, he replied "hearty, sir, never better." He reassured them that he had, "plenty fruits, plenty birdies, ten guanacos in snow time," and "too much fish."[97]

A month later Darwin wrote to his youngest sister, Catherine, that Jemmy "was quite contented," despite the fact that the year before, at the height of his indignation, he had said "my country people no sabe nothing – damned fools." Now, "they were very good people, with too much to eat & all the luxuries of life."[98]

Jemmy's Preference
Darwin and the others "were rather surprised, to find he [Jemmy] had not the least wish to return to England." In the same letter to Catherine,

FIGURE 5.3. This man looks like Jemmy Button in 1834 when Fitz-Roy and Darwin returned to say good-bye to him.

Darwin commented: "The captain offered to take him to England, but this, to our surprise, he at once refused: in the evening his young wife came alongside & showed us the reason." Soon after the meal, a voice announced in English: "Jemmy Button's wife." Fitz-Roy noticed that she was the good-looking young woman in Jemmy's canoe, his second wife, the young sister of his first. The shawls, handkerchiefs, and gold-laced cap she received did nothing to calm her fears. She waited anxiously for the return of her spouse to the canoe. Then Tommy called to him in a loud voice, "Jemmy Button, canoe, come!" But she kept on crying until he appeared on the deck. Finally Jemmy and his "tribe" departed in their three canoes laden with gifts, promising to return in the morning.

Matthews' Preference

The next morning, 6 March, following breakfast on board, Fitz-Roy and Jemmy had a long conversation and the former decided not to try to persuade Matthews to remain in Wulaia. Matthews had been on the *Beagle* the entire year and had expressed no desire to be left in Wulaia. Fitz-Roy realised that such a job would be too much for him.[99] Thus Fitz-Roy had to give up his plan to Christianize the Fuegians.

York's and Fuegia's Farewell to Jemmy

Jemmy told Fitz-Roy that York and Fuegia had returned to their own country some months before in the large plank canoe York had built. At first he simply said that they were very happy when they departed, loaded with presents, but he added, "York very much jaw... pick up big stones... all men afraid."

Later he confided in Fitz-Roy and Darwin that York and Fuegia had escaped in their large canoe during an incursion of the Oens-men (see below). Afterwards York and Fuegia returned and persuaded Jemmy and his family, including his mother, to accompany them "to look at his [York's] land." So they all went, York and Fuegia in their large canoe and the others in three canoes, as far as Devil's Island, at the junction of the Northwest and Southwest Arms and Beagle Channel. York's brother and their "Alikhoolip tribe" were waiting there. That night Fuegia, York, and his tribe robbed Jemmy of nearly all his "things" while he was sleeping, leaving him totally naked. Then they "stolen off," back to their own "country."

Fitz-Roy was indignant at this "last act of that cunning fellow." Darwin called it "an act of consummate villainy." They now realised that York had decided to be let off in Wulaia (in January 1833), calculating that he would obtain more presents there than had he been taken to his own country, and that he had built a large canoe to transport "his ill-gotten gains." Darwin remarked that York "appears to have treated Fuegia very ill." However, Fitz-Roy thought that "Fuegia seemed to be very happy, and quite contented with her lot." Jemmy asserted that she helped to "catch [steal] his clothes, while he was asleep, the night before York left him naked."

Meanwhile the Oens-Men Had Attacked

"The much dreaded Oens-men came in numbers" soon after Fitz-Roy had left Wulaia on 14 February 1833. Darwin identified them, now on 5 March 1834, after listening to Jemmy's story. "They clearly are [were] the tall men, the foot Patagonians of the East coast." Recall that Darwin used the term "Patagonians" for the Selk'nam as well as the Tehuelche. Here undoubtedly he was referring to the former. Fitz-Roy should be quoted here.

Jemmy told us that these Oens-men crossed over the Beagle Channel, from eastern Tierra del Fuego, *in canoes which they seized from the Yapoo Tekenica*. To avoid being separated they fastened several canoes together, crossed over in a body and when once landed, travelled over-land and came upon his people by surprise, from the heights behind Woollya. Jemmy asserted that he had himself killed one of his antagonists.

The Yapoo Tekeenica from whom the Oens-men seized the canoes were probably Yahgans in the area of Ushuaia Bay. If so, this time they didn't join forces with the Selk'nam to attack the Yahgans in Wulaia although apparently they did later (Chapter 9). Note also that these Selk'nam could paddle the canoes, even though they were "foot people," not navigators.

When these "dreaded Oens-men" appeared on the horizon, Jemmy and his family fled to Button Island, taking all of their "valuables" that they had time to collect. They let them steal whatever was left in Wulaia though Jemmy killed one of them. He told Bynoe that after this last attack, he settled on "his own island," Button Island, because it was safer there than Wulaia and had sufficient food.

Fitz-Roy thought: "They [the Oens-men] had doubtless heard of the houses and property left there, and hastened to seize upon it – like other 'borderers.'" That is, the "borderers," the Yahgan enemy, as well as the Selk'nam, were anxious to rob the Yahgans in Wulaia of the gifts given to them by Fitz-Roy. To avoid confusion note that while the "bad" neighbours attacked Jemmy's group early February (1833). before Fitz-Roy had returned to Wulaia, the Oens-men attacked them after Fitz-Roy had left Wulaia, after 14 February (1833). The movements of the Fitz-Roy group were watched closely by all the Fuegians. The news had even spread to the Selk'nam, on the other side of the cordillera.

I return now to 6 March 1834, to the farewell. Byrnoe strolled around Wulaia with Jemmy and Tommy as they pointed out where the tents had been pitched the year before. Jemmy told Bynoe that he had watched the gardens "day after day for the sprouting of peas, beans, and other vegetables," but even so his countrymen trampled over them. The three large wigwams had been deserted after the first frosts because they were too high, too cold to inhabit during the winter.[100]

Farewell Jemmy

Fitz-Roy felt that Jemmy's family was pleased by his return and ready to cooperate with "men of other lands." The first step towards civilisation had been taken. However, Jemmy was "but an individual, with limited means." The attempt to establish a mission with just the three Fuegians was "on too small a scale...[nonetheless] I cannot help still hoping that some benefit, however slight may result from the intercourse of these people, Jemmy, York, and Fuegia, with other natives of Tierra del Fuego. Perhaps a ship-wrecked seaman may hereafter receive help and kind treatment from Jemmy Button's children."

Fitz-Roy wrote this homage to Jemmy:

That Jemmy felt sincere gratitude is, I think, proved by his having so carefully preserved two fine otter skins, as I mentioned; by his asking me to carry a bow and quiver full of arrows to the schoolmaster of Walthamstow, with whom he had lived; by his having made two spear-heads expressly for Mr. Darwin; and by the pleasure he showed at seeing us all again.

The final moment of 6 March had arrived. Fitz-Roy appeared to be sad to leave the Fuegians forever more. "As nothing more could be done, we took leave of our young friend and his family, every one of whom was loaded with presents, and sailed away from Woollya."[101] And Darwin wrote these moving lines:

Every soul on board was heartily sorry to shake hands with him [Jemmy] for the last time. I do not now doubt that he will be as happy as, perhaps happier than, if he had never left his own country. Everyone must sincerely hope that Captain Fitz Roy's noble hope may be fulfilled, of being rewarded for the many generous sacrifices which he made for these Fuegians, by some shipwrecked sailor being protected by the descendants of Jemmy Button and his tribe! When Jemmy reached the shore, he lighted a signal fire, and the smoke curled up, bidding us a last and long farewell, as the ship stood on her course into the open sea.[102]

FIGURE 5.4. Jemmy Button and family bidding farewell to the *Beagle* crew, whom they will never see again.

And here is the text by Loren Eiseley, a Darwin scholar:

His [Darwin's] account of Jemmy Button and the last signal fire lit by the latter in farewell to his white friends as the *Beagle* stood out to sea contains the pathos of great literature.... Charles Darwin came close to envisaging the problem of culture as he bade good-bye to his Indian shipmates. It is perhaps too much to expect of one man in an intellectually confused period that he should have solved both sides of the human mystery, or have distinguished clearly between the biological and the cultural. On that day in his youth, however, in a great surge of human feeling, he stood very close to doing so.[103]

The Third and Last Visit to Tierra del Fuego

After bidding good-bye to Jemmy and his family in Wulaia, they sailed directly to East Falkland Island, for the second and last time (10 March to 7 April 1834), as related above. When they left the Falklands, after their second visit, they proceeded to southern Patagonia, near the entrance to the Magellan Strait, and took a whaleboat up the Santa Cruz River to the foothills of the Andes.

On 16 May (1834), they anchored off Cape Virgins at the very tip of the continental mass, at the entrance to the Magellan Strait. They spent almost two weeks there, "beating about the entrance to the strait, obtaining soundings."

Once in the strait, on 20 May, they stopped over in Gregory Bay, but "our old friends the Indians were not there." Sailing towards Port Famine a few days later, they rescued two "worthless vagabonds" in a pitiful state though in good health. They had deserted a sealing ship and joined the Patagonians, the Tehuelche. Darwin commented: "They had been treated by these Indians with their usual disinterested noble hospitality."[104]

Farewell Alakaluf

The *Beagle* remained in Port Famine the first week of June 1834. Fitz-Roy noted that the Fuegians (Alakalufs) "twice came & plagued us. As there were many instruments, clothes, and men on shore, it was thought necessary to frighten them away." He ordered the crew to fire "a great gun" towards them from a distance. Darwin related: "The first time a few great guns were fired, when they were far distant. It was most ludicrous to watch through a glass the Indians, as often as the shot struck the water, take up stones, and as a bold defiance, throw them towards the ship, though about a mile and a half distant!"[105]

Fitz-Roy sent a boat closer to them and ordered his men to fire musket balls near but not aim to kill. Hiding behind trees, the Alakalufs fired arrows after every musket discharge, which always fell short of the boat. Darwin noted in his diary that "the officer pointed to them & laughing made the Fuegians frantic with rage (as they well might be at so unprovoked an attack); they shook their very mantles with passion." When they saw the musket balls cutting through the trees they fled in their canoes. Fitz-Roy chased them in a whaleboat but soon desisted. Later another group approached the *Beagle* and was driven into a little stream. The next day Fitz-Roy sent two boats and drove them further away. Darwin seemed less amused this time.

It was admirable to see the determination with which four or five men came forward to defend themselves against three times that number. As soon as they saw the boats they advanced 100 yards towards us, prepared a barricade of rotten trees & busily picked up piles of stones for their slings. Every time a musket was pointed towards them, they in return pointed an arrow. . . . I feel sure they would not have moved till more than one had been wounded. This being the case we retreated.[106]

Fitz-Roy and his crew, like other well-armed jokers, sealers, and adventurers, enjoyed taunting the Alakalufs, mocking their efforts to fend off attacks. This was Fitz-Roy's and the *Beagle* crew's final farewell to the Fuegians.[107]

The "Destiny" of the Alakaluf

By 1900, the Alakaluf had been almost "wiped out" by the diseases they caught from outsiders and the alcoholic drinks they were offered and later sought. Among the small groups that remained, some pieced together their lives, working for their Chilean neighbours, selling fish in the markets in Chiloé and Punta Arenas. At times they sold fish and baskets, from their canoes, to seamen and tourists in passing ships. A community of Alakaluf, who prefer to be called Kaweskar, live in Puerto Eden, on Wellington Island, in about the middle of the Pacific archipelago. Nine or ten speak their language as well as Spanish. Several are college graduates as sophisticated as any anthropologist. They are determined to develop their Kaweskar identity and not let it drown in the deep waters of the fiords.[108]

1834–1836: The Long Voyage Back to England

The *Beagle* sailed through the recently surveyed Magdalena and Cockburn channels and entered the Pacific on 10 June 1834 and, on 2 October 1836, docked at Falmouth, near Plymouth. Thanks to the scholarly work of the last decades, this part of the voyage is well known.[109] On the last pages of Darwin's third volume of the *Narration of the Surveying Voyages of H.M.S. Adventure and Beagle* and his often cited book, *The Voyage of the Beagle*, he wrote "On the 2nd of October we made the shores of England; and at Falmouth I left the *Beagle*, having lived on board the good little vessel nearly five years."[110]

Home At Last

Keynes added: "That same night, and a dreadfully stormy one it was, Charles took the mail coach home to Shrewsbury, where he arrived after two days on the road. After a joyful reunion with his father and sisters...."[111]

And Janet Browne: "He walked into The Mount [Shrewsbury], just before breakfast on Wednesday, 5 October, five years and three days after leaving home. 'Why,' said his father, 'the shape of his head is quite altered.'"[112]

From Then On...
Soon thereafter Darwin visited his brother, Erasmus, in London, and went to Cambridge to greet Professor Henslow, who had been such an essential friend and support during the long voyage. Back in London, he met the great geologist Charles Lyell. From then on, he contacted the variety of scientists involved with the specimens he had sent to Henslow.[113]

Forty Years Later, Darwin Recalls His Voyage
The voyage of the Beagle has been by far the most important event in my life and has determined my whole career.... I have always felt that I owe to the voyage the first real training or education of my mind. Looking backwards I can now perceive how my love for science gradually preponderated over every other taste... the sense of sublimity, which the great deserts of Patagonia and the forest clad mountains of Tierra del Fuego excited in me, has left an indelible impression on my mind. The sight of a naked savage in his native land is an event which can never be forgotten.[114]

Fitz-Roy Back in England
Fitz-Roy undertook the laborious task of compiling the first volume of the *Narrative of the Surveying Voyages of H.M.S. Adventure and Beagle*, which was partly written and signed by King. In 1839 he completed his volume, the second of the *Narrative...*, and his *Sailing Directions for South America*. He checked the numerous coastal sheets, plans of harbours and views brought back from both voyages. His charts and his sailing directions were still in use in the 1970s. By then the Instituto Hidrográfico of the Chilean Navy began publishing a very extensive series of extremely detailed maps as well as sailing directions (*Derroteros*), that

have outdated some of Fitz-Roy's. Darwin's biographer and granddaughter, Nora Barlow, felt that Fitz-Roy had never received due recognition for his contributions.[115]

And... The Beagle

The "heroic little ship...the good little ship" was taken on another expedition to Australia the following year, under the command of Wickham. She then served as a coastguard and, from 1847 to 1870, as a "collier," transporting coal. Finally, as Keith Thomson discovered, at the age of fifty, she was ignominiously sold for scrap.[116]

6

1838 to 1843: United States and Great Britain Antarctic Expeditions Encounter the Yamana

The encounters of the Yamana with the United States and the British expeditions to the Antarctic region were incidental occurrences. The captains and crews of the two expeditions met the natives when, for one reason or another they stopped over in Tierra del Fuego either going to or coming from the Antarctic (it was not yet known as a continent). The Yamana became actors in these great events because they were curious about the outsiders and went to meet them. Neither expedition proposed to study them, as a French expedition will some forty years from now (Chapter 13).

1838 to 1842: The First US Expedition to the Antarctic; Its Formation and Objectives

During the 1820s, wealthy Yankee sealers, discouraged by not having located more rockeries in the southern latitudes, began lobbying the federal government to finance and organise an expedition along the shores of the Antarctic. The commercial whalers were not involved because by 1788 they had already penetrated the great Pacific (Chapter 2).

In 1828, the US Congress authorized such an expedition, but only with one ship. When it was finally organised ten years later, it was comprised of six ships with Lieutenant Charles Wilkes as commander.

The crews of the six ships totalled only 440 men, including twenty-five "scientifics" and two artists. They were all young men; Wilkes, at age forty, was the oldest. "We are all in the spring time of life," commented Midshipman William Reynolds.[1] Among the scientists, James Dwight Dana will become one of the United States' greatest geologists.

The fleet, or squadron, that departed from the Virginia coast in August 1838 consisted of the following ships:

1. *Vincennes*, the flagship, a 700-tone sloop (three masts) of war carrying guns on one deck
2. *Peacock*, another sloop of war, 559 tones
3. *Porpoise*, a 224-tone brig (two masts)
4. *Flying Fish*, a smaller two-mast schooner, to be used as a pilot boat and tender attentive to the needs of the three larger ships
5. *Sea-Gull*, the other schooner, also a pilot boat and tender
6. *Relief*, the supply ship, which accommodated some of the scientists and artists[2]

It was one of the last grand sailing expeditions and the first US scientific voyage to explore the Antarctic region, the shores and islands of the Pacific, and to return by circumnavigating the globe.

The sealers and their financiers were of course not familiar with the problems the scientists were seeking to solve. They were concerned mainly with the commercial interest of locating prey. Some supporters were keen on testing the "holes in the poles" theory proposed by John C. Symmes Jr., a self-styled "Newton of the West." The heartbeat of his "holes" theory was based on four hypotheses: His first – the earth is hollow. If so, the second hypothesis – entrances to its interior might be found in the holes, which, the third hypothesis – the hole might well exist near the North Pole. If so, the fourth hypothesis – why not also near the South Pole? Therefore the expedition could reasonably be expected to discover at least one hole near the South Pole, to the embarrassment of the scientists, who must not have wanted to waste the expedition's time and funds as well as jeopardize their reputations on such a surrealistic quatralogy of hypotheses.

Quite aside from the expedition's commercial commitments and an assignment in the Fiji Islands (see below), its scientific objectives (excluding the holes) were of the utmost importance. The geographers were very anxious to have the Antarctic region charted and surveyed. The geologists, geophysicists, and meteorologists felt committed to discovering whether the south polar region was like the north polar region, only pack ice, or if, beneath the south polar region's ice and snow, lay a continent, a land mass, earth, soil, dirt. They also hoped to gain a better understanding of the fluctuations of the compasses. By then it was known that the compasses responded to forces emitted from two magnetic poles. The English navigator Captain James Ross had recently located the North

Magnetic Pole, about a thousand miles (1,852 kilometres) from the North Pole. If the South Magnetic Pole could be located, this would answer certain questions concerning terrestrial magnetism, and greatly facilitate navigation by helping to solve the problem of the fluctuating compasses. By then, the geophysicists had assumed that the South Magnetic Pole was not at the South Pole or even very near it.

Captain Ross will appear in the Antarctic shortly after Lieutenant Wilkes, hoping to locate the South Magnetic Pole, and to explore the area – a real challenge.[3]

Wilkes will stumble upon another rival: Captain Jules-Sébastien César Dumont d'Urville, the commander of a French expedition, who had similar objectives in addition to setting up the French flag wherever he might. Urville was already famous for having acquired the Venus de Milo for France in 1820. Thus United States, England and France were vying to claim the honours of discovery in a virtually unknown area, perhaps even of a seventh continent, at the bottom of beyond.

In addition to the motives of the military, the scientists, the artists, the sealers and the would-be Newton, there was considerable enthusiasm among the public, whose patriotic fervour moved them to contribute funds to this extravagant undertaking. Despite their generous support and although Congress had authorized it in 1828, the latter was extremely slow to follow up such a costly endeavour. Congressional controversies went on for ten years concerning the expedition's plan, its objectives, its routes, the selection of the scientific staff, the number and types of ships, and so on. Finally the day and place of departure were set: 18 August 1838, from Norfolk, Virginia.

Wilkes' Expedition – A Success, Stunned by Failures

The instructions given to Wilkes were demanding. The task of fulfilling them was aggravated by the dangers of navigating in virtually uncharted seas with a leaky and poorly equipped fleet. Charles Erskine, one of Wilkes' seamen and author of *Twenty Years before the Mast*, was outspoken: "The English admiral's [Ross'] ships, the *Erebus* and *Terror*, were unlike the Frenchmen's [Urville's] and our ships. They were so strongly built that they were forced through a thick belt of ice two hundred miles into an open sea beyond. Our ships would have been completely destroyed before they could have penetrated one quarter of the distance."[4]

Jean-René Vanney, the French marine historian, affirmed: "None of the vessels [Wilkes' six] were prepared for the difficult tasks which awaited them." Accidents and adversities were inevitable. The most devastating, in human terms, took place on 1 May 1839, when the *Sea-Gull*, one of the pilot boats, went down with a crew of fifteen men, after departing from Orange Bay near Cape Horn. Three of the other ships – the *Relief*, the *Flying Fish* and the *Porpoise* – fared better, but not better enough. Wilkes sent the *Relief* home from Australia the following November, because it could not keep up with the rest of the squadron. Not everyone believed his motive: some contended that the reason was to rid the expedition of several officers, the "supposed trouble-makers." The *Flying Fish* had to be sold in Singapore and the *Porpoise* went aground in July 1841 at the mouth of the Columbia River, northwestern United States. The crew were saved but not the ship, nor the scientific collections. Minor and not-so-minor incidents were numerous. For instance, the gun ports of the warships were poorly fitted and leaky. On 4 March 1839, near Weddell Sea, the temperature had fallen to 28°F (2.2°C). Wilkes complained bitterly that his men were suffering from the "inferior" clothing the government had purchased at great expense.[5] Wilkes added: "This was the case with all the articles of this description that were provided for the expedition."[6]

A crew of exceptional stamina and a highly gifted commanding officer were required for such a difficult four-year mission with such defective ships and equipment. Herman Viola portrayed Commander Wilkes as "having the vision, intelligence and determination to do the job. He gave the expedition its distinctive stamp. Aloof, stern and resolute, he drove himself even harder than he drove his ships and men. His sense of mission and national pride dictated high standards of performance and accomplishment."

Of the 440 men of the original crew, fifteen had drowned, 127 deserted, including officers, in addition to eighty-eight seamen and officers who were sent home by Wilkes, and the two assassinated by Fiji natives. Only two of the original six ships with less than half (208 men) of the original crew returned to the United States in June 1842. Wilkes was certainly not uniquely responsible for the diminished fleet or for the desertions, miseries, and dissatisfaction of his men, but his personality, "aloof, stern and resolute," must have created floating nightmares for the crew. In view of the expedition's serious impediments, its extraordinary accomplishments were undoubtedly due to the perseverance of the scientists, artists and crew, most of whom did their very best, as Wilkes did, however "aloof" he apparently was.[7]

In *Magnificent Voyagers*, a rather recent publication of the Smithsonian Institution, Herman Viola recalled some of the expedition's little-known feats, though the last cited (in italics below) is disputed.

In less than four years, this gallant naval squadron of six small ships surveyed 280 islands and constructed 180 charts, some of which were still being used as late as World War II. The Expedition mapped eight hundred miles of the coast of the Oregon territory; it explored some fifteen hundred miles of the Antarctic coast, *thereby proving the existence of the seventh continent.*

Assume for the moment that Wilkes did prove the existence of the seventh continent, as affirmed above by Viola (see below note 12). The thousands of specimens and native objects gathered and the numerous drawings and paintings, both natural and cultural contributed to the first scientific collections of the recently founded Smithsonian Institution and of the National Museum, both in Washington, DC. The scientists and artists did a great deal to promote the incipient profession of the natural sciences in the United States. However, the entrepreneurs of the sealing industry were "disappointed" to say the least. In 1952, Raymond Rydell commented, "Though he spent part of 1839 and 1840 in the Antarctic, Wilkes uncovered nothing to encourage the sealers."[8] Recall (Chapter 2) that by 1830 the seals in the Antarctic had been largely exterminated.

The documentation the scientists brought home was enormous: 4,000 zoological specimens, about half of which were new species, and more than 50,000 plant specimens, including almost 10,000 different species. They also collected numerous fossils, minerals (and gems), corals and rock samples as well as thousands of indigenous artistic and utilitarian objects. The artists, the scientists and Wilkes himself had made superb drawings and paintings of native people, landscapes and seascapes, flora and fauna.

And Vendovi, the brother of a Fijian king, had been captured. Wilkes had orders from the navy brass in Washington, DC, to proceed to the Fiji Islands and capture those who, five years earlier, had assassinated ten crew members of an American ship. In 1840 Wilkes' squadron spent three months there. The king of Rewa (one of the main Fiji Islands) and his court were invited on board the *Peacock* and held hostages until the king handed over at least one culprit. A month later Vendovi, the king's brother, was delivered to the *Vincennes*. According to Wilkes, Vendovi confessed to taking part in the assassinations. While the expedition was still there, the natives of Malolo, another Fiji Island, killed two officers who had gone ashore, one of whom was Wilkes' nephew. Wilkes retaliated; two principal towns of Malolo Island were destroyed and about eighty Fijians killed for these two officers. The eighty Fijians may have been partially or completely innocent, but this is beside the point. More to the point, the Fijians were taught a lesson and Wilkes had a culprit – Vendovi.[9]

Arrival and Controversies

After four long years, on 10 June 1842, the *Vincennes*, the flagship with Wilkes at the helm, sailed into New York Harbour. Upon docking, Vendovi was rushed to the nearest naval hospital, where he died three days later. The *Peacock* arrived three weeks after Wilkes. Recall that the expedition had rendered imperial justice in Fiji, had made prodigious scientific contributions, and had brought home natural and cultural treasures. But were the expeditionaries hailed as patriotic benefactors, upon their arrival (in June 1842)? Much to the contrary: Wilkes and his weary scientists and seamen met a disinterested public, an unfriendly Congress, and doubts concerning their accomplishments in the Antarctic region. The probity of the commander himself was questioned; he was subject to two court martials owing to accusations by several of his junior officers, all of which further "clouded the Expedition's notable achievements." Eleven charges were brought against Wilkes, though he was only found guilty of "illegally punishing, or causing to be punished, men in the squadron under his command." Wilkes' punishment consisted of a public reprimand by the Secretary of the Navy, which took place on 7 September 1842.[10]

Even his claim to have discovered the seventh continent was questioned during his lifetime. It is no exaggeration to say that he was furious with President John Tyler. He was outraged that a court martial had refused to recognize that he had discovered that the Antarctic was a continent: earth, not simply ice and snow. He expressed his deep resentment as follows: "There never was so dastardly an attempt to persecute me, as well as to deprive the Country of the honor and glory it had obtained.... It was a diabolical attempt to do injury and wrong to gratify political spite on the former administration of [the then President] Mr. Van Buren, but the nation was silent under it."[11]

But did Wilkes, in January 1840, sailing from New Zealand, "discover" that the area of Antarctic was land mass, a continent, and not simply coastal islets, scattered patches of rocks, and enormous mass of ice packs? Admittedly there was a fine line to be drawn. Was he the first to report and furnish convincing proof that the Antarctic region was a continent – solid earth – even though it lay far beneath all that snow and ice? Or was he deluded by the mirages that give the appearance of land? Moorehead explained: "The mirages in the Antarctic had a clarity that was almost beyond belief, and made it difficult for an explorer to know whether he was seeing land or not." Wilkes and his men were not able to go ashore because of the impenetrable ice barrier, so the sightings were taken from his ship. Moreover, a really extraordinary coincidence occurred: the sightings were registered the same year, month, and day – 19 January 1840 – as those of Admiral Dumont d'Urville, the famous French explorer. Did Urville make the discovery a few hours earlier or ten hours later than Wilkes? Or is it possible that three days earlier, on 16 January, two of Wilkes' midshipmen sighted "distant mountains" from the *Peacock* and simply failed to note their observations in the ship's log? Apparently the question is still pending, as is whether Wilkes or Urville or neither should be credited with this discovery.[12] No one doubted, however, that Wilkes was the first to call that frozen expanse "the Antarctic Continent." Wilkes "defeated" Urville in the naming game. Not only the continent but also fifteen hundred miles of coast, along which he sailed, is now called Wilkes Land. The names of Urville and Adélie, his wife, only designate localities along the shore of Wilkes Land. A penguin was also named for Adélie. These were meagre rewards for Urville, but really tragic was the destiny awaiting him, his wife and son. The three were killed in a train accident a year or so after returning to France.

Moorehead suggested that the Russian explorer Baron Thaddeus Bellingshausen, in 1820, may have been the first to have reported that the Antarctic is a continent. Moorehead recognised Bellingshausen as a great admirer of Cook, saying that his "reports were always sensible and illuminating and bring to a conclusion the work of discovery which Cook began half a century before." And more to the point, according to Moorehead: "The Russians crossed the Antarctic Circle early 1820 and two weeks later they almost certainly caught sight of the Antarctic mainland – probably the first ever to do so."[13]

Almost ninety years will pass before the United States sends a second expedition to Antarctica, under Admiral Byrd.

Wilkes Published a Great Deal
Despite the resentment that Wilkes felt for the unjust and ungrateful treatment he had received from President Tyler and his peers, he spent many years, between 1847 and 1849 and after the Civil War to 1874, preparing the findings of the expedition for publication. First he completed his own reports in five volumes and an atlas. Then he edited all the rest of the

expedition's reports that were published in no less than twenty volumes and eleven atlases. But even this amazing production became a target. Wilkes was said to have assumed the authorship of the twenty volumes that were largely the work of the scientists, His name "might better have appeared as compiler, a more modest office, but an honorable one if competently performed," according to William Stanton. Wilkes was shielded from further accusations by dying in 1877, three years after completing this monumental publication. Once he ceased to be "a thorny public figure, [he] was hailed posthumously for his great Antarctic achievements," according to another scholar, Walker Chapman.[14]

Having so briefly traced some outstanding attributes of the expedition, we turn now to this expedition's "encounters" with the Fuegians.

The Haush Greet the Expeditionaries

When the fleet of six ships weighed out from Virginia in August 1838, Wilkes ordered Lieutenant George M. Colvocoresses to proceed with the supply ship, *Relief*, to Orange Harbour, Hoste Island, near Cape Horn and to begin preparations for the expedition to the Antarctic. Five months later, the *Relief* stopped over in Good Success Bay on the way to Orange Bay. Wilkes, who was not present, wrote part of the text much later, drawing from the *Relief*'s log. Colvocoresses also published his experience in a book: *Four Years in a Government Exploring Expedition*.

On 23 January (1839), the day after he entered the bay, Colvocoresses sighted several natives hailing his ship. When he and other crewmen reached the beach in three armed boats, fourteen – or seventeen according to Wilkes – unarmed Haush came running towards them, suddenly stopped, placed their hands upon their breasts as a welcome greeting, and for some unknown reason pointed to the ground. Then they started shouting *cuchillo*. The crew thought *cuchillo* was a native word, a kind of salutation. Actually the Haush were asking for knives, *cuchillos* in Spanish. The old man, the chief, repeated *cuchillo* as he advanced to salute them, first patting his own breast several times and then likewise to each of the crew, one by one. Perhaps among them were the four who had encountered Darwin and Fitz-Roy seven years earlier in December 1832 (Chapter 4).

The *Relief*'s crew were not aghast at their appearance, as Darwin had been, although Wilkes wrote, that they were "filthy and disgusting." As in 1832, all the native men, except their chief, were young, well formed and good-looking. One of the tallest was over six feet. Their hair was cut short on the crown, and a narrow border of long hair was kept in place by a band made of the skin of an albatross. (The haircut was a sign of mourning.) Each wore the usual knee-length cape of guanaco fur and just one sandal – supposedly I assume, because one is sufficient to grip the soil when descending a hill. Their front teeth were worn down, especially those of the old man; and their faces painted with red and white clay. Wilkes added that they were "entirely different from the Petcherais [meaning the Yamana] whom we saw [would see] in Orange Harbor." Colvocoresses noticed that they were admirable mimics and that they "appeared to understand" some words in English. They refused to accept tobacco, whiskey, bread and meat and made known that they wanted nails, and pieces of hoop-iron, as well as knives. Wilkes, from Colvoresses' log, added that their food consisted mainly of shellfish and fish, for which they used a thin slip of whalebone as a hook. Shaking their heads, they declined to come on board the ship, despite the offers of more presents, "as if they feared that we intended to carry them off by force" (see below).[15] The Haush still welcomed strangers, although by now they had become apprehensive.

Encountering the Yamana

Following two days in Good Success Bay, 25 January, the *Relief* headed for Orange Bay. On the way, having crossed Nassau Bay, the ship entered a large, beautiful bay surrounded by undulating hills covered with ever-green foliage. They called it Relief Harbor, which is not on the Chilean maps I consulted. It probably corresponds to Scotchwell Bay located just north of Orange Bay. A canoe approached the ship, carrying three men, a woman and a child. "Upon invitation two of the men came on board without manifesting the slightest hesitation or distrust." The woman, who remained in the canoe holding her three-year-old child, was only clothed in a small piece of sealskin, despite the cold weather. She was "no better looking than the men and appeared to take an equal share with them in the labours of the paddle." The two men bartered their bows and arrows for clothes, which so greatly pleased them that they immediately put them on and delighted the crew as "they moved about with strut-ting affectation of dignity, and gave themselves a thousand consequential airs." Colvocoresses was astonished by their accuracy as they imitated the tunes of a flute and a guitar that the crewmen played for them. They spoke in a whisper to each other, often bursting into loud laughter. But when they discovered they were being watched, "they looked as grave as judges, and said but little." The crew learned that they used their spears to kill seals, which abounded in the nearby bays.

When Colvocoresses and other seamen went on shore the next day, yesterday's friends, "immediately commenced jumping up and down, which is their mode of expressing friendship." One of them had a pair of yesterday's "pantaloons" tied round his neck. Their conical log hut (a wigwam) looked neat and comfortable. The floor was swept clean, and a large fire was burning in the centre, over which hung a string of fish. Nearby some shells were carefully laid out on clean leaves. The woman, who had been given a blanket the day before, had fled with her child and didn't return.[16]

The following day, probably 27 January (1839), the *Relief* sailed into Orange Bay with no problem, thanks to Fitz-Roy's sailing directions, which Wilkes praised highly.[17] Five men and an old woman approached the vessel in a canoe twenty-five feet (7.6 metres) long and three feet (0.9 metres) wide. Note that this Yamana canoe was remarkably long, as the maximum reported by John Cooper was twenty feet (6 metres).[18]

The six natives remained in their canoe, exchanging spearheads and shell necklaces for pieces of iron and handkerchiefs. When they were motioned by the sailors to come on board, a "rather good-looking youth" was the first to climb on the deck, and the other four men followed rapidly. The old woman, who remained in the canoe, was said to be "extremely ugly." The black and red vertical lines painted on her face did not enhance her appearance. Later they were seen fishing in the kelp for a while; then they returned to their "bee-hive hut." Colvocoresses visited them, and noticed the clay floor and that the fire in the centre was situated a few inches below the level of the floor.[19] He was one of the few outsiders to recognise that the bee-hive hut, despite its pitiful appearance, afforded an adequate shelter, nearly impervious to wind and snow, and that being so close to the ground, it conserved the heat.

The last day of January, Colvocoresses and six seamen rowed to nearby Burnt Island. While making observations of the tide, they greeted the men of the beehive hut, who were busy gathering berries. Besides mention of the disagreeable weather and the variety of birds they shot there, he reported nothing more about these Fuegians.

The Fleet Meet the Yamana in Orange Bay
The other five ships pulled into Orange Bay during this week (17–25 February) when the preparations were completed "for a short cruise to the Antarctic." Most of the crews were shocked upon seeing "savages" for the first time. Some pitied the "poor naked savages" shivering at their side, others admired their "handsome fish spears," ten feet (3 metres)

long, each tipped with a whale tooth. One midshipman recognised, "some ingenuity" in the construction of their canoes and their low oval huts, and blamed their "abject misery and wretchedness" on the "chilling, desolate or dreary country where even civilization would be of no avail."[20]

Wilkes was in Orange Bay between 19 and 25 February. Having read Captain Cook, he also confused these Yamana with the "Petcherai Indians," the Alakaluf, along the north shore of Magellan Strait. Wilkes thought they were "an ill-shaped and ugly race" and that it was "impossible to fancy anything in human nature more filthy." Apart from these and other unflattering remarks, he noticed a pile of mussel and limpet shells that was nearly as large as the hut it fronted and was amused that they were so pleased to receive pieces of red flannel, which they tore into thin strips and wound around their heads, giving the effect of turbans.

He deduced that they were seen only in their canoes and in their shoreline huts because Hoste Island's hinterland consists of almost impenetrable mountainous terrain carpeted with "quagmires" (bogs), thick forests cluttered with dead trees and dense undergrowth of thorny bushes. As he noted, they rarely ventured inland except to gather or cut firewood and to extract bark to make canoes and pails.

Charles Erskine, mentioned above, related that while in Orange Bay they saw many Fuegians who "were highly delighted and surprised at everything they saw." But he did his bit to perpetuate the defamation of them. Obviously paraphrasing Darwin, he wrote: "The Terre del Fuegians seem but little above the brute creation, and are the lowest in the scale of humanity." But Erskine is not the only one to do so. In 1968, David Tyler, though a professor of history, wrote these comments about the Orange Bay Yamana who greeted the Wilkes expeditionaries: "A few rather shy, unprepossessing-looking and uncivilised-acting natives made their appearance."[21]

The United States' First Attempt to Explore the Antarctic Area
As mentioned above, in January 1840, US expedition sailing from New Zealand, Wilkes discovered, or thought he did, that the Antarctic region is a continent. For their first trip to the Antarctic, a year before, on 25 February (1839), they set out from Orange Bay but only spent ten days there because of adverse weather. Wilkes, in the *Porpoise*, led the squadron. The four ships reached the islands off the Antarctic Peninsula, then sailed on to the large bay, the Weddell Sea, where they were forced to turn back on 5 March, daunted by an imposing ice shelf in the bay. On this first exploration they were unable to explore the Antarctic. Viola

clarified: "The weather was so bad the ships could not sail in company, and most of them returned without accomplishing anything. Wilkes, however, found enough indications of land to justify a more extended attempt the following year."

For this first voyage there was only one scientist present. The other twenty-three scientists, who did not go to the Antarctic, were probably disappointed when Wilkes told or ordered them to board the *Relief* and proceed in the opposite direction, to the Magellan Strait and then on to Valparaíso, the site of the next rendezvous. Wilkes, however, promised them that they would go to the Antarctic during the second "cruse" the following year. During this first expedition to the Antarctic, the *Vincennes*, the flagship, remained in Orange Bay to survey the area. This time the crew did admit that they were disappointed.[22]

Meanwhile in Orange Bay with the Yamana

Wilkes is the only source, although he was not present, for the following events (late February and March 1839), which I call eight scenes. Wilkes must have gathered his information from the logs of the *Vincennes'* crew.

First Scene: A Music Session

In Orange Bay, soon after most of the expedition had departed, three canoes came paddling towards the *Vincennes* carrying several families, including a one-week-old baby. Two of the men came on board and bartered their spears, a dog, and "rude native trinkets" for goods, not mentioned. They were only interested in the ship's carpenter, who was busy boring a hole with a screw-auger through a plank.[23] Their blasé attitude was compensated by their good humour. "They were very talkative, smiling when spoken to, and often bursting into loud laughter, but instantly settling into their natural serious and sober cast."

It occurred to the crew to test the accuracy and range of these "truly astonishing" mimics by asking them to repeat the scales played on a violin.

One of them ascended and descended the octave perfectly, following the sound of the violin correctly. It was then found he could sound the common chords, and follow through the semitone scale, with scarcely an error. They all have musical voices, speak in the note G sharp, ending with the semitone A when asking for presents, and were continually singing.

Their extraordinary ear for music was undoubtedly part of their ability to mimic. However their chants, like those of the Selk'nam, were ignored by outsiders until Charles Wellington Furlong and Martin Gusinde recorded some of them and the German musicologist Erich von Hornbostel analysed and commented upon them.[24]

After awhile their mimicry began to annoy the *Vincennes* crew, as it "precluded our getting at any of their words or ideas." For instance, when one of the crew pointed to his nose, to inquire the word for it, "they did the same. Anything they saw done they would mimic, and with an extraordinary degree of accuracy."

Second Scene: "Children for Sale" and a Look in a Mirror

When the two men came on board the *Vincennes*, the women, as usual, remained in the canoes. "They never move from a sitting posture, or rather a squat, with their knees close together, reaching to the chin, their feet in contact, and touching the lower part of the body. They are extremely ugly." Although they appeared to be very fond of their children, they were said, on several occasions, to offer them for sale to the crew for a trifle. I suggest that the crew misinterpreted the women when they held up their babies or young children while making some sort of gesture. Like the much vaunted "sale" for a button of Jemmy Button, these women would probably have refused to sell their children for any thing the navigators could offer (Chapter 3).

Their small, well-shaped hands gave the impression that they were not accustomed to hard work, which is contrary to the usual observation of the women doing strenuous labour. Wilkes also reported that the husbands, being exceedingly jealous, made their wives "hideous" with paint and smut. One had been made so repulsive that when she saw at herself in a mirror the sailors held up to her, she burst into tears "from pure mortification."

If the husbands deliberately made their women hideous by painting them, such a tactic was at times justified. Later on there are reports that some of the sealers raped the Fuegian women. However, at this time there was no such danger. The officers even offered to paint them, using the usual back, white and red paint. "This delighted them very much, and it was quite amusing to see the grimaces made by them before a looking glass."

Third Scene: Jim Orange's Week on Board the Vincennes

One of the young men, whom the crew called Jim Orange, was invited to sit at the ship's dinner table. After a few lessons, he used the knife and fork with much dexterity. "He refused both spirits and wine, but was very fond of sweetened water. Salt provisions were not at all to his liking, but rice and plum-pudding were agreeable to his taste, and he literally crammed them into his mouth."

Following this tasty meal, in good humour he sang *hey meh leh*, while dancing and laughing. After being washed several shades lighter and dressed in a seaman's garb, he attended the divine service. Greatly astonished, his eyes were riveted on the chaplain reading from "the book." He may well have imagined that the book was talking to the reader, as Weddell's audience had (Chapter 2). After a week, Jim Orange became bored, was taken on shore, "and soon appeared naked again."[25]

Fourth Scene: A Fashion Show

The crew was "extremely anxious" to please their guests. Jack (Jim Orange) directed the show on the *Vincennes* for the crew and the public of natives that were "not disposed to allow any difficulties to interfere in the fitting." Jack slit down the back of the jackets that were too tight across the shoulders. If a pair of trousers that was too small around the waist, Jack made it fit in the same manner, "and in some cases a fit was made by severing the legs."

The star model of the show was a woman in one of the canoes. When an old coat was given to her, she thrust her feet through the sleeves and succeeded in squeezing into them. "With the skirts brought up in front, she took her seat in the canoe with great satisfaction, amid a roar of laughter from all who saw her."

Fifth Scene: With a Jolly Scientist

That early March 1839, when three canoes appeared again and some of the men went on board, Couthouy, last name of one of the scientists, a conchologist (a specialist in marine mollusks), "hoping to break down their reserve," took one of the natives by the hand, "singing, waltzed him around the deck." The native followed both steps and notes exactly. Arm in arm they "figured away" to the amusement of the onlookers. Couthouy was aware that some of the officers and crew would find such an exhibition "excessively ridiculous." But he had a purpose: "we must, to win confidence...unbend a little...& consent for a time to be all things to all men."

Sixth Scene: The Life They Led

The Fuegians' main food was limpets, mussels, other shellfish and fish, which were found in great quantities in the kelp. Some seals "are now and then taken among the kelp." Also during March, the crew noticed the men building a temporary hut on the shore of Orange Bay, which took them only about an hour, while the women remained in the canoes. "The little children were seen capering quite naked on the beach, although the thermometre was at 40 [°F]." When the hut was finished, the women went on shore to occupy it. "They all seemed quite happy and contented."

Seventh Scene: Visiting the Natives at Home
Some time during March, two members of the *Vincennes'* crew, Tom Waldron and Joseph Drayton, one of the artists, visited the natives. Upon landing, a man greeted them and seemed anxious to communicate with them. "He pointed to the ship, and tried to express many things by gestures; then pointed to the south-east, and then again to the ship, after which clasping his hands, as in our mode of prayer, he said, 'Eloah, Eloah,' as though he thought we had come from God." This interpretation of the native's gestures recalls similar conjectures made by D'Arquisade in 1715 and Weddell in 1823 (Chapters 1 and 2).

Once on the beach, Waldron and Drayton joined in the welcome ritual by jumping up and down with their hosts, who repeated their welcome by taking hold of their arms, facing them, and jumping two or three inches from the ground, while keeping time, "to a wild music [chanting] of their own." The greetings completed, the two guests crept through a small entrance and saw the women, "squatted three deep behind the men, the oldest in front nestling the infant." The women were holding out small pieces of sealskin towards the fire to trap the heat. Then they pressed the sealskins to their bodies, an ingenious method of warming themselves. This is all that was told about the visit.

Eighth and Last Scene: An Unexpected Bye-Bye
The families left Orange Bay at the end of March, before the rest of the squadron had returned. They took off with pieces of the *Vincennes'* wind sails, which had been scrubbed and hung out to dry along shore. Wilkes observed: "They are much addicted to theft, if any opportunity offers." The pieces of sail must have been spare ones, as there was no further mention of this loss.

Wilkes concluded that "they do not want" thanks to their diet of shellfish and fish, which abounded in the bay, and some seals, berries and wild celery.

Wollaston Islanders Please Wilkes

After being obliged to leave the Antarctic on 5 March, Wilkes in the *Porpoise*, perhaps with one or more ships of his squadron, headed towards Le Maire Strait and, from 17 to 20 March stopped over in Good Success Bay, apparently without seeing anyone there. Then while sailing back towards Orange Bay, he spent a few hours on the Wollaston Islands.

Recall Darwin's judgement of six Wollaston Islanders just five years earlier. "These were the most abject and miserable creatures I anywhere beheld.... Viewing such men, one can hardly make oneself believe that they are fellow creatures, and inhabitants of the same world."[26] On 30 March (1839) Wilkes had a different impression of the six Wollaston Islanders he encountered. Two old women, two young men and two children were singing *hey meh leh* in a canoe as they approached his ship. "The expression of the younger ones was extremely prepossessing, evincing intelligence and good humor." They quickly climbed on board and "ate ham and bread voraciously, distending their large mouths, and showing a strong and beautiful set of teeth." After they had tied the usual strips of red flannel around their heads, one of the seamen played a fife for them. Wilkes was enchanted.

They seemed much struck with the sound.... We found them, also, extremely imitative, repeating our words and mimicking our motions. They were all quite naked. *I have seldom seen so happy a group. They were extremely lively and cheerful, and any thing but miserable*, if we could have avoided contrasting their condition with our own.... Their heads were covered with ashes, but their exterior left a pleasing impression. Contentment was pictured in the countenances and actions, and produced a moral effect that will long be remembered.[27]

This was indeed a joyful greeting and farewell. The difference between Darwin's and Wilkes' impressions of six Wollaston Yamana is striking, perhaps partly because Darwin was simply observing them, looking at them, while Wilkes and his men played a fife for them and joked with them. More contrasts of "encounters," with identical people (though not always the same individuals) will occur in the following chapters.

The Antarctic Squadron Back in Orange Bay

From Wollaston the *Porpoise* returned to Orange Bay on that same day, 30 March. Erskine seemed glad to meet the Yamana again, about whom he had written with such contempt. "We had no sooner come to anchor than we were visited by the natives. They are great mimics and are very fond of music. Our fifer played for them 'My Bonny Lad,' 'Sweet Home,' and 'The Girl I Left Behind Me.'" They did not react to these songs, but when the "The Bonnets of Blue" was played, they kept time to the rhythm.[28] Like true musicians, the Yahgan had discriminating taste.

The three other ships arrived in Orange Bay during the following days. In April the *Sea-Gull* and the *Flying Fish* departed heading for Valparaíso. But as noted above, the *Sea-Gull* "became exposed to heavy blasts and high Seas" and sank, with her crew of fifteen men.

The *Vincennes* and *Porpoise* were the last to leave Orange Bay on 20 April 1839. The squadron, now reduced to five ships, reunited in Valparaíso and sailed up the Pacific coast, on to new adventures. In January and February of the following year, the expedition made its second and last trip to the Antarctic, referred to at the beginning of this chapter, when Wilkes coincided with Urville. After circling the globe in June of 1842, the *Vincennes* and the *Peacock* docked in New York Harbour, having completed the most outstanding expedition ever, for the United States, thanks to the scientists, the artists and the crews but Wilkes' troubles were not over, as noted above.[29]

1839 to 1843: A Famous British Arctic Explorer Is Assigned to the Antarctic Region

The British appointed Sir James Clark Ross, their most competent "man for the task," to explore the Antarctic. He had joined the Royal Navy at the age of twelve. Six years later, in 1818, he was further schooled by Admiral Sir John Ross, his uncle, and by Commander William Edward Parry during the expedition in search of a northwest passage to the Pacific. He participated in three more Arctic expeditions, between 1819 and 1833. During the latter, he and his uncle travelled with the Eskimos and studied their mode of living in that extreme climate, far colder than Tierra del Fuego. In 1831 they became famous for having located the North Magnetic Pole, at 70°51' north latitude. It has since shifted several miles northward.[30]

In 1839, Captain Ross hoped to locate the South Magnetic Pole as well as survey and explore the Antarctic coasts. His expedition, like Wilkes', lasted nearly four years, from 1839 to 1843. Although Wilkes and Urville preceded him to the Antarctic, Ross had the great advantage of his detailed knowledge of polar navigation given his long experience in the Arctic. His two ships were also far superior to Wilkes', his crews were highly trained, and he was able to offer them excellent care.

Ross made three explorations in the Antarctic. I will only refer to his first, early in 1841, when he discovered one of earth's most amazing phenomena, the Ross Shelf, also named the Great Ice Barrier, the gateway to the South Pole. This discovery will remain a major achievement in the annals of Antarctic exploration. The outer extremity of the Ross Sea is partially blocked by a great ice barrier, an immense ice wall, called the Ross Shelf, which rises 150 to 200 feet (45.7 to 60.9 metres) above the sea, is nearly 400 miles (740 kilometres) long on its seaward side and more than 700 feet (213.3 metres) thick. This is hard to believe; however it is true. Stephen Pyne emphasised the crucial importance of this discovery. "The Barrier was the ne plus ultra of maritime exploration. Once the pack [the Barrier, the Ross Shelf] was breached, the open Ross Sea brought a party as close to the pole as possible anywhere around the circumference of Antarctica."[31]

Thus the Ross Shelf became the green light indicating the shortest route to explorers hoping to reach the exact geophysical point of the South Pole. Approaching a small island (now called Ross), Ross and his crew were again overwhelmed when they saw flames and black smoke spewing from a snow-covered volcano 12,467 feet (3,800 metres) high at the edge of the Great Barrier, just beyond Victoria Land. "Never had man contemplated such a spectacle." He named the volcano Mount Erebus and its smaller dormant twin Mount Terror, after his two ships.

These astounding discoveries were made in January and February of 1841. On 2 February of that year, Ross also reached 78°04′ south latitude and broke Weddell's "non plus ultra" of 74°15′ south latitude, which had surpassed Captain Cook's 71°10′ south latitude.

Ross' two other Antarctic explorations also greatly contributed to knowledge of the coasts, although the South Magnetic Pole eluded him, as it had Wilkes and Urville. Almost fifty years later, it was located by Ernest Shackleton.[32]

Ross Meets the Yamanas near Cape Horn

Ross chose Saint Martin's Cove as the best anchorage in the area, having read a report by one of his officers as well as Weddell, Webster and Fitz-Roy. It seems strange that Ross' contacts with these Yamanas were so superficial, despite having remained almost two months in the cove (from 19 September to 6 November 1842). The Yamana failed to ignite his curiosity, even though he found their company "joyful." Perhaps he was comparing them with the Eskimos, whom he greatly admired. He was more interested in the flora, encouraged by the presence of Joseph Dalton Hooker, a gifted botanist. The latter, only twenty-two years old, was the assistant surgeon and naturalist of the expedition. He eventually published six volumes on the flora collected during this expedition, achieved great fame in scientific circles and became Darwin's devoted friend and ally.[33]

Ross and his crews kept busy during those two months, measuring meteorological, hydrographic and magnetic phenomena besides studying the geology, flora and topography of Hermite Island. But the setting depressed him.

In Fuegia these wild scenes are rendered gloomy and . . . positively forbidding, by the almost total absence of animated nature, and by the clouded sky, constant storms, and vexed ocean, added to the silence which is only broken by the hollow voice of the torrent and the cry of the savage.

While Darwin drew analogies between the Yahgan and animals, Ross favoured a metaphor of gloomy nature. "Like the degraded and savage native, who wanders naked among the bleak rocks and almost equally uninviting woods of this miserable land, these plants may be justly considered the hardiest of their race in the southern hemisphere."

Ross and his men sighted a fire at the head of the cove the evening of their arrival, 19 September. The next day, while he and one of his officers were being rowed ashore, three natives shouted *Yamma Coyna* from a canoe. Ross recognised the words as a friendly greeting. As if they were expecting visitors, they pointed to "the most convenient spot for us to land, for the surf was heavy on the beach." A while later they passed by Ross' ship, paddling rapidly out of the cove, again shouted *Yamma Coyna*, motioning that a storm was approaching, "by signs that could not be misunderstood."[34]

Small parties of natives, camping at the head of the cove, often visited the ships. Robert M'Cormick, an officer of the expedition, noticed their "very crooked, spindle-like, and ill-shaped legs." He also inspected a bag made from the skin of a duck and lined with the feathers, also another bag or container made of kelp, that no one had noted before. He was pleased by the natives' good nature, inoffensive joyous manner, and again by their singular talent for mimicry.[35] He realised that they were "inured" to the climate, especially when he saw them walking knee-deep in snow on some of the coldest days with only a small otter skin as protection. Although Ross considered them to be degraded savages, he and his crew enjoyed singing, dancing and joking with them and showered them with gifts that were useful with two exceptions (see below). The crew entered "into every kind of fun, for which seamen are so famous." One morning on the shore, the sailors were trying to show the natives how to wash their faces with soap, but as the soap made their eyes smart, they washed their feet and hands instead. The seamen "then powdered their hair with flour and decorated them with ridiculous ornaments, the natives greatly enjoying their altered appearance, heightened in no small degree by the present of a complete suit of clothes for each and many useful articles they got on board the ship: they went away in the evening rich and happy." Nearly all of the natives "had their long dirty hair removed, and expressed much satisfaction at their short crop, which greatly improved their appearance."

Ross also visited a bay he called Joachim, which was probably the nearby Maxewell Cove, where Brisbane had been seventeen years earlier (Chapter 2). A family of fifteen, the largest number of Yahgan Ross saw, was living on the beach. Several of the men paddled to one of the ships and climbed on board, while the women "employed themselves diving for sea eggs, or picking up limpets, which are their principal food." This is one of several mentions of the women diving for sea eggs (Chapters 1 and 5). Ross described three types of spears: those used for killing large seals, for smaller seals and for birds. He found them "not unlike those of the Esquimaux, but of very inferior manufacture."[36] The spears may have been inferior to those of the Eskimos, though adequate for their needs. The Eskimos had to contend with a much harsher environment. While they were still in "Joachim Bay," natives from a nearby island paddled a canoe to the side of Ross' ship. Hiding their bows, they refused to barter their three arrows with points of obsidian, much less their white dog. Why they came is not stated. Once the men were back on shore, Ross or one of his crew observed them going directly to their neighbours' wigwam and sitting in a circle around a fire, "without speaking a word or manifesting any expression of satisfaction." An hour or so later they joined their women, who had remained in the canoe, and paddled away. This seemed like peculiar behaviour but Ross and other outsiders did not know that the Yamana did not greet each other (Chapter 5). The Yamana were very formal about greeting etiquette: one should be respectfully silent. The visitors had possibly come to see their neighbours on an errand about which Ross had no way of knowing.

He, like Captain Cook and others, was repelled by the "intolerable smell" of their bodies, smeared as they were with red ochre mixed with whale or seal oil. When he called the Fuegians "an indolent race," he was obviously thinking of the men who threw "the labour of paddling the canoes and collecting shellfish upon the women." Like Darwin again, he sympathised with the women and found the Yamana language so unpronounceable that, as usual, communication was by gestures.

The crew planted vegetables for them, trusting that they would appreciate them, which they didn't. They released several pairs of rabbits, hoping that they would multiply, as rabbits usually do, but they couldn't in such an environment. For their own table they shot woodcocks, quail, waterrails and upland geese, but the "less fastidious Fuegians" asked the crew to shoot their favourites: loggerhead ducks, kelp geese and cormorants, which they seemed to prefer in a putrid state.

Their conduct throughout the whole period of our stay was peaceable and inoffensive and their cheerfulness and good temper rendered their presence agreeable to us rather than otherwise; and, from the number of useful presents they received in the shape of knives, axes, saws, and all kinds of carpenters' tools, fishing-lines, hooks, and a great variety of other articles, I trust our visit will not have been without considerable benefit to them.[37]

The day before departure, Ross brought two natives on board, who "walked about the decks dancing and singing and eating biscuits, seemingly quite happy."[38] With this jolly farewell, the explorers weighed anchor on 6 November 1842 for the Falkland Islands where Ross will meet the would-be missionary Allen F. Gardiner, his wife and two children (Chapter 7).

7

1848 to 1851: Allen F. Gardiner Searches for Heathens and Finds the Yamana

The Yamana Are Still Cheerful

The Yamana were even joyful with strangers, though shy and fearful on occasion. They were prone to make off with something useful they saw on board the ships they visited but they shared their "ill-gotten gains" with kin and friends. They had left Wilkes' and Ross' ships, returned to their routine, probably exchanging impressions for days on end about those hairy white-skinned men in tremendous canoes and no women. They fell asleep, perhaps laughing as they mimicked the strange sounds the sailors had spoken and hummed the melodies of their songs.

The days passed, one then another, as the time was approaching for the next visitor. He will appear in 1848, not as a bartering navigator, a jolly sailor, a sealer killing their favourite food, or a curious naturalist – none of all these.

This next visitor will dominate the scene long after his final agonising months. Despite his sincere intentions, he will appear as a forewarning. After his death shadows will fall across the land as a hurricane rises on the horizon. The hurricane will gain force, uprooting those thousands of years of the Yamana's existence, attacking them with strange sicknesses until, a century later, all that will remain will be the scattered memories of a few survivors.

Allen F. Gardiner Is His Name

He had been a distinguished naval officer. Following the death of his beloved wife and child in 1834, he retired from the British Navy to dedicate his life to the heathens. That year, at the age of forty, he embarked upon an odyssey that took him to strange lands and a stranger destiny.

His odyssey was fraught with obstacles put in his path by wars and revolutions, by Christians of other denominations, by his impulsive nature, plus a large dose of faulty judgements. He was sustained by his tenacity to "leave no stone unturned" for the salvation of heathens.[1]

Gardiner Seeks Heathens

First in South Africa

Gardiner's search began in 1834, when he sought to convert a certain tribe of the Zulus known to be heathens. Shortly after arrival, with the help of a Polish friend, he acquired (probably rented) two wagons pulled by thirty oxen, plus seven horses and their riders, an interpreter "and all the necessary personnel." He contacted the tribal chief, but conflicts among the Zulus made it impossible to pursue his mission at that time. During the first interval in 1836, he returned to England, where he married for the second and the last time. His bride, Elizabeth Marsh, accompanied him back to South Africa. A loyal and devoted wife through the turbulent years to come, she was the sister of Reverend John W. Marsh, his biographer and great admirer. During three years (1835 to 1838), Gardiner attempted to work among the Zulus. Finally, in 1838, the tensions among the Dutch (the Boers), the British rulers, and the native Zulus convinced him that God had not intended that he pursue his mission there.

Argentina, Chile and Bolivia

Leaving his young wife at home, Gardiner sailed to Argentina for the first time, that same year. In Buenos Aires he found that the warfare "between the Buenos Ayreans and Pampas Indians" precluded any possibility of friendly relations with the latter. He went on to the town of Mendoza, crossed the Andes to Chile, and sought contact with the Huiliche and Araucanian (Mapuche) Indians. There he encountered difficulties with emissaries of the Chilean government, with Indian chiefs and with a "popish priest." He gave up Chile and proceeded to Bolivia, but Bolivia turned out to be a "popish country." His meeting there with "semi-barbarous and suspicious people" convinced him, early 1839, to alter the plan he had in mind for them.

New Guinea and the Papua People

February or March 1839 found Gardiner in Valparaíso, Chile, from there he sailed in June to Sydney. Arriving in September, he continued on to Indonesia, intending to visit Papua in New Guinea. He had to obtain authorisation to do so from officials in Indonesia. Two months later he was still in the town of Dili, Timor Island. Finally, about June 1840 on the island of Java, probably in Jakarta, he was officially refused permission to preach the gospel in New Guinea.

Back to Chile

As the Papua were out of the question, in early 1841 he returned to Valparaíso. There he distributed Bibles while waiting to sail to the island of Chiloé, where he arrived in May. In 1841, he intended to visit a tribe in the Andes, however a Catholic priest, who remembered having met him in nearby Valdivia, in 1838 or 1839, prevented him from hiring the necessary guides. In September he was back in Valparaíso, from where he embarked on other journeys "with no greater success." Then "Farewell to Chili" – the title of a poem he wrote as he departed for the home country.

The Tehuelche Indians, Back to England, Then to Argentina Again

At the end of 1841 Gardiner arrived on East Falkland Island with his young wife and two children, who remained there for the next ten months, waiting for him to return. In March of the next year he engaged a schooner and sailed to the Magellan Strait with the intention of catechising the Tehuelche Indians in southern Patagonia, Chile, hoping that they would prove less rebellious than the Mapuches.

In March or April of 1842 he camped on the north shore of the strait in San Gregorio Bay, where eight years before Fitz-Roy and Darwin had purchased guanaco meat. Although he found only a few Tehuelche, he stayed on until September or October, when he moved down the coast to a place called Oazy Harbour. There he was well received by other Tehuelches. Encouraged, he planned to return to England and seek financial support from the Church Missionary Society to work in Oazy Harbour. On the way back to England, he stopped off on East Falkland Island and joined his family, who were waiting for him. There, in 1843, he received financial aid and encouragement from the Artic–Antarctic explorer Captain James Ross (Chapter 6).

Back in England, having failed to obtain the support of the Church Missionary Society, the most active Protestant missionary society in England at the time, he postponed his return to Oazy Harbour. He returned alone to Argentina for some months in 1843–44, earning some money by selling Bibles and other religious materials in Córdoba, Santiago del Estero, and Tucumán.[2]

Gardiner Organises a Missionary Society in England, Returns to the Tehuelche, Then Back to England

Home again, in 1844, he realised that the Church Missionary Society would probably never finance his mission among the Tehuelche, so he appealed to sympathetic pastors of the Anglican Church and other charitable persons. With them he organised the Patagonian Missionary Society, later renamed the South American Missionary Society. He was appointed the first secretary of this society, which continues to be active today, though no longer in Tierra del Fuego.

Early 1845, he returned to the Tehuelche, accompanied by the catechist Robert Hunt. They found the Tehuelche in Oazy Harbour, where he had been well received in late 1842. This time the chief sought to deprive him of his provisions, especially the six bottles of cognac he brought along for medicinal purposes. With "suicidal amiability," the historian Armando Braun Menéndez wrote, Gardiner offered the cacique a taste of the cognac. In the midst of "tribulations," a Chilean warship, the *Ancud*, appeared in the harbour. Gardiner and his companion were invited aboard, where they must have felt relieved to find themselves among friendly people. But soon, on board the *Ancud*, Gardiner met the Catholic priest known as Padre Domingo, to whom the Chilean authorities had entrusted the spiritual direction of their aborigines. The Tehuelche were then definitely discounted. Anyway the *Ancud* was headed west, in the wrong direction, so Gardiner and Mr Hunt stayed on in Oazy Harbour. Shortly luck was with them. In March 1845, the British ship *Ganges* entered the harbour, heading in the right direction.[3]

In June, back in England, he informed the newly organised committee of the Patagonian Missionary Society of his current plan.

> I have made up my mind to go back again to South America, and *leave no stone unturned*, no effort untried, to establish a mission among the aboriginal tribes.... They have a right to be instructed in the gospel of Christ.... This I intend to do at my own risk, whether the Society is broken up or not. I therefore beg of you to fund the money which belongs to the Society.... Our Saviour has given a command to preach the gospel even to the ends of the earth. He will provide for the fulfilment of His own purpose. Let us only obey.[4]

Such a request could not be easily ignored. With funds from the Society, Gardiner sailed from Liverpool to Montevideo in September 1845 with the intention of going on to the "Gran Chaco." But fate determined otherwise: there was warfare there: England and France against Argentina and the latter against Paraguay.

Bolivia Again and on to England

Gardiner decided to try Bolivia again, this time accompanied by Federico González, a young Spanish Protestant. They rounded Cape Horn and disembarked in Cobija, Bolivia's only port, in February 1846. From there they continued on horseback up the Andes to the town of Tarija, where they settled for some five months, visiting nearby Indian communities. Gardiner explained that "though the Government [of Bolivia] was tolerably enlightened, the ignorance, intolerance, and vices of the clergy were incredible, and their influence sufficient to frustrate any attempt of so-called heretics to enlighten the Indians."

Opposed by the Catholic clergy again, he interviewed the president of Bolivia, who reassured him that the way was open for his missionary work among the Bolivian Indians. By 1847, encouraged by the president, he returned to England, hoping to persuade his Christian friends and the Patagonian Missionary Society to finance a mission in Bolivia. He also intended to send aid to González, who had become seriously ill and was waiting prostrated in Potosí, though "comfortably settled."

An editorial in the magazine of the Patagonian Missionary Society commented, in 1859, that Gardiner's attempt, from 1834 to 1847, to redeem the heathens, "was made *eminently* useful in the cause of Christ. But, at the same time, we confess that his apparent want of success . . . led many to suspect the wisdom of his plan of operations. And this certainly caused many persons truly interested in Christian Mission to withhold their support."[5]

Where Next?

In February 1847, Gardiner was still in England, fifty-one with a wife and five children. Thirteen years had passed since 1834, and his efforts to locate heathens had failed. Eric Shipton, in his excellent book *Tierra del Fuego: the Fatal Lodestone,* commented that by then Gardiner's "modest fortune had been squandered in this fruitless effort." He planned his next move more carefully. From his reading of Fitz-Roy and Darwin, he learned that some docile natives, untarnished by the "popish priests," inhabited a no-man's-land called Tierra del Fuego. They spoke some English, and "though most thievish in character, they were neither wantonly cruel, nor cannibals, like the natives of New Zealand." In 1847 he made up his mind to try those natives.[6]

Gardiner's First Encounter with the Yamana

To further his new objective (of converting the Yamana) Gardiner lectured throughout Scotland and England and collected some funds, mostly from "indifferent spectators." Again he obtained the backing of the committee, the governing council of the Patagonian Missionary Society. Reverend Marsh commented: "If he found it difficult to urge the Committee forward, they found it impossible to keep him back: nothing could stop him." The meagre funds he finally collected were only enough to outfit a small expedition. His equipment consisted of a decked boat twenty-one feet (6.4 metres) long, a whaleboat, a dinghy of eight feet (2.4 metres), two tents, supplies for six or seven months, and a pair of goats.[7]

He hired four sailors and engaged Joseph Erwin of Bristol, a ship's carpenter training as a catechist, who was to become his loyal friend through all that was to come. Early January 1848 they departed, with the equipment and the two goats, from Cardiff, Wales, on the *Clymene*, a small passenger ship, destined for Peru. Lucas Bridges commented: "Gardiner doubtless hoped to make contact with Jemmy Button's party, but an ocean-going merchant vessel [the *Clymene*] could not be expected to go in as far as Wulaia, so he was landed at Banner Cove, Picton Island. The plan was foredoomed to fail."[8]

The *Clymene* did not land them right away on Banner Cove, Picton Island, but rather on nearby Lennox Island. After two days, on 25 March, Gardiner, Erwin, and three of the seamen took the whaleboat to explore nearby Picton Island. They arrived there quite rapidly where Gardiner soon found "a snug and spacious cove," which he named Banner Cove, inspired by a verse in Psalm LX: "Thou hast given a banner to them that fear thee, that it may be displayed because of the truth." The name Banner Cove appears today on all detailed maps of Tierra del Fuego.[9]

That evening they camped at the entrance to the cove, on the island that he called Garden. (Later it was written as Gardiner in his memory.) The next day they set out to return to the *Clymene* in Lennox Cove, but they headed into a heavy squall. After fifteen hours, they landed on the north shore of Lennox Island at some distance from the cove where the *Clymene* was anchored. Having camped there that night, the next day, following a frugal breakfast, Gardiner read Psalm XXI: "In thy strength the king rejoices, O Lord; and in thy help how greatly he exults."

They had to reach Lennox Cove on the far side of the island, where the *Clymene* was waiting. Although the storm had calmed down, they were not able to launch the boat in the raging surf, so they secured it on the shore and struck out on foot. Through tangled undergrowth, sinking knee-deep in bogs, they hiked along the coast for three days until they sighted their ship: "Sail, ho! from a rocky height was joyfully cried out, by one of the foremost of our party."

Soon after they had climbed aboard the *Clymene*, eleven Yahgans in two canoes came to visit. It was here that Gardiner first met the docile, hopefully some English-speaking natives. Not English, but barter was their means of communication. They offered fish and shell necklaces for some trifling articles that did not please them. "It was evident that they set a much higher value on clothes [which they didn't receive]."

Among those who came on board, Gardiner noticed a lad and a little girl who had "an expression of much intelligence, nor were any of the party wanting in observation." They looked intently at the sailors hoisting casks containing water and shouted their astonishment when a sailor climbed the "fore rigging."[10]

So far so good. The next day, near the end of March 1848, the captain headed the *Clymene* toward Banner Cove, retrieving the whaleboat on the way. Gardiner was pleased with the cove, sheltered as it was from the prevailing winds by Garden (Gardiner) Island, with plenty of firewood and abundant fowl and fish.

"Only one factor marred the otherwise agreeable prospect: the very object of their quest, the Fuegians," Shipton commented.[11] While they were setting up the tents at the entrance to Banner Cove, seven natives appeared. They felt the texture of their visitors' clothes while pulling at the buttons and "vociferating at the same time the all-comprehensive word 'yammer-schooner.' . . . Their behaviour, as soon as they found that our respective numbers were nearly equal, was very unceremonious, amounting to rudeness." It was fortunate, Gardiner wrote, that his equipment had been stored away in a tent. He probably anticipated such behaviour, if he recalled from his reading Fitz-Roy and Darwin that they had similar experiences with the Yahgans along Beagle Channel in January 1833 (Chapter 5).

As night approached, he appointed one of the crew as a watch. Despite the watch, the natives attempted to enter the tent where the equipment was stored. Nothing came of the incident, but Gardiner was apprehensive, because he had planned to establish the mission station then and there. The *Clymene* would weigh anchor on the morrow and the next ship would not arrive from England until six or seven months later. He pondered the inconvenience of being constantly on guard and the likelihood that other Indians would join those there already. If this happened, their situation might well become uncontrollable and threatening. He reconsidered: "The attempt to locate among these barbarous people must be conducted gradually and cautiously." Rapidly, though reluctantly, he changed his tactics. "A Fuegian mission must of necessity for the present be afloat." He quickly made up his mind to return to England and procure two large decked boats, one to serve as a house, the other for supplies, and a small boat for landing. In this manner he would have free access to the natives from the houseboat, and avoid the dangers of settling on land.[12]

With a heavy heart he ordered that the equipment be reloaded on board the *Clymene*. Before embarking, Gardiner and the others took a walk to the interior of Picton Island. They enjoyed the view of a wide expanse of fresh water surrounded by large trees, many fowl, wild celery, currants and cranberries. In the distance they noticed several canoes paddling from the Main Island (Isla Grande) towards the shore of Picton Island. While returning to Banner Cove they watched the fur seals swimming about. Recall, for future reference, that Gardiner now noted an abundance of fish in the fresh water (small lakes). He released the pair of goats and a kid, born on the *Clymene*, hoping that the little family would increase by the time he returned.[13] As they sailed away on 1 April 1848, Gardiner strained his binoculars back towards the Banner Cove, trusting that "ere long, by the blessing of God upon our exertions at home, a Mission upon a suitable footing, may be established there, and the banner of the Cross displayed."[14]

Gardiner and his crew disembarked in the southern Peruvian port of Payta, where he sold his mission property at a public auction. The four sailors finally got passage up the coast to Callao, the port of the capital Lima, and from there reached home. During the five weeks Gardiner and Erwin had to wait for another boat, they rode on horseback through the country selling and giving away Bibles and tracts and meeting many people, among them some sympathetic priests. Four months had passed by the time they reached home, early August 1848.[15]

Home – Preparing to Return to the Yamana

Two years, 1848 to 1850, were spent in England. Shipton observed Gardiner's dilemma "Though he chose to regard his recent exploit, not as a failure, but as a valuable reconnaissance, it was not so easy to induce others to see it in this light."[16] Nor would it prove easy to persuade his public to loosen their purse strings. Undaunted, Gardiner took to the road again, lecturing and requesting funds, while urging his public to join the Patagonian Missionary Society. Reverend George Packenham Despard, an enthusiastic supporter, became secretary of the society in 1850. Despard is a name to remember. A generous lady from Cheltenham, Jane Cook, contributed the large sum of 1,000 pounds. A river near the dramatic events to follow will be named for her. Gardiner began preparing his expedition back to Banner Cove with "feverish haste," confident that he could finance it with such a donation, sundry contributions, and his own savings.[17]

The historian Arnoldo Canclini, explained that even with all the donations and what remained of his own fortune, Gardiner still lacked sufficient funds, that the four boats he could afford would prove completely inadequate for navigating in the Fuegian waters. Canclini understood that because of his lack of funds, he could only purchase two small boats, dinghies, to serve as tenders, and two larger boats, each measuring about twenty-seven feet (over 8 metres). Named *Pioneer* and *Speedwell*, they were equipped with sails and oars, but the hulls were made of iron and the iron roofs on the undersides of the decks "condensed the vapour and kept a perpetual rain dripping on the berths and floors." This inconvenience would prove extremely trying later.[18]

Six Volunteers

The first volunteer, Joseph Erwin, already engaged as a catechist, was elated at the prospect of this new mission: "Being with Captain Gardiner was like a heaven upon earth, he was such a man of prayer." The second, Dr Richard Williams, a thirty-three-year-old surgeon, abandoned his professional career to join the mission. A devout Wesleyan Methodist, he had spent his spare time preaching and catechising. Perceptive and sensitive, Williams will become as devoted to the cause as Gardiner. These two will also become my main "informants" during the trials that await. John Maidment, another catechist, was the third volunteer; a former waiter who had been recommended by the Young Men's Christian Association. The others, Badcock, Bryant and Pearce, three pious Cornish fishermen whose first names were also John, offered to man the boats and declared that, "where he [Gardiner] was ready to lead they were ready to follow." Three very nice dogs completed the crew.[19]

Though he admired Gardiner's courage and tenacity, Shipton sensed "an element of madness" in this new venture:

Twelve years of frustration and futile endeavour may well have unbalanced his mind; it is less easy to understand how he can have inspired his six companions with the same total disregard for reason. . . . It must have been abundantly clear before he left England that when he landed his party at Banner Cove his position would be no better than it had been on the previous occasion, nearly three years before. His two launches, Speedwell and Pioneer, were no more suited to act as a mobile base than had been the cutter and whale-boat he had then.[20]

Departure on the Ocean Queen

On 7 September 1850, with the equipment aboard, the seven missionaries sailed from Liverpool on the *Ocean Queen*, a rather large vessel. Henry Cooper, the captain, was bound for San Francisco with merchandise and emigrants who hoped that there would be some gold left in California. Reverend Marsh, Gardiner's brother-in-law, who probably saw them off, was reassured. "Seven warm hearts parted on that day from all they loved, but they were not depressed; they were cheerful and happy . . . having coolly made up their minds to dare anything for Christ's sake."[21]

Gardiner's Last Mission

Arrival in Banner Cove

Following a three-month crossing, the *Ocean Queen* arrived in Banner Cove on 5 December (1850) and found the natives busy chasing porpoises. Except for Gardiner and Erwin, the others were seeing natives for the first time. Note, in this quotation, how Dr Williams' impression of them became radically transformed as he approached them.

Whilst scarcely discernible with the naked eye, we heard their stentorian voices, shouting "yammer schooner"; amazing indeed, is the power of their voice. . . . It seemed incredible they could be human beings, . . . *On a nearer inspection, however*, I could trace in many of them, indeed I may say in all, the lineaments of the noblest humanity, and features expressive of benevolence and generosity, though, as it were buried deep in deplorable ignorance, and abject want . . . now my heart swelled with emotion full of pleasure and satisfaction. . . . I hailed the prospect with a degree of rapture.

Despite the rapture, later that day Williams was possessed by foreboding; the fatigue and the "weakness of the flesh" that he could not quiet, "yet I felt a firm and quiet resolution if need be, to sacrifice the flesh to the cause of God and humanity."[22] Gardiner's and Williams' diaries reveal how the faith of these two deeply religious men differed in their interpretations of the messages of the Christian God who was conducting them towards that greater cause.

The *Ocean Queen* remained in Banner Cove for two weeks (until 18 December). This time Gardiner and his associates had ample time to settle in the cove, supported as they were by Captain Cooper and his crew.

On the second day, 6 December, in Banner Cove, Gardiner and a few of his companions examined a tiny island named Round, in front of the cove. While Gardiner was taking "possession of it, by reading the 72nd Psalm and prayer," five Yahgan men came to greet them, knelt beside them, and joined them in prayer. Gardiner and the others must have been pleased, as certainly their gesture augured well for their mission.

Round Island was found to be too rocky, so they went to the much larger Garden Island, later Isla Gardiner, that shields Banner Cove from Beagle Channel, where Gardiner and Erwin had camped when they first came to the cove, two and a half years ago. Now they and the others set up two tents on the inner coast of Gardiner Island, facing the cove, on the tiny inlet Gardiner had named Tent during his first visit. Despite the lack of drinking water, Gardiner Island had the advantage of being much smaller than Picton. He reasoned that it might not be visited often by the natives. Even so, he and Erwin were no doubt pleased that the natives they met there now were "very civil" and that their little family of three goats had increased to seven or eight.[23] All looks well that begins well.

Having cut down some of the trees, they erected a rude storehouse. That night they slept in their two tents on Gardiner Island. The next day, 7 December, they built a fence of tree trunks around the tents and storehouse, leaving a small opening. Early that evening, three of the men who had joined them in prayer greeted them again shouting *yammaschooner* as they slid along at a great rate towards the entrance to the storehouse. Despite this rather menacing behaviour, the missionaries felt no reason to fear them because they had seemed friendly enough. They were laughing and imitating every word Gardiner and the others spoke. As evening advanced, he motioned to them to leave, which they did, carrying the few articles given them. Though reassured, that night each man took his turn on watch for two hours.[24]

The next day, during the Sunday morning service, the same three men returned and simply stood at the entrance. They remained quiet until late that afternoon, when they were startled by the mournful yelling of women in the nearby canoes – which, Williams realised, was caused by their apprehension that their foes were approaching. The three men made signs to the missionaries not to follow them, grabbed their spears, and departed in haste to meet the possible intruders.[25] The three men soon returned with strangers and, though the former were still peaceful, the latter were not. Gardiner was visibly annoyed. "[Their] rudeness and pertinacious endeavour to force a way into the two tents, and to purloin our things, at length became so systematic and resolute, that it was not possible to retain our position, without resorting to force, from which of course we refrained." He was aware that the fence could be forced at all points. But who were these intruders?[26]

"Jemmy" and the Oens-Men

Among the strangers who arrived was "an old acquaintance," whom Gardiner called Jemmy. Although he was not mentioned during their one-day stay two and a half years ago, Gardiner and Erwin had possibly seen him or perhaps Gardiner simply called him "an old acquaintance," as a manner of speech from his reading of Fitz-Roy, without confusing him with the real Jemmy Button, whom Gardiner planned to seek but never did. From December 1850 on, Gardiner and the others always wrote about him simply as Jemmy without quotation marks, though I use them to distinguish him from Jemmy Button. Gardiner's "Jemmy" would prove to be more of a leader than the real Jemmy and usually less compliant and less sympathetic to outsiders. Williams was impressed by these strangers, whom he portrayed at length as:

altogether a different people to the others their faces were quite blackened over, and they were sturdy and audacious in their bearing, and as we soon found, impudent and uncontrollable; unlike the former, they were ready to resent every check made upon their importunate demands, and resisted us in our endeavours to keep them in check, looking at us with a most contemptuous and malign look. . . . *They were very well made, and really good looking men*, but for the diabolical passions and malignity expressed in their countenances; like the others, they had the crown of the head cropped quite close, and the forepart like a circlet of long hair hanging over the face; like the others too they were *perfectly naked except the guanaco skin, which hung loosely over their shoulders and back.*[27]

This text indicates that the strangers were Oens-men, Selk'nam, as the reader may already have guessed (Chapter 5). They had crossed Beagle Channel in canoes probably paddled by their allies, the eastern Yamana, with "Jemmy" as their "ringleader," who may have been a Yamana-Selk'nam mestizo. Note that they knew that Gardiner and his men were there only four days after they had arrived. Probably everyone nearby, on both shores of Beagle Channel, had already seen or heard that another enormous "canoe" had dropped anchor in Banner Cove, somewhat like the *Clymene* they probably had seen two and a half years ago.

Five of the new arrivals were soon prying into everything. The original three Yahgan who accompanied them to the missionaries' camp became less "civil" than they had been and even tried to force their way into one of the tents. The missionaries feared that they were about to be attacked. That Sunday night, each of the seven kept watch for two hours. Williams, on duty, seemed depressed while explaining his feelings to himself:

Now that I was alone in the dead hours of night, surrounded by the dark thick masses of wood on the one hand, and the rippling waters on the other, with the rain pouring down in heavy showers, overcome with the fatigue of the day.... I could not overcome the weakness of my weak frail heart, and felt oppressed; the time of my watch hung heavily upon me.

At 4 AM Monday, 9 December, it was still raining heavily when two of the natives with blackened faces (the Oens-men) startled John Bryant while he was on watch. Gardiner, Williams and Maidment awoke and rushed to his side. Gardiner was troubled that with "Jemmy" as their leader, "It was no longer possible to keep them from entering the enclosure, and we were obliged to stand in the entrance of the tents, to prevent their forcing their way in."[28]

That morning, when Maidment sat down on a water container, perhaps to rest for a while, "Jemmy" pushed him off the container and took his place. Although Maidment was much larger than "Jemmy," he did not take offence at the insult. Then "Jemmy" tried to pull John Bryant's boots off his legs, but Bryant resisted and "Jemmy" gave up. After about two hours, all the natives left but they soon returned with others. Their conduct became "so utterly contemptuous, all but bordering upon hostility, that it was quite manifest we could no longer stay on shore." Gardiner thought it prudent "to strike the tents and return to the vessel" – to the *Ocean Queen* nearby – although Maidment and Williams remained confident that the Almighty would protect them from all possible difficulties and trials.[29]

A Tribute to "Jemmy"

Williams was much taken, perhaps fascinated, by this arrogant "Jemmy," whom he sensed might become a formidable enemy.

In this man there was a remarkable degree of intelligence, and he was very well formed and featured, powerfully made, and most active in his habits; unusual energy and quickness of mind were very perceptible in him. But all this was for evil, and not for good; he was the ringleader... in some measure as chief. There was a most daring and determined spirit in this man, and what was very striking also in him, was a display of pride and consequence, exhibited in his rejecting with contempt anything of a trifling character, whilst he showed a sound judgement in appreciating anything of a useful nature. Upon one occasion he passed back a preserved meat can, which the others always gladly accepted, and unless it was a knife, or a nail, or something of the sort, which was given him, a withering smile passed across his lips. If we might judge of him by the working of his features, his opinion of us was altogether contemptuous; and we often imagined... we could discern thoughts full of an assured triumph over us at some time or other, when an opportunity should present itself.

It would seem that this "Jemmy" would become a troublemaker. However, apparently he did not, according to the diaries I consulted, published by Despard. The original hand-written diaries might reveal more texts about "Jemmy" than the diaries published by Despard.

Williams assumed that the two attractive women in his canoe were his wives. He noted how "Jemmy," despite his arrogance, treated his wives:

But both women were very fine made persons, and really good looking; each one had an infant at their breast. I have been greatly struck with the quiet, and easily abashed deportment of these young persons, and with their utter subjection to their master. Jemmy however appeared to treat these kindly, and whatever light articles we gave him, as beads, and so on, he gave them to these companions.[30]

Where to Safeguard the Provisions?

Gardiner feared that the strangers, the Oens-men and "Jemmy" (who arrived with the three Yahgans on 8 December), were sufficient in number to attack whenever they pleased; besides, they might soon be joined by more "equally turbulent" men. He insisted that it was no longer possible to protect their property, and that they must return to the *Ocean Queen*, at least until their two large boats could be readied. The next day they built a wigwam on the shore of Banner Cove, probably at Cape Cooper, named after the Captain of the *Ocean Queen*. Here Gardiner intended to bury the provisions they would need later, under the floor of a wigwam, "so that our thievish friends will have little idea of the treasures hidden below."

How to Learn to Talk to Them?

Gardiner and Williams (and probably the other missionaries) complained that it was impossible even to begin learning their language. When they asked the meaning of a word, the natives always answered by "vociferating *yammer schooner* or by imitation of our own words, which they articulate most correctly."[31] The missionary Thomas Bridges will become the only outsider who learned to speak Yamana fluently. A few of the other Anglican missionaries also spoke Yamana (Chapters 11 to 13).

Dr Williams Entertains New Friends

There are no reports in their diaries from 11 to 13 December. During these days "Jemmy" and the other strangers (the Oens-men) had obviously departed without more ado and all became quiet again.

Gardiner and the others remained on the ship or at least slept there. The next day, Saturday 14 December, Williams and Captain Cooper went on the gig, a small boat, taking along the three Yamana acquaintances and their families. (These three had joined Williams and Gardiner in prayers, with two others, on 6 December, kept close to them afterward and joined the strangers, the Oens-men with "Jemmy" on 8 December.) When Williams invited his first guest on board, he rigged him out in trousers, shirt, stockings, a coat and a cap. The two others arrived with their families in two canoes and were treated with the same courtesy. They cruised nearby for several hours and then went ashore, probably to the newly built wigwam (mentioned above) and cooked a penguin Williams had shot. One of them sliced the bird with a knife, lent by Williams and shared it "pretty equally" with his companions. Williams also shot a bald-headed vulture, probably a condor, and gave it to his guests to take home. He was beginning to feel at ease with these three families, and this was promising.

A Startling Discovery
A few days later, while walking inland, on Picton Island, Williams noticed that fish were scarce in the fresh waters (the small lakes) near the cove. Then he recalled that Gardiner had told them that there would certainly be plenty of fish in the area because they had been so plentiful when he was there over two years earlier (though not at the same season). Williams suddenly realised that Gardiner, having mistakenly anticipated an abundance of fish, had not provided an adequate store of animal food in the supplies brought from England.[32] He probably shared his concern with his companions, but the subject was dropped, distracted as they were by celebrating Captain Cooper's birthday on 17 December on board the *Ocean Queen*. The missionaries slept on board again that night. The next day they retired to their two boats, which were anchored nearby.[33]

Gardiner's Faith
Although Gardiner was still worried about the safety of their provisions, he felt that all was well. Everyone expressed "cheerful endurance." Engrossed in meditation, he wrote: "when we look upon these poor degraded Indians, and consider that they are, like ourselves, destined to live for ever, we yearn over them, and feel willing to spend and be spent in the endeavour to bring to their ears, in their own tongue, the great truths of the gospel of salvation."

He then composed a poem, which began:

> At length on bleak Fuegia's strand,
> A feeble, but confiding band,
> In all our impotence we stand,
> Wild scenes and wilder men are here,
> A moral desert dark and dreary,
> But faith decries the harvest near.[34]

On Their Own

That day, 18 December, the *Ocean Queen* was readied to continue her voyage to the promised land, California. Captain Cooper bade a fond farewell to the seven missionaries, wishing them the protection of the Almighty for their "most laudable enterprise." The crew gave a watch, a ring and a pencil case to Williams as a "slight testimonial of his many good qualities and services rendered on all occasions." Maidment received a ring and a pencil case for "his general kindness and readiness to assist in any case of emergency in the trying time we have had during our passage."[35] No mention was made of presents for the others.

When the *Ocean Queen* was about to weigh anchor, Williams was filled with trepidation. "There was a heaviness on my spirits, and my heart was sad that night, in a way that I scarce ever felt before." Williams had a tender heart, coupled with a fine though tortured sensibility. Gardiner also regretted the *Queen*'s departure and expressed his last thanks to Captain Cooper for the kindness and attention he and the others had shown him.[36] A year or so later, Despard, the secretary general of the Patagonian Missionary Society, recalled: "On the 18th of December the gallant barque took her departure onward to California, and our mission party were launched forth on that sea of troubles...." Shipton praised Captain Cooper for keeping the *Ocean Queen* an entire fortnight in Banner Cove, "in this outlandish place. It may well have been because of his natural reluctance to abandon his former passengers in such an obviously precarious situation, though there is no evidence that he tried to persuade them to change their minds."[37]

The morning after the *Ocean Queen* put to sea, one of the missionaries' boats, the *Speedwell*, struck against the rocks, damaging her rudder and losing her anchor.[38] This was the first nautical mishap.

Two "Disappointments": Both Catastrophic

At the end of December 1850, Williams noted the scarcity of fish. This was the first disappointment. "The other disappointment, arises from the circumstance of our having left our stock of powder on board the ship so that we can no longer supply ourselves with ducks and geese, of which there are plenty here." These two "disappointments" will prove catastrophic. The historian Braun Menéndez remarked: "What an original destiny awaits the missionaries. The first six months of the campaign to evangelise the Indian will have to be spent avoiding the Indian."[39] Isolated in this remote land, with little reserve of ammunition and meat, surrounded by "poor degraded Indians," Gardiner pondered again on how to initiate his mission.

Gardiner's Three Plans

Perhaps they should go on to Button Island, find the real Jemmy, and persuade either him or some of his relatives, to come to Banner Cove. If this were to fail, they could go still farther west and bring back several boys from a different tribe (Alakaluf), because those from the same tribe might well become spies. Then again, Gardiner thought they might be able to take several lads to Staten Island or East Falkland and, after learning their language, return to Banner Cove "under more favourable circumstances." Future missionaries will carry out one of these plans (Chapter 8).

The Most Urgent Problem

Find a really secure place to hide the provisions was a must. There was not enough room to store them in the two boats, and it seemed inadvisable to stow any in the vicinity of Banner Cove. So they hauled the stores onto the two boats. Gardiner decided they must transport the supplies across Beagle Channel, to the south coast of Isla Grande, which for some reason he thought was not visited by the natives. There they could also work on the boats, already in need of minor repairs, unmolested by curious onlookers. They had the advantage of the long summer days. By 21 December, the summer season was beginning. A bit later, daylight would last until about 1 AM and night only about four or five hours.

A "Disaster" and Two Near Catastrophes

On Thursday, 19 December, the day after the *Ocean Queen* departed, Gardiner gave instructions to transport the provisions to the opposite shore of the channel. Williams, Erwin and Badcock boarded the *Speedwell*, while Gardiner and the other three climbed into the *Pioneer*. Both boats were off to a fine start, but the *Speedwell* got tangled in the kelp near the coast and was in danger of crashing against the rocks amid a roaring swell and a strong wind. Williams became alarmed. "Destruction now indeed threatened us, and poor Erwin was almost beside himself." This was the first "near catastrophe." After four tedious hours, they managed to get the *Speedwell* ashore, on the ocean side of Gardiner Island, where its occupants passed part of the night, sleeping soundly for a few hours. No natives bothered them. "The Lord is our shield," Williams affirmed. At dawn, about 4 AM on Friday 20 December, at high tide, they manoeuvred the *Speedwell* back into the Banner Cove, having decided to forego crossing the channel.[40]

Meanwhile the *Pioneer*, towing both dinghies, was crossing Beagle Channel when somehow the dinghies floated away. According to Braun Menéndez, this was a "disaster." Now they had no dinghies to take them to shore, and because the boats were very heavy, owing to their iron roofs, the missionaries would have "to enter the icy water up to their waists and drag the boats on shore" each time they disembarked.[41]

The *Pioneer* crossed the channel diagonally (toward the west) about 17 miles (31.4 kilometres) from Banner Cove and landed safely. Weary of waiting for their companions in the *Speedwell*, Gardiner and his men found shelter that night, 19 December, in a snug cove that led through a narrow channel to a beautiful expanse of water. They named this lovely spot Blomefield Harbour (now Cambaceres Bay). No natives appeared that evening, though the next day they saw an old wigwam and other traces of inhabitants. As the *Speedwell* was nowhere in sight, they hastened to return to Banner Cove without burying any provisions. Sailing the entire day in a choppy sea against an east wind, they pulled into Banner Cove at dawn and rejoiced when they discerned the *Speedwell*.

The trip on the *Pioneer* back and forth across the channel convinced Gardiner and his mates that their boat was "not altogether fitted for sea, at least [not] for rough weather, having no scuttle on her fore hatch-way, and leaking very greatly from one of the bolt-holes in the knee of the bulk-head." This was not good news; nonetheless, Gardiner was highly gratified to have found an excellent harbour, Blomefield, with no natives, where he could repair the *Pioneer* and bury the provisions.

Losing no more time, that Saturday, 21 December, both boats headed for the newly found retreat. This time the *Speedwell* got ahead and lost sight of the *Pioneer*, and found Blomefield when it was still daylight. Then Williams and the others cruised nearly all that night along the coast of Isla Grande (the north coast of Beagle Channel) searching for the *Pioneer*. Now it was *Speedwell*'s turn to hasten back to Banner Cove and search for the companion ship. When they arrived at 6 AM on Sunday, Badcock sighted the *Pioneer*'s masts and flag flying. Gardiner shouted to them: "All is right, but had you not come all would have been wrong." Why did Gardiner greet them in such an alarming manner? Later he explained that he and his men had been on the *Pioneer* the whole day Saturday until 2 AM Sunday, trying to cross the channel. Something had gone wrong with the *Pioneer* (not noted in his journal), so early Sunday they returned to Banner Cove with the aid of their sweeps (long oars used to propel or steer).[42] This was the second "near catastrophe."

"Jemmy" Appears Again

But still, why such an alarming greeting? Gardiner went on to relate that with just a few hours' sleep, in the early dawn of that Sunday, they had been awakened by two voices: the notorious "Jemmy and his almost equally troublesome companion" were threatening to come on board the *Pioneer*. Bad luck would have it that their boat had been grounded by the high tide and there was no escape. The intruders' threats made Gardiner and the others so nervous that they prayed desperately. Their prayers were heard and the would-be attackers quieted down. At that moment Badcock, in the *Speedwell*, sighted them. This was why Gardiner was so alarmed and relieved. Soon all seven missionaries were safely together again on the shore of Banner Cove. "Jemmy" and his cohort had simply disappeared.

Presently five or more other natives (Yamanas) were sighted, walking towards them along the beach. The missionaries, their guns loaded with some of the remaining ammunition, advanced to meet them, "when within a few paces we knelt down upon the beach, and committed ourselves to the mercy and protection of our heavenly Father." The would-be aggressors stopped, stood still, without uttering a word, while the praying continued. The would-be aggressors "seemed to be held under some degree of restraint." Again the prayers proved effective. As these natives were peaceably inclined, they were handed buttons and knives. Later Gardiner sent Erwin to build a raft as an auxiliary to help escape, just in case. Later still, while all seven missionaries held their Sunday service, the natives close by remained quiet and subdued.[43]

So far nothing alarming had happened, though it seemed as if something had or might. Williams' journal affords details of the next crucial days from 23 December, though not for every day, to 4 January.[44]

More Unwelcome Arrivals

On Monday, 23 December, the missionaries were still in Banner Cove. As the boats could not be secured with the ground tackle, they returned in the boats to Tent Cove, on Gardiner Island, which was opposite the natives' favourite camping spot on the shore of Banner Cove. That night the natives hung up white streamers (probably bark) on their canoes and painted themselves white "which we understood to mean hostility." At 4 AM the missionary on watch blew the alarm whistle and all hands rushed on the decks, prepared for the worst. Three canoes with only eight passengers in all, including men, women, and children, were advancing towards them. They "shewed no actually hostile spirit; certainly they in no way did anything hostile, but we rather anticipated they would." The missionaries did not give them anything because they had been troubled by having been awakened by them. The would-be aggressors soon paddled away into Beagle Channel. This same Tuesday, 24 December, Gardiner was determined to return to Blomefield to bury the provisions. Williams convinced him that they should not attempt it, given the condition of the boats. That evening, therefore, they buried all their surplus on Gardiner Island.

A Quiet Christmas

On Christmas Day they intended to repair a leak in the *Pioneer* but failed to do so. The dinner was a treat, with servings of some preserved meat and wheat meal dough with a few raisins in it. Williams added: "We enjoyed it as much as any epicure in England." No natives were around. The next day the neighbouring Yamana visited them in "a very friendly manner," bartered their small fish, and continued on to their wigwams opposite the missionaries. Later Williams and the others were surprised that the natives left their wigwams so quietly. Were they planning some mischief? Or had they simply gone fishing? If Williams was nervous, probably his companions were likewise. By now they were interpreting the natives' every move as an indication that they were planning an attack.

The only annotation for Friday, 27 December, is by Gardiner who noted that the missionaries made a mooring anchor with extra pieces of chain attached to a case full of stones with which they secured both boats; but the force of the waves threw the boats against each other so the anchor was not much use.[45]

No notations at all in either journal from 28 to 30 December.

Settling Down in Banner Cove?

On 31 December, Williams wrote that they were getting into "something like settled habits, as respects our new quarters, and altered circumstances" in Tent Cove (Gardiner Island), so apparently they were planning to stay there, at least for a while. This day he and the others were worried because there were "literally" no fish to be had except the tiny ones the natives caught. They were also still "puzzled" about how their gunpowder could have been forgotten on the *Ocean Queen*. They realised that the two casks of preserved meat Gardiner had brought along, and the one of pork, purchased on the *Ocean Queen*, would prove to be scant provisions for seven men for the coming six months until June, when the relief ship was scheduled to come from the Falkland Islands with supplies.[46]

Gardiner's journal takes up again on 1 January 1851, when the missionaries anchored the *Pioneer* in the high tide on the shore of Tent Cove in order to patch her leak when the tide descended, but they were not able to repair it. The next day they planted potatoes near their wigwam, obviously for future consumption. Then, on 3 January, they pulled the boats up to the shore, for added protection, and moored them again with the case full of stones.[47]

But were they preparing to remain in Banner Cove? Apparently they were but then changed their plans because the natives had not returned to their wigwams after 26 December. Williams and the others still thought they might be up to some mischief. "After some days had elapsed and we found the natives did not return, we began seriously to think that possibly they might be gone for the purpose of increasing their numbers, so that they might overpower us when they come back."

The missionaries were probably undecided about whether or not to settle in Banner Cove. They would have preferred to stay there because their future converts camped nearby and at times seemed friendly. Moreover provisions had been stored in Banner Cove, and this was where the rescue ship should come in June. But then again, they were wondering if the natives were about to attack.

The Fatal Day

On Saturday 4 January, an attack seemed imminent. Williams reported that at about 7 AM, even though "Jemmy" and families, who were alongside of them in Tent Cove, were friendly enough,

we found *that others*, to the number of eight canoes, *were coming in his sight* [Gardiner's binoculars]; and as there are usually two men, and sometimes more in each canoe, we knew their strength was greatly superior to ours. Captain Gardiner got his glass to bear upon their movements, and he plainly enough saw that they were come [coming] purposely for an attack upon us, as they were well provided with their war spears; and moreover they were taking in stones off the beach, the most certain evidence of their hostile intentions. *No time was now to be lost, and with all speed both boats were got under sail.*... As it was, we were able by God's good and merciful care, to get out before they had time to assemble themselves together around us.[48]

Writing on 6 January of the events of Saturday 4 January, Gardiner interpreted the Yahgans' tactics. When the women were paddling, it was part of their plan to feign a friendly attitude, as the natives knew the missionaries were armed (they still had some ammunition). When they offered to barter, it was also to catch them, the missionaries, off guard and then attack.[49]

As they approached, the eight mentioned above by Williams, they separated into three detachments, and this, Gardiner deduced, was part of the plan to disguise an attack. Three canoes were farthest behind. The other three canoes advanced round the point at the east entrance of Banner Cove (Gardiner Island is in front of the west entrance). The other two canoes had returned near the natives' wigwam, on the shore of Banner Cove, opposite the missionaries' camp (Tent Cove, Gardiner Island) where the missionaries were waiting to see what would happen. Gardiner counted two men in each of the eight canoes, sixteen men in all, some of whom he recognized. He imagined that there were even more canoes, more than the eight, out of sight but close by. Meanwhile, "Jemmy" and others, in one or two canoes, were offering the missionaries fish in a friendly fashion in Tent Cove. These were accepted and some articles were given in return. However, Gardiner was convinced that their purpose was also devious. He stated that, "Jemmy" looked "anxious and somewhat alarmed."

When Gardiner saw that the three canoes that had been farthest behind were also rounding the point and approaching, he ordered his men to prepare to leave. In his own words:

On perceiving the 3 last canoes rounding the point, I gave directions to prepare for leaving the cove, as there was every reason to apprehend that so large an assemblage of natives (we counted 16 men, and probably more were in the neighborhood) was for some hostile purpose and not for friendly traffic, as the people alongside the canoes were evidently desirous that we should regard it. They commenced by offering us fish for barter, which of course we accepted, giving them some articles in return. Jemmy was in one of the canoes, but he looked anxious and somewhat alarmed.

No attack had occurred. The preparations for the departure were rapidly though quietly taking place. Then Gardiner turned his binoculars on the natives on the shore of Banner Cove opposite them and distinguished men from two of the canoes, had bundles of "long war spears" in the sterns of their canoes. When he saw that these men had begun passing the baskets of stones to each other, stones they had just gathered along the beach, "The order to cut the cable was instantly given, and as readily obeyed..."

But at that moment the missionaries had difficulty getting their two boats clear of each other, because they had been lashed together to enable their sails to draw. Once the boats were disentangled, "the *Speedwell* almost got grounded but in a few minutes the men pushed her into deeper water with the oars and poles." The boats advanced so slowly with the light wind that the missionaries were surprised at not being followed and attacked. They looked back and saw that, instead of pursuing them, the natives were busy trying to catch hold of the raft that Erwin had made, which was floating there, having been cut away from one of the boats in the haste to depart. Once out in Beagle Channel, Gardiner thanked the Lord for having frustrated the attack.[50]

If the Yamana had been preparing an immediate attack on the missionaries, as Gardiner assumed, why didn't they pursue their enemy? Williams was convinced, by 26 December, that the natives were not to be trusted; that property was a great source of excitement to their cupidity, and that "the art of dissimulation is very perfect among them." When they were few in number, "their demeanour was quiet enough," but when they were equal in number, "matters were altogether altered." Now (on 4 January) they were superior in number: sixteen men in the eight canoes, plus "Jemmy" and his companions in with them in Tent Cove and only seven missionaries. Why didn't they attack? Was it because of their fear of guns?

They Flee

Williams first credited a breeze, then God's "good and merciful care," for their escape. Gardiner suspected that "there was much of design and skilful planning in the whole affair." He felt sure that the natives knew that they, the missionaries, had anticipated the attack, so they had not carried it out immediately because of their dread of the guns. He concluded that "we should all soon have fallen under their weapons."[51] This is a significant remark (see below).

Williams noticed "the marks of disappointment and chagrin" on the faces of some of the natives as his and Gardiner's boat passed beyond their reach. He also thanked God for their escape. Then Williams also thought that their small supply of ammunition turned out to be an advantage. "Had we been well armed, and come to open conflict with them, our chance of success had been poor; but to resist them and to do them harm, would have been as great an evil, and as deeply to be regretted by us, as our receiving bodily injury from them, and would have occasioned a double necessity for flight."[52] Also recall this comment by Williams for what will follow.

Is This the Whole Story?

Neither Gardiner nor Williams mentioned outright aggression on the part of the Yahgans. But were they in fact preparing an attack? Did the missionaries do them any "harm"? The historian Canclini asked: "What did occur?" And answered: "We do not know exactly."[53]

Thomas Bridges wrote the following amazing text. He was the most prominent member of the South American Missionary Society, and super-intendent or director of the mission in Tierra del Fuego from 1870 to June 1886. After he retired, he visited Hyades briefly in Paris, in 1886. Then he may have given Hyades the text quoted below. The words in parenthesis were probably inserted by Hyades. I added those in brackets. Note that this is not the original text, which I could not find, but rather my trans-lation from the French, which Hyades translated from Thomas Bridges' English.[54] This text is quoted here. I use italics in the middle of the first paragraph for emphasis.

The Mission, first named "Mission of Patagonia" afterwards "Mission of South America" was founded in 1850 by Captain Allen Gardiner, who disembarked on Picton Island (the East entrance of Beagle Channel), among the completely savage Fuegians. He was accompanied by a doctor, a catechist, a workingman carpenter and three fishermen from Cornwall; he had two boats full of supplies and construction materials. *After having killed one or several Indians, in order not to be obliged to massacre the others, he [Allen Gardiner] had to relocate on the north coast of Beagle Channel*, at Spaniard Harbour, about twenty-five miles from Banner Cove, that lovely bay on Picton Island where he first had the intention of settling. (The entire expedition died of hunger and sickness in Spaniard Harbour before the Fuegians could have arrived to destroy them.) I [Thomas Bridges] am convinced that if these missionaries could have made themselves understood by the Indians, the latter would have been agreeable and devoted neighbours: the circumstances decided otherwise, but the Fuegians should not be severely blamed. Even had the good missionaries given them gifts, without doing them any harm, they were an incomprehensible enigma for the Fuegians. These Indians who, in reality, are eminently sociable, mix with familiarity in any meeting, go with great liberty into any hut, and live in a perfect equality, could not comprehend the authoritarian, disagreeable, and suspicious attitudes of their strange visitors. Seeing all that these strangers brought along, they were irritated by the obvious intention of the newcomers to keep all those coveted treasures for themselves. Moreover, the missionaries kept to themselves, as a group of bachelors. This had great importance for the Indians, who were all married and had never heard of a group of men living without women. The Fuegians therefore believed, entirely naturally, by intuition, that the missionaries had hostile motives. Insofar as the Indians were few in number, by prudence they appeared to be friendly; but as soon as they felt they were sufficiently numerous to be the strongest, they became insolent, aggressive and determined to profit from their numerical superiority, ready, in effect, to kill these harmless missionaries, with the sole objective of ridding themselves of these completely strange and questionable individuals. In this circumstance, there were only two ways of staying in the Fuegian territory: be two or three times more numerous, from the beginning declare war on the Indians, kill several, and then live in isolation in their country – or share with good grace all their supplies with the Fuegians, adopt the mode of life of the Indians, and live among them as equals.

Thomas Bridges' words that Gardiner had killed one or several "Indians" (Yahgans), cannot reasonably be doubted. Recall that Gardiner and his men were surprised that the "Fuegians" were more concerned with catching the raft than pursuing them. They wanted to get rid of the missionaries, even kill them with "the sole objective of ridding themselves of these completely strange and questionable individuals" according to T. Bridges as quoted above. When one or more of their men had been killed, I suggest that they realised that despite their superior numbers, they couldn't defeat the missionaries with their slings against firearms and were satisfied that they had fled, so they didn't pursue them.

But why did Bridges give this text to Hyades? Bridges, a devout and committed Anglican and an outstanding member of the missionary society founded by Gardiner, would certainly not have given it to Dr Hyades or to anyone if he had not known that the killing had actually occurred. But he may not have imagined that it would ever be published. Actually it was published (in 1891) seven years before he died, but in French and in a scientific series of eight large volumes, so he probably did not see it. Apparently Hyades did not realise the importance of this text, as he made no comment concerning it. He may not have asked Bridges' permission to publish it. Part of the same text was published in Spanish in 1902 by the Salesian missionary José Maria Beauvoir.[55] However, none of the authors I consulted for this book referred to Beauvoir's article or to Hyades' text when discussing "Gardiner's tragedy," which is to say none mentioned that Gardiner had killed one or several Yamanas before fleeing from them.

Was There a Conspiracy of Silence?

How did Thomas Bridges learn about the killings? He arrived in the Falkland Islands in 1856, when he was about thirteen years old. As of

1858, he worked and lived with the Yahgans in the Falkland mission. In 1863, he went to Tierra del Fuego for the first time, made many trips to Ushuaia during 1870 and 1871 and settled there with his family in 1872. Therefore he had frequent and prolonged contact with the Yahgans and probably heard about the Gardiner episode from them. The killing episode may have been noted in Gardiner's or Williams' journals and deleted by Despard for publication. As noted above, some days were not recorded or are missing in both diaries. But some pages of his journal were swept away by a high tide on 18 February 1851, and Gardiner may not have rewritten them (see below). Then too, Gardiner and/or Williams may not have recorded the killing in their diaries.

Whether or not they did record them can be discovered only with the originals, which may not be complete either. However, there may have been a conspiracy of silence on their part, possibly by Despard and the later missionaries. In any event, there was not a conspiracy of silence on the part of Thomas Bridges because he gave the above text to Hyades.

The question has not been answered and must await further research. However, the missionaries did engage in a conspiracy of silence later on (Chapter 8).

As I mentioned above, Bridges' entire text was published only in French and was partially quoted in a bulletin that was not often consulted, that of the Salesian missionary Beauvoir, written in Spanish in 1902. This might explain why the authors who wrote about this incident ignored the killing of the Yahgans. Most of them declared that they actually attacked the missionaries or threatened to do so and obliged Gardiner to flee from Banner Cove. Nonetheless, although the missionaries felt they were in great danger, there is no evidence that the Yahgans attacked them. That very day, 4 January, even the dreaded "Jemmy" had been peaceful, nor were any of the Gardiner group reported wounded by the Yahgans on that day or before. As I mentioned, it would be unreasonable to suggest that one and all of the authors who described the episode deliberately omitted the references to the killing – that there was a conspiracy of silence on their part. But a definite bias does seep through most of their writings – that the Yahgans were the "bad guys" who, by their hostile behaviour, forced Gardiner to flee.[56] Shipton did raise a doubt.[57]

Through Gardiner's reading of Fitz-Roy and Darwin (both published in 1839), he could have anticipated the manner in which the Yahgans would act and the likelihood that some would appear threatening and then calm down, and that they might try to steal whatever appeared useful to them at the moment. Apparently he was impressed by Matthews' experience in

Wulaia. But he also read that Fitz-Roy and his group had a good relation with the real Jemmy and with the other Yahgans in Wulaia, except the old men (Chapter 5). Thus Gardiner had a guide to inform him of what to expect, which he seems not to have understood or simply ignored. His behaviour may be partially explained by his nervous temperament and his series of faulty judgements resulting from his lack of comprehension of the situations he was facing, which finally led to the killing of one or several Yamanas, as quoted above.

They Escape

When they felt safe in Beagle Channel, having fled from Banner Cove, they brought the *Pioneer* and *Speedwell* together and the men exchanged some provisions in case they should be separated later. They repeated their thanks to their "gracious God." Then Gardiner stated yet again that they should head for Blomefield. Williams thought he had already convinced Gardiner that it would be too perilous to attempt to go that far because of the condition of the boats. Williams prevailed, though according to Gardiner: "Had the wind permitted we should have gone to Blomefield Harbour." Once Blomefield was out of the question, they set sail to search for a closer harbour on the far side of Picton Island. But the wind came to a "dead calm." As they lay moored in the kelp in the channel, they thanked the Lord again for their "merciful deliverance."[58]

Williams was worried. They had "devised nothing that had issued in success," and now they "seemed to be getting disastrously crippled." Navarino Island was close by but had "the disadvantage of being peopled thickly with the natives." Even so, a light breeze sprung up, favouring Navarino, so they headed that way, west, to Beagle Channel. About midnight, a calm set in again and the boats remained immobile in the channel for about three hours between Picton and the east coast of Navarino. Then a heavy gale stirred and the wind and tide shifted, so they decided to go in that direction, south, and try for Lennox Cove, perhaps also because Gardiner and Erwin had been there during the first trip in March 1848. They arrived there late that day, 5 January (1851).

They Camp in Lennox Cove

As they were manoeuvring into the cove, two "Fuegian dogs" barked at them from the shore. Nearby they saw a well-built wigwam fronted by an enormous pile of mussel shells but no inhabitants. By evening both boats had secured their anchors in the cove, though violent gusts of wind obliged them to remain in the boats that night. The next morning Gardiner, in the *Pioneer*, was really nervous: "a more anxious and perilous night I have never passed." The next day while they were attempting to ground the boats, the *Pioneer* was driven onto a reef of rocks and so seriously damaged that it took them eleven days to repair it; this is why they remained in Lennox Cove for so long. The *Speedwell* was dragged on shore with no problem. By 10 AM on Sunday, 6 January, all were safe on the beach.[59] Although Lennox Cove was not very inviting, it was somewhat sheltered from the storms and, hopefully from the natives "for some time at least."

Besides repairing the *Pioneer*, they had to wait for the "spring tide" to look for a better refuge, though at first Williams was concerned that "if natives come we can't flee from them." (Perhaps they were fearful of being pursued and attacked by the Banner Cove Yamanas.) A few days later, Williams restored his faith and felt unusually elated. "Friday, January 10th, eleven p.m. I bless and praise God that the day has been, I think, the happiest of my life, at least I don't remember a day when my happiness was more full, if so complete."

Williams may have felt such a strong emotion because they were safe, at least for the time being. While they were repairing the *Pioneer*, from 6 to 17 January, Gardiner became increasingly anxious: "We never had been in so perilous a situation" – that is, vulnerable to attack by the natives. On 12 January, a canoe hauled up near the "well-built wigwam" but departed the next day. Williams was relieved: "We were well pleased to think they had not perceived us." Several days later two men and a few women and children did visit them and returned during the following days. While Gardiner simply noted that they appeared friendly, Williams was enthusiastic. Not only were they very quiet and docile, but also "one of the men [was] very good looking, with good feelings exhibited in his peaceful and pleasant looking countenance." Then Williams made these revealing comments:

It seemed quite unwarrantable and uncharitable to think evil of him, or to suspect he would do us harm. The child they brought with them was a very interesting little vivacious fellow. The father was most careful of him, and scarcely allowed us to handle him, fearing it might do him injury. He was well wrapped up in skins . . . conspicuous in the Fuegian character [is] their fondness for their children.

Williams was more giving than Gardiner, ready to acknowledge when the Yamana were friendly and perhaps wondering if any of them might attempt to avenge the deaths of "one or several Indians." The other missionaries were confident in the company of the visitors, though as usual they suspected "that they might go off for others." These were the only natives they met during nearly two weeks in Lennox Cove.

On 18 January, Williams lamented their "utterly helpless state," and he thanked God for keeping "the Fuegians unapprized of our situation." The *Pioneer* had been repaired and was afloat and the *Speedwell* was in good shape.[60]

Departure From and Back to Lennox Cove

A few days before, Maidment had been walking along the shore several miles south of the cove and had seen an attractive bay, which they later called Mercy Cove.[61] So following Maidment's recommendation, on 18 January, they set out for Mercy Cove, sailing or rowing along the shore of Lennox Island. Near a cluster of small islands they passed a group of natives among whom they spotted the two families that had recently visited them in Lennox Cove. All were busy fishing and trying to kill a seal until they noticed the strangers in the two boats and began shouting loudly to them. Five canoes, paddled by the men, took off in pursuit of them, "with a velocity that exceeded all our previous thoughts of their skill." Nearing Mercy Cove, the missionaries feared that the five canoes would catch up with them and that they would "be at their mercy [hence the name of the cove]." They avoided their pursuers by turning around and heading back to Lennox Cove, where they arrived at dawn Sunday 19 January. That same day Gardiner, still fearing that they might be overtaken, gave the order "to get under weight again." He thought of going to nearby Cape Rees (near the present town of Port Toro), on the east coast of Navarino, or to Blomefield.

With luck they might arrive at either place in time for the Sabbath service. The weather was fine, but soon the wind died down and, while tacking, the two boats collided. The Speedwell's bowsprit, a long pole used to keep the bottom of the sail stretched, fell into the water and sank, together with her jib (her sail). This loss was so serious that Gardiner decided to go back to Lennox Cove. As they were entering the cove, the wind stirred and a hurricane threatened, so both crews quickly ran out their anchors to avoid the rocks near the shore. Then a tremendous storm broke. One of the anchors dragged, but the kelp secured it and the other boat. For hours they held on in the kelp, the waves raging about them, the dark clouds pouring down cold pelting hailstones amid a deluge of rain. Finally they got ashore in Lennox Cove on Sunday.[62] But it was either too late or they were too drenched and tired to hold the Sunday service on 19 January.

Back to Blomefield?

The next day, with fine weather, they were off again in the two boats when Gardiner gave the order to head for Blomefield. Williams seems weary when he wrote this monologue: "I made no objection however to it, indeed I gave no expression whatever to my thoughts. . . . Repelled as we had been upon three attempts to reach Blomefield, or to get there together, I could not help but feel it was not God's will." Later he recalled that "after leaving Lennox Island, we again, to my surprise, were directed thither [to Blomefield]. I could not help but feel pained and grieved. I felt it to be sinful thus to go in the face of conviction, and of the leadings of Providence."[63]

His interpretation of "Providence" contradicted Gardiner's. But on to Blomefield, as the latter ordered. Passing by Cape Rees on the east coast of Navarino, Williams longed to stop over in that "snug cove" which seemed to invite them. "Nothing however, would do but Blomefield, so on we went as soon as the wind sprung up." By 8:30 PM (20 January) they had crossed Beagle Channel and were nearing Blomefield when three canoes paddled towards them. Among the occupants were "some very fine men," including one from Banner Cove, "a member of the league organised against us." However, they were not threatening and did not detain them. When they were close to the shore of Blomefield, they sighted several fires and such a large party of natives that Gardiner gave up Blomefield again. Williams recalled, with vehemence: "Our going to Blomefield Harbour was now a vain and useless thing altogether; it was clear we should have no rest nor quiet there, and equally clear they would soon accumulate an overwhelming force against us, and overpower our small and weak party."[64] This was the fourth time Gardiner had ordered them to go there. Williams was brewing a deep resentment against him.

Waiting in Beagle Channel

Searching for a place to camp overnight, they steered in the direction of Banner Cove. As they floated "becalmed" in the middle of the channel, another canoe approached them. Williams recognised an "intimate associate of Jemmy, the great concerter of the attacks upon us, and our most troublesome acquaintance." Just why he thought of "Jemmy" in these terms is not clear. "Jemmy" had not threatened to attack them, so far at least, according to the published journals. "Jemmy's" mother was in the canoe "looking as pleasant as ever." So obviously they had met her before, perhaps as had been noted in missing pages of their journals. Williams brooded: "Thus being driven out of every place . . . it being quite impracticable, in the crippled state of our boats to beat about and dodge off and on from place to place."[65] They gave up returning to Banner Cove also, thinking, "the hue and cry would go forth and they would all be around us again very soon."

On to Spaniard Harbour

A short while later, Williams felt comforted by Gardiner's praying. "Never did the Captain appear to more advantage," Gardiner had reasserted himself. Now he was determined, "the Lord willing," to proceed eastward, and endeavour to reach Spaniard Harbour (Puerto Español).[66] This harbour was some twenty-five miles (46.3 kilometres) down the coast from their position, tucked in the west corner of a very large bay later called Aguirre. He made this decision as a last resort on 20 or 21 January. Throughout his texts, he wrote that his fate and destiny were in the hands of God. As Blomefield was out of the question for a while at least, now he spoke as if the Lord was indicating where they should take refuge as an alternative. Shipton commented on their attitude: "It seems rather that they were inspired by a pious resignation, amounting to a kind of spiritual exaltation, which made them determined, even eager, to accept their fate."[67]

Lucas Bridges' familiarity with the zone and its inhabitants would have helped them a great deal had he been born on time. "Spaniard Harbour was well chosen, for so desolate is that country and so exposed the coast that it was seldom visited by either canoe or foot Indians." Notwithstanding, Lucas questioned the wisdom of this decision. "The prevailing winds here are from the south-west, which might have persuaded them to make for the Falkland Islands, for they certainly had compasses and Gardiner must have been an expert navigator. That they did not attempt this we can only attribute to the fact that they expected a relief vessel within six months [nearby in Banner Cove]."[68] However, had they gone on to the Falklands, there would have been no need for a relief vessel to pick them up, because it was scheduled to leave from there. Perhaps Gardiner thought that the Falklands were too far away, given the condition of their two boats.

Sailing or rowing toward Spaniard Harbour, the night of 23 January, they landed near Cape San Pio (coast of Isla Grande) for water and wood. A while later, as midnight was approaching, they camped in the bay later called Sloggett.

They Settle in Spaniard Harbour (Aguirre Bay)

By noon the following day, 24 January (1851), with fine weather, they had entered the harbour. Williams was relieved. "We now hope we were got to a place of refuge, where we might for a time at least have rest from our wanderings." The next morning he took a walk and was delighted by the meadows, valleys, the copses of trees and the mountain range beyond: "I began to think that even Tierra del Fuego . . . had in itself natural charms and beauty." He knelt, overjoyed that he would bring knowledge of the Saviour to the "poor inhabitants of the land," and gave thanks for His blessing and favour. Despite these declarations Williams was less inclined than Gardiner to relax on the conviction that divine guidance sufficed. He thought that humans also had to do their share. Apart from their different temperaments, this contrast between the two may have a source in their affiliations: Williams the fervent Wesleyan Methodist, Gardiner the ardent Anglican.

Finding it difficult to get ashore where they were, a few days later they continued along the coast of Spaniard Harbour to a nearby cove, which Gardiner named Earnest, in the "earnest hope of the fruit which we trust will in due time, by the blessing of God, attend our humble endeavours in behalf of the inhabitants of these islands."[69]

They were still in good health. Perhaps this explains their optimism upon arrival, which seems excessive with winter approaching, and little food and less ammunition (to be used to hunt whatever they might find there). However, as Lucas Bridges suggested, they seem to have regarded Spaniard Harbour as a temporary refuge, safe from the natives, until they could return to Banner Cove, where they had buried food provisions and they could wait for the rescue vessel, scheduled to arrive in June. The prospect of returning to "enemy territory" (my term) must have seemed potentially dangerous to them.

By the end of January, a heavy gale stirring outside the bay made them feel all the more snugly protected in Earnest Cove. Williams was still elated. "We were all ashore washing our linen, having a general purification, the first for nearly five months . . . all the day long on Friday, I never felt happier." Never again were they to enjoy such idyllic days.

The Pioneer Is Wrecked

Early that morning, 1 February, the sea rolled heavily into Earnest Cove. First the soaring waves plunged over the *Speedwell*. Williams was surprised when the waves swept over his cabin. "I could scarcely credit my senses, another, and another thump, and another sea breaking in over us, confirmed in the fact that something not looked for had happened."[70]

Gardiner ordered the men in the *Speedwell* to cast off her hawser, a heavy cable for mooring, and ride the waves dragging her anchor. But then the *Pioneer*, swept by another heavy surge, smashed into a huge rock on the shore and was very severely damaged. Gardiner was resigned, trusting only to save provisions floating about. Through it all Williams was consoled by the thought that he might have been worse off at home. "I have often . . . being wetted by a shower of rain in England, experienced more depression, more discomfort than all that I felt upon this occasion." Despite the heroics, this near hurricane on this first day of February had smashed the *Pioneer* nearly in half, ruined it, making it obsolete. This was the worst boat disaster since the loss of the two dinghies. Most of the clothes and blankets were scattered in the water and along the shore. The men gathered all they could, put them out to dry, and later stored them in a nearby cavern. The cavern was almost thirty yards (27 metres) deep, so only extraordinary tides and gales swept water into its depths. The men also located a dry spot inside the cavern where they slept for a few nights.

Although early February was midsummer, it began to snow persistently during the next few days, with rain and hail. Williams, probably like his companions, remained undaunted; God had spared them. He had provided them with an asylum. He had avoided irretrievable damage being done to their property and protected them from being exposed to an "irruption of the natives." All this optimism was also sustained by their plan, now agreed upon, to return to Banner Cove, despite the risks, and wait there for the vessel that would rescue them in June. For the time being no mention of saving heathens. Here they felt safe from being "hunted about from place to place, and chased like a hare by the hounds." Off and on they seemed convinced that the Yahgans might take vengeance.

A few days later, as the cavern proved to be excessively damp for sleeping, they found an alternative. They hauled the wrecked bow of the *Pioneer* farther up the beach and pushed it against the stump of a large tree. By stretching a piece of canvas over the wrecked boat, they made "a very comfortable sleeping apartment," though it was still within the reach of a heavy high tide. Thus the *Pioneer* was converted into an "apartment." That was fine, but now their other vessel, the *Speedwell*, had to be safeguarded. Shortly after the February storm, Williams and the others moved the *Speedwell* from Earnest Cove to a nearby shore where it was more protected. That day or the next they walked back to Earnest Cove to visit their comrades (my term) near the *Pioneer*.

The following days the weather was "most gloomy and violent," the ground "like a sponge" and the shore flooded by streams flowing from the highland. They spent the day in the cavern, and at night Gardiner and one or two others slept in the wrecked *Pioneer* at Earnest Cove, while Williams and the rest of the men slept in the *Speedwell* down the coast. On 8 February Williams wrote that it was almost impossible to sleep in the cabin because of the noise and violent shocks of the waves. But he was confident: the rescue ship would arrive in June and afterwards the mission would carry on according to the new plan. Gardiner had now made it clear that once the rescue came, he would "use every effort," back in England, to procure a schooner of eighty or a hundred tons, take some Fuegians to the Falkland Islands, learn their language there and only then return among them.[71] This became Gardiner's master plan (my term). Now they "only" had to survive five months until the rescue boat arrived. They were convinced that Gardiner's plan for the Yahgans could not be initiated until they returned to England, as noted above.

"The Old Man"

Apparently they had all agreed to Gardiner's plan; yet a while later, after the eighth of February, Williams referred to Gardiner in his journal, for the first and only time, with these startling lines: "One feature remarkably prominent in my experience during this time has been, as it were, the grinding down of *the old man* with his high mindedness, his self-will, and his love of self and of ease. Every thing has conspired together to give him a severe blow, would that it were his death blow."[72]

How could Williams profess such admiration for Gardiner, as he had in the near past and would again, and yet express such a loathing of him as "the old man"? Perhaps because of the tensions that Williams was enduring, incensed by Gardiner's obstinacy to proceed to Blomefield and above all by his failure to consult or inform Williams about their mission (see next quote). This second text leaves no doubt: the "Captain" and "the old man" were Gardiner. Had Williams lived on, he might not have permitted the above or the following texts to be made public.

When first I cast my eyes upon the work before me, and viewed the natives of Banner Cove, it was with a profound ignorance of the means whereby so great a work was to be accomplished, *having no clue whatever to any plan that had been submitted to my understanding . . . I was in darkness, for in this the Captain consulted not with me*, neither did he propound his plans to me more than the momentary intimation which preceded some new step, which the exigency of the moment had given birth to, and therefore *as far as my judgement went, I saw nothing practicable or feasible*; but I committed the direction of our affairs to Him who, I was sure, would wisely and beneficently order all things by His providence, and that He would send the light which should be for our guidance, in the very midst of our present thick darkness. A very short acquaintance with the natives confirmed the unfavourable report, which such writers as Fitzroy, King, and Darwin, had given of them.[73]

Here Williams appealed to Him, as if He were not communicating with Gardiner. Williams bitterly complained that the latter, "the Captain," from the beginning, had excluded him from the plans for the mission. His deeply felt resentments against Gardiner took the form of a loathing expressed in these texts. He was waiting for "guidance," for "light," not from Gardiner but from Him, from God. But meanwhile, the outrage and the acid complaints against "the old man" and "the Captain" spread to the Fuegians, whom he blamed for the failure of their mission. Williams felt betrayed by them, the very people for whom his love of Christ had inspired him to embrace the ultimate sacrifice. In this third text, which follows, he also evoked Gardiner's repeated insistence on returning to Blomefield as the most revealing evidence that Gardiner's obstinacy would have endangered their very lives. Williams was shrouded in darkness.

From the commencement therefore all was darkness as far as the means to be used went, in carrying out our object: when it was proposed, or rather more correctly speaking, when we were ordered to go to westward... to Blomefield Harbour, as upon four several occasions they were, to a part where the natives were more numerous... they would have had an easy and speedy access to us, and where from the nature of the harbour itself, we should have been in the utmost jeopardy of our lives, had we been attacked by them, I was clearly and decidedly of the opinion that we were running into the very midst of danger; *but I opposed not the order given, but I did admire the goodness of God in his providence, in keeping us from going there.*[74]

Williams' abiding faith revealed to him that the "Divine Will" had opposed Gardiner's determination to go to Blomefield. Here again the two men's faith as God's emissaries collided.

Gardiner's Journal Is Swept Away

Aguirre Bay, where Spaniard Harbour is located, is not along Beagle Channel. It is entirely exposed to fierce storms, southwest winds – as Lucas commented above – and currents directly from the Antarctic. Here the missionaries were at the mercy of the great forces of nature, all the more so being poorly equipped, undernourished, unfamiliar with survival techniques and struggling with spiritual turmoils. On 18 February, an unusually high tide swept into the cavern, carrying away precious items: Gardiner's annotated Bible, his books and his personal and most valuable manuscripts. Sometime afterward Gardiner rewrote some of the lost days of his journal. At least most of his warm clothes were returned by the tides.[75]

Scurvy

February was passing – a monotonous succession of days – their health slowly deteriorating, their energies dwindling. Williams was the first to become ill. On 22 or 23 February, he was struck with rheumatic fever. A week later, when he had somewhat recovered, then Maidment and the others began suffering from the same. Erwin was laid up with a "very painful carbuncle, on his left wrist," which Williams attributed to the vegetable diet. They caught some small fish with their net at the end of February. Meat from the stock was shared twice a week; only Erwin received a daily portion. The days were slowly becoming shorter, the nights longer. Gardiner was wounded on the back of his head by a sharp pointed rock protruding behind his bed in the wrecked *Pioneer*. A fire broke out in a shelter where they had stored some provisions.

On 12 March, Williams declared that he was recovering from his "excruciating pain" and "considerable feverishness," thanks to medicines and Maidment's kind nursing. But soon again he was in a "poor weak state." About then he realised that his symptoms were scurvy: "pain and great lassitude felt in the limbs, with spots and discoloration of the skin, disorder of the bowels, and bleeding of the gums." Scurvy, the disease most dreaded by seamen, from which Captain Cook had protected his men and which Williams, as a physician, identified only too well. On 17 March, Badcock, Erwin and Maidment were likewise afflicted. Gardiner evoked "gracious God.... On Him alone I rely for help." They caught fish and killed sleeping sea birds "occasionally."[76]

Back to Banner Cove

As Gardiner had killed one or several natives, the missionaries must have been reluctant to return to Banner Cove, but they urgently needed the food buried in the cases there. They, or Gardiner, would have to decide whether to remain there or to leave a message indicating where they could be located when the supply ship was scheduled to arrive in June. On 18 March, Gardiner decided that they must return there and immediately.

The next morning was sunny and beautiful. The seven men crowded into the *Speedwell*, whose heavy cargo made the boat "out of trim," top-heavy. Once in Beagle Channel, the sea became "angry" and the boat nearly capsized. The following day they pulled into Reliance Cove, near Cape San Pio, where they had stopped over on 23 January.[77] The next day or the following, Gardiner and Maidment felt strong enough to walk some sixteen miles (about 29 kilometres) to and from a river nearly opposite Banner Cove, probably Moat River. They hoped to find a more suitable cove to anchor their boat more securely, but they didn't. The others rested, meanwhile, during the three days the boat was moored in Reliance Cove.

On 22 March, the seven men set out to cross Beagle Channel. Navigating that day and night, they reached Banner Cove at dawn the following day, a Sunday. They took this incredibly long time to cover the fifteen miles (about 27 kilometres), crossing the channel at a diagonal, because of the very rough sea and the downpour of hail and snow. Then too, the boat, "with its disproportioned deck load," was in danger of sinking. Williams wrote of his great weakness, exacerbated as he was in the cramped cabin and by the incessant rolling and rocking of the boat. Doubts assailed him. Satan assaulted him as he strove to pray. Following this spiritual turmoil, he relaxed on the buoyancy of his faith and feared not death, neither by scurvy nor by the "Fuegians' jagged, notched war spear nor their deadly sling." Also he was "quite affected by the kindness of the Captain."[78]

When they anchored in Banner Cove, on the inner coast of Gardiner Island, at dawn 23 March, a small group of Yahgans shouted, greeting them from their wigwam on the shore of the cove and crossed the narrow stretch of water in two canoes to visit the newcomers. The missionaries realised that they had never seen this noisy, friendly party of five men, five women and three children. Despite this reassuring welcome, they were perturbed. Williams reported: "We now of course expected to behold the face of Jemmy, and his redoubtable associates, our late sworn and mortal foes, and that we should have similar trials to go through once more."[79]

Just why Williams always associates the enemy with "Jemmy" is not clear, perhaps because parts of Gardiner's journal (and his also) were lost during the February storms. The visitors, the thirteen natives, were said to be more squalid than those from whom they had fled. Even so, the missionaries were agreeably surprised by them, trusting that their "old acquaintances" would not join them. They held the divine service in hail, rain and snow that Sunday. Williams felt consoled despite the weather, his fear of "Jemmy" and feeling sick. "Sweet is the presence of Jesus, oh! I am happy in his love." The same friendly thirteen visited them for a short while the next day, 24 March. All was quiet. Gardiner and the other men, who were well enough, walked to the Tent Cove site nearby, where they dug out the barrel of pork purchased from the captain of the *Ocean Queen* but left the two casks of biscuits. Apparently that day or early the next, the friendly families departed, probably to replenish their fish supply, as they had bartered many fish for nails.

They searched Gardiner Island for the goats, in vain. Gardiner concluded that they had been killed by the natives. "This is a sad disappointment, as fresh meat is now so essential for those who are sick." They put the cask of pork on board the *Speedwell*.[80] The fish they had purchased from the families sufficed for a few days.

The Messages

It is not clear to me just when Gardiner decided not to wait in Banner Cove until June for the supply vessel. In any event, they did not prolong their stay there, despite the friendly natives they had met. Once the decision was made, they had to leave the messages. Three days after their arrival, on 26 March, Gardiner wrote the following on paper:

We are gone to Spaniard Harbour, which is on the main Island, not far from Cape Kinnaird. We have sickness on board: our supplies are nearly out, and if not soon relieved, we shall be starved. We do not intend to go to Staten Island, but shall remain in a cove on the west side of Spaniard Harbour until a vessel comes to our assistance. N.B. We have already been two months in Spaniard Harbour, finding the natives hostile here. Signed and dated March 26th, 1851.[81]

They enclosed the original and two copies in three separate bottles and "sunk" the bottles at the eastern and most accessible entrance to Banner Cove, at Cape Cooper, Picton Island. Then they erected boards above the bottles on which they painted the words "Look Underneath." The same or similar messages were painted on three nearby rocks.[82]

Many years later, at different times Captain Martial, Lucas Bridges and others saw one or more of the messages on the rocks that by then had been repainted several times by passing sealers or later by the Anglican missionaries. Lucas noted: "On the dark, flat face of a large rock at the entrance to Banner Cove painted in white the following legend, which, to my knowledge, was renewed from time to time for over fifty years: 'Dig Below Go to Spaniard Harbour March 1851.'"[83]

Williams and Badcock were too weak to keep watch. The others, though feeble, did so. Gardiner was perturbed, anxious to leave. "It is not to be expected that we shall be permitted to remain here long in quiet, and the next attack on the part of the natives will no doubt be conducted with great stratagem, probably with a more numerous party, and perhaps during the night."[84] Gardiner was still worried that the Yahgans might avenge their kin, killed on 4 January.

The Enemy?

The next day they heard voices while they were busy painting on the rocks. Their worst premonitions seemed justified. Suddenly four canoes of "Jemmy's party," apparently Yahgans, landed nearby, though he was not among them. Noisy and turbulent as they were, they exchanged a few fish for pieces of iron hoops. Shortly some of them proceeded to sever the rope that attached the raft to the *Speedwell*, but they didn't succeed in stealing it. These Yahgans were really interested in that raft. When the missionaries had returned there, on 24 March, somehow they had retrieved it and tied it to the *Speedwell*. Erwin had made the raft, and it had been left in Banner Cove when they fled on 4 January. Despite the bartering and the distraction of the raft, Williams was alarmed:

Amongst them were some of our old acquaintances, and doubtless they are but the harbingers of the whole of our evil disposed former associates.... we expect that to-morrow others will arrive.... the Captain proposes for us to start the first thing in the morning, for Spaniard Harbour again, the only place where there is rest for the soles of our feet.[85]

These Yahgans camped on the west shore of the cove, on Picton Island, below Gardiner Island, in or near the wigwam which had just been occupied by the previous families. Gardiner did not want to risk attempting to recover the two casks of biscuits buried on Gardiner Island. He remarked that "it would be imprudent to land there in the face of so evil disposed a party as those who are now here, and we know not how soon they be found by others." To make matters worse, heavy squalls and rain persisted most the day.[86]

The last night in Banner Cove, 27 March, Maidment and Gardiner kept watch, four hours each. About 1 AM the natives were heard striking wood. Could this be a signal for an attack? They were never known to be up before three or four in the morning. From 1 to 4 AM, the hammering on the tree trunks continued. Surely, they reasoned, these were signals to others to join them. Williams reported that men were standing up in the canoes near the *Speedwell*, bellowing, vociferating, vehemently gesticulating,

as if to make us sensible by the very force of their actions, and the loudness of their voices of what they were saying... in the midst of this was the chirruping sound of a child lisping "yammer schooner" intermingled with the fitful wail of a poor starving infant; here human nature is seen in its most degraded, wretched and depraved aspect. When will it please the Lord to deliver them from their deplorable ignorance and darkness?

Williams seemed exhausted in body and soul. If this second group were seeking to avenge their relatives killed by Gardiner, his premonition was accurate. He and the others had to leave.

They departed, at 4:30 AM, trailed by the natives, with only a light breeze, Maidment and one of the Cornish fishermen pulling hard on two oars. Suddenly the pursuers turned back. The missionaries probably peered over their shoulders wondering if they were still being followed. Gardiner recalled these moments.

In all probability there was a reinforcement near, so that had we postponed our departure but a little while longer, we might have been attacked by numbers, and the result in our enfeebled condition would have been most disastrous. The Lord has been very merciful to us, and heard our petition.[87]

Soon they were in Beagle Channel. The beautiful morning and the light winds augured well. Williams cheered up: "Every thing at present looks propitious to our having a favourable run." They crossed the channel with no problem, but that night, passing through troubled waters along Sloggett Bay, Williams lay in bed and heard the captain exclaim: "It is a wonder we were not capsized."

Back in Spaniard Harbour

When they reached Spaniard Harbour the following afternoon, Williams was becoming increasingly perturbed, if his incessant appeals to the Almighty may be thus interpreted. "How are we driven about . . . for God is not the less present because clouds and darkness are round about his throne and hide his guiding hand from our view."[88] Even though they had additional provisions, they languished, suffering from exposure, rheumatism and scurvy. Slowly starving, they huddled over a portable stove whose weak flames were kept lit with the last supplies of alcohol. Braun Menéndez commented: "They would have been much better off if only they had observed how the Indians managed in a similar circumstance."[89]

By 1 April, Williams was in pain, though reassured by God's presence. "But as I, day by day and night by night, lie here, what a world, unknown to the world, do I live in! God is indeed about my bed, and spies on all my ways, and his countenance is over me for good. How blessed is the thought." Eight days later he complained of the severe cold, the gloom and the heavy hail and rain. Badcock again shared the *Speedwell* with him. "Badcock and I are companions in afflictions. We get no better, but worse – the disease slowly progressing." Cold air and wind swept through the only opening in their cabin. "If to obviate this, we close the door altogether, the vapour from our breaths accumulates on the iron roof of our deck, only a few inches higher than our pillows and drops over us and trickles down on our beds in such quantities that we find it very troublesome."

Their immobility and lack of appetite, even for the boiled pork, increased their discomfort. Byrant, who attended them, was also showing signs of scurvy. Again they asked one another if the relief vessel would come as scheduled (in June). Williams was worried. "The Lord is with us, and will not fail us in our need; but our extremity will be his opportunity."[90]

The Hurricane of 12 April
Sweeping in from the Antarctic that day, a hurricane tore at the wrecked *Pioneer*, while the *Speedwell* was nearly swept onto the shore. A few days later, fearing that the hurricane would strike again, they moved the *Speedwell* about a mile farther down the bay to the mouth of the newly named Cook River, near where it had been in early February when the *Pioneer* was wrecked.[91] As before, Gardiner and Maidment remained in Earnest Cove, sleeping in the wreck of the *Pioneer*, while Williams, Erwin, Badcock and the two other Cornish fishermen took shelter in the *Speedwell* at Cook River. The two groups maintained frequent contact, thanks to the men who were still strong enough to walk the mile that separated them. The next day Williams was revived by the ethereal beauty of the surroundings, despite his longing for a more human world.

Dreary and desolate as was the scene, I could yet feel pleasure in the grandeur and magnificence of its very wildness... with the wind howling around, the sea roaring over the sand-bank close by, the air filled everywhere with falling snow, and with that peculiar sense of lonesome isolation which a bleak winter scene conjures up in the mind, suggesting our need of relative and social connections, there was still a sense of the sublime truly pleasurable.

Badcock's scurvy took a turn for the worse: swollen legs, discoloured, painful gums, frequent loss of blood and declining strength.

Winter Sets In
As the cold weather took over, Williams yearned for the vessel "that shall bring us succour." During the long autumn nights of May, the *Speedwell* afforded some protection against the storms, which this year

were severe. Williams and Badcock were bedridden, in darkness even during the day, relieved only by the light of a candle. Occasionally there was an interval of moderate weather, which cheered them, as did the company of their healthier companions, Erwin, Bryant and Pearce. The tapioca was replaced with rice. The preserved pork was nearly consumed. As Williams and Badcock drew upon the last bottle of gin, in flashes of desperate joking they toasted to each other: "The sooner gone, the sooner the ship must come!"[92]

On 2 May, Gardiner and Maidment trapped a fox, which they shared with their *Speedwell* companions. Besides this *bonne bouche* (Williams' expression), they dined on a penguin and a shag (a cormorant), both caught by hand on shore. Williams complained again of the dripping from the iron roof, of the pools of water on his "Mackintosh spread," and the bed wringing wet. On 7 May, recalling that just eight months ago they had departed from Liverpool, Pearce read one of Wesley's sermons, called "Repentance in Believers." Williams and Gardiner continued writing in their diaries, although Gardiner too was "in much weakness." With his usual style of understatement, on 12 May, he noted: "With the exception of the sick, we are with reduced rations.[93]

At the end of May, their only fish net was torn. Though it was soon repaired, a week later the ice ripped it again, this time to shreds. They could no longer catch any fish, however small. Gardiner explained to himself why this new disaster had occurred. "Thus the Lord has seen fit to render another means abortive, and doubtless to make His power more apparent, and to show that all our help is to come from Him."

About then Williams wrote for the first time of his "beloved ones," his mother and sisters, whom he would "shortly meet" in heaven. He and Badcock read and reread the Bible, humbly beseeching their Lord, grateful for the trials of their souls and bodies. By 11 June, Erwin was ill, and Maidment soon afterwards.

The next day, Williams, gravely afflicted by scurvy, was again exuberant. "Ah, I am happy day and night. Asleep or awake, hour by hour, I am happy beyond the poor compass of language to tell." Despite his exaltation or because of it, he sensed that they were all condemned to perish, even the captain. "All hands are now sadly affected. Captain Gardiner, a miracle of constitutional vigour, has suffered the least; and, if I listened to his own words, he is still none the worse, but his countenance bespeaks the contrary. Would it were not so!"[94]

A day or so later they killed ten "fine ducks" with only two shots, so thickly were the birds settled on the water: two welcome meals.[95] The following day, the shortest of the year, it was still snowing. Pearce sat in the *Speedwell* with the two invalids. Williams had wrapped his aching fingers in clothes. "His mind was beginning to wander," his biographer Hamilton noted. Williams' last words in his journal, a dialogue between himself and another self, are quoted here entirely.

When I left Burslem [his home, now part of Stoke-on-Trent, central England] on the mission, it was with a secret confidence I should see the salvation of God. Oh, my soul hath beheld it. "But the greatest trouble, some would say, is not over yet. You have but a week's provision more, even at the rate you are now living at, and no certain expectation of a vessel's coming in that time!" "Yes, this is so; but I have a certain and sure expectation of deliverance in that time." To-day is June 22; for I believe it is far advanced in the morning. We shall see. He that believeth shall never be confounded. Here I rest my hope. The Lord's will [will] be done.[96]

Resigned to the "Lord's will," he lingered on for two more months. The few supplies, which Gardiner probably shared with the others, remained in the cavern.[97]

Had the supply ship come to Banner Cove then, during June, as scheduled, with thirty casks with provisions for them that had already arrived in the Falklands, the seven missionaries would have been saved. So the "destiny," that caused their deaths was the delay in the delivery of provisions (see below). If everything that happens is credited to destiny or the "Lord's Will," "What must be, must be," as some famous philosopher surely said.

John Badcock, the First

Lying beside Williams, John Badcock turned toward him asking him to join him singing. With loud voices both sang the 202nd psalm of Wesley's Collection: "Arise, my soul, arise, Shake off thy guilty fears. . . ." A few minutes later, Badcock ceased to breathe. When Gardiner was told of Badcock's death, he remarked, "The first martyr joined his creator." According to Erwin's journal, his was "a miserable death of starvation and scurvy, but a thoroughly Christian." Maidment came from Earnest Cove to bury him that day or very soon thereafter.

The six remaining struggled to save themselves and each other, seeking anything edible – wild celery, seaweed, mussels, limpets, dead fish thrown on the shore by the high tides. But scurvy was gaining on them. By 2 July, Williams was delirious. Twenty days later, Bryant, weakened as he was, walked the mile to visit Gardiner in Earnest Cove. He told him that Williams was "wonderfully supported, both in body and mind. The Lord has been very gracious to him." Bryant was doing his best to comfort Gardiner.

By the end of July, the candles were burnt out and the last garden seeds consumed. Shellfish and wild celery could still be found. Gardiner cooked some mushrooms in water on the portable stove.[98] A week later he recalled the day he had left his home country. "On this day eleven months we left England for this country, and have been graciously preserved through many dangers and troubles. The Lord in his providence has seen fit to bring us very low . . . but all is in infinite wisdom, mercy and love."[99]

Joseph Erwin, Then John Bryant

The six men were agonising during the weeks after Badcock died. Then loyal Erwin, who had accompanied Gardiner on his first mission here, died on 23 August, in or near the *Speedwell*, at Cook River. Bryant who had returned there, died within the week. No other details were found about Erwin's and Bryant's last days. Pearce, very weak and overwhelmed with affliction for the loss of his two brothers of adoption, remained with Williams in the *Speedwell*. About this time Gardiner wrote farewell to one of his daughters and his eldest son, whom he bade to carry on his work.[100] This son, Allen M. Gardiner, will heed his father's last words (Chapter 8). Gardiner was now alone in Earnest Cove. Maidment had gone down the coast to Cook River where, despite his weakness, managed to bury Erwin and Bryant in the same grave, on 29 August. Soon afterwards he found his way back to Gardiner, who had been confined to his bed since 14 August.[101]

Williams and Pearce

About 28 August, Williams died, apparently on the beach, followed by Pearce in the *Speedwell*, probably on 2 or 3 September. Nor did I find any details about their final days.

Maidment

Somehow Maidment made his way from Ernest Cove to the nearby cavern, the first days of September. There he succumbed alone, on 3 September or the next day. Despard reported that, though enfeebled from hunger and disease, Maidment had traced "in trembling lines [in a notebook], in the damp cave where he abode, the expression of his joy in the Lord and his confidence in his love 'as sweet to know' in the chastisement from which he suffered."[102] He had struggled to enter this "damp cave" and die there alone.

Gardiner wrote, that very day, surprising details about Maidment's kindness to him, not knowing that he had already died, and added: "I tasted nothing yesterday. I cannot leave the place where I am, and know not whether he [Maidment] is in the body or enjoying the presence of the gracious God whom he has served so faithfully."

Gardiner Is the Last

Gardiner wrote extensively in his diary on 3 September, continuing from the above quotation: "I am by his abounding grace, kept in perfect peace, refreshed with a sense of my Saviour's love and an assurance that all is wisely and mercifully appointed, and pray that I may receive the full blessing which it is doubtless designed to bestow."

By 6 September, he imagined that Maidment was already "in the presence of his Redeemer, whom he served faithfully." That day of his death, Gardiner managed to write these trembling lines to Williams, who he thought was still alive. "Yet a little while, and though . . . the Almighty to sing the praises. . . . throne. I neither hunger nor thirst, though. . . . days without food. . . . Maidment's kindness to me. . . . heaven. Your affectionate brother in. . . . Allen F. Gardiner. September 6, 1851."[103]

Why Hadn't the Provisions Arrive?

Samuel Fisher Lafone, an English merchant living in Montevideo, had been contracted by the Patagonian Missionary Society to send a six months' supply of provisions to Banner Cove at the latest by June 1851. He dispatched the supplies from Montevideo early in January of that year, but the ship was wrecked on Staten Island. Lafone waited five months or so before engaging another ship. In May or early June the captain of this ship considered the area of Picton too dangerous to navigate in the winter so nearing Tierra del Fuego, he returned to Montevideo.[104] This captain and Lafone are responsible for not delivering the provisions as agreed upon, at the latest by June, although they had no way of knowing that the missionaries' lives were at stake.

Aftermath

Captain Smyley Arrives

Finally an experienced North American sealer was hired by Lafone, about early October, to deliver the provisions. This sealer, William Horton Smyley, had been sailing in these waters off and on since 1827. His name will become very familiar as Captain Smyley, the owner of a fast schooner called *John E. Davison*. On this occasion he was accompanied by Luis Piedra Buena, a sixteen-year-old Argentine, future sealer, and an energetic patriot. They headed directly for Banner Cove where, six weeks after Gardiner's death, they saw painted on the rocks: "Gone to Spaniard's Harbour." They found his message in one of the bottles. "The Indians being so hostile, we have gone to Spaniard's Harbour." In a severe storm, they sailed on the next day, 22 October, to the mouth of Cook River.

Smyley explained why they were unable to reach Earnest Cove and wrote of locating the *Speedwell* near Cook River, as well as the corpses of Pierce, Williams and Badcock. He apparently did not see Erwin's and Bryant's grave. Although he considered it his duty to make a further search, he failed to go to Earnest Cove because of the hail and snowstorms. He explained: "I can scarcely believe that the remainder [Erwin, Bryant, Maidment and Gardiner] is alive, but yet I have no evidence of their death, and it is my duty, it is every one's duty to make a further search."[105] He certainly reported his find to the British authorities in the Falklands. At least part of his report is quoted by Despard in his book *Hope Deferred, Not Lost*, to which I have so often referred.

Luis Piedra Buena, the young seaman, was profoundly moved by this scene of desolation. "The seamen weep because they are always brothers in their misfortunes."[106] Three months passed and no one went to Spaniard Harbour despite Smyley's harrowing report in October. No more was heard from Lafone.

The British Admiralty Comes to the Rescue

Captain Morshead had been Gardiner's fellow officer in the British Navy and was highly motivated by this assignment. As commander of the British Admiralty corvette *Dido*, he was accompanied by Reverend Armstrong. They had not been informed about Smyley's trip, so they assumed that the missionaries were still alive. They took along the thirty casks destined for them, which had arrived at the Falklands in June 1851, those which Lafone should have delivered. After searching for Gardiner and the others around Staten Island, they sailed on to Banner Cove on 21 January 1852, read the messages and proceeded to Spaniard Harbour.

The next day they found Gardiner's body near the wreck of the *Pioneer*, the remains of Maidment in the cavern, portions of Gardiner's diary, other papers and sundry objects strewn all about the shore. The following day they located the wreck of the *Speedwell* and, according to Morshead, "the remains of two bodies, which I conclude to be Mr Williams (surgeon) and

John Pearce (Cornish fisherman)." All the objects found were collected and carefully preserved, including Gardiner's and Williams' journals and Maidment's notebooks. Pieces of Erwin's notebook had been taken to the Falklands by Smyley. Thanks to Morshead, the seven were buried or reburied with military honours, late January 1852.

Had the Indians Come?

Although Smyley wrote that Pearce might have been killed by an Indian, because of the scar on his head and neck, there is no evidence that the Indians had approached the missionaries during their stay in Spaniard Harbour or after they had died. Neither Smyley nor Morshead reported traces of them, nor was their presence, or the sight of them, mentioned by the missionaries in their diaries during those seven months. Captain Martial, commander of the French expedition to Cape Horn some thirty years later, wrote: "The boats and numerous clothing which were intact would seem to prove that the Indians had not visited the sites for a long time."[107]

It is significant also that the Fuegians did not steal the missionaries' leftovers after their demise. But why didn't they come to aid them? The Haush probably had been nearby, as Spaniard Harbour was their territory. During all these months, they must have peered at the missionaries through the underbrush. They were usually peaceful and friendly to outsiders. Why didn't they offer help? The Yamana also certainly knew they were languishing there. Why didn't they bring them something – fish, for example? Perhaps they didn't because of the experiences they had had with Gardiner. The natives may simply have been afraid to approach them.

The News Hits London

It was not until 29 April 1852 that news of the tragedy appeared in the *London Times*. Soon other newspapers and magazines, such as the *Illustrated London News*, featured the story. It became a cause célèbre. Readers were stupefied. Sympathisers and members of the Patagonian Missionary Society were disheartened, discouraged and certainly asking: Is it reasonable to attempt to convert those Fuegians? Is it possible? Rather than risk more tragedies, it seemed preferable to many contributors of the society to support missions in Africa or some other continent where they were so badly needed. Why go so far? What about London's poor in the slums? "There is sufficient heathenish at home; let us attend to these first of all," appeared in the *Times* of May 1852. The *Voice of Piety* reported that the prestigious Church Missionary Society still refused to collaborate;

"too much to be done at home." Donations for the Patagonian Society slackened.[108]

Although public opinion was scandalised, a nucleus of determined "souls" proclaimed Gardiner a martyr, and the other six as well. In the logic of the missionaries' doctrine, nothing could happen without signifying the Divine Will in some way or another. Therefore their deaths were those of martyrs. Such was God's way of advancing the cause. He had, so to speak, been obliged to sacrifice these seven pious men in order to save the souls of thousands of Fuegians.

Admiral Sulivan's "Wonderful Deaths"

Thirty years later, in 1881, Admiral Sulivan, reflecting on the tragedy, applied the logic of the doctrine of Divine Will forcefully.

Had the Mission simply failed for a third time [the first – Fitz-Roy's attempt with young Matthews, the second – Gardiner's], it would have been very difficult to get people to take any interest in the work again; but *those wonderful deaths* and the *wonderful* journal preserved from the weather although it lay on the beach for months, awakened *wonderful* interest in the work, and with the blessing of God it was revived and continued with remarkable success, chiefly through the energy and faith of the Rev. G. P. Despard.[109]

Braun Menéndez paid the seven men this homage. "So much misfortune inhibits the historian from making a critical judgement of Gardiner's expedition, and of the errors committed by these devout, though mistaken men."[110]

8

1852 to 1858: The Missionaries Carry On; Jemmy Button Is Located

"The Mission Shall be Maintained"

When the news broke in Bristol in April 1852 of the deaths of Gardiner and the other six martyrs, Reverend George Pakenham Despard proclaimed: "By God's help the Mission in Tierra del Fuego shall be maintained." Rekindling the mission's resolve and hoisting the banner of "Gardiner the Martyr," he was supported by the Committee of the Patagonian Missionary Society and admirers. Despard, originally a pastor in Nottinghamshire, had been the secretary general of the society in Bristol since March 1850.[1]

Gardiner's last plan for a mission involved taking small groups of Fuegian (Yahgan) boys to the Falkland Islands, teaching them English and the rudiments of Christianity, while learning their language, and only then proceeding to establish a mission station in Indian territory, Tierra del Fuego. This plan was backed by Admiral Sulivan, now president of the committee, and other distinguished public personalities, including Admiral Fitz-Roy.

Sympathisers travelled throughout England and Scotland raising funds in memory of the "seven martyrs" in fulfilment of Gardiner's testament. Selections of his and Williams' diaries were read and discussed whenever and wherever possible.[2]

Save the Indians = Save the Castaways

Appeals for funds by the society were also made in the name of seamen whose vessels had been wrecked at that end of the earth. The public was told that castaways had been and would be in imminent danger of attack from the "savage inhabitants" unless these were converted. Moreover, future survivors of the wrecks would be sorely in need of a refuge where they could be cared for by the resident missionary and/or sympathetic English-speaking natives.

By then, 1852, the traffic around the Horn had increased more than could ever have been imagined. The discovery of gold in California was the cause. In 1849, during nine months from April to December, 549 ships "rushed" past or around the Horn. Some passengers arrived at their destination – San Francisco – where they tried their luck at digging or, more prosaically, offered their varied services in exchange for the diggers' nuggets. Other passengers and crews were not so lucky.

Despite the dangers, the Cape Horn route was still preferred to the Strait of Magellan. The 16,000 miles (29,635 kilometres) that had to be navigated from New York to San Francisco usually meant three months for the fast-sailing clippers; the slower ships took five to six months. The marine historian Marthe Barbance affirmed: "The competition for speed was born on the Cape Horn route." More recently the historian Paula Marks estimated that the rush to the California goldfields in 1849 attracted 90,000 "stampeders" from the United States, most of whom sailed around Cape Horn.[3] Not all the captains and stampeders made it to the golden land. Some left wrecks and cargos of hopes and bones along the coasts of these treacherous seas. But with the innovation of steamships, during the late 1850s, the cape route was all but abandoned by the commercial traffic in favour of the Magellan Strait. Steamships were usually able to navigate the most dangerous part of the strait (the western half), which had been a major problem for the sailboats. Even so the Cape Horn routes continued to be preferred by the captains of clippers or large sailing vessels (Chapter 2).[4]

By 1 August 1854, the "yacht of the Mission" was completed and baptised *Allen Gardiner*. Now confident and fortified in their determination, Reverend Despard, his collaborators and supporters were optimistic. The Patagonian Missionary Society advertised in the *London Times* for an experienced captain to take command of the vessel. The ad was answered almost immediately.

Captain Snow Is Hired

A certain William Parker Snow, thirty-seven years old, applied. Among his credentials, the decisive one was his experience of three years navigating Cape Horn "in good form." The society declined his offer to work free of charge but agreed to his request that his wife be allowed to accompany him as a non-worker, not officially connected with the mission though willing to aid it by helping him. He explained: "I was appointed to the post for the term of three years, to do everything with the vessel that in my judgement might be necessary towards the great object in view."

On 19 October 1854, during the farewell meeting in Bristol, Captain Snow received his written instructions. He was given complete authority as captain of the mission yacht. As soon as a mission station was established on the Falkland Islands, he was to proceed to Wulaia, accompanied by a clergyman and/or catechist, to search for Jemmy Button, highly recommended as the best contact for the missionaries, from their reading of Fitz-Roy and Darwin. Upon termination of Captain Snow's contract, he and his wife were to be sent home to England "free of expense."[5]

The Mission Yacht Sails for the Falkland Islands

Captain and Mrs Snow sailed from the inland port of Bristol into the north Atlantic aboard the brand new *Allen Gardiner* on 24 October 1854. The schooner had two masts, weighed eighty-eight tons and was about seventy feet (21.3 metres) long. It was armed with two small cannons and supplied with a twelve-months' supply of provisions. Snow was permitted to select the crew, although he was ordered "to employ no one but strictly religious men belonging to the Church." Finally, his crew consisted of two mates, four seamen, a cook and a cabin boy. All were recruited as devout Christians except the cook, a Hindu; and perhaps the good-natured cabin boy, called Bunning. There were also five passengers, including Mrs Snow. The devout passengers were Garland Phillips, a catechist; Dr James Ellis, a young surgeon-missionary; besides a carpenter and a mason also chosen for their piety but whose names were not mentioned. The latter four formed the "land party" and were assigned to construct a mission station in the Falklands.[6]

Snow, a religious man himself, was (initially) sympathetic to the objectives of the society, as undoubtedly was his wife. He was also a man of the world: besides having sailed three times around Cape Horn, he had joined a search expedition for the lost Arctic explorer Sir John Franklin. Snow had been a beachcomber in Australia and had met the native peoples there. He had also been an assistant to Thomas Babington Macaulay (1800–59), a well-known "Whig" (like Darwin) whose *History of England* was (is still) considered a masterpiece. Undoubtedly these experiences and adventures endowed Snow with a world-view that the missionaries lacked. He was also endowed with a passionate nature, open to new experiences with strange people, which rendered his Fuegian adventures exemplary though eventually self-defeating.

During the three months of ocean travel to the Falklands, Snow became annoyed by the "arrogant piety" of several crew members and passengers. He was especially irritated that his crew lacked knowledge of navigation and were more occupied with daily prayers than with keeping the schooner afloat.[7]

The Mission Rents Keppel Island (West Falkland)

That January 1855, shortly after their arrival at Port Stanley (the capital since 1844), East Falkland, Snow, probably in consultation with his two missionary passengers, selected Keppel Island, off the north shore of West Falkland Island, as a suitable site for the mission station. Soon thereafter the British authorities in Port Stanley received orders from the secretary of state for the colonies to allow the society to rent "unoccupied land on Keppel Island at 8 shillings per acre" for one year, later extended to twenty years. This island is a treeless expanse of bogs and tuft grass, six miles (11 kilometres) long and four miles (7 kilometres) wide, located about seventy miles (130 kilometres) by boat from Port Stanley.[8]

The contract having been signed by Captain Snow, construction of the station began early February 1855. During the following nine months everyone was busy building and settling down while Snow sailed to and from Keppel and Port Stanley for supplies and several times to Montevideo for the mail and other errands, including a search for a clergyman, which came to naught.[9]

Captain Snow Seeks Jemmy Button

Snow's assignment, as of October 1855, was to locate Jemmy Button and persuade him to allow some of the Yahgan boys to be brought to the Keppel Island mission station, as the martyr Gardiner had planned. Although he was aware that he was not about to enter the paradise of Rousseau's legend, he may not have realised that he was venturing into a world where hostilities prevailed among the Yamana themselves.

First Stop: Spaniard Harbour

On 11 October, nearly a year after leaving England, Snow and his wife departed on the *Allen Gardiner* with Garland Phillips, whom Snow referred to as Mr Catechist. The crewmen mentioned by name were Bunning, the cabin boy; Ali, the Hindu cook; and the seamen, Jones, Griffin and William Boyd.[10] Dr Ellis remained on Keppel, in charge of the "land party."

Word had gotten around in Port Stanley that the Fuegians were savage cannibals, to be given old clothes but not to be trusted. The sealers told stories about their mimicry, how disgusting they smelt, how they donned any old clothes every which way, that the women stayed in their canoes, and that with their painted faces they really looked funny. How could anyone comprehend such "savages"?

Hardly anyone thought about the natives. How did they know where such men came from in their immense canoes that almost seem alive? Why were some generous, even funny and friendly, while others were not at all? Why such disgusting hairy faces? Why were they all wrapped-up from head to foot? Where were the wives? Why did some give away food, clothes but others were really stingy, when they had such heaps of dead seals? Why did they kill herds of the seals even whales? What did they do with all of them? They couldn't eat so many. The strangers were a mystery to the natives.

Only Snow and Phillips had read Fitz-Roy and Darwin; but most of the crew had read the recently published *Hope Deferred not Lost,* by Reverend Despard, their superior, who was still in Bristol. As this book includes Gardiner's and Williams' journals, they approached Spaniard Harbour with a tense awareness of all that had occurred there just four years earlier. Upon arrival, Snow and Phillips recited passages from the Bible and they all sang hymns, including one Gardiner had composed. Then they nailed a commemorative tablet on the tree nearest the grave of the seven.[11]

Snow was aware that most of his men were alarmed at the prospect of navigating in the Fuegian waters. They had been warned in Port Stanley that the natives were "cannibals and that no vessel like ours ought to go alone." Despard's book had depressed some of them, though it had made others "arrogant and presuming." Snow did his best to counter these feelings by assuring them that the presence of his wife on board was a guarantee that he would not risk any unnecessary dangers. He admonished them "to show yourselves as men; and if there be any doubt or fear amongst you, now throw it overboard, trusting honestly and implicitly in your captain."[12]

Snow Meets the Yamana in Banner Cove

Snow's narration brings us closer to the Yamana than the writings of the previous outsiders, because he came with his wife and because both were surprisingly free of the superiority bias. He had "no hesitation in saying that, by her presence and good feeling, she was of great benefit to the mission."[13] Mrs Snow was the first white woman known to have met the Yahgan in their home territory. The natives must have been pleased to know that at least one white man had a wife.

Approaching Picton Island, sailing towards Banner Cove, Snow was "surprised and delighted" as he looked ahead. The setting seemed far superior to what he had imagined, and the beautiful day with its gentle breeze favoured the occasion.[14]

The Yamana they were about to meet probably remembered or certainly had heard about the white man and his six friends who stirred up so much commotion and killed one or more of them, just five years earlier. Although Snow might not have known about the killing, he was aware of Gardiner's conflict with the natives there.

Suddenly "stentorian voices" of three men shouting "*yamma scoona*" rang out from a canoe being paddled swiftly toward them by two women. The men in the canoe continued shouting, frothing at the mouth while making wild gestures with their arms. Snow thought they appeared "savagely indignant at our having violated the quiet of their native waters." But soon they were "laughing and mimicking" the newcomers. Snow was relieved. "They were fine, powerful-looking men, each in a state of savage nudity, and though shaggy as regards their uncombed hair, and otherwise repulsive, I could not help being greatly surprised at finding them so superior to what I had been led to expect the Fuegians really were."[15] He was probably recalling Gardiner's experience there. Phillips was less impressed, though at close range he found that "They were not so hideous-looking as the plates in Capt Fitzroy's book represent them."[16]

Snow noticed a "really good looking" woman in a canoe holding up her baby. With a winning smile and plaintive voice she repeated *yamma scoona*, meaning she wanted something for her baby, her *pauca nine*. Mrs Snow handed or threw her little presents, for which she smiled while uttering *Cutta-cutta, Cutta-cutta* to her baby. "Her attachment to her child was evident; and whatever was given to her for the child she immediately put around its neck, or about its person." The man with her was obviously her husband. Snow immediately realised that he was Gardiner's "Jemmy" not Jemmy Button (Chapter 7).[17] Then one of the seamen cried out: "There they are, the natives are coming off!" as two canoes paddled up to the yacht. Three of the men climbed on board, responding to signs of welcome from the captain. Young Bunning was "quite free and humorous with them." They patted his stomach first and then all the other stomachs while "wishing for everything they saw."[18]

One of the three on the deck was a rather old man, who struck them as the "cunning wizard of his party," walking about the deck "as he did with something like an independence and contempt in his manner." Another of the three was "Jemmy," Snow clarified, "there was nothing in him to cause dislike or dread. Neither he nor his comrades did aught on this or other visits to make us even be cautious of them."

They listened "with much attention" when the captain played his concertina, joined by Phillips and some of the crew singing the doxology hymn, a set form of words praising God.[19] Snow showed them a looking glass, dolls and other items for them to choose what might please them most. None took their fancy except some of the toys and gilt watches. They had a few things worth bartering for: bone spears, rush baskets, slings and a skin cape. Snow was pleased that they were "very fair and honest in their dealing with us." If they received an article that they thought he did not intend for them, they immediately returned it to him, whereupon he reassured them by giving the same object back to them. At sunset he made signs that it was time to go to sleep. When they departed, he was reassured that his manner with them had proven correct.

Thus ended this our first day amongst the haunts of these dreaded savages.... And how truly gratifying it had been to me I need hardly mention. I was amazed. And even now [after he had returned to England] I cannot help looking back to it with wonder! There was a total absence of everything that could make us afraid of them; and to express in words all that I experienced of delight and joy at this friendly meeting would be more than I can fitly do.[20]

Can they have been Gardiner's "enemies"? Snow knew that at least one was – "Jemmy" – and perhaps others also. Nocturnal shadows were shading the sky, so to ensure their safety, Snow ordered the crew to keep watch on deck in two-hour shifts until 8 AM. The following day, after breakfast, they went on a sort of pilgrimage to Tent Cove on Gardiner Island, where Snow read some "beautiful and touching lines" by Gardiner from Despard's book. They prayed for blessings for their labours and for the directors and supporters of the Society. Then they located the site of Gardiner's notice "We are gone to Spaniard Harbour," inscribed on the rocks.

When they crossed over in the yacht back to the shore of the Banner Cove, the natives rushed away as if to hide.[21] Snow beckoned to them from the deck, "intimating that we were friendly and in reply they invited us on shore; but here I hesitated." He was worried about leaving his companions on board, especially his "poor wife," and the possible danger of an attack by the natives with their slings, which he had read about in Fitz-Roy's account. Even so, he made up his mind to go ashore alone. Before leaving he gave orders to the first mate that if "an accident" occurred (meaning if the natives killed him), they should return immediately to Port Stanley and deliver the schooner to the authorities. He admitted to feeling "palpitations of the heart" as the yacht advanced to let him off, toward the "score of naked savages, yelling and making the most terrific noise imaginable." He stood on the deck and "made the usually understood sign of patting the stomach as an indication of friendly feeling." He had made up his mind that the best way "to win their confidence and respect is to place confidence in them, and show you do not dread their power."

He jumped into a small boat and rowed to the shore, where he found himself surrounded by "wild-looking creatures, shouting, frothing and gesticulating," laying hold of him in a way that made him "pause a while, and hesitate as to their intentions." The buttons on his jacket, his handkerchief and other things, "were handled by them somewhat roughly and the stunning noise they made, all talking together, confused me for an instant." But the chips were down, he could not turn back, so he followed them to their encampment, chattering as fast and lively as they (though in English), and patting their backs lustily as they did his.

In a few moments he "was perfectly at ease, seated on a fallen tree, amidst the whole family." The only inhospitable hosts were the growling, ferret-like dogs, which the men shooed away. He knelt to pray and his hosts knelt beside him. Then he capered about, singing with them, confident that he had won their hearts. Sure enough, they motioned him to enter their large wigwam. As he entered, a place almost free from the smoke was pointed out to him. He counted twenty-two people squatting around the fire.[22] Snow was not only courageous; he also proved that his confidence in humanity was authentic.

Meanwhile the crew, Phillips, and Mrs Snow in the yacht were becoming anxious. When the captain disappeared into the cluster of trees they heard confused noises and clatter from the wigwam. Everyone was wondering what was going on. Phillips and two crewmen went on shore in the other small boat, leaving the ship in charge of Bunning. When they came to the wigwam, they understood that the captain was inside. Phillips gestured that he wanted to enter, but the two oldest women and several men blocked his way. However he realised that his fears were groundless when his hosts began vigorously patting him and the two crewmen on their chests. One burly man took him in his arms and gave him a hearty, "by no means agreeable" squeeze that he thought best to receive with good grace. "I was like a feather in his grasp," he wrote. All the while the natives incessantly repeated *yama-schuma* (yet another spelling of the usual greeting), pointing to various articles of his outfit while mimicking his every word and movement. Despite these effusive greetings, Phillips was still not allowed in the wigwam. Later Snow imagined that he had been privileged to enter the wigwam because they had seen his wife, who was still on the ship.[23] In reality they had no way of knowing just who was her husband (see below).

Having settled in the wigwam, Snow began writing to provoke a reaction. The onlookers were so astonished that they begged him for his "magic wood." Several began scribbling, and he inferred that it would not be as difficult to teach them "as it is supposed."[24] Phillips, still outside, noticed the young women nearby who "had a most lively and interesting cast of countenance, and exhibited, in a greater or less degree, a large amount of intelligence." But he was especially pleased with the "pretty-looking little fellows." If only they were washed and clothed they could be petted and caressed by anyone fond of children. "Their little faces were round and plump, the teeth white, and eyes jet black and sparkling." While Phillips was romping on the grass with one of the little fellows, his parents kept a watchful eye on him, though they enjoyed seeing the amusement of their little son, "whose laugh rang through the trees right merrily." Thus ended Phillips' first encounter with the Fuegians, the Yahgans.

After dinner, when Snow and the others had been reunited on the yacht and were sailing nearby, the natives paddled a canoe trying to keep up with them, so Snow decided to tow it. They were overjoyed as their canoe cut rapidly through the water. "The novelty of the whole affair, fairly convulsed them with laughter," despite their fear of turning over. When the fun was over, all were safely back on land "amidst an incessant chattering of unintelligible jargon."[25]

After the canoe tow, Snow returned to the wigwam with his wife. They were greeted by expressions of pleasure. The women especially welcomed Mrs Snow, surrounding her and exclaiming *maquisce* (meaning unknown to me) in loud voices. They were very concerned that she not be inconvenienced by the smoke. Mrs Snow gave the name of Anunciata to an especially good-looking girl, about fifteen years old who had painted her face with black and red ochre. She, like the others, including the men, wore a sealskin.[26] Meanwhile Phillips was peeping through the wall of the hut. Even though he was still not allowed to enter, he was delighted with the hospitality shown to Mrs Snow and wrote: "This is another proof of the kindness of their disposition, and that savages though they be, they possess a politeness and amiability which sometimes are not to be found amongst many who are considered to have advanced to a high state of civilisation."[27]

Snow noticed heaps of mussel and limpet shells near the wigwam, residues of many a meal. Later he tasted a fungus, which when "young" had the appearance of a small salmon-coloured apple. He rather liked it, but Phillips thought it tasteless. This fungus, or mushroom, flourishes on the beech trees. Mentioned by Fitz-Roy and Darwin and named *Cyttaria darwinii*, it was later called Indian bread because it was such a favourite.

The Visit in Banner Cove Is Prolonged

Snow had planned to spend only a day or two in Banner Cove, but finally they remained a week. He went ashore daily, accompanied by Phillips or his wife, whom the natives were always pleased to see. Once he shot a bird for the women, which they cooked in ashes, as they did everything else. The cooking was fine, but hygiene was another matter. "They apparently have no idea of cleanliness, never wash themselves; vermin were swarming about them." Two men he measured were less than five and a half feet (1.67 metres) tall, and most were robust.[28] As the days passed, the good-looking Anunciata won their hearts. Again he noticed the Fuegians' fondness for children and that the dogs also claimed a large share of affection. Commenting on what Fitz-Roy and Darwin had heard about the natives' cannibalism, he added, "but of this I have no proof."

Snow was aware of the disdain some of his crew felt towards the natives. Several sneered when they saw him socialising and capering round in a circle with them, the children screaming with joy. When the first mate gave one of the adult natives a thrashing, Snow quickly reprimanded him for breaking the ship's rules. However, the second mate and the three of the crew never offended them. During this visit Snow even thought of proposing to the Society that he and his wife be assigned to live in Banner Cove for twelve months.[29]

Phillips was pleased when he was finally allowed into the wigwam with the captain and Mrs Snow. After a while, Phillips left the wigwam and went to the beach, perhaps to breathe some smoke-free air. There he came across "Jemmy" and his mother. Although Phillips had read that, according to Gardiner, "Jemmy" was a dangerous and formidable subject, he greeted him in a friendly manner. Then he knelt down, motioning to "Jemmy" and his mother to do likewise, which they did, while he pointed towards the heavens. As the three rose to their feet Phillips felt exalted, perceiving "on the dark features of these natives an expression of awe and wonder." This was his first act as a missionary.

On 24 October, the anniversary of their departure from England, they returned to the ruins of Gardiner's camp in Tent Cove. Phillips read the joyous 96th Psalm: "O sing to the Lord a new song; sing to the Lord, all the earth. . . ." As they were about to leave, two couples paddled across the cove to see what was going on. Mrs Snow gave one of the young women a needle, cotton thread and a little bag and began showing her how to sew. Meanwhile Snow and some of the crew had gone to shoot birds. The natives made signs to Phillips implying that Mrs Snow was his wife. Hereupon he clarified, by signs, that "the lady in question was the property of the captain." Phillips handed a tin pot to Bunning, when he offered to go into the woods to search for drinking water. As Bunning and his Fuegian guide trotted through the brambles, the latter suddenly stopped, peered on the ground, thrust a stick into the soil, "and then with a grunt of satisfaction turned and scraped up the earth until he came to water," pronouncing water in perfect English. When they returned with the pot full, Bunning reported that he had had "a charming unintelligible chat" with his companion.

On the day they weighed anchor, the natives gathered to bid them farewell. Phillips hoped they had made a favourable impression and expressed a longing to return with a missionary and "help to sow the good seed among them."[30] The visit to Banner Cove had been a stunning success for all concerned. The contrast between Snow's and Gardiner's relations with the same people highlights the decisive importance of the outsiders' attitude and behaviour, as did the encounters of Darwin and Wilkes with the Yamana on Wollaston Island (Chapter 6).

On to Wulaia

They set off heading for Wulaia, hoping to find the real Jemmy. Instructions from the Society's committee in Bristol were not to pass through Beagle Channel but to take the longer route through Nassau Bay. As Snow started out in that direction, a heavy squall obliged him to seek refuge in Lennox Cove. Approaching the shore, the crew saw smoke, an almost sure sign that natives were nearby. Towards evening, when the wind abated, sure enough a little family came to greet them. The men were "really very fine specimens of the human race." One especially good-looking man patted and hugged Snow, "rather too close to be pleasant," then led him to a beech tree and gathered the favourite fungus, which he ate by the handfuls. Snow tasted one, but now, like Phillips, found it excessively insipid.

On a nearby small island, probably Ormeño, they saw smoke again and went to discover who might be there. They were not disappointed when they met a man, his blind mother and three sons. Their wigwam was prettily situated in a small valley, surrounded by evergreens. This man also impressed Snow as being very different from "the notion we have of the Fuegians." He was erect, powerfully built and like his sons "wore nothing round him." Later Snow gave him a shirt. Two of the sons came willingly on board and received presents, but soon the youngest one began crying despite Mrs Snow's soothing. The father shouted from the shore, making signs to return his sons. Although Phillips urged Snow to keep them on board and take them back to Keppel, Snow refused and returned them to their father. Later he explained at length:

I did not consider it at all prudent to do anything rashly, as the catechist [Phillips] tried to urge me, in taking these poor boys away.... I saw upon the instant the risk was too great. I do not mean present risk, but risk to the future. It would, nay, I feel convinced, it will be ruin to the mission if any abduction of these poor ignorant natives takes place. They cannot understand the reason; they only know, or care to know, that their children are taken from them by the white man; and *very probably some sort of retaliation will occur....* I infer that it will be not only most unchristian but a dangerous plan to attempt taking any of the natives away. If the Mission wishes to be successful let it go amongst them as I did.

Finally, a missionary did "go amongst them" (Chapter 11). This strong moral stand by Snow was far more courageous in this epoch, when it seemed almost righteous to seize a native child for its own good. The next missionary took the risk of consulting the parents although a future missionary never heeded his example (Chapter 14).

On the morning of 30 October 1855, Snow steered the yacht from Lennox Cove into Nassau Bay where another heavy squall burst upon them as the sea became a "boiling maelstrom, bitter cold, snow, sleet, rain, wind." The yacht was so strained that he steered back to safe anchorage in Goree Road (between Lennox Island and Navarino Island). "Indeed no one can well describe the tremendous force of some of the gales of wind experienced in these places." Then he resolved to risk the Beagle Channel route to Wulaia despite his instructions to the contrary. On a beautiful first day of November, they entered the channel and came upon a scene "so truly charming to the eye – that one could hardly fancy oneself on the waters of Tierra del Fuego."[31]

Snow found that "many parts of Tierra del Fuego are far superior to anything generally represented by the early voyagers." The ship sailed through the narrow passage called Mackinlay Pass, then beyond the clay cliffs, passing flocks of penguins and the lofty peaks of Navarino Island. Having sighted fires on the south shore, Snow gave orders to camp there for the night, hoping to meet the natives who had been following them in several canoes, but none appeared. They awakened to another lovely day, 2 November. The local natives gathered on the coast of Navarino Island, and were intently watching the ship, while others were rushing from a distance to join them and get a better view of the strangers. All were completely nude, looking "wild and shaggy," grasping their long spears while shouting *yamma scoona*. But the yacht moved on, as canoes from both shores emerged, the natives shouting with all their might, and making signs to the ship to stop. But it sped ahead in a good wind until, a short while later, the wind died down. Snow lamented: "A calm is worse than a gale, without wind I could help myself comparatively but little if, as I soon found, the natives came off to us in numbers." Several crewmen grabbed the long oars and paddled the ship as fast as they could, but the natives were out-paddling them. Snow decided that he had best "use all precautions against being boarded by the dark and ferocious-looking beings that flocked around us." It seemed evident to him that most if not all of them had never before seen such a ship or such strangers. "Astonishment was depicted on their features."[32] More than twenty years had passed since Fitz-Roy and Darwin had been seen in the channel.

Oens-Men and Yamana Surround the Yacht

Snow gave orders not to allow anyone on deck or to let rope or anything else hang over the sides. About eight canoes were surrounding the ship. He thought from reading Fitz-Roy and Darwin that those on the starboard side were probably Jemmy Button's dreaded Oens-men (Selk'nam), from the north side of the channel, from Isla Grande, because they were "more bold and daring than the others" and "considerably more ferocious" than those on the Navarino side of the yacht. (Although the Selk'nam didn't normally inhabit this coast of the Isla Grande, they may have come down there, and borrowed canoes from the Yamana, because they had heard that strangers were arriving.) He gave strict orders not to allow those Oens-men on deck. He insisted that they were "much more warrior-like in appearance than our friends at Banner Cove." Two of the oldest among them had their hair plastered down with a white "substance" (clay), and they chattered so rapidly that "they foamed at their mouths like the froth of an angry sea." He was relieved to see two women with them, "for while the women remained I did not much expect there would be any attempt to attack us." Hoping to get on friendly terms, he bartered buttons and ribbons for shell necklaces, two spears and a "sunfish" which was thrown on the deck to add to the bargain. Despite his orders to the crew not to allow these Oens-men on board, he motioned them to climb on, which they did willingly. Although they picked up bits of iron and other objects that struck their fancy, "yet the same honesty in bartering was evinced here as at Banner Cove." However, when they left the ship and climbed back into their canoes, two of the older men began making such a clamouring noise, "demanding something from us," that Snow decided to outdo them. "I therefore took the speaking trumpet, and made a much greater noise than they. This had the desired effect. From a daring vociferous cry they fell to laughing, and seemed pleased that I made myself on a par with them – becoming, afterwards, quite as talkative, but not quite so bold."

His initiative had made the fearful Oens-men laugh. Nevertheless, he had the cutter and the other boat hoisted as high as possible "so as to be above their reach." When they began making furious noises again, he shouted through the trumpet and "ordered the cutter to be suddenly lowered as if it were going to fall upon them." This stopped their chattering, for a while.

Those on the port side (the Yahgans), were quiet and smiling. As they "had nothing to say to the others [the Oens-men], I imagine they were a totally different tribe." Even their children seemed astonished as they gazed at the ship and the captain.

By noon there was still not a breath of air and the ship lay immobile. Snow paced up and down the deck and "chatted" with the natives (Yahgans) now on board, while leaning over the starboard rail from time to time to catch a glimpse of the faintest ripple that would mean wind for his sails. He was nervous, not because of the calm or the Fuegians but because he was in Beagle Channel against the advice or orders "of an eminent naval officer," probably Sulivan, the director of the Society's committee. To calm his nerves and relieve the monotony Snow played his concertina, to the great delight of those on the south side (the Yahgans). To observe their reaction, Snow ignited some matches, which alarmed them; and when he turned on a signal light, they were even more astonished, though not fearful.

The Oens-men created more excitement when about seven of them began struggling to climb on board the yacht from their canoes without using the rope ladder. To avoid any "unpleasantness," Snow gave the order to shove the canoes away, but to no avail. He was determined to keep them at bay. As if turning his head towards his readers, he explained: "It would never do to take the 'dreaded Oen's-men' with us into the country of Jemmy Button . . . at all hazards we must get rid of these gentlemen." At that moment a faint breath of breeze from the north came to the rescue, then a breeze from the east. As the ship gained momentum, Snow mocked his would-be pursuers: "Too much for you, my Oen's men, is it? and you, too, more gentle Southerners."

Snow's clownish theatrics amused the Yahgans as well as the obtrusive Selk'nam. He had the ability and intelligence to improvise harmless tricks to distract potential aggressors.

On they sailed on through the channel, hoping to anchor at Wulaia before dark. As they veered south into Murray Narrows, they sighted figures in the distance gliding about in a wooded cove. Suddenly canoes appeared from all directions as voices rang out like a united shout: *Yamma scoona, Yamma scoona.* As they exited the narrows they discerned two small islets, then a much larger one, Button Island. More canoes darted out from the shore and several came in sight ahead.[33]

Button Island and a Real Surprise

Fires were lit on the islands, probably as signals. Seeing a crowd on the shore of Button Island, Snow was struck with the idea that perhaps Jemmy, if alive, might be there, instead of in Wulaia, about five miles (9 kilometres) farther on. As he hoisted the British colours, two canoes came paddling towards the schooner, while about a hundred natives gathered around their large fires on the promontories of the nearby cove.

Here Snow paused to tell the story of Fitz-Roy, of Murray's great discovery and of Jemmy Button. He was critical of Fitz-Roy for having taken the natives to England and bringing only one missionary on his return trip, although he expressed admiration for his survey of the narrows and the channel as one of the best ever made "of a coast generally admitted as the wildest and most tempestuous to be anywhere found."

When one of canoes was nearing the yacht, he hoisted the Union Jack farther up. Late this 2 November, Captain Snow stood on the raised platform of the deck shouting "Jemmy Button. Jemmy Button."

To my amazement and joy almost rendering me speechless – an answer came from one of the four men in the canoe, "Yes, yes: Jam-mes Button, Jam-mes Button!" at the same time pointing to the second canoe . . . [to] a stout, wild and shaggy-looking man standing up . . . "Jam-mes Button me! Jam-mes Button me!", shouted the newcomer; "Jam-mes Button, me: where's the ladder?" And the next moment Jemmy Button – the very man himself – the protégé of Captain Fitzroy – the one upon whom the mission rests so much of its hopes – was alongside, well and hearty, and giving me a welcome in broken words of my own tongue! . . . The next instant he . . . was on the deck of the "Allen Gardiner," shaking hands as heartily and as friendly as if he had known us for years.[34]

The crew were almost as surprised as Snow.

To hear their own language spoken by one of those very men upon whom they looked with so much contempt. . . . Twenty-three years had not obliterated the knowledge of our tongue, imparted to this poor child of nature by kind and friendly hands in England! . . . "Jemmy," said I, after the first few words of friendly greeting were over, "Jemmy, where good place for ship here?" "Yes, yes, plenty good – all here – that place me," he replied. . . . He was easily recognised from his resemblance to the account given of him in Captain Fitzroy's narrative. He was . . . quite naked, having his hair long and matted at the sides, cropped in front, and his eyes affected by smoke. The same words used by Captain Fitzroy to describe Jemmy are applicable now, as well as of his wife, who was also (this being his second wife and a very young woman) "good looking," and seemed to be much attached to Jemmy and the children.

Snow was not alarmed when at least sixty or seventy men surrounded the ship, although he cautioned his crew to be alert and not to allow any of them on deck. "Some 'bad men' were amongst them and he [Jemmy] pointed out one or two of the canoes as belonging to those 'bad men.' I did not, however, notice anything about them worse than the rest; and so long as they remained quiet, save the occasional 'yamma scoona,' I only took favourable notice of them."[35]

These "bad men" were undoubtedly Jemmy's Yahgan neighbours, who lived on both shores of Beagle Channel. Had they been the Oens-men, Snow certainly would have noticed that they were very different from the others as he had earlier this day along Beagle Channel.

When Jemmy was told that there was an "Ingliss lady" on board, he asked for clothes. As he was putting on the trousers, he said "want braces." Meanwhile Mrs Button was calling "Jamus! Jamus!" loudly and frequently, from a canoe, rapping hard against the ship's side with her paddle. She was greatly alarmed that Jemmy might be taken off again, somewhere far away.[36]

Following Jemmy's instructions, Snow took the ship into the cove. He lowered a boat to take a sounding of the depth of the water and discovered that it was not safe, but for that one night he decided to take the risk. The wind began blowing hard from the north, and a rock projection was much too close to the ship for comfort. Despite the dangers, he held the ship there.[37]

The Request

Snow posed the burning question, the motive of his mission, "in every possible and attractive form, both as regarded the adults and the younger branches, but a decided and positive negative was the reply from one and all." On the same page, he repeated that both he and the catechist (Phillips) asked Jemmy "if he, or any of his boys, would accompany us only a little way." Again they got a "positive negative."[38]

When Phillips returned to Keppel in the yacht the next month, he explained: "I have talked in English with Jemmy Button. He was very loving to me, and said, putting his arm round my waist, 'You very good man.' I wanted him to let me have his little boy for our missionary station, but he would not. I have made a proposition to the Committee to let us bring Jemmy, with his wife, girl and boy, to Cranmer [the Keppel Mission]. There will be so many advantages attending it."[39]

So no Yahgans were taken to Keppel in that November 1855. Snow deliberated:

Therefore, if I were to hear of ten or of fifty Fuegian boys as being at the mission station in the Falklands, I would never believe, until I knew that the Fuegians had learned our language, that those poor lads had gone there as only a religious society ought to let them go, namely, with a full and perfect knowledge of what it was for. Evil must not be done that good may perchance, and only perchance, come.

These thoughts carried him still further: "Savages they may be: degraded, miserable wretched beings! But they have hearts as well as we; and their way of thinking may be the same as ours on the question. Let us then go to them; not inveigle them to us."[40]

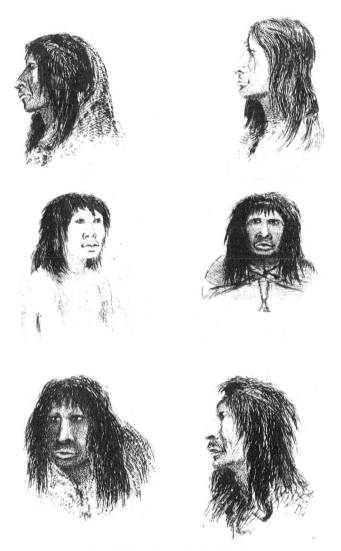

FIGURE 8.1. Six Fuegians sketched by Fitz-Roy.

Jemmy Sees Fitz-Roy's Drawings

Snow showed Jemmy the drawings by Fitz-Roy in the book he had brought along. "The portraits of himself and the other Fuegians made him laugh and look sad alternately, as the two characters he was represented in savage and civilized, came fore his eyes.... Which he thought he did not choose to say; but which I inferred he thought was gathered from his refusal to go anywhere again with us."

Jemmy spoke "with grateful feeling" of his stay in England and the voyages on the *Beagle*, recalling the people whom he had especially liked. In his own words:

Yes: me know – Ingliss conetree [country]; vary good – you flag, me know (meaning that he had understood the British Ensign that I had hoisted on the main); yes: much good – all good in Ingliss conetree – long way – me sick in hammock – vary bad – big water sea – me know Capen Fitzy-Byno-Bennet-Walamstow [the boarding school near London] Wilson [a clergy man, Chapter 5] – Ingliss lady, you wife?.... ah! Ingliss ladies vary pretty! vary pretty![41]

Snow inquired several times if any vessel or European strangers had been here since Captain Fitz-Roy. Jemmy replied: "No: – no ship – Capen Fitzroy, you."

He questioned the wisdom of giving Jemmy presents to the exclusion of the others and wondered if Jemmy's acquaintance with the English had given him some kind of superiority. But if so, he added, such superiority did not deter some of his countrymen "either by persevering solicitation, or, perhaps, by force, to get from him the presents I had made."

At dawn the next day Jemmy returned to the yacht, followed by a hundred or so others who appeared eager for gifts. Snow was sure that Jemmy could be trusted, though "his brothers and his countrymen were inclined to something like coercion with him."[42]

The latter are important comments because some of the missionaries, such as Thomas Bridges considered Jemmy a "great impostor" and thought that he had profited from his contacts with the English to promote himself (Chapter 9).

An Incident

While Captain Snow was waiting for the wind to stir, he distributed farewell presents to Jemmy, his family and the others. But Jemmy's brothers were not satisfied with the presents and began trying to pull off Snow's jacket and even unbuttoned his vest repeating: "Ingliss come – Ingliss give – Ingliss plenty." The tensions mounted but Snow remained calm. "To be surly with them I knew would not do; to show myself at all afraid would be equally bad; yet to act in any way that would cause those canoes full of savages to board us would be most unwise. I therefore moved toward Jemmy, who, however, could not or would not prevent his brothers' and companions' rudeness."

The last sentence highlights Jemmy's pacifism, even his lack of courage, his failure to aid Captain Snow. These texts are also relevant with respect to Jemmy's authority in his own group. Snow declared that Jemmy was not a chief "or the highest in authority amongst the natives." He had noticed an old man, with his hair plastered over, who seemed to have greater authority than Jemmy. A real crisis concerning Jemmy's leadership will occur four years later (Chapter 9).

Seeing that Jemmy did not help him, Snow decided to frighten the brothers and their companions, so he gave the order to "loose sails." At the moment the anchor was hauled up, "the effect I had anticipated was instantaneous. One and all, but Jemmy first, in answer to repeated calls from his wife, and after an affecting farewell, scrambled back over the ship's side as they saw her slowly moving, while a Babel of tongues and cries resounded everywhere about us."[43]

In retrospect again, recall Gardiner, who finally fired upon Yahgans and fled. Snow, also felt intimidated, but he neutralised the dangers that were latent in this situation, as he had with the Oens-men earlier that day.

Commenting on the above incident, Snow recommended that for future visits, the mission vessel should be equipped with auxiliary power in order to make a quick getaway if necessary.

Snow was with Jemmy only the evening of 2 November and the following morning. Although he told Jemmy that he would return in about six weeks, at the time he felt that he might never see him again. He composed these moving lines as he bade Jemmy farewell.

I waved my cap to the poor fellow; and that was the last I saw of Jemmy Button, the partly civilised Fuegian, the man of many hopes, of much talk, and of great name in getting an interest in the mission, while it brought large sums to the account, yet none the less a nude savage like his brethren....I did fancy the recollection of what he had learnt in England would have made him use a skin or some other article of clothing. But after all, it may be that we would do the same.... We like to be clothed; they do not, preferring the greater freedom which the absence from all external covering to their bodies gives them.[44]

Snow was again exceptional as one of the few outsiders who put himself in the Fuegian's "niche" as Darwin did with the African slaves in Brazil (Chapter 4). Yet Snow was unable to prevail upon Jemmy to accompany him "only a little way," much less to allow the male children to be taken there without their parents. Nor could Phillips convince Jemmy to let the children go.

Was Snow reluctant to insist that Jemmy accept his proposal to come to Keppel or least allow some male children to come? If so, was it because of a legal statue? H. E. L. Mellersh, Fitz-Roy's biographer, suggested that his reluctance was at least partly motivated by an "Alien Ordnance" of the Falkland Islands' statute laws, formulated to protect the natives of Tierra del Fuego as well as those of Patagonia, from being taken out of their homeland against their will. Mellersh stressed its importance as follows:

There was a local Alien Ordnance which might well be held to have been contravened if there was any suggestion whatever that the natives had not come entirely at their own free-will, that they had been kidnapped. There was also the undoubted fact that any captain of a vessel bringing in natives would be held directly and personally responsible for their welfare and might be chargeable to manslaughter should they die. Though this unexpected development was not to deter the missionaries, it did deter Captain Snow from pressing Jemmy Button too hard.[45]

Three years later, Gardiner's son would make another attempt. When Snow wrote his two volumes (back in England), he had distanced himself from the illusions he had entertained concerning the Anglican mission. "Familiarity with the naked savages of different lands would, I believe, do more to lessen particular immorality and vice than millions of sermons probably ever will or can."

But now, in early November 1855, the failure to recruit at least a few male children, was a stunning blow to Snow and to the Patagonian Missionary Society.

Mission Failed: Back to the Falklands

Having weighed anchor from Button Cove, they passed within view of Wulaia, where there was "not a living inhabitant in sight." As they sailed down Ponsonby Sound into Nassau Bay, a heavy gale from the southwest almost caused the ship to heel over; so they headed, tacking the wind, to the secure anchorage again in Goree Road. The next two weeks Snow explored the area of Wollaston and Hermite Islands, often seeing deserted "wigwams but no inhabitants." This puzzled him. He thought that they were probably hiding, afraid to approach his ship.[46] During the sixteen years since Wilkes' visit (in March 1839) the Yamana may have been badly treated by sealers and learned to avoid contact with any sort of vessel.

About 10 November, while rounding Horn Island, where the Yamana had never been reported by Europeans, they saw smoke rising from the narrow beach close to the cape. Snow thought it might come from the natives or perhaps wrecked mariners. He tried to approach the beach, but the strong winds made the manoeuvre impossible. As if shouting to invisible Fuegians or castaways, he wrote: "Fuegian if you be, or – God forbid! poor wrecked mariners. . . . Already are we heading off to sea;

and the mountain waves come rolling on in almost one long even line against us." The smoke obstructed their view, so they could not identify the figures moving about on the beach but as no trace of a wreck was noticed, Snow concluded that they must have been natives.

Safely back in Lennox Cove, he was again disappointed not to see any natives. He imagined that the family they had met recently, at the end of October, had departed because the father feared that he might take away his two sons.

Everyone aboard relaxed in Lennox Cove, exhausted as they were from the days of rough sailing around the Horn. Before dawn on 20 November, the ship departed, heading for the Falklands, advancing slowly. Although the sea was calm, the heavy swells moving forcefully toward the shore made navigation difficult. Snow dreaded those heavy swells even more than gales. He manoeuvred the yacht cautiously through the Le Maire Strait, confronting the usual riptides of contrary currents.[47]

Captain Snow's "Welcome"

Returning to Keppel on 22 November without any Yahgan boys, he anticipated trouble. As he expected, discussions became animated in Port Stanley and in the Keppel Mission. "Why didn't you bring at least a few boys, some Fuegians? Why didn't you do as ordered?" Some of his detractors thought he had not been persuasive enough, while others blamed Jemmy for being ungrateful for all the favours the English had showered upon him. Finally the news reached Bristol and the secretary of the Society, Reverend George Pakenham Despard.

Nine Months Later: Despard Takes Over

In August of the following year, 1856, Despard, the senior missionary, arrived in the Keppel Mission and soon afterwards fired Snow, leaving him and his wife stranded in Port Stanley. Despard violated the contract, which stipulated that the Society would pay for Snow's and his wife's return to England. Snow was sorely offended.[48] Mellersh wrote: "But whatever the provocation, Despard certainly treated Snow and his wife shabbily. Their passage money home was refused.... Snow managed to procure a passage home, where he set about suing the owners of the *Allen Gardiner* for wrongful dismissal."[49] Mellersh was sympathetic to Snow and felt that he had failed to defend himself as he should have, even though he had Sulivan against him for sailing through Beagle Channel to

Button Island, against orders. Also Despard was legally a part owner of the *Allen Gardiner* and therefore entitled to dismiss him. Nevertheless, Mellersh insisted, "the judge was sorry for Snow, whom he called a gallant seaman and an honest man and The Times' leading article seized on the fact that the unhappy captain had been quite unable to control his emotions in court."[50]

So ends this episode in the life of Captain William Parker Snow, this "gallant seaman," gifted with an uncanny sense of people, including Australian aborigines as well as Fuegians, whose company he really enjoyed. He was surprisingly free of prejudice, courageous, loyal to his convictions, unusually perceptive though impetuous and perhaps tactless while trying to defend himself. One of his personal chagrins was his failure to honour his promise to Jemmy Button.

"I told Jemmy; informing him that I should be back there again probably in about six weeks more; but the Society itself chose to prevent me, and, by the jealousy of the individual who was coming out [Despard], stopped all my future work."[51]

A fortune had been spent by the Society's headquarters in Bristol on the construction and voyages of the *Allen Gardiner*, the salaries and/or expenses for the Society's and mission's personnel and on the installation of the station in Keppel, which, after almost two years, had produced no results. Echoes of the discord between Snow and Despard did not reassure the authorities in Bristol.[52]

Despard was, nonetheless, exhilarated, early that June (1856), because he had been appointed as the director of the mission in Keppel and he thought that the Society was getting along just fine. "Our funds have wonderfully increased, and the formation of thirty-one Auxiliary Associations in England, Ireland and Scotland, both proves the spread of interest, and promises ample support."[53] On the eve of his departure for the Falklands he spoke of the arduous work ahead.

It will be carried on among probably the most debased of heathen tribes.... They are not well disposed to white men, and for good reason, for the white man passing along their shores has subjected them to every kind of bad treatment: he has shot them down for his amusement, saying "come, let us have a shot at those niggers." They have been killed by the men of science, who thought they had nothing better to do, than ... to put them to death, for the sake of bringing their dead bodies over to Europe and dissecting them.[54]

His last sentence is defamatory, that "men of science ... put them to death" is entirely an error, as far as I know. However, "dead bodies" were taken to Europe. Janet Browne mentioned a "solitary pickled corpse brought home in a barrel from the first Beagle voyage [which] was dissected at the Royal College of Surgeons."[55] Later, in 1883, two skeletons of the Yamana were taken to Paris for study (Chapter 13). All these Yamana had died of sickness. They were not killed by anyone.

Despard arrived in Port Stanley in August 1856 with an impressive entourage: his second wife, five children including an infant, two governesses, a house servant and furniture, even a piano. William Bartlett, the future manager of the Keppel Mission, came with his wife, and a carpenter, plus three missionaries. One was John Ogle, who was later dismissed because of his "independence of actions." Another, the catechist Charles Turpin, will stay at Keppel for years to come. Note the third was young Allen Gardiner, the son of the martyr, who will play a crucial and surprising role in the events to come.[56] A certain Dr Ellis, concerning whom I did not find much information, may have been a resident of Port Stanley. He joined the missionaries for a short while (see below).

Thomas Bridges

Among Despard's five children were two adopted sons. The youngest was Francis Jones, just ten years old at the time, who died two years later at Keppel. His story was not reported in the sources I consulted. The other orphan, Thomas Bridges, then thirteen years old will achieve a most outstanding missionary role in decades to come. At the age of about three, he had been rescued while crying, abandoned on a bridge in the port of Bristol. The little boy was well dressed but spoke no English, nor did he know his name, so he was baptized as Bridges (plural). His parents were thought to have been Belgian or French and to have perished in one of the plagues so frequent at that time. The missionary Phillips, who knew him well at Keppel, appraised him as "a very affectionate lad, he loves everybody, and I do believe everybody loves him."[57]

The Testament of the Martyr Is Honoured

In compliance with Gardiner's plan Yahgan boys – not girls or adults – should be brought to the Keppel Mission, taught the basis of the Gospel, some English, and the rudiments of civilising conduct. They should work there for the mission but also benefit from the experience once they returned home. Besides teaching the boys, the missionaries should acquire knowledge of the native language from them and eventually accompany them back to their homeland, where a mission station should be established in their territory. Meanwhile, the Keppel Mission should become a self-sustaining sheep and cattle farm and thereby free the society from the need to collect funds in England and elsewhere.[58] Despard was confident that all would go well, partly because "Happily for us, and (I trust) eventually for the poor Indians, the Falkland Islands are now under the British flag."[59]

Gardiner's Son Meets the Yahgans

From August 1856, during the next eight or nine months, Despard was busy settling in with his family in the Keppel station and organising future work. Early in 1857 he sailed to Montevideo to find a replacement for Snow and to recruit another pious crew. A certain Captain Bunt and a crew were hired. They are rarely mentioned in the mission bulletin or elsewhere.

Towards the end of March 1857, Despard departed for Tierra del Fuego in the *Allen Gardiner* with the new captain and crew, Dr Ellis and young Gardiner. Note that some confusion might arise because the latter had the same name as his father except for the middle initial. From now on he will be distinguished as "Gardiner's son," "young Gardiner" or simply "Gardiner" if the context is clear.

The final destination was Banner Cove, which young Gardiner was probably keen on visiting because of his father's experience there. Now, in 1857, they confronted such rough weather crossing over to Tierra del Fuego that that they took refuge in Good Success Bay for several weeks and then stopped over in Spaniard Harbour. Twenty years later, in 1877, Gardiner evoked the homage he had rendered there to his father.

I had the melancholy pleasure in the course of my Fuegian cruise of spending eleven days in Spaniards' Harbour. It was with singular feeling of solemnity that I read the Scriptures in that dark Fuegian cavern, where these Mission journals were indited [written], the recovery of which . . . were the providential instrumentality for reviving our Society's Mission work in Tierra del Fuego.[60]

The last week or so of April 1857, Gardiner and the others went on from Spaniard Harbour to Banner Cove, where they stayed for six days (not described). Then they continued on to Blomfield Harbour, where Gardiner's father had relentlessly insisted they return (in 1850 and 1851) despite Dr Williams' objections. Now they bartered peacefully there with the Yamana. Young Gardiner commented, "They seemed highly delighted at getting into such close quarters with us and their dog was soon quite friendly, and even so far forgot himself as to wag his tail."

Young Gardiner was unusually fond of dogs, as will become evident soon. The schooner sailed south, down to Lennox Cove, where two canoes with about thirteen natives approached the ship. A bit later, Gardiner and the others visited them in their wigwam, where he exchanged a duck they had shot for two young terriers. He noticed that these dogs were well adapted to travelling in canoes, much better "than the big Patagonian dogs." He named his dogs Jenny and Bob, the latter in memory of Robert Fitz-Roy, and became very attached to him.

The next day, 9 May, they returned to Banner Cove and stayed for two weeks with the same people they had seen or met on their first visit. Now, they were invited into the wigwams. The first time into a very large one occupied by twenty-six people, three dogs and puppies. A space was made for Dr Ellis to sit down and probably also for Despard and Gardiner. Their hosts were friendly though a bit intrusive. The women constantly motioned for gifts for their babies. "The man seated next to Ellis ran his hands over his coat several times, exclaiming '*Yammer schooner tiee.*'" He probably wanted the buttons on the coat. Ellis decided that the ornament he had already given to one of the children was a sufficient gift for all of them, which did not please the women. Later the men cut and loaded lumber for the construction still being done on Keppel (one of the objectives of this trip). These "Fuegians" (Yamanas) were amazed by how rapidly the crew cut down the trees with their steel axes. Two of the men helped carry the lumber to the ship and were paid with fishing lines, knives, clothing and scarlet comforters, which they much appreciated. Ellis noted that these two men, who afterwards sat down around a fire with them, were "very quiet and friendly."[61]

Just as Williams had observed when he first sighted the Yahgans in this same locality (Chapter 7), Ellis also explained why foreigners had such negative impressions of the natives when they first saw them and why these impressions often changed when they saw them at close range.

The first impression is one of disgust; the naked form, the long matted hair, which increases the apparent size of the head, the dirtiness of the person, and the strange uncouth gestures, all contribute to produce an unfavourable impression. The women particularly appear very ugly. But as the eye becomes accustomed to the naked form . . . the impression of ugliness wears off, and some appear even good looking.

Ellis, as a doctor, noticed that the eyes of some were constantly oozing, and that they wiped away the liquid with their long hair, that others had boils and eruptions on their heads, that several women were blind in one eye, that another had a wry-neck (torticollis), her mouth drawn to one side, and that an elderly man had a "cadaverous paleness." All in all not a very healthy group in Banner Cove. But Ellis, Gardiner and Despard were pleased with their "docility and friendliness."[62] This first trip to Tierra del Fuego in 1857 was obviously intended to familiarise Despard with the natives and above all Gardiner, who had probably already been selected for an important assignment. Dr Ellis apparently departed afterwards from the Falklands or stayed in Port Stanley, as he is not mentioned later.

Young Gardiner Is Assigned to the Most Difficult Task

It is no coincidence that the martyr's son was selected to take the leading role in the next assignment. Despard requested or appealed to him to succeed where Captain Snow had failed: convince Jemmy Button to allow some of the male children to be brought to Keppel, in fulfilment of his father's plan.

The Two Versions of Gardiner's 1858 Trip

This trip will last a little over two months, 20 April to 24 June. There are two versions of this trip. Both are by Gardiner himself and both were published in the mission magazine. The early version consists of selections from his journal which were published in *The Voice of Pity* in 1858.[63] Unfortunately I did not inquire about his original hand-written journal, which may be available in some archive in London or Bristol. The second version is a transcription of a speech he made twenty years later and was published that year, in 1878, in the same magazine, which had meanwhile changed its name to *South American Missionary Magazine*.[64] By 1878 Gardiner was probably in his mid-forties and had been ordained. Unfortunately he died at the end of that year, in Natal, South Africa, where he had gone to work as a missionary. If more data can be found, his biography should be written. In the following pages he emerges as a truly exceptional human being and missionary.

Both versions (of 1858 and 1878) are cited or paraphrased here as five episodes of this trip: from 20 April to 16 June when Gardiner leaves Wulaia. He returns to Keppel on 26 June.

20 April–18 May: First Episode: 1858 Version

On 20 April 1858 young Gardiner departed with the missionaries Charles Turpin, John Ogle, Captain Bunt, the crew and his dog "Bob" in the *Allen Gardiner* yacht. Six days later they reached Good Success Bay (Le Maire Strait) where they were "very thankful for shelter from a heavy gale." On

7 May they left there and arrived near the entrance to Spaniard Harbour the following day "but encountered such a heavy squall from the Bell Mountain, that the schooner could not carry canvas to get in; so Capt Bunt kept her away for the night. Providentially the wind shifted in the morning to a more favourable quarter, so that we reached an anchorage off Lennox Cove."[65] (They arrived on Lennox Island on 8 May.)

Lennox Island Monday [10 May] A canoe came this morning from the direction of Picton Island. . . . Two more canoes came over early to-day (Tuesday) [11 May] in a dead calm, and all occupy one wigwam – twenty-five, including children. This afternoon I visited their wigwam, and took a sketch of them, seated round their fire, and afterwards helped them haul their canoes up into the bushes for the night, the tide being very high on the beach. They put kelp down as a soft road to run them on, to protect the bark from being injured by the pebbles.

The next entry is nine days later:

Fuegian Wigwam, May 18th. Whilst writing this, a party of fifteen Fuegians are surrounding me closely. The fire too makes the wigwam unpleasantly warm, and the dogs' are barking incessantly, including my faithful dog "Bob" who evidently considering himself my special guardian accompanied me to the wigwam, in a very fierce frame of mind. The old woman sitting on the opposite side of the fire has lost an eye. One of the men is very busy, making a basket of rushes, and bargaining with me to give him a knife for it, when it is finished. Only six out of the number are new faces; the rest we saw last year.

20 April–18 May: First Episode: 1878 Version

The only date mentioned in this version is 6 May. Young Gardiner spoke (the "1878 version") during the twenty-seventh annual meeting of the South American Missionary Society, on 6 May 1878.[66] Following preliminary remarks, he began speaking about his meeting, exactly twenty years before, on 6 May 1858, because of an extraordinary coincidence of dates. (Note that as usual my words in the quotations are in brackets and those in Gardiner's text [in the SAMM], are in parentheses.) He stated:

Looking back into my journal, I find that it was upon this very day, the 6th of May, in the year 1858, that I attended a Meeting in Tierra del Fuego. That Meeting was like the present Meeting, influentially attended; for all the Fuegians from Picton Island and Lennox Island were present. On that occasion the same duty devolved upon me, which it has been my lot this afternoon, viz., moving the first Resolution. . . . They [the Yahgans] all spoke with eagerness on the main point and they all spoke at once, until after a protracted conference unanimity prevailed and our proposal was negatived. Considering the great trouble and expense undergone by the Society in preparing the Keppel Island institution for the Fuegian children, this refusal was exceedingly discouraging, more especially as it came from the natives of two islands (Picton Island and Lennox Island) admirably suited for our Society's objects. The whole matter had been most carefully explained to the natives. They had examined the cases of clothes sent out from England for their children at the Falkland Home. Sheep and goats had been promised them, on the return of their children to Tierra del Fuego, also vegetable and garden seeds. The children were anxious to come, but, nevertheless, we could not secure the consent of their parents.[67]

These two days – 6 May 1858 and 6 May 1878 – inspired Gardiner to make an analogy between the members of the Missionary Society, whom he was addressing on 6 May 1878, and the Fuegians of Picton and Lennox Islands, to whom he had spoken on that very day twenty years before on Lennox Island.

Recall according to the 1858 version they were still in Good Success Bay on 6 May but, in this 1878 version, on 6 May 1858 Gardiner held the meeting on Lennox Island, as quoted above. In the 1858 version there is no text whatsoever about the meeting on Lennox Island. According to this 1858 version, Gardiner did not arrive on Lennox Island until 8 May. This is a serious omission, not simply an error. Recall that one of the main purposes of the mission magazine was to diffuse, uphold and support the work and projects of the Patagonian Missionary Society, later called the South American Missionary Society. The refusal of Yamana parents to allow their children to go to Keppel, despite the gifts and the children's desires, was obviously considered adverse publicity for the society at that time. Their refusal substantiates Captain Snow's aversion to taking only the children to Keppel without their parents' consent. Also, the above quotation provides conclusive evidence of young Gardiner's moral stance: he did not even consider trying to lure the children on the ship and taking them to Keppel without their parents' consent, as Phillips had suggested to Snow. Gardiner was forthright in his attempt to persuade the parents to allow their children to be taken to Keppel (for a limited time) by calling a meeting of the parents of Picton and Lennox to discuss his proposals and he respected their decision. This fine quality of Gardiner will appear again in the near future.

22 May–1 June: Second Episode: 1858 Version

Between 22 and 25 May the schooner, the yacht, was anchored in Goree Road, where the crew waited for a wind in order to continue the voyage. Gardiner described the surroundings, the landscape. No event of any consequence is reported for these days. On 26 May they stopped over on Wollaston Island, having failed to reach Packsaddle Bay. Two days later they went ashore on Wollaston "to look for a watering place. We walked a long way before finding any. It was rather a break neck affair." Again nothing of consequence occurred: no natives mentioned.

There are three Wollaston Islands – Grevy, Bayly and Wollaston proper; the shores of Gretton Bay include all three islands.

In Gretton Bay, on 31 May, a Sunday, two canoes came to visit them. One was about eighteen feet (5.4 metres) long, the longest Gardiner had ever seen, and it carried two fires. The next evening [Here Gardiner refers to Monday, which was 1 June though at the end of the page, his next entry is 1 June, so there is a confusion of dates here.] This day, [probably May 31], at 8 PM, when it was already dark, canoes came again alongside the schooner. Then Gardiner and a few of his men took the schooner's whaleboat to visit people in wigwams nearby. The natives followed, paddling as hard as they could, but failed to catch up with them. At intervals Gardiner, in the whaleboat, waited for the natives because he needed them as guides to visit natives on the shore. After pulling about three miles, they came to a very sheltered harbour, where they saw smoke rising from a wigwam. Gardiner and Turpin entered the wigwam and were seated by the fire, surrounded by about thirty-five natives, including children. One of the men seated next to Gardiner was shivering and warming his hands by the fire. "He felt mine, to see if they were cold too." Gardiner noticed the dogs, patted the puppies, looked at baskets and bark cups hanging from the support poles and saw a bed of moss in a corner. The visitors exchanged some presents for a few fish and a basket.[68] This visit took place on the shore of Gretton Bay. On 1 June they continued towards Packsaddle Bay where they "landed" the morning of 2 June.

22 May–1 June: Second Episode: 1878 Version No Mention

2 June: Third Episode: 1858 Version

The next encounter, as published in 1858, related that on 2 June they arrived in Packsaddle Bay, on the coast of Hoste Island (near Orange Bay), where they remained a week. Three canoes approached them when Gardiner was in a boat going to the shore. "They were a gloomy looking company altogether, quite surly at times, and disposed to be quarrelsome, making signs for no one to approach their wigwam. And when the boat [Gardiner's boat] landed after dinner, Captain Bunt told me at one time he thought they were going to attack them [Bunt and his crew]." That morning Gardiner had purchased a canoe from the natives in exchange for three items: an axe, a large Crimean cloak and a coloured blanket, which very much pleased them. But when he and Captain Bunt tried to hoist the canoe on board, it slipped and sank. "Fortunately the natives did not see the catastrophe." After dinner Gardiner "went on shore with the natives in their canoe, and visited their wigwam."

They made no objection to my coming in, perhaps because I was alone; and as one of their party was sick, and huddled up in a seal skin by the fire, it accounts for their unwillingness yesterday for any one to come near the wigwam. They had a tremendous fire, and seemed in high spirits at having got my axe. The oldest man amongst them astonished me rather by commencing to sing in their outlandish way, his voice getting high, when he suddenly stopped, and by way of a climax, I suppose, seized hold of my hair. I did not return the compliment, but tried in a social manner to divert the current of his feelings; and very soon after this little demonstration whistled to my dog, who was racing about the premises, glad to get out of the vessel, and cleared out. I ought not to forget to mention, that this morning a canoe was alongside when we had prayers, and the natives pointed up to the sky; but when the hymn was sung, the women burst into tears.[69]

This is all that was reported, apparently on 2 June.

2 June: Third Episode: 1878 Version

From Picton Island they sailed to Wollaston Island an anchor in Gretton Bay. Here Gardiner does not give a date. It probably was on or about 2 June as noted in the 1857 version. Having arrived in the schooner in Gretton Bay "fine" canoes visited them. (Gardiner probably was thinking of the three canoes mentioned in 1858.) These Fuegians asked or told them by gestures to accompany them across the peninsula to their huts. "Hoping to create a favourable impression," Gardiner and some of the crew followed them in the whaleboat. Having reached the shore, Gardiner ordered his men to leave their weapons in the whaleboat but told the man who stayed in the whaleboat to keep it afloat outside the kelp. Then Gardiner and his men (except one who remained in the whaleboat) continued on foot, following their guides to the wigwams. It was almost dark when they saw natives in the distance, standing by fires outside the wigwams. In some way "the manner of the Indians" leading them to the wigwams suddenly changed and seemed threatening, so Gardiner and his men rushed back to the whaleboat. The natives followed them "with their spears" and rushed towards the whaleboat, but Gardiner and his men got away safely. "The Fuegians launched six canoes with great rapidity, and, owing to the fires in the canoes [by then it was dark], we could watch their proceedings without our own course being perceived. We lost no time in getting clear, and as our boat [the *Allen Gardiner*] under sail could beat their fastest canoes, they soon returned [went home]."[70]

Gardiner and his men were able to flee and avoid a confrontation. However, he did not say why they were threatening to attack him and his party. Neither does the 1858 version explain why these Yahgans were so hostile to these visitors, when usually, as we have seen, they greeted strangers, especially if they were not commercial sealers, in a friendly manner. I assume that for the 1858 version selections were made from his journal of two visits to the wigwams and that it relates the first visit, which was not mentioned in 1878. While the most aggressive, the last one, when Gardiner and his men were pursued, was obviously censored for the same reason mentioned above: it would not have been good for public relations.

9–15 June: Fourth Episode: 1858 Version

Having stayed a week in Packsaddle Bay, until 9 June, the mission party sailed on to Wulaia that same day, where they were greeted by a man in a canoe near the coast. When Gardiner inquired about "J's" (as Gardiner usually wrote Jemmy Button's name in his journal) whereabouts, the man indicated, probably by gestures, that he was on Button Island. Later, about two hours before dawn, Gardiner noticed that a canoe had departed from Wulaia. At noon, 10 June, it reappeared with four other canoes coming from Button Island. "J" was not there, but his daughter and her husband were. The husband was "one of the most intelligent looking Indians we have seen." Gardiner gave them a few things, while showing them far better ones, and repeating "Jemmy Button." This had the desired result. The next day, 11 June, as quoted from his 1858 diary:

About 9 A.M. four canoes were seen rounding the north point of Button island, and coming across the sound.... As soon as they were with in hailing distance I called out, "Jemmy Button," and a native stood up in the foremost canoe and replied, "Yes Sir." In a few minutes more he was alongside, came up the ladder, and shook hands.

Over coffee, bread and butter Jemmy inquired about Captain Fitz-Roy and was very pleased for a gift Bynoe had sent for him: a box of carpenter's tools. Jemmy's daughter also showed that she appreciated the presents she received for paddling back and forth to fetch her father. Jemmy took the crew to the spot where Fitz-Roy had the huts built for Matthews, York and Fuegia in 1833. Again from his 1858 journal:

It was a very pretty scene, nineteen canoes scattered about the cove; the natives, some cutting wood, some repairing their wigwams with green branches, others lighting their fires. It was surprising to see the dexterity with which they handled their rude axes. One of them J. [Jemmy] said, was given him by Captain Fitzroy; so it must have been in use for twenty years. It was a very big one originally, but is worn down almost to nothing.[71]

When Gardiner asked Jemmy to take him for a ride in his canoe, he immediately told his wife to haul up their canoe to a rock. They embarked in style, Mrs Button manoeuvring the little "flotilla with much precision." While canoeing, Jemmy told his host of a tragedy that happened a "long time ago" and a "long, long way off." A ship with white men fell amongst the natives and they were all killed, though not by his people, Jemmy insisted. (I found no other reference to this incident.) Gardiner continued and wrote that on 12 June Jemmy and his little son attended "our family worship." At that moment or a bit later,

He [Jemmy] volunteered to come with us himself, with his wife and three of his children. To try if he was serious, I proposed to him to send his canoe on board, to which he replied, "Very well;" and Capt Bunt had it hoisted on board, fortunately without any damage to it, to J's great satisfaction. Whether he really is coming, I cannot pretend to say; but he leaves his present on board. All J's tribe are here now, and are very civil, both on shore and when alongside the vessel.

On 15 June, still the 1858 version, Jemmy and his family were on board and the yacht set sail for Keppel. Their relations followed them a little way in their canoes but the wind died down, and "the schooner had to be towed back to the anchorage." Gardiner remarked that he was not sorry for this delay, "as it gave J. an opportunity to retract, if his resolution was shaken." The next day they left Wulaia.[72]

9–15 June: Fourth Episode: 1878 Version

Only the events and explanations in the 1878 speech, which were omitted in 1858, are cited here. Gardiner did not mention Jemmy by name in his 1878 speech and referred to him as "the Fuegian who, in his childhood, had been taken to England on board H.M.S. Beagle." In his 1878 speech clarified why "the Fuegian" agreed to go to Keppel in 1858. "Through his [Jemmy's] advice we amended the Society's proposal so as to take several families with their children, instead of the children alone. He volunteered to bring his family at once as an example to the rest if we would wait one week for him to obtain the consent of his tribe."[73]

His speech continued, with italics added:

The day before we sailed [15 June], a large force of Beagle Channel Indians came over to attack the Mission vessel, and endeavoured to secure the co-operation of the Navarin Islanders. We immediately shifted the schooner from her almost land-locked position in Woollya Cove to the outer roads. *During this manoeuvre the Channel Indians shouted to the Navarin Islanders for their help to capture the vessel. The hostile party of sixty canoes* that approached us now were the same which massacred our Mission party, one survivor excepted, and captured the vessel in the following year, 1859 [see Chapter 9]. On that occasion, however, the Navarin Islanders unhappily joined them. It was lamentable to notice the countenances of these Indians under the diabolical influences which seem to rouse the savage by sudden paroxysms from a state of apathy to what I can only call homicidal mania. The boldest seaman on board recoiled in disgust from the fearful sounds which these Fuegians made continuously for four hours. It resembled rather the continuous roaring of wild beasts than human voices, and most of the men were foaming at the mouth in their wild excitement.

At sunset the missionaries responded to their continuous "roaring" by firing "brass carronades with blank cartridges, sent up sky-rockets, and burned Bengal lights, which illuminated the ports." This impressive display had the desired effect, "and overawed by these strange sights, the Fuegians ceased their furious cries and paddled away into the gloomy darkness of the Beagle Channel."

Sixty canoes, as quoted above, may seem exaggerated, but an even greater number of canoes is reported the following year in Wulaia (Chapter 9). It seems clear to me that Gardiner's term "Channel Indians" refers to the "hostile" neighbours of Beagle Channel (Chapter 5). Concerning the number of canoes the Yahgans might have been able to assemble for an attack it is also relevant that Murray reported that, in April 1830, he saw near Murray Narrows "upward of a hundred canoes...in one day" (Chapter 3).

Young Gardiner was able to handle the aggression of the Yahgans (the "Channel Indians" and their Navarino allies) without fatalities and without fleeing from them, in contrast to his father's inability to cope with them (Chapter 7).

Note that following Jemmy's advice, Gardiner amended the Society's rule to take only male children to Keppel so as to be able to take Jemmy, his wife, with three of their children there. Recall that the 1858 version simply stated that Jemmy volunteered to go to Keppel with his family.

Gardiner may also have offered to take Jemmy, his wife, with their three youngest children to Keppel because of the 6 May meeting on Lennox Island, when the parents refused to allow their children to be taken alone to Keppel. Then too he certainly knew why Captain Snow had failed to convince Jemmy to go to Keppel just three years before. Note also that Jemmy asked for "the consent of his tribe" to go to Keppel, which was not mentioned in 1858 either.[74]

16 June: Fifth and Last Episode: 1858 Version
They departed from Wulaia 16 June but did not arrive at Keppel until 24 June because of the "very rough weather . . . our Fuegian family were not sick, as I expected."

16 June: Fifth and Last Episode: 1878 Version
The day after the aggressors left, on 16 June 1858, with little wind, the *Allen Gardiner* departed for Keppel, moving slowly under the "towering cliffs" of Button Island, followed by an escort of ten canoes. Jemmy and his family "looked anxiously at their friends in the canoes," who responded to the three cheers from the crew with much friendly gesticulation. Gardiner "felt that the first link of the Mission chain had been ultimately fastened in this hitherto neglected region of Tierra del Fuego."[75] They arrived in Keppel on 24 June as noted in Gardiner's 1858 journal, on 26 June according to the 1878 version.

In Retrospect
The Anglican mission magazine omitted the following four events (of three "episodes") of Gardiner's 1858 journal, which were mentioned in his speech and published in 1878, by the same magazine.

1. In the First Episode, 6 May: the meeting Gardiner held during which the Picton and Lennox parents refused to permit their children to be taken to the Keppel mission
2. In the Third Episode, about 2 June: the threatening pursuit by the Yahgans of Gardiner and his crew in Wollaston Island (Gretton Bay)
3. In the Fourth Episode, 9 June: the concession Gardiner made, following Jemmy's advice, by offering to take Jemmy and his family to Keppel instead of only Yahgan male children
4. Also in the Fourth Episode, 15 June: the threatened attack of 60 canoes of the "Channel Indians" near Wulaia against the mission yacht

These omissions are too coherent to assume that they were left out in 1858 for lack of space in the magazine. Therefore, it seems obvious that in 1858 the editors censored these four "events" of Gardiner's journal. As I mentioned above, such events would give the impression to their readers that the missionaries were not welcome in Tierra del Fuego. But if so, why did the editors of the same magazine publish the four events mentioned above in 1878, without censoring them?

Several possible answers come to mind. One, that twenty years later the editors did not recall the contents of the 1858 article or had not read it. Also, the 1878 text, only three pages long, is one of five speeches, all of which appear in very small print and do not strike the casual reader as important. Another possibility, or hypothesis, is that with the passage of time, the Society was no longer concerned about the opposition that the missionaries confronted in Tierra del Fuego or did not approve of the former censorship and therefore published Gardiner's entire 1878 speech, aware that it revealed the censorship of the 1858 article. I am inclined to accept the last mentioned hypothesis. However, the probability of serious omissions in this magazine should be kept in mind in treating it as a reliable source, even though it remains an historical document of inestimable value. I should add that I was given full liberty to consult the magazine by present church authorities and employees in Buenos Aires.

Gardiner departed, from the Falklands soon after he returned there with Jemmy and his family, perhaps back to England and then perhaps on to South Africa where, twenty years later, he will spend his last days.

9

1858 to 1860: The Yamana Visit the Keppel Mission; Massacre in Wulaia

Jemmy and Family at the Keppel Mission

Following a rough passage of ten days from Wulaia, the *Allen Gardiner* arrived on 26 June at Keppel Island. Despard's feelings ran high, his heart sang with joy and hope: Jemmy Button, his wife and three children had arrived to stay for a while, hopefully months. "It lays the bridge for constant traffic between the Fuegians and us. It secures good treatment for our Missionaries from his tribe."

Despard's wife, Francis, was equally exuberant as she peered out of the door of her house at the *Allen Gardiner* pulling onto the shore:

I ran quickly to the house door, from which we command a fine sea view, and there, truly, was the stout little craft . . . with all her sails hoisted, and her two flags flying. . . . Soon after, Captain Bunt and Mr Turpin were seen finding their way up to Sulivan House, with the joyful news that Jemmy Button, with his wife and three children, were on board. Then arose a shout of joy and praise among us.[1]

Despard discovered Jemmy's real name – Orundelicone (meaning unknown), that he spoke English intelligibly although with few words, and that he vividly recalled Fitz-Roy, Bynoe, Bennet, Sulivan, a certain Bob Craig and seven others, not named by Despard. Later Jemmy spoke of St. James' palace and quoted the words King William IV had said to him over twenty years ago. Despard again failed to note Jemmy's words. He did quote Jemmy's reply about his Christian learning:

Yes, Jesus Christ die. I go tell my people: good man please good God, lazy man, bad man. Working man, good man. You working man. I like Wilson [the pastor at Walthamstow in 1832], he very good man, very good. Captain Fitzroy talk much of God up in heaven. Good man go there (pointing to the sky); bad people go down there (pointing to the earth). *I try teach my people long time, no understand. No God in my country.*[2]

348

Jemmy did not appear to be an Anglican enthusiast. He came with his first wife, whom Fitz-Roy and Darwin had met, twenty-four years before (in 1834), and their three youngest children, including a baby boy. The rest of his family remained on Button Island: their three oldest children, Jemmy's youngest wife, her baby and a young daughter. The only property he brought along was the family canoe. His eldest son was taking care of his favourite dog.

Jemmy confided in Mrs Despard that his younger wife "cry much" when they left. She was younger than Jemmy, who was about forty. Mrs Despard thought the first Mrs Button was "very ugly, but not frightful." Jemmy said he called her Tucoo: later he clarified that her real name was Lassaweea, though at Keppel she was known as Jamesina. A twelve-year-old boy, nicknamed Threeboys, was the oldest of the three children at Keppel. He acquired this curious name from the missionary Turpin in the following manner. Jemmy had misunderstood Turpin's question when he asked the name of this son. Thinking that Turpin had asked him how many sons he had, Jemmy replied "three boys." Turpin, perhaps as a joke, began calling the lad Threeboys, and this name "stuck" with the missionaries and ever after. His real name, Wamme-striggins (*striggins* is a suffix indicating male gender), was never or very rarely used at Keppel.[3]

The Despard couple found him to be very intelligent. Mrs Despard gave an example: when her husband offered to shake hands with Threeboys, he extended his left hand. Her husband having corrected him, Threeboys immediately turned to his sister and showed her which hand was the shaking-one. She was about eight years old and was soon called Fuegia instead of Passawullacuds or Passawulla. Years later she was known as Hester (Chapter 14). The baby, nine or ten months old, was called Anthony (Tony) at Keppel. It was derived from his Yahgan name – Annasplonis.[4]

Despard assigned Turpin to be Jemmy's guardian. He took such a lively interest in Jemmy and his family that Despard hoped he would become the first missionary in Tierra del Fuego. But this was not to be. Despard treated his guests in the "very best manner." An abandoned brick store was made into a dwelling for them, complete with a board floor, a tight roof, a comfortable bed and plenty of blankets. The house had a chimney so they could have a fire all day if they so desired. They could cook their own food, which was selected to please them. As they would be near the beach, they could gather shellfish and, in calm weather, fish in the kelp from their canoe.

Despard was pleased that Mrs Button washed the children every morning and that Jemmy swept out his house daily. He was also polite: knocked at the door, scraped his shoes and always said good-bye and "thank you sir." When he was introduced to Mrs Despard, he inquired: "Dat your wife? Vary good gal; vary fine gal." Jemmy was recovering his English and remembered some words in Portuguese he had heard in Río de Janeiro.[5]

Despard found Jemmy quite willing to repeat words in Yahgan and was pleased when he had "collected a couple of dozen." Thus began the linguistic annotations that eventually would grow to 32,432 words, thanks mainly to Thomas Bridges and his principal informants Okoko, Lucca and Sisoi.[6] Despard contended that there were no words in Yahgan for God, spirit, soul, mind, heaven and hell. Later Bridges found the corresponding terms for all these concepts except hell, which was nonexistent in the minds of the Yahgan until the missionaries warned them about it.[7] Mrs Despard thought that it was difficult to learn words in their language because Jemmy and his family did not like speaking it in the presence of the missionaries; and when they did, they did so in a whisper. One day in September, while Despard was reviewing his Yahgan vocabulary, Jemmy patted him on the arm saying: "You know more my country talk than me Inglis."[8] Then he asked Jemmy: "We go live in your country, people kill us?" Jemmy replied: "No, my people not kill, not steal. Bad people Oens-men steal."[9]

Jemmy's Family

As their stay of almost five months was drawing to a close, Despard's enthusiasm for them had not dwindled. He thought the baby, Tony, then about fourteen months old, was the best-looking of all the Buttons, though he scowled too much.

Master Anthony Button grows apace. He walks alone, and is a perfect Firelander in miniature – naked all, save that a small cloak hangs over his shoulder. His hair extends in a shock, like a patent *Ramoneur*; and he stands erect, with a stick, like a spear, in his hand.... Tony has quite taken with Mr Turpin: puts out his hand for a shake, and if in his father's arms, cries to go to him.

Jamesina, Mrs Button, was "inquisitive, touchy, musical, loquacious; kind and attentive to her children; with quick ear and correct utterance, and ingenious." She listened intently to a duet being played on the piano while visiting the Despard family, about a month before they departed. This new experience made her curious to know where the music was coming from – the book which the players were looking at?, from the players' fingers, moving so rapidly over the keyboard?, inside the piano? "She peered very inquisitively about to discover the secret." Her questioning recalls other Yahgans' reactions when they heard Weddell reading the Bible (Chapter 2).

Little Fuegia, the daughter, was very active, affectionate and docile. Despite her very bright face and pleasing expression, her features were not as attractive as her brother's, according to Mrs Despard. Once she offered two flowers to Emily (Despard's daughter), pronouncing their native names.[10]

Threeboys resembled his father except that he liked to work. He was rather short, stout, very affectionate, easily trained to labour, "the harder and heavier the better, quick in apprehension and in learning language, very observant and imitative, and inclined to be clean and neat in person." He played with Despard's children and helped them in their garden. Turpin had not been able to teach him to read, but he spoke English very plainly, considering the short time he had been at Keppel. A day or so before they departed, Turpin asked him: "What will you do when you go back to your country? You will get no bread, no coffee, no sugar." He replied quickly: "Plenty of eggs, plenty of fruit; God make."[11]

Jemmy Pleases Almost Everyone

Despard commented that Jemmy "has a very pleasing look; and with his hair cut, and clothes clean, and well put on, would be looked on as a very respectable-looking dark gentleman." Despard thought he was "very sensitive to slights, not revengeful, nay, affectionate, courteous, cleanly, orderly, saving; has good memory...not verbal; slow of comprehension; unobtrusive; rather taciturn and, eschewing hard work; religiously inclined."

Always present during the daily and Sunday services, Jemmy repeated the Lord's Prayer on his own and even tried to sing the doxology. He counted the weeks as churches; one week ago – "one church ago." Turpin had difficulty dissuading him from what might be called an anthropological approach to religion: "They [Jemmy in particular] imagine it [Christianity] to be a custom of a different nation, instead of a privilege and a duty of every fallen man."

One Sunday Despard asked Jemmy if he had understood the words of the morning service. "Yes Sir, God – everywhere; Jesus Christ came down from heaven, died." Hereupon he mentioned Despard's father, whom he had heard had been "killed by frens [friends]" in a war. He also asked about his brother who was a soldier, how many brothers he had and if his mother was still alive. Despard eschewed these questions. "I tried to recall him to more important topics, by showing him the Hebrew Bible, and speaking about Adam and Eve."[12] Evidently Despard did not want to treat Jemmy as a personal friend, despite his appreciation of his many qualities.

Despard was impressed by Jemmy's pride. "One of our men's wives shut out his family from her house, as much through fear as anything. He never went thither again, though he would often go next door, under the same roof." Again, when someone accused his wife of stealing palings for fuel, Jemmy retorted: "I not steal; my wife not steal; I not stay Keppel Island; I go home; come ship. No, me not steal." It was all a mistake: Mrs Button had not stolen the palings, they had been cut and given to them. He became very upset when Despard asked him to leave little Fuegia with Mrs Despard to be brought up as their daughter. He "only quieted when he got me [Despard] to confirm Mr Turpin's assurance, they would all go back together [to Button Island]."

Despard seemed to enjoy telling stories about Jemmy, as for instance when, he brought a bouquet to Despard's wife. "Some days ago he saw a pot of flowers in our room, so he started off and got a great bunch of the finest, pinkest halcyon flowers, and sent them up to 'Lady,' as he calls Mrs D." And he offered fish. "Today he speared, for the first time, two large fishes. He immediately hastened up, out of breath, to our house, knocked on the door, 'Here's fis [fish], Mr Despard.' Of the other [fish], he gave half to his friend, Mr Turpin."[13]

Like Darwin, Despard noted Jemmy's vanity. He brushed and washed his coat so frequently that after a few months' wear it still looked clean. He washed his caps and comforters until they shrank and fell to pieces. He wiped his shoes before he came into Despard's house and then would lay his cap where it would not rest on any one else's. "At table he eats very noiselessly, and drinks and eats slowly and little." All of this highly pleased the missionaries. Jemmy was "the only gentleman of leisure in the place." But this was not a compliment: the quality least appreciated was his disinclination to work. "Mr Button . . . paid me a visit; remarked my work to be wet and dirty, but certainly made no offer to help. J. B. employed his time looking at a large book of pictures." This was a little too much. The next day Despard reminded him: "Jemmy every one work here; you no work." He replied: "Yes, Sir, I clean knives." Despard then informed him of what had to be done. "Ditching, gardening, fencing, painting, carpentry, shoe-mending, and tailoring. Then I am domestic tutor, theological professor, linguist, chaplain, &c. The Lord made these employments beneficial!"[14]

Evidently Jemmy was not a partisan of the "Protestant ethic." Work was not a divine obligation, leisure was more in harmony with gentlemanly manners. When he saw Despard entering the garden, he hastened to the gate, holding it open until he passed, wishing him a good evening, though he refrained from going into the garden (to work). When Turpin returned very weary from a day of hard labour, Jemmy insisted on making his fire and boiling water in the kettle for his tea. "J. B. never receives anything without a 'Thank you, sir, or ma'am' and a motion of the hand to the forelock. He is very careful in a room not to push past any one; he waits patiently till they give him space.... If offered cake out of a full plate, [he] selects the smallest piece."

Once Jemmy noticed that Turpin handed one of the mission workers a chisel with the edge foremost and reminded him that people in England always turned the handle foremost.[15]

The Visit – A Triumph

An anonymous article in *The Voice of Pity* lauded the comportment of the Button family during their stay at Keppel.

The cleanliness, and gentlemanly bearing of James Button; his courtesy, and grateful appreciation...the quiet and affectionate behaviour of his children – their intelligence and docility: the change effected in the appearance of his wife, so striking as to cause her to be called, on her return to her home "English-woman" – form a combination of evidence in favour of our attempts to civilise the Fuegian tribes generally, which cannot be made light of. The present results are too manifestly indicative of success to admit of serious dispute.[16]

Their visit was almost a total success. It augured well for the future mission in Wulaia. The Button family had gained such approval with no special evangelistic effort on anyone's part. Jemmy and his family were certainly pleased to share these months with the missionaries. His pride in his appearance had changed radically at Keppel (as it had in England), yet his personality remained unaltered. He sought to please his hosts, but without becoming a worker. He was pleasant and sociable but had threatened to leave if he or his wife continued to be accused of stealing.[17] It became evident to the missionaries that his ability to adapt yet maintain his dignity was clear evidence that his mental capacity was equal to that of any civilised human being. Darwin was aware of this quality in Jemmy but he failed to comprehend its fundamental message. Despite future tragedies, most of the missionaries retained special esteem for Jemmy, his family and their descendants until the very end (Chapter 14). However, Jemmy was not Thomas Bridges' favourite, to say the least.

A Sad Farewell

Having spent four months at Keppel, they were preparing to return home in early November 1858. Despard would accompany them for his first (and only) trip to Wulaia. In Montevideo, earlier this year, he had contracted another captain for the schooner, Robert Fell. His "seagoing" credentials were ideal: five years working as a missionary to seamen in England. The catechists Phillips and Turpin were to be part of the group, in addition to the carpenter, Mr Jackson (or Johnson). The cook's name was not mentioned at this time; later it proved to be Alfred Cole (or Coles). His role in the coming events will make him famous. The names of the other members of the crew were not yet given. Young Gardiner had departed, back to England, never to return, but Bob, his favourite dog, was not one of the passengers.[18]

After they departed, a nostalgic Mrs Despard wrote to a friend:

I cannot tell you how very sorry we were to see him [Jemmy] and his family take their departure, or how much we miss them now that they are gone! During their stay here they behaved extremely well, never doing anything to offend or annoy. Sometime after talking, he [Jemmy] would look at me; and then, tapping me on the shoulder, he would suddenly exclaim, "I like you, and you vary good gal; work much, vary much, always work all day; in my country gal no laugh, no talk, work vary little, stay in wigwam, fish sometimes." I said, "Jemmie, will you come back to us?" He would not promise, but replied, "Perhaps, bye and bye, me no tell now!" The Fuegians are very curious, and naturally watch all you do; they like to touch and feel everything they see, but never offer to steal; they are also very idle. The little girl, "Fuegia," as we used to call her, was really a pretty little dark-eyed child, so gentle and modest, pleasing, and affectionate. She and her mother, and the babe (which was a cross little fat thing) used to come up here whenever they liked.... They would follow me into the kitchen and watch me cooking the dinner and washing the clothes, baking, &c. and would then go to their hut and try to imitate all they had seen me or others do. Little Fuegia would spend hours with our children; and when I entered the room, she would run toward me and throw her arms round me, and put her face up for a kiss.[19]

Such was her farewell to the Buttons.

Homeward Bound

First Stop Banner Cove

Leaving Port Stanley they sailed on the *Allen Gardiner* on 16 November. Jemmy and his family were accompanied by Captain Fell, his crew, Despard, Turpin and Garland Phillips.Through a rough sea, nine days later they reached Banner Cove, which Gardiner's father had named in 1848, Captain Snow and Phillips had visited there in 1856 and young Gardiner the following year (Chapters 7 and 8). Now, 26 November (1858), four canoes, with twenty Fuegians aboard paddled up to their yacht as its cable was running out. The Button couple had speedily enveloped themselves in all their clothes in layers from the worn-out to the new. They were definitely not to be seen naked. That very morning Jemmy consented to have his hair cut again "in the fashionable round crop, and looked very genteel." Here Despard translated the often repeated expression *yamma schoonas* (yet another spelling) as "Friend, very good man," though it was nearly always a bid for gifts.

A canoe crowd, in one of the canoes, asked Jemmy in Yamana: "What, countryman, you there in English ship?" He replied but in English: "I come from far way-off land." He refused to speak his own language. As the chatter flowed on and on Despard heard a kinship term, Jemmy explained that his eldest son's wife was from Banner Cove, and that her sister was there, in one of the canoes hailing him as her "sister's father-in-law." This was proof, Despard concluded, that there was marriage at least between two families on Button Island and Banner Cove. Through the commotion and bustle of bartering, Jemmy maintained "a quiet, gentlemanly manner, was very kind to them, got up presents for them of his [own] accord." He even gave away some of his prized possessions, though not the knife secured around his neck. He protested: "No, no, I only have one. Mr Despard he gave me," as he patted his benefactor on the shoulder. Mrs Button was rather "crusty" with the visitors on board: "nasty vulgar people, with naked ribs and dirty faces." Despard, on the contrary, found that the two men who came on board were "pleasant looking." Each was given a shirt, trousers and a necktie.

Despard profited "now and then" from Jemmy's lessons in Yahgan and from listening to the "Picton dialect," which was somewhat different from Jemmy's. Despard spotted a young woman he had seen on the previous trip, who had slipped away with a shawl and "broke the contract of barter." After a few hours of bartering from the canoes to the deck, the natives departed, having declined the biscuits, saying that they were not food for men, meaning, Despard imagined, that only rats liked them.

Later, on shore, some twenty-five people greeted them in a large wigwam. Despard was pleased by the welcome.

Such a gathering at the wigwam – old women, young women, two of them wives and mothers at fifteen, and really *pretty* – boys, girls, infants, men, grandads, all smiling, laughing, talking together to welcome the Pallillowa (Englishmen). . . . There was a good deal of mocking our English, and trying their Tekeenica [Yahgan], and we got on so far toward a reciprocal understanding, as to make out that they thought us well-dressed good people, and would like to possess an equally good outfit.

The catechist Phillips and Captain Fell made the usual visit to Gardiner Island, with prayers and a consecration to the seven martyrs.[20]

Blomefield Harbour

The following day they crossed Beagle Channel to Blomefield (Cambaceres Bay), where the senior Gardiner had been so intent upon hiding the provisions in 1850. Men in three canoes came paddling rapidly toward them shouting vociferously. These "noisy people," kept jumping up and down in their canoes, wildly throwing their arms up in the air, while beating the water with their paddles.

They received some knives, which they really wanted, and accepted used clothes and blankets in exchange for spears. Despard noted that, "their confidence immediately increased in our good will toward them, and the *Yamma Schoonas* were fired off at a great rate." As the yacht pulled out of the bay, men in other canoes paddled toward the ship, but finding it impossible to reach, they shouted and bellowed in rage and disappointment. These men were the eastern Yamana, whom Gardiner had so feared.

Navarino Friends

The schooner swung back toward Navarino Island and late that afternoon reached a bay opposite the far end of MacKinlay Pass. Despard waxed eloquent: "Oh that some day, these beautiful shores may be covered with teeming villages, and the name of Jesus resound."

Following prayers, Mrs Button, who "had command of the deck," was accompanied by Bob, young Gardiner's dog. She called out in English, "canoe come," as four canoes were seen approaching the ship. Jemmy recognised several old friends and bartered more of his Keppel treasures with them for baskets. Mrs Button acquired a large one for "lady Mrs. Despard" and Jemmy another for "what you call – Ho, yes Miss Hanlon [Hamilton, the governess of Despard's children]." He promised other new baskets for Despard's two daughters. Despard was pleased by this demonstration of the Buttons' generosity, as he was by Jemmy's gifts of knives, clothes and even a six-inch spike nail to "his destitute countrymen." Nails were as precious to him "as rubies and diamonds."

The visitors' carefully painted faces attracted much attention. Captain Fell was enchanted with a "fine looking man" who came on board despite his fear, "not knowing but that his life might be in danger by us, and at the same time willing to run the risk to get his *yamma schoona* gratified." Fell was so pleased with the man that he kept saying to him: "You are a very fine fellow." The latter, though he did not understand a word of English, sensed its meaning, and repeated: "You are a very fine fellow." Mrs Button further assured him that he had nothing to fear on board while she helped him fit into his new white shirt. "Jemmy Button too seemed fond of him, and wished to let him share his apartment to sleep." He declined the invitation because, he explained (as translated by Jemmy), his two wives and a child were waiting for him on shore. He promised to return in the morning. Jemmy said he had seen him at least five times in Wulaia. Captain Fell became wary, seeing the Buttons' friend so well fitted out and the others leaving with almost nothing. He imagined they might be jealous, so he motioned them to return. When they climbed back on the deck, he tied strips of another white shirt round each of their heads, "which in their estimation made them both grand and noble." Early the next day, a Sunday, 28 November, the visitors appeared again on the deck. No bartering was permitted on the Sabbath, but the guests seemed to enjoy hymn singing with the crew. The men in two canoes were spearing porpoises, "standing up and posing their spears in the fine, calm, sunlit basin."

Suddenly Jemmy recognised Tish-pinnay, a friend, an old man with a blind eye. When Despard inquired how he lost his eye, Tish-pinnay explained, by gestures and with Jemmy's help, that he had cried so much when a friend died that his "eye ran away in water all over his cheek." Finally Jemmy became "tired of the incessant *yamma schoona* from those in the canoes, shouted to them to go ashore (as if saying go home or "get lost")." Captain Fell and the crew laughed at him because he was not aware that he was shouting in English. He became so utterly annoyed with his countrymen that he shoved both hands in his jacket pockets and left the gangway.

That afternoon everyone took a walk along Navarino shore and found "an enchanting winding fresh-water lake about a mile long" and another nearby equally pleasant. Despard was again delighted and thought this whole place far superior to Banner Cove for its beauty and for its agricultural potentials. Advocating emigration (though he did not specify of whom), he repeated Jemmy's expression when speaking of his homeland "plenty water, plenty clear land, plenty grass, plenty geese," adding "and a fine salubrious climate."

Oens-Men Appear

Later that afternoon they had only sailed eight or ten miles (15 to 18.5 kilometres) beyond the pass (beyond Gable Island). Nearby they anchored in a sheltered cove on Navarino Island. Soon a dozen or so canoes accosted them, the men appealing for clothes, knives and necklaces. Some sixty persons in four of the canoes surrounded the schooner. Jemmy's people "very quite modest fellows" were in two of them while several "ill-looking fellows," the dreaded Oens-men, had paddled the other two canoes from the opposite shore (Isla Grande).

This scene recalls Captain Snow's drama in 1856, when he had the peaceful Yahgans on his portside and the rambunctious Oens-men on his starboard, though this time the latter departed quietly.

Despard's "Advice"

Despard remarked that the great need of the natives was knives and other edged tools and regretted not having brought along iron hoops. He added significantly: "In their present mode of life clothes are of little service." But the advice implied in this comment was never heeded, either by Despard or his successors. On the contrary, they gave great importance to clothing "the naked savages" with used apparel from England. Giving such clothes to the natives will be severely criticised as one of the main causes of the Yahgans' demise. Above all, these garments were likely carriers of diseases. Then too, while being worn by the Yamana, they often became wet and cold, so instead of protecting them from the inclemency, the clothes increased their exposure to it. During the first contacts, these clothes did not do much harm because the Yahgans tore them to pieces, to share them with their comrades, or wound them around their bodies in ways that were not intended and inadvertently allowed air to circulate. Later Despard, despite his "advice," vaunted the missionaries' clothes policy. "I think there is now scarce an individual, out of one hundred and seventy here, who has not a garment of some kind."

Back to England?

The next day the schooner's sails were damaged by strong winds and Fell had to backtrack late that night to the point of departure of the morning. When Jemmy saw the ship turning around, he became alarmed. "What you call this? You take me back to England? This [England] not my country." Despard and Fell must have reassured him that they were simply backing up, as no further comment was recorded.

Despard became aware of the rapid, unpredictable alterations in climate, so characteristic of this area. He also remarked on the sparse population along Beagle Channel, as not over 200 on both sides. This number seems far too small given the quantity of natives seen along the channel during these years.

Almost Trapped

While waiting to get under sail, the first day of December, one of Jemmy's countrymen who was in a canoe alongside the ship confided in him that someone on Button Island was threatening to kill his "big boy" – his eldest son Querentze. Jemmy decided to take his family to the shore to check on the threat. Threeboys was very reluctant to go but consented when his father shouted "Come" and Despard also urged him on. Fuegia was also urged to go. Despard observed that Jemmy and his family, climbing down the ladder into the messenger's canoe, looked "like a family of ourselves." Twelve canoes escorted them to shore. Sitting on the bank, Jemmy began conversing with a numerous "deputation." After a few minutes he stood up and waved a branch to Despard and the crew, who were leaning on the rail of the deck looking in his direction. He continued waving the branch, as a signal to send a boat right away to take them back to the schooner. When he realised that Despard and the others were not paying attention, he quickly gave one of the men nearby a waistcoat as payment to canoe him and his family back to the schooner. Once they were on board, Despard inquired: "Well Jemmy, why did you not stay?" He replied forcefully: "Bad men, wanted me to cooshie (sleep in French); wanted to steal all my close [clothes] . . . tried to cut great piece off my wife's shawl. All story [a lie] about my son. I stay, very well, sir; go up [to my] country with you."

The bad men tried to induce him to take a nap in order to steal his clothes and were about to cut off a piece of Jamesina's shawl. Then Jemmy realised the story about his son was a lure to entice them to come ashore in order to steal their clothes. When they were back on the schooner, Threeboys and Fuegia, relieved to be out of danger, "were smiling, laughing out their joy." That evening Jemmy confided in Despard: "Mr. Despard, by-and-bye you see my son [Querentze], my brother [probably Tom]; you tell them pray God make good men – no steal. I tell them you [are a] very good man – very kind – Churchman."

Tish-Pinnay, the Aristocrat

The next day one-eyed Tish-pinnay, Jemmy's special one-eyed friend, was in his canoe, along with three other canoes, following the yacht as it slowly advanced down the channel toward Murray Narrows. When they had anchored the ship to camp for the night, Tish-pinnay attracted the attention of Fell and Despard, not because of his one eye but because of his nose. Despard let his enthusiasm soar:

> He possesses such an aristocratical nose, that Capt F. gives him the *soubriquet* of "Duke of Wellington".... All honour to Tish-pinnay (cui lumen ademptum), he knows how things ought to be, and keeps them so. Moreover, he has free course among the Beagalians; for he is now in one canoe, now in another, as the humour or view of convenience takes him; but, *wherever*, full of talk and *sound reasoning*, (as a man with such a nose must be).[21]

Tish-pinnay was endowed with an aura of respectability because of such a singular correspondence, a harmony, between his nose and his personality. He undoubtedly merited such flattery, short-lived as it will prove to be.

He and the others remained in their four canoes; they did not follow the crew to their camp, nor did they "molest us in any way." They lingered on all the next morning alongside the yacht. Despard imagined that they were curious, "to see the ways and doings of such strange Pallill-awa [Englishmen in Yahgan]." He longed "to know what they say and to speak to them, and fancy they have the same feeling, for I hear '*yapee-mata*' on their lips very often, meaning 'Converse with us.'"[22] He and Fell noticed that among Tish-pinnay's laudable qualities, he knew how to dress correctly and how to keep his jacket in one piece and "wear it *a la mode*."

However, about then Tish-pinnay climbed on the deck, without being invited or asking, while the man beside him had been invited. Now the latter had risen into Despard's good grace as a "fine-looking" man, "pleasing in countenance, and quiet in manner." He was given a coat and a headdress. Captain Fell was more emphatic: "A better formed man I think I never saw . . . [Grateful] for whatever little presents were bestowed, without pressing for more." Now Fell contrasted his gentlemanly manners with Tish-pinnay's, "who kept poking his ugly, because dirty, face over the ship's rail, breaking the quietness of the moment by shouting '*yamina schoona*.'" Fell imagined that differences existed "in the constitution of their minds.... Doubtless in this long neglected land, there are minds which if cultivated, could accomplish great things." Tish-pinnay had definitely tumbled into Fell's disfavour. But when, Fell learned that the handsome, quiet, well-mannered gentleman was Tish-pinnay's son, he was astounded and somehow his train of thought led him to Jemmy, "one of the dullest of his race." Then Despard also expressed his growing dissatisfaction with "Poor Jem." He was not only "very stupid as interpreter – he understands neither them nor us... when we tell him to say something to them, [he] persists in using his broken English."[23] This was the first time Despard spoke in harsh terms about Jemmy. Captain Fell, however, was known to express very conclusive thoughts about those who either pleased him or did not and to modify a most fervent opinion from hot to cold.

Wulaia, the "Celebrated City"

Passing beyond Murray Narrows, Button Island opened to their view. Jemmy was "sadly disappointed" when the yacht did not anchor there. For some reason Despard had decided that Button Island was not a suitable place for a mission station, though he had never been there and now only saw it from the deck. On 4 December they pulled into "the long-desired Woollya."[24]

Besides taking the Button family home, two other purposes of this visit were to recruit male candidates for Keppel – if they were married also their wives, and to begin the construction of a mission station (house and garden) in Wulaia. Thus Despard planned to eventually convert the natives to Christianity here in Wulaia. This was to be accomplished with the facilities of the mission station and the help of the young men to be trained at Keppel.

Despard imagined that Wulaia was indeed an ancient settlement as he glanced at the circles of high shell mounds with deep depressions in the middle, where wigwams had once stood. However, as they strolled about "the celebrated city," they only saw "six miserable wigwams," and no one was there to welcome them. Jemmy was chagrined, even mortified, having so often boasted about his home country. An old woman ran by them carrying a water container made of tree bark in one hand and a stick in the other. Fell and a few others followed her and peeped into her wigwam, assuring her of their good intentions. Her dwelling, which was about three feet under ground, impressed Fell because it had to be entered "just like rabbits or rats entering their respective holes." He concluded that the people here and their wigwams were much inferior to those on Picton Island. Finally "Dr Button" (Jemmy's uncle, a renown *yakamush*, shaman) caught up with them, having seen them from his canoe as they passed by Button Island. Dr Button, also referred to as "the old gentleman," was wearing a piece of a used shirt. Perhaps because of his undignified apparel, Jemmy seemed ashamed of him, though he introduced him to each visitor, including the members of the crew, beginning with "This Mr Despard," while Dr Button repeated each name after him. When he came to Captain Fell, Jemmy put his hand on Fell's shoulder saying "This Capt Fitzroy – Capt Fell," correcting himself.[25]

The Button "Clan"[26]

That evening Despard and his companions met thirteen of Jemmy's close kin, including (1) his oldest brother Tom and (2) Rachel, Jemmy's youngest wife (Jamesina's sister), whom Despard esteemed as "the best looking and most intelligent young woman here." She was holding (3) her baby girl and stood beside (4) her other daughter, the nine-year-old Makuall-kipin (the suffix is usually spelled *kipa* – the general word for "woman"). Despard also met (5) Jemmy's mother-in-law (the mother of his two wives), (6) Querentze, Jemmy's oldest son "a very intelligent lad, though too pale and thin," (7) his pretty wife, Lookal-ké (suffix a misspelling of *kipa*) from Banner Cove, and (8) Harry, the "tall strong man" was Jemmy's seldom mentioned second brother. Also present were (9) Laus-in-Kelder (this name is entirely misspelt), Jemmy's and Jamesina's oldest daughter, whom Despard thought "plain," and (10) Loolé, her handsome husband. (11) Tellon, Jemmy's oldest brother-in-law was an important guest (his wife, Jemmy's oldest sister, is never mentioned and may at this time already have died). Those present in addition were (12) Squire Muggins, Jemmy's nephew (who was to obtain notoriety very soon), and the sociable (13) Dr Button. Among the absent were Jamesina, her three youngest children (who had just arrived from Keppel), among others.[27]

While surrounded by these relatives, Jemmy whispered to Turpin: "Capt Fell give other man clothes, no give my countrymen clothes? What do you call that?" Fell overheard and replied: "Jemmy this late night; Monday me got plenty of clothes, and give your men clothes." (It's no wonder Jemmy spoke pidgin English, as both Fell and Despard "pidgined" to him.) Jemmy, "greatly pleased" with Fell's reply, bowed to him and saluted him in the "man-of-war fashion." Without waiting, Fell untied one of his Buenos Aires boxes of clothes and served Dr Button first, then the others. Jemmy thanked Fell again "with a polite bow after each person served." Meanwhile Despard observed that all were very quiet, and that kin should not say goodbye to one another, nor greet each other when meeting.[28]

Okoko Appears

Jemmy became Captain Fell's interpreter; no one else was available. Fell wanted to know more about a lad of fourteen whom he had invited on board. Jemmy informed the captain that the lad was a close relative, that his home was on the opposite coast (of Ponsonby Sound, Hoste Island), that his mother was a widow, and that his name was Ookokko-wenché (*wenché* is a suffix indicating male). The youth, subsequently called Okoko (the spelling varies a great deal), will become a loyal and devoted ally of the missionaries.

Fell was extremely pleased with Okoko. Once washed, clothed in a sailor's suit, fed, and given a blanket, he became "quite exhilarated, went walking about the decks in great glee." When his brother Silagelish, a year older, appeared in the evening, Despard declared: "Thus have we two hopeful youths in tow for Crammer [Keppel] on the first day."[29]

The next "church day," service was held in the ship's cabin and attended by Okoko and the four Button brothers. Jemmy had inquired if he might come with Threeboys and Querentze, so that the latter "see how Englishmen prayed to God." They all came and heard a sermon from the Gospel according to Luke (verses 40, 47 and 52).

Despard observed that the natives in Wulaia had remained quiet the entire day, including those in twelve canoes who had just arrived. Monday was also quiet, even though there were "about thirty Firelanders squatting about us at the time." The yacht crew, helped by some of them, began laying the foundation of the future mission house. Jemmy started building a wigwam for himself and later carried his precious chest, other furniture, and gifts from Keppel to his half-finished wigwam. This scene recalls Fitz-Roy's first visit to Wulaia with Darwin and the three Fuegians, January 1833.

Fell's Labour Policy

That afternoon Jemmy complained that he had not received biscuits for breakfast; "What do you call that, no biscuit, no nothing, to eat?" Fell's response was immediate: "No work – we no can give biscuit." He clarified to his readers: "We are not unkind to poor Jemmy, far from it." Then he explained to his future workers that Jemmy had been their guest at Keppel, waited on hand and foot, and well provided and that that regime had expired. Now back in his own country, Jemmy and his countrymen had to obey the apostolic injunction: "If any will not work, neither shall he eat." The message was not wasted. That afternoon Jemmy and his brothers hauled trees, the following day they stripped bark for the frame of the mission house. They were paid a number of biscuits corresponding to the hours of work. Fell was reassured. "It would be a great blessing if we could, by such means, get them to acquire habits of industry."

Okoko's Mother

About 7 December, Okoko's mother appeared in her canoe, "crying and bawling in a most impassioned manner." Outraged, she demanded the return of her son. Finally she won. Okoko was divested of his fine clothes and taken home. Despard commented disdainfully: "The dear, delighted mamma kept up an incessant and sharp volley of scolding all the way back to the landing, whether because Okoko had run away, or because we were unlawfully harbouring a witless minor, I can't say." Despard was probably thinking that the missionaries might be accused later by the Falkland authorities of "unlawfully harbouring" a minor, as Mellersch wrote that Captain Snow had feared (Chapter 8).

When Querentze, Jemmy's eldest son, offered to sleep in the schooner, Despard agreed and invited his wife on board as well. He had already noticed her because she was "a good-looking young woman, with brown curling hair, like a gypsy girl," and because of her fishing gear: only a baited string weighed down with a stone.[30]

The Labour Policy Again

Captain Fell clarified that the "Firelanders'" increased efficiency of hewing and chopping down trees was due to his latest reform: pay them after each task, after each haul, instead of at the end of the day. Fell was convinced that his innovation had remedied their habit of sitting down after each haul. Even so he admired their hability with the axe and their strength. Despard was also impressed when they "carried very heavy burdens through thorny bushes and across a swift and deep brook, such as I could not carry nor even lift." The workers were also kept busy on board the yacht, repairing sails and on shore marking the reefs and bands for the sails. Despard was the first to admit that the pay – the biscuits – were "rather musty from age."

To supplement the biscuit diet the natives ate large quantities of "unwashed and raw" dandelions, which, Despard observed, "they relished very much." He announced that Darwin had made a mistake: the birch fungus was not the only vegetable Fuegians ate; they also relished dandelions.

Fell also became aware that the biscuit pay was somewhat stingy, so he substituted clothes for it, but not before separating the pay clothes from the best clothes that were destined for the natives who were to be selected as the next contingent to be taken to Keppel. When he saw that most of what was left for pay were old rags, he commented that they were "quite good enough for our purpose." Despard agreed with Fell, that the rags were "good enough to bring the Firelanders into the use of clothes." Fell did not "expect that the garments would fit the person to whom given, but still they were of value to them, and we wished to get their labour in return." The reader might have the impression that Despard and Fell were unabashed labour bosses, which perhaps they were.

Another Fashion Show

Despard was no doubt gratified that even young lads agreed to chop down trees and carry wood in exchange for Fell's "Buenos Ayrian garments...mere rags." Despite the rag pay, the workers' mood changed when twenty of them became "very merry, and yet in no wise impudent or noisy." Their attention was focused on the fashion show (my term, see Chapters 2 and 6 for others). It began when one worker was forcing himself into a pair of small boy's "unmentionables" he had just earned, while another was pulling his "pay," a waistcoat, over the torn piece of a blanket. Having wiggled into the waistcoat, he tossed the piece of blanket over it. A third worker had thrust his head through the armhole of a vest while the rest of it was left, "hanging gracefully over the left shoulder." An old lady was manoeuvring into a flounced black-muslin gown and finally managed to squeeze into it, though the trail of the gown was left dangling in front of her. "This droll figure excited more shouts of laughter." A "fellow" who received a petticoat was no other than the former aristocrat Tish-pinnay, "on whom we all look with suspicious eyes." He had already slipped into a black frock coat, but his long legs were left bare, so he pulled the petticoat over the black coat, his head peeping through. While observing the "show," Captain Fell remarked that he hoped to give better clothing by and by. But through it all he remained convinced that: "We must expect difficulties and scope for the exercise of patience in breaking them out of lazy habits, such as sitting by fires in the different wigwams all day, not moving hand or foot until hunger necessitates them to go on the beach for mussels."

Fell Is Mystified

Fell failed to comprehend the Yahgan "way of life" – for instance, the egalitarian concept that work was to be done when necessary for the "worker," his or her family, other kin and friends. There were no bosses in their system of living.

Their Regime

The neighbouring kin-related families were apparently grouped into five so-called districts, each claimed a certain territory and in each a different dialect was spoken. The families moved within their "districts" to the same or nearby campsites year after year. For instance, the "Button clan" moved from Button Island to Wulaia quite constantly. Apparently the districts were neither endogamic nor exogamic. Marriages occurred within and between the "districts." For example, Jemmy's parents were both from the "Central District," while Qerentze, Jemmy's eldest son, was married to the good-looking Lookal-kipa from Banner Cove, the "East District."[31]

As the natives frequently moved from one campsite to another they kept their material belongings to a minimum. They hunted, fished and gathered to obtain their basic food and there was little left over when they canoed to another campsite, as only small amounts of food were transportable. The exception was the campsite near a beached whale, when they became sedentary often for months at a time, depending on the number of mouths to feed and the size of the "gift of nature" (my term) (Chapter 2).

In this sort of economy, labour was at a minimum because there was no accumulation of food or goods and no privileged class or elite that organized labour – and that had to be fed, clothed and provided with luxuries. The Yamana men's work did not entail daily tasks for hunting, the manufacture and upkeep of the canoe, making tools or gathering firewood (which the women also did). The huts were built rapidly and the sturdier wigwams were often simply repaired. However, the women worked every day caring for the children and because of the need for "the daily bread" and the frequent canoe paddling. They had to fish and gather shellfish, eggs and other edibles constantly. After the seals and whales became scarce, from about 1780 to 1830 (Chapter 2), the women had to supply almost all the food, and worked long hours. Partly because there were far fewer seals to be hunted and whales to be butchered, the men had more leisure time than the women. However, the hunting–gathering system of living traditionally (normally) required less labour for both women and men than other economic systems because of their nomadic or semino-madic existence: minimum "baggage," everyone working and no elite. Hence the notion of an "original affluent society" proposed by Marshall Sahlins.[32] As long as hunger did not strike, such a system allowed ample time for ceremonies, games and (for the men) to take it easy.

"Affluent" though they may have been, their hunting–gathering way of life was more exposed to periods of hunger or even starvation. The preservation of whale meat and other edibles (such as mushrooms) was only a temporary safeguard against famine. They were more vulnerable to the contingencies of the weather than the farmers whose settled life usually provided at least some food in storage.

The Fuegians appeared to be poverty-stricken to outsiders because they had no surpluses. They did not need much clothing; their greatest ally was fire. Their luxuries were necklaces, feathered headgear and the like. In preparation for their ceremonies, they expended considerable labour on the construction of a ceremonial hut, painting their bodies, making masks and other ritual paraphernalia. These were necessary luxuries.

Captain Fell and Despard understood that were the natives to be useful to the missionaries, they would have to be disciplined to work for a boss, whoever he (she or it) might be.

Polygamy Not Such a Sin?

Despard was informed on 9 December: Jemmy was a "trigamist" not just two but three wives and that they were sisters. Although Despard found polygamy repugnant to the ideal of conjugal felicity, "we should wonder things are not even worse." Such tolerance contrasts with the attitude of the future head of the mission, Thomas Bridges, an impeccable mono-gamist. Jemmy promptly denied having three wives. He clarified that he had only two and that the other was his sister.[33] In effect, all reliable sources agree that Jemmy had two wives who were sisters, Jamesina and the younger Rachel. He also had two sisters, Tellon's wife (or widow) and the unmarried one (in 1858), who was living with his family, hence the confusion of wives and sisters.

The Oens-Men Again

When twelve canoes arrived Sunday, 10 December, Despard noted: "At noon, twelve canoes, altogether quite a little fleet of 'Anchinché' [not identified] and other people, came into port, but beyond a yamma scoona, en passant, they took no notice of us, but went up and moored to the kelp off the town." Phillips reported that only six canoes had arrived. In any event they departed soon afterwards.

Later that day, Jemmy relaxed: the bad men had left, they were "too much cheek people" (the expression Jemmy used for noisy people he did not like).[34] But Despard identified them: "The main body of the Oens-men took themselves off, as they found for the present our visit and benefactions are not for them." He also noted that he heard them say *yamma scoona*, a Yahgan expression, which would indicate that Oens-men were accompanied by some other "bad men." Fell noticed that these canoes belonged "to quite a different tribe," that their behaviour was very different from what it had been in Beagle Channel (even though the Oens-men had left the ship quietly then, see above). Perhaps Fell was thinking about the commotion they had provoked with Captain Snow, which Phillips probably told him about, that as it may. Fell thought that these Oens-men were quiet "like the people of Jemmy's country." Nonetheless, according to Phillips the "six canoes of Oen's men took their departure with much shouting and gesticulating, returned by some ill-disposed persons on shore." They had remained in the vicinity for five days, apparently without contacting anyone in Wulaia. No one made any further comment concerning them. Perhaps Despard was distracted by the variety and size of the fish he saw, by the red-breast geese on the shore and the pretty parakeets.[35] But why had these men come, parked near Wulaia, and remained there by themselves for five days? Maybe they were observing the scene for future reference. If so, they saw that the missionaries were building a house, obviously to take up residence there, in Wulaia. Eleven months from now, early November (1859), a much larger group of Ones-men will appear, at first without provoking alarm (see below).

More Dirty Faces

On 12 December, a Sunday, the weather was "squally," so the divine service that otherwise would have taken place on shore was held on board the yacht. Present were Jemmy, Threeboys and Tom, Jemmy's favourite brother, who appeared with his face painted white. Despard objected to his "dirty face" and told him to wash it. Tom retorted that Despard's face was also dirty, referring to his beard. Captain Fell felt sorry for him. "Poor Tommy, with his long untidy hair, held down his head all the time of the service; while Jemmy, with his Sunday coat buttoned up, sat at the foot of the table, having a more respectable appearance."

Despard also objected that Mrs Button (probably Jamesina) had gone fishing on this Sabbath day, but by that time she was far away.

Volunteers for Keppel

On 15 December 1858, despite the reprimand from Despard, Tommy announced that he would go to Keppel with his young wife. He had recited many new Yahgan words for Despard who was so impressed that he decided that Tommy was much more intelligent than Jemmy. Tellon's son, a boy about twelve years old, also offered to go to Keppel. His name was Luccaonchee, Lucca for short. Lucca's mother, Jemmy's sister, had apparently died, as noted above. Lucca will become another "important person" (my term).

That afternoon the men and boys were still working on the mission house. Despard clarified that the house was not just for the missionaries, that it was also to show the natives, "a very improved style of dwelling, and quite within their capacity to make." He must have been gratified a few days later when Mrs Button (Jamesina) slept in the mission house "even without roof" and had found it much warmer "than their own *uccers* [wigwams]."[36] It *was* warmer, in December, and during the following summer months but not in the winter (see below).

The Working Mass

According to one of the bosses (Despard), the six most active labourers working on the house on 16 December were Okoko (who had returned), Threeboys, Querentze, Pinoense (Tom's oldest son), Squire Muggins (spelled variously, Harry's son), as well as the youngest, Mammerstriggins (Jack for short, Dr Button's son). Despard qualified the others: "J. B. is lazy, Lulé [or Loolé, his son-in-law], lazier, and old Dr Button the laziest." A page later he decided that J. B. and Lulé were lazier than Dr Button.

The next day Captain Fell reverted to the biscuit-wage but began a free hair-cutting service as if to compensate for the biscuit-wage. While directing the work on the house, Fell noticed that the women were busy gathering grass for caulking. Despard exclaimed: "The people are a merry, laughter-loving lot, poor things!" Again he was impressed by the men's strength, this time by Tom's, as he carried a tree "two of us can just lift" with more ease than a sportsman his gun. He was doubly gratified to see more washed faces.

Rebellion of the Masses, Almost

The workers requested a raise: two biscuits for transporting a shoulder load of bark. The bosses flatly refused the request, attributing it to greediness and laziness. Jemmy retaliated: he refused Fell's service as his "hair cutter."

The Proper Name Problem

Two days later, 18 December, the missionaries could call nearly every "Firelander" by their names, that is the short pronounceable ones they were giving them, usually an abbreviation of their Yamana names, such as Okoko and Lucca, or, in English, such as those of the four Button boys (my term). At times the missionaries reverted to their Yahgan names. For instance Garland Phillips called "Threeboys" Wammastriggins and his sister "Fuegia" Passawullah. He also called Okoko "Robert" for some reason and Lucca – "James." The Yahgan workers had it easier, as their bosses' real names were short. Only the carpenter's name, Jackson, proved a little difficult, so they called him Carpinton. The next day Jemmy announced that he had become a grandfather for the first time, of a girl. Despard wanted the baby named Sophia, after some faraway mission friend. Her father (Querentze) agreed; anyway she would be given a Yahgan name. They would acquire a third and a fourth later, such as Okoko became George (as well as) Despard when he was baptised. When this occurred their former names were discontinued. All this renaming creates problems for the researchers.

The Doctor of the Weather

Dr Button, Jemmy's uncle, became the centre of attention a few days later. Despard identified him correctly as a *yaccomosh* (usually spelled *yekamush*, a shaman), adding the epithet "Doctor of Weather." This is also correct as predicting and controlling the weather was an attribute (or obligation) of the *yekamush*. Despard noted that his "operations" were audible – not visible. From his "laboratory wigwam" Dr Button was heard moaning, having a fit of crying while "curing the bad weather." Actually he was chanting, probably to induce a trance and request or beg the outer forces to improve the weather. He emerged from his laboratory with a "very self-complacent look," his face "elegantly lined with fine streaks of red," his eyes banded with white paint. Despite this elegance, Despard and/or Fell received him with an expression of "disgust – for his dirty face," telling him to wash it.[37]

The few days before summer (21 December) brought much snow and storms. Despard consoled himself. "Well, things are balanced – on my former visit we found summer weather in winter." He was recalling his visit to Banner Cove, in March and April, autumn of 1857 (Chapter 8). The missionaries and their men, confined to the ship because of the weather, received "nine gentlemen" on board. Among them was Tom painted with a "doctor's diploma," red and white on his cheeks. He was "politely requested" to wash it off before boarding, which this time he did cheerfully.

Christmas Day

For "the first Christmas dinner in their lives," the one-room mission house accommodated fifty-one "Firelanders." The male guests were assigned to one side of the room, the females to the other. Four great plum puddings and a tin of molasses sauce were placed in front of them. Following the prayers, blessings and singing led by Captain Fell, a few managed to consume three helpings, the others a small piece of one portion. Soon two buckets of cold water appeared for all faces and hands.

Then ensued the serious business of recruiting those (in addition to Tom, his wife and Lucca) who had already expressed their desire to go to Keppel. Jemmy collaborated by saying to each, in Yahgan this time, "*Oh-he* Keppel Island" (come to Keppel Island) and answering for those who agreed to go, "*Ow-a*" (yes). The latter were "bidden to come aboard on Monday to be purified [washed] and dressed." The new recruits finally totalled eight adults and a child. The recruitment completed, Despard and the crew went boating to a nearby island. Having climbed to the top of a hill, they were awed by the view, reaching far down Ponsonby Sound toward Nassau Bay. Despard exclaimed: "I have never seen anything to surpass this place for effect of wood, lawn, mountain, island, inlet, sea-green, white, blue, brown, black in combination."

Come Sunday, Jemmy did not show up for the service but Tom did and was given dinner – of biscuits. Despard again complained of Jemmy as a poor language informant, trusting that, besides Tom, there would be other efficient linguists among the new recruits. After tea on the yacht the missionaries went on shore to visit the elders, Tellon and Dr Button, but they failed to understand their conversations because Jemmy and Tom were absent.

More Disputes

An eruption of dissatisfaction occurred on Monday, 27 December. On shore, Fell met three people he would have preferred to avoid: first, Mrs Button (Jamesina) "attacked him with a volley of words [not recorded]." Then Dr Button "seized him by the vest, and forced it open to his shirt, and vociferated his disappointment in not receiving better clothes." Finally Jemmy joined in, contrasting the generous gifts of Fitz-Roy with those Captain Fell had distributed. The latter soothed the three as best he could by inviting them to the ship and giving biscuits to two and a blanket to the "irate medico." The sometimes gifts, sometimes rag wages, and/or biscuit wages, must have confused them. Captain Fell was becoming increasingly unpopular.

On 29 December, Despard wrote that these people were self-willed, capricious as grown spoiled children, "requiring great patience, firmness and an undaunted spirit" to manage them. Jemmy had breakfast on the yacht and assured Despard that the party, already selected, were still determined to go to Keppel, with the understanding that they would be returned to Wulaia "by-and-by." But Jemmy refused Despard's request to allow his thirteen-year-old daughter (Jamesina's daughter, seldom mentioned) go there, the reason being that she would cry too much away from home. He also declined to allow his younger daughter (Rachel's eldest daughter) to go there, because she was only about nine and likely to cry even more. Dr Button made the same decision for the same reason for his son, Mammerstriggins (Jack), whom Despard "earnestly desired because so intelligent." However, he sympathised with the "tender parental feeling in their rude breasts."[38]

The next day unidentified visitors arrived in a canoe and proceeded to pull the bark off the mission house to get the nails by which the bark was fastened to the walls. Despard kept calm, commenting that he hoped they would leave the frame intact until the missionaries' next visit, when the bark could easily be replaced.

December in Wulaia a Success

Come the end of the year, Jemmy dined on the yacht for the last time and informed Despard that his youngest brother, Billy Button, wished to join the Keppel group with his wife. They had no children. Despard agreed, thinking it advisable to take the two brothers, Tom and Billy, so as to "strengthen the Button alliance."

Despard appraised their stay in Wulaia. During the nearly four weeks among the some 170 natives (residents and visiting neighbours), there had been no breach of amity and no case of dishonesty. They had learned many native words and the Firelanders some English. He and the others had mixed with the natives with "no fear or hesitation, never taking weapons ashore." The missionaries were aware of the natives' repulsive "habits" and their "ignorance." They had made "many an attempt, not all unsuccessful, to reform the one [the habits] and remove the other [the ignorance]." Assured of the success of this visit, Despard informed his readers that "a beginning of the Mission, in direct intercourse with

Firelanders, has been made." And lastly, on the first day of January 1859, he wrote: "We have left our boat undefended on their shores; have left our vessel for hours with only 'cook' [Alfred Cole] on board, and have no reason to regret our confidence."[39] Despard will have ample "reasons to regret" just ten months later, but now, on 1 January 1859, he had reasons to be confident of the future.

The Second Group of Recruits
This Keppel contingent was completed shortly before departure on 1 January. It consisted of three couples, one with a little daughter, and two youths. All the eight future pupils (and the child) were kin by blood or marriage to Jemmy. The following appraisals of the recruits are Despard's.

1. Tom Button, alias Makuallan (spelled differently, too many times to mention): the eldest and stoutest of the party, has an agreeable English countenance. He greets the missionaries with a ready smile and helps them in their attempts to use his language. He is a professed Yacco-mosh [shaman], can exert prodigious strength under burdens, though he soon exhausts himself.

2. Tom's wife, Wendoogyappa or Wendin-gy-appa: age about seventeen, is the favourite of the women: very short and broad, when well dressed is good looking even to an English eye, affectionate, merry and mercurial.

3. Billy Button (Macall-wenche or Maccool-wence): the youngest Button, whose countenance is just an ordinary face.

4. Billy's wife (Wyeenagoewl-kippin or Watch-winna-kipa): age about twenty-five, very broad face, small eyes, very bright and expressive of intellect, wears a constant smile, sets much value on personal cleanliness, strong and willing to help in women's household work. Her mind gives her the command of her sisters.

5. Squire Muggins, otherwise Schwaiamugunjiz or Schway: Jemmy's nephew (Harry's son). With a word he would help, very intelligent, passionate, but sly, the most light-fingered of the party, so that the approach of Schway is the signal for gathering up and placing in safety the small articles lying about.

6. Squire Muggins' "rib sole" (wife) Oodothelewyll-keepa or Wyruggel-keepa: the third young woman in this list, seventeen or eighteen years old, a pleasant face, ready to work, but like her husband light in the fingers.

7. Kitty: their daughter, about three years old, is full of friendliness and sprightliness. I add: Her extraordinary name, written by Despard as Wy-atte-gatta-mootoo-mowl-keepa, or as Kiatta-gatta-matta-mowky-keepa. (The latter spelling reads like Italian, Spanish, Italian, English and Yahgan in this order. Kiatta and gatta are not a long way from Kitty, her nickname.)

8. Lucca (Luccaenche, Tellon's son, Jemmy's nephew): about twelve years old, is able to become pettish and sulky, not playful though he enjoys a good laugh, does not take kindly to work with the hand, but he is quick in the letters, a nice, intelligent lad, and a good candidate for Keppel.

9. Okoko (Ookokkowenche): age about fourteen, whose mother finally permitted him to go to Keppel. His countenance is beaming with intelligence, good humour, and mirth. He has excellent ideas about cleanliness and is so ambitious to become white that he washes very often, in the hope of washing the brown out of his complexion.

"The elect for Keppel" were on board, with no baggage, that is, no used clothes, canoes, slings or dogs. Many Wulaia residents and visitors paddled out to the yacht and received "parting gifts" (besides the usual sugar and slices of pork). Tellon asked Despard to take special care of his little boy Lucca, while patting him affectionately. As was customary, afterwards Tellon took no notice of his son, nor Lucca of his father. Jemmy said good-bye to the English passengers and crew, naming each, though not to his kin.[40] The same etiquette was the rule for departures as for arrivals.

January to October 1859: The Second Yahgan Contingent at Keppel

After five days of stormy weather they anchored at Keppel on 5 January. Everyone was well. The next day the new arrivals scouted the island for edibles; admired the horses, cows, pigs and goats (all of whom they call *muma* (a word for guanaco); and pronounced them all "good food" but not to their liking. They located a colony of penguins, killed a dozen chicks, gathered some large sweet limpets, built a fire and cooked supper. The missionaries spotted the smoke rising in the distance, fearing that the entire island might ignite. Three days later they decided that the habits of these new arrivals were "too gross." They were denied free access to the missionaries' homes, which Jemmy and his family had enjoyed, and were entrusted to the "superintendency" of Phillips in the morning and of Turpin in the afternoon.[41] Four months later Mrs Despard wrote an evaluation of the pupils.

The men are idle, but the women are willing to work. They are very fond of music. . . . They now begin to know that Sunday . . . is a day different to others in the week . . . 1st because they join [singing hymns] . . . 2nd because . . . they have on clean clothes; and lastly, because they get a good and large plum-pudding. . . . They seem to have some glimmers of religion. . . . When we look at these poor creatures, and see them sitting at our table, and behaving in a way that would do honour to Christians, clothed, and in their right minds, and anxious to do right; and then think that . . . more than four months ago, they were running wild in their native woods, both men and women, and boarded the Mission ship in a state of perfect nudity.

The condescendence of Mrs Despard was unfailing. But she did make two original comments: that the Yahgan language very much resembles Italian and that "both goats and chickens seem to take kindly to the language [Yahgan], and are obedient to the command."[42]

By July 1859, plans for the future were being discussed. Tom said he would bring his son Pinoense to Keppel. Despard proposed to take Lucca and Okoko to England. They readily assented and suggested that Threeboys and one of Lucca's cousins would also like to go. Finally the next director would make the trip with Threeboys and three other young Yahgans (Chapter 10).

The three young wives at Keppel complained that Despard had invited them and their husbands only once for tea, while Okoko and Lucca had been invited every Sunday. Despard had a very good impression of these three young women. First of all, they never failed to say "thank you." Why, given their polite manners, they were invited only once to tea, is a mystery. When it was Tom's turn to have tea with the Despards, he spoke of Captain Fitz-Roy, York Minster, and Fuegia Basket (whom he called by her Alakaluf name). He also cited words for "most articles of food and furniture" in English. But Despard became disappointed in Tom despite his English and sweet nature. He was not the reliable interpreter Despard had hoped for, nor was he "over industrious." Lucca and Okoko had become his favourites. On 24 August he wrote: "These lads are patterns of good behaviour and gentlemanly manners. Neither of them would take a second piece of cake at tea, nor some fruit tart, though they like sweets well."

Both lads had been assigned to live with the Phillips couple, who had become very attached to them, as is evident in the following text by Phillips, the missionary, written in September:

Both my wife and myself regard them with much affection. . . . A more industrious, good-tempered boy than Ookokowenche cannot be found, I am sure in England; and he is of such an affectionate disposition. . . . Luccaenche is not of so warm and generous a nature, but is, nevertheless, a very good boy. He has such a keen sense of the ridiculous, that he is perpetually caricaturing some one or other. They are both of an inquisitive turn of mind . . . and are continually asking the names and uses of things that meet their eye, and always attentively listen to what I relate of the fine old country. Little Lucccaenche will sometimes come to my wife's side, put his hand in hers, and ask her all manner of questions about England, and then enter into a long account of what he will do by-and-bye.[43]

The affection of Phillips and his wife for Lucca and Okoko was not lost on them (see below).

On 17 September the *Allen Gardiner* arrived at Keppel from Montevideo, with Captain Fell still at the helm. Fell had also gone to Buenos Aires, where he had not been as cheerfully welcomed as in the past because of the political turmoil there. He returned to Keppel with his wife and child, his younger brother as chief officer, a North American sportsman with Arctic experience and three young "Swedish seamen." In reality the three were not Swedish, though they were from northern Europe.

On the day before departure, from Keppel 27 September, Phillips related another incident concerning Okoko. "Mckoo-allan [Tom] came down to the peat-field this morning and displayed some ill-humour against Ookckoowenshey. . . . The poor lad [Okoko] took it all most patiently. If it were not that he would like once more to see his poor old mother, he would fain stay in Keppel Island."[44]

The Keppel Pupils Return to Wulaia

After nearly nine months, the young guests were "very desirous of returning to their own people."[45] Keppel had meant a lot of work. Tom and the younger men were assigned to the vegetable garden and carpentry. They also cared for the cattle and sheep with Bartlett (the manager at Keppel) and young Bridges. The women were kept busy sewing and housekeeping. All were obliged to be present during Sunday Church, to repeat the prayers every day, appear for "instructions in the rudiments of Christian truth," for classes in English, and to teach Yahgan to Despard, young Bridges and Turpin. To relax, they went on long walks, played games and at times had tea with their missionary friends. Probably by early September 1859, Despard had decided that it was about time to return these nine "Firelanders" to their homeland.

Despard was optimistic about their visit, almost as much as he had been about the months Jemmy and his family had spent there. Also last December, in Wulaia, he had been encouraged by the work accomplished with the local Fuegians, aided as he was by Captain Fell. The mission house had been built. Now eight more adult Fuegians had been at Keppel nearly ten months. To say the least, their morals and habits had vastly improved. Okoko and Lucca had made great progress, and Despard had annotated a thousand words in "Tekeenica" (Yahgan).

The First Search

Fell had been informed that certain articles of the "ship's company" were missing. He searched all the Fuegians' bags on the morning scheduled for departure from Keppel, 28 September. Later Fell explained, "several stolen things were found.... They [the natives] made a great noise, persuaded that their things, which they valued so much, would all be lost. Old Billy [Button] roared out, I suppose with grief and one of the women sat down and cried.... Schway-muggins claimed his box, which he hoved into the sea when the search was going on."[46]

Billy Button and Squire Muggins were very offended by the search precisely because they were guilty. No stolen items were found in Lucca's or Okoko's bags or in Tom's.[47] Phillips strongly protested against the search, even though he knew that some tools had been stolen. "To do wrong is one thing; to be found out is quite another. And to many, the latter is by far the more painful of the two. The Fuegians are very jealous of their character for honesty; the more so, perhaps, as it stands sometimes in peril."

Phillips thought it best to minimize the incident. "The demonstration speedily subsided and all went smooth again." After the search, everyone on board was told to return to shore because of bad weather. On 4 October, two days before the *Allen Gardiner* finally departed from Keppel, Despard remained confident, minimised the thefts; praised Tom, Lucca and Okoko; and especially the three young women.[48] By this time he knew that Billy and Squire were very offended by the search. When, on 6 October, the *Allen Gardiner* finally sailed from Keppel into Port Stanley, the temper of these two men was still such that both Fell and Phillips "were warned by several friends in Port Stanley to be on their guard."[49]

Why did Despard stay in the Keppel station? Why didn't he accompany Phillips and the others to Wulaia? This was not explained. He must have decided that his presence was not needed. Like Phillips, he was not concerned that Billy and Squire had stolen a few tools. He had entrusted Phillips with the direction of this "expedition." The main objectives of the trip were simple enough: return the nine to their homeland, inaugurate the mission house and recruit the next group for Keppel.

Also why didn't Thomas Bridges accompany the Fuegians back to Wulaia? He had good reasons to go. He was about seventeen and spoke Yahgan more fluently than any of the other missionaries. Many years later, his son Lucas Bridges explained: "My father was greatly disappointed, but it was decided that it would be better for him to remain and continue his studies at Keppel Island."[50]

Captain Fell, again in charge of the *Allen Gardiner*, was increasingly assuming more responsibilities, aided as he was by John Fell, his brother, the second officer. The entire crew totalled eight men. The carpenter Mr Jackson (or Johnson), had arrived with Despard (in 1856). Phillips thought well of him: "an orderly, industrious and clever fellow; seems thoroughly to understand his business, and able to turn his hand to various and multifarious occupations." The cook Alfred Cole (or Coles) had been on the previous trip to Wulaia, was also part of the crew. The four new recruits (Fell had hired in Montevideo) were a North American – old Mr Hugh Mac Douglas (or M'Dowell), the ship's sportsman, a dead shot, besides being an excellent seaman with Arctic experience. The other three were the young seamen said to be Swedes, but many decades later their true identify became known: John Johnssen, a Dutchman; Brown (first name not given), a Scot; and August Petersen, a Norwegian.[51] Despard liked them all. "The new crew are certainly the finest, nicest-looking set of men we have had yet in the schooner."[52] The entire party totalled eighteen: Phillips, eight crew members and nine Fuegians.

Despard Instructs Phillips

Despard didn't mention bringing other Fuegians back to Keppel in his instructions to Phillips, although he probably told him to do so. He did specify that the yacht should proceed rapidly to Wulaia and return at least in time for the next mail leaving Stanley for England, by late December 1859. Anticipating a friendly reception, he wrote that they should "spend two or three days there on shore, in the house erected during my last visit there." Work should be done on the garden. Captain Fell was supplied with biscuits "for the encouragement to the natives." Phillips should spend every day with them, take notes on their language, rehearse the usual hymns, and give presents to the Keppel boys' relatives. The most significant instruction will prove to be the following: "I look to you to undertake the services in the *Allen Gardiner* and would advise, when the weather allows, that you should have the morning and evening Sabbath service on shore, so that the natives might attend and be roused to inquiry."[53]

Fifty-three years later, Mrs Winn, Despard's youngest daughter, declared that in addition to her father's "general instructions," others had been given to Phillips: "He [Despard] specially cautioned Mr Phillips... that if there was any gathering of natives from other parts he was not to hold service in the little building [the mission house], but on the Allen Gardiner. These directions were not followed."[54] As they were embarking from Keppel for Port Stanley, the lads (Okoko and Lucca) bid a fond good-bye to Mrs Phillips, "with many regrets," and received her gifts of clothing for their relatives. Four days later, the nine Fuegians (including Kitty) went ashore in Port Stanley, dressed in their best and were "lionised" by the residents. Mrs Smyley (the wife of the famous North American sealer Chapter 7) and Mrs Sweeny, (the American consul's wife) "were very pleased of the opportunity" to see the young women (the three wives) and to give Kitty "sweet stuff" and the warm gaiters and the woollen coat they had purchased for her in a local store. They were all escorted to another lady's home, where they received gingerbread nuts. "Flocks of cottagers" hurried down to see them off, with more little presents.

The Departure from Port Stanley Is Again Delayed
The day before departure (10 October), Phillips wrote to Despard (who had remained in Keppel):

It is very clear that the natives thought very highly of their "lionising," yesterday, for, to-day, they have frequently told me and others that they do not want to go [home] to Tierra del Fuego, but to England. [They said] "Tierra del no good." ... I am thinking, however, that did we take them at their word, the fit would not last long, but they would be very angry at not returning to the southern shores [their homeland].

[Note that he added:] I hope to send you a full account of our doings by the next mail, which leaves here on the last of December; but I post this now in case we fail in getting back so early.[55]

Waiting out a series of gales off Port Stanley, they finally "weighed anchor" on 25 October. After an uneventful trip, they arrived in Wulaia on the first day of November 1859.

The Eventful Week in Wulaia

Tuesday: 1 November
The *Allen Gardiner* anchored off the coast of Wulaia. No one went ashore until the following day. However, according to Fell, they reached Wulaia the next day at noon.[56]

Wednesday: 2 November
Fell searched the Fuegians' bags again (the first search took place on 28 September), while they were still on the yacht, and found stolen knives, handkerchiefs and a harpoon. Only Squire Muggins and Billy resisted the search. Later the cook, Alfred Cole, explained: "They were very angry, and Schwei [Squire] Muggins caught hold of Captain Fell by the neck on the gangway where the things were. Captain Fell knocked him off of him. And then Schwei Muggins, and the other man, Billy Button, with their wives, got into the canoes without their things."[57] Later Okoko insisted that when Captain Fell found Hugh Mac Douglas' new harpoon in Squire Muggins' bag, that Squire only pushed him off, but that he did not strike him. Even so, he and Billy Button were more furious with Fell than they had been during the first search.

When Captain Fell went ashore, he noticed Jemmy Button "naked, and as wild-looking as ever.... It was almost too trying to behold him. It seemed to prove that all our labours with him had been thrown away. Something entirely different to what has been already done, will have to be taken in hand, before the natives will be benefited."[58] Fell was increasingly assuming the role of a missionary.

Thursday: 3 November
While the crew were cutting wood, Phillips and "his boys" worked in the garden almost the entire day. Fell added: "the natives went on shore, and Schwya-muggines got his clothes in the evening."[59]

This day or the next "about seventy canoes arrived and some three hundred natives had assembled." Phillips and the crew mixed freely with them "as they had done on former occasions."[60] Note that the arrival in Wulaia of such an extraordinary number of canoes, carrying about 300 men, did not alarm anyone.

Friday: 4 November
The seventy canoes may have arrived this day. Fell wrote that his crew continued cutting wood and that "Our natives too lazy to get their house

covered in."[61] Perhaps he referred here to the mission house. Cole reported later that Jemmy came on board the *Allen Gardiner* this day "and was much displeased at not getting many things as soon as he expected."

Saturday: 5 November

The woodcutting went on as usual though Fell noted that: "Crew at the wood. Natives rather troublesome alongside." Cole commented fifty-three years later, in 1912, that during this week "the natives visited the ship from time to time, and were allowed up the ladder a few at a time."[62]

Sunday: 6 November; the Crisis

Half-past ten: the entire crew (except Cole, the cook), and a number of "Firelanders" including Jemmy Button gathered in the mission house for the service, which was about to begin. Cole remained on the yacht preparing the midday meal. As the yacht was anchored a short distance from the beach, the men went ashore in one of the ship's boats. As usual they were not armed. Later Cole declared:

Soon after, when the Crew had got into the [mission] house, *I saw two natives taking the boat's oars into a wigwam. I thought there was something up in a moment.* The next thing I saw was our men running out of house for the beach, and the natives following them with clubs, and big stones, flinging stones in all directions, and making a dreadful noise. The [mission] house was about a dozen yards from the beach. When they got to the beach they were all knocked down, except *Mr Phillips and another, a Swede, one of the sailors, who tried to launch a canoe*, then Billy Button took up a stone and flung a stone at Mr Phillips, which hit him on the side of the head, and he fell in the water. I saw Captain Fell and his brother killed, they were side by side on the beach. I could distinguish them quite plain. I saw them all killed but old Henry [Hugh Mac Douglas]. The boys told me he was killed in the [mission] house.[63]

Cole, the only survivor, clarified, in 1912, that the sailor with Phillips was Petersen, a Norwegian (not a Swede), and that both were killed with clubs in the water as they were trying to escape.[64]

Mrs Christian, the sister of the two Fells, declared (in 1912):

On Sunday, November 6, the Service took place, the cook, Alfred Coles, being left in charge of the ship. The company were on their knees at prayer, *when some 300 natives armed with clubs and stones rushed upon them.* Poor old Henry, the boatswain was killed on his knees, and the others fled from the hut and made for the boat. My brothers covering the retreat, back to back, were killed together. The natives plundered the ship, and, strange to say, spared the cook's life. . . . Robert was 31 years of age, and John 29, and were good sons. Mother always wrote to them.[65]

Phillips' brother published, in 1861, essentially the same account and added: "Mr Phillips reached the water's edge, but at the moment he had his hand on the boat, he was struck on the head by a stone, and fell stunned into the water; but the natives dragged him out, and killed him on the spot."[66]

Mrs Winn, Despard's daughter, insisted, also in 1912, that the directions her father gave to Phillips had not been followed:

Consequently when the natives saw them all safe in the [mission] house, they took the oars out of the boats to prevent escape and then struck the party down with stones and clubs. Humanly speaking, the massacre would not have taken place, if the warning had been taken at the *unusual number of strange natives* who had come in their canoes the previous day.[67]

Cole told Despard later: "Our Fuegians [the locals in Wulaia] were with the rest in the attack, but Ookokko ran up and down and put out his hands crying."

Eight men had been killed: Phillips, the two Fell brothers, the three "Swedes," Hugo, the North American artic hunter and Jackson, the missionaries' carpenter.

Alfred Cole Escapes[68]

When Cole realized that all the eight men were dead, he started for the stairs to go below for a gun; but fearing that the natives would overtake him, he changed his mind, seized three small loaves of bread (that were nearby), threw them into the gig, and loosened the cords that held it alongside of the ship. "I lowered the gig, and jumped into her and went away towards the woods; I landed and ran into the woods. The natives were close after me."

He fled without a gun. A canoe started after him, but he kept ahead, paddling with all his might. When he landed on the nearby shore, the loaves of bread fell from his grasp. Without stopping to pick them up, he dashed into the woods and climbed a tree. He couldn't see any natives but did see that his gig had been towed away but that they had not followed him into the woods. He probably waited a while, hidden in the tree, then made off running through the forest towards the east (the interior of Navarino Island).

During four days through open country, Cole survived on berries, and saw many guanacos and flocks of upland geese. At night he made a shelter with branches and grass but couldn't light a fire because he had no matches. He could still hardly believe what had happened. After four days, he came to a river but couldn't ford it, so he followed it down to the sea (to Ponsonby Sound) and headed north (toward Wulaia), along the coast, living on raw mussels and limpets. As he couldn't make a fire, he was wet nearly all the time. He stayed along the coast, hoping that a boat would pass. But none passed during twelve days. Then he sighted two canoes coming around a point, hailed them and one stopped. "I was so weak and exhausted from want of food that I cared little whether the natives killed me or not." He warmed himself by the fire in the canoe. Tellon's eldest son (Lucca's brother) was in the canoe along with eighteen or twenty other natives of "that tribe." None had been to Keppel but they had seen him on the yacht, near Wulaia, the year before. A while later they landed and took off all of Cole's clothes, except his belt and his one earring, and they tried to pull out his beard. A man in a canoe was wearing a sweater that had belonged to one of the men who had been killed and another had on Captain Fell's blue coat. They shared their food with Cole. But he was miserable, especially the first days, because he was naked and had a boil under his ear, which was very painful. They took him to a group of huts a couple of miles away and fed him. They divided his clothes (left in the canoe) among them and "gave me a coat of paint instead." He stayed with them for ten days.

Cole Waits in Wulaia

In Wulaia he found "Jem" (Jemmy), Tommy and their families but not a quarter of the people who had been there before. They were all friendly to him. Squire Muggins and the others brought him some clothes, including Captain Fell's boots. Jem gave him stockings and other things. Tommy returned his trousers and someone else one of his caps (taken from the yacht after Cole had fled). "I lived with them pretty well on shellfish, fish and mussels. Sometimes the men would go out at dawn and come back by sunrise, with a great load of fish &c. They treated me as one of themselves." He went a dozen times on board the *Allen Gardiner* during these two months in Wulaia. It was a "mere wreck." Every bit of iron had been removed, from the deck lights, from the poles, from the wheel, and even from the sails and the gaffs (parts of the masts). The cabin steps had been torn up. There was nothing left of the yacht except the hull and spars (the masts).

"Boys of the tribe" told him that Jemmy Button and the others went on board the *Allen Gardiner* the evening after the massacre and that Jemmy had slept in the captain's cabin (denied by Jemmy in his deposition). There was no one living on board when Cole returned to Wulaia. One of the natives had found a musket and powder in the ship and, with "shot" and percussion caps that Jemmy and Tommy had taken from the yacht, Cole went shooting geese with them. "When I gave them two or three geese, I was a very good fellow." Jemmy used his English to explain "things" to him. In the evening the men and boys played at wrestling and knocking each other about, but during the day they loafed or slept. At times Cole went canoeing with them and once they went to Button Island. He also went swimming with the women, who could beat him at it. Tom's wife was "the kindest of the women." He often went to the scene of the massacre and for days on end searched for the corpses, but without success. Thus he passed the time until 6 February 1860 (see below).

Meanwhile at the Keppel Mission

Despard, at Keppel, was expecting the *Allen Gardiner* to return by late December 1859. But why did he wait until early February before sending a ship to inquire about Phillips and the others? Fifty-three years later (in 1912), Mrs Winn, his daughter, explained the delay. There was no communication between Keppel and Port Stanley (some 70 miles or 130 kilometres away) except by the mission's small schooner, which was not at Keppel during those months. Despard was so anxious for news from Wulaia that he was about to make the 300-mile (556-km) trip in a whaleboat to Wulaia. Then a small schooner came to Keppel, which he took immediately to Port Stanley, hired Captain Smyley and chartered Smyley's boat, the *Nancy*, to proceed to Wulaia.[69] Why didn't Despard go with Smyley to Wulaia if he was so worried that Phillips and the others had not returned? This question was never answered.

Cole Is Rescued and Jemmy Volunteers to Go to Keppel

On 6 February, Alfred Cole must have been excited and relieved when he sighted the *Nancy* on the horizon. Thirty-nine canoes paddled out to greet the new arrival. Smyley was certainly perplexed when he saw only Cole waiting on the beach.

Despard reported: "James Button willingly (no cheating nor compulsion was used) takes him [Cole] to the *Nancy*. James B. goes on board [the *Nancy*], walks into the galley (forward), stands inside of it, whilst A. Cole tells his tale to Smyley, whom J. B. knew to be a friend of Fitz Roy, and a fighting man, from Stanley."

Having heard the gruesome details from Cole, Smyley learned that the bodies of the victims had been buried nearby, but he could not take time to search for them.

According to Despard again: "Smyley ascertained, through J. Button, that the *Allen Gardiner* was still afloat." It had been almost entirely ransacked, but steadied by a submarine rock near the shore and its hull and spars were sound. "He saw the garments of our people on them, shilling, and half crowns slung round their necks.... The boats were recovered through James and Tom Button's interventions. The latter behaved admirably well, watering, and wooding for the *Nancy*."

Later Okoko told Despard that a group of natives, searching for treasures, broke (destroyed) whatever was left (they couldn't use) on the ship, and then lit fires on the deck (to sink the yacht). Then the "Woollya people" went on board (put out the fires) and agreed not to sink the ship because the "Englishmen would not be so enraged if they should find their ship whole and that she would be fitted up again."[70]

Smyley decided that the vessel could be towed back to Port Stanley but he didn't have time or equipment to do so then. He planned to return to Wulaia later, to search for the bodies, and to tow the *Allen Gardiner* back to Port Stanley.[71] He hastened back to Port Stanley, arriving four days later, 10 February, with the dreadful news and the two witnesses: Cole who was impatient to return to Port Stanley, and Jemmy who volunteered to go.[72]

Jemmy in Port Stanley

Lucas Bridges commented "that cunning fellow, Jimmy Button, went to Captain Smiley and asked to be taken to Keppel Island – a trip that, up to then, he had persistently refused to make." Note that Lucas apparently forgot that Jemmy and his family had been in Keppel five months, the year before (1858). He called Jemmy "cunning," as if he had some hidden motive for volunteering to go to Keppel.[73]

When Smyley arrived at Keppel on 10 February and told Despard the terrible news, Despard wept and prayed for forgiveness: "Pray ye to the Lord not to lay this sin to their charge. Weep not for the dead, weep for the living."[74]

Jemmy remained in Port Stanley, almost two months, until early April 1860. He presented his "deposition" (testimony) on 12 March to Mr Moore, governor of the Falkland Islands, and J. R. Longden, the colonial secretary, in the presence of Reverend Charles Bull, the colonial chaplain at Port Stanley. (See Appendix below for J. B.'s entire deposition.)

One can imagine Jemmy's despair during these two months in Port Stanley: his failure to prevent the massacre and the accusations of Cole, waiting alone, wondering what would happen to him. Later, after

12 March, Mr Moore, as the governor of Falklands, made the legal decision concerning Jemmy's innocence or guilt (see below).

Who Was Guilty?

Cole Accuses Jemmy

During his deposition on 10 March 1860, Cole stated:

My belief is that the cause of the massacre was, that Jemmy Button being jealous that he did not get as much as he thought he had a right to, and *that he was at the head of the whole proceedings.* As to what became of the bodies I don't know. The boys told me they were cast into the sea. They also told me they saw Jemmy Button fight. I did not distinguish him from the rest. I could not tell [distinguish] him, I could only tell Billy Button.[75]

Jemmy Testifies

Jemmy asserted that he was in the mission house when the attack started, that he remonstrated against the killing but feared "the violence of the people" and for his own life, that he saw the Oens-men kill Captain Fell but did not see the others killed. He attributed the massacre to the Oens-men, that they had threatened the local Yahgans in Wulaia were they to attempt to prevent them from attacking the missionaries. (See his deposition below.)

The Authority in the Falklands

The governor of the Falklands, Mr Moore, did not credit Cole's accusation against Jemmy. He concluded, in March, that Despard's arrogance and bad judgement had caused those events.[76] Thus Jemmy was officially declared innocent. In early April he returned to Wulaia with Smyley (see below). Despard must have been chagrined by Moore's comment, which apparently was not an official accusation. His troubles were just beginning, however (Chapter 10).

Reverend Charles Bull, colonial chaplain at Port Stanley, explained why he also supported Jemmy:

I may add my own impression, that Jemmy Button did not take part in the awful tragedy, though afterwards he joined in the plunder; but his kindness to Alfred Cole, and his coming voluntarily on board the "Nancy," prove that it was not a premeditated act. I believe it [the massacre] to have been revenge, for what the natives deemed insults.... [77]

Okoko

Okoko, who was present but did not see the actual killings, said that the three women who had been recently at Keppel cried bitterly after the massacre.[78] The missionary who succeeded Despard, Reverend W. H. Stirling, wrote: "James Button and Thomas his brother, [were] men whose character Ookokko ever vindicates from guilt concerning the massacre."[79] Despite Okoko's presence on the scene, he was never interviewed by the colonial authorities in Port Stanley.

The Bridges' Opinion of Jemmy

In 1879 Thomas Bridges declared: "He [Jemmy Button] would not tell the people what he had seen, but made capital of their ignorance and his knowledge by keeping it to himself. He only became the greater impostor, and assumed a pompous conduct towards his fellows, and did not a whit of good." Thomas Bridges may have felt a deep dislike toward Jemmy mainly because (I suggest) he never really attempted to convert his people to Christianity. Lucas Bridges affirmed: "It was subsequently established beyond all reasonable doubt that Jimmy Button had been the chief instigator of the massacre." This statement appears in his book *Uttermost Part of the Earth*, probably still the most widely read work in English and Spanish on Tierra del Fuego.[80] It has often been taken as authority since 1948, when this book was first published. Lucas may have been influenced by his father's dislike of Jemmy Button.[81]

Later, the Majority of Authors

Among the well-known authors, Gusinde stated that Jemmy Button did not appear to be responsible for the assassinations. Hyades and Shipton concluded that the massacre was motivated by the anger of the Fuegians upon being searched by Captain Fell in Wulaia.[82] However, the majority of authors consulted held Jemmy responsible for instigating, staging or leading the massacre.

The anthropologist Lewis Burgess, who carefully read my text, commented:

The Europeans were unable to fathom the Fuegian psyche and were ignorant of Fuegian facial and body language, gestures and expressions. They could not see what was coming: their overwhelming sense of superiority and ethnic arrogance made it impossible for them to see the Fuegians as human beings worthy of respect and their massacre was due to this as it was due to the rage of the Fuegians, which they unwittingly incited.[83]

The Missionary Society

The considered opinion of the committee of the Patagonian Missionary Society was published as editorials in the 1860 issue of *The Voice of Pity*. The authors of the June editorial did not doubt the facts in Cole's declaration. They agreed that Jemmy shared the plunder and that one of the men (certainly Billy Button) who had been recently at Keppel took part in the attack. Then they declared: "But we feel convinced that the Oen's men [the Selk'nam] were the real movers in the matter, and we are willing to believe that the Button, or more correctly the Tellon, tribe became accessories through an overpowering temptation."

The authors of the editorial in the next issue agreed with the British chaplain who acquitted Jemmy "of every thing except sharing in the plunder" and reiterated "that the Oen's-men, who had now left Woollyah, were really the prime movers in the previous fatal attack."[84]

The committee of the Patagonian Missionary Society reasoned that by the day of the massacre, the missionaries (Phillips and Fell) were alert enough to have been able to discern any symptoms of "disaffection," had it existed, and would have taken the necessary precautions, or they would have held the service on the ship. On the fatal day the behaviour of the natives was not in the least conducive to any suspicion of danger. The editorial specified: "In fact, we regard a too generous confidence in the natives by our missionary brethren to be the true source of the late disaster."[85]

Despard

The following year, Despard wrote: "I am firmly persuaded that our natives were not, save it may be in two persons, Billy Button and a Yahgan named Happi-Aurnersh [not identified], engaged in the massacre, before to plan, or after to execute, it."

Then Despard advanced the argument that if the Navarino Islanders had "engaged in the massacre," they would have killed Cole, removed every trace of the massacre or pillage, burned the ship, and claimed that it had gone long ago to York's country, Alakaluf territory. Despard was sure that they would have been believed, that further search for the yacht would have been made, and it would finally have been concluded that the entire crew had perished at sea. Despard continued: "They were innocent or idiots – the last they are not.... Ookokko varies in his tale of the massacre to-day. He told me Happi-Aurnersh held Fell down; many men killed him. I asked their names; there were so many he could not tell." He concluded: "Our readers will remember that the Chaplain at Stanley, who had an opportunity of examining J. Button after the massacre, acquitted him of participation in it, and we see no good reason to do otherwise."[86]

Among Others
Everyone had an opinion. Admiral Sulivan, an outstanding member of the committee, insisted that he had warned Captain Fell, time and again, in Port Stanley and by mail, that it was too soon and too dangerous to establish a mission station in Wulaia. Sulivan implicitly blamed Fell for the disaster and attributed it to revenge on the part of the natives against the white man who had treated them so badly. He added "we mean to benefit them. [If so] It's folly to settle on their land without a knowledge of their language."[87]

Also Reverend Stirling, though a "latecomer" – the successor of Despard – esteemed that covetousness "possessed the whole multitude" but that "another and fiercer tribe gave occasion to this sudden attack." He added: "After the massacre some of the local Yahgan had a share in the spoils (clothes of the victims, coins and objects taken from the schooner). However six victims were buried by them without having been despoiled."[88]

My Hypotheses
I agree with Mr Moore (the governor of Falklands), Reverend Bull (the chaplain at Port Stanley), Despard and the editorial of *The Voice of Pity* that Jemmy was not the instigator, and that the "Oens-men" (the Selk'nam) with the assistance of Billy Button and Yahgan allies carried out the massacre. I briefly review the "evidence" for this hypotheses.

1. On 15 December 1832, Jemmy asked Fitz-Roy to fire on the "Oens-men" as they passed the Atlantic coast of Tierra del Fuego (Chapter 4).

2. Later, on 22 and 23 January 1833, Jemmy told "many long stories" about the Oens-men attacking his people. Fitz-Roy noted Jemmy's stories, adding that the Oens-men hiked over the cordillera in groups of fifty to a hundred to the shore of Beagle Channel, where they seized canoes belonging to the Yapoo (probably the Ushuaia Bay Yahgans) and crossed over to Navarino Island (Chapter 5).

3. On 14 February 1833, when Fitz-Roy returned to Wulaia, Jemmy told him that "strangers" had attacked Wulaia (on 7 February). These were certainly the Beagle Channel Yahgan neighbours, the "bad men" not the Oens-men.

4. The Oens-men did attack a few weeks later in February 1833 after Fitz-Roy had left Wulaia (on 14 February). Then Jemmy killed one enemy and he and his family fled to Button Island to be out reach of these "dreaded Oens-men." Jemmy told Fitz-Roy that the latter had seized several canoes from the "Yapoo Tekeenica," had fastened them together and had paddled to the south shore of Beagle Channel, from where they hiked to Wulaia.[89] The "Yapoo Tekeenica" were certainly the Yahgans in the area of Ushuaia Bay. Just how the Oens-men seized their canoes is not stated (end of Chapter 5).

Follows the evidence that some or many Yahgans did not support the missionaries.

5. In May 1858 young Gardiner arranged for a meeting on Lennox Island of the Yahgans of Lennox and Picton Islands and asked permission to take some of their male children to the Keppel Mission for a limited time and offered the adults many useful presents. Recall that "They all . . . spoke at once, . . . and *our proposal was negatived, this refusal was exceedingly discouraging. . . .* "(Chapter 8).

6. From there young Gardiner went on to Wollaston Island, where the local Yahgans threatened him and his men.

7. Then, on 15 June 1858, while still off the coast of Wulaia the "Beagle Channel Indians" attacked young Gardiner with sixty canoes. There is no evidence that the Oens-men were among them, in June 1858, though they may have been (also Chapter 8).

8. Late in December, also 1858, when Despard, Phillips and Fell took Jemmy and his family back to Wulaia, natives came in six or twelve canoes and camped near Wulaia. Despard identified them as Oens-men who "took themselves off, as they found for the present our visit and benefactions are not for them." These Oens-men saw that the missionaries were building a house for themselves, not just wigwams, as Fitz-Roy had in 1833. No doubt they and the channel Yahgans also knew about the episode of January 1851 involving the father of young Gardiner (Chapter 7).

The channel Yahgans and probably the Selk'nam were aware of the movements of the *Allen Gardiner* since Snow had gone to Button Island in November 1855. By 1858 both groups had ample reasons to believe that the missionaries had plans in mind and that, in November 1859, they had come to settle in Wulaia.

9. This year (1859), as related above, the third or fourth day of November, seventy canoes arrived with 300 "natives," who immediately mixed in freely with everyone and "showed no hostility whatever." These numbers may seem amazing. They imply that

in 1859 the "Beagle Channel Indians" (and I propose, the Oens-men) organised a crew of paddlers, mostly four men to a canoe. The 300 number does not seem exaggerated. Also recall that when Jemmy told his "long stories" about the Oens-men's invasions into Yamana territory, he said they came over the cordillera in groups of from fifty to a hundred in the time of "red leaf," or autumn (September to November [Chapter 5]). Therefore they could have hiked over the cordillera in October 1859 and joined the Yahgans in Ushuaia and Navarino and together mobilised 300 men and seventy canoes.

I propose that the "hostile party" (which killed Phillips and seven of the crew of the *Allen Gardiner*, except Cole) was composed not only of Jemmy's "bad" neighbours on Navarino Island, and the Yahgans on the north shore of Beagle Channel (in area of Ushuaia), but also, as Jemmy declared in his deposition (see Appendix below, answer 4), the Oens-men – the Selk'nam. This would mean that the Selk'nam and Yahgans of Ushuaia crossed Beagle Channel, where the "Navarin islanders" joined them and, with a fleet of some seventy canoes and about 300 men, des-cended Murray Narrows to attack the missionary party in Wulaia.[90]

Most of the local Wulaian men did not show active opposition to the attack, though Okoko and the women did, as noted above. Some of the local Yahgans took part in the plunder of the yacht, wore the victims' clothing, and hung coins around their necks, however they did bury the eight victims and were helpful to the only survivor. It seems clear that the local people were not the "instigators," nor was Jemmy. Moreover, given Jemmy's usual reluctance to assume leadership, it is not surprising that he was not capable of attempting to counter it once it began.

The weapons were clubs and stones, which the Yahgans usually employed, while the main weapon of the Selk'nam was the bow and arrow, which is not mentioned. In any event, as the killing took place so rapidly and at very close range, the bow and arrow could not have been used.

Revenge for the two inspections by Captain Fell (at Keppel and Wulaia) of Billy Button's and Squire Muggins' bags was certainly a motive for the former to kill Phillips, but there is no indication that Squire Muggins was involved in the actual massacre.

Plunder was an obvious motive. (Jemmy was even "plundered" by his own family [Chapter 5]). Were there others? The Oens-men and the channel Yahgans could not very well have been driven by revenge, simply because their previous contacts with the missionaries along Beagle

Channel were quite peaceful, even though they provoked Snow in 1855 (Chapter 8).

It was one thing to plunder the missionaries, and quite another to allow the strangers to settle in their land. The channel Yahgans may have felt not only the temptation to plunder the strangers but also threatened by their occupation of Wulaia, because it was close to their territory. If so, it is not surprising that, once assured of the support of a powerful ally, the Selk'nam, they organised to attack the missionaries with full force the first week of November 1859.

However, except for plunder, why the Selk'nam? Until the early 1880s, they had little contact with outsiders (sealers) and none with the Anglican missionaries in their own territory. The contacts of the Selk'nam with them along the coast of Beagle Channel were incidental and quite peaceful. So why would the Selk'nam want to kill the missionaries? Beside the usual desire to plunder, it may be proposed that the Selk'nam had calculated that they would also be invaded, which in reality they were, though not by the Anglican missionaries.[91] Briefly, I propose that although plunder was a motive, the strategy: "defeat the invaders before we are defeated by them" (my term) was more important.

During the years following the 1859 massacre, neither the Yamana nor the Selk'nam will make any other attempt to attack the missionaries or to plunder anyone. But, from 1864 to 1868, the Yahgans will resist to accept the missionaries' teachings, and abandon their traditional way of life (Chapter 10).

Since the 1624 massacre of seventeen Dutch sailors (Chapter 1), the Fuegians were never known to attack outsiders until November 1859. It may never be known for sure whether or not the channel Yahgans and the Selk'nam hoped, by the last massacre, to eradicate the missionaries once and for all from their land. But if they did, the continued and insistent presence of the well-equipped missionaries forced them to recognise that the strangers were there to stay, as of 1869 (Chapter 11).

Appendix: Jemmy Button's Deposition in Port Stanley

The Patagonian Missionary Society was aware that the Colonial Office in the Falklands did not favour their evangelising project. An editorial of 1860 in the *Voice of Pity* expressed concern that the missionary society was being held responsible for the massacre by the colonial authorities for their improper treatment of the natives in Wulaia.

In reading the following deposition, presented on 12 March, it should be borne in mind that Jemmy Button spoke as a prisoner in the hands of those who had the power to condemn him. His first desire was to get back home. In his "deposition" that follows he very strongly expresses this desire and protested against a return to Keppel.

It should also be remembered, moreover, that his examiners had no knowledge of his language, there was no interpreter and their questions were framed in terms of their suspicions or preconceived opinions. If they imagined, for instance, that the massacre was attributable to improper treatment of the natives by the missionaries or enforced residence at the mission farm at Keppel, they would, as a matter of course, ply Jemmy with questions calculated to bring out a confirmation of such suspicions. Making allowance of his natural desire to go home and not to Keppel, the editorial, in the *Voice of Pity*, saw little in Jemmy's statements but what the Patagonian Mission Society was disposed to regard as truthful. And the editorial insisted that "knowing the readiness with which he formerly came to Keppel, and the kindness with which he was treated there, we are entitled to give to his alleged dislike to go to that island a prospective, and not a retrospective, interpretation."[92]

As stated above, it will become evident that many of Jemmy's replies were to questions concerning his attitude towards the missionaries for having brought him to Keppel in the first place, rather than to inquiries about his role in the massacre. This partly explains why his testimony is so incoherent as published here. Also, it is apparent that he had considerable difficulty in understanding the questions and probably difficulty expressing himself clearly in English, especially in such official surroundings. The secretary's inability to understand his replies, let alone clarify his English, was also responsible for his incoherence. However, the *Voice of Pity* did not publish the entire deposition. Unfortunately only one of the questions put to Jemmy is cited, though the others can be deduced from his answers, which may not be completely published here either.

The text of his deposition is copied below without alterations except for replacing the word "stop" with three dots. "Stop" apparently was inserted when the secretary failed to understand his answers. I also divided the text into nine questions. The words in parentheses are in the text. His answers are followed by my interpretations and comments in brackets.

"*Colonial Sectary's Office, Falkland Islands. March 12, 1860.*

"In the presence of Governor Moore, the Colonial Chaplain, Captain Smyley, and the undersigned James Button, Terra-del-Fuegian, states."

1. [No question recorded]

   J. B.: "I staid at Keppel Island four moons with wife and children. Did not like to . . . don't want to; don't like it. Despard say, go back,

Jemmy, you're old, your children…would like children to…at Woollya; want to go back with you (Captain Smyley) all like to go back Woollya."

[J. B. stayed at Keppel from 24 June to 16 November 1858, with his first wife and three children. He did not like to do something, but he did not say what it was. He does not want to stay at Keppel now. Despard said he was too old to stay at Keppel. Despard wanted his children to stay there, but J. B. wanted his children to remain in Wulaia. As Captain Smyley was present, he spoke directly to J. B. when he said he wanted to go back to Wulaia with him now. By "all like to go back Woollya," in the last sentence, J. B. probably meant that all his countrymen who had come to Keppel wanted to go back to Wulaia.]

2. "Mr Despard ask you to go to Keppel?"

J. B.: "Mr Despard said, go two time to Keppel, two time a year Woollya; no work at Keppel. Cask of water a big tub at Keppel; spear fish at Keppel, no catch seal, catch fish, big fish."

[Here perhaps J. B. referred to Despard's plan to bring people from Wulaia to the Keppel Mission twice a year. "No work at Keppel" probably means that he was not obliged to work when he was at the Keppel Mission. The "cask of water" may refer to the water available for him when he was at Keppel. While he was there he did not catch any seals but fishing was good.]

3. [No question]

J.B.: "I did not see them search the bags; our country boy very angry boy when Despard look in bags."

[This sentence is evidently in answer to a question concerning the search of the bags on the yacht on 1 November. Here J. B. confuses Despard with Captain Fell, as Despard was not present during either search. By "country boy" as J. B. rarely used the plural in English, he probably meant the two adult men (Billy Button and Squire Muggins) who were angry when the search was made.]

4. [No question]

J. B.: "Owen's countrymen killed Captain Fell; all same as Patagonians, bow and arrow men. My country in small channel, others from big waters; my country at Woollya, theirs near Patagonia. Owen's country boys say we no kill you, you go away we kill them. Captain Fell was killed with stones, by Owen's country. I see Captain Fell killed; carpenter; another man saw one killed; I no see Mr Phillips killed."

[The "Owen's," are the Oens-men, Selk'nam – similar to those in Patagonia, the Tehuelche, bow-and-arrow men. "Big waters" is probably the Magellan Strait, which J. B. had seen passing by it in the *Beagle* in December 1832. His "country" is on the small channel, meaning Beagle Channel or Ponsonby Sound. The Oens-men said that they would not kill him if he would "go away" but that they would kill the men on the yacht. He saw Captain Fell killed with stones by Oens-men. Someone else saw the carpenter killed. He did not see Phillips killed.]

5. [No question]

J.B.: "I put four in the ground; I no see the others. I will show Captain Smyley."

[After the massacre J. B. buried four of those killed. He did not see the other corpses. Later, when he returned to Wulaia with Smyley in early April 1860, he and Tom showed Smyley six burials. Smyley did not move the graves. Much later the bodies were given a Christian burial in Wulaia (Chapter 11).]

6. [No question]

J.B.: "I no see no one live; I think one get away in the field, run away. I bury Captain Fell, and the Carpenter, and two other Swedes. I no sleep in schooner, run about on main land; no more sleep, run about. I have been all round island, no see white man; we look for body Captain Fell, my brother say, all by ground near house, my brother dig."

[Following the massacre he did not see the "one get away," that is Alfred Cole. He thought he (Cole) ran into the countryside. J. B. identified the four that he buried. He did not sleep on the yacht (as Cole had testified). He searched all around the "main land," Navarino Island, for Cole. He did not sleep because he was searching for the "white man," for Cole, but failed to find him. They looked for Captain Fell's body and others who apparently had been buried near the mission house and later Fell's body and others ("all" in the last sentence) were dug up and buried again by J. B. and his brother, undoubtedly Tom.]

7. [No question, although the secretary wants J. B. to identify the languages of "tribes."]

J.B.: "Every tribe speaks differently, woman at Woollya is keepa; my tribe has fifteen canoes (counting on his fingers) plenty canoes other side over water plenty. York people no speak Woollya; Owen's country no speak (Lennox Island described) they no speak."

[Jemmy J. B. gave the word "Keepa," often spelt kipa, as an example of the pronunciation in the Wulaia dialect (it was employed as a suffix on female proper names, as a noun signifying woman). While his tribe has fifteen canoes, those on the north side of Beagle Channel, undoubtedly the eastern Yahgan, have "plenty," meaning more canoes than his tribe. York (Minster) does not speak the language spoken in Wulaia, nor do the Oens-people speak his language. The reference to the speech on Lennox Island is not clear and obviously incomplete.]

8. [No question]

J.B.: "York's country two ships broke long time ago; York man eat man, scratch country."

[Jemmy speaks of two shipwrecks in York's country, on which occasion the Alakaluf ate some of the castaways. "Scratch" has no meaning here, and is an error of the secretary, though "scratch country" may have meant that he searched for the shipwrecks.]

9. [No question, but apparently its subject was the Yahgans' attitude about being brought to the mission station at Keppel.]

J.B.: "My brother perhaps go back to Keppel; I had plenty of it, no want go back; been away three times; countrymen perhaps go back (accompanied by look to say no, afterwards added) my countryboy no want to go back to Keppel."

[His brother, undoubtedly Tom, may agree to go back to Keppel, but he, Jemmy, does not want to return there. "Away three times" refers to having been once in England and now twice to Falklands. "Countrymen" and "countryboy[s]" may refer to all those of Wulaia, who may go back to Keppel. Then changed his statement saying that they ("countryboy" probably meaning his people) do not want to return to Keppel.]

"Taken down the day and year before mentioned, from Jemmy Button's lips, as far as he could be understood, or made to understand the questions. (signed) J. R. Longden, Colonial Secretary, [and] Charles Bull, Colonial Chaplain."[93]

1860 to 1869: The First Devastating Epidemic; The Missionaries Seek a Location; Four Other Yamana Visit England

Despard Continues as Head Missionary, Until...

Early April (1860), Captain Smyley returned to Wulaia with a double crew and Jemmy, who had been declared innocent of instigating the massacre by the British authorities in the Falkland Islands as well as by the Anglican missionaries. He was eager to return home after two months in Port Stanley. He will not appear again until three years later.

Smyley and the crew spent a week in Wulaia, amid ice and snow, preparing the pillaged schooner to be towed back to Port Stanley. Jemmy and Tom showed Smyley the burial site of six victims, of the 1859 massacre, near the foot of a rock beyond the settlement. Smyley left them untouched. Dogs had devoured the other two corpses.

On 11 April, when Captain Smyley was about to leave Wulaia, towing the *Allen Gardiner*, Okoko announced "that Keppel was his country – those were his friends there – Mr Despard was his friend." Smyley gave him two days to reconsider. Then Okoko assured him that he had not changed his mind. Smyley requested that he announce this wish before all the people in Wulaia. "He did so; gave away his canoe, and came off." Okoko boarded Smyley's schooner with his wife Cammillenna-keepa, (later written Gamela). Both were about sixteen years old. This was to be the third visit of the Yahgans to Keppel.

When Smyley arrived at Keppel, on 12 April, with Okoko and Gamela, Despard was overjoyed: "I regard the coming of these persons here as a smile of God upon us." When he installed them in one of the cottages, Okoko turned to him saying: "Nice warm house, thank you." In the days to come he frequently repeated: "Poor Fell – poor Mr. Phillips."[1]

Despard renewed his determination to pursue the objectives of the mission. He had at least three reasons to be encouraged by the presence of the young couple: in 1859 Okoko had shown his loyalty to the mission during his ten months' stay in Keppel, both he and Gamela were innocent of the slightest participation in the massacre and after the massacre Okoko had volunteered to return to Keppel. Their arrival was also symbolic, a reassuring link to the past and an inspiring promise for the future. Despard was enchanted.

Ookokko is happy as he can be, and never talks of returning home, nor does his wife. Every day they are each side of me learning their lessons in reading, and I do heartily thank God for the privilege, and could have cried tears of hope the other day when Ookokko pointed out the name of Jesus everywhere on a page of inspiration.

A few days later he became even more exhilarated:

We were not overthrown in 1852 [1851], when Gardiner perished so miserably... nor shall we be overwhelmed now with so much, very much, still ours: so many associations, so many friends, such funds, a Station, property, vessels, boats, stores, experience, language, natives. Send out an army of working Missionaries; your superintendent can find places for them. The Lord of Hosts is with us. The God of Jacob is the God of salvation to the ends of the earth.[2]

Despite his impassioned evangelical stance, the following year, on 25 July, after five years in Keppel, Despard left for England with his family and servants on the renovated *Allen Gardiner*. They never returned to Keppel. The committee of the Missionary Society in Bristol had called him back. But why, following such an auspicious renewal of the mission work with the Okoko couple and his progress in learning the Yamana language? Despard himself had obviously planned to remain at Keppel as superintendent. He did not mention, in his published diary, any motive for resigning from his post, even though, many years later, Lucas Bridges wrote that he "had given up in despair." This is apparently not true. The assumption imposes itself that the Society somehow associated him with the massacre, though without holding him responsible for it. Back in England, he continued for a while as an active member of the Patagonian Missionary Society, newly named the South American Missionary Society. Later he migrated to Australia and became canon of the cathedral in Melbourne, where he died in 1881.[3]

Thomas Bridges, and the Bartlett couple, who had come with Despard in 1856, remained at Keppel. Young Bridges, who had been carefully trained by Despard, was put in charge of the station until the new super-intendent was to arrive two years later.[4] At that time Bridges "had already acquired a degree of serenity and quiet self-confidence rare even among mature people of the most secure background."[5]

The day the Despards departed, Bridges seemed depressed. "I felt some-what lonely in going up to my quarters, but I am one that rather likes quietness and not much company."[6] Years later, his son Lucas wrote with pride: "Richard Mathews had failed and fled, Allen Gardiner had died of starvation, Garland Philips had been struck down and perished in the sea [during the massacre at Wulaia], George Pakenham Despard had given up in despair. One man alone remained to carry on the great work, and that man was Thomas Bridges."

12 April 1860 to Early March 1863: The Third Yamana Group in Keppel

Okoko and his family remained in Keppel for these three years. Lucas noted that Okoko and Gamela were "a talkative and laughter-loving pair, in this way he [Thomas Bridges] was able to unravel the mysteries of their intricate yet beautiful grammar [of the Yahgan language]."[7] In May 1862 their second child was born. Bartlett, now the administrator of the mission farm, was very taken by Okoko's wife. "Camelena was very kind and attentive to me when I was poorly, and I have done all I could for her, for I like her very much. She certainly is a very quiet, gentle woman, very unlike the others that were here [in 1859]; she is also very clean and tidy."[8]

Bartlett also appreciated Okoko. "I would rather have Okokko to work with me than half the English lads." But he acknowledged that Okoko had a quick temper. Once when he was in a "great passion with Mr. Bridges, who could do nothing with him," Bartlett took him into the garden to work off his steam, reassuring him that Bridges was his very good friend while warning him that God would be angry were he to give way to his violent temper. For the first time Okoko seemed troubled. "God does not answer my prayer now as He used to. Mr. Bridges tells me, if I pray, God will give me a new heart, and He hasn't done it."[9]

I pause here to clarify to the reader that three visits to Keppel have been noted (the third being that of Okoko and his wife, Gamela) and that four more visits to Keppel will occur (in this chapter), as well as attempts by the missionaries to establish a station in Tierra del Fuego.

The New Superintendent

Reverend Waite Hocking Stirling offered to take Despard's place as superintendent of the Keppel Mission. He was the best candidate, if only because he had served for six years in England as secretary general of the Patagonian Missionary Society. In January 1863, he arrived aboard the *Allen Gardiner* with his wife, two young daughters, a servant, his brother Tom and three missionaries: Jacob Rau (a German), and the other two identified by their surnames as Lett and Andrews (both probably British). This same year the latter two were assigned to the newly created mission station in Carmen de la Patagonia, a little town at the mouth of the Rio Negro. Rau remained at the Keppel Mission for two years.

Stirling was also pleased with Okoko: his good English, pleasant manners and joyous laughter. Then too he was impressed by Bridges' progress in learning Yahgan. At that time Bridges had been on bleak, treeless Keppel Island for seven years. He had probably often dreamt of Tierra del Fuego, that "mysterious world of forests and channels and mountains beyond the south-western horizon."[10]

Wulaia Visited for the First Time Since the Massacre

Okoko and Gamela were the only contacts the missionaries had with the Yahgans during almost three years (since April 1860). Early in March (1863), Stirling and Bridges sailed on their first trip to Tierra del Fuego, accompanied by Okoko, his wife, their two children, the captain and a crew. Okoko and Gamela were very anxious to return to their homeland, if only for a visit. Stirling will seek to renew contact with the natives in Wulaia and to create "a good understanding" with them, for which he will rely heavily on Okoko and Bridges.[11]

Sailing the roundabout way to Wulaia, via Nassau Bay, they stopped over in Packsaddle Bay, Hoste Island. Two women paddled up to the schooner, with three children and a man. Okoko greeted them cheerfully and they listened intently as Okoko and the others sang, from the deck, their favourite hymns: "From Greenland's Icy Mountains" and "Praise God from Whom All Blessings Flow." Stirling was pleased with the singing. He considered this, his first encounter with the Yahgans "at home," very favourable. The Okoko couple were "as well conducted, and quiet, and fair in their dealing, and modest in their behaviour, as the most fastidious could require." On shore the same natives requested an encore, so Okoko and Bridges complied. Thereupon they both explained, in Yahgan, the objectives of their mission and asked the only adult man present if he would like the oldest boy there, his son, to visit Keppel to be instructed there.

Urupa Is Recruited

The father, Umchumpalahgun, usually called Chingaline, consulted his son and then gave his consent. The fourteen-year-old lad, Uroopatoosaloom, Urupa for short, seemed pleased. His full laughing eyes inspired Stirling to compose the following amazingly introspective text.

Full of gentleness and good nature is this Fuegian lad, as far removed from a savage as I am.... The fact is, I went to Tierra del Fuego screwed tight up in my prejudices or pride, or both, to view my own superiority.... To my surprise I found myself wondering at the evident resemblance to myself which these savages presented, and then struggling to convince myself that they must be worse than they seemed to be. But I think I have learnt... to observe in fact the Apostolic precept – "honour all men," than to cherish exaggerated notions of our own superiority and their degradation.

Will Stirling apply his declaration of intentions during his stay with the Yamana?

Chingaline feared that the missionaries' food on the ship would not be acceptable for his son, so he supplied fish and a cormorant for his dinner. Chingaline was invited on board to witness Urupa being washed and dressed. "The boy looked extremely well, and made a far from unnatural appearance among the ship's company." Before leaving, Chingaline gave instructions that his son should not go ashore at Wulaia, as the people there were not friendly. Then he paddled back to the shore in the wind and rain, leaving his son in the care of the missionaries.[12] Stirling was impressed that Chingaline had entrusted his son to strangers, "yet he mistrusted his own countrymen, belonging to a neighbouring clan, distant but twenty miles" (37 kilometres).[13]

Wulaia: Three Years after the Massacre

When they arrived at Wulaia the following day, 28 March 1863, no one was there. They went ashore anyway and inspected the ruins of the mission house where the fatal attack had begun in 1859. Two hours later, twenty-nine canoes appeared and others followed "containing on an average not less than five persons." Most were "eager petitioners for gifts." Among the crowd of some 200 natives were Jemmy and his brother Tom, "men whose character Ookokko ever vindicates from guilt concerning the massacre...." Stirling invited these "privileged persons on board," together with Jamesina (Jemmy's eldest wife), Lucca (Jemmy's nephew), Okoko's brother and one or two others.[14]

"Since the massacre at Wulaia the natives had lived in constant dread of reprisals," according to Lucas Bridges.[15] However, they did not appear to fear reprisals nor did Stirling appear to be harbouring feelings of animosity towards them, nor toward Jemmy, whom he called James. Recall that he had not given credence to Cole's declaration against Jemmy (end of Chapter 9). Bridges and Okoko were anxious to establish friendly feelings with the Wulaian residents. Jemmy and Tom seemed happy to see them.

Okoko stood on the deck addressing the large assembly of natives gathered in their canoes and on the nearby shore. This was the first time a native Yahgan preached to his countrymen in their own tongue. Stirling was pleased that his tone of voice "was unaffectedly earnest and many attentive eyes and ears were fixed upon him." Okoko's reception also augured well for the mission's success.

Rumours had circulated in Wulaia that the missionaries had killed Okoko and his wife in retaliation for the massacre. Stirling protested: Okoko's and his family's presence here was proof, not only that they were alive and had been well treated at Keppel but also of the mission's "honourable purposes and good will." Okoko lost no time telling his people about God, how Jesus Christ died for them, that good men go to heaven and bad men to hell. And if they were good, the missionaries would teach them many things and by and by they would have goats and sheep and gardens, the same as on Keppel Island. Stirling was utterly gratified.[16]

The next day Stirling, the captain and Bridges went ashore, escorted by Tom and Jemmy. Stirling was again pleased because none of the natives begged or stared at them. Above all he was well impressed with Bridges' knowledge of Yahgan and with his "very strong desire to be a messenger of Christ to these people." He promised Jemmy tools on his next visit if by that time he had restored the "now too-celebrated hut" and had prepared a pile of wood to be taken back to Keppel, where wood was so scarce. Years later, in a lecture Bridges said that a few days after he arrived in Tierra del Fuego (Wulaia), for the first time after the massacre, 300 to 400 natives had been present.[17]

Recruits for the Fourth Visit to Keppel

Okoko and his wife had planned to return to Keppel, and Urupa had obtained permission to go there from his father. Although the mission schooner remained in Wulaia only four days, five more volunteers, in addition to a baby, had been recruited. Three who had been to Keppel during the fatal year of 1859 had volunteered to return: Lucca (Okoko's special friend), Tom Button, his wife Wendoo (Wendoogyappa), now about twenty-three and their baby. Besides these, Threeboys had permission from his father to return to Keppel, having spent five months there in 1858. The other recruit was Pinoense, Tom's oldest son by a former wife. Stirling thought he was a "good natured looking lad." Despite Tom's age, close to fifty, Stirling accepted his offer, thinking that he desired to act as a sort of guardian for the youths, meaning Urupa, Lucca and Threeboys. The two couples, the baby and the three promising lads augured for a real success for the mission in Keppel and eventually in Wulaia.

On 1 April (1863), as Jemmy cheerfully towed the *Allen Gardiner* from the shore, his canoe fastened ahead of the schooner, he "begged three cheers" in memory of "auld lang syne" as a farewell gesture. Stirling and Bridges sang, complying with Jemmy's wish, as the vessel sailed away.[18] This was the last time they would see him.

Threeboys, and the entire Button family, impressed Stirling very favourably. "It is but the simple truth to say that he [Threeboys] would pass for a European anywhere; his good looks and intelligent countenance are beyond dispute; and it is a remarkable fact that James Button and his children are manifestly in possession of the best looks of the Woollya tribe."[19]

All the recruits except for Urupa were Jemmy's kin. Stirling clarified that no single women were invited, nor would they "be permitted by the natives of Tierra del Fuego to come under our care."[20]

Tehuelches at Keppel

Meanwhile at Keppel, three Patagonians (Tehuelches, now known as Aónikenk) had been brought voluntarily from the Province of Santa Cruz, Argentina. They were identified as the Capitanejo, a mocking term for "captain," about sixty years old; his daughter Mariquita, twenty-two years old; and his son, Belonkon, eighteen. Although the Tehuelche were good-humoured and polite to the Yahgan Keppelites, they "did not disguise the superiority of which they were conscious."[21]

April 1863 to Mid-February 1864: The Fourth Visit to Keppel

Stirling insisted that the recruits be subject to a more rigorous discipline than Despard had applied during the previous three visits (the Button family in 1858, nine others in 1859 and Okoko and Gamela from 1860 to 1863). He thought that the group in Keppel just before the massacre had been "most imperfectly instructed."[22] With the help of Bridges, the daily tasks were to be supervised and carried out in a strict sequence: awake at the sound of a bell, three meals at given hours, and, during the day the men and boys should work in the gardens and with the cattle and sheep. The distribution of the stores was to take place in the afternoon. Religious instruction and services at certain hours, morning and evening weekdays, to be announced by the sound of the bell, and so forth.

The new arrivals (Urupa and Pinoense) had a series of surprising experiences, some amusing. They had never seen animals of such uncanny tameness as the horses and they quickly learned to ride them. The cattle running wild reminded them of the light-footed guanacos; pursuing them on horseback relieved the monotony of the routine. The meals were something else: such an abundance of vegetables and scarcity of meat and fish were not to their liking. The closed houses were nothing like the well-ventilated wigwams. The clothes could no longer be torn apart and shared or worn just any old way. The missionaries' incredible mania for routine and cleanliness were felt. This was a new life for Urupa and Pinoense, yet they easily fell in with the discipline. The old-timers also took the stricter schedule in their stride, as if they had anticipated it.

The climate at Keppel was healthy – invigorating – and everyone was getting along fine. Being gifted mimics, the new recruits quickly picked up common words in English. At first the English lessons amused them. There were frequent smiles on the part of the more advanced pupils, especially Okoko and Tom, who possessed a more facile utterance than Threeboys. Bridges, who was trying to increase his knowledge of Yahgan, found that it offered no means of translating concepts about "God, and the gifts of His Son, and of His kingdom." Then, or shortly afterwards, Stirling decided that the basic Christian instruction had to remain in English.[23]

From Pagan to Christian

Stirling and Bridges were not aware of the Yamana's legacy. Even so, Bridges was right, the concept of the kingdom of God must have seemed very strange to his pupils, and not translatable. The Yamana moral precepts did advocate atonement, but not in the figure of the sacrifice of the son of an all mighty. According to the Yamana doctrine, the human being was not born a sinner, although he or she might become an evil person. Watauineiwa was a sort of "all mighty," an abstract power that manifested itself in different natural forms and determined, or was responsible for, the death of the individual. At times the Yamana were furious with Watawuineiwa, particularly for taking the life of an innocent child.

The Keppel pupils (my term) understood that they should perform certain rituals to honour the supremacy of the Christian god. Watawuineiwa had not set down a code of rules that humans were obliged to respect lest they become sinners. Their two culture heroes, the Yoalox brothers, symbolized radical alternatives. The elder Yoalox was the intransigent idealist. He aspired to create an eternal paradise on earth: no work, enjoyment of the products of nature, no suffering and ultimately no death. In contrast, the younger Yoalox was the pragmatist. He advocated certain rules similar to those taught by the Protestants: work was not only necessary but also uplifting, the obligation and privilege of every adult to the community, suffering was inevitable and death was the inexorable result of the human condition. Finally the younger Yoalox prevailed, seduced the beautiful Máku-kipa and fathered the first human beings.[24] When allusions were made to such "superstitions," the missionaries turned a deaf ear. They failed to realise that the Yahgan moral concepts were similar to their own. They also ridiculed the Yamana holy men, the shamans (*yekamush*), in whose bodies and spirits good and evil engaged in endless struggles. In effect their shamans were not compatible to the Anglican pastors, whose ideology was dogma. It occurred to Stirling that the Keppel teaching might make the "pupils" unfit to live as they had been brought up. But he was reassured that this danger would be overcome by the "natural affection of these natives for their people." Nevertheless, Stirling did feel that Okoko should not be detained in Keppel, away from his people, "lest by a too long separation he should lose his influence for good over them."[25]

The Fourth Group Returns to Wulaia

Okoko and Gamela had been in Keppel almost four years, since April 1860, except for the brief visit to Wulaia in 1863. On 17 February 1864, they and the six other adult Wulaians, who had spent over ten months in Keppel, were to return home. Stirling, Bridges and the German missionary Jacob Rau would accompany them. Just before they headed home, Wendoom (for short), Tom Button's wife, gave birth to a girl, her third child.

Okoko and Gamela had made preparations to settle in Wulaia. Upon arrival there they will be given the seven goats and the four sheep, which were all boarded on the *Allen Gardiner*. A large stock of grass as fodder was taken in case they should be delayed along the way. Okoko had packed most of his belongings in a zinc-lined trunk recently sent from

England. He made it clear to Gamela that in their new home she was not to wander about in a canoe fishing but be an English wife: stay home and care for their children.

There was great excitement preparing for the homecoming, "all was cheerfulness, and mirth." Old garments were repaired, new and warm clothing and other necessities had been selected from the store in Stanley. Stirling hoped that the axes, spades, saws and knives would "introduce a new era of industry into their own land." The boys, now young men – Lucca, Urupa, Pinoense and Threeboys – were full of joyous energy. Stirling was touched by their enthusiasm for returning to "the rude privileges of the wigwam, and bark canoe." They were to see their families and friends, exhibit their treasures and tell tales about their life in Keppel.²⁶

On route they enjoyed some "glorious sunny days," and the natives saluted them with fires all along the coasts. About ten days after departure they reached Packsaddle Bay (Hoste Island), where head winds prevented anchorage, so the captain took refuge in nearby Gretton Bay, Wollaston Island, Nassau Bay. There some fifteen friendly natives in two canoes cut grass for the goats and sheep in exchange for "some small presents." The next morning six canoes of the Wollaston Islanders were tossing about in the rough sea trying to reach the ship. The wind was blowing so hard towards the shore that the captain hastened to depart, leaving the Wollaston Islanders frustrated in their canoes.

The Most Dreadful News

It was already dark when the yacht moored in Packsaddle Bay, about 4 March (1864). Three canoes paddled nearby but did not approach the ship until the next morning. Urupa and everyone else on board were looking out for his father. They were told that he was some miles away, so a reward was offered to fetch him, but no one could locate him. The natives who finally did come on board told them that a few months after their last visit "a fatal malady" had struck here in Packsaddle and in Wulaia and that "large numbers of the people" had died. Threeboys heard that his father was among them, Tom Button learned that his three brothers had died (including Jemmy), Gamela that all of her relatives had perished, Lucca that his uncles and cousins had succumbed, and Urupa that his mother also had died. Tom Button came to Stirling more than once saying: "Mr. Stirling, I very unhappy." The missionaries and crew were asked not to mention the names of those who had died. "Grief took possession of our lately happy company of natives." The saddest of all was Threeboys.

As soon as the news of the catastrophe was known they headed for Wulaia, arriving 7 March in a dark and drizzling rain. As the vessel approached a burst of loud and melancholy chants echoed the tidings of death. There had been a malignant sickness no one could identify. Old and young had been swept away. Most of the survivors had their hair cut short on the crown, a sign of mourning. Although they still petitioned for gifts, their manner was in a "less exacting spirit than of old, a pleasanter manner in asking, a more gracious tone." Stirling found it remarkable that the sickness occurred subsequent to the massacre and after their last visit, which had been "a pledge of the forgiveness of their enemies, which Christians can show." Now it seems that Stirling did hold the Wulaia inhabitants partly responsible for the massacre, despite his expressions of friendly feelings toward them.

The next day a canoe with eleven persons aboard came alongside the ship. Mrs Button was among them, Jamesina, as Despard used to call her. "Her face was visibly impressed with sorrow; and, pointing with her finger towards the sky, she gave me [Stirling] to understand by looks more than words, the cause of her grief, and how great it was."

Later, still in Wulaia, Stirling paid this homage to her. "I have felt a very lively interest in the poor woman; for she waits for me daily, when our working party lands, and in broken speech, we manage to engage each other's attention for a while." Jamesina's deep distress was shared by others, especially by her son Threeboys. Stirling also noticed how proud she was of her children and again remarked on the exceptional good looks of the Button family.[27]

Jemmy Button had passed away, sometime between late 1863 and early 1864, from the epidemic that took so many lives. Nothing like this calamity had ever occurred before, so far as is known.

Origin and Spread of the Epidemic

It spread beyond Wulaia and Packsaddle Bay, undoubtedly to Button Island and probably to other areas. There may have been commercial fishing ships (for seals) navigating in the vicinity at the time, though no report of them has been found. Further research is obviously necessary. The only known foreigners in the area were the missionaries. The question of contagion is difficult to establish, mainly because a healthy person may be an agent. In any event the epidemic was not endemic; outsiders had brought it, certainly unaware of the terrible calamity they had created. Everyone in Wulaia and many in Packsaddle had lost their beloved ones. The Keppel residents had been lucky.

Thomas Bridges' estimate of 3,000 as the "original" population of the Yamana, before this first recorded epidemic, can be accepted for the moment. Likewise it also seems reasonable to assume, with Bridges, that during this epidemic the Yamana population was reduced to approximately 2,500.[28] Stirling's estimate, published in 1867, is similar. His account of the difficulty or impossibility of calculating the Yahgan population with precision is certainly relevant.[29]

Given the scarcity of data on this epidemic, it may have combined with other diseases and lasted for some years after 1864 – for example, on Button and Keppel Islands.[30]

Okoko Hopes to Settle on Button Island

After hearing the overwhelming news and witnessing the grief it had caused, Stirling decided to visit Button Island, the "Buttons'" favourite camping ground. He took a boat with Bridges, Okoko and Pinoense and went ashore in front of a narrow valley, walled in by precipitous granite rocks. Nearby they spotted an old fur seal with her offspring, who poked its little head above water "but took no pains to wake up the drowsy lion [the mother]." When they shot and wounded her, she leaped into the air "and with a fierce plunge disappeared beneath the deep water." The natives were "disappointed. That seal would have been a prize for their people." No one felt sorry for the seal or her pup.

The visitors strolled about inspecting the island with several local boys, looking for a suitable place for Okoko to build a house. Stirling recognised the little harbour where Captain Parker Snow had discovered Jemmy in November 1855. Recall that Jemmy had asked Despard to establish the mission here when he returned from Keppel in November 1858 (Chapter 9). Okoko also preferred to settle here instead of Wulaia. Pinoense promised to help him plant a garden and tend his seven goats and four sheep. "Pinoiensee is a good, honest fellow, very good-tempered, and while on Keppel Island very industrious." He excelled in gardening and the use of the needle, though "not quick in book-learning." (See his photo in Chapter 13.) Stirling was glad that he was so willing to aid Okoko and promised him that if he continued to do so, six more goats would be brought for him on the next visit.

While walking about the island they came upon a funeral pyre on which, they were told, Jemmy's body was placed while the family awaited the return of Tom from Keppel to submit it to flames. No account of his burial has been found.

The local boys distracted the visitors by offering them a taste of fungi, telling them that there were six different sorts of fungi, edible during much of the year, so that at least one was nearly always available. Berries were also abundant and varied. While listening to the boys and tasting the fungi, Stirling thought that the natives were not so badly off after all. Okoko praised Button Island for its good soil, verdure and water. He really wanted to settle there, but then Stirling decided that Button Island was inappropriate for Okoko and for the mission station because it lacked an open space for development. Later he selected a site for Okoko in Wulaia, near the ruins of the mission house.[31] Okoko had to obey.

Six of the 1859 Victims Are Buried

Back in Wulaia, Lucca guided Stirling and Rau to a deep cavern under a cliff where six of the massacre victims had been buried shortly after 6 November 1859. They easily identified Phillips and Captain Fell but not the others. The bodies had been placed under rocks and stones to prevent the "foxes" from devouring them. They were probably dogs, as foxes are not reported on this island, Navarino. The bodies were still clothed and "not even their pockets had been rifled." Stirling was perplexed as to why Cole had not located them during the two months he was here. The remains of the six were placed in a single coffin and buried again near the site of the massacre, and a large wooden cross was mounted over the grave. Stirling prayed and evoked the sacrifice of the victims there and again on the ship as they hung the flag at half mast.[32] The other two corpses had been placed in a shallow grave shortly after the massacre but had been devoured by dogs. Later the coffin was reburied on the grounds of the Ushuaia Mission.

Threeboys Needs Company and Lucca a Wife

Urupa had not seen his father in Packsaddle, nor did he go ashore to Wulaia in early March 1864, when the victims of the terrible epidemic were being mourned. His father, Chingaline, came in his canoe all the way from Packsaddle to this unfriendly territory to fetch Urupa, because he was worried about him being so young (about fifteen) and away from home for nearly a year. When Chingaline was sighted paddling toward the yacht, the four with him were recognised as his younger son, a nephew, the latter's wife and her young sister. He pulled alongside the yacht, climbed on board, and saw that Urupa was well and contented with his stay in Keppel. However, it was clear to Stirling that Chingaline wanted to take him home immediately. Despard had had the same problem with Okoko's mother five years before, in January 1859. And like Okoko, Urupa was an obedient son. He fetched his property and everyone on board said good-bye to him, regretting that he had to leave, as he had won everyone's affection. Threeboys asked Stirling in a tone of real sorrow: "Uroopa, a nice boy, I plenty like Uroopa, he not come back? Perhaps ship go to Packsaddle?" Chingaline departed, certainly relieved to have his son back and probably gratified to be dressed in a soldier's uniform, which had been given to Bridges in Port Stanley by a soldier whose time of service had expired.

Meanwhile Lucca, on deck, was staring at the young sister who was sitting in Chingaline's canoe waiting to depart with Urupa. The captain of the *Allen Gardiner* noticed Lucca staring at the girl and asked him: "Why not speak to her? Ask her to marry you?" Lucca replied seriously: "O yes, I plenty like woman, but Mr. Stirling no speak." Stirling overheard, and said as if to himself: "This is a new responsibility [for me]. But in truth I am strongly in favour of taking young married couples to Keppel Island."[33]

Lucca, about fifteen years old, longed for a wife, and Stirling longed to set matrimonial affairs right. He noted: "The young men are too often glad to pick up derelicts, while their sires adorn their wigwams, and propel their canoes with the fairest faces, and choicest arms in the community. Lucia's [Lucca's] fortune hangs in suspense."[34]

Pinoense had found a wife, the last young "damsel" available in Wulaia. Another young woman, unhappily married, longed so hopelessly for Pinoense that she took her canoe, without a fire, and went alone to Button Island. After several days two canoes were dispatched to search for her. She was probably located.

The Women Who Favour Polygamy

Stirling noticed that many of the older men thought it undignified to perform hard labour and managed to take young women as their second or third wives. In Wulaia he saw the young men willingly carrying logs and wood, their naked bodies forcing their way through the thick brush (Tom also, although he was not young), so he had the impression that the division of labour according to age and sex was strictly adhered to: the older you are, if you are a man, the less you work. He thought this was fine, though he realised that the women, young and old, had the worse deal. They were exposed to hardships in the cold "when they have to wade in the water in search of mussels, or to moor a canoe to the kelp, or set it free."[35] The young women were often obliged to marry older men and work full time (see Chapter 14). The old widows who espoused a young man had to paddle the canoe, and this could be exhausting. However, an older married woman had an advantage: she could be relieved of much labour if her husband found a younger wife (or wives), so she favoured polygamy.

An editorial in *The Voice of Pity* elaborated on this theme as another example of these natives' ignorance of God.

An elderman will be found often to possess two young wives in addition to one his equal age; while a young man will often be allied to a woman his senior by forty years. . . . These customs . . . offer in the very outset many difficulties to those who approach them as Christian missionaries. The teaching of the missionary at once touches the whole fabric of their social life.[36]

The "Double-C Strategy"

The missionaries were convinced that the "whole fabric of their social life" had to be transformed in order to convert the natives – that Christianity could not be meaningful to a people who clung to such "depraved habits." In order to Christianise them, the missionaries felt they had to civilise them, among other "bad habits," convince them – one wife for each man. So Christianity was not just faith and prayer, it was a way of life. The missionaries employed what I venture to label "the double-C strategy": Civilise and Christianise, which for the Fuegians meant uproot and reroute. This radical strategy will be rigorously applied and at times resisted.

Okoko and His Family Settle in Wulaia

Okoko agreed to settle down in Wulaia (March 1864), even though he preferred Button Island. Rather rapidly a two-room hut and goat shelter were built by the crew and friends in Wulaia. About that time Gamela gave birth to their third child, a boy, and the family settled into their new abode.

On 20 March, Stirling and others went to bid farewell to Okoko and found him cooking fish for breakfast. He and his family had been given a generous supplement of food to see them through the winter. As they could not leave enough to feed a family of five during the entire winter, Stirling feared that "both Ookokko and his wife would be thrown back upon canoe life, to the neglect of the children . . . and all that concerns the future introduction of civilised manners."[37] Stirling was already applying "the double-C strategy."[38]

April to October 1864: The Fifth Visit to Keppel

While still in Wulaia Stirling encouraged the male children to approach him. One day he was followed by a boy, about eight years old, who had lost his father, Harry Button, and probably also his mother in the epidemic of 1863–64. He seemed to be searching for a surrogate father. The child offered Stirling a piece of fungus, asking (in English) if he might go to Keppel with the others. When Stirling retired to a quiet place in the woods to read, this "young ally" found him again and sat beside him. "Looking into my face with a look that would fain penetrate my inmost thoughts, he asks, if I will be his good friend." The child recited words in English that he had learned from his father, who had picked up English from Jemmy. The boy pronounced "horse," "cow," "sheep," "boat," "spoon," "towel," "soap," "potatoes," "turnips" and "pig" in English. The last word greatly amused Stirling, for there were no pigs anywhere, not even at Keppel. He was captivated and decided to take the child back to Keppel with him. Mamastugadegenjes, his name, was too difficult to shorten, so from then on he was called Jack.³⁹

Lucca and Threeboys asked to return to Keppel, especially the latter, because his father had died. His mother, Jamesina, confided in Stirling: "Threeboys very sorry (sad, she means, because of his father's death). Threeboys go Keppel Island; again come [home]."

The selection for the fifth round of Wulaia candidates for Keppel was completed. The child, Jack, was among them, as were Threeboys (for his third visit), Sisoienges (Sisoi for short), who was going for the first time, and Lucca, although he had not given up the "young sister" he hoped to marry. The three others from Wulaia were not named. In all seven had been selected so far.

Pinoense wanted to return to Keppel with his new wife, but Stirling told him to stay on to help Okoko. However, Tom Button wanted to stay in Wulaia with his family, fortunately for him, because Stirling felt that he had not assimilated the "Christian truth" and that his mind was "very dark." For example, he often asked Stirling "What will become of me [after death]?" But Tom was grateful for the kindness the missionaries had shown him and more so now, when he received food supplies for staying home. Rau, the German missionary, liked Tom; even though he had not been a steady worker, he had usually been ready to serve and even worked voluntarily in the garden.⁴⁰

Stirling was pleased. Having spent two weeks in Wulaia, by 21 March 1864, nothing had been stolen, the weather had been fine, the natives "quiet and friendly." The foundations of "Christian civilisation in these hitherto savage parts" had been laid.

Besides these satisfactions, the seven recruits from Wulaia had been carefully selected. Also, an assortment of Yahgan "treasures" had been collected (by barter and gifts): spears, slings, sealskins, fire stones, baskets, a bow and arrow, a trap made of whalebone and sinew, four paddles and best of all, a large canoe, eighteen feet (about 5.5 metres) long, which finished off "in a jaunty-looking point at either end."[41]

Reception in Packsaddle

On the return trip to Keppel, they stopped off in Packsaddle Bay for three days. Among the fifteen canoes in the bay, only eight visited the yacht. Stirling found the people aloof, even though some requested to go to Keppel, including Urupa's father, Chingaline. Stirling was surprised but refused to take him because he was applying the former rule: no parents. Disappointed as he may have been, Chingaline agreed to let Urupa return and even to allow his younger son join the Keppel group. Apparently Urupa had convinced his father that he had benefited from his recent stay of ten months in Keppel. But there were no clothes left over for Urupa's brother. Stirling, in his report to the mission magazine, appealed to his readers to send "good corduroy for trousers, and some strong stuff for coats and jackets [instead of the usual worn out or unsuitable clothes]."

The "young sister," Lucca's choice for a wife, consented to go. Lucca had found a wife in Packsaddle but Urupa, now that he was about sixteen years old, had not. His pleas to a young woman had been in vain. She was "mistrustful of strangers" and refused to accompany him.[42] With Urupa, his brother and Lucca's wife from Packsaddle plus seven from Wulaia, the ten were off for Keppel (the fifth visit).

Farther on, the yacht anchored off New Island (in English on the Chilean maps) where a "sheep run" was going on. The governor of the Falkland Islands had lately brought the sheep, perhaps the first in Tierra del Fuego. The governor had also been "making an inspection of the islands." The British were aware or assumed that Tierra del Fuego was still a "no-man's-land." Although Captain Juan Williams had taken possession of the Strait of Magellan for Chile in 1843, not until 1881 was the area south of the strait officially attributed to Chile and Argentina.

Life at Keppel during the Fifth Visit

When the *Allen Gardiner* arrived back at Keppel, everyone on board was greeted by the Bartlett couple and their five children. Mrs Stirling was particularly taken by Jack. "Poor child! he has no parents of his own, and . . . and seems to be looked upon by the whole tribe as a sort of adopted child. He often comes up to our house."[43] Like her husband, she found that the term "savage" could not be applied to "the four lads" (Jack, Threeboys, Urupa and Sisoi). She died a few months later of a prolonged illness. Her two young daughters remained in Port Stanley until mid-1869, when their father took them back to England.[44]

Soon after the arrival, Urupa, his brother and two of the younger recruits from Wulaia came down with pleurisy, which was particularly dangerous because it often led to pneumonia. They had been sick for three weeks with pains in the left side, trouble breathing and bad coughing. All recovered except Urupa's brother and Bartlett's baby. Mariquita, the Tehuelche, who had been well and full of merriment, was seized with apoplexy and also passed away at this time, despite Stirling's brother's efforts to save her.

The four lads mentioned above (Jack, Threeboys, Urupa and Sisoi) lived with Bridges, Rau and Huniziker (another missionary). Bridges was fast perfecting his study of Yahgan with the new-comers. He was also their English teacher, interpreter, evangelist, instructor for farm work, friend and helper.

The boys had a busy life with "gentle discipline." They did not complain except once, at midnight, because rats were running over their faces. They took a great interest in farming except digging up potatoes. To start them on the job, Mr Bartlett would throw a potato at one of them, as a signal for the "potato fight." They valued everything that might possibly be of use to them. Pieces of iron served as knives, worn coats were made into caps using a plate as a pattern. They learned to ride horseback and were clever at lassoing sheep. They were having fun except when they were homesick. They often spoke of their "own land" and what was going on there at certain times of the year. "Now my countrymen plenty eat whale. . . . Now my countrywomen plenty catch fish. . . . Now my country people plenty eat mussels." The nostalgia and disciplined routine were mitigated by the pleasure they took in each other's company. Rau eavesdropped on them once while they were laughing about a blackbird's peculiar behaviour. He often heard them singing together as they went about the daily tasks.

Lucca and his wife (not named) may have taken their vows by now; the missionaries probably would not have allowed them to cohabit otherwise. They shared a house with the other couple from Wulaia, about whom very little was written. Although the two wives discharged their household duties satisfactorily, Lucca's wife did not live in harmony with her new husband and probably longed for her home in Packsaddle. Bridges was confident that the couple would become reconciled by and by. He had great hopes for Lucca, who had been in Keppel with Okoko just before the massacre, the second visit (Chapter 9). He excelled as a farmer and was rendering "the services of a paid workman." Almost every evening he drove the cattle quite a distance from the mission into their enclosure. He was always willing to help and was more reliable than the other three.[45] As Okoko had taken Jemmy's place, Lucca will take Okoko's, though not for long.

Bridges and Eight "Pupils" of the Fifth Visit Return to Wulaia

After six months in Keppel, eight of the Fuegian contingent departed in late September 1864 without Urupa's brother, who had died of pleurisy, and Jack, the orphan, who remained in Keppel with Stirling. This time Bridges and Rau accompanied them: Lucca, his unhappy wife, Threeboys, Sisoi, Urupa and three others not named, plus the crew and fourteen goats. Even though the *Allen Gardiner* took the shortest route to Wulaia, via Beagle Channel, the trip lasted two weeks. No natives were encountered on the way, perhaps because of the devastating effects of the 1863–64 epidemic. When they arrived in Wulaia, only a few people were seen.[46] Stirling planned for Threeboys, the Lucca couple and Sisoi to settle down there with Okoko, Pinoense and Tom, who were waiting for them. If all went well, there should be enough Christian natives in Wulaia to guarantee the success of the mission station there.

Okoko Is Troubled

During the week in Wulaia, Bridges and the others planted a large garden. An old man there was dying of cancer, which Bridges said was common among these people, though rarely mentioned by him or anyone else. Okoko was not present when they arrived; however, they noticed that he had taken good care of his goats – three had been born and he had killed only one for food. He and his family had been there over seven months, from March to October (1864). Pinoense had helped him; he had built a bridge of logs over the nearby river, although he, his wife and his father Tom were living on Button Island.

Within a few days, Okoko and his wife but only two of their children boarded the yacht to greet Bridges, all dressed in "clean and tidy clothes . . . as civilised persons." Okoko was distressed as he told Bridges what had happened during these months. A week before the yacht arrived, their baby boy had died, so they left Wulaia. It was customary not to remain in the place where a loved one had passed away. Their youngest living child, a daughter, was "fearfully thin, so much so, that all expressed astonishment that she still lived." Okoko himself had been seriously ill during the past months and had not entirely recovered. Tom Button had a grown daughter whom he tried to persuade Okoko to take as a second wife, and Tom became very vexed when he refused at first. Now Okoko told Bridges that Tom had tried to frighten him and his family by saying that "the Foot Indians [Oens-men] were coming overland to fight and kill them." Later Okoko admitted taking Tom's daughter and another young woman as temporary wives. His worst problem, beside the death of his baby, was "the lawless state of the natives," who stole many of his belongings and provisions and, even more disturbing, – they refused to listen to his Christian teachings. He often spoke to them "of God, and had rehearsed to them those Bible stories he had heard; some listened, but others ridiculed him."[47] Later Lucca confided in Bridges about Okoko's serious problems.

[Okoko] had often spoken to his people of God, of heaven and hell, and what sort of people should live in them: his people being very proud and bad would not listen, and were sometimes very angry, and said that Ookokko told lies; that as he had never seen nor heard God they would not believe, that man and all things had ever been as they are, without beginning and therefore without a Maker. One man said, he [Okoko] pretended to be Jesus Christ; some were afraid to be in hell . . . some threatened to kill Ookokko, but were afraid to.[48]

Okoko had a very hard time during these seven months in Wulaia as a preacher, a father and as a husband.

Okoko Stays in Wulaia

Bridges, as well as Stirling, very much wanted these first Fuegian Christians to set the example for the others in Wulaia. This time Okoko and his family, Pinoense, Tom and his second wife, Wendoo, remained in Wulaia, in addition now to Threeboys and Lucca.

November 1864 to April 1865: The Sixth Visit at Keppel

After the week in Wulaia, Bridges departed for Keppel (19 October), with part of the sixth contingent (see below): three new recruits (not named) and Sisoi (second trip). Bridges was probably glad to see that "No less than 40 canoes, and certainly 240 persons" came to see them off. When the *Allen Gardiner* stopped over in Orange Bay (near Packsaddle), seven canoes came to greet them; among the passengers was Chinagaline (Urupa's father). He allowed Urupa to go back again to Keppel, despite the death of his younger son. Bridges selected, from the crowd in the seven canoes, two older boys (to be mentioned later) and their young wives, which made five from Packsaddle plus four from Wulaia, all "of a very teachable age" to be taken to Keppel. By early November they arrived at Keppel. Recall that the majority of the "veteran Keppelites" (my term) had stayed in Wulaia: Okoko and family, Threeboys, Pinoese and family, Lucca and unhappy wife and Tom Button and family.

Bridges worked as usual with the boys, learning Yahgan and teaching them to write in English. He remarked that two of them could count to 100 and "make a very fair attempt in writing." They all very much enjoyed singing, especially "From Greenland's Icy Mountains." "They are all very useful here, and generally work regularly and well," and everyone was in good health. The five months passed without drama. In March (1865), Stirling left for Wulaia with all the pupils; only Jack remained in Keppel as usual, now with Urupa.[49]

The Sixth Keppel "Pupils" Return to Wulaia and Find a Disaster

Upon arrival in Wulaia (April 1865) Stirling heard some good news: "The gardens were unmolested, extra ground having been put under cultivation, and well fenced in." The bad news was really bad: Okoko and his family were even worse off than the year before. Their house had been set on fire and burned down, with all of their belongings destroyed. Three natives of Wulaia had set it on fire while Okoko and his family were away fishing, just a few days before Stirling and the others arrived. And the neighbours had killed all five of Okoko's goats.

Okoko was even more distressed because his daughter had suffered burns and his Bible and prayer book had been consumed in the fire. They had been printed in phonetic characters that he could read and there were no copies in Keppel. The fire had also destroyed the clothes that belonged to the other "protégés" (now Stirling's term). The situation was so critical that Stirling decided to take all "the most hopeful of our old friends" back to Keppel.[50]

Exodus from Wulaia

Stirling now realised that Okoko and his family had to return to Keppel as well as the others who had stayed in Wulaia: Threeboys, Lucca (reunited with his wife) and Pinoense and his young wife. Those who had just come from Keppel – Sisoi, as well as the two young men from Orange Bay (near Packsaddle), Tyashof and Yecif and their wives – were also told or advised to go back again to Keppel. These two couples had recently been at Keppel. In all, twelve adults, "the most hopeful natives," returned to Keppel with Stirling.[51] All the mission protégés except Tom Button and his wife Wendoo (Tom was considered too old and not very useful anyway) were taken back to Keppel, where Urupa and Jack were waiting for them. All the Christian Yamana, nine men and boys plus five wives, were now at Keppel. Thus the second attempt to establish a mission basis in Tierra del Fuego had failed.

Having arrived at Keppel, Stirling expressed optimism: "Our voyage to Tierra del Fuego was quick and prosperous, extending over five weeks." Despite this declaration, he had to admit, if only to himself, that while the first attempt to establish a mission station in Wulaia had failed, terminated in the massacre of 1859, now this second attempt, with settled Christianised natives under the guidance of Okoko, had also failed. As of April 1865, none of the fourteen promising disciples remained in Wulaia or Packsaddle.

All the "Pupils" Stay at Keppel the Seventh Visit

I repeat: "All the Christian Yamana, nine men and boys, plus five wives, were now in Keppel." A total of fourteen adults: the four youngest men, to be mentioned later, and the five young couples: Okoko and Gamela, Lucca with his unhappy wife, Pinoense with his happy wife, who had recently borne a son and Tyashof and Yecif and their wives from Orange Bay (near Packsaddle). Most would remain at Keppel for two years, from April 1865 to May 1867. The five couples were in the best of health. They had to accommodate to the stricter discipline implanted by Stirling, which Bridges and the other missionaries also had to respect: no more separate houses for the couples, daily English classes, Bible and prayer meetings after and between meals. The labour was again tending the tame and wild cattle and horses, calf-catching, peat-hauling, stacking, draining, digging, stream-weeding and pointing of stone buildings. Okoko and Gamela also worked with Bridges on his dictionary, as they were his favourite informants.[52] Bridges was optimistic. "The natives are, and have been, well behaved, contented, industrious, willing to learn, and be taught, regular in their attendance at prayers.... they know there is a hell to flee from, even the wrath of an offended God, and a heaven to flee unto and to gain, even the love of God."[53]

Bridges was increasingly assuming a paternalistic attitude toward his pupils, though he was only a few years older. But despite the progress, he was aware that "Okoko has asked many questions, and has shown great concern to be satisfied of the truth of the facts he hears stated, as though he felt their consequence."[54]

Okoko's Spiritual Crisis

Following Okoko's devastating experiences in Wulaia, his faith in the evangelical teachings had been profoundly challenged. About eight months after returning to Keppel, early in 1866, he was even more perturbed. His questions and requests, which were addressed to Bridges, express his disturbing search for the truth of the Scriptures and for their reality.

I have converted the original text into the first person but otherwise it is authentic. Though his questions are addressed to Bridges, Okoko seems to be pleading with his inner self, revealing, as he does, his deep anxiety and his troubled commitment to his new faith.

Okoko: "How should I act and what should I say supposing a man should offer me his daughter as a wife? This was the case before with two men, both of whose daughters I lived with as my wives together with Camelena [Gamela]."

Okoko: "Are you certain that Jesus rose from the dead?" Bridges observed that Okoko considered "this point, if established, a seal to the truth of all the rest that he had heard."

Okoko: "Are you certain Jesus will return to the earth to make the good happy, and the wicked miserable?"

Okoko: "If I repent and ask Jesus to forgive me, and to be my friend, and save me, are you sure He would hear and grant it?"

Okoko: "If I ask God to make me good, peaceable and wise, will He surely hear me?"

Okoko: "If someone should quarrel with me, how should I act?"

Okoko: "If my brother should be killed by a man, how should I act?"

Okoko: "Tell Lucca, Pinioia [Pinoense], Threeboys, and Uroopatoosh [Urupa] to help me teach my people. If only I teach them the strange truths I have learned, they will despise what I say, and despise me, as they did before."

Okoko: "Write out some prayers for me in my own language, so I can use them."

About this time, 12 January 1866, Bridges commented:

He frankly acknowledged he had a bad temper, being passionate, and he lamented he quarrelled so much with the other natives, and he wished to be reconciled to Tirshof, and asked him to forgive him for some quarrel he had needlessly with him some time since. This may give you some idea of his state, and doubtless with me you will say, and rejoice that this man is not far from the kingdom of heaven.

Bridges concluded: "I am much more satisfied with his character than I was, and think him much more capable to hold his ground among his people than he was."[55] Apparently Bridges was not able, or did not wish, to seize this opportunity to assuage Okoko's despair. Little did he imagine that more trying times were ahead for Okoko.

Stirling Takes Four "Keppel Youths" to England

Stirling chose Threeboys, Urupa and the younger boys, Sisoi and Jack, to accompany him to England, partly because they "were free from engaging alliances, young, healthy, and capable of being easily stowed away in the *Allen Gardiner*." They had been together in Keppel during the last visit, the fifth (in 1864) so they were already "pals" (my term). Threeboys, now about twenty years old, especially was pleased to visit the country where his father had been so many years before. He and Urupa, who was sixteen or seventeen years old, were among the most advanced Keppel pupils. Sisoi, about eleven years old, was known for his intelligence and sympathy, and the youngest, Jack, was Stirling's favourite.[56] Stirling's two daughters were left in Port Stanley, in the care of their affectionate governess. The Reverend and his four pupils will be away for almost two years, including the voyages, from July 1865 until June 1867. His motives for the trip, other than strictly personal, were to demonstrate, with the help of his four disciples, that the efforts of the mission had produced their fruits. He also planned to refit the mission schooner and hoped to collect always needed funds.[57]

In August 1865 they arrived at the mouth of the Avon. Then they sailed up to Bristol, where the four disciples were vaccinated. The latter were astonished and delighted at "the wonders and varied scenes of civilisation." On 13 September, they were presented at a meeting of the British Association in Birmingham, and later they visited the Crystal Palace in London. During their entire stay they were well received in the homes of friends of the mission throughout England and Ireland and took part in many meetings, speaking in Yahgan and singing hymns. "Their good manners and happy dispositions and alert attention attracted everyone." The committee of the South American Missionary Society stated that their presence in England marked an epoch in the work of the mission. Stirling was proud of God's and his own achievements, though less inclined to acknowledge those of his four disciples. He stated solemnly: "It was no light task to have reduced their confused speech to a grammar and to have taught savages to live civilised lives. But best of all there was evidence that God's mighty Spirit was working in the hearts of people sunk in the depths of barbarism."[58]

Heads Examined Again

During the disciples' presentation at the meeting of The British Association, it occurred to someone to have their cerebral capacity measured. The task fell to a certain Dr John Beddof, a "foreign associate of the Anthropological Society." The measurements were taken on all four, though those of the two oldest, Threeboys and Urupa, were the most significant because their cerebral capacity was considered fully developed. The results of the study must have dumbfounded the savants, left them speechless and perhaps humbled them, even Dr Beddof, who reported: "In the two elder boys, in whom the head has attained its full dimensions, most of the measurements *are above the averages yielded by the population of Bristol and its neighbourhood.*"[59]

Macdonald, Stirling's biographer, affirmed: "Dr. Beddoe [Beddof]... examined their heads phrenologically with remarkable results. Savage born and bred, though they were, they were better shaped and sized than those of the average people of Bristol and neighbourhood."[60]

Rather recently, Canclini commented: "Today all this provokes a smile, but at the time it caused a sensation, as the Fuegians, who were assumed not to have any [cerebral] capacity whatsoever, had such notable measurements in some aspects superior to the Europeans."[61]

Stirling observed that the four boys attended a Bible class "without showing any inferiority to the English boys who belong to the same class...."[62] Here he might well have said that the Fuegian boys were superior to their English classmates, as they had to assimilate a still unfamiliar religion in a foreign language.[63]

Shortly before the disciples embarked for home (December 1866), they were presented to the members of the South American Missionary Society. They created a sensation by their neat appearance, their quiet modest bearing and their singing with propriety in English, "How Sweet the Name of Jesus Sounds" and "There Is a Happy Land." After describing the lives of the Fuegians in their homeland, Stirling clarified: "The feeling against Europeans, arising from past maltreatment chiefly by the Spaniards, was being overcome in favour of the English."[64] Stirling was mistaken or disingenuous. During the nearly three centuries from 1578 (or 1624) to 1866 (when Stirling spoke) the Yamana had very little contact with Spaniards, Chileans or Argentines. Except for the Dutch in 1624, their contacts, up to 1866, were mainly with English navigators, Darwin, English-speaking sealers and English missionaries.

At Keppel

As the months passed at Keppel, the five young couples were becoming anxious, waiting for the *Allen Gardiner* to return from England to see their friends and be taken home.[65] By the end of that January 1866, the couples were all tiring of the routine. They longed to know what kind of life their four countrymen were living in England, whether, as in Keppel, "under rules, of working so long, learning so long, eating at such times, &c, &c., or as in their own land." They were overjoyed to receive a letter from Threeboys (not found).[66] Nor did I find any texts about the four concerning their adventures in their mentor's homeland except when Threeboys and Urupa went out alone in London and commented that finding the way through the streets of London was less complicated than finding the way through the forests of their own country.[67]

Urupa's Last Voyage

Stirling and his four protégés embarked from Bristol on the *Allen Gardiner* for the Falklands sometime in January 1867. The boys were probably eager to return home, after the year and four months travelling throughout England and Ireland, giving lectures and being applauded. Three had been in good health, but Urupa had come down with tuberculosis. His condition worsened during the unusually long voyage (sixty-seven days) and the stormy weather from Bristol to Montevideo. There Stirling realised that Urupa was seriously ill and had him taken ashore. Now he finally admitted that clothing had a harmful effect on the health of the Fuegians. "Fuegians, who for generations lived exposed lives with no clothing, fall an easy prey to pulmonary disease if they adopt the clothes and ways of civilised man; and Uroopa arrived at Montevideo far gone in consumption."

Urupa was attended by a doctor and his three friends kept him company during the nine days the yacht remained in Montevideo. As he did not improve, he was taken back on the ship, which was kept in port for another nine days, lest on the trip to Port Stanley, "the tossing about and inadequate care should kill him at once." Reduced to a skeleton, Urupa, "bore his sickness with great patience." He was baptised John Allen Gardiner, as a special honour, while still in the port. Later Stirling wrote that Urupa was "the first baptised native of Tierra del Fuego . . . the first fruits of . . . that spiritual hero who laid the foundation of this Society when he perished at Spaniard Harbour."[68]

The journey from Montevideo to Port Stanley, which normally took three days or so, took eleven in the midst of some of the worst weather the seamen had ever experienced. Stirling was present when Urupa was dying. "He had calmly distributed his few articles of property, making me his executor." While telling this to Stirling in a tone "which seemed full of sweetness," Urupa added "if Jesus takes me." Once he said "that he was troubled with bad dreams, and feared to go to sleep." Stirling tried to comfort him and commended him "to Him who 'giveth his beloved sleep,' and he seemed hopeful and refreshed." When Stirling asked him: "How do you know you love Jesus?" Urupa replied: "Because I feel it." His last words came when he woke from a nap saying: "I have been to sleep. I have seen Jesus. Jesus loves me. Dear Jesus." One of the seamen was profoundly moved: "I wish I was as ready to die as that lad, he is a good innocent lad." Urupa passed away in the early dawn of 2 April 1867, the day before they pulled into Port Stanley. Three days later he was buried there in the little mission cemetery. Stirling: "I rejoiced to believe he had departed to be with Christ, which is far better. He himself realised this most fully. . . . It was life, not death, that triumphed. We must rejoice, not mourn, here."[69]

An editor of the mission magazine noted "the happy death of the first baptised Fuegian convert . . . " and asked the following question: "Is not such a death as Uroopa's a recompense for all the labours bestowed on the poor natives of Fuegia?" The editor replied to his own question: "We are sure it is thought to be so by Mr. Stirling." Thereupon an appeal was made to the readers to help Stirling with their prayers, exertions and alms.[70]

To rejoice at the death of a young person seems incongruous with the Christian doctrine of piety. Certainly the Yahgans would not have rejoiced. The death of a child stirred their wrath against their "Almighty," Watawineiwa.

Once Urupa had been buried in Port Stanley on 5 April 1867, they went on to the Keppel Mission, where their Wulaia friends (the five young couples) were so eager to see their countrymen. They remained nearly five weeks. On 9 May, Stirling, Threeboys and Sisoi, together with most who had stayed on at Keppel, boarded the yacht to sail on to Wulaia. Bridges, Okoko (without his family), three of the other married men, Lucca, Tyashof and Yecif with their wives and children, all returned home. Only Jack (who just returned from England), Gamela, her two children, Pinoense and his wife and child remained in Keppel.[71]

Note: this round trip, Keppel–Wulaia–Keppel (9 May to 22 June 1867) will not be narrated chronologically because two extraordinary events that took place during this trip will be highlighted: the first with Urupa's father and the second with Threeboys. Only then will the entire round trip: Keppel–Wulaia–Keppel be summarised.

Urupa's Grieving Father

Urupa's saga does not conclude with his burial in Port Stanley. On the return trip from Wulaia to Keppel, the yacht stopped over at Packsaddle Bay in June (1867). Suddenly four canoes appeared. In one of them a man was standing, "shouting and wildly gesticulating and aiming a spear in a threatening way." The man was Chingaline, Urupa's father. Somehow he had heard that the missionaries had killed his son and he had come to seek vengeance. He was "very violent, and maddened with rage and grief." His younger son had died in Keppel of pleurisy a few years before and now Urupa, also with the missionaries. Stirling immediately called to Chingaline to come aboard. "He refused but the friendly tone of Mr. Bridges won him." Bridges spoke to him, in Yahgan, of Urupa's fine qualities, how greatly he was liked by all, how kindly he had been tended during his illness, that he was buried in the mission cemetery, and "of the resurrection, and of the happiness of those who love and serve God." The bereaved father also wanted to know about his son's property. He was given Urupa's axe, knife, pannikin, suit of clothes and blanket. Chingaline's desperate grief impressed Bridges. "Poor Chingaline showed real, heartfelt sorrow, and sobbed deeply and shed many tears. Okokko and Threeboys were then called in, and they both spoke comfortably to poor Chingaline."[72]

A few days later, when the schooner was about to depart from Packsaddle Bay, Stirling seemed to have forgotten his emotions when Urupa was dying on the ship. Contrary to Bridges, he was annoyed by Urupa's father.

Chingaline again manifested much anger and displeasure; but the people here are emotional and excitable, and allowance must be made for that want of self-control and that slavish addiction to doing the right thing in the estimation of his countrymen (and the right thing down here is very often to make a noise – so violently do the words rush to their mouth)... which is characteristic of savages at least.

Threeboys had stayed beside Urupa during his long illness, was present during his last moments, had wept when he died and now he tried to comfort Chingaline. Little did Threeboys imagine, Stirling commented, that "within three weeks he was himself a corpse."[73] Stirling's words here are also singularly crude.

Threeboys Dies on Board

Recall that following Urupa's burial on 5 April, the *Allen Gardiner* had stopped over in Keppel for over a month, as mentioned above. Then, on 9 May, Bridges and most of the Keppel pupils got on board to return home. The first day out, Threeboys was "very subject to headaches" and had a pain in the chest. After an unusually long trip because of the stopover in Banner Cove (see below) and snowy weather, they anchored off the shore of Wulaia on 22 May. During the ten days there, Bridges became aware that Threeboys needed medical attention; so he resolved, and Stirling must have agreed, to take him back as soon as possible to Port Stanley. In early June, when they left Wulaia and sailed on to Packsaddle Bay, they met the distraught Chingaline, noted above. Despite his illness, Threeboys talked to Chingaline about his son "frankly and with a feeling which did him credit, which was very important to the bereaved father."[74]

By then Threeboys was seriously ill, though Stirling thought that he was, "only slightly, being about as usual, and looking as stout as ever." But a few days after leaving Packsaddle, Threeboys was confined to his cot. Stirling detained the yacht in Banner Cove, "dreading the effects of the vessel knocking about at sea when the poor lad was so ill." His chest pain became violent and permanent, "unyielding to any treatment." The intense pain broke down his spirit, and several days later, "sickness ceased and delirium supervened, the pain still continuing, but gradually moving lower down." As soon as the wind calmed, Stirling ordered the captain to "bear away direct for Stanley, to secure medical aid." For five days they "buffeted about at sea." The third day out, 19 June, Threeboys was dying while Okoko attended him "very kindly." Then, during his dying moments, Stirling baptised him as George Despard, whom Threeboys remembered so well. In his delirium he talked and shouted for hours. "Yet nothing offensive escaped his lips, while frequently in his unconsciousness he would repeat the Lord's Prayer, or a line of a hymn, or text, or a fragment of the Creed. One night abruptly, but with a rich, deep, and most solemn tone, he exclaimed, 'I believe in one God, the Father almighty.'"

It was not easy, Stirling thought "to ascertain the full force on his heart of the teaching he had received." But his dying words "never before seemed to me so marvellous, and I shall never forget the effect upon me."[75] Bridges paid him this tribute. "All on board are very sorry; he was such a useful and sensible lad."[76]

Threeboys died at sea, on 21 June 1867, just as Urupa had, the day before the *Allen Gardiner* entered Port Stanley. He was buried beside his friend in the mission cemetery.[77] Perhaps their graves have been located.

More than a century later, Arnoldo Canclini did not share the compassion of Bridges and the others. I translated, from his 1980 book *Waite H. Stirling. El Centinela de Dios en Ushuaia*, this text as follows:

But the son of Jemmy Button died the day before arrival [in Port Stanley]. There he occupied a place next to his friend Urupa. The episode was very painful, nevertheless, looking back at the efforts of Fitz-Roy on behalf of his father, three and a half decades before, to his treason and death without repentance, that [the death of Threeboys] had an aureole of triumph.[78]

A vengeful God striking an innocent young man for the "treason" of his father seems to me outrageous and unchristian. What is more, Canclini's contention that Jemmy Button had been guilty of "treason" contradicts the declarations of Jemmy Button's innocence by the Anglican pastors (Chapter 9).

A postmortem examination, at Stirling's request, revealed that Threeboys' death was caused by disease of the kidneys called Bright's disease.[79] Of the four lads Stirling had taken to England, Jack and Sisoi were still alive.

Backflash: 9 May to 22 June 1867: The Round Trip Keppel–Wulaia–Keppel

Among those who were returning to Wulaia on 9 May 1867, recall that dying Threeboys, and Sisoi were on board, with those who had joined them at Keppel, among whom was Okoko, who came alone and planned to stay in Wulaia only while the yacht was there.[80] The yacht, having departed from Keppel 9 May, took six days just to reach the Strait of Le Maire, some 250 miles (463 kilometres) away, owing to stormy weather. In the strait, "a great number of fur seals kept us company for a long time." The next day, 16 May, they anchored in Banner Cove for several days, enjoying pleasant weather, gathering berries and praying. Threeboys was suffering increasingly.

Friendly Oens-Men in Banner Cove
Later, four canoes arrived "in no great hurry, and there was much less vociferation than on former occasions." Then Bridges learned that those

who had arrived were the "Foot Indians" and that some of the Yahgans knew their language. Stirling referred to them as "the bold and more warlike Foot Indians" and as Oens'men, using Jemmy's expression. But the contact was peaceful. These Oens'men, the Selk'nam, had seen the *Allen Gardiner* sailing along Beagle Channel during past years. He added, "they have expressed the desire aloud that we would visit them."[81] After the 1859 massacre, the Selk'nam were apparently resigned to the presence of missionaries in Tierra del Fuego. Stirling and Bridges will attempt to contact them later (see below).

Sickness on Button Island

The yacht sailed on through Beagle Channel and down Murray Narrows to Button Island, arriving there on 21 May. That evening Lucca's relatives came alongside the ship and told of many deaths, probably the aftermath of the 1863–64 epidemic. Bridges observed: "The natives are in a sad unquiet state.... Every succeeding visit more deeply distresses me with a sense of their wretchedness." Stirling was less critical when he noticed that the Button Islanders "were greatly pleased to see their friends; the pleasure was mutual," and that no ill will was caused by the long delay, over two years, in returning there.

The following day they sailed on to Wulaia accompanied by twenty-five canoes. There was already snow on the ground. Stirling remarked that in winter the natives kept very close to their special quarters (Wulaia and Button Island).[82]

Lucca in Wulaia

Lucca was anxious to settle in Wulaia with his wife and child, and to tend goats and a garden. Despite Okoko's devastating experience, he felt sure that he would "be able to lead a civilised and civilising life among his people." His Keppel countrymen spent the next three days building a wigwam and goat house for him, aided by the neighbours, who visited them more than Lucca liked. Besides the goats, he was given a dog to hunt guanacos and provisions for four months "if he can keep them."

As Threeboys' health was deteriorating rapidly, Bridges tried to speed up their tasks in order to get him back to a doctor in Port Stanley. Sisoi, who had been in England, had become very attached to the missionaries and wanted to return to Keppel with them, but his father was "unable to appreciate the advantages his son has when with us. We are all very sorry for poor Sis." He remained in Wulaia with Lucca and Lucca's still unhappy wife and child.

Having spent over a week in Wulaia, the yacht weighed anchor, heading back to Keppel, with Threeboys, who was very ill. In addition, Stirling had brought five new recruits: a couple with their child and "two nice boys," whose names were not given. That day the yacht stopped off in Packsaddle, where Urupa's father showed his outrage because of his son's death, while Bridges, Threeboys and Okoko tried to soothe his grief.

Then Tyashof and Yecif and their wives got off the yacht in Packsaddle Bay. They had been at Keppel for more than two years, since March 1865. The latter's father wanted Yecif to remain home. Certainly he feared that his son might die, like Urupa and his brother. Bridges lauded Yecif's mental capacity and trusted that he would become "disgusted at the low habits of his people." The latter remark, so often repeated by Bridges, expressed his disdain for the Yahgans as a people, despite the affection he obviously felt for the individual Yahgans he came to know. In this respect Bridges' and Darwin's attitudes were quite similar. By this time Threeboys was gravely ill. The day after he died, on 21 June (1867), the yacht reached Port Stanley.[83]

June 1867 to January 1868: The Third Attempt, with Lucca, to Establish a Mission Station in Wulaia

Recall that by now two attempts had been made to set up a mission station in Wulaia: one before the massacre of November 1859, and the other with Okoko and his family, from March 1864 to March of the next year when all the "veterans" (my term) were returned to Keppel. Sometime between April and May 1867 Stirling had resolved to make a third attempt, this time with Lucca, his wife and child.

Meanwhile, some three months after the arrival back in Keppel (in September 1867), Gamela gave birth to a daughter and was well, but Bridges was in bed with rheumatic fever, the Yahgans were ill and Bartlett also. Stirling reported: "Rheumatism, sciatica, neuralgia and other rheumatic affections flourish in the Falkland Islands.... Never since its formation has the Station been visited by so much sickness and suffering." The sicknesses were not epidemics, not yet. Stirling was convinced that they "would increase the strength and confidence in one another, and would enhance their trust and confidence in Him as they recognised His great mercy in healing them."[84]

That December (1867), the *Allen Gardiner* set out again from Keppel, to see how Lucca was getting along. By now he had been six months in Wulaia. Stirling went with Bridges, taking Okoko, his family, Pinoense, his wife and child and this time also young Jack, all of whom were to settle again in Wulaia, this time with Lucca. On board were the usual small herd of goats and other provisions.

Lucca, his wife and child had been in Wulaia since the previous June. But six months later, in January 1868, when Stirling and the others arrived, they found that Lucca had confronted difficulties. These were not described in the mission magazine I consulted, except to note that his wife had returned with their child to her home near Packsaddle, leaving Lucca alone. Apparently the couple was never reconciled, nor had Lucca succeeded in setting up the mission. Stirling explained that Threeboys' friends had been "naturally much distressed to hear of his death, and for the most part they have kept in retirement from the ship." However, he believed that they were "fully satisfied of our good faith and kindness" and added that he and Bridges distributed among them tools bought from the money received from the sale of Threeboys' belongings. However, Lucca had failed to establish himself in Wulaia. This new fiasco had to be admitted. The 1863–64 epidemic, Jemmy's premature death like that of so many others, had greatly affected the remaining residents in Wulaia. Then Okoko's preaching had outraged many. Later Threeboys' death had apparently created a real animosity toward the missionaries. Lucca's failure seems almost inevitable. To all concerned it must have been distressing to recognise that the local Wulaian residents did not want the missionaries or their protégés to settle there. All hope of installing the mission in Wulaia was given up, forever more.

January 1868: Lewaia, the Fourth Attempt to Establish a Mission

On 3 January 1868, most of the "Kepplers" in Wulaia (Lucca, Okoko and family, Pinoense and family and Jack) with Bridges and Stirling, sailed north, up Murray Narrows to Lewaia (sometimes spelt Laiwaia) on the northwest "corner" of Navarino Island, along Beagle Channel. Here Stirling had decided to try again to establish a mission station.

Bridges cited the advantages of this locality: many islands nearby abounding with mussels, excellent fishing grounds, land very suitable for cultivation, deciduous birch trees for firewood and berries – a favourite of the natives. Besides, it was well protected from the rough waters of Beagle Channel. Stirling was equally enthusiastic. He found the climate "more genial than the Falklands. What is more, you can go in a boat to some pretty sheltered sunny creeks to pic-nic, while the white turbaned peaks of the mountains look down on you from the clouds."[85]

The two missionaries, their Kepplers and the *Allen Gardiner* crew camped in Lewaia for three "churches" as Jemmy would have said. They all pitched in to build a log house with three private rooms and one common room, destined for the two families (of Okoko and Pinoense), and the two "bachelors" (Lucca and Jack). The Yahgans who lived here periodically arrived in canoes and helped to complete the house. Each worker was paid the usual biscuits, in addition to eggs and a knife when the job was done. The workers also aided the crew carrying wood to the ship to transport back to Keppel. Bridges was again impressed with their strength and their manner of playing and living together, although a bit later he reverted to his usual comment of "the wretchedness of these people, owing solely to their own folly and wickedness, which necessarily arises from their ignorance of God."[86] No matter how charmed Bridges might be with his experiences with the people, he could not free himself of his conviction that they were wretched pagans.

It occurred to Stirling to request that a little canoe be made for children in England, with little paddles, spears, a basket, reed rope and a bucket. "By-and-bye I shall get some made as models, about two feet long and . . . send them to England for sale." This is the first mention of miniature canoes being made for export. Later the Yahgans made them to sell to the seamen, and they were still being made in 2009 for tourists by the few remaining Navarino Yahgans.

Recalling Lucca's problems and that Okoko's house had been burnt down in Wulaia, Stirling decided to have his house made of iron when he would finally settle here.[87] He preached during the "three churches" in Lewaia, Bridges translating each sermon into Yahgan. On the second "church," Stirling preached in the new log house to some sixty "poor and ignorant" people of Lewaia. At this time he penned these memorable lines: "They used to think we were not born into the world like themselves, but were of a different nature, and dropped down from some other world, or escaped from the waters of the ocean."[88]

Tom Button came to visit Lewaia on his own. Stirling still thought he was not much of a worker, though friendly and peaceable, but even so:

He regards himself almost as belonging to the ship. Amongst his people he likes to get a little respect for himself by magnifying his fancied influence with us. So he talks to us in English (i.e., his English) before his friends, that he may seem knowing and of superior quality.

These comments by Stirling recall those by Bridges about Jemmy (Chapter 9). On the last Sunday in Lewaia, 19 January, Sisoi arrived with his father from Wulaia. Stirling approved of Sisoi as he observed him washing in Beagle Channel before coming to the divine service. But he was less impressed with his trousers, which dated from his trip to England, worn so thin that he could hardly hold them up. Then he was pleased to hear Sisoi singing a hymn in English and reciting the Lord's Prayer, "full of tenderness and beauty."[89] The Argentine historian Canclini was also impressed by what he had read about Sisoi and noted that his talent for singing was very much appreciated by Stirling and later by Bridges.[90]

All in all, the three-week visit had been encouraging. The new residents were left with goats, biscuits and other provisions to supplement the food they knew how to obtain. The local natives had cooperated, had heard three sermons in Yahgan and the locality had much to offer.[91] What more? Nothing more; Lewaia seemed ideal.

Two Last Visits to Lewaia

Stirling visited Lewaia a second time, accompanied by Bartlett and thirty goats for the Keppel settlers. Then, for some unknown reason, he began to doubt that Lewaia was adequate and apparently began looking for another site (Chapter 11). But the plan for Lewaia had not been put aside, because Bridges visited there later in September, with twelve goats, seed potatoes and turnips, with the obvious intention of supplying the Keppel disciples. Then Bridges reported that the latter had passed a "very trying" winter and that some of the children had died "under the hardships and privations."[92] Much later his son, Lucas Bridges, gave more information on how serious difficulties had been for these Keppel settlers in Lewaia:

The Laiwaia [Lewaia] settlement on Navarin Island, had been started in January, 1868, with Okoko, Pinoi, Lukka and Jack. After Jack had left [probably returned with Stirling in April 1868 to Keppel], the others had been overwhelmed by the jealousy of their poorer fellows. There had been fighting, and at a nearby spot a man had certainly been killed. George Okoko, head man of the settlement, had had his house burnt down when he was out fishing.[93]

The death of some of the Keppel children, hardship, jealousy of the local people, fighting, a man killed and Okoko's house, probably the log communal house, burnt down were more than sufficient reasons to give up the plan to establish a mission station at Lewaia. Just who was killed and why there had been fighting was not explained.

Lewaia: the Fourth Failure

Later Stirling explained that Lewaia had been unfit for a permanent station. The port was too narrow, the soil too poor for gardens, it lacked good wood nearby and good water was scarce.[94] He and Bridges had previously chosen Lewaia precisely because all of the above mentioned had been judged really "good." The real motives for abandoning the site were those given by Bridges and later by his son Lucas, quoted above. By September 1868 the problem had to be faced: where to establish a mission station?

"Those Who Follow Me Shall Be Redeemed"

Despite the resistance the missionaries were finding among the Yamanas in Wulaia and Lewaia, Bridges seems to have gained even greater confidence in the sanctity of his mission, as evidenced in the following text, written in October 1868, one of the most utopian declarations of the entire Anglican–Fuegian enterprise.

Over fifty individuals have been brought over from their own country to Cranmer, our Mission-station on Keppel Island, where they have enjoyed regular religious instruction, many of them have been taught to read and write, have been taught the art of cultivating the ground...[and] have grown attached to civilized life. Many of these have for many months enjoyed the means of grace in their own language, and have heard the Gospel...Sunday after Sunday...and hundreds of the Indians in Fireland have from the lips of their own countrymen heard the chief doctrines of Divine revelation they have learnt to trust, love, and respect us, they know our object in coming to them, and they look upon us as friends.[95]

Was he hallucinating while declaring his faith in the mission's project, or simply making a plea for greater support from his readers?

Bridges' Seven Months in England

By 1868 Thomas Bridges had been on Keppel Island almost thirteen years and was now about twenty-six years old. Probably sometime after April 1868, when Stirling realised that the establishment of a station in Tierra del Fuego would be delayed, he urged the Society's committee in Bristol to grant Bridges permission to return to England. There he should be ordained in the Anglican ministry, be treated for his health problems and select a few men of Anglican persuasion for the work in Tierra del Fuego.[96]

Late October 1868, Bridges embarked alone from Port Stanley on a ship of the Royal Navy, arriving in Plymouth in January. He took along three bark canoes for children, which measured eight feet (2.4 metres) by twenty-two inches (56 centimetres).[97] In mid-January he met the members of the Committee and later spent months lecturing. Once he had been ordained as a deacon by the Bishop of London, the Committee appointed him superintendent of the mission in Tierra del Fuego, under the direction of Stirling. Bridges interviewed various candidates for the mission work and selected two (see below). Toward the end of his stay, a young woman, Mary Varder, came from the nearby village of Harberton to attend his lecture in Bristol. She was fascinated by his account of the Horn archipelago and of the wild people who lived there. After the lecture she asked him to tell her more. They fell in love and a few weeks later, on 7 August 1869, were married in Harberton, the residence of the bride's family.[98] Two days afterwards, they departed via Southampton for the "Land of Fire." On 18 September in Montevideo they met Stirling, who was on his way back to England, and received encouraging news from him about a new station that had recently been founded (Chapter 11). The Bridges couple arrived in Port Stanley in early October 1869.[99]

Appendix: Darwin's Questionnaire Sent to Bridges

In a letter dated 6 January 1860, Darwin had sent thirteen questions to Thomas Bridges, while collecting material for his book, *The Expression of the Emotions in Man and Animals* (published in 1872).[100] Bridges answered eight of the first ten about October 1860.[101] As the eleventh question, concerning the domestication of the Fuegian dogs, and the last two, inquiring about wild pigs and cattle on the Falkland Islands, were not answered; they are not quoted here.

1. Darwin: "Do the Fuegians or Patagonians, or both, nod their heads vertically to express assent, and shake their heads horizontally to express dissent?"
   Bridges: "The Fuegians do nod their heads vertically, to express assent; and horizontally to express dissent."
2. Darwin: "Do they blush? and at what sort of things? Is it chiefly or most commonly in relation to personal appearance, or in relation to women?"
   Bridges: "They blush much, but chiefly in regard to women, but they certainly blush also at their own personal appearance."
3. Darwin "Do they express astonishment by widely open eyes, up-lifted eye brows and open mouth?"

Bridges: "They certainly express astonishment by widely opening their eyes, by raising the eyebrows, and opening the mouth."

4. Darwin: "Do they evince anger or fear by the same expression of countenance and actions as we do?"

Bridges: "They evince anger with the same signs as we do, with an angry face, which becomes pale. They stamp their feet, and walk about abstractedly, and if very angry they cry, and inflict pain on themselves."

5. Darwin: "When out of spirits or dejected, do they turn down the corners of the mouth?"

Bridges: "When out of spirits, they evince in it the very same manner as we do."

6. Darwin: "Do they express contempt by the same gestures as we do, namely, by turning up nose and puffing out their breath or even by spitting?"

Bridges: "They express contempt by shooting out the lips, and hissing through them, and by turning up the nose. To spit at one is the highest mark of contempt."

7. Darwin: "Do they sneer, which is chiefly shown by turning up the corners of upper lip?"

(not answered)

8. Darwin: "Do they frown when trying to understand anything or considering any difficulty?"

Bridges: "They frown greatly when deep in thought, as I have frequently seen."

9. Darwin: "Do they ever shrug their shoulders to show that they are incapable of doing or understanding anything?"

(not answered)

10. Darwin: "What ideas of feminine beauty have the Fuegians? Do they admire women with strong American cast of countenance, or such as at all approach Europeans in appearance?"

Bridges: "The Fuegians consider a woman a pretty one, who has a round face, who is slender, yet compact, and strong. And it is very certain that the nearer a person approaches to the Caucasian race, the most beautiful, for what European females they have seen, they decidedly looked upon them as beautiful."

Darwin commented on the above answer: "I cannot but think that this must be a mistake, unless indeed the statement refers to the few Fuegians who have lived some time with Europeans, and who must consider us as superior beings."[102] Except for the last, Darwin was probably gratified by the answers Bridges gave, which confirmed his theory, elaborated in *The Expression of the Emotions in Man and Animals* that people the world over generally express emotions by the same sort of gestures.[103] For the readers who do not have Darwin's book on hand, I found three references to Bridges that quote his answers to questions four, six and two in this order. Darwin commented on number two. "This latter statement agrees with what I remember of the Fuegian, Jemmy Button, who blushed when he was quizzed about the care which he took in polishing his shoes and in otherwise adorning himself."

1869 to 1880: The Missionaries Settle in Tierra del Fuego; The Yamana Attempt to Adjust

January to June 1869: The Fifth Attempt to Establish a Mission Succeeds

Otatosh the Diplomat

In April 1868, when Stirling was still in Lewaia, he met a Yamana youth, later known as Otatosh from Ushuaia Bay, who happened to be visiting there. Later, when Stirling wrote to his daughters, and stated that Otatosh had brought him to Ushuaia Bay. "The Liwya [Lewaia] and Wollya [Wulaia] people are jealous and angry because I have come to settle here [Ushuaia Bay]; but these people are very pleased...this part of the country, which is Otatoosh's, and which he highly praised. I have found it deserving of the praise he gave it."[1]

Stirling went to the large bay of Ushuaia, that April or later in 1868, because Otatosh "had highly praised" it. Apparently he examined the bay to his satisfaction, guided by Otatosh, who introduced him to his countrymen. After their troubles in Wulaia and Lewaia, Stirling would certainly not have embarked in Ushuaia Bay early January 1869 as he did and gone directly to the suitable site, with the assurance that the local Yahgans would receive him, had he not been there before and decided that a mission could be established there.[2] It is also significant that Otatosh later received Stirling as his baptismal name.

Ushuaia Bay was certainly appreciated by the native people as a place of beauty and plenty. This was the Yamana heartland: imagine Ushuaia Bay as Paris, Beagle Channel as Les Champs Élysées, and Wulaia as Fontainebleau – all Yamana territory.

Yayoshaga of the Mythical Matriarchy

Even though Ushuaia was not a place of pilgrimage, the Yahgans may have guarded it with a certain awe for the great transformation that was thought or imagined to have occurred at the western entrance to the bay, in a place they called Yayoshaga (*shaga* signifies "canal," but I have not found the meaning of *Yayo*). According to the myth, the women of ancient times had reigned there in full force. They were supreme – well organized as a matriarchy. This theme may well have been part of very ancient Patagonian tradition, as it was also known to the Selk'nam and probably the Haush.

According to the Yamana version, the dominant matriarch was Hanuxa, the sister-in-law of Lom (or Lem), the "Younger Sun-man." She was also the wife of his brother, Akainix, the Rainbow-man, a great shaman. The men finally revolted against the women, led by Lom. Most of the women were killed and transformed into animals. The men kept the innocent young girls and female babies. The physical force and ingenuity of the males had vanquished the female-powered society. One version of their myth relates that after being vanquished by the men, during that "great revolution," Hanuxa, the chef matriarch, escaped from the *Kina* (the sacred hut of the women). Transformed into the moon, she took revenge by causing a flood, probably because of her power to control the tides. All the people drowned "except for the few who were able to save themselves on five mountaintops [called Five Brothers], where the water did not reach."[3] When the flood subsided, they returned to Yayoshaga, and thus the Yamana people were reinstalled in their territory, under the rule of the men. Victorious, the men installed a male-dominated society, a patriarchy, which is not a myth.[4] The Selk'nam especially and even the Haush were also patriarchies, probably since very ancient times.

Thomas Bridges visited the site of the vanquished matriarchy while on a long walk during his second trip to Ushuaia Bay in July 1870. He wrote: "The celebrated lake at Yiu-uoh-ah-ga [Yayoshaga], with which is connected the Indian tradition of the deluge. It is about six miles from the settlement [of his Anglican mission]" (referred to again in Chapter 15).[5]

Why in Ushuaia Bay?

Otatosh led Stirling to Ushuaia Bay, but why was Stirling convinced that a mission station should be established there? Bridges explained that this bay was sheltered and timber and grassland were abundant. So far it sounds like Lewaia; but he added significantly that it was "easily approached by the whole Yahgan tribe from east, west, and south." The historian Canclini also offered an answer: "it is the largest and safest bay in the entire zone, in the centre of the Yahgan's habitat."[6]

When Otatosh and his people were still masters of their destiny the Bay of Ushuaia had been overawing: a broad expanse of forest reached far up from the coast to the snow line of the five towering jagged mountains framing the bay as if guarding its back flank. These are the five "brothers," where the mythical Yamana found refuge during the great flood. Beech trees stood high along the shore line of the bay and rumbling streams glided down the mountains, forming cascades before sliding into the bay. The water of the bay was secured from the throbbing currents of Beagle Channel by a protective peninsula and its outer islets. Shellfish thrived along the rock-bound coasts. Seals and penguins made special trips there to feed on the seasonal influx of sprats (a small fish). Herds of guanacos descended from the mountains, munching the vegetation as they wandered through the forest. Sea and forest birds mingled, and a whale, fleeing from pursuing orcas, could find refuge there; not for long, however, if it was wounded and became stranded on the shore. Then the Yamana would feast upon this "gift of nature" (my term) for weeks or months at a time.

When Stirling arrived the mounds of shells, bones and refuse appeared like the walls of ancient dwellings where the former wigwams stood among the recent wigwams. The catechist James Lewis, in 1873, like the more recent settlers of Ushuaia, used these "heaps of garbage" to fertilise their gardens. Lewis stated with pride "that the unsightly heaps of refuse shells, &tc, about our dwellings and neighbourhood will soon, most of them, be turned into turnips, etc."[7] Thus the "ancient city" began to be recycled, first by the missionaries, then by other settlers and finally by archaeologists, who treasure these "heaps of refuse" because they contain artefacts and remains of the food that this "original people" (*pueblo originario*) had consumed.

How to Settle These Restless Fuegians?
Stirling's plan was to set up the mission station with the help of Otatosh and his loyal Keppel assistants, who would exercise "direct and constant influence on the natives."[8] Given the previous difficulties, he had to make sure local Yahgans cooperated. Moreover, he wanted his house to be made of iron, to prevent it from being burnt down by enraged natives, as had happened to Okoko and Lucca in Wulaia and Lewaia (Chapter 10).

He faced yet another problem: how to keep these natives in one place, in Ushuaia Bay. It was as if he had to trap these wild birds, build cages and provide food in order to preach, teach and lead them up the path to earthly salvation and possibly to eternal grace. How was he ever to civilise and Christianise them if they continued their habitual coming and going in pursuit of their daily substance, their incessant visiting of relatives and friends, perpetually canoeing around the bay and up and down the coasts of Beagle Channel? How could he deal with these restless savages?

Before the end of January he thought to try charcoal burning, timber cutting and a little commercial sealing to employ and settle them. Yankee and British sealers had preceded him and almost cleaned the rocks of seals, but they had missed a few; others escaped and some had returned.[9] Stirling was not the first to upset the traditional mode of the Yamana in the bay and along Beagle Channel; the sealers were. Although they came only temporarily, they succeeded, like midnight thieves, in stealing the Yamana's favourite food and frightening the women.

"These People Are Very Pleased"

Stirling sailed into Ushuaia Bay on 7 January 1869 in the *Allen Gardiner* with his adopted son Jack (who had become his "housekeeper") and Jack's wife, "a mere girl." Otatosh was there, greeting him, together with Okoko, Lucca and a new Keppel pupil Wageradegom (Woguri for short). Okoko and the others had moved to Ushuaia after their log house had been burned down in Lewaia.

Although Stirling had learned some expressions in the Yahgan language, he depended on Jack and his other Keppel friends to communicate with the locals. He wrote to his daughters that "these people are very pleased, and call me 'our countryman,' and never refuse to do any work I have yet asked them to do."[10] However, these people, the local Ushuaians (my term), failed to appreciate the favouritism shown to the Keppel intruders, Okoko and the others.

First a Dinner, Then a Tea Party

In any event, Stirling's arrival was peaceful. Shortly afterwards, his "little room," eight by nine feet (2.4 by 2.7 metres), was built, probably with material brought in the schooner. On 14 January, the *Allen Gardiner* departed and "God's sentinel" was on his own. The yacht was scheduled to return a month later. On the eve of its departure, Stirling invited his Keppel friends and Otatosh to dine. During the dinner party, while he and his guests were peacefully chatting, one of them noticed two eyes peering through the window. Soon they discovered that the eyes were those of "a great thief, of violent temper, a woman killer" by the name of Urupuwiah who was, as Stirling expected, a *"yekamoosh"* (shaman). After a while the "thief" tired of peering and departed. Having dined, Stirling's friends went to fetch his baggage, left on the landing place about a half a mile from his hut. While they were gone, an "Indian file" of women appeared and informed Stirling that a fight was going on at the landing place. Moments passed while Stirling determined his course of action. His mind made up, he advanced toward the site of the problem. From the brink of an embankment he saw "natives rushing to and fro, brandishing clubs, and spears, and axes," and heard them shouting wildly.

The Keppelites, his dinner guests, were being attacked by the Ushuaians "excited to jealousy against them," led by none other than the peeping-thief, Urupuwiah. "The moment was critical." Stirling descended firmly and rapidly toward the shore. When the ringleaders saw him, they beat a hasty retreat to their wigwams. Even at a distance, his appearance "had worked a marvellous change." He was confident: "I knew, once for all, that I had an ascendancy over them which was of priceless value. Strong, therefore, in the sense of an acknowledged authority, I proceeded to the wigwams of the ringleaders, there to rebuke them for their violence and to examine into its cause."[11]

Stirling was not timid. Having declared that he was now "an acknowledged authority," he explained that Urupuwiah, the peeping-thief, had maliciously misinformed them, that a tea party invitation for the fifty Ushuaians was for the morrow and not now, which was the dinner for his protégés, the Keppelites (my term). Peace was restored.

He had "issued invitations" to some fifty local adults for a tea party, which was to be held the next day (15 January), Stirling's birthday. That day a fence was rapidly installed in front of his one-room hut. He invited his guests to pass into the enclosure. Forty-six adults were seated and offered slices of his beautiful birthday cake, which Mrs McClinton, who was taking care of his daughters in Port Stanley, had made for him. They also feasted on biscuits, potatoes and "treacle" (molasses) and enjoyed the tea with sugar "immensely."

The Peeping Troublemaker Again
A few days later Urupuwiah was in a great rage, gesticulating and foaming at the mouth, because Lucca had slammed a door in his face. Stirling was doing his best to keep him in "cold shade." He was jealous of the Keppelites and said many bad things about them.

This peeping *yekamush*'s son, Muga-tella-shinges, was Jack's assistant. Stirling caught Muga-tella-shinges stealing biscuits from a box in his room. This story takes an unusual twist because Jack's young wife was waiting at the door to receive the stolen biscuits. "The little vixen, quite unabashed, simply laughed, as if utterly unconscious of shame; but the boy [Muga-tella-shinges] seemed ashamed and grieved; still the girl's laughter seemed to carry him away, and he tried to laugh too."

The laughing had hardly ceased when Jack appeared on the scene. While Stirling was informing him about what had just happened, the two culprits overheard him and laughed again. However, Muga-tella-shinges later approached Stirling and vowed never to steal again, holding his head back to keep the tears back. Stirling was so moved that he almost kissed him and was doubly pleased when he learned that Jack had already taught him the Ten Commandments, in Yahgan.[12]

No More Trouble?

Several more days had passed when Lucca discovered that his "beautiful American axe," a recent gift from Stirling, was missing. Stirling himself had not lost a single thing except a teacup full of sugar. Despite these losses, he declared: "The Ushuawian people are not supposed to be thieves." Nevertheless, Urupuwiah had stolen Lucca's axe, besides tools from the yacht, which somehow the thief hid on his head, perhaps under a crown of feathers such as the *yekamushes* use when they need the support of invisible powers. Stirling recovered the tools from Urupuwiah's head in "an unceremonious manner." That humiliation prompted him to confess to all of his sins.

The Beloved Sisoi

Word came soon that Sisoi longed to join Stirling and his Keppel friends in Ushuaia. Like Jack, Sisoi had been to England with Stirling but afterwards had remained in Lewaia to please his father. Lucca told or reminded Stirling of Sisoi's wonderful purity of character and sweetness of temper. Lucca added that Sisoi greatly loved his father, "and would rather wait patiently for his father to let him come willingly [to Ushuaia], than force his way back to us." Stirling was touched and said: "My heart is full of love for him."

Stirling – Not Complaining

The routine was functioning: prayers and catechising before breakfast and in the evening, daily work on his hut and garden, fencing, cutting wood for export, charcoal burning and cooking. By then Stirling was installed, satisfied and wrote enthusiastically to his daughters, wishing they might see

the fowls quietly pecking away in front of the house, and the clothes hanging on the line; the orderly stacks of firewood; and my little hut neatly railed in . . . a neatly thatched fowl-house; and beyond a well dug garden, a zig-zag fence round it . . . in the morning and evening certain natives of Tierra del Fuego [arrive] some with clothes, others scarcely clothed, yet coming at a stated call to Christian services.

If only his daughters could see all this they would be "very glad that the way had been so far prepared for the spread of God's love and truth in these uttermost ends of the earth." As the days passed, Lucca and Jack showed Stirling their mode of wrestling, while the women, with their lines in the kelp, brought him plenty of fish. Stirling was not complaining.

A month had passed, everyone was friendly, even though the day before, 6 February, a fight had begun that might have led to serious disturbances. The aggressive party, "being in the minority, and not belonging to this place, threatens to return with a party of foot Indians [Oens-men] to drive us all out." However, Stirling had no fear, nor apparently did anyone else. It was simply a rumour.

Another Theft

A few days later, 13 February, Stirling was overjoyed thinking that the *Allen Gardiner* was due to return with supplies and news from Port Stanley. He looked around for the cord to hoist the mission flag to greet the schooner, but the cord was not there. It had been stolen. The suspect this time was none other than Squire (or Schwin or Schway) Muggins, who had been in Keppel and in Wulaia that fatal first week of November 1859 (Chapter 9). Stirling claimed that he had taken "a leading part in the massacre, [and besides was] a noted thief." Be that as it may, he was now Stirling's canoe maker and declared his innocence of the cord theft. Stirling decided to "put on the screw" and peremptorily challenged him: "Schwin, unless you go, and go quickly, and fetch that line you stole from the flag-staff, just look out. The *Allen Gardiner* is at hand – no biscuit for you – no knife." Schwin objected again: "I didn't steal it." Stirling: "Yes, you did, somebody saw you." Schwin: "Who saw me? Who?" His countenance revealed his guilt. Off he went and, to everyone's surprise, except Stirling's, he returned half an hour later with the cord in hand.[13]

The Novelty – Wearing Off "a Little"

Life went on, though not as usual. That summer and autumn, January to June 1869, the weather was fine and the rivers and bay were well supplied with fish. But it proved difficult for Stirling to direct the natives' attention to "industrial pursuits." The mission settlement in Ushuaia should be self-supporting. He promised the Yahgans who were drawn to him and those arriving from other parts of the bay "steady work under my direction, food sufficient for their wants." As will become clear, he and the other missionaries could "supply" good words but only a small number of natives with "steady work" and "food sufficient." As winter set in and the fish migrated to distant bays, Stirling became aware that the novelty of his presence "wore off a little, and had less force." Now he decided that the best employment plan for the "aborigines" was cutting down trees and preparing the trunks and long branches, for sale in Port Stanley, where lumber was so scarce.

A New Pay Policy

The *Allen Gardiner* brought provisions from the Falklands for Stirling and for the natives he employed. Instead of distributing the food, the main payment, to his employees once their work was completed, he decided to have it cooked in his hut and portioned out at intervals to those who had earned it, so they could consume it then and there. He adopted this policy "because the number of friends increases in the wigwam in proportion of anything available worthwhile."[14] Thanks to his new policy, the workers were able to consume (eat) all they had received as pay without sharing it with their families or friends. Stirling was aware of "the custom of the people to divide their supplies of food with those about them." This they had learned from childhood and youth during the long Chexaus ceremony (Chapter 15). Stirling had not heard about this ceremony but he did known about its teachings, that "they should be generous in the distribution of food to their needy brethren. A seal is always divided at once. . . . If a guanaco should fall a prey to the natives, this great prize must be shared by all." Even though he didn't know about their traditional teachings, he thought that it might be "invidious" on his part to refuse the food they earned to "their friends at home." But the Yahgan workers themselves wanted "to get out of the difficulty [of sharing], they wished that they might have their meals daily in my hut, which was agreed to." This is why he had decided to offer them cooked food in his hut.

This accommodation of individual consumption, of the pay on the spot, though made at the request of the workers, accelerated the dissolution of the ties that were so essential to the Yahgans' way of living. Their relations of redistribution and reciprocity were being severed. The workers themselves were caught up in a process they could not control, and by their attitudes they too hastened the pace of disintegration. Stirling explained to them that in his home country and the Falklands, it was different. "There we had rulers, who punished the bad and protected the good. Here [in Ushuaia] everything was upside down."[15]

It was becoming evident that turning everything "right side up" spelt the doom of the natives' entire culture, even without all that was to follow (Chapters 12 to 14).

Those First Six Months

Stirling was satisfied that, during his six months in Ushuaia (January to June 1869), he had succeeded in establishing an Anglican mission among the natives of Tierra del Fuego.

A year later, Stirling wrote about these six months and the "degraded and wretched condition of the Fuegian Indians... without God in the world, and sunk to the lowest state that our humanity admits of." Yet on the next page he described the manner in which the women and their husbands were always "delighted" to furnish him with fish, even late at night, and sometimes in snowy weather. "In fact I have great reason to speak favourably of the kind disposition of many among this poor people." While insulting the Fuegians, he could not resist telling how much they delighted in serving him. How could they be at that "lowest state" and be so kind, and self-sacrificing?

He also insisted that among the Fuegians "religious sentiment has never found any form of expression. The heart and intellect here are indeed benumbed and deadened." Moreover, outside the family, he found that the relationships were doubtful, if not hostile; the bond of a common language or even of the tribe was no guarantee of friendly feelings.[16] Like Bridges in 1876 (see below), Stirling viewed the Yahgans as sunk in "the black hole" (so to speak). He was unaware that his presence was intensifying tensions and envy among them by creating competition to obtain missionary food and goods. The next year he also recalled:

I had come down to teach this people, to teach them with authority, to induce them to abandon many of their established usages, and to impress upon them, by the whole weight of my influence, a deference to the Divine law. Consequently, I *was appealed to as law-giver; I was expected to act as judge, jury, policeman, and often executioner.* As foreman of works. As a minister of Christ.[17]

Suddenly, during these six months, in lieu of a new sort of *yekamush*, or a gift-giving navigator or a target for petty-thievery, the Yahgans had a self-proclaimed law-giver. To whom did Stirling refer when he wrote: "I was appealed to as law-giver" and "I was expected to act as judge, jury,

FIGURE 11.1. Thomas Bridges, approximately 25 years old.

policeman?" Who appealed to him to assume these enormous powers of social and individual control? The Ushuaians is the obvious answer. But could they have forfeited their traditional freedom, sacrificed the mode of living they had developed during so many generations, handed over their entire gestalt to an utter stranger?

Bridges Becomes Director of the Ushuaia Mission

Having returned to Port Stanley and Keppel in June, Stirling sailed for home with his two daughters in August 1869, while Bridges was busy being married and departing from England (Chapter 10). Going in the opposite directions, they met in Montevideo in September. Back in England in December, Stirling was appointed Bishop of the Falkland Islands with jurisdiction over the Anglican churches in all of South America. This appointment, a great honour, would entail long absences from Keppel and Tierra del Fuego. Thomas Bridges, as of 1870, would assume virtually complete authority over the mission in Tierra del Fuego. Stirling visited the mission, in Ushuaia and Keppel Island, during the years to come. He died in 1923 at the age of ninety-four and was buried in the cathedral of Wells, near Bristol.[18]

Bridges, Newly Wed, Returns to Keppel

In October 1869, Bridges and his bride arrived in Keppel and were greeted by Mrs Bartlett, a young Yahgan named Cushinjiz (later called James) from Gable Island and Jacob Resyeck (or Resyek) among others. The latter was a "Christian sailor," a native of British Guiana, who had arrived that year. Although Thomas Bridges regarded him highly, Lucas thought he was "so taciturn as to give the impression that he was either deaf or simply morose."[19]

In November 1869, Bridges was gratified by the conduct and decent aspect of the seven Yahgans at Keppel, including two young couples from Gable Island. They were engaged in the usual labour, supervised by Resyeck, who was rapidly learning Yahgan.[20]

The two catechists selected by Bridges in England had arrived with him in Port Stanley: John Lawrence and James Lewis, their wives, and Willy, the Lewises' son. Late 1869 into 1870, Bridges was tutoring them in Yahgan and all were well in Keppel.[21]

Meanwhile at the Ushuaia Mission

William Bartlett, who had come with Despard and young Bridges in 1856, had directed the new mission after Stirling departed in June 1869 until the next director (Bridges) was to take over. Bartlett helped Otatosh plant a garden and assisted the four Keppelites now established in Ushuaia, mainly Lucca, young Woguri, who had greeted Stirling in January 1869, and Pinoense, Tom Button's son, who had arrived with his wife. Okoko and Gamela apparently had gone back to Lewaia, though they returned to Ushuaia from time to time.

An Innovation – A Mission Store

Bartlett was given permission to open a store in the settlement and supply it with clothing, tools, bread, flour, sugar, rice and "treacle" (molasses). These goods, used as wages for the natives, could also be obtained by bartering the skins of fur seals, otters and guanacos.[22] The store created an additional fissure in the Yahgans' social structure, as if draining its vital force, by inserting a purely impersonal economic factor in the network of their social relations. No money, or not much, flowed in and out of the pockets of the Yahgans, though it did from the visiting sealers to the missionaries, who paid cold cash for the goods they bought. From time to time the Yahgans sold their pelts to the sealers for cash, however little.

During this interlude (June 1869 to March 1870), the Keppel graduates and probably Otatosh had installed about 170 stout posts in the ground, fenced in 150 yards (137 metres) on one side of the garden, tufted areas around the cow barn, hoed the potato patches and cared for the goats.[23]

March 1870: Bridges' First Trip to Ushuaia

When Bridges departed in the *Allen Gardiner* for Ushuaia, nine months after he had returned with his bride to the Falkland Islands, he was about twenty-seven and had been appointed director of the Ushuaia Mission.

The day after the yacht stopped over in Banner Cove, twelve canoes appeared carrying about seventy people. Bridges thought they were "the most wretched looking of any Indians we have yet seen in Tierra del Fuego." They may have looked "most wretched," but were they? Not according to Bridges himself, as quoted by his son, Lucas, for the same visit: "Father went on shore and spoke to the natives. Father writes, 'All the canoes seemed well supplied with fish and the Channel teemed with bird life.'"

Having departed from Banner Cove, sailing along Beagle Channel they stopped along Gable Island where Cushinjiz-James, who was on board, decided to remain in his own territory, Gable Island, and look around for a wife. James was known as "an intelligent, energetic, and tidy youth." He was taken ashore "with a box of goods and injunction to spread the Bible story and the good precepts he had learnt."[24]

Sailing on through MacKinlay Pass, they also stopped beyond Gable Island, where Bridges recalled that Stirling had heard, in Ushuaia, that these Indians "entertain evil intentions towards us." In effect, Bridges found them to be "very clamorous and rude." So he spoke to them "very sharply and firmly." Then he gave them some geese and penguins' eggs from the Falklands, with the result that they "became very much ashamed and quiet."

People in faraway Rous Peninsula (southern Hoste Island) were also "reported to have uttered threats against us, moved by the like feelings." Nothing came of these rumours either. As noted in Chapter 9, after the 1859 massacre, the behaviour of the Yamana as well as the Oens-men was never outwardly aggressive, never life-threatening, though from time to time individuals became angry with the missionaries and others may have felt resentment or a latent hostility toward them.

When the yacht pulled into Ushuaia Bay on the lovely day of 29 March 1870, Bridges, seeing the bay for the first time, was excited. "It is a most suitable place for our first mission station in Tierra del Fuego. It is central, has excellent harbours, plenty of water, and an endless supply of wood, a fine extent of excellent pasture and tillage land; the people also are friendly and desirous for improvement."

Later he explained the mission settlement was named Tushcapalan, meaning "the Kelp island of the Flying Loggerhead Duck," while the name "Ushuaia" referred only to the bay.[25] However, I will use the term "Ushuaia Mission" to refer to Tushcapalan.

The next morning, 30 March 1870, Otatosh and two of the Keppelites (Lucca and Wogur) greeted Bridges. A new Yahgan recruit, Samuel Mateen, was with them. He was found to be such a good worker that two of his three wives were overlooked. He will reappear twelve years later, when Captain Louis Ferdinand Martial, the French explorer, will be very pleased to meet him (Chapter 13).

Okoko and his family had come from Lewaia the day before because "very lately" their home had been set on fire – again for the third time (once in Wulaia and now twice in Lewaia). Okoko's strength of character and resolve to assist the missionaries "had brought him to the front, and he was now the leading figure in Ushuaia."[26]

The *Allen Gardiner* brought materials for the "Stirling iron house," which Stirling never inhabited. Bridges and his helpers began digging the foundation for the new house. During the following week, in early April, there were "only about forty Indians" in the bay, probably including the Keppel settlers named above. As Bridges planned to return to Keppel shortly and then go back to Ushuaia four weeks later, he assigned work for his five Keppel assistants to be done while he was away: finish the foundation of the "Stirling House," cut and place the rails and palings around the other three sides of the garden and dig up more land. He told them that he could not give them sugar, tea, coffee, raisins and the like because "the Mission could only supply them with necessaries; that if they want these things they must purchase them [in the new store]."[27]

Bridges Obtains "Full Permission to Take Possession"
Shortly after he arrived for his first visit, the end of March 1870, Bridges sent word to all the natives that they were to meet him after dinner for

a serious matter. The weather was beautiful and apparently most of "the forty Indians" came on time and sat down on the grass. Bridges knelt before them and prayed to God to make him wise. Then he stood up and gave his speech in Yahgan, summarised in his words as follows:

I got full permission from the natives of Ushuaia to take possession of any land for house and gardens. Next time I intend giving them something as small acknowledgement. I told them plainly that should they get tired of us *they must not expect to drive us away and get the land back*, that the land belonged not to this or that one, but to him or them who lived upon it, cared for it, fenced and made use of it; and that if we [the missionaries] should go to the trouble of fencing, planting, and building on the land, that the land became ours. I told them that in England all the land was privately possessed, whereas *here no man could point to any piece of land and say "that is mine."*[28]

Please reread the above quote. Note that the arrogance of his speech strikes an alarm. It certainly didn't fall on deaf ears. What could these "forty Indians," the majority of whom were Ushuaians, have understood by this statement? Bridges must have utterly confounded them. Did they grasp or even sense its implications for their future, even though he spoke to them in their own language? No discussion, no questions were reported.

Like Stirling before him, Bridges moved in on the inhabitants with the self-assurance of his religious affiliation: he (Bridges) had the right to possess their land because he was occupying it for the Anglican Mission, for God's mission. He chose to ignore the fact that the land belonged to the Ushuaians, the members of the lineages that camped there.

Two years later, Bridges reaffirmed: "We obtained full permission from the people of this part to settle here; and to take possession permanently of certain land for building on and for gardens."[29]

Despite Bridges' declaration, I found no evidence that the Yahgans in Ushuaia had granted their land to Anglicans nor did they or the Selk'nam grant their land to the Argentine government when it "took possession" of half of the Isla Grande nor to Chile when it claimed the other half in 1881 (Chapter 13). These appropriations recall Denis Diderot's fiction of a rebuttal given to the French, by a Tahitian sage: "So this land is yours? Why? Because you set foot on it! If a Tahitian should one day land on your shores and engrave on one of your stones or on the bark of one of your trees, 'This land belongs to the people of Tahiti,' what would you think of them?"[30]

Herman Melville, like the French encyclopaedist Diderot, supported the idea of the Tahitian "noble savage" and was passionately anticolonialist.

And Diderot, like Melville "was not concerned with fairness in the Christian sense; he thought the original crime of the European intrusion had put all subsequent talk of fairness out of court."[31]

When Bridges departed a week later, many boys in the Ushuaia area wanted to go to Keppel. Bridges chose only one, a nephew of Jamesina (Jemmy's first wife), "a well-grown, good looking youth."[32] They stopped over in Gable Island, where James came to meet them and was "still decently clothed," although he had given away most of his new outfits. He gave Bridges a basket for his wife, "seemed happy, and had no wish to return to the Falklands." At the next stop, in Banner Cove, another youth, Ascapan, was picked up. He had first gone to Keppel in January 1868 and was known as a quiet and good worker.[33]

More Trips to the New Mission

Bridges made additional trips to the Ushuaia Mission before he took his family there in September 1871. In July 1870 he arrived with 10,000 bricks for the cellar walls of the Stirling House and stayed on for two weeks. The Keppel natives worked well on the house, despite the snow.[34] On the next trip there (his third) in October of that year, he remained for five weeks. Then he was accompanied to Ushuaia by James Lewis and Jacob Resyeck, the two new missionary assistants, and by two native couples, who had been in Keppel a year or more and who were let off on Gable Island. Together with James, they were to form a nucleus of Christian Yahgans on that island, the first outpost or branch of the Ushuaia Mission.

Arriving in Ushuaia Mission the next day, they found that eighty-two Yahgans, including Sisoi, were doing the basic work for the mission from 6 AM to 5:30 PM for two daily meals and afternoon tea. But before Bridges departed, he told Lewis and Resyeck to employ only seven of the eighty-two after he left. He advised the other seventy-five to hunt and fish as usual.

Bridges gave necklaces to the women and girls and distributed bags of biscuits and commented: "Nothing of consequence was missing of the house materials so long left under native care." In mid-November 1870, he returned to Keppel, leaving Lewis and Resyeck in the new mission and taking along three other Yahgan youths.[35]

On New Year's Day 1871, Lewis faced a situation which will become increasingly critical during the years to follow. "No charity for the unemployed was the best teacher." Some Yahgans reverted to traditional pursuits, which often meant taking a canoe, if they had one, to search the coasts for food. Others were begging, stealing and surviving somehow or not. Lewis was frank when he noted that only those employed received "anything [something] from us (a restriction which has done more to dispirit their innate mendicancy than endless dissuasion would have done), and even the seven [Keppelites] employed have had but a very poor allowance indeed."[36]

Bridges, back again in the Ushuaia Mission on his fourth trip in mid-February 1871, held three tea parties on consecutive days: for the men, for the women, and for the children, in this order. Twenty-three men and youths came to the first party, twenty of whom were identified as four bachelors, seven monogamists, five bigamists, three trigamists, and one quadrigamist.[37] For the second party, the guests were thirty wives of twenty men plus one who was either a widow or a young "Miss." Not receiving the "couples" together mitigated the impact of polygamy.

During the usual "religious and moral instructions," Bridges paraphrased portions of St. Luke's Gospel in Yahgan and taught the responses for grace of the commandments.[38] A schedule was being established. Bridges obtained fish from the Indian women and Resyeck took care of the thirteen sheep recently brought from the Falklands. Together they made almost daily visits to the wigwams. Bridges excused himself for not detailing these visits: "It would be useless and monotonous to make further extracts from my journal, each day's work being so similar." He departed in the *Allen Gardiner* for Keppel at the end of May, as usual with a cargo of lumber.[39]

Shortly after Bridges sailed away, a barrel of bread was stolen from the cellar of the Stirling House. This time Lewis expressed concern for the bread thieves, hoping that "generous subscribers will not begrudge for once, at least, a barrel of bread to the poor fellows, who, hunger-pinched in a barren land, and just entered on a sharp winter, took advantage of an opportunity for obtaining at least one substantial meal in their lifetime."[40]

A Whale Comes to the Rescue
Mid-May to the end of September 1871, mostly winter, brought hardship to those who were unemployed. Lewis wrote that those who were employed "have worked readily and cheerfully during the four months for their food only, which latterly was necessarily a short allowance." Toward the end of that winter, a young whale was stranded in an inlet nearby, "furiously lashing the water with its tail and fins." Lewis joined the men, who with an old sword-bayonet were stabbing the young whale

repeatedly behind its blow hole. "After much furious struggling, the poor animal died." Lewis was amazed that the "poor fellows," who usually avoided even a splash of clean water, now jumped into almost freezing water, "nearly up to their armpits, and applied themselves as I had never previously seen them do; a fire was soon made on the spot, some strips of blubber frizzled thereon, and were eaten with a gusto."

Canoes from all around were paddled to the scene. As long as "a bit of whale remained to be obtained by coaxing, importunity, or bullying, not a woman would stir to get a mussel." The first arrivals, who had done the butchering, tried to conceal blubber in a little stream nearby, "which the late-comers soon discovered, much to the loss and sorrow of the owners." Whether they liked it or not, the first-arrivals shared their prize. The men made spearheads from the bones and fishing lines from the sinews. A few hours later, "not a vestige of flesh or bone remained on the spot, save the liver, not eaten as a rule by the natives."[41] A stranded whale had always been a great treat and now saved them from real hunger.

1871: The Bridges Family Settle in Ushuaia

Less than two years after Bridges returned from England with his bride, having made four trips to Ushuaia, the time had come for them to settle in the new mission station with their first child, Mary Ann, now a year old. They departed from Keppel in late August 1871, filled with zeal for "evangelising and civilising this destitute, degraded, but well inclined and naturally pliant and tractable people."[42]

This fifth trip to Ushuaia was a strain on everyone, especially Mrs Bridges. Instead of the week or less that the voyage normally took, this one lasted five weeks, to 30 September.

Leaving Keppel, they pulled anchor from Port Stanley, and had "a very prosperous run across" to Good Success Bay, but there they waited out the storms for almost a month, much to the discomfort of Mrs Bridges. There is no mention of going ashore or of seeing the Haush.

On 24 September, about a month after leaving Keppel, the yacht pulled into Banner Cove. Eric Shipton, the explorer, related this episode as if he had filmed it.

That evening when the exhausted crew had retired to rest, Thomas and Mary Bridges were alone on deck gazing over the quiet water of the lagoon to the twilight forest beyond. Almost too weak to stand, she clung to her husband's arm and whispered, "Dearest, you have brought me to this country, and here I must remain; for I can never, never face that voyage again."

The "miserable state of these people" deeply affected her.[43] What had made the Banner people so miserable in these last years since Captain Snow's and young Gardiner's visits (Chapter 8)? Or was it misery in the eyes of the beholders?

A week later they entered Ushuaia Bay. As the yacht was slowing to a halt, Mrs Bridges was on the deck gazing at the women fishing from their canoes. Some paddled up to the side of the ship, offering fish and limpets to the crew in exchange for knives, biscuits or sugar. When Mrs Bridges and her baby were rowed ashore, all seemed strange to her, even frightening. Dark figures, draped in otter skins or almost naked, "stood or squatted, gazing curiously at the little boat as it approached the beach." She walked about a quarter of a mile beyond the shingle beach, among the "half-buried hovels made of branches roofed with turf and grass" up to "a small hill covered with thorny brush." Arriving at the summit, she entered the Stirling Iron House, where she was to spend most of her long life. Lucas remarked: "It looked very lonely perched up there all by itself."

Later she discovered that the "hovels" smelt strongly of smoke, decomposed whale blubber and refuse. Lucas added with a tone of heroic nostalgia:

Thus did a tiny, but resolute, party take up their abode in the Fuegian archipelago, a collection of islands...covering an area of two hundred miles from North to South, and three hundred and sixty miles from east to west...surrounded by from seven to nine thousand primitive children of Nature, the Fuegian Indians.[44]

Following their arrival, Bridges established a longer routine for the workers: 6:30 AM to 8 PM. In October 1870 it had been from 6:30 AM to 5:30 PM. The allowance for breakfast was now a pound of navy bread; if tea or coffee were not available, the bread was increased. For lunch, a pound of beef and two pounds of potatoes were allotted to each man; for tea, another pound of navy bread. This daily five pounds of food for each worker was to be shared by his family. So much bread and potatoes were not a very welcome diet for these Yahgans, who had been accustomed to fish and meat.

On Sunday two services were in order, then school instruction by the catechists.[45] I comment: "Sermons, praying and hymn-singing were nothing like old times, with the dramas of the Kina and Chexaus ceremonies (Chapter 15)."

Ten days after their arrival, the yacht sailed back to Keppel. As Bridges assumed the direction of the mission, the compassion he showed for

Urupa's bereaved father and for dying Threeboys was almost gone. At times he expressed pity for those he met or knew who were hungry or critically ill and gave them food, though never ceased to reprimand the others for their idle habits and sinful ways.

The die was cast: life would never be the same again for the Yahgans in Ushuaia Bay or, eventually, elsewhere in their country. The explorer Shipton evoked their "way of life," which was so quickly melting into the past.

The people were singularly free from drudgery; they were strangers to heavy, repetitive toil; there was a great variety in their daily occupation, and many of their tasks demanded a high degree of dexterity and cunning. . . . There was no government to dictate their actions and no tribal chief to extort tribute. . . . Though Europeans found their climate harsh, they themselves were superbly adapted to meet the rigours.[46]

1872: Their First Year in Ushuaia

This summer, January to March (1872) was perhaps the highest mark point the mission will ever attain. There was employment for the local Ushuaians as well as the Keppelites. Food was available and no sickness was reported. The missionaries were busy organising and instructing, while the natives were "softened, respectful and receptive," for the most part.[47] They were off to a good start, but was it "a good start" for the Yamana?

Stirling, now a bishop, arrived at this time, his first visit since his departure in June 1869. He was overjoyed: "a Christian influence was extending itself over the hearts and minds of some of the natives."[48] However, he insisted that they must consolidate and expand the work. The Ushuaia Mission should become the training station for native evangelists and for a boarding school for children, while station tributaries should be established. Stirling was full of plans and overjoyed.

Naming, Baptisms and Instructions

During Stirling's stay in February and early March, thirty-six Yahgans were baptised, including Okoko, who became George Despard, the name that had been given to Threeboys. The wives were given equally suitable names, such as Eleanor Stirling. From now on their baptismal names, often only the first, are usually used in the mission journal, making identification even more difficult. All this English naming loosened their kinship and territorial ties as their language was being overtaken, which was indeed the purpose of the "Christianise and civilise" strategy. Stirling had decided that the Bible instruction should be in English, and Bridges seemed to agree, despite being fluent in Yahgan.[49]

A Group Marriage

That summer of 1872, Stirling presided over the simultaneous marriage of seven couples (unfortunately not identified). They took their vows in the open air, surrounded by the mission "crew" and 150 countrymen (including women and children). The brides wore dresses of print materials brought from Port Stanley. The *Allen Gardiner* crew made wedding rings out of sixpence coins. The brides were crowned with wreaths of flowering shrubs arranged by the captain, his wife and the mate. The steward was kept busy baking the seven wedding cakes. This must have been an amazing and an emotional spectacle, one that would never be forgotten or ever repeated.

Prayers

The day before Stirling departed, he yielded to Mr Lewis' suggestion and attended an evening service to be conducted in the native language. Stirling reported:

First there was a hymn; then George Despard [Okoko] offered up a prayer in his own language so calmly and earnestly, that I was astonished and greatly moved in heart. Then Stephen [Lucca] prayed for three or four minutes with almost equal force and sweetness. There was a second hymn, follow by warm, heartfelt utterances in prayer; first by William Bartlett [Wagurii], then by John Marsh [Sisoi], finally by Allen Gardiner [Pinoense] . . . all the prayers were mingled with confession of sin in themselves.

Stirling was also "greatly moved" by Okoko's "resolution to lay himself out more than ever to teach his people Christian things."[50]

Economics Rears Its Ugly Head

Bridges remarked in March (1872) that Port Stanley was "a very convenient market" for pressed wool, potatoes, other garden products, as well as butter and cheese made by the wives of the missionaries and some of the Keppel wives, besides the lumber. Three acres were already cultivated and over eight fenced in.[51]

Even so, by winter and early spring (June to October) there was little work and less food. Instead of the daily five pounds of bread last year, "One biscuit to each a day was a help, and a sufficient inducement to secure a very full and regular attendance in all weathers." A biscuit a day was starvation pay, as the missionaries certainly knew. They also knew that it was a "great blessing" for the natives when they could trade in the mission store for "wholesome food" in exchange for their seal and otter pelts. Note that the mission store offered them more than the "private purchasers," the sealers. About then Bridges sent thirty-four skins to sell in Port Stanley. The Ushuaia Mission was beginning to resemble an old-style feudal farm.

Christmas

It was a fine day. The service was attended by 124 natives. Having heard Bridges' sermon, they prayed and sang. Then they were invited to his front yard, where some presents were given away and others exchanged for bone spearheads, fish lines, baskets and the like. A serving of pudding was passed around to each guest. "They were all very pleased, and their conduct throughout was decent and exemplary." Of the 124 attendants, all but six took to their canoes soon afterwards to go home elsewhere.

1872 into 1873

During the six months (spring and summer, October 1872 to March 1873), the routine was unfailing: sermons and doctrinal instruction, prayers and hymn singing, constructing, gardening, fencing, tending the cattle, lumbering and so on. The original six or seven Keppel families were still there, as were approximately twenty Ushuaians. The floating population varied from more than 130 to only a few families. For example, near the end of January 1873, thirty-six canoes arrived, and all but three left a few days later. These visitors, including those who were seeking employment, came mainly from neighbouring Lapataia, from the large Yendegaya Bay, Lewaia and probably other sites along Beagle Channel and the Narrows.

Biblical Messages

During a prayer meeting in 1872, Pinoense (Tom Button's son, now named Allen Gardiner) spoke of sins, his own and his people's, and of his fear of God. Lewis reported: "He alluded to the massacre of the missionaries at Woolia, and said that the missionaries should no more be molested; that they who were now Christian brothers would protect them, and tell them whenever any evil was premeditated to them."

James, from Gable Island, offered a more original message, which would have pleased Darwin because it was all-encompassing. He asked

God to help them pray and be merciful "not only to their relatives, but to all men; not only to all men, but to the dogs and birds, not to torment them." James had abandoned Gable Island and come to settle in Ushuaia Bay with his wife and baby. The missionaries trusted that he would return to Gable or elsewhere as a catechist or, if not as "a useful and influential person": – that "ere long" he would repay the mission for the "extra trouble taken with him."[52]

Okoko visited people in their wigwams, "talking to them of all he knew concerning the future worlds." He knew that some had listened attentively "whilst others would not."

Were They Understood?

Bridges was anxious to acquaint the natives with the gospels according to John and Luke in Yahgan, despite Stirling's preference for English. Initially Bridges may have favoured John's gospel because his messages are not overly steeped in biblical lore and John uses symbols and metaphors drawn from common, universal experiences, such as water, light, life and the word. "In the Beginning was the Word, and the Word was with God, and the Word was God." This may be a notion not easily understood by some Christian beginners, but it probably did not seem at all strange to the Yamana. They would have quickly grasped the concept of Jesus' signs: that he converted water into wine, that he cured a sick child by his father's faith in him, that he gave sight with his spittle mixed with clay to a man born blind. The Yahgans, especially the *yecamush* shamans, were accustomed to symbolic and abstract notions, and virtually everyone "knew" that certain physical objects were endowed with curing power. They trusted and had faith in their own holy man, their own *yecamush*, though not necessarily in the *yecamush* "next door." Some were probably captivated when Jesus, "the holy man," affirmed "that every one who sees the Son and believes in him should have eternal life; and I will raise him up at the last day."

Difficulties might well have arisen when Jesus declared that "he who eats my flesh and drinks my blood has eternal life, and I will raise him up at the last day." This message, coming from Jesus himself, must have sounded very strange to the Yamana. It must have stretched their symbolic imagination a bit too far, as they knew that their people had been accused of cannibalism. But they probably easily understood why the evil official Jews, the enemy, sought to kill Jesus. Even so, as Bridges pointed out, they could not understand why Jesus agreed to dine with a personage such as Zaccheus, a tax collector for the Romans. Bridges had to explain what a tax collector did and "what the taxes were for, and the necessity of persons paying, and for others to receive taxes." With respect to the Scribes' questioning Jesus about the tribute due to Caesar, Bridges told them who Caesar was, and how "one country had subjugated others, and how it became necessary to obey foreign governors, and submit to foreign taxation, which the Jews so rebelled against." Some of the Yamana may have felt subjugated by "foreign governors," the missionaries, although they never paid taxes, not to the missionaries or to their shamans. In all likelihood this story's impact was diluted and may have confused them.

Once, a lively conversation ensued in the schoolroom on the merits of the medicine men, the *yekamush*. Two *yekamush* were there and performed "in the presence of a large number of witnesses, in order to refute our denial of their powers.... They signally failed."[53] Bridges' cavalier disregard for the Yamana shaman was incurable.

During a sermon in September 1872, Bridges spoke at length that "Jesus Christ came into the world to save sinners," a phrase that the Yahgans repeated many times, after Bridges. Then he told them "what class of sinners they were." There had been adverse weather that day and the day before, very unfavourable for the natives to secure their usual sustenance, so each of the 110 sinners were given a biscuit. Bridges concluded his sermon on the sin theme, warning them "to seek reconciliation with God before it was too late."

Sin as misguided behaviour was not strange to the Yaghans, because their myths, full of moral teachings, were recited and discussed during the great Chexaus ceremony; but everyone being born a sinner was not part of their moral code. The Yamana, like other Fuegians, held the individual and often the family or the lineage responsible for misconduct of one of their own kin, but sin was not an intrinsic human failing. Human beings were not born sinners.

Certain Christian messages resounded, echoing the Yaghans' own ancient code and exemplary stories in their mythology and day-to-day life, while others were undoubtedly discussed among the Yahgans themselves, mainly the Keppelites, seeking to cultivate the seeds of the Christian lessons. The Yahgans had probably always been passionate examiners of their own beliefs, wondering, for instance, why innocent children were condemned to die. They spent much of their leisure time around the fire philosophising, as Bridges had noticed.

The six most reliable converts at Ushuaia – George (Okoko), Stephen (Lucca), John Marsh (Sisoi), Stirling (Otatosh), James (Cushinjiz) and a certain Joseph – were informed that Bridges wished to give them special lessons that would prepare them to instruct their fellow countrymen. Among the six, Okoko and Lucca had already learned to instruct, the hard way.

The day after the Bridges' second child, Despard, was baptised, 22 July 1872, the natives were treated to pudding in the clean and respectable cow house. Fifty-three adults and thirty-four children heard the proud father's brief, cheerful message. Two years later, Bridges recalled that many Ushuaians professed special affection for Despard because he was born at Ushuaia, their "base camp," as the archaeologists might say.[54] Such special affection for Despard is a beautiful example of the strength of the Yamana's identification with their home territory: even if you are not one of us by tradition and race, we love you because you were born in our land (lineage territory). Apparently the natives of Ushuaia still considered that land their own, despite Bridges' declaration to the contrary (see above).

1873: An Eventful Year

In late February 1873 the *Allen Gardiner* had brought a special passenger, Mrs Bridges' sister, affectionately called Yekadahby ("little mother" in Yahgan), who became a permanent member of the Bridges household. That year the Lewis family was assigned to Keppel and a few months later John Lawrence and family settled in the Ushuaia Mission, where he will continue working long after Bridges retired in 1886.

"Gifts Are . . . to Be Avoided"
During the first month of 1873, Bridges wrote that "the supplies of food have been scarce," although it was summer and there were plenty of potatoes. A certain Tispinjiz killed a large fur seal and supplied his family and friends for a few days. But most of the families were already eating the *anachik* fungus, dried by fire.

In early March, twenty-six natives received half-acre plots for their gardens, and the mission exported sixteen fur sealskins and six otter skins. Bridges specified: "A very strict account shall be kept of all the Society's property, and we have long since avoided gifts to the natives. . . . Gifts are in every way to be avoided." The used clothes that kept coming in were destined to pay for labour or to exchange for the skins.[55] The epoch of seduction was over. The serious business of running the mission with Protestant discipline was being enforced.

How Can They Become Self-Sustaining?

Bridges reported that in October 1873, early spring, the mission some-times employed twenty natives "for days together" but seldom for more than six months of the year. Everything in the mission was expensive, and the climate required "nourishing food." He wished that the mission could employ the natives at a cheaper rate. However, a few sentences later, he remarked that "the work is now carried on cheaper than formerly" because the things the natives formerly received gratis they now largely paid for. He trusted that, in the future, the mission would not have to employ so many natives, as they became more "self-dependent."[56] Just how they could become self-dependent was a mystery. Their existence had been predicated on a seminomadic routine and on a network of mutual aid, reciprocity of labour and gift giving, which the missionaries were determined to destroy. Bridges recognised that although the mission sta-tion was supporting the missionaries, it was not developing sufficiently. Even the twenty-six natives who had received half-acre plots in early March were not or no longer permanent residents. "None of the natives are really *resident* here.... the ordinary number of men more resident here than elsewhere is about 20; their wives, 28; their children 35; and occasionally this number is doubled. Sometimes only 2 or 3 men are here, and the people often make long absences."[57]

Lewis, who was still residing at the Ushuaia Mission (from 1870 to 1873), painted a devastating picture of the winter months. To keep the fire lit day and night the "wretched axeless Firelander" had to dig the dead wood out of the snow or break it off from trees with his bare hands. Most of the edible sea birds and fish had migrated to more congenial haunts. Only one hunter out of four or five succeeded in killing a guanaco. The foods available were limpets and mussels from shallow waters, which were mostly acrid and full of seed pearls, and a few scarce and taste-less fungi could only be obtained by laborious tramping through snow three feet deep. Lugging these "miserable substitutes for human food," the provider would return exhausted to his wretched wigwam and its "wretched inmates half suffocated with smoke and reeking odours from bodies besmeared with filth."[58]

The Keppel Regime Is More Relaxed

Meanwhile at Keppel (April 1873), the old and new recruits were liv-ing peaceably with the routine of prayers and "school, except at such times when they are not otherwise engaged." They were busy during the summer season shearing sheep, often working from 4 AM to 9 PM.

"Notwithstanding feeling a little tired, they enjoy the time very much," according to Lawrence. They were given extra clothing and provisions from the store during the shearing and "as we may deem necessary for them, and which we think will compensate for their labour." They were allowed a half-holiday each Saturday.[59]

Fuegia Basket Appears in Ushuaia

Bridges and others were surprised to meet the famous Fuegia Basket, now at least fifty years old. Fitz-Roy and Darwin had last seen her in Wulaia in February 1833 (Chapter 5). She arrived "yet strong and well" with a group from Lushoff, her mother's territory along the Southwest Arm of Beagle Channel. Bridges commented, "how very pleased many in England would be to hear that we had seen her...." Fuegia and her family remained in the mission area for six days. She came with her new husband, who was about eighteen years old, a native of Lushoff. Such a young husband was not exceptional, as noted above (Chapter 10). Her party was a border people – more Yahgan than Alakaluf – though she was more Alakaluf than the others. Her mother was a Yahgan, her father Alakaluf, from Atisimoon, on the outer coast. When Fitz-Roy captured her and ten other Alakalufs in February 1830, she had been camping with her family near the outer islands, on Burnt Island, her father's territory (Chapter 3). In 1842, Fuegia had greeted the crew of an English vessel in the Strait of Magellan, saying: "How do? I have been to Plymouth and London." And nine years later she and York were recognised, also in the Magellan Strait, by the governor of the Chilean settlement (Punta Arenas), who had probably seen her previously.

Now, in May 1873, Bridges found her, "as dark, spiritually, as any of her people," and "very uncommunicative." This is a strange comment, because according to Bridges himself, she conversed a great deal. She told him and the others that York Minster's real name was Asinan, and that years ago he had been killed in retaliation for the murder of a native in Lushoff. She spoke to Bridges about her daughter and son, both now adults, and other family members. She recalled a "Miss" Jenkins, with whom she had stayed in London (the wife of the school-master north of London), as well as the *Beagle* and Captain Fitz-Roy. Although her religious training had faded, she repeated several words in English, probably to please the Reverend, and was happy to meet his children. Bridges noticed that although she spoke Yahgan, her original language was "Alooculoof." He observed her in the Bay of Ushuaia. "Whilst here she was much occupied, like the other women in her canoe, fishing for mussels, and the weather was very cold, and deep snow on the ground."[60]

Okoko Is Losing Favour Again

During these years (1870 to winter of 1873), Bridges and his colleagues may have felt encouraged because they had settled in Ushuaia Bay quite successfully. However, at the same time the Yahgans were becoming increasingly affected by the disruption of their tried and proven system of living, while the missionaries could not offer them viable alternatives that would enable them to adjust or even survive under the new regime. Concerning the loyal Okoko, Bridges wrote: "George Oococoo knows most and reads best, owing to his special individual teaching during his long residence at Cranmer [Keppel], from 1859 to 1864; but Stephen [Lucca] and others have much better abilities and learn faster than he, so that he is losing his pre-eminence."[61]

Okoko was falling out of grace. By now he like the other Keppel graduates had become so acculturated, so identified with the Protestant mode, that it would have been almost impossible for them to revert to the ancestral ways. Their world was changing too rapidly and too definitively.

The Mission – A Trading Post

The Yamana were increasingly coming to trade from greater distances. Bridges referred to a man from beyond the Northwest Arm near Chair Island (Darwin Sound) and a party from Gordon Island (between the Southwest and Northwest "Arms"), who came to barter their seal or otter skins, which was a "very great incentive to the natives to resort here."[62]

Lawrence Settles in Ushuaia

The two couples who had come with Despard in 1856: the Lewis couple were assigned to Keppel, while John Lawrence, his wife Clara (and young daughter) were assigned to the Ushuaia Mission in September or October 1873 to replace the former. Very soon Lawrence noticed the baptised natives were "submissive, calm, and solemn in manner" and did not paint their faces with different sorts of clay when in mourning. The others still did so and their "yells and cries were almost inhuman." But he assured his readers that such absurd doings were "becoming obsolete." He was pleased with the behaviour and singing of the children. They were being taught English, arithmetic, and other useful lessons. Several mothers requested to be present in a class when their children were being taught.[63]

Although Stirling had decided that English was to be the lingua franca and taught to the children, the adults who had not been to Keppel had a hard time learning it. Bridges continued conversing and preaching in Yahgan while the other missionaries were learning it as best they could. The Yahgan mothers, very like mothers today in our primary schools, were concerned about the language being used and the instructions their children were receiving.

The "Evil Custom..."

Toward the end of 1873 (late spring), Bridges was worried that many natives "in our very presence have suffered often and much from want of food and fuel." They could not gather mussels because of the severe weather, and the winter fungi were very scarce. The mission assisted them with soups, vegetables and tea, but having a limited supply for themselves, they curbed "the tendency to yield to the wants of the people." Those who had turnips and goats consumed them sparingly. He was consoled by the following thought: "It is well they should sharply feel the evils of the wandering, thriftless life they lead, making no provision for the morrow, that thus they may be stirred to exert themselves in providing for the future, and to give up their present evil custom of living one upon another."

He chose to ignore that their "evil custom of living one upon another" made life possible during the severe climate. However, he may not have been aware that the missionaries themselves had created the natives' problems with their unpredictable supplies and their off-again on-again work offers and now-and-then handouts. The natives were encouraged to come to the Ushuaia Mission but told to look after themselves. Bridges disapproved of their mutual dependency.

One would think that these people were very independent, but in reality they are very dependent one upon another. They are constantly giving, and receiving, and interchanging; and few have independence enough to object to a proposal from a friend, though, after the proposal is closed with and effected, they will grumble enough to others.[64]

Bridges was bold in criticising and accusing his protégés. He was equally bold in assuming that he was endowed with a divine infallibility. Referring to this period, Lucas echoed his father's attitude. "The Yahgans lived for the day, taking no thought for the morrow, much less for something that might happen to them after they were dead."[65]

What might happen after death is a difficult subject. The Yamana forefathers had meditated for centuries on the nature of the *kashpi*, the soul or spiritual essence. A Yamana, Nelly Calderón Lawrence, even though she was Lawrence's daughter-in-law, confided in Gusinde in 1921: "The ancient Yamana, also my own father and I myself, we never believed that we all will meet again after death.... The empty talk of the missionaries is false, they want to deceive us."[66] Nelly was thinking, I will guess, of the usual biblical vision of paradise or hell after death, not of the *kashpi*. According to my reading and conversations with the last knowledgeable Yahgans, the *kashpi* did exist eternally, though it did not "live" eternally.

1874: Lawrence Is Alarmed

Early the following year (1874), Lawrence became aware of the real hunger and poverty of the people surrounding him. Most were clothed "as our means will allow," but the others only had a skin to cover their shoulders. Desperate for food, they would try to sell back to the missionaries things they had previously received from them. As they noticed and observed the supplies of food and goods arriving from Port Stanley, destined for the missionaries, they felt all the more deprived and could not comprehend why they were so poorly recompensed for their work, besides being constantly reprimanded for their idle, sinful ways.[67] The missionaries sensed the potential danger of this situation and attempted to thwart any aggression it might provoke by distributing food and clothing on certain occasions.[68] Yet in fact there was no sign, since the massacre of 1859, that the Yahgan or the Selk'nam (the Oens-men) ever contemplated attacking them, much less expelling them from their land. However, individuals did bitterly complain and even insult them. For example, in early February 1874, six canoes arrived with a man by the name of Lasaprlum who brought two sticks of firewood to sell to Bridges and a canoe to sell to Lawrence. Bridges politely refused the sticks, explaining that he already had a large supply of the same. Lasaprlum became "very angry, and abused me, and said I was like one of his countrymen, and not like a Palelmwa, i.e., Englishman. He accused me of being proud, and making myself very important, and a great many other things."

Lasaprlum had no better luck trying to sell his canoe to Lawrence. Bridges remarked: "He went away very angry, having behaved to Mr Lawrence worse than to me." A few weeks later there were over 130 natives in Ushuaia, "all daily eating considerable quantities of turnips." Bridges remarked that they had been variously and busily employed.[69] They were employed, but could they survive on turnips?

By mid-March 1874, the end of summer, the ground was covered with snow. Bridges distributed bread to the natives who had not received food for their work. One morning, at 7:30 AM, he and the other missionaries noticed a man up to his waist in the water trying to kill a penguin, and several women and children picking up "miserable remnants of mussels" as they waded through mud and water in the wind and driving snow. He reasoned that they seldom even had a supply of firewood, mainly because of their dishonesty and their begging and "distributing" habits. Despite these accusations, he pitied them, wishing that "regular work and food could be obtained for all."[70]

Bridges had no patience with polygamous men. He severely reprimanded John (Sisoi), one of the Keppel four, who had been to England with Stirling and by now had become Bridges' preferred linguistic informant. He was scolded for having an extra wife and deprived of his employment for two weeks "for example's sake."[71] But the example didn't "take," as noted further on.

"Why Don't They Steal More?"

What a strange question. On 23 April 1874, a fine day, Bridges reproved several natives for stealing turnips, but he was grateful that they respected the missionaries' possessions and thought it strange that they did not steal more than they did. "We often times wonder that with so little power to repress or punish, we are so little troubled by the audacity, stealing, or vice of the people. We realise in our happy, peaceful, circumstances the good hand of our God."

He thanked God, not the Yahgans. Sisoi assured Bridges that there was less quarrelling and fighting than previously, that they no longer gave free rein to their passions. Bridges assured his readers that even the *yekamush* were ashamed to carry on their "very ridiculous practices."[72] Less stealing and quarrelling, less free rein to passions and more ashamed shamans were all indices of submission, and that "civilisation" was taking a firmer hold.

Whales Again to the Rescue

Fortunately a bonanza appeared during the last week of April and there was no more need for turnips. Gusinde reported that almost every man and woman along Beagle Channel had gone to finish off the whale in the vicinity of "Age," probably Agaia-waia, a place along the coast of Ponsonby Sound about forty miles (74 kilometres) from Ushuaia.[73]

Bridges had reported on the event. A few days after so many natives had left, more than ten canoes returned to Ushuaia Bay, each carrying, "a share of the poor whale, which literally was killed by inches, having received into its body somewhere about a hundred spears." The whale, a young female about eighteen feet (5.48 metres) long, had been wounded two days before (perhaps by an orca). Hardly had they recovered from their stomach aches, from overindulging, when a week later three more whales were beached in the same locality. These had been wounded or even killed by swordfish and "whale beaters" (orcas). Then yet another whale was reported. Thus five whales were butchered during these few weeks. Everyone in Ushuaia Bay, except the missionaries, reeked of whale oil; even their hair was plastered with it. In mid-May, the canoes were still returning, laden with their whale booty. Again many complaints of stomach aches were heard.

The vital importance of whales as food is highlighted here. The over-eating may be a symptom of the anxiety that hunger produces. The disruption of the Yankee maritime commerce caused by Civil War in the United States, as well as the loss of the market for whale oil beginning in the 1860s, had severely affected the industry (Chapter 2). By this time, in the 1870s, whales were again seen along shores of Tierra del Fuego.

Winter – Hunger

A few months later (1874) Bridges was having trouble with the natives thrusting themselves into his yard, hoping to get some food. "I had to use much firmness in clearing the yard again and again. "Two days later the beggars, the unemployed, let him know that he was being too stingy with clothes and food. He acknowledged that "This feeling on their part is very wrong, yet very natural. Seeing large supplies come [on the *Allen Gardiner*], the desire for possession is strong." It was not so much "the desire for possession" as the desire to eat.

The missionaries and their families consumed most of the supplies from Port Stanley, so there was little left over for their hungry proselytes. Bridges gave notice that during this winter he would require very few workers, but that with the return of working weather he would employ more.[74]

The Death of Jack

Lewis mentioned the recent death in Keppel of Ucatella (not identified) and of Jack, who was probably about twenty-two. The only comment I found was that his death made a deep impression on the minds of "our

Indian brethren."[75] Jack had been Stirling's favourite since 1864, when he asked Stirling to be his father. He was the youngest of the four "lads" Stirling took to England (1865–67) and the very first to accompany him as his "housekeeper" when Stirling founded the mission station in Ushuaia Bay in 1869 (Chapter 10). It is strange that no more comment was made about his death in the article cited. Stirling may have done so elsewhere.

1875: Bridges Views Their Mode of Living

Bridges wrote a sort of ethnography of the Yahgans in April 1875, almost twenty years after he came to Keppel. He wrote less vehemently on the subject later.[76] His view of their culture at that time throws more light on his attitude and behaviour toward a people with whom he was spending his life in order to rescue them from heathenism, sin and eternal damnation. The text is too long, seven pages of small print, to be paraphrased; only nine of its key concepts are partially quoted here:

1. Parents universally take no pains in the education of their children . . . save it may be a little instruction.
2. The native never punishes his child because he has *done wrong*, but because he has troubled him.
3. In fact, in all the duties of life the heathen . . . is so selfish, so immoral, so unreasonable, so foolish, as to forfeit each other's regard, the affection of their children, and the confidence of all men.
4. Fear is the powerful agent, fear of man, fear of death. . . . Society . . . each clan [supports] its member, guilty or not guilty.
5. The wandering habits of the natives result in making them servile to each other.
6. Their dwellings . . . no seclusion, no exclusion; natives in and out of each others' dwelling all day long, squatting close up to each other, women with their arms round each other, and so walking about, and the men, too. . . . This horrible looseness prevails through everything.
7. A general absence of confidence, faithfulness, and love is everywhere apparent. There is a great show of friendship, but little sincerity.
8. When they sell skins or other things to us, they aim to do so unknown to their fellows, in order to keep what they receive to themselves.
9. So given are the people to exaggeration and lying. . . . Each side invariably clears itself and condemns the other.

. . . *I think I have now said enough against the people*; is there nothing I can say for them? Yes, much. Compared to what they were, the change is great, and influences beneficially in a thousand ways – in what it does, in what it prevents.[77]

What can explain or elucidate this vision of the Yahgans as a people? Feeling such contempt for them, why did he spend eleven more years, until he retired in 1886, trying to evangelise them? His response is in the last sentence quoted above; they were redeemable. Perhaps he had in mind a passage from the gospel according to Luke, which he translated into Yahgan, verse 5.27: When Jesus' disciples asked him "Why do you eat and drink with tax collectors and sinners?" Jesus replied: "Those who are well have no need of a physician, but those who are sick; I have not come to call the righteous, but sinners to repentance."

"The greater the sins of the sinners, the greater the merit of the redeemer" may explain Bridges' acrid vision of the Yahgan as a people and his determination to pursue his mission.

Encounters with the Haush

Bridges, like Darwin, was not a racist, however severely he reprimanded the Yahgans and scorned their culture. For example, he was not severe with the Haush, whom he called Onas or Eastern Onas. He first met them in late September 1875, when the *Allen Gardiner* was detained for nine days in Good Success Bay during a trip to Ushuaia. They hailed the crew so vigorously from the shore of the bay that Bridges and others went to meet them: twenty-two (twelve adults) Haush, even poorer than the Yahgans, clad in old, worn guanaco and fox skins, and unarmed. Two women spoke only Yamana. The men were anxious to trade their "beautifully made" flint and glass-pointed arrows but not their quivers. Bridges preached to them in Yahgan (the two women and probably some of the others understood) and remarked: "They lead a very hard life . . . and they need a friendly hand and Christian teachers to help them out of their low estate." He was so impressed with them that he wrote: "Our own people are far more suspicious than the poor races who we disdainfully and wrongfully call 'savages.'" Perhaps he wondered if he should have evangelised the Haush instead of the Yamana.

An Orphanage – A Necessity

That same year, in early October (1875), Bridges returned to the mission, having been absent for two months (probably in Punta Arenas for medical treatment). Then he was informed that only seven or eight natives had been regularly employed among the 200 who had come to the mission at different times. Lawrence told him that many were sick, most were hungry and that two children had died. "The natives, much driven by hunger, were very importunate in coming to him [Bridges] in order to get something to eat." Of the seven or eight employed, three were men, while four or five were women making shirts. This is the first mention of factory-like labour in Ushuaia. These women were envied by the others "and certainly were much better off." Some of the unemployed were

busy repairing their miserable canoes, preparatory to departing on the morrow.... As usual, they were full of woeful accounts of their hungry state, and of the difficulties of getting food; how they had awaited my return; how they had continued to attend the meetings in the school room, and so on. Then they asked me for something to eat, *they were hungry and weak*.

Bridges explained that he could not feed everybody, that he was very sorry. Upon leaving he gave bread to two women, one old and the other in bad health, in exchange for a basket. He visited Mecuygaz, who was an invalid and very weak, though glad to speak to him. The natives who accompanied him there troubled Bridges by their begging "and made civility a cover for their covetousness." Two years later, Bridges reported that Mecuygaz had died of his long illness but had "received many kindnesses from his people, many of whom have given fuel, and gifts of food which they could ill afford to give."[78]

The missionaries were having great difficulty dealing with the dependence of the Yahgan on them, which they had not anticipated but, however unintentionally, had created. Bad times certainly were not unknown before the missionaries took over, but then the people knew what to do, where to look to assuage their hunger, even though some may have died during severe scarcities. But now they had nowhere to turn.

That winter and early spring of 1875, hunger was taking on proportions of starvation. Sickness was increasingly reported, though not yet as an epidemic. The number of parentless or abandoned children was mostly the result of the high mortality and of the disintegration of their kinship and mutual aid systems.

By 1875 an orphanage was being completed, in charge of Robert Whaits, a carpenter, wheelwright and blacksmith and who had come to the Ushuaia Mission from Keppel with Bridges. His wife and young daughter arrived later.

Tushcapalan, Almost a Village

The main road ran up a hill from the shore to the summit and was dominated by the Stirling House, the home of the Bridges, with flowers and fruit bushes in front and a kitchen garden at the rear. On the right-hand side of the road were houses of corrugated iron lined with wood. The first was the home of the Lawrence family, farther up the road was the Stirling House. Just beyond it the structure of the orphanage was being built, and behind it a carpenter's shop with a forge. Behind the forge was a smaller house that served as a church, schoolroom and meeting place. Last in line were the cowshed and its yard, a woodshed and outhouses.

The kitchen garden of the Stirling House was planted with swedes (turnips), other vegetables and in some years potatoes, which did not flourish. The Bridges' great standby was rhubarb, "which did very well indeed." Strawberries, currants, gooseberries and raspberries also grew quite well.

On the other side of the road stood a row of huts and three model cottages, also of corrugated iron, owned or rented by the "most civilised" Yahgans, who had constructed them under the direction of a missionary. Each of the latter had a little fenced vegetable garden, and the front doors were flanked with beds of flowers.

The "slums of Ushuaia" (Lucas Bridges' expression), were located on the far side of the bay, in the forest, completely separate from the mission compound. Here the native Ushuaians camped in their wigwams with their heaps of refuse of shells, bones and other garbage, which in time formed a protecting rim around the "humble dwelling." The present city of Ushuaia, with its 60,000 or more inhabitants, is located in that slum section of the bay. Lucas commented, with a nod to future archaeologists: "Along the Fuegian coast in centuries to come the site of many a simple prehistoric village will still be as clear as Stonehenge, for there will remain ring after ring of shell and bone . . . to show where generation after generation of Yahgans once had their homes."[79] It is too late now; the Yahgan Stonehenge is no more. The new Fuegian urbanites (mainly Argentines and Chileans) have used the rings of shell and bone to fertilise their gardens.

1876: On the Way to Punta Arenas

Passing beyond Brecknock Peninsula in March (1876), on its way to Punta Arenas, several canoes reached the *Allen Gardiner*. Bridges was delighted to find the natives (probably Alakaluf) so friendly. He thought they might be hostile because he had been told of "a recent collision with an American schooner," probably a sealing ship, during which natives had been killed. These natives may not have known about the murders; in any event they were not resentful. They were anxious to sell their sealskins for money, presumably Chilean currency.[80]

Bridges remained alone in Punta Arenas now for some six months, from March or early April until late September 1876, probably again for medical treatment.

Tea Parties

Meanwhile in the Ushuaia Mission (mid-1876) Mrs Bridges invited the children to a tea party in celebration of her wedding anniversary, 7 August. "The poor little things looked very cold and hungry." Ten days later the Lawrences gave another treat to "all who were lawfully married, the seven couples married the year before." First Lawrence reminded them of their duties, and then Okoko preached: that his countrymen were so poor, so foolish and so unthankful, like dogs, compared to the missionaries, because the latter loved the Saviour. Okoko also spoke of the plentiful supply of good food the missionaries had, but that they were not able to create food, as the Saviour had done in creating the five loaves. "Jesus was able to supply all their wants."[81] His last sentence reads like a veiled appeal to the missionaries to act like Jesus.

When Bridges returned to Ushuaia, in early October 1876, he noticed much sickness, as he had the year before. "The chief symptoms were first sharp pains in the stomach, followed by blotches, which quickly suppurated, and formed scabs similar to smallpox. It attacked its victims in rapid succession, so that twenty-five were sick at one time, and in real need of the assistance of the Society."[82] There was no doctor in Ushuaia Mission to diagnose the sickness, but it was very probably a sign of an epidemic disease.

This Christmas, 1876, attracted 246 natives, including forty-two babies, for the distribution of clothing. As word spread, the number of natives who gathered for the Christmas presents increased year by year.

A Wreck Off Hoste Island

Early in January 1876, the *San Rafael*, from Liverpool bound for Valparaíso, caught fire and was abandoned near Cape Horn. The crew escaped in two boats and lost contact with each other. About a month later, those in one boat were rescued in the Pacific by a New Zealand vessel. The other boat landed at the extremity of Hoste Island, Rous Peninsula.[83]

In mid-April, a convoy of Yamanas in canoes brought the news to the Ushuaia Mission: ten castaways had died of starvation. They were wearing clothes of the dead and offering English sovereigns for sale. Cushooyif, the leader of the convoy, told the story: he and his wife had first seen signs of survivors, months before, but were afraid to land because of the surf, so they left in search of help. Later Cushooyif returned with other men and found two of the crew still alive, though so weak that they were unable to walk. "One still retained his senses." They tried to carry him to their canoe. He drank a few sips of water and tasted the cooked cormorant they offered him but was too weak to eat or even to be moved. He beckoned them to take what they chose. The other was nearly dead by then. The natives left, as they could do no more for the men and were in danger of being stranded there because they could not haul their canoe ashore on the steep rugged coast. The wretched weather prevented their return for several days, and when they did come back, both men were dead. They took some of the clothes strewn on the shore but did not touch the ten corpses.[84]

When the news was heard in Ushuaia, Captain Willis, two seamen and four Yahgans left on the *Allen Gardiner* and located the site two miles (some 4 kilometres) beyond Black Cape (Punta Negra), the very dangerous pass at the southwestern extremity of Hoste Island that Fitz-Roy had warned navigators against in 1830 (Chapter 3). Captain Willis was amazed that the castaways could have landed on such an exposed coast. He found a letter written by the captain, James McAdam, forty-one days after they had been on that "desolate island," when he knew that he and his wife would not survive. It was addressed to his stepson and was published by Lucas Bridges.

The bodies lay in an orderly fashion, well clothed, near piles of other clothes spread out along the shore. Willis explained that the Yahgans who had tried to save these people had never been to the Ushuaia Mission "but were able to tell us they saw the dying man pray," and they repeated his last words: "Lord Jesus Christ." He noted that though these natives were "covetous," they had been "kind and affectionate."

Moreover:

They did not take anything off the corpses . . . tears fell from their eyes, while their hearts bled for the woes which befell the white men. . . . During the past month many thoughts have arisen in my mind. Might not these nine [ten] sufferers [of the *San Rafael*] have saved their lives had they no fear of the Indians, who are reported to be warlike, and even cannibals, and which is decidedly false.[85]

Captain Willis was aware that the affectionate behaviour on the part of the Fuegians toward the two dying castaways contradicted the often-repeated warnings to seamen about the dangers of encountering Indians who had not been to the mission. Willis was sympathetic to them, as he will be to the victims of the sealers and later to Bridges (Chapter 13).

The following year Bridges received twenty pounds' worth of new clothing from the Board of Trade in London, sent "through the generosity of

Her Majesty's Government," to distribute among the Indians who had brought news of the *San Rafael* disaster "and behaved with humanity toward the distressed seamen."[86]

Soon afterwards, thirty canoes arrived at the Ushuaia Mission to receive Her Majesty's gift of clothing. About 310 men and women assembled in front of Bridges' house. Despite the crowd, he discovered that "some who were entitled to a share had not come" because they were afraid to pass certain islands where unfriendly countrymen lived.[87] One-third of the case of clothing was put aside for those who had been afraid to come. There is certainly more to this story than I have noted here. For instance: Why did so many Yahgans claim the reward, and even more were afraid to come for the reward when only very few actually assisted the two dying survivors? I can guess that they were all kin and friends of those few, but I do not know. More information may be available.

News of the Button Family
The first the bad news: Anthony Button, the baby that won the hearts of Despard and Turpin in Keppel in 1858, died in his early youth, "not joyfully in Christ, but in tranquil peace, free from fear." That same year, 1876, there was good news: one of Jemmy's daughters appeared at the mission with her beautiful four-month-old twins. Bridges reported that she "was very pleased with a little food, and some articles of clothing for her babies given her by my wife."[88] This is the last mention found of her and her twins.

Querentze, the oldest son, had died two years before. His sons were eight and ten years old at the time. The elder, named Willie Beckenham after his sponsor in England, had "a very interesting intelligent face." The other, James Fitz-Roy Button, was sponsored by Mrs Fitz-Roy and officers of H.M.S. *Beagle*. And the Button saga continues. Apparently Thomas Bridges had an abiding interest in this family despite the contempt he had expressed for Jemmy (end of Chapter 9).

1877: Nature Comes to the Rescue Again

That summer (1877) dense masses of sprats (a tiny fish, species of herring) appeared along the shore near the mission, creating a great stench and even greater "excitement among the natives." Swarms of mackerel, flocks of birds, herds of seals and many other marine fauna rushed to prey on the tiny fish (as already noted in Chapter 2). For the previous five months there had also been an unusual abundance of winter fungi, the great stand-by. Bridges was probably relieved. "The health of the people is now good, but at the best they are wanting in vigour and soundness."

Climate and Sickness

During the unusually mild winter of 1877, the men were busy hunting guanacos and the supply of fungi and fish was bountiful, so the health of the natives improved. Yahgans from the west (toward the Northwest Arm) sold Lawrence over 180 sealskins, which he resold in Port Stanley. In September and October the weather changed "owing to the trying winds, [which] prevented them from obtaining fish." The Ushuaia Bay was so rough and the temperature so cold that thousands of birds died. That same month, October, eighty-five natives were baptised (the record so far), but again "much sickness . . . chiefly resulting from want." In November six people drowned who were spearing sea-gulls by torchlight in Ponsonby Sound when a heavy southwest gale overturned their canoe.[89]

Ascendancy over the Yamana

During these months Stirling docked in Port Stanley and went directly on to the Keppel Mission, where he was pleased to see Lewis and meet the sixteen pupils, some of whom had been there several years. They were "most friendly." At that time, December 1877, he made the seminal declaration that the mission's ascendancy over the Yahgan tribe was "morally complete."

1878: Search for the Oens-Men

Encouraged by such success, Stirling proposed (in 1878) to contact "other tribes not so friendly, and not so docile, I fear, owing to their having been exposed for generations to the attacks of foreigners."[90] This is an obvious reference to the Selk'nam. By then, Europeans in Punta Arenas had begun negotiating with the Chilean government to acquire enormous tracts of land on Isla Grande, Selk'nam territory. These were the best pastures for sheep in the entire area south of the Magellan Strait, which would soon, in 1881, fall under the sovereignty of Chile and Argentina (Chapter 12). In 1878, Bridges and Stirling made an excursion on horseback into the area, hoping to contact the natives there. They sighted herds of guanacos, a great variety of birds, smoke from encampments and dogs, but no natives, who undoubtedly were hiding.[91] Stirling and Bridges never encountered the Oens-men, but Lucas did, and for years off and on, from about 1900 until the 1940s.

Heathens Are Drawn to Ushuaia

Bridges reported in March 1878 that the number of "heathens" visiting the mission from other islands varied from 170 to ten or twelve. On Christmas Day 1878, more than 340 natives came from all around for the yearly clothing distribution, sent from Valparaíso as well as England. One man took his bundle of clothes in such a discontented manner, because he expected to receive more, that Bridges called to him and took back his bundle. Many women were turned away empty-handed. They were not happy either and said they would not come for the distribution of bread the next day. However, nearly all showed up.

Later Bridges informed his readers that eleven natives owned a total of forty-nine to fifty head of cattle. Then he appealed for support of the mission by gifts and prayers. Employment was a favour: it could be denied as a punishment for sins of various sorts, especially polygamy. "Also, if persons employed are insolent or dissatisfied, as they often are, as a punishment, employment is withdrawn."

About this time Bridges made the strange observation that while some of the heathen who came to the Ushuaia Mission from the south and east, the Cape Horn area, were "miserable specimens of humanity, being unnaturally dwarfish," and lost flesh as they aged, they kept in good health; others, on the contrary, who kept "full flesh" and were still strong and quite young, suddenly passed away. This apparent abnormality is probably a sign that infectious diseases were spreading, but not to the Cape Horn area. Bad colds affected the natives much more than the missionaries and often "engendered the seeds of consumption, so prevalent among the people."[92]

The Circle around Ushuaia Is Closing

During his many outings in late April and May 1878, Bridges, with five Yahgan friends, went to Lennox Cove to rescue the survivors of a wreck who were said to be nearby in two boats. But when they arrived, the castaways had already left. They had probably made their way to the Falklands. During this outing, Bridges and his Yahgan "pals" (my term) stopped over on Picton Island, where they met a few Lennox natives who were visiting there because a whale had been recently stranded. They were carrying immense quantities of whale meat and offered chucks of it to their countrymen in Bridges' boat. Bridges spoke to them of God and invited them to come to his Ushuaia Mission. They told him that their Gable Island neighbours "dissuaded and kept them back" from going to the mission, because they were trying "to keep the eastern [the Ushuaia Mission] trade in skins to themselves." Bridges remarked that "The natives of Gordon Island acted much in the same manner toward the western natives."[93]

The Gable and Gordon natives were encircling Ushuaia, trying to prevent other Yahgans from flooding the Ushuaia skin-market, in order to maintain the higher prices for their own sealskins and monopolise the mission trade in skins.

Bridges' Passion for Boating

Bridges' passion for sailing and rowing was such that almost any pretext sufficed for him to set out on the water, accompanied by a few Yahgan friends or workers and often by one or more of his three sons. Lucas wrote that "he was never happier than when steering a sailing-boat. . . . At such times, with his hand on the tiller, he would start singing for sheer joy." However, Lucas added, he was known to be reckless "and even the Yahgan crew sometimes refused to go out with him."

During these years the mission magazine offers many accounts of Bridges' outings. He felt exhilarated to confront the dangers of the weather, to admire the beauties of nature and scout for castaways as well as to recruit young men to go to Keppel. He would greet and preach to the Yahgans along the way and admonish them not to plunder wrecked ships or rob the survivors. He usually remarked that the natives along the way were "very friendly," pleased to see him and his companions, offering them shelter for the night, food and advice on the best routes to take on the morrow. Once he stopped over very near Cape Horn on Deceit Island, where the Yahgans told him that vessels, probably sealers, occasionally visited these islands. Bridges concluded: "We found them very poor; they had no axe, bucket or clothes, but had good mantles of otter skins, and were all well to do and vigorous looking."[94] Again, they were poor in the eyes of the beholder. Not subjected to the mission, they were able to adjust to the lack of seals.

Hunting Cormorants

As Bridges sailed by high cliffs where shags (cormorants) nested, he undoubtedly was told where Yamana had fallen and been killed or severely injured. The four species of cormorants in Tierra del Fuego were highly valued because of their "good weight of flesh." The *Phalacrocorax magellanicus*, called the rock cormorant, makes permanent nests in cliffs. "No place is so exposed to wind and weather but those hardy birds find there a place of rest and safety."

The hunter of these cormorants chose a dark and windy night, counting on the darkness and the roar of the wind to drown the noise he made while approaching their nests. He was quietly paddled up to the base of a cliff. Then he climbed the cliff, holding a torch of dry bark and a stick, and struck a bird with the stick, seized it with both hands and killed it as quietly as possible by biting its head or twisting its long neck. If another bird was aroused, the others would hear him and scatter out of their nests, though the glare of the torch would usually stupefy those close by.

If a cliff where the cormorants were nesting could be reached only from above, the task was more hazardous. Then the hunter descended the cliff, bracing himself as best he could and tied to a long thong, the extremities of which his companion on the top of the cliff held tightly. Once the hunter had killed a bird, he tied it to the thong dangling from his waist. When he had killed several, he signalled to his companion by pulling on the thong; they would then haul up the dead birds. Many accidents occurred: the sharp rocks could cut the thong, or the hunter might slip or lose his balance while climbing or killing. If so, he would plunge into the sea below, drown or be badly hurt. If his wife or helpers were in a canoe below, they would pull him out of the water. If a gale obliged them to leave, often they would be unable to return for days. If the hunter had no helpers below, even if he was not badly hurt, he might drown, as most of the men could not swim. Bridges heard of many distressing cases "when the men have had to drink shag's blood, and to eat them raw," and nearly perished from the cold.

Other birds were more easily killed: the hunter hid in a little bower near the nest of loggerhead ducks, imitated their cry and simply seized them. Sea birds were also caught in their nests, at night with the aid of torchlight.[95]

Sealers Kill Some Yamana

Then an event occurred (early October 1878), which would stir up arguments for years to come as to how many Yahgans were killed and who had provoked the sealers. A schooner named *Rescue* met a group of natives in Gretton Bay, off the largest Wollaston Island, who went on board and were killed by the sealers.[96] Soon after the event, Bridges, who had probably heard the captain's version of the story, went to the scene of the "fatal collision ... to hear what the natives had to say."[97] Arriving in Gretton Bay and seeing no one there, he and his men sailed on to nearby Herschel Island, where he met a group of natives he had never seen. "They occasionally visit Horn Island, and live chiefly on seals and birds." (This is another notice of Yamana on Horn Island.)[98] When Bridges returned to Gretton Bay, he sighted the Yahgan survivors of the *Rescue* "quietly gathering shellfish" at low tide. Bridges sat down nearby and "spoke to them of the wickedness and folly of such conduct, and showed them how, if they did not give up their wicked ways, they would soon all be destroyed." That same day a canoe approached the side of his boat "containing a handsome Indian ... and his wife, equal in form and stature to himself." He was impressed by their good looks, but when they asked for food, he was not pleased. He told them that he was not sent to "fill their stomachs or cover their backs, but to teach them how to please their Maker, and how to obtain His favour and blessing. They were offended." They paddled away and certainly had learned a lesson: avoid the missionaries.

Then Bridges preached to the survivors and kin of those killed by the *Rescue* crew about the love of God, offered prayers and told his readers that the survivors "were all freshly bedecked with paints indicative of the death by violence of their near relatives." He accused them of having "brought the trouble upon themselves by their wicked attempt upon the vessel." They assured him that they would not seek revenge.[99]

His attitude contrasts with that of Captain Martial, commander of the French ship *Romanche* (Chapter 13). Shortly before Christmas 1882, Martial stopped over in Gretton Bay. Two natives came on board and told him about the attack (Martial's guide translated from Yahgan to English); that the dispute was caused by the abduction of some of the Yahgan women and that sealers of the *Rescue* "had assassinated some fifteen of these unhappy natives who were objecting to the abduction."[100]

After relating the story to Martial, they became gay and confident, playing games and imitating the movements of the crew. But they had not forgotten the massacre. Seven years later, in 1889, the captain and crew of the *Rescue* returned to Gretton Bay and were immediately recognised as those who had killed their people. The missionary, Mr Burleigh, who was on the *Rescue*, had great difficulty calming them.[101]

Bridges Is Optimistic

Bridges was still convinced that agricultural pursuits, fishing and "a heartfelt appreciation of the goodness of God" were all that was needed to ensure the happiest life for these people.[102] He must have known by 1878, having spent eight years at the Ushuaia Mission, that it was virtually impossible for the Yahgans or anyone to develop agriculture because of the severe climate, the brief growing season and the inadequate soils. Only garden vegetables could be depended upon. Shipton's remarks are again relevant. "They [the missionaries] judged all conditions of life by their own standards...they were blithely unaware of the dangers of interfering with aboriginal tribes...to adopt alien customs and techniques...but there is little evidence that our present-day idealists are endowed with more wisdom and humility."[103]

A Young British Couple Arrive at Keppel

Leonard and Nelly Burleigh came to Keppel in 1878, apparently as volunteer lay clergy and Leonard as a teacher. I did not, however, find much information concerning their ten years at Keppel. Leonard wrote about the sickness there and sympathetic notes concerning eleven boys in his care, including one from Cape Horn, whose name was Asclenderlium, baptised Paul Gilbert.[104] The Burleighs will reappear dramatically in Chapter 14.

1879: Bridges Admires Their Language

At this time (1879), Bridges calculated that his dictionary would comprise at least 18,000 words. He wondered "how so depraved and miserable a people kept up their language, which is so comprehensive and regular." Despite his many expressions of this sort, in 1879 he wrote an amazing tribute to the Yahgans, describing their active social life, as can be appreciated in the following extraordinary text:

This [their language] can only be accounted for by their living in public and not shut off in family seclusion. Thus they always moved about in company, and four or more families would crowd into a single wigwam. The children heard every subject spoken of, came into contact with hundred of persons, and were living constantly hearing the lively discourse of many persons. Thus these poor people knew intimately more persons than most people do who live in civilised communities, and heard and took a share in much more conversation than is common with a reading and fully occupied society.

A few pages later he overwhelms the reader again with his enthusiasm for their rich language. "The structure of Yahgan is unique, and wonderfully erected, *and is alone proof of the divine origin* of these poor remnants of humanity who have preserved it."[105]

Although Bridges resisted giving credit to the Yamana for almost anything, even their language, he did acknowledge his informants' patience. He asked them to pronounce the same words "so frequently, that they have called me deaf."[106]

Sisoi, the Favourite Linguistic Informant

In 1870 Bridges had praised John Marsh (Sisoi) for his "good mental power, a good clear voice for singing and speaking a very accurate English." Three years later he repeated that Sisoi had "a good voice for singing and pronouncing."[107] Sisoi was still working on the dictionary in 1878, when he took "to himself a second wife." Bridges promptly discontinued his service. But "there is no one so able as he to satisfy me as regards the meaning and construction of words and sentences," so he directed "the girl" to leave Sisoi promptly. She obeyed and the dictionary got off to another start.[108] So did Sisoi later.

Bridges' dependence on Sisoi became more evident when he, with some members of his family, went to Punta Arenas for six weeks. He took Sisoi along and continued working on the dictionary between visits to the doctor, for himself and for Sisoi. This visit will be repeated later on (Chapter 13).

In 1881, Bridges was pleased to receive from Port Stanley the first publication, 500 books, of his translation of Saint Luke's gospel into Yahgan, as he called Yamana. The literate Yahgans were very interested to read their language in print for the first time. He decided to sell it to them "rather than lessen their sense of their value by giving [the books] away, or selling them at a lower price." He sold twenty-two advance copies to them at one shilling each.[109]

His monumental dictionary, which finally contained 32,432 words, first published in 1933 and reprinted in 1987, will remain for all time a gift of Bridges and his informants to humanity. Unfortunately the language has not been studied since then by a trained linguist. A really profound knowledge of the language is required to analyse and clarify Bridges' dictionary.

Bridges' Dreaming

By early August 1879, the winter in Ushuaia, though not severe, "was long and very trying. The people have manfully bestirred themselves in hunting guanaco, but with very poor success." He and the other missionaries hired "much labour out of sheer pity in getting firewood sawed up, though we all had a good supply." Despite the hardships, Bridges remained convinced that the natives in or around the Ushuaia Mission were "in a most contented and hopeful state," desirous of living as Christians in peace.

The mission orphanage was inaugurated on 22 March 1879 by the Whaits couple, who complained that the sixteen orphans in their charge were deceitful and naughty.[110]

1879–1881: The Bridges Family Visit England

Having seen Dr Fenton several times in Punta Arenas, Bridges was advised to go to England to be examined for possible cancer of the stomach. Soon afterward he returned to Ushuaia and the entire Bridges family, the five children and aunt Yekadahby, set out for old England (late 1879). Upon arrival, they visited Harberton, where Mrs Bridges must have been thrilled to be reunited with her family, whom she hadn't seen for nine years. Bridges, despite his illness, travelled about lecturing. A year and a half later, on the eve of their departure in March 1881, he pronounced a farewell speech to members of the South American Missionary Society, among whom were the loyal Despard and potential donors. Optimism reigned. After stating that there were 180 baptised natives, including children, and thirty-six "communicants," he asserted: "The presence of the Mission had decreased the death-rate, and *there was not the least probability of the race dying out.*"[111]

In 1880 Bridges appealed to his audience and readers on four long pages. He repeated his original figure for the Yahgan population of about 3,000. Apparently he forgot that he had estimated that some 500 had died from the 1863–64 epidemic.

He stressed the need for funds to build a church with a capacity for 500 people and a school for 200 pupils. He stated:

There are seldom less than 150 Indians there and often over 300. In the course of a year from 1,000 to 1,500 persons visit the settlement, coming for all kinds of purposes – to barter skins, purchase tools or clothing, grind axes and spades, &c. and carry away seeds and plants for their own cultivation; and with these also, we trust, some of the good "seed of the Word"....

Civilisation was taking over Christianity. The "double-C strategy" was applied now in terms of investments besides funds for the mission He appealed to his audience to invest on both shores of Beagle Channel where there was "much available land for pasturage and tillage, good arbours, plenty of wood, fair fishing grounds." Ushuaia was "a very favourable spot for the development of our Christian and civilising work, and well deserves to be more developed for the wants of these too long neglected but deserving people."[112]

Nearing Home, a Surprising Encounter

While Bridges and his family were returning from England in March 1881, sailing beyond Brecknock Peninsula in Alakaluf territory, a man in a canoe, Lahwahr, approached the ship and told Bridges that he had been shot in the head twice by a sealer a few years before. Bridges examined his scars and commented that the attack was "utterly reasonless and wicked on the part of the whites." When he urged these canoe people to live in peace and virtue, "Lahwahr told me that I should teach my own people first to behave themselves properly."[113] Bridges must have been startled by this comment. He was not accustomed to being challenged by a Fuegian.

Meanwhile the Sealers

The Bridges had been absent during twenty-one months, from September 1879 to May 1881. Lawrence reported that in February 1880, many sealing vessels had come into Ushuaia Bay and that a crew of sealers had wounded two natives deliberately. He and Captain Willis were not able to identify the sealers or their boat. That winter, a Yahgan who had been wounded by another crew of sealers appeared at the mission. The victim seemed like "a very quiet, harmless, poor fellow." Others were also being shot at by sealers. Willis became alarmed and wanted the owners of such vessels to be held responsible for shooting the natives.[114] However, some of the captains of sealing ships employed the Yahgans because of their knowledge of the prey and of the location of rockeries, and treated them fairly, as for instance Captain Lynch, a North American, and two other captains (not named).[115]

By 1879 to 1880 many Yahgans were arriving from other localities eager to see "new things," to trade their seal and otter skins and beg for "a little biscuit." If Lawrence refused to comply, "they say I do not love them, seeing we have plenty compared to their poverty."[116] He was troubled by not being able to share more of his own supplies with those in need.

12

1881 to 1882: First Signs of Epidemics; Alakaluf Kidnapped to Europe; Last News of Fuegia Basket

Bridges' Return

Welcome Home

After a year and nine month absences, Bridges and family arrived in Tushcapalan on 15 May 1881. Lawrence, Whaits and "a considerable party of natives" were there to greet them. Bridges was delighted and felt that the tenor of their salutations was "We have missed you very much; have long desired your return, and are very glad you have now come back." A bit later he was still elated. "Surely we have here a happy home, and we were surprised to find all things and the buildings so well kept."

Soon he noted that the natives who carried their luggage from the shore were "much in want of food [and] are very desirous of a job."[1] This was the first sign that all was not so well.

The next day he visited the orphanage, which "now shelters twenty-five happy inmates," from five to sixteen years old. Whaits, who was still in charge of the home, did not seem to agree that they were "happy," because he complained that he and his wife, "had many difficulties to contend with their unruly and strong-passioned charges."[2]

Bridges appealed to his readers again to adopt orphans by sending funds, promising to write to each who did. Then he observed that none of the natives' gardens produced anything worth mentioning because "they are too ready to attribute their ill success to the bad weather, little suspecting that half of it is owing to their idleness... it is folly to help those who won't help themselves."

Even though his health may have deteriorated, he was his old self again, scolding the natives even more forcefully: "I show them plainly what the inevitable consequence must be to them if they continue idle, thriftless, lawless, and immoral livers and wanderers and which have befallen hundred of thousands of similar people in many lands, even diseases, poverty, sin, and final extinction."

He explained to his readers that the usual residents had to disband because of the scarcity of mussels, limpets, crabs, fish, "the important winter funguses" and the fuel supply. They had to go where these supplies "are comparatively plentiful and handy." He rejoiced that they did go. "Of one thing I am happy to assure you, that these will exert a good influence wherever they go, and many." Here he seems to recognize the failure of the mission, but not his responsibility. His converts should return to their old way of life. He had "nothing to employ them on worth mentioning, no workshops, no materials." Because of the weather that season "we shall employ very little indeed."[3] This was the bad news.

A few days later, during his first ten days at home, "a feed of porridge" alleviated the hunger of 134 natives, including fifty-two children. The following Sunday the services were attended by only forty or fifty natives, and the weekday meetings averaged about twenty-six, all men. He discovered that "Many of the people complain of poor health." Two men were afflicted with cancer and many others had died. Nevertheless, "Certainly native life at Ooshooia is far more happy, moral, and wholesome than elsewhere."

In England, he had not been able to sell many of the baskets the women had made. No one would buy them except as curiosities because of their "tedious workmanship." However, he remained convinced that it was preferable to take them in exchange for the clothes rather than give away the clothes for nothing at all.

The long letter quoted here, dated 25 May ten days after he arrived, illustrates Bridges' flagrant contradictions. He recognised that food and fuel were scarce and that the mission could only employ few natives but accused them of being "idle, thriftless, lawless" and urged them to go elsewhere, where (despite all their defects) they would "honour God by obedience, good conduct, and worship." Even though he must have been aware that many of the natives in Usuhaia were sick and of the others who had died, he insisted that "native life" was happy there. Did he write in this manner to reassure his readers? Or did he really believe what he wrote?

Lawrence Is Worried

Lawrence obviously expressed his true feelings when he wrote that the natives were desperately trying to survive, even though he refrained from criticising the mission's policies. As of 12 May, three days before the

Bridges family arrived, most of the people were too poor to purchase much from the store; seals were scarce because the sealing vessels carried so many away. They could obtain imported food and clothing only by working for the missionaries "whenever we can employ them." Towards the end of this winter (August 1881), Lawrence was worried on two accounts: Bridges' health and "much sickness and many deaths among the natives, at Ooshooia."[4]

The sealer Captain Lynch again tried to alleviate the hunger of the natives by giving the missionaries "a sack of beans and 600 lbs. of flour." Bridges also received clothing "and other things" from England. Again he thanked the donors by name (this time twenty-two women and one man) as well as from "kind friends in Valparaiso" for sending thirty-four packages of food. The *Allen Gardiner* also brought "a very large cargo; all the framework for the buildings, all our private goods and stores from Sandy Point [Punta Arenas] and Valparaiso." The shipment included a new whaleboat and 500 "little books," his translation in Yahgan of Saint Luke's gospel, which he offered to sell to the natives who could read.

About then Bridges recognised that "The young men, who grow up here, not being taught to make canoes, when they get wives, keep them and themselves very ill provided, to our great grief and disappointment." So he still assumed that he and the other missionaries were in no way responsible for this loss of their traditional ability to make canoes. He complained of a "relapse of his old complaint" (cancer) and added: "A medical man would be of great importance here."[5] He could go to Punta Arenas for treatment, but where could the natives go? Six years would pass before a missionary with medical knowledge arrived.

First Signs of an Epidemic

Finally Bridges did become alarmed because "great numbers of people have died . . . chiefly of congestion of the lungs, and the mortality is still going on, though much abated." A tuberculosis epidemic was killing them, as Dr Hyades will soon reveal. Then Bridges assumed that the epidemic was due to the "badness of the climate," while Lawrence attributed it to contagion from the sealers.[6] Lawrence may have been right, because at this time they were the only other foreigners in the area.

Bridges insisted that the mortality had been "very decidedly less [in the Ushuaia Mission] than among those at a distance." He remained convinced that "the adoption of clothing and civilised ways and order of life and food is beneficial to the health of these natives even as to ourselves... it is foolish of people to say that savage races find civilised modes of life destructive."[7] In the following year, Dr Hyades will seriously contest these statements (Chapter 13).

On 1 January 1882, Bridges again assumed that "the changes in the general life of the people is perceptibly great and happy, and should be a great cause of joy and praise to all the servants of Jesus Christ." Yet three paragraphs below he repeated: "There has been much sickness and death since I last wrote." He and the other missionaries were "very desirous of stirring them up to self-supporting energy, showing them that this is their duty and honour, and that they might thus become very happy people."[8] The missionaries had been doing their utmost to make them abandon their "wandering savage" ways and now he urged them to do exactly that, now when the young men no longer knew how to make canoes. They offered some assistance to Otatosh and the six or seven resident Keppelites for their gardens and now for cattle. After his eleven or twelve years in Ushuaia, he became discouraged with the gardens, and it occurred to him that "Cattle rearing and sheep must prove the only remunerative occupation of the people in time to come." Even the "three model cottages" were not serving as models.[9]

Neither the gardens, nor the cattle, nor the contributions from sealers such as Captain Lynch, nor gifts from England and from Chile sufficed for the Yamana resident in Ushuaia. Thirteen years after January 1869, when Stirling settled there for six months, the missionaries were still not able to convert the nearby area into a productive enterprise and occupy the Yamana as partners or employ them as workers. Yet following his retirement in 1886, Bridges established a sheep farm of his own, down the coast from Ushuaia, which was to become very successful for his family (Chapter 13).

During the early 1880s, as the conditions worsened, competition among the natives for the mission market increased, even among those who had never been to the Ushuaia Mission, mainly to sell their seal and otter skins. News came in November 1881 that the Haush, the "Eastern Ona," near Valentine Bay had massacred a small number of Selk'nam, the "Western Ona," because they [the latter] tried to monopolise the trade with Ushuaia. "And yet they [the Haush] have never visited us."[10] This is the second news (see Chapter 11 for the first news) of the economic impact of the mission beyond Ushuaia and the only report of the usually peaceful Haush killing anyone.

Otatosh's Last Wish

In February (1882), Bridges reported that the health of the missionaries and their families was "fairly satisfactory. But among the natives there continues much sickness and frequent deaths." He was concerned about their Christian faith: "Of one and all I may say they knew the Gospel, but I knew not the degree of comfort and grace they derived from it." Then he mentioned three "very ill indeed and not likely to last much longer.... they are obedient to the faith and cheerfully submissive to the will of God." One of the three was Otatosh.

Otatosh, now called Stirling Maacole, was about thirty, had befriended Stirling in Laiwaia in 1868 and presented him to his countrymen in Ushuaia. Thanks to him, Stirling had been able to establish the mission there (Chapter 11). Otatosh was among the original six or seven Yahgans in Ushuaia who aided Stirling, though he had never been to Keppel. And afterwards, through the years, he had been an unfailing supporter of the missionaries. In midwinter 1880, he wrote a letter, phonetically in Yamana, to Bridges in England. Lawrence also highly esteemed him as "one of the most intelligent and persevering men in Fireland."[11]

By mid-February 1882, when Otatosh became very ill, Bridges asked him if he wanted to risk going to Port Stanley for medical treatment, with Dr Hamilton, warning him that he might die away from home. Otatosh replied with heroic frankness: "It is all the same to me whether I die here or there." That morning, 14 February, he lost a large amount of blood from the nose and was taken to Port Stanley.[12] Late March 1882 Stirling wrote that although Dr Hamilton had been very zealous on Otatosh's behalf, "after some five weeks of great suffering," he had succumbed.[13]

He died from tuberculosis, which will be diagnosed as an epidemic by Dr Hyades, in November 1882. A monument will perhaps be built in Ushuaia in memory of Otatosh, the first Ushuaian Christian, for his dedication to the missionaries and for his heroic death.

Encounter with the Haush

By the third week of May 1882, the missionaries were probably relieved for a distraction from Otatosh's death and that of many others. The schooner *Golden West* (*San José* by another name) had pulled into Ushuaia Bay, coming from Punta Arenas. Among the passengers were three important Italians: Lieutenant Giacomo Bove and two scientists, Domingo Lovisato and Carlos Spegazzini.[14]

Bridges was grateful to "these gentlemen," who were very helpful to everyone connected with the mission. He accompanied the three Italians in the *Golden West*, with a crew of twenty-two, to Sloggett Bay, Haush territory, taking along two of his sons – ten-year-old Despard and Lucas, eight, as well as two Yamana men. On the way to Sloggett they picked up another man, on Snipe Island, by the name of Paiwan, who spoke some Haush and was familiar with the Sloggett area. Bridges hoped that he might serve as an interpreter if they met some of the "Eastern Onas," whom Lucas correctly identified as the Aush (Haush).

As the anchor was being lowered in Sloggett Bay near a shore bordered by "unscalable cliffs," a gale suddenly struck them and the ship crashed against the rocks. Bridges grabbed little Lucas by the wrists and swung him towards the shore, where he fell into the kelp seaweed and two of the crew dragged him to the foot of the cliffs. Despard clung to his father, who also hurled him to safety. Once everyone was on the beach, Paiwan and the two other Yamana scaled the cliff, lit fires, in the snowy scrub of dwarf beech trees and set up camp with the provisions the crew had managed to salvage. Soon Lucas was playing with his toy magnet, which curiously attracted a mass of black sand. He saved the sand as a souvenir. Several years afterwards the sand was found to contain gold dust (see below).

After camping for five days, the mate and some of the crew departed in the whaleboat saved from the wreck and arrived in Ushuaia Mission three days later. Within the week, Captain Willis returned in the *Allen Gardiner* and rescued the anxious castaways. Shortly after the whaleboat had left, Bridges and the others noticed smoke signals farther down the bay, beyond an "unfordable river." The next morning two well-built, tall, powerful men clad in guanaco skins appeared near their camp, having forded the river on foot, over the ice. "Bold fellows they must have been, for they might easily have been received with a hail of bullets." Bridges had warned the captain of the *Golden West* to control his men and not to fire on the newcomers. "They came in style, painted and in their best attire." Bridges and Paiwan went to meet them and escorted them to the camp. Soon nine or ten men and boys, who had stayed behind to see how their elders were received, were reassured and joined them. Standing around the campfire, several men offered their well-made bows and arrows, indicating, by gestures, that they wanted knives in exchange. Bridges passed out bread to them, motioned them to sit around the fire and began conversing with those who knew enough Yamana to translate for the others. Paiwan helped with his scanty knowledge of Haush. Lucas noticed the legs of the men were covered with the bleeding wounds that, he was later told, were self-inflicted signs of mourning.

Bridges and his sons accompanied the visitors back to their camp, where fifty Haush, including women and children, were waiting. They were also very muscular and tall except for a few of the women, who were much shorter than the others. Soon Bridges discovered that the shorter women were Yamana, wives of the Haush. Their camp consisted of nine shelters made of guanaco skins and branches, one for each family, unlike the huts of the Yamana, who lived more communally. Bridges was told that they sometimes used caves or overhanging rocks as shelters. Their aspect was "pleasing and imposing," clothed as they all were in guanaco furs from head to foot. The men wore conical pieces of blue-grey fur tied around their heads and fur moccasins. One of the men was blind and another somewhat lame. It was evident that they led a hard life. When Captain Willis returned in the *Allen Gardiner* and rescued the castaways, two of the "most friendly and trusting" Haush accompanied them back to Ushuaia.[15] The "gentlemen of the expedition," the three Italians, were very favourably impressed by the Haush, as they would be by the Yamana at the mission, and treated them generously.[16]

The text quoted above is one of the few descriptions of the Haush. Recall Darwin's encounter with them the third week of December 1832 (Chapter 4) but then only with men. Haush-Yamana couples were rather frequent for two reasons: because they were neighbours and because they were both peaceful people, in contrast to the Selk'nam. However, it must have been a trying experience for the Yamana women to adapt from sitting for days paddling a canoe to hiking for days loaded with camp equipment. Bridges would never meet them again, though this is not the last news of them.

A month later Bridges sent several Yamana in a whaleboat from Ushuaia to the site of the wreck to recover the salted meat and other provisions that had been saved from the wreck. They were found just as they had been left. The Haush had not touched them.[17]

The Epidemic Acquires Greater Force

After Bove and his companions departed from Ushuaia, in June 1882, Bridges announced "with much sorrow the death of many natives, owing to a widespread sickness, among them affecting chiefly the mucous membranes of the throat and lungs." However, he was still unaware or could not imagine that the sickness was an epidemic. He terminated his letter attributing the mortality, as usual to the natives, "to their poverty, carelessness, and vice, and chiefly, I fear, to the latter cause."[18] Although Bridges was utterly incapable of confronting the crisis, Lawrence was aware of the dangers, as noted above.

That winter, June 1882, the men were hunting guanacos, trailing them in the snow. The fish had been very plentiful "in this fine bay [Ushuaia]," where thousands of penguins and gulls came to prey on the fish, but soon adverse weather prevented catching any more. By then the Yamana had only a small number of seal and otter skins to offer for sale to purchase food.[19] The missionaries were aware that they sold their skins in their mission store because they were given a better price than the sealers offered. It had been their policy to pay them for work and skins with food and used clothing. But by mid-July 1882 they were paying cash for some work. Bridges stated that they received two pence a log and had cut 4,000 logs, which were ready for shipment.[20]

By then, the deaths were increasing at such an alarming rate that Bridges could not "account for this present state of things. There had been seasons before of serious illness, followed by long intervals of good health." But now there were fifteen cases of "dangerous illness." The month before, four had died in the orphanage, including Jemmy Button's two grandsons, mentioned in the last chapter.[21] Dr Hyades, who will appear on the scene in November 1882, learned from Bridges that seventeen children had died in the orphanage during this same year, from April to June.

The clothes of the half-yearly distribution were portioned out to about 146 persons. Bridges' advocacy of (European) clothes was embedded in his mind like a moral fortress. "Being dressed, they are protected to a large extent against the cold, are able, with comfort and propriety, to attend our meetings, and being clothed promotes among them wholesome feelings of self-respect and decent conduct."

William Barclay, the author of the preface to Thomas Bridges' *Yamana–English Dictionary* and free of any personal bias, wrote one of the most authoritative texts on this subject and on the entire policy of mission. Published in 1926, it merits extensive quotation.

From the standpoint of ethnology, the effect of the Christian missions in breaking down accepted frontiers; in the introduction of new rites to celebrate marriage and death; in the substitution of mixed food for a purely fish or meat diet; in the learning of new crafts, such as gardening, and the dropping of the old, such as canoe-making or flint-working; all this has produced a social upheaval in aboriginal Fuegian life . . . some of the most sweeping changes have been brought about by the introduction of European dress.

FIGURE 12.1. 1882 or 1883: Robert Whaits (right) and his wife (left) with eighteen orphans of the Anglican Ushuaia. © musée du Quai Branly.

Yet the harmful effects they produced were logical enough.... The rain, running off a hardened and grease plastered skin left no after-effect; but when the Yahgans sat fishing all day in their canoes in damp clothes they caught a chill at once. Their more orderly appearance (according to European notions) and the improved shelter afforded in winter by permanent wooden huts were dearly purchased in exchange for rapid infection by consumption, influenza, smallpox and measles ... it would have been better to have allowed him [the Yahgan] to remain cold and hungry but healthy. In place of attempting teaching these Indians to plant turnips in the water-logged Fuegian soil, their natural genius as fishermen might have been turned to catching and preserving the shoals of sardines, mullet and shellfish which abound in the Beagle Channel. A sufficient food-supply would thus have been secured without altering their diet. The conviction, common to all proselytising sects, that the regeneration of an Indian can only begin when he dons the clothing of his well-wishers is so deeply seated that it usually dies out only with the Indian himself.

Only a few stragglers remain of the thousands who, listening to the white man's talk of peace, found it only in unremembered graves, about which the winds and waves of Fuegia intone their endless requiem.[22]

Barclay's last sentence is one of the most poignant texts ever written in memory of the Yamana. In my opinion Barclay wrote the most precise and conclusive statement concerning the effects of the mission's policies on the Yamana people.

The clothing handouts continued to the end of the nineteenth century and beyond, as Barclay also stated, often as wages or as recompenses for good behaviour, possibly contrary to the intentions of the donors, who may have preferred the clothes be given to the most needy. In January 1882, Bridges had told those who cut logs on the north shore that they would be supplied with clothes for themselves, their wives and children. Lawrence was applying the same principle. He distributed the "superior outfits in quality and quantity" to the children in school who showed progress in learning.[23]

Thomas Bridges' son Lucas affirmed that while "generous people in England, gave shop-soiled clothing, high-heeled shoes, worn-out tennis shoes, and flimsy garments, there was a great deal of useful clothing" in these shipments.[24] It cannot be assumed that even the "useful clothes" had been thoroughly cleaned and disinfected. The used clothes might well have been germ carriers, though not purposely infected. Fitz-Roy had alluded to the giving of "infected things" together with "intoxication" as insidious attempts to thin the numbers of the Araucanian (Mapuche) Indians of Chile.[25] However, I found no evidence that the missionaries or sealers intended to infect the Fuegians in this manner, even though, later, a few remaining Yahgans I knew declared that the whites, *los blancos*, had done so on purpose. Even if the used clothes had been germ-free, they hastened their death, as Barcley stated above.

Eleven Alakaluf Are Kidnapped to Europe

On 23 July 1882, Bridges welcomed the four Alakaluf survivors of eleven who had been kidnapped along the Strait of Magellan in August of the previous year. They remained in the Ushuaia Mission for seven months, where they recovered somewhat and were "evidently very happy."[26] Though Yamana were not involved, they witnessed the outcome of the kidnapping in Ushuaia. They certainly commented on it and probably imagined themselves in the place of their unfortunate neighbours.

A German sealer, Herr Waalen (or Whalen) residing in Punta Arenas, had captured the eleven Alakaluf (one couple with a boy child, two mothers and their babies, an adult single man, a young single woman and two youths). Whalen was said to have lured them on board his boat by offering food, probably at different places along the strait, because there was only one couple with a child among them, the two mothers were without their husbands and none of the adults were close kin. Although they were said to be Yamana, in reality all were Alakaluf. Waalen was obliged to give a bond, the equivalent at the time of 12,000 to 15,000 francs, to the governor of Punta Arenas as a guarantee for their return to Punta Arenas. There Waalen transferred them to a German boat, the *Phoebus*, bound for Europe.[27]

Waalen contacted a well-known showman Carl Hagenbeck, though he kept a close eye on his captives during the "shows," calling himself their guardian. Hagenbeck was a big-time entrepreneur on the European circuit of spectacular shows, first (in the 1860s) of wild animals and subsequently of exotic people. Both Hagenbeck and Waalen intended to make money by exhibiting these eleven Fuegians as savage cannibals in the principal cities of Europe. Waalen took along a canoe, bows and arrows and stone tools as props to give the impression of authenticity to his shows.

The first stop was Hamburg, but the captives did not descend until the *Phoebus* docked in Le Havre, early September 1881. Albert Geoffroy Saint-Hilaire, director of the Jardin Zoologique d'Acclimatation (Paris) was waiting for them and conducted them to Paris.[28]

The Captives in Paris

Upon arriving in Paris, the eleven were vaccinated and enclosed in the Jardin in the Bois de Boulogne, still today a popular park for Sunday strollers. The enclosure was furnished with the canoe brought by Waalen, a hut made of branches, prominently displayed bones and an open fire around which the captives huddled, thus creating a scene depicting "the savages – the primitive cannibals – of Tierra del Fuego."[29] They were covered with guanaco or fox-skin capes, although the men wore shorts so as not to offend the public.

Slogans such as "Come and see authentic Tierra del Fuego cannibals" circulated around Paris, announcing the big attraction. "Motionless for hours at a time, they occasionally glanced at the curious crowds pressed against the fence as if peering at some extraordinary animals." Now and then an onlooker tossed coins through the fence.[30]

During the three weeks they were on exhibit in the jardin, eminent members of the Société d'Anthropologie de Paris visited them and took numerous measurements of their bodies, while noting their behavioural and psychological traits.[31]

The Anthropologist Manouvrier Visits the Captives

Léonce Manouvrier was one of the few scientists who treated the Fuegians like human beings, not savages to be measured, observed and analyzed.

FIGURE 12.2. September 1881: Alakalufs in the Jardin Zoologique d'Acclimatation. Note the public behind the fence in the background. © musée du
Quai Branly.

They were demoralised and ill during the first days in Paris. Some leaned
against a wall of the hut until their legs flexed and sweat appeared on
their foreheads as they slumped to the ground.

During the first visit (September 1881), Manouvrier and his four colleagues found them sitting silently around the fire, holding on to the
small fox or guanaco skins that covered their chests, eating slightly
roasted meat with their fingers. The two children and the baby were
seated or held between the legs of their mothers, trying to tear apart the
pieces of meat they were given. The youngest mother, about twenty-two
years old, called Petite Mère, gave her baby girl to drink from her mouth
and was constantly covering her little shoulders with the small fox skin,
which kept sliding off. "A really sad spectacle," Manouvrier remarked.

The pustules from the vaccinations on the captives' arms were painful
and the swelling of ganglions bothered them. Manouvrier and his colleagues sat down among them around the fire and tried to please them by
offering them bracelets and necklaces. It soon became obvious that they
preferred useful things. One of the women made it clear to Manouvrier
that she would like to have a basket or a glass, and another asked for
a comb. Manouvrier thought Petite Mère was the most intelligent of the
eight adults. Later she learned to say *merci*. She graciously let her head

FIGURE 12.3. September 1881: The eleven captives in front of the house in the enclosure. Lise is standing on the far left. © musée du Quai Branly.

FIGURE 12.4. September 1881: Petite Mère and her baby, who died in Paris on 30 September. © musée du Quai Branly.

be measured, her hands and feet drawn and she encouraged the others to do likewise.

As the days advanced, the captives' health improved somewhat and they allowed the anthropologists to take some fifty measurements except of the genitals. It is not clear just what went on when the Fuegians were left alone in the evening with the guardians of the jardin. Manouvrier thought they might have feared the guardians, who taught them to be modest, and

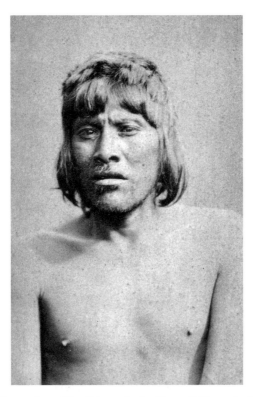

FIGURE 12.5. September 1881: "Antonio the Fierce." © musée du Quai Branly.

this explained, according to him, why they refused the requests to have their genitals measured. It is strange that Manouvrier could be so naïve, or perhaps he was being ironic.

Antonio, aged thirty-five or so, was less compliant than Petite Mère. The Frenchmen called him "Antonio the Fierce" or "the warrior." He showed his displeasure about being there by pacing in front of the anthropologists and the public while chewing on his guanaco cape and brandishing his bow and arrow. Perhaps to placate him and entertain the spectators, the guardians would hand him a long spear to aim at a bag filled with wood shavings. Antonio also demonstrated the technique of making an arrow point out of glass, for lack of silex. Although he cut himself twice with the glass, he took pride in his work and seemed pleased at the attention his work attracted.[32]

During Manouvrier's subsequent visits, while taking measurements, he began to think that fear or timidity dominated their behaviour. The public

FIGURE 12.6. September 1881: Catherine. © musée du Quai Branly.

threw them coins through the fence but perhaps because of timidity, they paid no attention to these offerings. But once they learned that the coins were money with which they could buy useful things, they picked them up. One of the photographers was annoyed by their disinterest in the efforts he made to distract them. "It was only with cigarettes, and above all boxes of matches, that I could gain their gratitude."[33]

During one of Manouvrier's later visits, Petite Mère and Catherine, the latter also a mother, in her mid-twenties, made fun of his beard and laughed a great deal when he twisted his moustache to amuse them. They, like the other Fuegians, thought hairy faces disgusting. But they were really shocked to see Manouvrier blow his nose into a piece of cloth and then put it in his pocket. He realised they were unhappy, offended by being the objects of a spectacle, but he found them gentle and sociable. They helped each other in little ways: the women by sharing care of the children, the men, when they had learned to smoke, by sharing the pipes they were given as well as the knives. They even became gay when they were not imposed upon and treated kindly.

FIGURE 12.7. September 1881: Henri. © musée du Quai Branly.

One day the administrator of the jardin took them to a circus. They understood the gestures of the clowns and laughed heartily at them, though they were afraid of the horses. Back in the enclosure, some days after the outing, suddenly they all turned in the same direction to look at something that caught their attention. It was the bus that had taken them to the circus.[34] Were they recalling those moments of fun and liberty? The two youths, Pedro and Henri, enjoyed the spectacle enormously, even though Henri was inclined to worry about their future.

Lise, whose name was also given to her by the guardians in Paris, was the youngest woman, about eighteen, tall, robust, seemingly healthy, and the only woman without a child. (See Figure 12.3 above, Lise standing on the far left.)

Piskouna and her husband, called El Capitán, were the oldest and only couple in the group. He was about thirty-five years old and she younger. Their child, a boy, was about three. El Capitán seemed to be very fond of his wife, staying close by her side and passing on to her any object that was given to him, even tobacco. She and their little boy were among the few survivors (see Figure 12.9, below).

Petite Mère's Baby Dies on 30 September

Was the death of the Fuegian baby considered so unimportant that it was hardly mentioned in print, or was it intentionally ignored to avoid embarrassment on the part of the "guide" (Herr Waalen) and the anthropologists participating in the exhibition? It is also strange that the cause of her death was not mentioned.[35]

The Ten Captives Are Taken to Berlin

In Berlin Rudolf Virchow (or Virchov), professor of pathological anatomy at the University of Berlin and a well-known anthropologist, made measurements of five of the captives. The other three adults refused to comply and the two children were not asked. By then Petite Mère and Catherine were sick. Lise was still well.[36]

On to Munich

From Berlin they were taken to Leipzig and then to Munich, where another anthropologist by the name of Bischoff made some "observations of the genital organs" (of Catherine and Lise) and other measurements of them. Bischoff commented that according to the "guardian" (their abductor Waalen), the women were much more sexually interested than the men and preferred white men and the *coit ab anteriore*. Why was Bischoff so "interested" and how did the "guardian" know all this? Although the Fuegians did not allow the French to measure their genitals, somehow Bischoff persuaded Catherine and Lise to allow him to do so. And he continued to measure Lise's genitals even after she died.[37] I found no account of her death or her burial except that she died in Munich. Bischoff corresponded with the French naturalist J. Deniker, who reported on his behaviour with Lise.

The Nine Finally Reach Zurich

According to the sources consulted by Peter Mason, after three weeks in Paris, **they were** taken to Berlin and then to Leipzig, Munich, Stuttgart, Nuremberg and finally Zurich. They were unhealthy or sick by the time they reached Zurich (18 February 1882). A month or so later four or five died, while they were housed in the Plattengarten Museum in Zurich. Petite Mère, Catherine, El Capitán and young Henri all died there. Young Pedro survived his comrades in suffering. Dr Hyades does not name them but does state that they died of measles complicated by infection of the

FIGURE 12.8. September 1881: Lise, standing; below, Petite Mère and her baby and Catherine and her daughter who survived. © musée du Quai Branly.

lungs and by syphilis. Mason, who studied such kidnappings in detail, pointed out that in Zurich "Hagenbeck intervened and decided to send the five survivors back home.... Antonio may have died on the voyage [back to Punta Arenas]."[38]

The Four Arrive at the Ushuaia Mission
After four or five had died in Zurich (Antonio may have died during the voyage), the four others were returned to Germany, put on a ship,

FIGURE 12.9. September 1881: El Capitán, Piskouna and their son. Piskouna and her son survived. © musée du Quai Branly.

and sent back to Punta Arenas where Schroder's agent (not identified) "took wise care of them" and sent them on the *Allen Gardiner* to the Ushuaia Mission. The four were Catherine's little girl, about three years old, Piskouna (El Capitán's widow) and her son, about four years old by then. The adolescent Pedro also survived.

Bridges welcomed them on 23 July 1882. They remained for seven months in the mission, where they recovered somewhat and were,

FIGURE 12.10. September 1881: Pedro, standing in front of the house in the enclosure. He was the fourth survivor. © musée du Quai Branly.

according to Bridges, "evidently very happy."[39] However, Dr Hyades, during one of his trips to Ushuaia, found them "morally very depressed."

Pedro pleased the missionaries by his energy and good looks. When Bridges talked to him and Piskouna, using his scant knowledge of the "Alaculoof" language, they were surprised and joyful, "laughing even to tears." This was the first time their language was spoken to them since they had been kidnapped about two years earlier. The next month, Catherine's little daughter fell in the fire in the hut where she and the others were living. She was "so shockingly burned as to render her detention at Oooshooia necessary." She was taken to the orphanage where "her burns were healing nicely." The last news I found of her was that she survived the epidemic of measles that struck Ushuaia in 1884 because she had been inoculated in Paris. Apparently she remained at the Ushuaia Mission.[40]

Three Return Home

In March 1883, Bridges escorted Piskouna, her son and Pedro in the *Allen Gardiner* back to their homeland, the east coast of Dawson Island (about the centre of Magellan Strait).[41] Pedro will appear again in the next chapter.

Much of the story remains to be assembled concerning the treatment these eleven people were subjected to by Waalen, the showman Hagenbeck and the French, German and Swiss anthropologists. Exhibiting "savages" and other "exotics" from the distant parts of the world had become a highly profitable business, drawing huge crowds in Europe and the United States. It was also a convenience for local anthropologists to study "indigenes" in their home cities without bothering about "fieldwork." As Raymond Corbey remarked: "Science, commerce, and imperialism went hand in hand."[42] Other Fuegians were to be kidnapped in 1889 (Chapter 14). This practice of exhibiting "exotic peoples" continued in the Paris Jardin d'Acclimatation until the 1930s.[43]

Recall (Chapters 4 and 5) that with the exception of Boat Memory, who died upon arrival in England in 1830, Fitz-Roy took far better care of the other three Fuegians (York, Fuegia and the Yahgan Jemmy Button) than most of the anthropologists did of the eleven Alakaluf fifty years later.

Meanwhile in Paris, after the ten Fuegians had been taken to Berlin for the next show and study, probably towards the end of October 1881, the recently departed ten became subjects of debate.

Members of the Société d'Anthropologie in Paris Discuss Two Topics

First: "These Fuegians Are Members of an Inferior Race, N'est-ce-Pas?"

They all agreed on the main subject of debate in the beginning: these Fuegians were members of an inferior race – the Mongolian "yellow race." But the debate soon got stymied: this little group was too heterogeneous; the individual components were not exactly all of the same race or even subrace. Several captives seemed to resemble the Indians of North America. Other scholars thought that some were more like the Eskimos. One of the captives was said to look like the Botocudos of Brazil or the Quechua of Peru. One of the anthropologists objected to all these hypotheses: if these Fuegians were dressed like everyone else, they would easily pass as Europeans on the streets of Paris except for the colour of their skin. So how to define them racially? No one seemed to agree.

Second and Last Topic: By What Criterion Are They Inferior?

Then the debate centred on the other problem: whose solution should clarify the initial one of race. Several criteria were proposed.

1. Their cephalic index (measurements and locality of bumps on the head) should certainly prove the point. But the study (in Paris) of four heads of the adult Alakaluf had revealed that they were somewhat superior to the average European. This was baffling; it seemed incongruous: there had to be an error in the measurements. So the cephalic index had been made again: this time of all eight adults. However, these measurements were all superior to those of the average Parisians.[44] The results may have discouraged the anthropologists, but whether they were surprised or confused was not stated. In any event, the cephalic index criterion was dropped. Perhaps these scholars were not aware that in 1866, Threeboys' and Urupa's heads had shown them to be superior to those of the average Englishmen of Bristol (Chapter 10).

2. One of the anthropologists, Monsieur Hovelacque, proposed that the Fuegians were inferior in their body proportions. Monsieur Topinard, his colleague, objected: "The *nègres* have the longest arms and thus are close to the apes, those of the European races are less long, and thus are further removed from the apes. Well, the arms of the Fuegians are even shorter than the Europeans."[45] So the Fuegians must be inferior in some other way.

3. Perhaps because they lacked curiosity. Everyone who visited them in the jardin had been impressed by their indifference. They were not interested in hardly anything offered, given or shown them. This might well be a criterion of inferiority. However, Monsieur Nicolas, one of the colleagues, objected: animals are curious, the guanaco is one of the most curious in the world. He insisted: "The Fuegians in their own country are not lacking in curiosity, but nothing here awakened their curiosity and this is not surprising." Nicolas pursued his argument: "Our civilisation is too noisy for these savages

and probably annoyed them rather than seduced them."[46] Thanks to Nicolas the curiosity hypothesis was eliminated.

4. That they did not value money might solve the criterion problem. But one or several of those present recalled that when the Fuegian captives understood what they could obtain with the coins that were tossed by the public through or over the fence, they caught them and their purpose right away. Enough was said to put aside this explanation.

5. Then one of the scholars suggested that gullibility (*crédulité*), or superstitious beliefs, might do as an inferiority criterion. Here Darwin was brought to the Fuegians' defence. He had written that they were not any more superstitious than the seamen on the *Beagle* and that they did not believe in the devil. Nicolas intervened again, adding that "even certain highly regarded scholars are very *crédules*."[47] Darwin's and Nicolas' comments sufficed to discard *crédulité*.

6. Undaunted, Monsieur Hovelacque, who thought that his criterion (number 2 in this list) had been too abruptly eliminated, now proposed that their weak hands might well be a sign of their inferiority, as civilised people are laborious and have strong hands. This idea was politely ignored.

7. Most of the specialists agreed that these Fuegians did not seem very intelligent, and certainly intellect was a sign of progress, and the lack thereof a sure sign of inferiority. But one colleague objected, suggesting that if Europeans lived in Tierra del Fuego under similar conditions, in a few generations they would become like the Fuegians. This argument was still being discussed until it occurred to another colleague (Manouvrier) that if Darwin had been a Fuegian, he would probably have excelled in a number of tasks and might have become a *sorcier* (a shaman). Again Darwin saved the day for the Fuegians' reputation, and lack of intelligence was definitely defeated.

8. Someone recalled that the "guide" Waalen had affirmed that the Fuegians had been naked when he first saw them. This time all but one of the colleagues agreed: nakedness could not serve as a valid criterion.

They are inferior, but why? The scholars could not put their fingers on the answer, though they recalled again that it was common knowledge, sound common sense, that the Fuegians' simple Stone Age culture was inferior, and hence the Fuegians were also inferior. Monsieur Nicolas, who had already intervened with several caustic remarks, was losing patience and almost ready to declare the entire debate null and void, commented: "From this point of view our Fuegians constitute a veritable anthropological paradox; and we have not been able to agree on the nature of their inferiority, which all of us admit in principle."[48]

Manouvrier Proposes

The criterion problem remained up in the air, floating around for thirteen years, until Léonce Manouvrier brought it down to earth by challenging the entire concept of inferiority, all of it, with this decisive statement:

Physically, there is no reason to consider the savage life of the Fuegian hunters and fishers as requiring a cerebral function less complicated than that of most of the Europeans. Like our uneducated peasants and workers, the Fuegians know how to perform difficult tasks to assure their existence; they know how to express their ideas in a sufficiently rich language. They can count only to 3, but this is no reason to suppose that their notion of numbers is limited to the distinction between 1, 2 and 3.

Manouvrier insisted: "A Frenchman or an Englishman of average intelligence is easily persuaded to boast about the progress in science, industry and art, though he himself be neither a scientist, nor an inventor, nor an artist in any sense of the word. Dressed in clothes he has not made, disposing of weapons and tools he could not possibly fabricate, he scorns the Fuegian shivering in his canoe, using a knife made from stone. However the Fuegian uses the weapons, tools and clothes that he himself makes; he eats the game he himself has killed and fish he has obtained." Manouvrier asked: "Where does this illusion of superiority come from?" He answered: "from the outer reaches of science, industry and art that the average civilised person uses and prides himself on, as if he himself had invented and created them when in reality he is only the consumer–producer (and the victim)." Among other comments, Manouvrier contested the notion of progress as implied to the notion of inferiority–superiority. He gave the division of labour as an example and declared: "The division of labour has enabled us to produce more and better collectively, but it has also resulted in an unfavorable condition for the individual development of our faculties in general."

Having read the articles published by Dr Hyades on the Yamana (see Chapter 13), he also commented: "Hyades, Bridges and other observers recognised the Fuegians' capacities to be instructed even though the conditions under which attempts were made to civilise them were obviously very bad."[49]

Manouvrier's deeply penetrating remarks were far in advance of the views of many of his contemporaries and are certainly pertinent today.

In Jennifer Michael Hecht's extraordinary book on this period in France, published in 2003 and entitled *The End of the Soul. Scientific Modernity, Atheism and Anthropology in France*, she refers to Manouvrier's funeral in 1927. Then Dr Raoul Anthony, who spoke on behalf of the Société d'Anthropologie de Paris, stated that, "it was beyond doubt that Manouvrier would one day be seen as one of the most profound thinkers of the end of the nineteenth century and the beginning of the twentieth." Hecht dedicated an entire chapter to Manouvrier and referred to him frequently throughout her book. She was aware that "This important anthropologist has received little attention from historians." Among many controversial themes, "Manouvrier championed aspects of both Darwinism and Lamarckianism and brought much positive attention to the theory of evolution in general."[50]

Three cheers for Manouvrier, as Jemmy Button might have shouted.

The Last News of Fuegia Basket

I turn again to March of 1883, when Bridges accompanied the three Alakaluf, survivors of those kidnapped in 1881, to their home on Dawson Island. While they were on board the *Allen Gardiner* sailing through Whale Boat Sound, the yacht slowed down as a canoe approached. The Alakaluf family in the canoe informed Bridges that Fuegia Basket was nearby on London Island and was ill. He went to meet her and found her surrounded by her daughter and "three beautiful children." Though very ill, she was "quite conscious." He spoke to her in Yahgan and she "silently assented to what I said, and appeared glad to see and hear me. . . . I was greatly pleased to see the care that was taken of the aged and sick woman. She was sufficiently covered up with garments, and her grown daughter appeared to be very kind to her, and of an amiable character."

This is the last news of Fuegia Basket, the plump merry girl who had so willingly trusted Fitz-Roy and let him take her to a strange land. She adapted well to that "new world" of experiences and, upon returning to her homeland, had lived as loving mother, always pleased to recall her English adventures with passing navigators and missionaries.

The meeting was marred only when Fuegia's son-in-law bitterly complained about sealers who had taken the sealskins he offered for sale and then refused to pay for them. Bridges commented: "They are treated most shamefully in this way. Knowing what we do, hatred must be bred in the hearts of these poor people by such unjust treatment."[51] On both occasions when Bridges stopped in Alakaluf country (to inquire about Fuegia) he had heard complaints of shooting or cheating by the sealers.

13

1882 to 1886: The French Arrive; Then the Argentines; The Epidemics Become Uncontrollable

The French Expedition Surprises a Yamana Family

When the "French boat" dropped anchor in Orange Bay (Hoste Island) on 6 September 1882, a seven- or eight-year-old Yamana girl and her family gazed up at it in wonder from their canoe. They had come from their camping grounds near Cape Horn (Wollaston Island) and apparently had never seen a European vessel before, although commercial fishing boats had passed near the area where they lived since nearly a hundred years before (Chapter 2). Her real name was Carrupale-kipa. Later she was called Julia. In 1920 she became Gusinde's principal informant for Yamana myths even though she hardly spoke Spanish (Chapter 15). Unfortunately she died in 1958 six years before I came to Tierra del Fuego. She talked to Cristina in Yahgan about her first impressions of the Europeans, which I recorded in 1987. Her story is translated here as closely as possible to Cristina's colourful Spanish:[1]

When the French boat arrived, she and her family were gazing up at it from their canoe, hidden under their sealskin covers. They did not know it was a boat [it didn't have its sails up]. The old people said that it was a cliff, a huge rock or floating island.

Recall that the Yahgans, who first saw Weddell's ship some fifty years before, imagined that it was alive (Chapter 2).

One of Julia's family said: "Gee we are already in springtime because, look – those birds [the crew walking on the deck] are already taking little blades of grass to make their nests." Some thought the sailors and the officers, with their white caps, were cormorants of the high sea, others thought they were *lakuta* [spirits of the sea]. The old people were afraid. The French sailors tossed presents for them into the water: sacks of flour, soap, biscuits, and sweets. The Yahgans fished them out and dragged them on shore.

[Cristina continued:]

They asked each other: "What are these things good for?" They opened the small sack of flour... and said: "This must be *tumap*, the white powder they used to paint themselves. So they took some and spread it on their faces, all over their bodies, even on their hair. They were pleased with it until it began to rain and it hardened on their heads. They said: "This cannot be *tumap*. Who knows what it could be?" So they threw it away [back into the water]. The next day they tasted the soap and said: "Bad." But while they were tasting it, one of them thought maybe it was for washing. Then they realised if they washed themselves they [the French] were not cormorants but people.... They thought the biscuits might be good as firewood so they burnt them all. They tasted the sweets, but as they had never eaten anything so sweet, they thought it might be poison, so they threw all the sweets back into the sea also.[2]

Cristina explained that afterwards, the Frenchmen showed them that the biscuits were to eat, not to be afraid of them, that they were not there to kill them. But, Cristina insisted: "Abuela Julia didn't like their food nor the whites – never."

The French Expedition

The French "cormorants" were the crew of the Scientific Mission at Cape Horn, while the "cliff" or "floating island" was the three-masted steam ship, the *Romanche*. This expedition formed part of the commemoration, later called the First International Polar Year, which took place for an entire year, from September 1882. A second International Polar Year took place fifty years later, 1932–33, the third in 1957–58.

For this First Polar Year eleven expeditions from European nations and two expeditions from the United States coordinated their research during that year. Eleven expeditions were established at different points around the Arctic Circle, while only two were assigned to the vicinity of the Antarctic, one of which was French, near Cape Horn, and the other German, on the South Georgia Island. The immediate task of the thirteen expeditions was to make simultaneous observations of the eclipse of the sun – that is, the passage of Venus in front of the sun, on 6 December 1882. Each team was committed above all to studying magnetism (the problem of fluctuating compasses), geophysics and meteorology. Also included in the program were hydrography, cartography, geology, botany and zoology. Anthropology was carried out by the French among the Yamana near Cape Horn and by the American expedition at Point Barrow (Alaska), with the Inupiat Eskimos. These two were the only expeditions located in areas of human habitation.[3]

FIGURE 13.1. The ship *Romanche* in front of Mission Cove. © musée du Quai Branly.

The Frenchmen Meet the Yahgans

The French expedition left Cherbourg in mid-July 1882 in the sturdy *Romanche*. As this ship was equipped not only with sails but also with a motor it was able to penetrate channels and inlets where sailboats had rarely ventured. Furthermore it carried a small motorboat, the usual whaleboats, a year's provisions of clothing, and some food, scientific equipment and prefabricated materials for structures to be erected at their destination.

On 6 September, the *Romanche* anchored in Orange Bay, Hoste Island, Chile, about twenty-five miles (40 kilometres) from Cape Horn. An inlet within the bay, later named Mission Cove in honour of this expedition, was selected as its base.

The crew took a month and a half to install the prefabricated buildings that housed the men and the scientific instruments.[4]

Captain Louis Ferdinand Martial was the commander of the expedition. The entire crew totalled 140 seamen, including twelve officers. Two civilians from the Museum of Natural History, Paris, joined the expedition at different times. The personnel were divided into a marine group and a land group. Captain Martial and his crew formed the marine group, while Dr Paul Daniel Jules Hyades was in charge of the land group, which remained in Mission Cove during most of the year, September 1882 to September 1883.⁵

During the year the land group was in Mission Cove, the Yamana made frequent visits there. Dr Hyades encouraged them to come so that he might measure and make plaster casts of various parts of their bodies, including their heads. It may seen odd that some of the natives agreed to submit themselves to the ordeal of the plaster casts. According to Lucas Bridges, they complied only because his father prevailed upon them to do so, otherwise they "would never have allowed themselves to be smothered with a thick coating of plaster of Paris."⁶

Hyades estimated that from thirty to forty Yahgans lived in the bay off and on and that a total of 300 or 400 came at different times during the year the expedition was there. He was aware that they were worried when they thought that the Frenchmen were settling down on their territory – that they could not understand "what our intentions were." He realised that this was natural enough.⁷

Despite the intrusion, the native inhabitants (the Yahgans–Yamana) expressed hostility toward the Frenchmen only once (see below). During his first week in Mission Cove, Hyades wrote that these Fuegians were healthy and surprisingly vigorous but were the most deprived and brutish of all humanity.⁸ He soon changed his mind about the latter.

When the *Romanche* crew first saw fifteen Yamana in two canoes paddling toward the ship, they tossed biscuits to them from the deck. About then "Julia" and her family first saw "the French boat," as related above. Captain Martial also found it "difficult to imagine a more miserable example of the human species." Later, when he realised that they had been judged too harshly by previous navigators, like Hyades, he changed his mind about them.⁹

Sealers Are Rescued

One day in September the sealing vessel *Thomas Hunt* sailed into Mission Cove from nearby Packsaddle Bay. The captain, whom the French called Mr Eldred, was the American Captain Eldred Lynch, who the year before had donated food for the Yahgans in the Ushuaia Mission. He came to request the ship's physician, Dr Hyades, to treat one of his men who was sick, and while he was there he showed Captain Martial, on a map, the localities of the best anchorages in the region and told him and Hyades about the Yahgan, whom he knew quite well, having been in the area for seven years. Three weeks later, Lynch returned to Mission Cove from the offshore islets, Idelfonso, where he and his men had killed ("harvested," is the usual expression) about sixty fur seals a day, while two years before Lynch claimed that they had harvested 500 a day. Hyades called this "a massacre." On the Diego Ramirez Islets, Lynch had just harvested 300 seals and had rescued eight desperate castaways who had been there for four months. They were waiting for their ship, the American sealing vessel *Surprise*, nearly starving, and by then were convinced that their captain had abandoned them forever. Lynch left them off at the Ushuaia Mission on his way to see Hyades and Martial.[10]

A few months later, Bridges reported that the eight rescued sealers had helped the missionaries a great deal and had taken the orphans in a whaleboat three times around the bay. In December, when they boarded the *Allen Gardiner* for Punta Arenas, the orphans and everyone else were sorry that they left so soon.[11]

Lynch had also informed Martial and Hyades that sickness at the Ushuaia Mission was taking an alarming toll, especially among the children.[12] But two months will pass before Hyades goes to the Ushuaia Mission.

The French Are Off to a Good Start

During the first days, early September 1882, the Yahgans in Mission Cove observed the French closely as they unpacked their equipment and assembled their prefabricated buildings. They helped the crew to salvage sheets of wood that had fallen from the ship. Martial was confident that his crew and the natives would get along fine. Meanwhile he was busy rectifying certain mistakes made by officers of the *Beagle* (in 1830) on the hydrography of the bay. Martial's handouts of biscuits had begun and would continue for the next twelve months. His cook kept baking a generous supply of them.

Captain Martial's Only Interpreter

The day after the *Romanche* arrived, on 8 September, a canoe approached the ship and a young Yahgan climbed on board without asking permission, started speaking English, requesting to see the captain. When Martial appeared, the visitor asked for a book in English. One was handed to him and he proceeded to demonstrate his ability to read it, said good-bye and left. The next day he returned and offered his services to Captain Martial.

Martial needed an interpreter, so he agreed, and the new recruit was promptly washed and given a sailor's outfit. This photograph (Figure 13.2) was probably taken then. He was a lively extrovert with a style

FIGURE 13.2. 1882: Yekaif, Martial's translator, outfitted as a French sailor, looking very serious with two of his kin on board the *Romanche*. © musée du Quai Branly.

all of his own. He introduced himself as Yekaif, short for Yekaifwaianjiz, and explained that the sealers had taught him English. Lucas Bridges, who knew him quite well, thought of him as a tough and hardy lad and said that he was from the outer coasts, where he had been working for sealers.

A few days later the *Romanche* sailed out of Orange Bay north to the tiny island Packsaddle, then named for its twin towers of basalt, some twenty-two yards (20 metres) high, which from a distance resembled a packsaddle. Yekaif and a few crewmen climbed the highest tower, took bearings and made a small pyramid of rocks to commemorate their visit.

The Frenchmen noticed the evergreen beech trees (*Nothofagus betuloides*) growing near the base of the towers. Yekaif explained that his people, the Yahgans, used the bark of this tree to make their canoes. A large number of seals were lounging on the rocky coast of the island and great flocks of cormorants were nesting in the nearby islets. This island had belonged to the families of Chinagaline, Urupa's bereaved father, who had probably passed away by then, as he was never mentioned after the death of his son Urupa in 1867 (Chapter 10).

Early January 1883, Yekaif suddenly announced that he was leaving the *Romanche* to join Bridges in Ushuaia. Martial was annoyed and attributed his decision to "the changing, mobile character of these natives." Yekaif explained later that he quit because he suspected that the Frenchmen would take him to some faraway place, like Fitz-Roy had taken Jemmy Button in 1830 (Chapter 3). Later Yekaif overcame his fear and accompanied Martial on his fourth exploration (see below).[13] Lucas Bridges recalled Yekaif's French: "He soon learned a number of spicy French exclamations to add to his stew of Yahgan, Spanish and English."[14]

And the Photographs?

The photographs taken during this expedition are perhaps the earliest and certainly among the best of the Yamana before civilisation and the missionaries upset their "way of living." Two officers were assigned to this task: Jean Louis Doze was part of Martial's team, and Edmond Joseph Augustin Payen worked with Hyades. Fortunately Payen's photographs identify most of his subjects by their real names, probably noted by Hyades.[15] He was certainly at Payen's side, telling him just how to pose the natives for his anthropological study. This explains why many are posed: front and profile, hardly ever relaxed or smiling. This may also explain why most of the subjects are naked. The fact that the photographer had to cover his head and the camera with a dark cloth and to tell his subjects not to move for a minute or so must have also made them uncomfortable.[16]

The most popular portraits, taken by Payen, are those of attractive, almost nude young women, especially the beautiful Kamanakar-kipa, and the handsome Athlinata. They are often reproduced in publications about Tierra del Fuego and as postcards, usually with no indication of when, where or by whom they were taken and without names. However, it may have been more for aesthetics rather than science that the young women were posed facing the camera, with only a small triangular piece of leather tied around the hips with a cord as a pubic cover. The women hardly ever (or never) appeared outside of their huts with such a scanty covering. When they were being photographed entirely naked, they always covered their pubic area with one hand. Almost everyone usually wore seal or otter skin capes, though the men were not modest about appearing naked. They did not need much clothing, as they were much more resistant to the cold than the Europeans, were invariably smeared with seal or whale fat for protection, and were often near a fire in their huts or near the fires burning in their canoes. However, the photographs taken at Mission Cove (Orange Bay) do perpetuate the false image of the Yamana as "nude savages in the fierce climate at the end of the world." And, as already noted, the Yahgan men often left their capes in their canoes when they boarded the ships or hid them when they greeted strangers, fearing that they might be stolen, so they were often nearly naked when they were on the decks of ships.[17] The almost inevitable first question people ask me about these Fuegians is: "How did they, so naked, resist such a cold climate?" My usual short answer is: "Well, they knew how to protect themselves from the cold and to avoid the wind; besides, genetically, having lived there for some 6,000 years, they were conditioned to the climate. Besides it was not usually so terribly cold there either" (see end of Chapter 2).

As Martial was not concerned about Hyades' anthropological interests, his photos, taken by Doze, are not posed in the same manner. Instead, the subjects were told how to pose by signs, usually by one of his officers, as in Figure 13.3.

Hyades's favourite models, Kamanakar-kipa and Athlinata, are shown further on.

"Dr Hyades Was Untiring"

He was in charge of the land group that remained at the base (Mission Cove, Orange Bay, Hoste Island) most of the year, to September 1883.

Hyades was keen on meeting the highest standards of physical anthropology of the time, with its great emphasis on posed photographs, measuring and making plaster casts of all parts of the body. This was standard practice for physical anthropologists at the time, largely abandoned later. Despite his outstanding qualities, both intellectual and humane, Hyades was not fully aware that he was missing some essentials of the Yamana culture, such as their ceremonies, shamanism and oral traditions. Like Darwin, he asserted that the Fuegians were not very superstitious and that they did not have any religious notions.[18] The latter affirmation

FIGURE 13.3. 1882 or 1883: A couple and child on board; on the right an officer indicating to them how to pose. © musée du Quai Branly.

stands contested if religion is to be defined as the belief or conviction that supernatural beings or forces determine or influence the course of human existence. Over fifty years later, Gusinde published extensively on Yamana religion, ceremonies and shamanism.[19]

Although Hyades often treated the Yahgans for their different ailments, his gamut of study went far beyond his professional duties. The volume on the Yamana is number 7 of the Mission Series, which he published with Dr J. Deniker, who was not a member of the expedition. Deniker wrote the first two chapters, analyses of anatomy and morphology, based on data given to him by Hyades in Paris. In five chapters of this large book, Hyades dealt with many aspects of Yahgan culture and with the epidemics. He often referred to Bridges' unpublished notes as *memoire inédit*, which Bridges may have lent him in 1886 in Paris, the year he retired. Hyades rarely cited the Yahgans he knew at Mission Cove. He did mention several who said that the mission in Ushuaia was a cemetery and that they did not want to live there. But his dependence on and admiration of Bridges as his principal source of information concerning the Yahgans did not soften his criticism of the Anglican mission or Bridges' idea about the origin of the epidemics (see below), even though he sometimes praised the "English mission."[20]

Hyades was an active member of the Société d'Anthropologie de Paris and continued his contact with the Fuegians, through correspondence with Bridges, writing about them until 1891.

Dr Hyades Diagnoses the Sickness in Ushuaia

On 10 November 1882, Bridges took the *Allen Gardiner* to Mission Cove to solicit the aid of the expedition's two doctors, Hyades and Philippe Hahn. He informed Hyades that fevers were ravaging the natives at his mission and that he urgently needed a diagnosis of the sickness, since all their treatments had failed, the natives were very alarmed and the missionaries were beginning to fear for their own families. That same afternoon Hyades accompanied him back to the Ushuaia Mission.[21]

Entering the Bay of Ushuaia, Hyades felt depressed by the atmosphere of the mission settlement.

An impression of melancholy imposes itself when one first sees the few English houses, all of material brought from Europe, installed in this sombre surrounding, as if lost at the end of the world.... This impression lingers when one disembarks and becomes aware of the natives...dressed as they are, possessing relatively comfortable huts and some even owners of well-kept gardens. But none seem any happier than the Fuegians we just left, naked in their canoes, going as they well please, in search of their daily sustenance.

Since the foundation of the mission in Ushuaia in 1869, it had never been visited by a medical doctor from Port Stanley or anywhere else.[22] Bridges did not or could not engage a physician to visit there, much less reside there. Otatosh was one of the few who were taken to Dr Hamilton in Port Stanley, though too late (Chapter 12).

Hyades was told that among the 150 Fuegians there, many had already died, even entire families, from April to June 1882, months before Hyades arrived. The illness had killed seventeen of the original twenty-five

FIGURE 13.4. Dr Hyades, second from the right, with the other officers, except for an assistant from the Museum of Natural History, Paris, seated in front, who stayed for only a few months. © musée du Quai Branly.

children in the orphanage. No more children were being taken there. The women who cared for their sick husbands or kin had come down with the same disease, and many of them had also perished.[23]

Upon arrival, Hyades attended the sick until midnight and the following three days, until 16 November, when he returned to Mission Cove. At Ushuaia, he performed four surgical operations without anesthetics.[24] He removed an eye of a patient, a man by the name of Palajlian. Lucas Bridges wrote: "Father records that the patient clutched his hand convulsively, but refrained from showing, even by a moan, any sign of pain."[25]

Postmortem examinations revealed to Hyades that the prevailing sickness was tuberculosis. The lungs and pancreas were full of tubercular deposits. Thomas Bridges explained: "The lungs were glued to the chest and ribs, were so disorganized as to be scarcely recognizable. The spleen also was equally affected. Of the fifty-four patients Hyades examined, thirty-three were consumptive, including fifteen bad cases. Two daughters of the missionary families were affected but survived."[26]

Thirty-three had tuberculosis at the Ushuaia Mission, whose population was 150 at the most. Many of the sick whom Hyades treated or saw perished before he left the following September. Tuberculosis had probably been introduced to the Ushuaia Mission in 1881, by visiting sealers, as Lawrence thought. The disease spread rapidly through contagion and secondary factors, such as the clothing mentioned above, the scanty diet, the closed quarters, etc. Hyades disagreed with Bridges that the diseases among the Fuegians were caused by the harshness of the climate and that those living in their primitive condition were more prone to diseases than those who lived at the mission. Hyades was unequivocal.

The harshness of the climate is admirably supported, from the physiological point of view, by the Fuegians living in their traditional surroundings, near where we lived [in Orange Bay] and we did not observe among them any death due to consumption (*phtisie*)...the natives who had been affected by the germ of tuberculosis during a visit to Ushuaia were rapidly cured once they returned to their nomadic life, continually in the open air, in their canoes and on the beaches.[27]

Nor did he agree with Bridges that the disease had always prevailed. He declared: "The Fuegians had no sickness associated with their race."[28] He explained: "When primitive peoples come into contact with whites they are not annihilated as a result of some fatal or mysterious law but rather because the diseases which the civilised peoples bring evolve in a virgin territory with incredible violence."[29]

He described the ailments of the natives he treated at Mission Cove during the year he was there; only one had tuberculosis and was getting better.[30] Some of the photographs taken by Payen there show children with bloated stomachs, who seem to have been suffering from malnutrition or intestinal troubles.

Bridges was probably aware that Hyades disagreed with him about the origin, causes and location of the diseases, but he was grateful for his medical aid to the natives as well as for vaccinating the four Lawrence children and his own youngest. He was probably proud that Hyades commented that while the natives in Mission Cove were persistent beggars, at the Ushuaia Mission no one had asked him for anything.

Dr Hyades was untiring in his efforts of investigation and relief, and was so very pleasant in all his ways. He greatly interested the natives in his attempts to speak to them in Yahgan.... He gives us reason to hope for the recovery, under arsenic, of many of the natives, and of putting them and us into a better state of health.

Bridges feared that, despite Hyades' assistance, the epidemic would not abate, and he trusted that it would be temporary.[31]

Hyades became aware of the dilemma the mission had created for the Yamana. He explained, very clearly, as follows:

More than one of those [Yahgans] who passed one or two years in Ouchouaya [Ushuaia] and through work and good behaviour acquired a little house, and a cultivated plot of land, suddenly, without regret, left all their possessions to resume their life in the canoe. These savages are aware that those who settle in Ouchouaya rapidly lose their habit of supplying their own needs by means of the traditional industries. Their sons no longer know how to make canoes, nor harpoons to hunt otaries or seals, and they find themselves dependent on the good graces of the English for their food. They also flee from Ouchouaya because the sickness there is more fatal than elsewhere, be it consumption or other imported diseases.[32]

By December 1882, Lawrence related that in that year "the continual sickness and mortality has exceeded anything of the kind previously known to us." He was grateful that a few had recovered since Hyades treated them and remarked that his "visit and indefatigable efforts to do good to all were highly appreciated.... It is the first and only privilege we have had of medical advice and skill at Ooshooia."[33] They desperately needed a resident doctor.

Bridges also agreed and hoped that a medical fellow worker would soon be assigned to the mission.[34] Four years later a missionary, Edward C. Aspinal, who had medical knowledge, finally arrived.

Despite Hyades' insistence on plastering heads and bodies, he was one of the most caring and interested observers of the Yamana. He was an exceptionally dedicated doctor, and though he usually relied on Bridges' unpublished notes, he wrote about the Yamana with originality and insight. "The dominant characteristic of this amazing people is the unconditional love of liberty and the hatred of any sort of constraint. . . . It may well be that this love of liberty, which is perfectly conscious, determines their preference for the savage life over and above the delights of civilised life."[35]

Although Hyades is not well known even in France, one might wonder why the historians and anthropologists have not cited his texts, such as the one above, to contrast them with the derogatory comments about the Yamana that are often used, even today. Could it be because many do not read French? In the following, Hyades highlighted the generosity of the Yamana and explained how such a society can be egalitarian and at the same time highly individualist.

This feeling may have its source in the absolute liberty and in the perfect equality which they enjoy, without chiefs, without wage-earners, without slaves and also in their accentuated egotism which contradicts their generous habits. The Fuegians . . . like to share whatever they have with whoever and all who are nearby and one cannot say that this is a consequence of possessing goods in common. Communal wealth does not exist in Fuegia land. Each possesses what he makes, obtains by fishing or hunting or what he finds on the beach. Even the little children are proprietors of whatever has been given to them. But it seems that above all the Indians desire to possess goods in order to give them away and for the pleasure of being generous.[36]

Nor was he mystified by their mode of greeting, which had baffled Darwin and Fitz-Roy: "The newly arrived person is always assured a place near the fireplace and a serving of food. But the welcome is always cold and silent, with a certain mistrust and if he [the newly arrived] has some provisions, he should share them with his hosts."

Moreover he insisted that the Yamana were not cannibals. "Whatever may be the tortures of hunger they may feel, the Fuegians never commit cannibalism."[37]

Athlinata, the Most Photographed

Hyades first saw him in early February 1883, in a bay not far from Mission Cove, after a curious incident. Hyades had just persuaded a young Yahgan, whose wife had recently died, to retrieve her corpse from the burial and give it to him. He was thinking of conserving it in alcohol

FIGURE 13.5. 1882 or 1883: Athlinata with his wife and two children. © musée du Quai Branly.

and taking it to Paris for anthropological study. His interpreter was a Yahgan who "spoke a little English." He more or less explained this to the grieving husband, who apparently did not oppose the disinterment.[38] (Later a photograph was taken of him in Mission Cove.) While Hyades was talking to the widower three canoes appeared in the bay with many men on board, among them one later known as Athlinata. Hyades' interpreter warned him that this native (Athlinata) was an influential person, so strongly opposed to the French expedition that he planned to attack them in Mission Cove during Hyades' absence. When Athlinata and his men landed nearby, Hyades ordered his men to board the whaleboat quickly, without the corpse. They camped nearby that night, their weapons on hand. The next day Athlinata and his companions had vanished, so Hyades returned to the burial site and took the corpse as agreed. (He published a photograph of her skeleton in the 1891 volume.)

It is not explained why Athlinata renounced his intentions to attack the expedition and why he later agreed to being immobile for hours while Hyades made plaster casts of various parts of his body. The plaster used

FIGURE 13.6. Athlinata posing with a harpoon. © musée du Quai Branly.

on Athlinata was defective, so all casts of him were thrown away. About then Hyades thought that he was "one of the most intelligent Indians in Orange Bay."[39] He became Hyades' favourite male model, as evidenced by the two presented here (of the seven taken of him).

Another photograph was taken of Athlinata some twenty-five years later, in 1907, when he was in his mid-forties, at the last Anglican mission on the Douglas Inlet, Navarino Island when the North American writer, Furlong, witnessed a dramatic scene involving the missionary and Athlinata (Chapter 15).

Kamanakar-Kipa, the Favourite Model

Hyades wrote with feeling about Kamanakar-kipa, the other star model (Figure 13.7). "This young woman was very intelligent, with a primitive grace and a natural spirit that distinguished her from her companions." The photograph below and the following are two of the eight taken of her by Payen.

Bridges wrote to Hyades in 1885 that there had been no case of measles in Orange Bay, and that all the Yahgans Hyades had known were healthy except "the two most beautiful young women of this group [Figure 13.8], Kamanakar-kipa and her friend Chaoualouch-kipa, [who] went to Ouch-ouaya, where they died of measles the same day."[40]

Just why they went to Ushuaia is not explained. They certainly did not realise that there was so much sickness there. Even though both were orphans, perhaps they had relatives there.

Pinoense, "An Accomplished Fuegian"

A year before he died, the often mentioned Pinoense was photographed twice, on Button Island, during Martial's last trip.[41] He was the son of Tom Button, a friend of Okoko, also a "Keppel graduate" (my term), and finally father of seven boys, all of whom died from the epidemics. He remained close to the missionaries most of his adult life (Chapters 9 to 11). Hyades may never have met Pinoense, but he published Bridges' text, quoted below, which Bridges may have written in Paris in 1886 when Hyades may have shown him this photograph (Figure 13.9).[42]

Bridges expressed a sincere admiration for Pinoense and sorrow for his and his family's untimely deaths in this beautiful eulogy.

He was in every sense, an accomplished Fuegian . . . a superb hunter. . . . His sweet and generous character made him popular among his own people. . . . He belonged to the Yahgan clan of Murray Narrows which, when he was young, consisted of fifteen families, now reduced to only two. . . . Pinouayentsis [Pinoense] made a good marriage and had seven sons but no daughters. . . . Of an even, amiable temperament though he did not tolerate being imposed upon by the other Indians. . . . He remained for several years with the other Fuegians who lived near us in Ushuaia but one day, tired of the continual routine of the Mission, he left us to return to the way of life of his own people, going from one place to another, devoted as he was to hunting. He was sufficiently instructed and his conduct sufficiently pure to merit being baptised in 1873 with the name Allen Gardiner Pinouaya. . . . His first great sorrow was the death of his faithful wife Elizabeth or Anagou, then followed the death of several of his children. Finally he became ill from an epidemic of measles [in 1884] which carried him away with his last son.[43]

FIGURE 13.7. 1882 or 1883: Kamanakar-kipa seated in the middle of a group seven girls. © musée du Quai Branly.

FIGURE 13.8. 1882 or 1883: Chaoualouch-kipa with her friend Kamanakar-kipa. © musée du Quai Branly.

Once the epidemics started spreading, there was no way the Yahgans could escape from them. Their shamans soon realised that their treatments could not help cure the sicknesses brought by the Europeans (Chapter 14).

FIGURE 13.9. August 1883: Pinoense, Tom Button's son. © musée du Quai Branly.

Captain Martial's Seven Visits and Explorations

Captain Martial made seven trips, during his assignment to the Cape Horn area, from October 1882 to August 1883, including three visits to Punta Arenas and met the Yahgans on several occasions. He and Dr Hahn, who accompanied him, were very concerned about them, though Martial's main interests were hydrography and cartography. He was also keen on locating suitable anchorages and moorages in the area. The three visits to Punta Arenas were purely administrative. I will only refer briefly here to his seven trips and explorations, especially with reference to his encounters with the Yahgans.

During his first trip (26 October to 30 November) on the way back from Punta Arenas, 15 November (1882), he stopped over at Staten Island and collected whale bones in Puerto Cook. A few days later he spent two days in Banner Cove (Picton Island) where he located Gardiner's inscription "Dig below, go to Spaniard harbour–March 1851" (Chapter 7). Sailing along Beagle Channel, at Gable Island he noticed the mission's "little village": several huts, a hundred or so resident Fuegians and a herd of about fifty cattle.[44]

The next day, 24 November, when the *Romanche* dropped anchor in Ushuaia Bay, Martial's first impression was agreeable. "The harbour of Oushouaïa is vast and secure; the depths are moderate and hold very well; the gusts of wind are not violent and it is well sheltered with winds coming from the west.... Beautiful forests cover the slopes of the mountains."

He was greatly impressed by a Yamana called Samuel Mateen, who politely greeted him in English. Martial described him as "vigorous and tall," and commented that he wore his European clothes with ease. His young wife had just given birth to their first baby: "[her] quiet and confident aspect contrasted in a striking manner to the sordid and troubled appearance of most of the Indians we saw." The couple seemed happy with their new life and had been living there for several years.

The well-being he was enjoying was entirely due to his intelligence and his work.... He showed us, in detail, his large garden where, with great care, he cultivated potatoes and turnips and possessed a dozen or so cows which supplied him with milk and cheese.... Mr Bridges, who accompanied me, interpreted when I asked him if [he] wanted to change his mode of living and return to the former existence. His response was frankly negative.... Samuel is an exception among his people even though next to his small farm, there were others which denote a considerable progress with respect to the past.[45]

Two years later Samuel died of a devastating measles epidemic. The fate of his wife and baby was not mentioned.

Martial learned then that the missionaries and their families totalled eighteen – four men, six women, and their children – and that sealers frequently came to the mission, mainly for the facilities it offered as a depot and to purchase supplies in the store. He estimated that about 150 natives lived there more or less permanently. Dr Hahn, who accompanied him, continued the care of the sick begun by Hyades. Hahn recommended cod liver oil and certain medicines that Bridges sent for to Punta Arenas, and Martial gave him medicines to help curb the epidemic of tuberculosis that Hyades had diagnosed a few days earlier. Bridges was also gratified when he learned that Martial had prohibited tobacco and liquor to the natives in Mission Cove. Later Martial expressed admiration for the progress realised by the mission, adding that it supplied a decisive argument in favour of the "*perfectibilité de cette race.*"[46]

While Martial was visiting the orphanage of the Ushuaia Mission, one of the dying girls, Gerty Wocimoon, was being tenderly cared for by an old native woman. Martial inquired by gestures: "Is she unconscious?" The woman nodded that she was. Little Gerty saw their gestures, became very excited, lifted her head and cried out (in English), "I am conscious," not wanting to give up hope of recovery. But the next day she died. Another orphan, also named Gerty, died shortly afterwards.

Probably to distract the people from tending the sick and mourning the dead, on 27 November Martial invited everyone on board his ship. The forty-four natives, Bridges and the mission teachers were delighted, "greatly interested" in everything they were shown, as the *Romanche* was the first man-of-war (*aviso*) to enter Beagle Channel.[47]

During his second exploration (14 to 26 December 1882) he surveyed the area near Cape Horn along the Wollaston Islands, where Doze took several photographs, including the one below (Figure 13.10). Shortly before Christmas (1882), the *Romanche* stopped over in Gretton Bay and met the kin of the fifteen apparently killed by the crew of the *Rescue*, as related in Chapter 11.

The third voyage (23 January to 20 March) while passing by islets near Packsaddle Island, he noticed that the fur seals had become very distrustful since the "relentless war" declared on them by the sealers, as Webster had commented over fifty years earlier (Chapter 2). Martial explained that fortunately seal furs had lost some of their appeal in the London markets and that exports to China had also diminished.[48] Despite the loss of markets and overkilling, there were still sealing vessels in the area.

During the last week of January (his third exploration), while Martial was again in Ushuaia, Bridges gave him some "human bones" that the natives had given to him, so Martial was told, "without any difficulty."[49] Then he met the Alakaluf youth Pedro, a survivor of the 1881 kidnapping. Dr Hahn treated Catharine's little girl for her burns, mentioned in the last chapter.

After leaving Ushuaia on 30 January, the *Romanche* crossed Beagle Channel from Ushuaia Bay and approached the creek called Awaiakihr on the north coast of Hoste Island. Three fires were lit on the shore to greet the visitors and, while their ship anchored nearby, forty-two natives in seven canoes paddled rapidly towards the vessel and received small gifts. Several canoes lingered on near the ship and Martial's attention was caught by a woman who was wearing a sailor's jacket, which looked very French. It occurred to him immediately that she had gotten it from a member of his crew, who had bartered it for an otter skin or something else, which was strictly forbidden. When an officer attempted to board her canoe to inspect her jacket, she plunged into the water and swam to

FIGURE 13.10. December 1882: Woman and girl from Wollaston Island, on board the *Romanche*. © musée du Quai Branly.

another canoe and was paddled away.[50] Martial was either embarrassed or furious, though he made no comment and let the matter drop. Curious coincidence: in 1833, Fitz-Roy had a very similar "encounter" in the same place (Chapter 5). History did not repeat itself because Martial took it all in his stride.

Martial's fourth trip (28 March to 1 May) was outstanding. By then Yekaif had overcome his fear of being kidnapped and came along as interpreter. This was the first scientific expedition to survey the entire south coast of Hoste and New Year's Sound, where the many French place names bear witness, though Martial encountered only a few natives along the way. Even though New Year's Sound had been populated by the Yamana and therefore had marine resources, it was too difficult to navigate even in a steam ship such as the *Romanche* and remains so today. Martial described it as "a large bay which penetrates about twenty miles into the interior of the land, in which there are numerous islands, groups of islets and rock [and fjords]. . . . The absence of routes of communications and its many dangers divest this great bay . . . of any utility whatsoever for navigation."[51]

In the area, they met a small group in Bay Claire (Bahía Clara), who hid in the forest when they noticed the vessel approaching. Yekaif located them by their barking dogs and reassured them of the Frenchmen's good intentions. Another group was in a bay called Ouftaténa (not on Chilean maps consulted) near Bay Claire. Martial thought they were the most primitive and most timid he had ever seen. However, some spoke a few words of English, which they had undoubtedly learned from sealers.

Exiting New Year's Sound, they entered Christmas Sound. Although Captain Cook, in 1774 and Fitz-Roy in 1830 had met many Fuegians there, Martial did not find any trace of them. The *Romanche* then continued through the Southwest Arm and down Murray Narrows. Passing the shore of Wulaia, they noticed some fifteen canoes and a hundred or so Yahgans, who were enjoying a *"pantagruélique"* whale feast. They signalled by fires inviting the crew to partake of their feast, but Martial ignored the invitation and sailed to Mission Cove. During this trip they had met Yamana twice feasting on whales, evidence again of their great importance.[52]

Back in their cove, Martial became outraged a few weeks later (mid-May) because some "bold pranksters" had stolen the whalebones that he had gathered on Staten Island. Once the culprits were discovered, he ordered that the hut where they had been living be burned down as punishment. It would not be surprising if the Yamana thought that Martial had stolen their whalebones in the first place.

During his next trip, the fifth (14 May to 5 June), Martial retuned to Ushuaia and Punta Arenas without encountering anyone on the way.

During his sixth trip (18 June to 3 July), in mid-June, he explored Wollaston Islands again and saw the wreck of a large ship, the *Oracle*, which had come from California with a cargo of wheat and was heading for New York by way of Cape Horn when a storm struck. The wreck had occurred after Martial's first visit to the area in December 1882, and castaways had been rescued in the meantime by a passing ship. He or one of his crew heard from a group of natives that they had given the castaways "wild strawberries," the only food they had at the time.[53] These Yahgans, like those who tried to save the two survivors of the *Rescue*, had had no contact with the mission.

Each time the *Romanche* returned to Mission Cove, the Yahgans came to receive food and old clothes. Despite occasional "petty thievery," relations with them remained friendly.[54]

Martial's final exploration, his seventh, lasted from 7 July until 20 August. Then he and his crew had completed the surveys begun on the previous trips and had explored (and surveyed) most of the area recognised later as Yamana territory. On 14 July, they stopped over at Button Island, where the Doze took photos of Pinoense, Tom Button's son, mentioned above and in previous chapters.

Adieu Terre de Feu
On 4 September 1883, the Frenchmen bade farewell to the Fuegians at Mission Cove and the missionaries at Ushuaia. Bridges thanked Martial for the building materials from Mission Cove that Martial gave him and expressed his gratitude to Hyades and Hahn for their medical aid.[55]

Aftermath
Soon after Martial returned to France he was assigned to command an expedition to China. Near Beijing in 1885, at the age of forty-nine, he contracted a fatal illness, and passed away there. The last three of his seven trips and explorations in Tierra del Fuego had been very summarily described in his log, and perhaps some of his journal was lost. Louise Jeanne Claire Spenner Martial, his widow, collaborated with Dr Hyades in preparing for publication of his notes and the log that were found as the first of the mission's eight volumes.[56]

The Ushuaia Mission Carries On

Shortly after the French expedition departed, Captain Lynch, in his vessel the *Thomas Hunt*, reappeared in Ushuaia Bay and gave the carcasses of forty or fifty young seals to "our hungry people," along with a load of flour and bread. More relief came a few weeks later when ten men Bridges had sent to the Evout Islands, near Cape Horn, returned with 200 penguins and a dead seal. Bridges warned the resident natives, who were killing their female cattle for food that if they persisted he would not give them any more. The tuberculosis epidemic had not abated. Of the twenty-six children who were in the orphan home in 1881, only three were still alive in 1884.[57] That June Bridges recognised: "The late mortality has been very widespread, and removed a large part of the people." (See this note for his population figures.)[58]

A few grew turnips and those who still possessed some cattle were selling them to buy imported provisions in the store. Lawrence reported that most of the people were wearing a piece or two of manufactured clothing that had lost their "original appearance." He complained: "We have daily to remind them of our inability to comply with their numerous requests and expectations, though it may seem but little for each one to ask. We have much of this unpleasant work to do."[59]

Again the Gift from Nature
Good news for the Yamana in September or October 1884; another whale came to the rescue. A sixty-footer was stranded in Ushuaia Bay, meaning food for weeks or perhaps longer. Then a little bad news for Bridges: a theft from his gardens by night. He "rebuked" "the evil doers" by refusing them employment.[60]

Stirling's Advice
Later that year Bishop Stirling visited Ushuaia and Keppel and announced that he would like the missionaries, upon retirement, to become proprietors of sheep farms, so as to prevent outsiders from exterminating the Indians, as the Onas (the Selk'nam) were being killed "under immigrant influence." He was right; the genocide against them had begun. At about this time (see below) concessions from Chile and Argentina were being obtained, mostly by a few Europeans in Punta Arenas and Buenos Aires, of immense tracks of land on the Isla Grande (Selk'nam territory), which were being converted into a few immense sheep farms.

Meanwhile, at Keppel in 1884, Stirling made no mention of sickness among the twenty young Yahgans, even though the winter was so terrible that many cattle and horses perished and sheep were found standing dead, their feet frozen into the ground.[61] This image of the sheep dramatises the suffering of the domestic animals in winter more forcefully than any other I found.

The Argentines Arrive

One calm day at the end of that September (1884), the Argentines sailed into the Bay of Ushuaia in full force. The Expeditionary Division to the

South Atlantic, under the command of Colonel Augusto Lasserre, made a surprise appearance with a fleet of six ships (three were cutters). The crews included thirty men who spoke some English. Lasserre proceeded to establish a subprefecture as the capital of the "territory"(not a *provincia* as the other states of Argentina) of Tierra del Fuego and the town, then named Ushuaia, was founded. The Isla Grande had been officially claimed by Argentina and Chile in 1881. The boundary ran in a straight line from Beagle Channel, twelve miles (19 kilometres) west of Ushuaia, up to very near the Atlantic entrance to the Magellan Strait.[62]

The epidemic of tuberculosis had somewhat abated when, on 12 October 1884, the official founding of Ushuaia was celebrated. Some two months later Lieutenant Félix Mariano Paz, the first governor, took office. Luis Fique, a merchant who arrived with this expedition, was the first Argentine civilian to settle permanently in Tierra del Fuego. Later, he will prove to be one of the best contacts with the Haush in Good Success Bay.

Bridges had several reasons to be thankful to Colonel Lasserre, who was treating him with the greatest consideration, and to feel assured that his fellow missionaries would be dealt with fairly under the new regime. When Lasserre sent two medical men to examine fourteen sick natives, Bridges remarked, "we were greatly pleased with the medical men's kindness and evident ability." At last there were "medical men" in Ushuaia, though only temporarily. Bridges was optimistic for the natives and for himself.

The natives will be more or less engaged to work for the party, and will be well paid; but in engaging them they [Lasserre and the subprefecture employees] will consult me. Thus everything appears most hopeful, and the natives are all well pleased.... Our cattle are now becoming profitable.... We supply their wants gladly to the limit of our resources.

Bridges imagined that the establishment of the Argentine subprefecture was about to solve the mission's and the Yahgans' problems. He was passing responsibility for the dreadful situation of the Yahgans on to the Argentines. The sealers had also created problems for the natives, but they did not count now. Bridges added: "Colonel Lasserre will also further our Mission's request for the land grant." Here he was referring to his request to the Argentine government for land for the mission, not for himself, not yet.[63]

His letter dated 30 October 1884, written in Punta Arenas, expressed his confidence in the will and ability of the subprefecture, and especially the colonel, to provide "great advantages" for the natives.

The prefecture has been so happily and wisely established, under the able parental care of Colonel Lasserre, that we rejoice sincerely over it, seeing the great advantages accruing to the natives, and to the Mission in consequence. Every assistance has been promised us, and much already given.... The regulations for the Sub-Prefect are in perfect accord with our work, and the good of the natives, to whom the Colonel will prove a father. We are full of gratitude to God for the favour He [God] has shown us.

Here again he was shifting the care for the natives from his mission to Lasserre, concentrating less on their future and increasingly on that of his family.

Bridges Takes Six Yahgans to Punta Arenas

In October 1884, Bridges made a round trip, Ushuaia–Punta Arenas, with Colonel Lasserre in the Navy ship *Parana*. He frankly stated, in his letter dated 30 October written in Punta Arenas, that he took six natives "to serve as domestics," that they had been "affected" by the pneumonia that was "raging" in Ushuaia before they departed and that one died during the trip.

I took Henry Lory to assist me as pilot, and we also brought six young natives to serve as domestics in the houses of the Colonel, and his sisters, the 1st Commander, and Dr. Alvarez. But these most unhappily have proved to have been affected by the pneumonia then raging at Ooshooia, and one of the children died on board (we buried him in Hope Harbour), and the rest are dangerously ill.... We hope some may recover.[64]

Recall that Henry Lory, the pilot, was also Yahgan. What finally happened to him and the five who were "dangerously ill?" Lucas explained that despite the medical attention in Punta Arenas:

Only one of the patients survived. Poor Henry Lory was among those who died. These six deaths from this virulent disease greatly worried my father, for before he had left Ushwaia in the Parana several of the natives complained, though no one had had the slightest idea that it would develop into anything so dreadful.

Five natives died: one on the way to Punta Arenas, then four others there in addition to Henry Lory, the Yahgan pilot. I found no mention of the survivor. It is hard to believe that Bridges took six young natives, who had been, or were already, sick to work as servants in this manner. But he did.

Thanks to Lucas, we also know that Doctors Fenton, in Punta Arenas, and Alvarez, the Argentine ship's surgeon, mistakenly diagnosed the fatal sickness as typhoid–pneumonia. Lucas' mother, his aunt, Mrs Lawrence and Miss Martin, her sister, "all decided that it was measles. None of the grown members of the Mission party, who had had measles in their youth, contracted the complaint, which goes to prove that this time the ladies knew better than the medical men." Measles had struck Ushuaia before Bridges left for Punta Areas with Henry Lory and the six other Yahgans.

The Most Deadly Epidemic Strikes

Lucas also wrote that, meanwhile in Ushuaia, "the natives went down with this fever one after the other. In a few days they were dying at such a rate that it was impossible to dig graves fast enough. In outlying districts the dead were merely put outside the wigwams or . . . carried or dragged to the nearest bushes."[65]

The measles epidemic gripped the population on 16 October (1884), while Argentine officials and crews were in Ushuaia. Even though none of them were ill, apparently they were the unwitting cause of this disastrous epidemic. It struck with lightning force and spread like wildfire, killed Karmanakar-kipa and Chaoulouche-kipa, among many others. Greatly alarmed, Whaits wrote, on 15 November 1884, to the editors of the mission magazine:

The day after they [Bridges and Lasserre] left nearly all the Indians here were taken ill of measles, so that in a few days, the whole population were stricken down at once, Mr T. Bridges' and Mr Lawrence's children included . . . all the children were down at the same time. Many of the people died in sickening before the measles came out, and others died of lung disease after the measles. We have now lost forty-three persons in three weeks at Ooshooia; but how far it has spread I cannot say, for it is as much as I can do to look after those near at hand.

Whaits was also worried because in his orphanage one little girl had died and a boy was still very ill. He added: "I can assure you it is very sad to see the poor things suffering so much, and not be able to help them."

The epidemic spread across Beagle Channel. Having heard that "two families" were suffering there, Whaits hurried across the channel with a certain Mr Gibbart on the *Allen Gardiner* to the north shore of Navarino Island. He did not specify exactly where they went to find the two families. Whaits was shocked, overwhelmed, by what they witnessed there. His testimony is probably among the most heart-rending accounts in the entire history of plagues. Whaits is quoted entirely.

At the first house we found eleven people sick, and one old woman who had recovered; they told us three had died, and pointed out several others who they said would die – among them a little boy, who held his arms out to me and said, "No, no, I am not going to die, Mr Whaits; do take me to Ooshooia with you in the boat, and then I shall soon be well." But the poor little fellow will die.

At the next place we found three women, a little boy, and a man trying to get to the canoe to come to Ooshooia. The man told us he had buried four, but was so weak that he could not bury the others who were in the house. We went in and found one dear little fellow on his back, not quite dead; he asked me for water, which I gave him; he died a few minutes after. Near him we found a man who I found was Leonard Burleigh's [baptismal name of a Yahgan] father, his mother having died a few days before. In the same house we found a man who had been dead for two days, and in his arms a poor little boy, not dead. When I took him away, he cried to go back to his father. We took him to Ooshooia, but he died on the way. But I will not write more of this sad picture, for in the midst of it all, our mercies have been very great.

Then Whaits commented that it would have been "much worse" if any "of us English people had been sick," adding that they remained well and helped the sick natives. Gusinde, who had other sources, added:

The epidemics spread to the north coast of Navarino Island and there also, the beach was soon covered with cadavers. Many of the sick certainly saw the foxes [probably wild dogs] coming out of the forest and devouring the cadavers, but no one was able to defend themselves against them or scare them away. A dying woman whose little boy was seated beside her, could not protect him. A fox attacked her and began to devour her when she was still alive. When her little son threw stones at him, the animal backed away. When his mother died, the child lit three fires as a distress signal and soon then a canoe came to his aid. Once he was in the canoe, the fox came out of the forest again, back to the cadaver of the woman and ate it.[66]

I am sure more testimonies could be found. A week later, Lawrence expressed his and Whaits' gratitude for the help with the sick natives from the crew of the *Allan Gardiner* and the employees of the Argentine government and was thankful that "our dear children are spared, and are slowly recovering." Lawrence concluded:

Though our trials have now been great, we are sure many of the natives, whom we have known and loved so long, such as Samuel Mateen, Leonard Burleigh [a Yahgan, not identified, named for the missionary], and others, *have passed away to a happier home*. What a privilege to speak and pray with them, and to know they were able to express their humble submission to the will of God, and their calm and peaceful confidence in Jesus, having a *joyful hope of triumph and victory* over death through the finished work of Christ.[67]

After all their suffering, such a "happier home" and "triumph and victory" may have sounded deceitful to the Yahgan survivors, as it did to Nelly Lawrence.

How Many Succumbed?

According to Lucas, the epidemic reached its peak about mid-November 1884; although when his father returned from Punta Arenas, a bit later "the natives were still dying fast." Lucas added:

It is astonishing that this childish ailment, contagious in civilised communities, yet seldom fatal, should wipe out over half the population of a district and leave the survivors so reduced in vitality *that another fifty per cent succumbed during the next two years*, apparently from the after-effects of the attack . . . the Yahgans, though incredibly strong, and able to face cold and hardship of every kind and to recover almost miraculously from serious wounds, had never had to face this evil thing [measles], and therefore lacked the stamina to withstand it.[68]

It was not stamina they lacked but rather medical aid. Later, Thomas Bridges wrote: "The measles . . . some seven years ago took away fully 70 percent of the people in the central district, Ushuaia and Beagle Channel."[69]

In 1886, he calculated the number of the "Yahgan tribe" as about 288 persons, though twenty days later he made "a census" of the Yahgan tribe that slightly exceeded 400 persons.[70] In reality Bridges had no way of counting them and had different impressions according to the news he received and his own observations.

Hyades wrote that the measles epidemic took half of the population of Ushuaia but that it had not reached Orange Bay, where he had been a year before.[71] Moreover, given the huge mortality in Ushuaia, Thomas Bridges was mistaken when he asserted that the health conditions of the natives (tuberculosis and measles) were worse beyond Ushuaia. In 1886, he made this other "mistake." "The natives must now stand or fall, they must meet temptation and resist it, or, like so many others, fail. . . . This is no country or climate for a roving life."[72]

Bridges had learned nothing. It was not temptation, or the climate, much less the roving life, that would make the natives "fail" but rather the continuing onslaught of unattended imported diseases.

Measles Strikes Keppel

Many of the boys who had been in Keppel and had returned to the Ushuaia mission had perished "in the late violent attack of measles." The news from Keppel itself was not more reassuring: several were on their deathbeds and others very weak and sickly. Among the dead was another of Jemmy's grandsons, a "good boy" for whom there were great hopes, who had been helpful in the school. His name was not given.[73]

And the Haush?

Nothing had been heard about the Haush, the "Eastern Onas," for the previous fifteen months, but "general opinion" was that all had perished from measles, according to Bridges.

Angela Loij, my Selk'nam informant, told me that the majority of Haush had been killed by sealers who shot seals and put poison in their bodies, leaving them for the Haush to eat. She said they didn't shoot the Haush because they lived in or near forests, where they could easily hide.[74]

Origin of the Measles

Lawrence thought the measles epidemic and tuberculosis had been introduced by people "from other countries" – that is, by the sealers. He also alluded to the presence of the Argentine envoys.[75] Sealers had been coming and going in and out of Ushuaia Bay probably years before Stirling established the mission there in 1869; but until October 1884, there had been no evidence of measles.

Bridges wrote, in a letter to Hyades, that following the establishment of the Argentine subprefecture in Ushuaia, the Yahgan population had been reduced from a thousand to five hundred. Apparently none of the men on the ships were sick at that time; nevertheless, according to the date and place of the first outbreak of measles, at least one of them was apparently the agent of the epidemic.[76] Darwin referred to several such cases "of the most malignant fevers having broken out, although the parties themselves, who were the cause, were not affected."[77]

The Worst Had Passed But...

Early in January (1885), Lawrence affirmed that the worst had passed; although some were still suffering, others were well and strong and "were, comparatively, in good health." But two months later, "Many have evidently only rallied for a time, and are gradually wasting away."

Mrs Hemmings, a missionary nurse who arrived in January, took over Whaits' job in the orphanage, which then housed another group of sixteen girls. Bridges had designated the orphanage in the Ushuaia Mission for girls, while the orphan boys were taken to Keppel.[78] Mrs Hemming complained of continued sickness in the orphanage after the measles epidemic began to subside. Five months later, in May 1885, she was grieving: "They [the orphans] are capable of being taught anything taught to English children, and it grieves me to see them droop and die." There were only eight girls (of the former sixteen) in the orphanage. She was anxiously awaiting the arrival of the missionary with medical training, Mr Aspinall, who would replace Bridges when he retired two years later.[79] "The worst" had passed but more was to come.

The Gold Rush Takes Off

Meanwhile, by 1885, in Punta Arenas the bars and cafés, street corners and park benches were full of men engaged in endless debates on the how and where to jump on the bandwagon leading to a quick and maybe great fortune. In the early 1880s, when gold was first reported in southern Patagonia (on the continent), many unemployed and employed men abandoned Punta Arenas to try their luck on the gold roulette. They headed either for southern Patagonia (Province of Santa Cruz, Argentina) or for the Chilean Fire Land (Isla Grande). Gold had become another contagious disease. In 1886 Captain Willis reported from Punta Arenas: "There is a mania here for gold-seeking: shepherds, labourers, shopkeepers, and sailors are leaving their occupations and going to Patagonia, washing sand for gold."[80] The more prudent stayed in Punta Arenas, preparing for business with the nugget gatherers.

Prospecting had begun, in 1881 in the Sierra Boquerón, the Chilean section of Isla Grande, where, according to the historian Mateo Martinic:

Within a short time, some two hundred men were panning the gold-bearing sands of the rivers.... This district had a large native population [the Selk'nam], which was bound to suffer the immediate consequences of the presence of such a large number of foreigners: the latter tried to get their hands on Indian women, leading to repeated acts of violence against the natives, with sad consequences for the latter.[81]

The most notorious prospector was Julius Popper, a Romanian engineer. He arrived, in 1886, on the Atlantic coast of Isla Grande, Argentina, with a troop of Croat immigrants, well equipped for any eventuality. Five years before, Lucas Bridges, still a child, had been playing with his magnet on the sands of Sloggett Bay (Haush territory) and had saved a little pile of sand in which he noticed sparkling dust, later found to be gold (Chapter 12).[82] The word had travelled and Popper had his own sources of information. By 1888 he was off to Sloggett Bay (Chapter 14).

Genocide Against the Oens-Men (The Selk'nam)

The richest grazing lands were on the upper half of Isla Grande (northwestern section), which had been mostly Selk'nam territory. During the 1880 decade to the end of the century huge tracts of land, up to a million acres were granted to just one person, José Nogueira, by the Chilean government. Somewhat later the Argentine government did likewise, granting land for sheep farms along the Atlantic coast to Europeans, some of whom were well-known merchants living in Punta Arenas and Buenos Aires.[83] These "pioneers" were given a free hand to "clean" the land of the bothersome Indians. The guanacos, the essential source of food and clothing for the Selk'nam, were being killed by the "pioneers" because they ate the sheep's grass and also provided food for the pioneers' dogs. Given the scarcity of guanacos, the Selk'nam killed the sheep to eat and also to retaliate against their enemies. Their enemies were the *estancieros*, the owners of the farms, and their henchmen, such as the notorious "Chancho Colorado" (Red Pig), a Scotsman working for the estanciero José Menéndez. The Selk'nam fought back with their bows and arrows, broke camp and fled with their women and children when they were attacked by the mounted, armed, henchmen. They had no chance against such an enemy. How many were slaughtered during this reign of terror remains to be documented.

Apparently the period of outright genocide lasted some ten to fifteen years, from the mid-1880s onward. But the most devastating of all the enemies were the white man's diseases, which, together with the genocide, provoked the demise of the Selk'nam as an autonomous people and culture. By the 1890s the diseases, the epidemics, spread to the confined quarters of the Salesian mission on Dawson Island, where Selk'nam and Alakaluf were taken as of 1889, and later to the second Salesian mission opened in 1897, near Río Grande. Here the missionary Padre José Maria Beauvoir (an Italian despite his French name) risked his career in trying to protect the Selk'nam. The genocide gradually subsided as the epidemics took force. The Salesian missionaries convinced the landlords that it was more humane to gather them in the missions. The landlords agreed and made donations to the Salesians. The Indians were dying of the sicknesses in the missions, so why bother killing them? The two missions had become loci of contagion, despite the best intentions of the missionaries. Some of those who were already sick fled from the missions, but they contaminated their healthy countrymen.

Julius Popper and Ramon Lista, an Argentine military officer, "explored" the Selk'nam home territory during the same year, 1886. Lista and his troops, during the two and a half months they were in Tierra del Fuego, killed some forty Selk'nam men and captured a number of families, which he shipped to Patagonia, far from their home, to "clean" the land of those "savages." Popper had the bad taste to have himself photographed in the act, triumphantly gazing into the horizon, with a dead Selk'nam at his feet still clutching his bow. Popper was not seeking to exterminate the Selk'nam; he "simply" shot them when they got in his way. Lista didn't have a camera, but he killed about forty, perhaps more than Popper. During those years (approximately 1884–1900), the Selk'nam population, possibly 3,000 individuals, fell to about 500, dispersed throughout Isla Grande.[84] Thus the Selk'nam ceased to exist as a viable culture with a prospect for the future.

The Yamana were not persecuted as the Selk'nam were, mainly because their homeland did not offer great expanses of grassland apt for grazing sheep. Also the main farm owners there were retired missionaries, Bridges and later Lawrence, not the owners of large sheep farms, such as the Selk'nam had to confront.[85]

The gold diggers killed some Yahgan and Selk'nam men who got in their way, but gold diggers were on their own, each working for himself, so they didn't implement a policy of extermination, as the businessmen–owners of sheep farms did.

Alakaluf and Selk'nam Escape to Ushuaia

In October 1885, the Anglican missionaries and residents in the brand new town of Ushuaia had an unexpected visit, according to Bridges, "a great surprise.... twelve fine men, as much Ona as Alacaloof, both in language and appearance... well clad in new guanaco hides and... well provided with good bows and arrows." The twelve men were seeking to bring their families to Ushuaia "because they can do so without fear of being shot, which is not the case in their own country [Dawson Island], and in Ona-land [Isla Grande]." They were guided to Ushuaia by young Pedro, a survivor of the eleven who in 1881 had been kidnapped and taken to Europe. Among these, three of the four survivors, including young Pedro, had returned to their home territory, Dawson Island, in March 1883 (Chapter 12). In 1885 Pedro led the party of twelve men (Alakaluf and Selk'nam) who had set out with their families to seek refuge at the mission and the new town of Ushuaia. During the weeks of hiking on the way, they had hunted guanacos for food. The women and children were unable to reach Ushuaia because "a large river and an almost untraversable district lay between their camp and Ooshooia." A few of the men went ahead of the families, as scouts seeking the best, the safest, passage for the women and children. Finally some arrived in Ushuaia and sought the help of the missionaries and the government to aid the families to cross the bogs and rivers that were detaining them. After much difficulty all the families finally arrived safely in Ushuaia thanks to the help of Bridges, his son Despard, two Scotch sailors and two Argentine captains. There they were kindly received by the ninety-six Yahgans (including twenty-eight children), "who were much interested" in the refugees. Soon the men began working. None of the refugees wanted to return to where the genocide had begun.[86] But they were trapped between the genocide at home and the epidemics in Ushuaia.

The Bridges Visit Their Future Sheep Farm

Early April 1884, five months before the Argentines arrived (see above), Bridges visited Gable Island and estimated that it could support two thousand sheep. He was planning his retirement, which would occur two years later.[87] In October 1885, the Bridges family looked over the land of their future farm, first called Downeast and later Harberton, after Mrs Bridges' birthplace. Bridges had chosen the area of his future farm, about forty miles (74 kilometres) east of Ushuaia Bay near Cambaceres Bay, and the former Blomefield Harbour, where the would-be missionary, A. F. Gardiner, was so set on burying his provisions (Chapter 7). The bay was renamed by Bridges for the president of the Argentine congress. The area was about 50,000 acres (20,000 hectares), fourteen miles (26 kilometres) along the coast of Beagle Channel and about six miles (11 kilometres) inland, which included a dozen offshore islands, the largest being Gable. Here there were "many sites of ancient Yahgan villages."[88] Bridges contacted his future work force, "a company of fifty-eight natives." Among them James-Cushinjiz, a Keppel graduate, worked for Bridges making enclosures for the sheep. By this time, October 1885, Bridges may have felt assured, by Captain Lasserre and his influential friends in Buenos Aires, that he would acquire a grant for the land from the Argentine government.[89] The latter did accord the land grant the following year. But the question arises: Did Bridges request "full permission from the natives" as he had for the land of the Ushuaia Mission in 1870? Probably not, because the natives no longer owned their land; the Argentine government did.

Okoko Returns to Lewaia

When the Bridges family returned to the mission a few days later (in October 1885) the loyal Okoko appeared. Bridges promised to transport Okoko's "few cattle" from the mission to "Livia" (Lewaia), on the north coast of Navarino, where Okoko was still determined to establish himself.[90] He had attempted to resettle in Lewaia since 1868, when his house had been burnt down for the third time. He obviously felt that Lewaia was his home. By mid-1886 Okoko was alone. The loyal Gamela and all but one of their children had passed away, apparently victims of the tuberculosis and measles epidemics. His last child, the eldest, called Cranmer (because he was born in Keppel), died that July 1886 at the age of twenty-seven.

Other Yahgans Sent to Punta Arenas, and to La Plata, Argentina

Despite the death of the five Yahgan youths and Henry Lory, whom Bridges had taken to Punta Arenas in October 1884, again in February 1886, with Bishop Stirling's approval, Bridges agreed to send a family of three to Punta Arenas "as servants." He reported: "Accordingly I sent Fred Beadle, and Lucy his wife, and their little girl Amy to our agent, Mr Stubenranch, and two lads to serve Mr Tonini in the Museum in the new city of La Plata."

This time the governor in Ushuaia, Captain Felix Mariano Paz, challenged Bridges: "As Governor I am the appointed protector of these natives; it is therefore my duty to see that none of them are deported from this country without authorisation from me."

Paz sought to "guard against the repetition of abuses which had arisen in the north [of Argentina] in the placement of natives in the service of the whites." He informed Bridges that his government desired "to secure the welfare of these natives, so that at least it might have the satisfaction of saving a remnant of the native races of its wide domains."[91] Despite these solemn declarations, Governor Paz allowed the little family to be sent to Punta Arenas.

Lawrence was worried about them. Their health began to fail in Punta Arenas and the couple were "unable to fulfill the duties of servants to their masters." Three months later, in April 1886, the family was returned to the Ushuaia Mission. Lawrence was thankful and they were "very glad to be with their own people again." He added, "and from a Christian point of view I think their advantages will be greater if they remain with us."[92] Lawrence was acting as a Christian, but was Bridges?

Governor Paz also allowed the two young Yahgans to be sent to the Museum of Natural History in La Plata, as quoted above. One of them, Maishkensis, known as Maish, arrived at the museum in 1886. Manuel Moreno, the director of the museum, and his family became very fond of Maish, and he worked in the museum preparing and classifying materials "with much ability." He learned to speak Spanish as well as some English and French and did not wish to return to Tierra del Fuego. But about 1892 he died in La Plata of tuberculosis, while he was still young.[93] I didn't find information about the other youth.

Latest News of the Haush

In February 1886, Dataminik, a native Haush from Spaniard Harbour (Aguirre Bay) living at the Ushuaia Mission, went home for a visit but did not find any of his people, the "Eastern Onas" (Haush). It was the "general opinion" that they had succumbed to the recent outbreak of measles.[94] However, some were still strong and healthy, at least in Good Success Bay. In 1890, Señor Fique, the subprefect there, was said to treat them kindly. Four years later, a few were taken to Ushuaia and were well received by Governor Paz. In 1896 Tenenesk, a young man, whose parents were Haush, became known to the outside world, thanks to Gusinde.[95] By then the remaining Haush men spoke Spanish and had begun working on the sheep farms, especially at Harberton. Less than a century later (1981), the last mestizo Haush, Luis Garibaldi Honte, drowned in the river Rio Grande. Thus ends the history of the peaceful Haush. They had received the Nodal brothers with open arms in 1619 and nearly all the outsiders who followed. Much remains to be published concerning them.

And the Buttons

By July 1886, consumption (tuberculosis), pneumonia, scrofula and very severe influenza were rampant in Ushuaia, though no longer measles. Jemmy Button's granddaughter, a little girl named Annie, died of tuberculosis. She was the eighth child of Hester and Philip Lewaia. Hester,

Jemmy's and Jamesina's daughter, had been called Fuegia when, at the age of about five, she had spent five months in the Keppel mission in 1858 (Chapter 9). By 1886, six of her children had already died of the epidemics, as had her husband, Philip Lewaia, and both of her brothers: the youngest, Anthony, in 1877, and the unforgettable Threeboys in 1867 (Chapter 10). Her first and only remaining child, George Lewaia, born in Keppel in 1869, was still alive in 1886. He and Hester survived the epidemics (see below). That year another of Jemmy's grandsons was alive, an adult known as Edmundo Button. A few years later (1890), Bishop Stirling awarded him a licence as a catechist and praised him for the Christian counsels he gave his people.[96] Apparently he and his wife died later, still young, probably also victims of an epidemic. So very few, if any, of Jemmy's descendants survived the epidemics.

The Governors and the Natives

The natives had to comply with the official regulations; however, they were viewed as special citizens. In 1886, Governor Paz was still trying to assume the missionaries' role as their custodian. In March 1887, some of Bridges' farm workers, twenty Onas and Yahgans, died on Picton Island after having eaten the poisoned flesh of a stranded swordfish. The government rescued those who survived. Bridges expressed his gratitude: "This number [twenty] would have doubled but for the kind and generous relief afforded."[97]

But in the town Ushuaia, as might be expected, with the presence of unattached men, the sealers and the newly arrived Argentines, the "vices" introduced by them flourished – mainly alcoholism and prostitution, including syphilis. Lucas Bridges was aware of the plight of the Yahgans who had survived. "What a change! Hamlets deserted; gardens overgrown with weeds; cattle slaughtered for needed food – or even sold for liquor or exchanged for a third-rate gun; but worst of all, a frightened, weakened tribe in mourning [because of the measles epidemic] . . . the old Mission was doomed."[98]

The new authorities were attempting to aid the Yahgans while enforcing no-nonsense rules of conduct. In April 1885, eleven young Yahgan men volunteered to join the Argentine "national service." But in June Bridges reported that they could not adjust to its restraints, so many had simply left. Some of them were imprisoned for a while and others were punished for various offences.[99] The Yahgan men who took second wives were imprisoned. No more monkey business: they had to comply to the new regulations as citizens of the republic.

A Yahgan Is Appointed Alcalde

About 1886, Governor Paz appointed a Yamana youth, Robert Yenowa (or Yunoowa), as mayor (*alcalde*) for a year, of the natives living in Ushuaia. As compensation, the government provided him with food rations, perhaps a salary and permission to fly the national flag.

As *alcalde*, Yenowa had to report any offence committed by his countrymen to government headquarters. Having been in Buenos Aires, he spoke Spanish and English in addition to Yahgan. He was known as one of the most industrious Yahgans in Ushuaia, despite his drinking problem. Lawrence had great hopes for him because he "manifested more ambition than the natives in general."[100]

In 1884 Yenowa had married Hester, ten or fifteen years older than he, after the death of her first husband and seven of her eight children, as mentioned above. Later Hester and Yenowa had two daughters. Despite his appointment as mayor, he continued drinking with the Argentines in town, much to the dismay of Lawrence. In July 1887 Reverend Aspinal (Bridges' replacement) valued him as the best-educated native alive, and he was "trying to be a good man," though he could not mange to free himself from *guaro* and tobacco.[101]

In April 1890 Yenowa broke two ribs in a saw pit where he was working, was not properly attended and developed "hypertrophy." During his two months of continuous bleeding from the throat and nose, Lawrence waited on him tenderly while he repented for not leading a Christian life. Hester was with him night and day, though she was pregnant and gave birth to her last child during this time. Yenowa died still young, not of an epidemic or because of his sins but as a result of his injuries in the saw pit.[102]

The life of Yenowa calls to mind the experience of the "natives" in the United States during their long periods of struggle, resistance and final defeat by the American army. While the governor of Tierra del Fuego appointed only one native to police his countrymen, the US government instituted a policy of training their "Yahgans" (American Indians) as soldiers and policemen to fight and control their own people. In 1890, Sitting Bull, a Lakota Sioux and an extraordinary leader of his people, was killed by a Sioux policeman. Yenowa killed no one, but as a native policeman and a victim of alcoholism, he resembled the Sioux policemen.[103]

Reverend Bridges Retires

Thomas Bridges resigned from the Anglican mission in June 1886, when he was in his mid-forties, despite the objections of his superiors and others in London and Bristol. His son Lucas commented: "Immediately there was a general outcry. Friends in the Falkland and elsewhere loudly expressed the opinion that he was heading straight for bankruptcy and deplored the fate that awaited his unfortunate wife and family." In these moments of most need, his loyal friend Captain Willis lent him his life's savings, 700 pounds, Lucas explained, "at a fixed rate of interest . . . when no one else would finance what they considered to be a crazy venture [the Harberton farm]." Later that year Bridges went to Buenos Aires, where he became a citizen of Argentina and received the land grant for his farm, Harberton, through the good offices of President Julio Argentina Roca. From there he sailed to England, where he purchased material needed for the buildings and equipment of his farm. He visited Hyades in Paris, probably sometime in 1886. Hyades noted this visit in his last publication in 1891 (p. 405) although I didn't find any mention of this visit by Bridges. He returned to Ushuaia in May 1887. During the following years, until he died in 1898, he was busy raising his children, administering his farm with the help of his sons, and his Yahgan and Selk'nam workers. He also continued conducting services in Ushuaia and presiding over baptisms and marriages between Yahgan women and Argentines, mostly employees of the government. Nor did he fail to admonish his workers for their indolence, disorder and vices.

The farm flourished through the years. For the Yamana life on the Harberton farm was preferable to the "vice-ridden" town of Ushuaia, where diseases were rampant.

Despite his shortcomings, Bridges was not a racist and he was obviously very fond of some of the Yahgans, as he called them, among them Pinoense, probably Okoko and others. Nevertheless he was often arrogant while preaching to them and at times his behaviour was really harmful. His religious conviction of their pagan inferiority may at least partially explain why he was incapable of comprehending or recognising the problems the mission had created for the Yahgans or of appreciating and fostering the merits of their traditional society.

These last years of Yenowa and Bridges are included here in order not to disperse them among the many events related in the next chapter, which covers the final decade of the nineteenth century.

1887 to 1900: Other Fuegians Kidnapped; The Unending Epidemics; "Is God Very Far Away?"

Bridges' Replacement

When Edwin (or Edward) Couplan Aspinal arrived at the Ushuaia Mission from England with Bridges in May 1887, he was surprised to find the natives "so intelligent, [and] very many of them so good looking." The next year he replaced Bridges, though in a somewhat different category. Bishop Stirling appointed Aspinal the general and medical superintendent of the Ushuaia Mission and its branches, with teaching responsibilities. Aspinal had been ordained and had medical knowledge, though he was not a trained physician. Lawrence continued as superintendent of the Ushuaia base station, as he had been since Bridges resigned from the mission in June 1886.

In September of that year there was still "very much sickness" – many cases of influenza. Almost every native was ill, including all but one of the sixteen orphans. Aspinal wrote to the committee in Bristol of hoping to save many lives, that he urgently needed more surgical instruments and medical books. Yahgans living on Gable and Picton Islands, survivors of the tuberculosis and measles epidemics, were being hired, mainly for shearing the sheep of Bridges' new farm. Others were scattered along the channel and some had remained in Ushuaia. The natives in the southernmost islands had not been affected by the epidemics.

As 1887 was drawing to a close, 150 natives from outlying territories came to Ushuaia for the usual Christmas distribution, many for the first time. Aspinal was pleased to have an average of twenty-six children in the mission school and again remarked on the natives' good looks, intelligent faces, neatness and polite manners. He noted that a growing spirit of independence was shown in their desire to make dugout canoes and build houses. Although he was discouraged because "much of

Bridges' work is not now visible, so many were swept away by the measles epidemic."[1]

More Gold Prospectors Arrive

As mentioned near the end of the last chapter, Julius Popper, the to-be-famous albeit notorious gold prospector, had heard that gold was to be had in Sloggett Bay; so off he went. While he was digging in 1888, the Haush, who had greeted Bridges, and the others six years earlier, did not show up. Sloggett's wide, level beach, about 300 meters long, soon proved to be the richest gold site in Tierra del Fuego and drew prospectors from far and wide. One of the newcomers was John Spears, an American journalist and an expert on gold mining. His words are worth gold.

The gold of Slogget Bay is marvellous gold. It is, as said, nugget gold as distinguished from gold dust. The traditional "nuggets as big as kernels of corn" are to be had there. I have seen them myself, and when one has seen a handful of such stuff he does not wonder that prospectors keep trying again and again, in spite of the fair certainty of death.[2]

The news travelled fast. Unemployed workers and destitute farmers, mostly from Eastern Europe and some from Chiloé, Chile, flocked into Punta Arenas. While the majority failed pitifully or squandered their nuggets in Punta Arenas, fortunes were enlarged by the sober capitalists – Mauricio Braun and José Nogueira among others. These "pioneers" owned boats, supply stores, bars and saloons in Punta Arenas, where gold dust and nuggets were welcome.

Once the Sloggett gold had apparently been exhausted, the restless diggers, now called miners, rushed to the nearby islands, mainly Lennox and New; where they sifted gold dust and nuggets from the sand, though it was less plentiful than at Sloggett.[3]

By 1889 the spurt of prosperity for some and the dreams of riches for others were beginning to peter out. Mr Ince, an artisan catechist, observed: "The gold fever is over. We hear little of it, only that men kill each other, and die in each other's embrace; ships are wrecked and all hands perish; men tied up, and their gold taken from them, and have to return penniless."[4]

However, it did not peter out until many years later. The surviving miners and some recent employees of Chilean and foreign companies outnumbered the natives in Tierra del Fuego. From the end of 1891 to February 1892, a company of fourteen Dalmatian miners extracted 150 kilos of gold on Lennox. The next year there were still about a thousand miners working throughout the entire area, also, according to the Chilean historian Mateo Martinic, mostly of Slavic origin. Spears noted that many of the emigrants had little or no sea experience and perished while "trusting their moorings to hold fast" or went under in the gales that "come every day in summer and every week in winter."[5] They were also known to shoot at the Yahgan men trying to defend their women. But the Yahgans usually avoided them, knowing that they were armed and hoping they would soon leave. The miners were a "gold sent," for Bridges. Lucas related: "By bringing us trade, it helped my father to establish the Harberton settlement with something more than the savings from a missionary's meagre salary." But Thomas Bridges was not an unscrupulous merchant. Once the word got around that there was no liquor and no tobacco for sale in Harberton, a great many of Bridges' would-be clients (mainly miners and sealers) went directly to Ushuaia, where they spent their gold and traded their pelts as they pleased.

Year after year, from the 1880s until the first decade of the new century, the miners penetrated almost every nook and cranny of the Yahgan homeland and part of Selk'nam territory, determined to get some reward for their miseries. They stayed for months in localities where the Indians normally camped, disrupting what remained of their lives. The sealers and whalers were less numerous and more transient than the miners, even though they were still destroying what was left of the Yamana's most precious food. To escape from the plague of gold seekers, many Yamana in the southern area of New Year's Sound fled to the mission station in Tekenika Bay (see below).

During these years, tons of gold were brought to Punta Arenas, to the joy of the big and small capitalists. It was said: "If this continues, it will be a second California." But it was only a mini-California, though at times nearly as rough. By 1902 there were only thirty men on Lennox Island, accompanied for the first time by a woman. A few years later, companies were formed by financiers in Punta Arenas and Santiago, but by 1910 the profits no longer justified the costs.[6] A few diehard prospectors continued, through many decades, into the twentieth century, sifting sand in remote streams of the once famed Tierra del Oro.

The Poor of London Worst Off

By late 1887 the measles epidemic had subsided, although other epidemics followed through to the end of the nineteenth century and beyond. These epidemics were devastating to the natives not only because of their lack of natural immunity but also because of their weakened physical condition, resulting from the drastic change in their habitual mode of living. Even during the unusually mild winter of 1889, food was so scarce that the girls in the orphanage were still dying, despite the dedication of Mrs Hemmings. The situation became so critical that she sent the orphan girls to live with Yahgan families. Some were taken to nearby islands, away from Ushuaia by their adopted families and returned in better health. Mrs Hemmings remarked that in a time of such scarcity, these people, "managed better than the poor in England.... Our poor people would be starving if similarly exposed."[7]

Her amazing comment implies that the Yahgans were more capable of finding solutions to such crises than the missionaries and the poor in England.

Other Fuegians Captured and Taken to Europe

At the end of 1888, again eleven were captured, this time Selk'nam, the former "Oens-men," and taken first to Paris, where they were exhibited as savage cannibals, and then to London. This time Maurice Maître, a Belgian whale hunter, kidnapped them along the Strait of Magellan, the Chilean coast of Isla Grande.[8] As apparently heavy chains were used to capture them, "like Bengal tigers," it is not surprising that during the voyage to Europe, one of the men was killed trying to defend himself and another died. So only nine were still alive when Maître took them to Paris and this photograph was taken.

While Paris Celebrates the Centenary of Its Revolution

In Paris Maître entertained the public by keeping his prisoners hungry and throwing pieces of raw horsemeat into their cage to show their voracious "cannibalistic instincts." The event could not have been less propitious: the Exposition Universelle of 1889 marked the centenary of the French Revolution. Its motto – *Egalité, Liberté et Fraternité* – was proudly echoed through the world. The celebration culminated with the inauguration of the Eiffel Tower, whose massive steel structure symbolised the industrial age. In the shadow of this great symbol, the Fuegian captives languished, confused and troubled. The news got around. Chilean representatives complained to the French Ministry of Foreign Relations.

On To London – the Third Victim

Given the complaints in Paris, Maître took his captives to London, late 1889 and exhibited them at the Westminster Aquarium as a family "whose savage customs were for a time the talk of the town."

FIGURE 14.1. 1889: In Paris, Maître on the left, holding a stick or whip, with nine of the Selk'nam he had captured, in cage in Paris. Two of the men had died on the trip to Paris (one was killed).

A woman whose name is not known is the epitome, the personification, of this entire episode. Her "infamous" story is highlighted by the indignation expressed by one of the British doctors. She became seriously ill in London. When Maître took the troupe on to Belgium, she was abandoned and "thrown to the hands of the English ratepayers – no one understanding her language, no one caring for her body or soul." She was sent to St. George's Infirmary, attached to the workhouse. Dr Webster, the resident physician, regarded the treatment of this woman as "infamous." A nurse reported:

When she came into the infirmary . . . she had on only an old rug tied on like a cloak, a rope tied round her waist, and a pair of slippers made of string. . . . She was filthy dirty . . . and she objected by every sound and sign she could make to being washed. . . . She would not eat or drink anything we offered her, and we did not know how to feed her.

A few days later they offered her "some partly-cooked beef, and for the first time her eyes brightened a little, and she ate of it." Alone, mortified and distressed, she died of an undefined illness on 21 January 1890. Dr Webster was outraged. "I consider it a most shameful thing . . . that these poor creatures should be permitted to be taken from their native land, and brought to this country, where they are almost sure to fall sick, when they are at once foisted upon the ratepayers."

Before Maître took the others to Belgium Dr Webster had notified the representatives of the South American Mission Society. They "left no stone unturned to procure their release and return to their native land." But their appeals were not responded to by the Aquarium directors, nor the Aborigines' Protection Society, nor the Chilean authorities in England, nor the Foreign and Home Offices. All this, "in free England! We have for months quietly tolerated what is, virtually a state of gross slavery," commented an anonymous author in the mission magazine.[9]

On to Brussels

Maître had felt threatened in London, so he fled, with his eight remaining captives, to his own country, Belgium. But the pressure there was such that he was arrested and nothing was heard of him again. The eight were exhibited for a few days on the outskirts of Brussels and then taken to jail, apparently for only a few days, because as indigent foreigners no one was responsible for them. Meanwhile two "disappeared" and the boy captive in Figure 14.1 was taken by one of Maître's assistants, who was later forced to surrender him to the Belgian authorities. Somehow the child arrived in Montevideo. The remaining five were sent to Dover and confined in a workhouse, where the South American Missionary Society again contacted government authorities. This time the Foreign Office requested that the Chilean representatives in London "take charge of their own subjects and send them back to their native land." Finally, on 19 February 1890, they were embarked in Liverpool on a ship bound for Punta Arenas. Two died during the voyage. The three who arrived in Punta Arenas were sent to the Salesian school and later to Dawson Island, where a Salesian mission had just been established.

On a boat from Montevideo to Punta Arenas, José María Beauvoir, the Salesian missionary mentioned in the last chapter, recognised a boy on board as a Fuegian, befriended him, and took him to the missionary school in Punta Arenas, where he found his three companions in misery. While in school, he became very attached to Father Beauvoir. A few years later, about 1896, Beauvoir took him to the Isla Grande (Tierra del Fuego, Argentina) while the second Salesian mission was being built near the incipient town of Río Grande, on the Atlantic coast. He became Beauvoir's principal informant for his study of the Selk'nam language and was baptised Luis Miguel Calafate, the name of a bush (*Berberia buxifolia*) whose berries were much appreciated by his people. More details concerning the Fuegians kidnapped (in 1881 and 1889) are known now thanks to the Chilean anthropologist Christian Báez and to the British anthropologist Peter Mason.[10]

The exhibit of Fuegian "cannibals" was only one attraction among many. In the 1890s, Buffalo Bill's Wild West Show exhibited North American Indians, among them Sitting Bull, in many European cities. Such shows and exhibits of exotic people from Africa, Asia and America were extremely popular and profitable in Europe and the United States from the 1870s into the twentieth century.[11]

Meanwhile at the Keppel Mission

Keppel (east Falkland Island) had become a sort of oasis. The measles epidemic of 1884 to 1885 had not struck there. Leonard and Nelly Burleigh remained in charge of the station until 1888, when they accepted a new challenge (see below). George Lewaia and his young wife were living with them. He was Hester's only surviving son, who had obtained a license as reader and catechist. He and the Whaits couple were responsible for the mission farm. By the end of 1893 there were twenty-one boys and older youths there. They "looked happy and contented" except one who was still recovering from an illness. They had schooling and Bible reading and were especially interested in learning to build sailing boats. True to their tradition, these youths were great mimics and close observers of all that was said and done.[12] Their spirit had not been broken.

The Missionaries Move Farther South

This year Bishop Stirling, aware of the precarious condition of the natives in the Ushuaia, decided that a mission had to be founded farther south (in Chile), beyond Ushuaia (Argentina), a swamp of contagion of all sorts. The mission could move but not the converted natives, who by now had to manage on their own. Stirling decided that the mission should be located on one of the Wollaston Islands, near Cape Horn, and have access to the heathens thereabout.

The Ushuaia Mission was to carry on under the guidance of Lawrence and Aspinal, whose efforts were limited to maintaining the services there and in the town of Ushuaia, not to converting heathens, because none were there and very few within reach. Those settled on the Harberton farm or who were employed part-time elsewhere were already civilised if not Christianised. The missionaries felt that they had to turn to the heathens living on the outer islands if they were to continue in Tierra del Fuego.[13]

In May 1888, Aspinal, Lewis (a missionary who had come with Bridges in 1869) and Leonard Burleigh set out in the *Allen Gardiner* to contact them. On the way they met Okoko residing alone in Lewaia and reported that he was "very well."[14] Okoko may have looked very well at that moment, but he probably did not feel that way. The tuberculosis and measles epidemics had killed his entire family: five children and his loving Gamela.

The missionaries continued on. Passing beyond Murray Narrows, they camped in Wulaia. Apparently no one was there. A while later, in Grandi Sound, they came across families in four canoes. Somehow Aspinal gained permission from one of the fathers to allow two of his children, "nice boys," to join him and be taken to Keppel.[15]

Sailing down Nassau Bay, they headed for Grevy Island, one of the Wollaston group, where they knew, from their web of informants, that they would find some Yahgans. They found forty-five to fifty almost "entirely untouched by civilisation" – except seven who had been to the Ushuaia Mission. The seven greeted Lewis, inquiring about his wife and two sons, and telling him about their families and who among them had died since they last met. Lewis saw that they were "wretchedly clad" but seemed strong and healthy, though not happy. They were grieving for two children who had recently drowned. The visiting missionaries held a service in a large wigwam, which Lewis recognised as the *Toomeecoo uchr*, called *Keena*, usually spelt *Kina*, "erected not to live in, but in which to perform certain initiation rites with the youths."[16] Lewis remarked that eighteen years before he had seen a very large Kina hut near Wulaia, and that such huts were "rarely seen now."

Having completed their exploratory visit on Grevy Island, still in May 1888, Aspinal took "on board seven of these people, who asked us to take them to Keppel." Their ages and names were not mentioned, neither was permission of the parents, assuming that they were children (see below).[17]

Later that year Aspinal obtained a concession for ten years from the Chilean government to establish a colony that would "lend valuable services to navigation in general, and chiefly to shipwrecked crews of the numerous vessels that are lost near Cape Horn."[18]

The Anglican Mission Settles on Bayly Island

By 1888 Leonard and Nelly Burleigh were well trained to confront the formidable challenge of administering the new mission station in such an isolated place. They had worked for ten or eleven years in the Keppel station and spoke Yahgan. They and their young daughter Katie set off, in mid-October 1888, on the *Allen Gardiner* from Ushuaia. Captain Willis, exceptionally his wife, and two sheep and two goats, accompanied them. No one was on Grevy Island when they arrived so Burleigh decided that it was preferable to establish the mission farther down the coast on Bayly Island, where some of the forty or fifty people they had met in May were seen camping. Willis and the crew remained at Bayly the first week, helping Burleigh clear a plot for a garden and build a wharf and a one-room house, twenty by ten feet (6 by 3 metres). Burleigh closed his first Bayly letter by assuring his readers that he and his wife were settled in their bright and comfortable home, very happy and hopeful for the future.

Their home may have been "bright" but the surroundings were not: a pebble shore backed by bogs and a ridge of barren hills, fronted by a narrow expanse of water across which lay the flat tail of Grevy Island facing Nassau Bay. If the landscape was depressing, the climate was more so, with its nearly constant rainfall, frequent violent storms and cold, windy days. Nearly a century later, in 1987, when I visited this forlorn site, remains of the wharf were still there. Several low mounds, where the

FIGURE 14.2. Burleigh preaching to the natives on Bayly Island: "Behold I bring you good tidings."

Burleighs' house and perhaps the wigwams had been, were covered by bogs. A few fragments of pottery of an English tea service were scattered about. The place was so forlorn that even the seagulls had fled. They must have been there because the location is named Surgo Seagull (in English) on the Chilean maps.

Here on Bayly (in October 1888) many of the forty or fifty natives were "fresh-comers," newly arrived from farther south. Mrs Burleigh found "the poor creatures in a dreadful state... [however] they seemed to be very friendly and eager to be employed by the Mission."

After listening to Burleigh's first service, the women and children gazed at the couple "aghast" for some minutes; then, for some reason, they all laughed. They approached the Burleighs as if they were an unknown kind of human being, touching and feeling their clothes "and wondered at everything they saw." Nelly told them in Yahgan: "We are your friends, and we have left our land and friends to come amongst you, to help you and to try to do you good."[19] Upon hearing this message, they threw up their arms shouting (in Yahgan): "All friends."

Eight months after they had settled in the new station, Leonard recalled that the years he and his wife had worked in the Keppel Mission had led them to expect "a lively time among the Southerners," but that anything they could have imagined then had been "far surpassed in [by] our daily experiences [in Bayly]." Just what he meant by "far surpassed" will become clear. Although he lacked the religious training of some of his colleagues, he was a deacon, a catechist and an expert carpenter.[20] He was endowed with a far more passionate and unsettled nature than would be expected, given that he had passed so many apparently uneventful years at Keppel. Nelly would prove undaunted; a dedicated worker, a usually compassionate companion of the natives and a loving mother and admirer of her "dear husband." No portrait of her was found. The illustration of Leonard in the Anglican journal shows a man who probably attracted the ladies.

A Bereaved Mother

Leonard informed the natives that he and his wife had come to stay and that he was gratified that they were well disposed to receive them. As soon as he had completed his greetings, a woman came forward with a request that, at first, seemed outrageous. In Yahgan she explained: "Two of my children [boys] have gone to Keppel, and it is only fair that I should have one of yours." Five months earlier, Aspinal, on nearby Grevy Island, had taken her two sons to Ushuaia without her permission. She asked for Burleigh's daughter, little Katie, in exchange. Her request was politely refused. Yearning for her two children, a week or so later the bereaved mother returned in her canoe and gave Katie a necklace of shells. This gesture portrays her grief more than words could. The incident ends here. I found no evidence of the fate of her children or whether they were returned to her, nor was her name given or those of her sons. Recall Captain Snow's objection to taking the children to Keppel without the parents' consent and the refusal of the Picton and Lennox parents, on 6 May 1858, to give their children to young Gardiner to be taken to Keppel (Chapter 8). Aspinal stated above that seven "people" were taken from Grevy to Keppel of their own accord, but he failed to add that among them at least two were children whose mother had not been consulted.

An Old Man Asks God to Come to Bayly

Soon a very ill and weak old man called the Burleighs aside and asked: "Where does God live? Is he coming soon to Wollaston?" Mrs Burleigh was not sympathetic: "This shows you how dark they are." But Leonard was glad for the opportunity to console the old man, who he thought might be preparing to meet the Holy Spirit. The following week the old man was even more debilitated, despite Burleigh's medication, and insisted again on knowing: "Is God very far away? And did I understand that He is coming down to earth again?" Two months later, he was still alive and continued to question Leonard about "where this God lived, and whether he was coming to Wollaston soon." When suffering a fearful agony, he "broke forth," praying to God to save his soul and imploring Him to take him to heaven. A bit later Burleigh discovered that he was "a most peaceable, good-living man, had one wife and three children, for whom he manifested great affection." When this discovery was made and when Burleigh realised that he was dying, he baptised him. "He passed quietly away some days later... "[21] Such a profound, disturbing anxiety concerning appeals for assurance of the reality of the existence of God recalls Okoko's crisis (Chapter 10).

Frustrations and Some Compensations

The Burleighs remained for three and a half years on the bleak shore of Bayly, complaining in letter after letter about the food and clothing that did not arrive from Ushuaia (some finally did) and their urgent need for a helper, any helper. The latter also arrived three months before they left. The Burleighs were frustrated by their attempts to grow potatoes or at least turnips in a soil where only watercress prospered. Firewood was scarce and the weather unmentionable. But through it all the couple remained firm, determined to save these heathens from themselves.

At times Leonard was slightly amused by the behaviour of his special nemeses, the four resident "old doctors," *yekamush* (shamans). But more often he was disgusted by their "ridiculous antics." Also, the other people often annoyed him. He was periodically desperate, hurt and repelled by their "frantic outbursts of savagery and passion," by their disinclination to "conform to what is good and right, by their stubbornness and bad temper when reproved." The daily scenes of cruelty he witnessed made him shudder. Even when the men worked they were unreliable, and when they hurt themselves with his iron tools he had to tend their wounds. His missionary zeal was being seriously tried.

Early on, many were stricken with blood poisoning from having eaten rotten "black fish." Two of the four, old *yekamush*, fully powdered and adorned with the appropriate feathers, did their best to cure or at least alleviate their patients' suffering by rubbing them and yelling (chanting) at them. On one such occasion the two "doctors" gave up and turned to Burleigh saying: "See what you can do." He stepped in and relieved the patients with emetics and other medicines.

Leonard also had to contend with the misconduct of three other men: one had taken an eight-year-old girl as his wife; another was abandoning his wife and child, intending to replace her also with a young girl; while the third, also married, was going off in his canoe with three very young women, leaving his wife and child to fend for themselves. Burleigh remedied the latter's misconduct right away: he quickly manned the dingy, and after a hard pull caught up with the canoe and brought the culprit and the three wayward young women back to the mission quarters. He felt "compelled to protest against, and grapple with, their evil doings. . . . Fortunately . . . I have since been thanked by certain of the natives for doing as I did . . . [against] these disgraceful child marriages." He had a large wigwam built close to his house where he assembled all the young unprotected girls under the care of a reliable native couple.

Despite such dramas, the first Christmas celebration was very enjoyable and all the guests (some sixty-two) were pleased and behaved "exceedingly well."

Natives from Hermite Island
Two days later a canoe appeared occupied by five men who had been camping nearby with their families and had recently come from Hermite Island. Later the men brought their families, that is thirty-two in all, to the mission. They were in fairly good health and "rich in paint, oil and blubber." A few months later, Burleigh sent them back to Hermite Island, telling them to stay there for two months. He handed them a letter that indicated the location of Bayly Mission and told them to give this letter to any shipwrecked survivors they might see or come across. Apparently he hurried them away at least partly because he lacked food and work for them.

Leonard . . .
By March of the following year (1889) Leonard was congratulating himself on the advances made with the natives and for not having shrunk from his duty to protest against their loose morals. Some of the men were becoming steady workers, and even though the women "generally come empty-handed some of them offered a small return" for the food they received. "I am getting together a nice supply of canoes, baskets, buckets &c. which I hope to dispose of for the benefit of the Mission."[22]

At times Leonard is really difficult to decipher. His moods flash on and off, bright and dim, not in ways that fit a pattern, as if some inner force were leading him in a direction that he barely understood. But perhaps this is simply an outsider's impression; his unstable temperament may have been the expression of the tensions he was trying to control.

With the passage of time, the "petty troubles" with the natives were no longer as irritating as they had been and he came to realise that these people were "of a very varied nature." Even though they shared the same routine experiences and the same tradition, their personalities were very different. Leonard and Nelly remained confident that little by little they would be led "out of their heathen darkness into paths of Christian virtue and happiness."

Some Hermite Islanders Return

About this time nineteen of the thirty-two from Hermite Island returned in a terrible state: no stranded whales, little to hunt and not even one shipwreck to report. The sealers and whalers had "cleaned out" the southernmost islands but none had wrecked. Nelly was very touched by a ten-year-old girl who had come to Bayly with the Hermite group. She was so frightened by Nelly that she kept running away from her. Later Nelly learned that she was so shy because the whites had killed her father. "No wonder the poor lamb was afraid of white people and ran away. She is such an engaging little thing, and always meets you with a smile. When the bell rings for prayers, these little things [this girl and others] wait for my husband, and sometimes he runs on first, and they follow, so delighted."[23]

Aspinal Visits Again

In mid-1889, Reverend Aspinal, this time with Henry Katanash, came for a visit. The latter was the Yamana youth who had accompanied Aspinal to England, where they had remained for six months, and had returned to Ushuaia in January 1889.

The Burleighs were overjoyed. Leonard introduced the visitors to his eighty residents. Another twenty were away and would return soon. Aspinal also learned that there were three to four hundred natives in New Year's Sound; some were said to be coming to the mission. He heard that "Burleigh's people are rather afraid of them owing to old feuds between them."[24] Finally none came to Bayly from New Year's Sound, though they would a few years later, to the next mission station.

More Trials and Some Amusement

Burleigh was running low on patience with the *yekamush*. One night in June 1889 (after Aspinal and Henry had left) he was summoned to see "a poor fellow" who had been ill for some time and was dying, supposedly. The four *yekamush* doctors kept propping up their patient in his bed as he kept sinking down. All four were "in full dress of paint and feathers, and yelling at the top of their voices and squeezing and punching him until the poor fellow had scarcely a breath left in him." Leonard despaired of intervening and passed on to the next wigwam. The following morning the patient told him he was feeling much better, that the "learned men" had extracted two large stones out of his face and a still larger one from further inside of him. Leonard accounted for his recovery otherwise: by the medicines and nourishing food he had given the patient before the four doctors' treatments.

One day soon thereafter, Leonard was walking by the same wigwam and heard a little boy crying bitterly. He discovered that an earache was the cause. One of the same four doctors was applying the "shouting remedy" into his patient's ear while shaking his body "as we should an apple-tree to make the fruit fall." This was done to revive the patient's hearing capacity. But it was too much for Leonard. He whispered to his colleagues that perhaps he might be of some assistance. The attending doctors nodded and stepped aside while Leonard applied warm water in a syringe to the aching ear. The boy felt relief immediately. "Strange to say," twelve of the onlookers suddenly complained of earaches and requested this new treatment, which Leonard obligingly administered to one and all. He added: "But time would fail me to tell one thousandth part of the curious things we see and hear, some very amusing and others quite as sad."[25] Stirling and Bridges never found any of the *yekamush* amusing; they would not tolerate them, and that was that.

Five months later, about the end of 1889, Nelly was relieved to report that the "old sorcerers were coming to Leonard when they themselves were feeling sick." Even so, she still complained of the noises these "horrid Yacamoosh" were always making.[26]

The Bayly Missionaries Know Better, But...

When there were about a hundred Yahgans there, in June 1889, Burleigh admitted that the handouts of used clothing were doing more harm than good, but that once they had begun there was no stopping them. The *Allen Gardiner* had just arrived (with Aspinal and Henry) but no clothes. It had been nearly ten months since the last distribution. "The lot of rough and heavy work" the men were doing resulted in so much wear and tear on their clothes that "there is scarcely a sound garment among them." Despite receiving clothes from the next trip, he expressed regret that "not a garment [was] in the place . . . most of the people will be worse off than when we found them, for they have given away their skin capes and will soon be without any covering; and as winter is upon us the outlook is very bad."[27]

Burleigh's candid recognition of the harm the used clothes had created recalls Despard's comments. Despite their awareness, nothing could stop the clothes handouts or use of them as pay. Despard never tried and it was too late for Burleigh to even attempt to alter this policy. His account of the hard work the men were performing, was rarely acknowledged by the other missionaries. It was in 1858 in Wulaia when Despard and Fell commented on the Yahgans' strength and goodwill while working and in Lewaia when Bridges was impressed with the natives' strength and their manner of playing and living together (Chapters 8 and 10).

The persistence of the missionaries in clothing the natives was only one aspect of their "double-C strategy." Burleigh was aware that the men were no longer going on their usual hunting excursions, nor were their wives going out to fish or to scour the beaches, instead they were waiting around for employment or handouts from him. He felt that they must not be "pauperised," yet "they must be fed and clothed" and recompensed for their work. He and Nelly had created the problems and, again as in Ushuaia, their hope fell back on the children.[28] Recent history was repeating itself, though not entirely. Burleigh, like Lawrence and Lewis, was alert to what was happening. Nelly even attempted to remedy the reliance on used clothes. Early 1890 she was teaching the girls to cut patterns for their own dresses.[29]

A Sign of the Future

Late in that year (1889), Burleigh had an experience foreshadowing an event that will occur several years later. Returning in a small canoe, he was almost on shore when "He was drifting away very quickly. The sea was terrific, and the whole heavens seemed like one large red light." Nelly was very alarmed. Two native women, seeing him in great danger, jumped into their bark canoe, and "dear me, how hard those poor souls did paddle." But the sea was too high for them to reach him. Meanwhile the other natives were frantically yelling at him, trying to direct him to the shore. An "old doctor" was raving at the elements, making such "hideous noises" that Nelly begged him to quiet down. Leonard was finally pulled "nobly" to safety by Yahgan men in another canoe. Once he was safely on shore, drenched but relieved, the old doctor said to him: "There, aren't you proud of your Wollaston sailors [the men who saved him] . . . and wasn't it brave of those two women to risk their own lives [attempting to rescue him]?"[30]

Stirling and Aspinal Arrive with Good News

When Aspinal visited the Burleighs again in 1890, he was accompanied by Bishop Stirling, who had never been there before. Some hundred natives were present, though only about half were residents. The others were moving about in the area.

Stirling considered that this small outpost was insufficient for "these scattered people...savages, and of the wretchedest type." He was convinced that there was "no inducement to the natives at a distance to settle on Bayly or Grevy islands. If we induced them to come there we should have to support them." He thought that Ushuaia and Keppel were still good stations and Downeast (Bridges' farm) a "beautiful place," but in Wollaston (the Bayly Mission) "nature is hostile." Then Stirling made a very significant statement: "Yet I say without hesitation, more sincere, cheerful and effective Mission work has never been done in Tierra del Fuego than by Mr. and Mrs. Burleigh on Wollaston Island." This was indeed maximum approval; he had declared their work superior to that of all the previous Anglican missionaries. The Burleighs must have been proud, though they didn't vaunt their feelings. This acknowledgement by Stirling of the Burleighs' accomplishments led him to propose they should be moved "to a more congenial part in Tierra del Fuego, say to Wollya [Wulaia], or that neighbourhood."[31] It is strange that he thought of Wulaia. The missionaries had rarely if ever visited there after Okoko's and Lucca's fiascos trying to settle there from 1864 to 1868 (Chapter 10).

Leonard Is Cheered

After the visitors departed (early in 1890), despite Stirling's praise and proposal to move the station to a "more congenial" place, Burleigh became depressed again. He was tiring of the "prevailing evil and ignorance of the people," their abuses and imprudence, the stubborn old women, the semicivilised natives who came to reside there in order to take advantage of their "less enlightened brethren." He was engrossed in such sombre meditations when the southerners (from Hermite Island) pulled onto the shore again. Then he became really downcast as he contemplated these new arrivals smeared with paint, grease and powder, their long tangled hair and nakedness except for a few rags. But suddenly his spirit soared as he heard his girl pupils spontaneously greeting these "wretched visitors," singing "While Shepherds Watched Their Flocks by Night."[32] What a beautiful gesture on their part!

A while later, in March 1890, some fifteen months after the southerners had arrived, Leonard was again finding the old people "troublesome lazy and wicked." This time he refused to give them any "advantage from the store." Obviously offended, they left in their canoes and stayed away for nearly a year. Burleigh's hope lay in his pupils and Nelly was becoming increasingly friendly with the women.[33]

Another Long Two Years

At the end of March, still 1890, Burleigh was thinking of the move to "a more congenial" place that Stirling had offered, but time was passing too slowly. A few weeks later he wrote of the ceaseless wet and stormy climate and of sickness on the increase. Moreover, his boats were in very bad condition and he had to discontinue "a little nourishing food" he was giving to the sick as he had hardly enough for himself and family. In one wigwam he visited that day the sick were in a "wretched state, drenched with rain... without fire."[34] Their ailment was unidentified, but so far no epidemics.

Aspinal Comes to the Rescue

Early October 1890, Aspinal became alarmed that the epidemic of small-pox in Ushuaia (see below) might have reached to Bayly. He borrowed a small sailboat with oars from the storekeeper, the old-timer, dependable Mr Fique, and set out on his fourth trip to Bayly. In two days he and his five young helpers covered the seventy miles between Ushuaia and Bayly. Upon arrival, they learned that the epidemic had not reached Bayly; only one man was sick though not from smallpox. But the provisions were so scarce that Aspinal gave Burleigh half of his own. On their return trip, having crossed Nassau Bay, his "plucky friends [the five Yahgans] were not to be beaten, and pulled on hour after hour."[35] Later Lawrence pointed out that such sailboats were in far greater danger than the canoes, which the natives were expert in handling, especially during the heavy squalls and sudden gusts of wind.[36] This was the first and perhaps the only time that the Yahgan canoes were recognised as in any way superior to sailboats.

Finally

In Bayly in early 1891, Burleigh, laid up with a bad cold, received word that two or three of the "learned doctors were very willing" to come and do their utmost to cure him. He declined with thanks. They came anyway, hovering around him to see "if there was a chance of a job."[37] Though he thanked them again, he was not exactly grateful.

By December 1891 there were fifty-one Yahgans in Bayly; only about half were children, which meant that there were proportionally few children. About then Bishop Stirling wrote that the mission really had to be moved to a new station, located fifty miles (ninety-three kilometres) northwest, in Tekenika Bay (as written on the Chilean maps), off Nassau Bay, on the east coast of Hoste Island. There they would be closer to Ushuaia; the climate was not overly severe; and contact would be possible with Fuegians from New Year's Sound via a portage trail to Tekenika Bay.[38] This was good news, but otherwise the routine continued for another six months, until May 1892. Near the end of their stay in Bayly, Nelly gave birth to their second child. She and the other mothers compared and complimented one another on their respective babies, as mothers tend to do.[39] The Burleighs had "survived" the three years and seven months in Bayly, from October 1888 to May 1892.

Meanwhile – Typhoid Fever Strikes Ushuaia

During the months from October 1888 to mid-1889, the Yahgans who had remained in Ushuaia were attacked by typhoid fever. Although known as "a filth disease usually caught from contaminated food and water," here, according to Lawrence, it was transmitted by a crew of one of the steamers from Buenos Aires.

Since the measles epidemic, which began in 1884, there had been nothing comparable. "It has passed through almost every native dwelling at the Mission station. . . . In some cases for many weeks they were unable to help themselves."[40] Aspinal was in England during this time, so Lawrence, his wife Claire, and Mrs Hemmings struggled to administer medicine and food to the most seriously ill.

At the biannual distribution early in January 1890, many of the hundred natives there failed to collect the handouts "owing to their illness."[41] This latter illness may have been caused by the lingering effects of typhoid fever. Otherwise I found no news about this "illness."

Five Centres of "Christian Life"

In 1890 Stirling noted five "nerve-centres of our active and beneficent system of Christian life": (1) what was left of the Ushuaia Mission; (2) the Bayly Mission; (3) Good Success Bay, where Mr Fique was officially in charge of the Haush – no missionaries there; (4) the Keppel Mission; and

(5) Bridges' farm.[42] That year fifty-eight natives were living and working at the farm, still called Downeast; again only about half were children. Bridges affirmed that although their health was faulty, the adults were strong and the children lively. But his son Lucas was not so optimistic: "They were a dying race, who seemed to know it. They certainly did the best they could."[43]

"We Are in the Midst of an Epidemic of Small-Pox . . . "

A year had not passed since the spread of typhoid when (early or mid-1890) Aspinal identified smallpox, "the least understood and most destructive disease in history."[44] He was outraged against Dr Mario Cornero, the second Argentine governor, appointed in April of that year.

Last time that the "Tye" [a ship from Buenos Aires] came down she brought a case of small-pox, which by the Governor's orders (although a doctor of medicine), was placed on the north shore [location of the town Ushuaia]; and notwithstanding my protest and request, all the natives were sent on board to get wood for the vessel to take to Buenos Ayres; the consequence is that already nine have died, and seven are lying sick with it.

Cornero had ordered the Yahgans to take firewood to the *Tye*, even though, as a medical man, he knew the dangers of contagion, and despite Aspinal's protests.

Aspinal vacated the church and put beds in it. Mrs Hemmings "nobly volunteered" to take care of the sick. He was hesitant to allow her to expose herself to the infection, but he had to accept her offer and leave her "in the hands of our gracious God." Then he spoke gratefully of his "fellow-helpers": Mr Ince and Mr Hawkes, who were digging graves and burying the dead in an effort "to save the natives from exposure to infection." Also Mrs Hawkes had "freely given herself to the care of the orphans and to cooking for us."

The orphanage had been kept in isolation from this epidemic, but mortality had been caused there by lack of food. In September 1890, when Aspinal returned from the Downeast (Harberton) farm, where he had vaccinated the Bridges family and the workers, he learned that twenty-three Yahgans in the mission and the town of Ushuaia had passed away from smallpox; that is, nearly one-third the entire native population there.

Then Aspinal gave a drastic order; burn all the "property accumulated by our own natives, much of it by their own industry." He expressed special gratitude for the help of Henry Katanash, whose little daughter was also ill with smallpox. "He is the only native I have allowed to help us, and we could not possibly do without him. He deserves the highest meed of praise for true unselfish Christian courage."[45]

The situation had become a catastrophe. Aspinal wrote later: "As far as I could I burnt everything that came in contact with the sick, houses, clothes &c, except the church, which I most thoroughly fumigated and disinfected." Thanks to Aspinal's policy, the epidemic was more or less controlled by September 1890, but the burnt-out survivors were more destitute than ever.

Then Whooping Cough

Typhoid fever and smallpox had been largely controlled when whooping cough was brought to Ushuaia (still 1890) this time by one of the children of an Argentine schoolmaster.[46] The surviving Yahgans were now fleeing Ushuaia, but, as usual, those who were already infected spread the disease to the parents or friends who received them.

When Aspinal returned to Ushuaia in November 1890 from his brief trip to the Bayly mission station mentioned above, he learned that three babies and a man had died from whooping cough. And there was dreadful news from his special friend and helper Henry Katanash. His little girl, Katie, recovered from smallpox but died of whooping cough. And a year later Lucy, Katanash's "beloved wife," succumbed after a long and sad affliction.[47] Henry did not survive very long either.

Whooping cough is said to strike early in life. "With fatality rates highest among the youngest, a hundred years ago [in 1895] it was a major cause of infant mortality around the world and may still grimly reap wherever people are too poor or isolated to get immunized."[48]

In 1893, during Peter Godoy's first year as the third governor of Tierra del Fuego, Argentina, he reported to the minister of the interior that in a radius of 600 *leguas* (2,400 kilometres), there was no medical doctor, pharmacy or anyone who might lend aid to save a life.[49] This is evidence of the central government's, Buenos Aires', disregard for the natives as well as their own people who lived there. However, there were doctors in Punta Arenas (Chile) and Port Stanley (the British colony).

Alcoholism

Diseases were not the only plagues. The "spread" of alcoholic beverages was almost inevitable since 1884, when the "outside males" arrived in the Argentine fleet; Lawrence was sorry to add (to write) that some of the heavy drinkers were English. In May 1891 he became alarmed: the natives were having even closer contacts with the newcomers, mixing with them with less shyness and fear, and were yielding to the "temptation."[50] Lawrence was powerless to prohibit or even limit the sale of alcoholic drinks to the natives, but he had not given up.

October of that year, in Ushuaia, Okoko made a stirring speech fulminating against the sin of alcoholism. He spoke in Yahgan, English and Spanish to a public as mixed as his languages – members of the Total Abstinence Society. He made a few verbal jabs at the "foolish *yecamoosh*," who were no longer in Ushuaia anyway, and at the people who had come to Ushuaia and made "plenty of trouble," though he added that some "Argentine people" were very kind to him. He also trod lightly while speaking of the Roman Catholic religion, asserting that although the Virgin Mary was not like Jesus, she was a "very good woman."[51]

Lawrence persevered with his campaign and in July 1893 appealed to the storekeepers, lamenting that "all the stores are drinking shops." Two years later, Governor Godoy prohibited the sale of intoxicating drinks to natives in Ushuaia.[52] Unless he had an army of sober inspectors, which he did not, his ruling could not be effective. In years to come, alcoholism, including heavy drinking among the male Yahgans and mestizos, provoked violent fights, some ending in death and serious abuse of the women (Chapter 15).

Influenza – and Lawrence Retires

The succession of epidemics lingered on and seemed unending. For the Fuegians in Ushuaia and along Beagle Channel, life on earth was drenched with suffering, though some still hoped for a better life "here and now." Following whooping cough, influenza was reported in 1892. It had also spread from the ships in Ushuaia Bay, first to the town and what was left of the mission, then to Navarino and the Harberton farm. Influenza, known as the flu, or even a common cold in its mild form,

can lead to pneumonia, especially for the elderly, the malnourished, or individuals stressed by chronic lung or heart problems. The viruses that cause flu are wondrously prone to mutate, making the manufacture of vaccines an annual crap shoot. Usually nothing to worry too much about, flu is nonetheless potentially capable of enormous havoc.[53]

Lawrence stated in 1892, as if he was too was coughing: "Some of the natives have died in various places...in Ushuaia, all along Beagle

Channel, and Tekenika, the new mission station." He was only consoled and strengthened by his faith in Jesus.[54]

Lawrence was evidently weary, very weary, of the insoluble problems. When he retired in 1892, he was concerned, like Bridges, about the future of his wife and five children. His appeals to the Argentine government for a grant to establish a farm were amply supported by his twenty-three years as a missionary in the area and his reputation based on his sincere dedication to the natives, Christians or not. But he had to wait. Meanwhile, a Frenchman who had recently arrived in Ushuaia, in 1893, was awarded a generous grant, by the local Argentine government, of forest land in nearby Lapataia. A few weeks later he appeared with more than forty men and a great deal of machinery, sheep and oxen. He immediately began erecting houses for his workmen and large sheds for the machinery.[55] All this accommodation for the newly arrived foreigner and nothing for Lawrence was outrageous. Lawrence, his sons and son-in-law had to wait five more years, until 1898, when they began to obtain titles for a farm measuring 25,000 acres, half the size of Bridges' farm. The site, originally called Shucamush and renamed Remolino (Whirlwind in Spanish), was midway between Ushuaia and Harberton. Arnoldo Canclini, Lawrence's biographer, told his story; from the time he arrived at the Keppel Mission in 1869. In 1902, he settled on his Remolino sheep farm even though he did not yet actually own it. Some Yahgans were employed, especially for shearing, and many continued visiting him for a baptism, a favour, his advice and company until his death in 1932.[56]

The Bayly Mission Moves to Tekenika Bay; the First Years

At last, in May 1892, the Burleighs transported their belongings from Bayly to the new site of the mission station, as Bishop Stirling had promised, a bay called Tekenika off Nassau Bay, on the east coast of Hoste Island. This name is derived from the word "Tekeenica," Fitz-Roy's mistaken name for the Yahgans (Chapter 3). (The missionaries often used Fitz-Roy's spelling of the word.)

As the Burleighs and their "old friends of Wollaston" were settling in, they were joined by other families from Orange Bay, Wulaia and New Year's Sound, so that within a month, by June, the population totalled over 200. The ground was deeply covered with snow, but the Burleighs' outlook was bright during the first week or two. With the increase of resident natives, the lack of provisions from Ushuaia became critical. In coming months the Tekenika station became the only refuge for the "poor hunted Indians" fleeing from Europeans, now mainly gold seekers and professional miners, who were spreading over nearly every shore in Tierra del Fuego.[57]

Influenza in the New Mission

Five months after the Burleighs had settled in the Tekenika Mission, the spring of October 1892, twenty or more boys came down with influenza, an epidemic, which had spread there rapidly from Ushuaia. The women were wailing over a boy who was very ill. A lady *yekamush* was performing "her heathenish rites upon him" when Burleigh was asked to assist. He was surprised that she acquiesced willingly. By now the *yekamush* were aware that their treatments were ineffectual to cure or even alleviate these new diseases. Leonard was increasingly solicited. He could hardly finish a meal or sleep without being summoned. Finally influenza struck him.[58] He recovered, though not from a depressed state of mind.

In September 1893, all except two or three in Tekenika were very ill. How many died is not stated. Meanwhile more people kept arriving in a wretched state from New Year's Sound.[59]

The Women Hike to a Stranded Whale

Soon afterwards the news that a whale had been beached in New Year's Sound incited the younger, still healthy women to return immediately to their home country. Most departed carrying a baby on their backs; each had a basket full of shellfish and some had torches to kindle a fire along the way. They walked for many miles in the snow over the portage trail to a fjord named Doze in New Year's Sound, located their canoes and paddled to where they had heard the monster lay. How the women cut and shared the whale meat and blubber, as there were no men in the group, is not reported, nor did I find any further news of how they made out.

Meanwhile clothes were distributed to those who worked and to the "poor, miserable-looking" natives who had come from New Year's Sound. The generous supply of clothes was more than enough for the twelve nearly naked boys in the orphanage. The donation had been sent from England by twenty-four women. Nelly wrote a note of thanks to each.[60]

Flight from Gold Miners

In mid-November 1893, about seventy more natives from New Year's Sound arrived at the Tekenika Mission seeking protection from "foreign traders." Nelly wrote three years later that some were carrying a dying woman. When they laid her down on the ground at the station, she asked them: "Where is Mrs. Burleigh?" When Nelly arrived, she begged her to take care of her two children "and love them for me, for I am dying." When Nelly received the "two wretched looking little objects," she was very moved.

> It took twelve days before we could get them clean; but very dear and intelligent children we found them. When they first saw us, and found that we were white people, they simply flew from us, and hid under the bed in the hut. We went down to tell the poor mother that we would love and take care of them, but she had passed away. The little girl Atumersurwyerheeper, I believe, has been a Christian for some long time, and now [April 1896] I get the news of her death.[61]

The seventy natives who had brought the dying woman had fled from New Year's Sound seeking protection in the mission from three large boats they had seen there. Leonard reported that they had "come over in droves; men, women, and children fleeing in terror from their danger to the station for protection." This news caused great alarm.

A few days later the three boats anchored about four miles (7 kilometres) from the mission. Some of the crew walked to the station and their leader asked Burleigh to take charge of one of the boats, which belonged to a mining company in Ushuaia, explaining that they were going farther on in search of gold and could not manage to take the spare boat. Burleigh reported that the men were "quiet and respectful."[62]

An Assistant Arrives

Leonard and Nelly must have been greatly relieved when the assistant – a young missionary by the name of Peter Pringle – finally showed up toward the end of that month, November 1893. He immediately got busy adding a room to the orphanage, where the girls could cook and wash. He even began building a small church and a schoolroom. A short while later he started a letter to his mother, telling her that the gold miners' real intention of coming "was to steal some young native women." They even had the "impudence to demand a house to live and to store their provisions, &tc. This was promptly refused." Then they erected a tent close to the mission, where they began menacing everyone. Nelly rushed all the women into the orphanage. "The Spanish villains came over as usual [several times] but found their intended prey gone." Fortunately most of the miners left in December; only two remained. One of these appeared carrying a rifle, with knives and revolvers stuck in his belt, and announced to the natives that he had come to kill the two missionaries.

But he desisted when Pringle sent word to him that he would come to see him. He ended this first part of his letter to his mother with these disturbing words: "You can image our anxiety night after night, and now tonight again we must be ready at any moment, as they will likely come up here after dark." Then he minimised the danger: "Never mind, mammie, I am all right, though not feeling very comical at present."

The next morning the two miners suddenly packed their tent and left. Everyone relaxed, but not for long.

A Dreadful Accident

A day or so later (23 December 1893), Pringle added in the same letter: "My darling mother, I can hardly write. Burleigh, poor fellow, was drowned in the Bay this afternoon, and now I am left alone. Poor Mrs. Burleigh is nearly distracted, and we are now sending to Ooshooia for help. May God help us and keep us in safety. Pray for us."[63]

In the "anguish of her heart" Nelly wrote a note to the missionaries in Ushuaia that very day:

My precious husband was drowned this afternoon in the Bay. I can say no more. He has been much worried with some miners who have just left, and today, Saturday, he wanted a little quiet and went in the boat here, and in some mysterious way he must have fallen overboard; I do not know. May God help me and my dear children. I have sent to ask Mrs. Hemmings to come to me. I will do all I can for these dear creatures while I am here, God helping me; but oh dear, dear, I cannot believe it. . . . God's ways are so mysterious, but all He does is in love.[64]

A month or so later Stirling gave these details of the accident. Following a period of much anxiety owing to the threats of the miners, Burleigh had gone alone, in the big mission boat, to look after some natives working on a far side of the bay. Suddenly a heavy squall had struck his boat, causing it to keel over, and the mainsail had fallen in the water. There had not been enough time for a canoe or another boat to rescue Burleigh before his calls for help ceased. He had perished in the deep water, caught in the "treacherous forest of entangled kelp weeds." Stirling told how the women tried to rescue him.

The conduct of the natives at the Station was, I am told admirable . . . that instantly . . . women threw off their garments and swam off to their canoes, moored many yards from the shore, in order to hasten to the disastrous spot to render aid. The tide was extremely high, which made the distance from the land to the canoes greater than usual, and caused delay; but every effort was made and every second turned to account in the eagerness to rescue their friend and teacher.[65]

For a second time the Yahgan women risked their lives for Burleigh, again in vain. Pringle told of another accident that occurred somewhat later: a mission worker, his wife, their child and a Yahgan woman had gone out in a canoe that had overturned. The Yahgan woman rescued the couple, though she was not able to save the child.[66]

Upon hearing of Burleigh's death, Mrs Hemmings and young Martin Lawrence (the missionary's son) rushed to Tekenika and found Pringle "a tower of strength."

Stirling Visits and Pringle Carries On

Five weeks had passed since Burleigh's death when Stirling appeared in late January 1894 at the Tekenika Mission. Little Kathie Burleigh was there to greet him, among the thirty or so children, all in mourning attire. They sang a hymn of welcome to him, composed by Kathie's late father, as she and the other children led the way to her mother's house. Stirling was aware of Nelly's profound distress. "In incessant and loving attention, and ministries to the children under her charge, and to the sick and troubled who came to her, she finds relief for the great grief which at first she thought would rob her of her senses."[67]

A year later, 1895, there were still many natives sick with influenza and one or more had died. Pringle was despairing as how to deal with all the problems – not only the sickness. He was discouraged by the men who, when they received a garment they had earned, decided that further work was useless and sank "into their usual listless life-is-a-burden state, lolling about – preparing for useless lives and early deaths."[68]

About this time, 1895, Aspinal retired from the Anglican Mission and became canon (church dignitary) in the town of Ipswich (in England or perhaps Australia).[69]

More Sealers Who Shoot to Kill

In early 1895 the rumour spread that the captains of boats passing from Punta Arenas to Ushuaia were given official permission to shoot any natives who got in their way. Lawrence wrote to the governor of Magallanes in Punta Arenas inquiring if the rumour was true and received a prompt denial. A few months later, in May, Lawrence learned that one or more of the crew of the sealing schooner *Henrietta* had fired on a Yahgan family as they paddled away from the vessel without selling their otter skins, wounding the woman in the knee and the child in the back. They were treated by the government doctor in Ushuaia. The mother recovered but the little girl died of her wound. Lawrence informed the governor about this "act of cruelty."[70] José Perich, a Chilean author, related the same event differently. The wounded woman had testified to Governor Godoy in Ushuaia there had been sixteen in the group, in addition to her family and herself, among whom twelve had been killed. Later Denis Forhasky and Pablo Ramírez, the two sealers who had committed the crime, were caught in their schooner and tried in Punta Arenas.[71] The punishment they received is not stated in the mission magazine, though it may have been in the Punta Arenas newspapers.

It is significant that at this late date some of the sealers continued killing the Indians, just for fun. Lawrence lamented: "In this our sphere of Christian labour we are sometimes tempted to think that our best efforts...have been almost in vain."[72] He seemed to be struggling, like the old man at the Bayly Mission, wondering why God had not come to Tierra del Fuego.

About this time Lawrence was reading a book that did not help his morale. He declared that the author, the US journalist John Spears who visited Tierra del Fuego (quoted in Chapter 13), wrote a great many false statements about the missionaries. It is true that Spears was not partial to them. When Lawrence told him that the natives had changed and become civilised, Spears was incredulous: "This change, instead of being a matter of congratulation, is one that should make every white man connected with it hide his head in shame, and every other one who sees it shed tears of pity." But like Lawrence, Spears was partial to the Yahgans, as he expressed here: "He [the Yahgan] delighted in what civilised people call the higher pleasures, the joys of good stories, witty sayings, quick repartee, and he had almost unlimited opportunity for cultivating the faculties which gave him greatest pleasure. How could such a man be hideous?" It is remarkable or curious that Spears, despite his few contacts with the Yahgans, wrote essentially the same phrases as Bridges had concerning their joy in discussing and conversing.[73]

The Nineteenth Century Is Closing

When, in 1899, Pringle returned from England with his bride to the Tekenika Mission, he found that, "the average daily attendance for the services in Tekeenica was only thirty-four (mostly men) in addition to the seven orphaned boys." The orphaned girls were in Ushuaia. The number of Yamana in Tierra del Fuego, at the turn of the nineteenth century was about 200, according to various sources. The largest group was in Tekenika.[74]

After a few months Pringle employed about twelve "lads" to do woodwork. But he discovered that the "lads have neither application or the intelligence necessary to produce even a rough class of work."[75] The Tekenika Mission had become the only refuge from gold miners, but the Yahgans were having great difficulty reconstructing their lives.

In the 1890s their homeland was being overrun by "outsiders." The historian Mateo Martinic documented this period concerning the Chilean settlements very precisely. The government in Punta Arenas was giving concessions for a number of years to the local emigrants to create cattle and sheep farms as well as saw mills. Companies were organised to exploit the remaining seals, crabs and fish. Wulaia was occupied by Austrians. On the east coast of Navarino a port called Toro had been established to accommodate the Chilean Navy and commercial ships coming from Punta Arenas. The area farther south was still being trampled over by gold miners and by sealers tracking their prey around the Horn, throughout New Year's Sound, and elsewhere.[76] During the last years of the century, Lawrence was aware that so few natives remained that "there is now very little for the Society to do amongst them."

During 1899, his final year in office, Governor Godoy kept insisting that the native children in Ushuaia be taught in Spanish and attend the government school where from thirteen to twenty children of the settlers were taught. Lawrence replied that there were no children of school age among the twelve mixed couples. Some of the young men could not find a wife among their own people, so "recently lawful marriages have taken place...between Yahgan men and Ona women." Lawrence referred to the latter as healthy, clean and strong.[77] But they had few children.

The new era for the surviving Yahgans had begun, the epidemics had abated but they had no home country. Most were still in the Tekenika Mission. Some were in Ushuaia looking for jobs or handouts or "shopping" for supplies, including wine and other necessities. Others worked part time at the sheep farms, sawmills and lumber camps or lived in small enclaves along Beagle Channel, but they too had to find employment during part of the year to supplement otter hunting and fishing.

The Keppel Mission Is Sold

In 1894, all the Keppel pupils, twenty-eight men and youths, began return-ing to Tierra del Fuego. Five years later, the Keppel Mission was converted into a commercial farm by the mission society in Bristol (apparently in agreement with the Falkland authorities), and in 1911 it was sold, fifty-five years after it had been founded (Chapter 8). Ten "Keppelites" married later, but only one couple had two children and another just one.[78] This very low birth rate had become usual among the Yahgans and the mixed couples and may have been a result of the lingering epidemics.

The President of Argentina Visits Ushuaia

The presence of Julio Argentino Roca dramatised the entry of Tierra del Fuego into the new century. Ushuaia, with its 250 inhabitants, did not have accommodations for the president's nearly 3,000 guests. Most of them dined and slept on their ships. Fifty or sixty natives came from Ushuaia to greet "el señor presidente" and witness the festivities, which lasted an entire week. They, the missionaries and their children must have been dazzled: "flags flying, bands playing, drilling, signalling with the electric lights, and the whole Bay of Ushuaia scanned by searchlights at night."[79]

As the Century Sinks into History

Influenza claimed fewer victims, though lung diseases and syphilis per-sisted among the young adults. Gusinde noted that the region around the Ushuaia Mission "was known among the Yamana as *welapatux-waia*, the bay of huge mortality."[80]

Like sparkling threads running through the tattered cloth of life, in 1894 Hester and her one son George were still alive. He was working with the last recruits at Keppel. That year he was reunited with his mother in Ushuaia. Lawrence, who witnessed the reunion, remarked that they were "very pleased" to meet after a separation of ten years. George passed away five years later.

Through the din of the long suffering, Hester witnessed the turn of the century. Fuegia, the bright young daughter of Jemmy and Jamesina in 1858 (Chapter 8) had become Hester, the mother of ten children and the loving companion of two husbands. Following the deaths of her first husband and seven children, she nursed and cared for her second husband, the father of her last two children, who were still alive in 1900, though very fragile. What became of them I do not know. Her encounter with her first-born, George, was perhaps the highlight of her last years. She died in 1900.

Okoko was about sixty, working on the Lawrence farm, and said to be the oldest Yahgan in Tierra del Fuego, the only survivor of the thirty-six who had been baptised in 1869. He had joyfully joined Despard at Keppel before the 1859 massacre and had volunteered to return there afterwards, in February 1860. He was the first native who preached to his countrymen. He and Gamela were the first to offer to establish the mission in Wulaia. He struggled to comprehend the Christian message, resisting the aggression, risking his life and mocking of his own people who were offended by his preaching. Later with Lucca, Pinoense and Jack, he persisted trying to set up a mission in Lewaia and then joined Stirling with his family in Ushuaia in 1869, when one was finally established there. By the time he died he had lost all of his family, except a grandson, to the fury of the epidemics.[81]

Jemmy was friendly with the missionaries but he resisted their messages. Through the years he recalled his English friends by their names, and sent them souvenirs of his friendship. Jamesina, Mrs Button number one, and her sister, Mrs Button number two, were Jemmy's devoted companions. Among their children were Hester and Threeboys. When Threeboys returned from his trip to England in 1867, he showed more anxiety for his dying friend Urupa and Urupa's desperate father, than for himself, while suffering from his own fatal illness. Sisoi became "famous" when he sang the Christian hymns in England (1867), but he loved his father more than the missionaries. After his father died he became Bridges' most essential informant for his extraordinary Yamana–English dictionary. Lucca, like Okoko, risked his life to convert his countrymen to Christianity. Apparently Sisoi and Lucca did not survive the epidemics. Urupa died loving Christ with no regret or blame.

Young Otatosh led Stirling to Ushuaia, presented him to his kin, and remained attached to the missionaries to the very end. They and loyal Jack, generous Pinoense and the everyday Tom Button should be honoured "for evermore," as well as the women who risked their lives attempting to save their sick husbands, Burleigh and others from drowning. The tragic deaths of Karmankar-kipa and her friend recall those of the many who died as babies, children and in the prime of youth. Athlinata, the "most intelligent native," took the blows aimed at a missionary though living in the most squalid mission station ever (Douglas, the last Anglican mission) amid swamps and alcoholics (Chapter 15). All were descendants of the original pioneers, of some 6,000 years earlier, in this the "Land of Fire."

This decimated population closes the last chapter of these hunter–gatherers, these so-called savages, who had lived for thousands of years in this desolate, magnificent country. By 1900, they had been brought into the fold of Christianity and civilisation. The "double-C strategy" had spent itself. Their culture was shattered, although fragments of it were nourished by those who had somehow survived. Many, mixed or not, cherished their ancestral memories and performed their great Chiexaus ceremony. They continued speaking their own language with each other and English or Spanish with "outsiders," among whom were their fathers or husbands (Chapter 15).

15

The Twentieth Century: Ushuaia, the Ancient
Yamana Campsite, Becomes a City

The Journey Ending

The Tekenika Mission

"The last Yahgans are dying out. The Alakalufs are almost extinct. The Ona...much shot down by the sheep farmers," the missionary Peter Pringle wrote in 1901.[1] The circle was closing, the curtain falling. Pringle became convinced that the work in the Tekenika Mission was nearly over because of the many deaths of infants, the few children who survived, the scarce food and even scarcer jobs for the adults. Everyone seemed to be "fast dwindling away," Pringle also.[2]

At that time some seventy Yahgans still lived in Tekenika. About a hundred and thirty were scattered: some in or near Ushuaia, a few on Lawrence's sheep farm, some who worked steadily on Bridges' Harberton farm. More were there for shearing, while most were living along the south coast of Beagle Channel (Navarino Island), some of whom boated to and from Nassau Bay and the Cape Horn area to fish or to hunt otters or seals.

Professor Roberto Dabbene, an Argentine historian, visited Tekenika in 1902, and affirmed that there were one hundred Yahgans there and that another hundred "were vagabonds around Cape Horn in a state of savagery or half-civilised in different parts of the archipelago, especially in several farms where they worked as peons." In Tekenika he noticed that most of the men were "decently dressed," but the women were not because fewer clothes were donated for them. He also noticed about seventy starving dogs. The number of resident Yahgans there varied from one month to another. As noted in the last chapter the Yamana population in Tierra del Fuego was about 200 at the turn of the century, according to the missionaries and most of the visitors.[3]

The Last Anglican Missionary

John Williams, the last envoy of the South American Missionary Society, arrived in Tekenika with his wife Judy from Punta Arenas, where he had been a chaplain. He replaced Mr Robbins, who had substituted for Pringle. Once established there, Williams' wife began teaching the women to knit stockings and make jackets for themselves, motivated by Nelly Burleigh's example (Chapter 14). Several months later Williams complained that the bad weather and high tides made it impossible for the natives to obtain food. Again a stranded whale came to the rescue. Thirty men left for the feast, but this time the whale only lasted a week. The boys in the orphanage were dying, the orphan girls were still in Ushuaia.[4] The next three years the condition of the boys and the other residents worsened.

And the Last Mission

In 1906 Williams organised the transfer of the mission (property, personnel and residents) from Tekenika to the Douglas River inlet, on Navarino Island, seventeen miles (28 km) south of Wulaia, along Ponsonby Sound. There the mission would be closer to Ushuaia and more protected from bad weather than in Tekenika. In Ushuaia what was left of the mission's facilities, for instance, the "girls' school," closed, and some of the Yahgans there went to the Douglas River station.

In 1987, Cristina and Ursula Calderón and I admired a small commemorative monument, dedicated to the Ushuaia Mission, below the site of the mission on the west side of the bay. As far as we could see nothing remained of the mission settlement on the barren hills beyond.

Furlong's Memorial Visit
Charles Wellington Furlong, a North American explorer and writer, visited the mission in December 1907.[5] He paid his fare there in a cutter, named Garibaldi for its owner, a well-known resident of Ushuaia. The owner sent the cutter there to barter with the mission residents for otter skins. The skipper was an Austrian trader and smuggler. His cargo consisted of washiki, the worse quality rum available in Ushuaia.

The skipper let Furlong off near the mission site in a small boat. He didn't enter the river leading to the mission but rather took the Garibaldi about a mile down the coast where he threw out his anchor. Furlong noticed three canoes full of Yahgan men were already rowing behind the cutter. Follows an example of Furlong's talent as a writer:

The Garibaldi was well stocked with the vile washiki, a poisonous, mind-inflaming alcoholic drink, and her skipper, like others, had no compunctions against first staling a chunkie's [derogatory term for Yahgans] mind and then his pelts. One could easily foresee the results of this visit.... They spent perhaps their season's catch of otter-skins for six bottles of washiki, and return with half of it, drunk, to a crazed, full-headed, empty-handed crowd, with still enough left to go the round with those on shore.

Furlong soon discovered that about seventy-five of the natives were resident there, though some forty men were absent, hunting off the Wollaston Island. He noticed the shell-heaps extending for almost a mile on both sides of the inlet, the refuse piles left by the Yahgans. Such mounds are usually composed of mussel shells mixed with bones of birds, seals and whales and occasional stone or bone tools, or fragments thereof or, now and then, human bones. These mounds were big: some ten feet high and forty feet in diameter. He wondered: "It must have taken centuries to bring about the vast accumulations of some of these Yahgan villages." An Australian anthropologist, who will come there later, will notice even larger mounds (see below).

Furlong, disdaining the platitude that human nature is about the same the world over, insisted that "it is the technique of existence that interests us: the novelty and surprise...." He sounds like Lévi-Strauss (see Introduction). He decided that "the Yahgans, as a people, are inherently intelligent." Even so, he couldn't resist calling them "children of nature" and "uncivilised people."

The day before he arrived, sometime in December 1907, two Yahgan men had been murdered in a canoe on the river, near the mission settlement. The woman who had been with them swam to shore and accused the surviving man, who was still in the canoe, of killing them. When Furlong descended from his boat on shore, he realised that the relatives of the two slain men were already mourning: "their hair cut in a round spot on top of their heads, with knives and mussel shells, or sharp stone." Their faces were painted with black charcoal and "white pigment from a shell-like composition picked up along the beach," all of which "rendered their expression hideous."

Athlinata Reappears

The search had begun to retrieve the two bodies from the icy water. The following morning, through a murky sky and drizzling rain a canoe appeared loaded with the bodies. For a reason not explained, but obviously part of the mourning rite, two groups of men started smashing one another's heads with heavy paddles, and aiming large stones at each other, yelling wildly, while the women cried and shouted. The dogs, going crazier by the minute, raced around the fighters, barking with all their might. This turmoil only lasted a short while. The serious fights began when some forty more Yahgans arrived in ten canoes from Mejillones Bay, Navarino Island, along Beagle Channel, because one of the murdered men was a kin of theirs. Then a "terrific brawl" began.[6] This was only a semblance of the former mourning rite that had become a brawl mainly because of the washiki.

At that moment, Furlong went to the tent he had put up when he had debarked, loaded his Winchester and headed for John Williams, the missionary, who was encircled by two men battering one another. In his own words: "Before reaching them I saw a blow aimed at his head, which luckily was intercepted by a Yahgan named Athleenatah [Athlinata of Chapter 13]." Williams motioned to Furlong not to approach. Later Williams explained that he feared that "a stranger's interference" would have made matter worse. By then Williams, aided by one of his mission Indians, had managed to separate the two who were battering each other and were trying to lug them to their wigwams. Furlong admired the missionary. "Mr. Williams and one Indian were hauling, dragging and half-carrying the more powerful of the two. With the courage and tenacity of a man twice his size, the plucky little missionary eventually landed his man turning him over to the none too gentle surveillance of the women."

Finally when "the camp was restored to some semblance of order," Furlong took supplies from his emergency kit and proceeded to bandage Athlinata's "ugly head gash and an open chuck," the wounds he had received. Athlinata was the "one Indian" who defended "Mr Williams."

Twenty-five years before (1882) Athlinata had done his best to accept the overwhelming presence of other outsiders, the French explorer Hyades and his crew. Later he got involved with the English missionaries. He probably realised that this new world imposed upon him and his people allowed no liveable place for him or them, the other survivors of the epidemics. Despite the miserable living conditions in the Douglas River Mission, he defended the missionary and was badly wounded. More information may possibly be found concerning him. Thanks to Furlong

FIGURE 15.1. 1907: Athlinata being bandaged by Reverend Willams, standing at his left, Athlinata's wife at his right. Douglas River Mission, Navarino Island. Courtesy of Dartmouth College Library, Rauner Special Collections.

we can recognise Athlinata as a hero who risked his life to save a missionary without harming his own people, who were attacking the missionary. Furlong took this photograph of Athlinata just after he had been bandaged.

The Next Visitor Is of Hierarchy

When Reverend E. T. Avery, the Catholic bishop of the Falkland Islands, visited the Douglas station the following year, 1908, he realised that the Yahgans had fallen into an abyss between two worlds. As many of the Protestant missionaries, he blamed the Yahgans for being "very weak morally," giving way "far too easily to temptation," and for their "tendency to pilfer." Besides the "men seldom go to Ushuaia without obtaining some of the fatal drink. . . ." He had no illusions.

For good or evil these people have completely grown out of their old way of living and yet the new way does not altogether suit them. Flour or biscuit, for example, is now a necessity of life to them. They cannot thrive now on the excellent mussels with which these southerly regions abound and which, as the old mounds of shells testify, furnished the food for their forefathers for ages. The present race is not healthy. The promising girls whom I saw in the Home [in Ushuaia] three years ago are dead. Thus the Mission, even in its closing chapters, remains an unsolved problem.[7]

Furlong Recalls . . .

Ten years later Furlong had not forgotten the Yahgans. He recalled the fatal error of clothing them, the "Christian haircut" that divested the Fuegians of their "best natural head protection in that frigid clime," and the plagues he identified as: catarrhal affections, measles, whooping cough, pleurisy, phthisis, pneumonia, scrofula, consumption and smallpox. He added these passionate though true lines:

Then came the trader and unscrupulous adventurer with their rotten rum and more rotten morals, and left in their wake some of the white man's vices syphilis and other virulent forms of venereal diseases. . . . During my visit to Fuegia in 1907–08 I estimated the total Yahgan population of those regions at 175. . . . today [1917] possibly not more than 100 remain.[8]

Julia (Carrupale-Kipa) Escapes

Cristina Calderón recalled Abuela Julia's testimony of her escape from the Douglas River Mission, probably about 1910. She paddled a dugout canoe for most of two months, accompanied by a faithful dog, around the large island of Hoste, some 280 miles (450 kilometres), camping along the coasts. She set out to the south through Ponsonby Sound, then along Nassau Bay, rounded False Cape Horn, somehow passed New Year's Sound, and the treacherous Black Point, steered up Christmas Sound, along the west coast of Hoste Island, then back through the Southwest Arm, to Beagle Channel where she finally arrived at her destination,

Sambutu (Mejillones Bay). Cristina vividly explains why Julia left the mission and how she survived the trip, translated from Spanish.

She left the mission at Douglas. She escaped. . . . It took her months, because that island [Hoste] is big. . . . The missionaries wanted to teach her to pray, but she didn't want to. They wanted to teach her to knit socks, spin wool, all that kind of work. They had houses separated, for the men and for the women. She didn't like all that either. They gave her those biscuits, she threw them all away. Those turnips that they planted, she didn't like those either. She didn't like coffee or tea, not even a drop. She only liked tea of the leaves or bark of red beech tree [Nothofagus Antarctica]. This is why she escaped. . . .

   She made the whole trip around the island and came back this way [to Beagle Channel] all by herself, paddling with a little paddle. When it was calm she went along fast. She kept a fire [in the canoe] on lumps of mud or bogs. She took along a dog who caught birds for her. She ate eggs and shellfish too and three mussels [choros] a day and some water, that was enough. Alone she couldn't kill a seal. She had some blankets that the gringos [missionaries] had given her.

I asked Cristina if Julia had been afraid. "No she was never afraid. She tied her canoe to kelp when she went [swam] ashore [to sleep]. . . .⁹

Why she took this very long route instead of going north through Murray Narrows to Beagle Channel, then over to nearby Mejillones Bay, was not explained. Perhaps she wasn't familiar with this shorter route because at that time she had probably never been in that area. She was from Wollaston, near Cape Horn. Or perhaps she went the long way to avoid the somewhat populated area to the north, fearing she might be taken back to the Douglas Mission.

Hermelinda Acuña also heard Julia tell about her escape from Douglas and commented: "She paddled all alone. She had a dugout canoe, made of one trunk. I myself saw that canoe."¹⁰

In 1920 Julia became Martin Gusinde's best informant because of her superior knowledge of Yamana myths (see below). She didn't speak Spanish, so Gusinde worked with four bilingual Yamana men as interpreters. After 1920 he never saw her again. When he returned to Mejillones Bay in 1922 she had left with her husband, also a Yamana, in a canoe, to visit her home territory, Wollaston Island. She died in 1958, six years before I arrived in Navarino Island.

Julia's undaunted fixation on her own lifestyle has a truly epic dimension. Surely someday it will be recognised as such. Her triumph of manoeuvring a canoe alone during almost two months through an uninhabited area is perhaps the most forceful homage that can be evoked to honour the Yamana women as expert and courageous navigators.

Emilia Also Holds on Tight

Ursula Calderón, also my friend and informant, knew Emilia well. Emilia had adopted her husband when he was an orphan child and later he and Ursula often took her travelling in their row-motor-boat around Hoste Island, through Yahgan and Alakaluf territory, south of the Magellan Strait. Ursula repeated several times that the abuelas Emilia and Julia were the last Yahgans to cling to the old ways, as if to a sinking canoe, struggling to keep it and themselves afloat. Emilia's real name was Kapumucus-kipa, probably a name in her birthplace, the Wollaston Island. Like Julia she spoke Yamana though later she picked up Spanish. She often told Ursula how "lovely" it was living in Wollaston "as they used to live." She had been taken to the Tekenika Mission when she was a child. She never liked the food "the English gave her." She didn't like bread, potatoes, rice, beans or cheese, not even guanaco meat. Probably about 1910, she married "a civilised" (un civilizado), a Christian Yahgan, twice her age, known as Charlie. He took her to live in Ushuaia when she was still wearing sealskins. He told her to put on the "pretty dresses" the missionaries gave him for her. But she didn't like those clothes. He would hide her sealskins and shout at her: "So you won't wear these dresses?" Ursula said that he hit her too, trying to force her to take off those sealskins. He would say: "You have these dresses that the mission, the gringos gave you, well, wear them. You always go around with these skins!" Then when he left to work she would take off the dress and put on her sealskins again. When he returned home, he would say: "So you put these on again!" Then she would wear the dress for a little while and when he left the next day, she would put on her sealskins again. Ursula said that once he got really mad and threw her sealskins into the fire. "From then on she had to wear the dresses. She still didn't like the food either but she had to eat it. What she liked was a seal meat, fish, and mussels, limpets, that was her food."[11]

Emilia's and Julia's "way of living" was more than clothes and food, more than a culture, traditions or customs; it was that red liquid that irrigates the body and the mind, that circulates and vibrates constantly, awake and while dreaming.

Ushuaia, a Penal Colony

At the beginning of the twentieth century Ushuaia had 250 inhabitants; twenty were policemen. The percentage of policemen might be high but they were not very busy. In 1901 Lawrence observed: "Ushuaia seems quieter now than of old, both at the Mission station and the Government settlement. There are more prisoners and ex-prisoners here than any other class of people. Natives are few."[12]

The next year Ushuaia was endowed with a military prison, in addition to the existing "Second Offender Prison" and a local prison. Colonel Lasserre had established the first military prison of Argentina, in 1884, on the far-away northeast coast of Staten Island, in a fjord or cape called San Juan de Salvamiento (Chapter 13). Five years later it was moved nearby to a fjord named Puerto Cook, in honour of the great explorer who had been close by on 1 January 1775 (Chapter 1). Staten Island was as distant as possible from the Argentine mainland but it was as much of a prison for the guards as for the inmates. The second most far-away place was Ushuaia. In 1902, it became the locality of the third prison, for the military offenders. At that time there were more military prisoners than civilians. The former performed a great deal of useful labour in Ushuaia and the guards lived in town.[13]

In 1902, when the sixty-nine Puerto Cook–Staten Island prisoners were escorted off the pier in Ushuaia they may have had mixed feelings about attempting escape at that moment, wondering what was happening to their fifty-one comrades who had escaped a few days before from the Puerto Cook prison when the transfer had begun to Ushuaia. A year or so later the Ushuaia prisoners would learn that most of the fifty-one convicts had perished: some drowned trying to row across the Strait of Le Maire, others managed the strait only to be killed fighting among themselves and later by the mounted police. The few survivors of the fifty-one were probably welcomed by their former prison buddies in the Ushuaia compound as they listened overawed to their amazing flight from the Staten Island prison, and especially how these few had managed to live through all that had happened.

In 1907 Furlong visited Ushuaia and "explored" the three prisons. "At the western end of the town, the Penitentiary and Prison for Old Offenders, or Civil Prison, raises its grey stone walls. Three kilometres eastward along the coast, beyond some boggy land, is the Military Prison. Here are harboured the criminals from the Argentine army."

By 1907 Ushuaia had a population of some 500 "souls" among which there were 260 prisoners "controlled by a meagre and insufficient garrison of fifty-six soldiers and a handful of vigilantes."[14]

In 1911 the military and civil prisons were merged though Ushuaia was still called a penal colony. "Political and social prisoners," mostly from Buenos Aires, were confined there at different times in 1911 and especially in 1930 (see below). Through the years the prisoners, dressed as zebras from head to foot, supplied most of the labour force for the town: chopping firewood, digging through the forests to open roads, building bridges, laying ties for a local railroad, installing sewerage and running water, street lights, "anything needed." All this development enhanced Ushuaia, the Argentine capital of Tierra del Fuego, and took some of the sting out her fame as the Argentine Siberia. The prison was also "famous" for the extremely severe punishments and tortures inflicted on the prisoners, despite the efforts against such treatments by more than one enlightened prison director. Nonetheless, a few convicts grew so attached to the town that they settled there when they were released. In 1947 the penal colony prison was closed by orders of the Argentine president Juan Peron. Since then, through the years, the prison buildings were used by the military. Recently part of the enclosure was converted into a fascinating museum, where full-sized portrait-mannequins of the prison's most famous or notorious inmates pose, seated or standing, in their assigned cells, whose doors are now open for the public to admire them. Among the prisoners so honoured are the legendary tango artist Carlos Gardel, who was said to have spent a short term there, and Professor Ricardo Rojas who is part of our story (see below).[15]

"Four Decades of Decadence"

Mateo Martinic, the often-cited dean of Magellan history, called this period, 1910 to 1950, the "Four decades of decadence and abandonment."[16] But life for the Yahgans and mestizos continued more or less as usual. During these years the Chilean and Argentine governments continued granting concessions of land, in former Yahgan territory, to new settlers and companies. Most of the lands changed hands more than once, or the proprietors went bankrupt and new ones sprang up, such as ephemeral coal mining companies and factories of different sorts.[17]

Christmas about 1912, thirty-six mostly adult Yahgans gathered on Lawrence's farm for a special service. He painted a "sad picture" of them and the others. He thought most of the men were dying of alcoholism. Many possessed firearms, and were killing one another when drunk or "through their careless handling of their weapons... and not a few drowned while in the same state." However, Lawrence was glad that now they were "rarely ill-treated by the foreigners," meaning the Argentines especially.[18] Lawrence was their faithful friend through the years as will be proven again, soon.

The problems were shifting – the epidemics did not appear again until about 1925 (see below). Some, especially the men, whose immune system had defended them against the epidemics, could not resist "the deadly temptation."

The last mission, on Douglas River, was falling apart. In 1916 Reverend Williams was "the most isolated missionary in the world." The mission was closed that year and with it the South American Mission in Tierra del Fuego. Williams and his wife returned to Punta Arenas while their three sons were granted the mission site in Douglas as their private property, which they managed as a sheep farm for years to come, like Bridges' and Lawrence's children, in compliance with Stirling's advice (Chapter 13).[19]

Even before the mission closed, many Yahgans had left it and were living on both shores of Beagle Channel, criss-crossing it as if it were one and the same country (actually by then the channel was the border between Chile and Argentina). Lawrence, aware that the natives had no place to call their own, obtained a concession of land, a reserve or reservation, for them in Mejillones (Mussels) Bay, on the Navarino coast of Beagle Channel.[20] This is where Julia reached her final destination about 1910 and passed away in 1958. About 1910 Yahgan and mestizo families were living there in wooden houses with zinc roofs. They kept alive by fishing, tending small herds of sheep, a few cattle and horses as well as working during the summer months on the missionaries' sheep farms and elsewhere along Beagle Channel. The men were often away for weeks or months at a time on the farms, or hunting foxes on Hoste Island, otters and the new generations of seals on the southernmost islands. The hides of these animals were sold in Ushuaia and the earnings spent there, often for you-know-what.

Father Gusinde with Julia (Carrupale-Kipa) and Nelly Calderón Lawrence

For his study of the Fuegians, Father Martin Gusinde benefited from the enthusiastic support of Dr Aureliano Oyarzún, the director of the Museum of Anthropology and Ethnology in Santiago, Chile. Gusinde arrived in Chile in 1912 and worked for years as professor in the German Liceo in Santiago, learning Spanish himself while teaching history and in 1916 spent two months among the Araucanos (Mapuches) when this photograph was taken.

During four trips to Tierra del Fuego, between 1919 and 1923, Gusinde first met the Yamana in 1919, returned in December 1920 to visit them

FIGURE 15.2. 1916: Gusinde in Santiago, dressed in his Mapuche poncho, three years before he began his work in Tierra del Fuego.

again when he worked with Julia. In 1922 he spent several more months with them, accompanied by his colleague Willhelm Koppers. During his fourth and last trip, 1923 to 1924, he visited the Yamana and the Selk'nam also again, said goodbye to Nelly in Remolino and spent two months with the Alakaluf.[21]

Gusinde met Julia in 1920 or early 1921, during his second stay among the Yahgans on Lawrence's farm, along Beagle Channel. He realised that she was the most knowledgeable of the Yamana tradition he met then and even afterwards. She spoke so little Spanish that he had to work with four bilingual Yahgans – Yamanas as Gusinde called them – to translate her recitations. The majority of the sixty-eight myths Gusinde published were told to him by Julia.

She had probably guarded her memory of the "oral tradition" because she resisted the "outsiders." She may have pictured the personages of the myths as if they were real while reciting them to whomever would listen, or while meditating as she gazed at the fire in her hut or at the birds who were the heroes and villains of her stories. Gusinde referred to his interviews with Julia as follows: "We were together day after day for long hours and thus I was able to collect the rich treasury of the Yamana."[22] But his favourite friend may well have been Nelly Calderón Lawrence who he met in 1919, while visiting Lawrence's farm. She was named Nelly in memory of Mrs Burleigh (Chapter 14). She was a Yahgan, Cristina's and Ursula's aunt, as well as the first wife of Fred Lawrence, the oldest son of the missionary. According to the historian Arnoldo Canclini, it was a marriage that did not especially please the members of the Lawrence family. However, apparently it was a happy one; in any event they had six children.[23]

Nelly was fluent in Spanish and English, besides her native Yahgan. Gusinde and his colleague Koppers highly esteemed her fine personal qualities. The former dedicated his original volume in German, on the Yamana, to her. In 1924 and 1925, another devastating measles epidemic struck Ushuaia again, the nearby area and inland, the Selk'nam-Ona territory. In 1924 a year after Gusinde had departed, Nelly succumbed, in her mid-forties, to the measles epidemic rampant in Ushuaia that year and the next, which in the Lake Fagnano region killed so many Selk'nam. Canclini reported that all of her six children died "victims of endemic pulmonary diseases," without leaving descendants.[24] However someone told me, I can't remember whom, that one of her male children survived, had gone to Valparaíso but never returned to Tierra del Fuego.

FIGURE 15.3. About 1920: Nelly Calderón Lawrence, Gusinde's most helpful Yamana assistant. Courtesy of Dr J. Piepke, Director of the Anthropos Institute, Sankt Augustin, Germany. Archive # GU 34.33.

Nelly (Figure 15.3) did not cling to the old ways as Julia and Emilia, even so she was the anthropologists' dream come true. She was articulate, trilingual, willing to share her knowledge of her people with outsiders she trusted and to convince others to do likewise, while unforgiving when recalling the horrors that had led to the extinction of her people.

The Yahgans from Then On

In 1958 the Mejillones reservation was transferred to a place called Ukika. The Chilean Navy tore down the houses in Mejillones, relocated the people living there and built better houses for them in Ukika, near the navy base of Puerto Williams, along Beagle Channel, at the mouth of the River Ukika. There, the Yahgans were still semi-nomads, now crossing Beagle Channel back and forth between Chile and Argentina, often with their families, in row or motor boats, from their jobs on the missionaries' sheep farms to the Ukika reserve. In 1973 a threatening military conflict between the two countries made crossing the border to Argentina difficult or impossible. The potential conflict was peacefully resolved in 1978 but the border restrictions continued.

During these years even women in Ukika who had married "foreigners" (Argentines or Chileans), were somehow still Yahgans, still Fuegians, Indians or mestizos. All the Yahgans, "pure" and "less pure," were different from the "pure" white adults whose parents had been missionaries, sailors, bureaucrats, owners or employees of sheep farms, sawmills, hotels, cafés and bars. They were different from everyone else. Since 1978 most of the Yahgans and their descendants who live in Ukika tend to remain in the Chilean section of Tierra del Fuego, except for occasional visits to Ushuaia.

Clemente, a Famous (or Notorious) Yahgan

By the 1930s, forty to seventy Yahgans remained. As the number of the "pure" Yahgans dropped, that of the mestizos increased by intermarriages. Those whose mother tongue was Yahgan vindicated their ancestral heritage but not as a mode of living, not like Julia and Emilia. During those years, most of the "pure" or not, usually the mother was Yahgan, performed the Chexaus ceremony, gathered mussels, canoed to the ancient campsites to fish and hunt and occasionally discovered a beached whale. Rosa Clemente, Clemente's granddaughter, recalled with pleasure: "Once two whales were beached in Eugenia [north coast of Navarino] and the men [from Mejillones] got seven big barrels of oil and sold them in Ushuaia and we all ate whale loin steaks and the fat fried like cracklings."[25] These Yahgans were sheep-farm workers, wore factory-made clothes, purchased outboard motors, ate potatoes and mutton and drank wine. Once a Yahgan woman complained to me:

They [the Yahgan men] liked wine too much. Some people died from fights and beatings, from the wine. When I was a child they really liked wine.... They beat the women. Grandmother Rosa once was all swollen from a beating. They were bad drunks. One almost killed another grandmother.... They drank a lot in Mejillones.... I knew this I was there. Now they [the men, in 1988] don't drink much.[26]

Rosa Clemente, who died in 1992 or 1993, recalled that when she was young in Mejillones: "We used to only speak Yahgan." She learned Spanish later in Ushuaia and understood English, thanks to her grandfather, Clemente. Her recollections of him are especially pertinent because he will appear later on.

My grandfather Clemente was taken as a child to the Malvinas [the Keppel
Mission], to the missionaries, the English. When he returned he was a grown
man. He could speak English, write and all that.... He read the Bible.... He
didn't speak in Spanish: in English [all the time] but never forgot Yahgan. He
knew all the Bridges [the second generation, Lucas and his siblings].... When
he came home he would throw himself on the bed and read the Bible. When
he came back from Malvinas he got married to an Ona and then my papa was
born.... When he became a widower, he married Rosa, an Alakaluf, and had
more children.... He died about 1975, and worked until his last day.... He
had a lot of Bibles. He read the Bible every day.... My grandfather was no longer
a Yahgan because he spoke English and was a Christian. He liked to tell us
about the sacred history of Our Lord Jesus Christ. He told us many stories about
all this.[27]

Despite Clemente's Christian enthusiasm he killed his second wife,
Rosa. She was Alakaluf and once her people found out, a group of her
kin searched for him in their canoes, to avenge her murder but apparently
never located him. In any event he died peacefully. All this occurred after
the 1930s, after he had met Sir Baldwin Spencer and Professor Ricardo
Rojas (see below).

The Last Kina Ceremony

The Kina was principally a male initiation ceremony, probably related
to the Selk'nam Hain celebration. Its essential thrust was similar to that
of the Hain. Nevertheless, the Kina ceremony was quite different from
the Hain ceremony. It had far more spirits than the Hain and was not so
emphatically "macho." The wealth of Gusinde's and Koppers' testimonies on the Kina has certainly enriched our knowledge and appreciation
of the Yamana culture.[28] But it is too complex to be even summarized
here. Moreover, none of my Yahgan friends had participated in a Kina,
nor did they know much about it. It was probably enacted for the last
time in the Mejillones reservation in 1922 for Gusinde and Koppers, who
contributed food for the participants during the six-day performance.[29]

And the Chexaus

The greatest Yamana ceremony was called Chexaus (spelt Chiexaus by
Gusinde). Given its communal character it is my impression that it had
"always" been for both sexes.[30] My three Chexaus informants, Cristina
and Ursula Calderón (Figure 15.4) and Hermelinda Acuña, often told
me in the 1980s that it had been the most joyful event in the lives of
their people before the destruction of their culture and even afterwards.
Therefore it is fitting that the two final Chexaus be evoked here, near the

FIGURE 15.4. 1988: The sisters Cristina and Ursula Calderón, Navarino Island, Chile.

end of this book. Hermelinda was initiated, in the last one, as a young girl in about 1933 while Cristina was taken into the sacred hut, when the next Chexaus was scheduled to begin about 1935, though she was not initiated, nor was anyone else.

Chexaus Symbolisms

The "Chexaus house," la casa Chexaus, symbolised the Yamana's close association with the sea. The hut, carefully built of branches and twigs for the occasion, evoked a rocky cave at sea level, the habitat of seals. It really did resemble a dark cave, filtered through by sunlight.

Hermelinda repeated several times that the interior of the hut was "real pretty," thanks to the painted slabs that decorated the walls. A large fire was kept burning in the centre and two or four smaller fires were kindled along both sides of it.

The adults wore headbands of white geese or seagull feathers that symbolised foam on the crest of waves. Formerly they were made of the soft white down of the albatross and the participants, both men and women, dressed in long strips of animal skins also decorated with white down, perhaps to represent rippling waves. The gentle oscillation of the sea was evoked by the back and forth movements of the dancers, as their costumes swayed in unison with the painted staffs that they moved rhythmically with both hands as they chanted. The staffs' designs were similar to those of the painted slabs of wood.

The "Watchiman"

The Chexaus had a male director, though the several "watchiman" (spelt as it was pronounced in Spanish with an "i" and always singular), were far more active than the director (Figure 15.5). In Yahgan they were called winefkar or winefkema, the word for albatross. They wore a crown of white albatross feathers and were daubed with red paint from the nose to the chin, representing the beak of this bird streaked with the blood of birds he attacked. Balancing on the dome of the Chexaus hut, these "watchiman" imitated the albatross' fierce cries in order to frighten the children who dared approach the hut. Each held a leather whip, twelve to fifteen feet long (3.6 m to 4.5 m), with which they would lasso any preadolescent boys, the "naughty boys," who dared approach the hut as well as any boy being initiated in the hut who was attempting to escape from it. They lassoed the naughty boys with their whips from the roof of the hut and scared them away. Normally the adolescent boys were treated in a dignified manner and were escorted into the hut by their elders. Ursula said that the "watchiman" were like policemen and spied on the children as far as they could see from the roof of the Chexaus.[31]

The Initiates

The Chexaus focused on training, "initiating," the adolescents of both sexes, who were called *ushwaala*. They were taught the behaviour expected of them as adults, and the everyday know-how they would need in the future. After the initiation ritual, an elder would often gather the male ushwaala around him and explain how they should live, much like the Ten Commandments, and recite the myths concerning the moral debates of the heroes of old, such as those of the two Yoalox brothers (Chapter 10). There was also a notable insistence on the spiritual force of trees that had been people before they were transformed.[32]

A boy, usually about fifteen years old when he entered the Chexaus, had already helped his father and uncles while they were busy with different tasks but he still did not distinguish the work from the play. He had to learn how to make and employ the tools and weapons and to become accustomed to the idea that he would be responsible for supplying his future family with the products of the hunt: seals (hides, meat and fat), certain birds (especially the cormorant) and so forth.

FIGURE 15.5. 1922: Yamana ready to participate in the Chexaus ceremony. At both extremes the two "watchiman" stand, holding their whips; Gusinde is in the back row. Mejillones Bay, Navarino Island. Courtesy of Dr J. Piepke, Director of the Anthropos Institute, Sankt Augustin, Germany. Archive # GU 32.65.

A girl candidate, twelve or thirteen years old, could already paddle a canoe made of bark, later a dugout canoe, could swim and perform most of her mother's tasks. But she was still a child, irresponsible and playful. The ceremony should transform her into an obedient, laborious, good-humoured young woman in preparation for becoming a wife and mother. The lessons had to be taught, not simply recited, so that the adolescents comprehended their meaning, and could apply them.[33] Cristina said that the Chexaus was a school where the pupils had to learn to obey. Hermelinda thought it was more like military service. Ursula insisted that in the old times, everyone, except the uninitiated children, participated in the Chexaus celebration because they always learned something. She exclaimed with enthusiasm: "The Chexaus never ended, people would take part in it until they died. The old people were welcomed because they knew so much and could teach the young."[34] Through this often-repeated ceremony, their heritage was kept alive.

The chants were sung constantly. At least one person had to be singing in the hut, day and night, from the beginning to the end of the ceremony, to keep the malignant spirits at bay.[35] Everyone had an assigned place inside the hut, where they sat and slept. The *ushwaalas* sat between their two sponsors, usually a woman and a man. They also moved about inside the hut, mostly dancing. The adults would sometimes leave the hut to go canoeing, to hunt birds or seals or to obtain other food, principally for themselves, not much for the hungry *ushwaalas*. If the ceremony took place at the site of a recently beached whale, they would have ample food for a long time, depending on the size of the monster. Ursula told me that where Abuela Emilia grew up, in Wollaston Islands, the people there were always "doing the Chexaus." Wherever there was a stranded whale, they saw the smoke signals, they knew there would be a Chexaus and whale meat to eat. "That was how the ancient people lived."

The ceremony loosened the family ties. The adolescents had been living with their small families and a few other kin travelling in canoes from one lonely campsite to another. During these ceremonies, the Chexaus as well as the Kina, the young people socialised with those of other families and had to obey the elders, not just their parents.

Disciplining the Adolescents

During the Chexaus the adolescents were constantly watched over by their two sponsors: to see that they drank water through the leg bone of a bird, not simply out of a container; that they scratched themselves, if need be, with a special stick, not their fingers; and that they held onto the painted staff tightly and not let it fall on the ground. When they were moving about inside the hut, they were told to insert the staff carefully in the rafters. Above all, they were cautioned not to trip or fall. The adults also had to be careful not to fall. Gusinde tripped and fell in the hut the last day of the 1922 Chexaus, and all hell nearly broke loose; the evil spirits were about to take control of the hut and Gusinde himself was in danger of losing his soul, his kashpi. An evil spirit could have kidnapped it. A yekamush–shaman came to his rescue by massaging his legs and probably chanting. Thus order was restored to the hut and Gusinde's kashpi returned to his body.[36]

The *ushwaala* were given very little to eat, a real punishment for adolescents. Early in the morning they were escorted out of the hut to a nearby river to wash a bit and were allowed a few sips of water from the shell of a mussel. Their mouths were painted red, with the imi. If they attempted to drink a lot, their sponsor would immediately notice the smeared paint on their mouths and reprimand or punish them.[37] The candidates had to learn to endure the privations they might be subject to later on.

The Boys Are "Scared to Death"

While one boy was being initiated the others were not allowed in the hut, and were sent to collect firewood or on some such errand. At the beginning of the ritual, the chosen *ushwaala* was pushed into the Chexaus hut, his head and face covered by an animal skin, later by a blanket. Though he couldn't see, he could hear terrible thuds, of the men huddled around the fire beating the ground with their fists, yelling and shouting to frighten him all the more. The boy also felt the structure of the hut shaking, as if the earth were quaking. He, himself, was shaking as he was led to the central fire and felt the heat of the flames. Suddenly one of the men threw off his head cover. At that moment he was "scared to death." Yetaite, the "evil spirit," had just sprung from the underground, through the flames and was staring at him. Aghast, the boy peered at the dreadful creature: its tangled red powdered hair, red face with white lines radiating from its mouth, its entire body painted white and long feathers dangling from its shoulders. The very minute this hideous Yetaite emerged from the underworld, the men screamed and pounded the earth with more force than ever. One of them discreetly stirred the fire until the flames were leaping higher and higher almost to the roof of the hut. Then the boy was ordered to fight with the Yetaite; to hit it with all his might. After struggling with it for several minutes, as if his life were in danger, the boy gathered his strength and gave it a terrific blow, or made the motion of doing so, and the Yetaite collapsed. Then one of the elders put his mouth to the ground and hollered a prolonged hu! meaning that the boy, the *ushwaala*, had been victorious, that he had killed the Yetaite. Another elder ordered the boy to inspect the motionless "corpse." The boy cautiously peered at the limpid body and soon recognised "it" as one of his own people. The impersonator sprang to his feet and became the boy's special sponsor for the remainder of the ceremony. A bit later the boy was told that this individual was an impostor, a false Yetaite. He was warned that the real Yetaite was very much alive, wandering about in the forest nearby, and would probably attack him when he was out there alone gathering firewood, or whatever.[38]

The girl *ushwaala* had to witness this terrible struggle, though she was not subject to any such ordeal. As the ceremony was held frequently, only a few adolescents were presented at a time.[39]

Throughout the ceremony the *ushwaalas* had to fetch water and firewood, always accompanied by an adult, to sweep the hut, in short, to do all the drudgery.

The Adults Are Possessed . . .

The young initiates did not enjoy the ceremony, but the adults did, immensely. It liberated them from their daily routine, from "housework" and other family duties. Food was brought to them by women who rotated preparing, and serving the meals and caring for the children. However, the main reason for their enjoyment was spiritual. During the evening the adults meditated in silent communion, concentrating while chanting. This calm, serene atmosphere might suddenly be shattered when one of the adults became possessed by his or her guardian spirit. The spirit was always that of an animal: a cormorant, different species of ducks, gulls, geese, or penguins, a fur seal, a sea lion – almost any familiar animal. While an adult felt possessed and was chanting loudly, the others joined in, imitating the voice of the guardian spirit, such as the song or quack of a bird guardian, the grunts of a seal guardian. The possessed person also danced, alone or with a partner, and at times all the adults joined together holding their decorated staff in both hands. The dance consisted of moving the staff rhythmically, horizontally or up and down, thumping on the ground imitating the sluggish trailing of a seal or prancing like the vigorous hopping of a bird. Thus each dance and chant was identified as being that of a certain guardian spirit.

The adults also freely expressed their feelings inside the hut by proclaiming their sadness, anxiety or contentment of the moment. At times someone would confess having wronged a friend or family member or, on the contrary, accuse another adult, who might be present, of having insulted or offended him or her in some way. In this context the ceremony might be compared to a group therapy session.[40]

Although Ursula was never initiated she enjoyed telling me about the Chexaus that took place in Mejillones Bay when she was a child, and there was plenty of food available. Potatoes and flour were brought from Ushuaia. Beef and mutton were on hand from their own herds. Guanacos could be hunted on Navarino Island where the Chexaus took place, birds were nearby along Beagle Channel. The young adults brought live birds in a bag and let them fly inside the hut, so they could be heard singing. "Afterwards their necks would be twisted and they would be sent to the kitchen to be cooked." In a separate hut several women cooked the meals by turns and took them to the "Chexaus house." Other women stayed in the camp nearby caring for the infants and young children who were watched to prevent them from going near the Chexaus. The adults in the camp shooed them away when they were talking about the Chexaus but Ursula would "hang around," so she heard bits of their conversations. "It was all a secret and we kids were not supposed to know anything about it."

Hermelinda Recalls "Her Chiexaus"

Hermelinda (Figure 15.6) is quoted almost entirely below because of the humour and emotions she expressed while telling me about her Chexaus, the last complete one that took place about 1933. She was about twelve then and was confined in the hut for almost two months, in Mejillones Bay where Ursula and Cristina also lived. Hermelinda explained why she was initiated so young. "I was punished because I hit my sister. My padrino [her sponsor] saw me hit her. My sister wouldn't do as I asked so I hit her, in the nose and how she bled! She was younger than I, but I hit her anyway. They caught me, and that was that."

They threw a blanket over my head, tied me up and dragged me to the Chiexaus house. Was I scared! I was punished for two whole months in that Chiexaus. At three in the morning I had to go look for firewood and get water [in the river nearby] in my bare feet, in May when there was already snow on the ground. We didn't use shoes then. I wrapped my feet in bags but I suffered all the same. Then I had to sweep out the hut. Milichic [a Yahgan] and his wife, Abuela Rosa, were my padrinos. She kept watch on me and warned me, "You had better do everything I tell you." The bed there was so narrow I couldn't sleep much – at all. Almost all day I had to sit looking at that stick, without moving my eyes from it.

FIGURE 15.6. 1988: Hermelinda Acuña showing me a basket she is weaving.

It was prettily painted. They made me wash my face [to wash off the paint] in the river every day but I wasn't allowed to drink. But I took in a few sips anyway. Abuela Rosa painted my face, and my knees down to the feet, every day. She painted my cheeks with a little stick, fine lines in red, white and black. I looked real pretty. I wore a headband of white feathers and they gave me another stick to scratch myself with. We had to drink water through the bone of a cormorant, only a few sips at a time.

I wanted to escape but Abuela Rosa warned me, "If you misbehave they'll keep you here even longer." From then on I did everything I was told.... I was really punished. It was like being in the army. I was always hungry. They'd give me a little piece of bread. Sometime they'd bring in a cormorant but they'd hand me just a tiny slice of it. We were two kids, being punished, Dionisio and me.

After a while I got bored, really. Then Abuela Rosa warned me again, "You have to stay quiet and behave." She would take me outside when I had to go.... Did I get tired of sitting all day! Finally I learned to chant but I hardly remember now. You had to chant and shout like they did. At times we had to dance, holding that painted stick in front, dance in a line around and around the fire. They'd [the adults] do the dance of the gulls, of the hawks, all different birds, dance like those birds, stirring up the dirt with their bill to get at worms, everything that that bird did.... Then we'd spread out our arms like the bird flapping its wings taking off. The same thing for seals, the same way they drag themselves over the rocks, and grunt just like they do.

That Chexaus house was painted real pretty [inside]. When I was there, there were at least twenty-five adults [she named twenty-one]... but only we two kids, Dionisio and me.[41]

The Last Chexaus

Cristina was younger than Hermelinda and of course could not possibly participate in the ceremony. She complained to me that the adults "wouldn't tell us anything about what was going on in the Chexaus house.... Even Hermelinda wouldn't tell me... they didn't even let us look toward the Chexaus.... I was afraid when they began and heard them... singing and shouting as they ran around the fire place inside the Chexaus."[42] That year, in May (probably 1934), Dionisio had to be initiated again, probably because the elders felt he hadn't learned enough during his first Chexaus the year before.

Cristina is the only recorded witness of this very last, probably thousands year old, ceremony. When the Chexaus had been going on about a month, Cristina recalled:

Dionisio was chopping down a big tree when it began falling. He tried to get out of the way but he ran the wrong way and it caught him right in the middle. He lived just a little while. When they carried him into the Chexaus, he died there. He never spoke. His brother was with him, so were a lot of the old people. Then they went to report to the Carabineros [rural police] and they came and said: "No more of this, ever because this boy died. If you go on doing this [the ceremony] more of you will be killed and if you do you'll all go to jail." This is why it was – never again.

The adults never dared present another Chexaus. The director, a Yahgan called Felix, realised that this was the only time the children could see the inside of the Chexaus hut and see how adults were participating in it, so he ordered them to enter the hut. Cristina recalled that Felix had told them: "Now you will see this last Chiexaus house. It will never ever be given again."

That's why we went; two boys, two girls and me. The Chexaus... was narrow and with a little door very low.... I had to go in, stooping way down.... Then I saw the painted sticks white with red rings. I saw all those who were there [the adults], their faces painted, each different. Each wore a head-dress of white geese feathers but they were dressed like every day. They danced for us holding on to that painted stick, in front. They chanted and imitated the birds when they take fight squeaking – like the geese of the beach... pecking at each other. As they were all painted I couldn't see who was who. Later I saw three or four men balancing on the roof of the Chexaus. They were the winefkar [the watchiman], all painted red and white with long feathers dangling from their heads. I didn't know who they were either. They were screeching like the winefkar [albatross] There aren't any of those birds around here. They are only on the high sea...

We saw all this. When it was all over Felix told us to go back to our tents. Then they began tearing down the Chexaus house. That was the last one, ever.[43]

Cristina, Ursula and Hermelinda led me to the wooded enclosure near the Mejillones reservation, where Dionisio had died and Cristina had entered the last Chexaus hut. As we strolled through the clearing that had faced the hut, they spoke again of the Chexaus, of Dionisio, Felix and others "who had departed."

The police orders forbidding its performance marks the end of the cultural expressions of the Yahgan. Eventually its written memory may incite a renewal of the Chexaus, though it would be difficult to re-enact for a public because it was such a "private affair." The adults' dancing and mimicking birds and seals would probably seem funny, picturesque or folkloric to the outsider, instead of expressions of profound emotions they undoubtedly felt.

Visits of Notable Outsiders

During the first decades of the twentieth century among the notable visitors were the frequently mentioned German anthropologist Father Martin Gusinde, the Englishman William Barclay, the Argentine historian Roberto Dabbene (who often quoted the North American journalist-turned-explorer Charles Wellington Furlong), and, among others, the archaeologist Samuel K. Lothrop, who spent a year in the area from 1924 to 1925. These visitors were very partial to the Yamanas they met and published studies concerning them.

Three others, also famous visitors, were a North American artist Rockwell Kent (Figure 15.7), and Sir Baldwin Spencer, the dean of Australian anthropologists, who was accompanied by his secretary Miss Hamilton. The other "visitor" was an Argentine historian and university professor, Ricardo Rojas, a political prisoner in Ushuaia. The writings of these three cast new light and shadow on the human landscape of the period, the 1920s to the early 1930s when the last Chexaus ceremonies were being held.

Rockwell Kent's "Rainbow Land"

Rockwell Kent's creativity ranged widely as an artist and as an author for his social awareness. In the art world he was known as a "stormy petrel." He is still famous in the United States. This text, written in 1942, sounds like today.

When I was a young fellow I was very much disturbed by there being some people with lots of money and lot of people with no money.... I am still disturbed by the fact that there are a few millions with no jobs, and that the world is rich in

FIGURE 15.7. 1923: Rockwell Kent in Tierra del Fuego. Courtesy of the Plattsburgh State Art Museum, Plattsburgh College Foundation, Rockwell Kent Collection. Bequest of Sally Kent Gorton.

resources and that people are starving to death, and that all of the people in the world want to live and yet a good part of the time they're busy killing each other. I take these phenomena of life very seriously. Consequently I rate even my being an artist and a writer by being heart and soul a revolutionist.[44]

Kent visited Tierra del Fuego from December 1922 to February of the following year. Though motivated to sail around Cape Horn, he was intrigued by Ushuaia: "a cheerful, friendly place where the town folks' simple lives are just as full of gaiety as those of some great capital, and, one may venture, just as barren of real happiness; and where the care-free convicts walk the streets about their work in scarcely guarded freedom."

He set out for Cape Horn in January 1923 from the Bridges' Harberton farm where he hired a guide, Captain Chistopherson "a mighty seal and otter hunter," who was familiar with "every rock and little anchorage" as far as the Wollaston Islands. "Chistopherson was a huge, calm man, a Swede. He spoke a broken English, softly...moved slowly, heavily; yet he was, somehow, the embodiment of latent energy and power." His mate was also a Swede. Kent rented a sloop, whose owner warned them that the engine "will never last to get there [to Cape Horn]." Kent took the risk and the two Swedes agreed.

Within a few days they got as far as Bayly Island (Chile), where otter-poachers were living, near the Anglican mission station whose director had been Leonard Burleigh, from 1888 to 1892 (Chapter 14). Kent irreverently recalled in a footnote that in Bayly he had been told about Burleigh's "carryings-on" with women in the Tekenika Mission, which "came to the knowledge of Mrs. B, and upset her terribly; it reached the ears of the bishop clear over in the Falkland Islands. It was too much. Official action was resolved upon – when suddenly, in the very nick of time, Mr. B. fell overboard and was drowned."[45] Understandably all this was not alluded to by Burleigh's missionary colleagues, but it was, with all due respect, mentioned by some of the Yahgans I knew.[46]

Kent and his two sea-mates were greeted on Bayly Island by a Yahgan man and one of the Argentine poachers. The latter and two other Argentines, who were in the hut nearby, were illegally in Chile. Garcia, the first Argentine Kent met when they landed, was wary of visitors, though he realised right away that these three could not possibly be Chilean inspectors or police: they were obviously foreigners. Equipped with gifts, two bottles of "fiery caña [rum] and a quarter of mutton," the visitors were led into the dark, filthy interior of "Vázquez' shanty." Vázquez, the other male Argentine, welcomed the three visitors. Young, rakish and handsome, he had committed a murder and been freed after a term in the Ushuaia civil prison. They were introduced to his wife, Genevieve, "a pleasant, pretty, brown-skinned, dark-eyed, slatternly Argentine fille de joie." Garcia, the first Argentine poacher they met, was a former inspector at the Ushuaia prison: age fifty, "blonde eyes with yellow whites, pot-bellied, whose great moustache mocked his baldness." He looked over the three guests with the "ferocious dignity of an imbecile." The fourth resident was Garcia's wife, Margarita, hardly twenty years old, the only other Yahgan. "Pathetically gentle, sweet and servile," she was nursing her three-month-old baby girl. Berté, the Yahgan who had greeted them, was not as beautiful as Vázquez, though stocky and powerful; he had spent twelve years in the "English mission" in Ushuaia. Later they were invited to Berté's solitary wigwam nearby, which proved to be "a very decent, tidy place."

Having settled in for the visit in Vázquez' shanty, Kent turned to Margarita, asking: "Are you happy here?" She replied, murmuring in English, "No – not happy," as she glanced at García "that sullen brute, her mate." Kent insisted: "Do you love him?" Hiding her face, she answered quietly: "Yes – I love him." Meanwhile Vázquez passed a cup of the rum gift to Kent, toasting him, "I consider artists, writers and musicians to be the greatest people in the world. I drink to your prosperity: salud." He touched Kent's cup and they drank to Victor Hugo and Tolstoy while Genevieve served more of the same. In the candlelight of Vázquez' squalid den "confronted by as villainous a crew as ever fought for pirate treasure," Kent sang "Genevieve, Sweet Genevieve." Vázquez was charmed. Margarita smiled as she nursed her baby, while García rolled his eyes at Kent, nodding sternly. Vázquez, enthralled by Kent's singing, threw off his jacket and danced wildly "disgusting, beautiful by the sinuous grace of his lithe body." Margarita laughed and Genevieve screamed with merriment. They shuddered playfully as Vázquez "with the long, keen bread knife in his hand," enacted the drama of the murder he had committed. Berté joined in the dancing "sodden with drink, some still-remembered war dance of his race." The latter is another example of Kent's wit. The Yahgan never danced before or after any "war." Through it all Margarita sat silently "her maternity in affecting a contrast to the drunken uproar.... How we got aboard that night no one could recall."

The next day, the three adventurers rowed ashore again, despite a strong wind and hangovers, to join their newly found friends on the "bog lands of Bailey Island." Kent and the mate climbed the summit of the island, 1,100 feet (335 metres) high, from where they beheld "the vast and fearful wonder of the region of Cape Horn."

That day they bid farewell to their hosts, weighed anchor heading towards Cape Horn, but on the way confronted the turbulent waters of Franklin Sound, beyond which emerges the great cape. Drenched as they were, they pushed ahead in the restless sea, all the more terrible because windless. The mountainous crests of the waves surging from the depths lifted and tossed the over-loaded boat, breaking over it and pouring down on its entire length. Finally Chistopherson, fearing being capsized, turned towards Kent, without smiling, and shouted, "We must turn back." Kent's illusion to reach Cape Horn sank to the bottom of Franklin Sound. His consolation may have been that while his illusion had perished, the crew and the artist had not.

That evening they got safely back to the Harberton farm. Other adventures awaited Rockwell Kent as he travelled north on horseback, across the Isla Grande, to the Atlantic Coast, through Selk'nam territory to the other sheep farm of the Bridges', named Viamonte, also in Argentina. From there, in one of the first model Fords, travelling on good roads, he reached the town of Porvenir, Chile, on the shore of the Magellan Strait where he took a boat to the opposite shore, to Punta Arenas. There he bid a sad farewell to Tierra del Fuego, his "rainbow land," with these last lines of his book. "And everywhere among the settlers poor or rich the traveller meets a warmer hospitality, more trust, more generosity than he'd find elsewhere in a lifetime."[47]

An Anthropologist Visits "Darwin's Tierra del Fuego"

The Australian Sir Baldwin Spencer (Figure 15.8), one of the most outstanding anthropologists of his generation, at sixty-nine, fulfilled his dream of visiting "Darwin's Tierra del Fuego."[48] His two books will undoubtedly remain classics in anthropology: one, *Wanderings in Wild Australia* and the other with his colleague F. J. Gillen, *The Arunta: A Study of a Stone Age People.*

When Darwin was in Tierra del Fuego, between late 1832 and 1834, the Yahgan culture was still almost intact (Chapters 4 and 5). But by 1929 only a few Yahgans knew and cared about the old culture. The population had dropped to about a hundred including the mestizos. Spencer was more or less aware of this but he was determined to visit Darwin's Tierra del Fuego and to shun a "straw-death." He set out in a cargo ship from England on 18 February 1929, accompanied by his secretary, Miss Jean Hamilton, who planned to study the native women. On 12 April they reached Punta Arenas, "a quite a picturesque little city, partly modern, with the really fine houses of sheep magnates built round a Plaza."

Three weeks later they boarded a passenger cutter, with a motor, for "a little settlement called Ushuaia," where Spencer heard there were two or three Indians. He was optimistic. "As winter is coming on, I may perhaps be marooned here for two or three months, but if there are any Indians, that will not matter." One of the passengers was Claude Williams, son of the missionary John Williams. Claude and his older brother Ken owned the sheep farm at the site of the last mission station at Douglas River Inlet. During the trip Claude invited them to his sheep farm where there were

FIGURE 15.8. About 1928: Sir Baldwin Spencer. Courtesy of The Royal Society of Victoria, Australia.

still some Indians. After four days in the cutter, they arrived in Ushuaia, which Spencer thought was "very picturesque." Unfortunately Spencer did not inquire about other Yahgans, nor was he informed about those who were still living in Mejillones Bay, just across the Beagle Channel from Ushuaia. Obviously Claude Williams did not tell him about them, nor had he read Furlong. Gusinde hadn't published yet, so if no one told him, Spencer had no way of knowing that the only viable Yahgan community was not on Williams' farm but rather in Mejillones Bay. Julia, Gusinde's star informant, was there also.

Losing no time, Miss Hamilton and Spencer set out for Williams' farm, where Claude had assured Spencer that there were several Yahgans, there or nearby, with whom he might work. Arriving the same day, they met Ken Williams. A few days later Ken went further down the coast, to fetch some informants for the visiting anthropologist. He returned with a Yahgan family: the husband known as George, his wife, several children, their dogs and cats. George proved to be "difficult to get anything out of and keen on getting as much as he can for nothing." He did recite some proper names and words in Yahgan, which Spencer carefully noted.

In off-hours, Miss Hamilton and "the Professor," as she usually called Sir Baldwin Spencer, took long walks. At times she referred to him as "the Great Man." They collected and classified shells, observed the birds, fed them bread crumbs and dissected a few. They searched for Yahgan arte-facts along the shore and in "kitchen middens," the large refuse mounds mentioned above by Furlong. Some of the mounds they measured were twenty feet (6 metres) high and apparently very ancient. Spencer reread Darwin's *Voyage of the Beagle* during the evenings, comparing his own notes on the plants and animals with Darwin's. He also read his other favourite author, Charles Lamb, and continued studying Spanish, draw-ing, photographing and writing in his journal. He complained of severe pains across the chest on 21 May, about ten days after they arrived in Douglas. He was feeling better a few days later, when another Yahgan family appeared: George's uncle Domingo, his two wives and five chil-dren, two "otter dogs" and a tame gull (see below). One of the children brought him a whalebone harpoon, which pleased him very much. Four days later, everything was "very dark and dreary and forbidding." By the end of May it was snowing, and when the snow melted it rained, dripping into Spencer's room. He gave up Domingo and tried to inter-view his oldest wife, known as a witch, a bruja in Spanish. In reality she was a yekamush, a shaman, as Spencer probably guessed, but she only spoke Yahgan and there was no interpreter nearby. Then he decided that this family could not help him learn about the "old culture." On 2 June he paid off Domingo, who was reluctant to lose such a "soft job," say-ing that he still might want them back to interview his oldest wife, the so-called bruja.

He was despairing of finding an informant who would do more than recite isolated words. He hoped to do original fieldwork, as he had with the "black fellows," his Australian friends. He wondered: "It looks much as if the only way to get anything out of the natives nowadays is by giving them drink."

A few days later the otter and seal hunter, Rockwell Kent's guide Chis-topherson, appeared from the islands around Cape Horn where he and his three companions had just spent two months. They were very disap-pointed because they had only gotten sixty otter skins. The Chistopher-son crew continued on, probably to Ushuaia. By 23 June, everything was frozen outdoors, including the clothes hanging on the line to dry. Even the water in the tubs indoors had to be chopped out.

At the end of June, the professor and Miss Hamilton set out from Williams' farm, again accompanied by Ken and his servant, for a settlement located at about the middle of Murray Narrows on the shore of Hoste Island. Called Yakashake, it was a stopping-off place for Indian otter hunters, between the southern islands and Ushuaia. Ken had told Spencer about an old Yahgan lady there who spoke a little English. He hoped to persuade her to return to the Douglas farm to translate whatever Domingo's wife, the "witch," might tell him.

Miss Hamilton commented: "The Professor was most anxious for our visit to be a success." When they arrived snow covered the entire settlement. Miss Hamilton was disheartened. "A more lonely looking place would be difficult to imagine." They saw a few huts and fenced-in corrals and noticed a corrugated iron hut tucked in a nearby wooded valley, which the professor was told he and Miss Hamilton could use as living-quarters. Old Juana, the Yahgan lady they were looking for, greeted them in a friendly manner in English and was soon cooking fish for their dinner.

Miss Hamilton was aware that the Yahgans did not fascinate the Great Man nearly as much as the Australian "black fellows." But soon he was drinking maté tea with them. Miss Hamilton wrote admiringly:

His neat immaculate appearance made a strange and attractive picture as he sat amongst these unwashed and unshaven natives, who though poor, slothful, and filthy with neglect, were given the same graciousness and quiet understanding courtesy, which he extended to everyone regardless of race or quality. His bright remarks produced low chuckles of enjoyment from the old woman Juana.

The visit was off to a good start despite the weather. The next day, the last of June, the professor commented that some of the younger generation there seemed ashamed of the beliefs of their ancestors. Their usual answer to his questions was Quién sabe? Who knows? Only the old Juana was of "any use scientifically." Miss Hamilton went fishing with her and noticed that, as she sat on a sheepskin on the floor of the row boat, she "appeared transformed into a witch – jabbering Yahgan to the fish as she moved her line gently up and down in the water, listening intently meanwhile." Juana explained that she was bewitching the fish onto her line. She was such good company and laughed so frequently that Miss Hamilton forgot her "first feeling of repulsion."

Early in July, Spencer was annotating Yahgan words, beliefs and customs. He noted that the Yahgans kept a gull, kalala, as a pet and took it with them on their boats where ever they travelled.[49] He must have been pleased when Juana "dramatically told her stories" and named birds and places in Yahgan. She confided in him that her father had killed all the frightful Hanufs (usually spelt Hanush), mythical monsters of the forest, near a lake in the mountains of Hoste Island during a terrible snow storm where her father had gone to rescue his son, whom the Hanufs had kidnapped.[50] She firmly believed this story and convinced Spencer that she was an authentic Yahgan.

Both he and Miss Hamilton were pleasantly surprised on 2 July by the arrival of another old Yahgan, Clements (spelt Clemente in Spanish, see above). He came with his Alakaluf wife Rosa and four children. They had been roaming "the solitary bays near Ponsonby Sound" searching for otters, to sell their skins in Ushuaia "for food or preferably drink." After two months of living on shellfish and hunting, they had only two otter skins and two fox skins to sell in Ushuaia and were hungry. The Swede Chistopherson had killed sixty otters, also in two months. Clements was decidedly on the losing side.

Juana agreed to accompany the visitors back to the more comfortable quarters at the Douglas farm and translate conversations of the "witch." Clements also promised to come back to Douglas a week later and talk to the professor, after selling his skins in Ushuaia. The Great Man was pleased, anxious to return to Douglas and to begin working with them. On 4 July, Miss Hamilton was relieved to see that he was in good health. "Certainly no one would suggest that he was not still young; so amazingly well he looks. . . ." But the very next day he suffered another attack, angina pectoris, worse than the previous one. It was a bad attack. She and Ken Williams were alarmed. Ken left for Ushuaia, only 18 miles (29 km) away, to bring a doctor, despite Spencer's insistence that hot bottles were all he needed. When Ken returned without the doctor but with medicines, the patient was "slightly delirious." But the following day he was again cheerful and keen on continuing his work with his new informants. Meanwhile Juana was going off in her boat every day to catch fresh fish for her guests. Two days later Spencer gave in to Miss Hamilton's urging and consented to return to Punta Arenas to be treated there, thinking to come back to the Douglas farm once he had recovered. On 14 July he said he was warm and very comfortable. A little while later "he sat up quite suddenly, and quite peacefully passed away." Miss Hamilton was overwhelmed. Ken and Juana were very grieved.

The schooner that was to take them both to Punta Arenas arrived at Yakashake the next day. On 17 July, two days later, Miss Hamilton bid a sad farewell to Juana. Then she and Ken placed Spencer's body in the schooner and with the captain and a small crew, headed for Punta Arenas. En route the captain got lost several times though he managed the most dangerous pass, at Brecknock Peninsula. While sailing up Cockburn Channel "the dreadful winds" they had confronted before had died down, but so had the engine and in the middle of the channel. Miss Hamilton later wrote that if they had put "the Professor ashore, I also went ashore." A more poignant testimony of her loyalty to him is difficult to imagine.

The schooner's engine couldn't be started. Ken convinced the captain to carry on and they all shook hands to stick together "whatever happens," implying that no one would abandon the schooner if a passing boat or canoe offered to rescue some but not all of them. The captain gave orders to three of his crew to tug the schooner in the small boat while two other men, with one oar each, rowed the schooner, Miss Hamilton at the helm. Two days passed and they were still in Cockburn Channel with only an occasional breeze to fill the sails. That day, 22 July, they exchanged a little meat and biscuits for two otter skins with a family of desperate Alakalufs, whose wigwam had been blown away by the "terrific hurricane." Shortly after the Alakalufs left, a furious gust of wind broke the mainsail and swamped the tow boat, but the wind carried them along at a terrific speed while the captain shrieked orders to his men. The next day they anchored near a lighthouse on the continent twelve miles (19 km) south of Punta Arenas. They telephoned from the lighthouse to Punta Arenas and rescue boats were quickly sent, but the sea was still in such fury that transferring the weary passengers and the improvised coffin to the boats proved to be hazardous. They had made 310 miles in nine days, which at the time a motor boat took three days. "Such storms have not been known in the South for the past nine years," commented the captain. Back in Punta Arenas, Sir Baldwin Spencer was buried on 26 July 1929 in the main cemetery of Punta Arenas. Ken's father, Reverend Williams, and a clergyman of the Church of England, presided over the intimate ceremony in the company of Miss Hamilton and Ken and probably the captain.[51] Sir Baldwin Spencer had shunned a "straw-death" in a Tierra del Fuego that was no longer Darwin's nor the Yahgans'.

The Third "Visitor"

Professor Ricardo Rojas (Figure 15.9) is the "visitor" whose "crime" was his opposition to the military coup that had taken over the Argentine government from the elected President, Hipolito Irigoyen, in 1930.

FIGURE 15.9. About 1930: Ricardo Rojas. Courtesy of Museo Casa de Ricardo Rojas, Buenos Aires.

Rojas was perhaps the most famous political prisoner taken to the Ushuaia penitentiary. This is saying a great deal, as quite a number of top-ranking former government ministers and intellectuals, who had also opposed the dictatorship, were confined with him. They were known in Ushuaia as the pharaohs. Carlos Pedro Vairo, the author of an excellent recent publication on the prison, stated that: "They were rather free. They only had to sign the Police Register daily. The pharaohs worked and studied. Rojas wrote with no stop."[52]

Professor Rojas had been the president of the University of Buenos Aires, probably in recognition of his literary creations and highly esteemed historical studies. He was also an ardent admirer of the Fuegians and advocated in favour of the indigenous peoples of the entire country. A brilliant defender of their rights, he praised their contributions in the struggles to achieve a lasting democratic republic for Argentina.[53]

For his "crime" of having courageously opposed the dictatorship, he was incarcerated in Ushuaia from January to May 1934. The notes he wrote "with no stop" became a book entitled *Archipiélago Tierra del Fuego*. In his "Preliminary Explanation" he stated: "I have written these pages in order to revise the Darwinian legend and reveal [divulgar] the truth about Tierra del Fuego."⁵⁴ In effect, his book is full of historical, statistical and ethnographic data in addition to recommendations addressed to a future democratic Argentina concerning how to improve this tierra maldita, Tierra del Fuego, for the coming generations and render justice to the original inhabitants. While he was still a prisoner, he sought to meet any native Fuegians he could contact in and around Ushuaia, hoping to learn about their "primitive mentality."

Only if we free ourselves from our pretension of being civilised and employ intuition can we approach the primitive mentality and its secrets by contemplating its culture from its interior.... The religion of the Southern Archipelago may well be the most ancient of the planet, conserved thanks to its insular isolation. Thus it has not been easy to comprehend.⁵⁵

One day in Ushuaia, Rojas heard that an Indian family had just arrived at the dock. Immediately he hurried there and was delighted to meet Darskapalan, better known as Clements, with whom Baldwin Spencer, on the eve of his death, had hoped to work, and the grandfather of Rosa Clemente. Rojas realised that Darskapalan was caught between his "missionised" faith and his ancestral convictions. He arrived with his son Augustín, a robust youth who resembled his mother, a Selk'nam.⁵⁶

Rojas invited Darskapalan to his room, offering him his only chair. He replied to Rojas' inquiries with "dignity and the wisdom of an elder." Rojas learned, for instance, about Kuanip, the culture hero of the Selk'nam, and the deluge, an episode of a Yamana myth. Clements also spoke about his otter hunting and mentioned his poverty. When Rojas insisted on paying him for the interview, he refused at first but finally accepted with tears in his eyes, exclaiming with melancholy: "You are a Christian gentleman," in English.

Rojas thought the regime in Ushuaia was "sterile" for the society and for the convicts. "After fifty years of sovereignty Ushuaia, according to the 1932 census, had 1027 inhabitants in addition to some 500 prisoners. The whites came to Tierra del Fuego to 'populate' it when in reality they 'depopulated' it, as there were more people here before they came."

Ushuaia had become a place of confinement for political causes, "a novelty which gives its history an unexpected laurel." Rojas penned his impressions of this novelty:

The street extends along the coast...symbolically from the prison to the cemetery.... During the day there is no traffic...and, at the night, the residents hesitate to venture outside because there is hardly any light, the paths are made to stumble over and for other reasons as well such as the climate. The police yawn because they are idle which is a sign of the virtue of the populace. The government building is almost always closed; the church usually without the faithful; the dock and the bay without boats. There is no industry. There are no roads, no centres of amusement. There is no culture.

Ricardo Rojas was an ironic sort of promoter of Ushuaia, as when he wrote that it was "populated by the best people in the country, and that, I say with a certain vanity, as now I also am a resident here."[57]

Ushuaia: The Former Yamana Camp Site Becomes a Busy City

The bay called Ushuaia by the Yahgans and the land surrounding it had been their camping ground, their Paris as I imagined. Here the mythological matriarchy was defeated (in Yayoshaga, Chapter 10). The city – Ushuaia – is flourishing as a famous tourist attraction, also due to the presence of the Argentine provincial government, its many offices and employees and important military establishments. Gone are the vegetable gardens cultivated by the missionaries and fertilised by the Yamana's shellfish mounds, Professor Spencer's "kitchen middens." Gone too is the missionaries' "village," in whose memory tourists can contemplate a small, figureless monument near the coast. Gardens and pastures are grown with the aid of chemical and natural fertilisers. Vegetables are tended in hothouses. Foreign- or Argentine-owned assembly factories and an ultra modern airport accelerate the creation of a modern economy, geared to export and the tourist industry. Tourists are drawn to Ushuaia's scenic beauty, its nearby fishing and skiing facilities, its five-star hotels and tours along Beagle Channel. Ushuaia today with its almost 70,000 inhabitants can also boast of an important scientific research centre known as the CONICET, fascinating museums, boutiques, bookshops, satellite saucers, social workers, all this and more except....

Ukika, the Yahgan Community

In 1995 some seventy-four people considered themselves Yahgan, fifty of whom lived in Ukika.[58] Ukika, located along Beagle Channel, borders on a town, a former navy base, Puerto Williams, Navarino Island, Chile. This proximity and enlightened government policy brought improved conditions for the Yahgans and mestizos: a nearby source of employment, and access to schools, also a renewed museum named in honour of Gusinde, a clinic, a library and so forth. Ships full of tourists occasionally dock there for a few hours on their way to Cape Horn or the

FIGURE 15.10. 1996: In the Museo Martín Gusinde, Puerto Williams, Navarino Island, Chile. Standing left to right: Hermelinda, a friend from Ukika, Cristina and Ursula. I am seated in front.

Antarctic. Some of the Ukika residents weave baskets and make miniature canoes, like the ones Stirling commissioned in 1869, which they endeavour to sell to tourists seeking a souvenir of those intrepid navigators.

But a longing for Mejillones Bay, the former reserve, lingers on. In recent years the Calderón sisters and others obtained permission from the government to build summer homes in Mejillones Bay, hoping to recreate a semblance of their ancestral heritage, without abandoning Ukika and the facilities offered in Puerto Williams. Ursula Calderón's dying wish was to spend her last days in Mejillones. Her daughter Julia complied and took her there in 2002, shortly before she passed away. Only Cristina still (in 2009) speaks Yahgan, because Rosa and Hermelinda have also "departed." Cristina, her family and other Yahgan descendants who live in Ukika are aware of the need to valorise their ancestral tradition.[59]

And Finally

The abyss in which the Yahgans were trapped in the last mission station, on Douglas River, has been bridged; the present-day Yahgans are full-time Chileans and their Indian ancestry enhances this identity. Through these four turbulent centuries, their forefathers and mothers emerged onto the scene of written history, but finally nearly all were deprived of a future. Some resisted the new settlers like Julia and Emilia while others tried to comprehend the missionaries and apply their Christian messages such as Okoko, Lucca, Threeboys, Urupa, Mamastugadegenjes (Jack), Sisoi, Pinoense and Otatosh.

During thousands of years, they had confronted the perils of canoeing in this "end of the world" and the challenges of securing their "daily bread." They experienced the excitement of the Chexaus, of a beached whale, the joy of being together as Rosa, Cristina, Ursula and Hermelinda recalled with such pleasure.

Through it all Jemmy Button emerges, not as a hero, not like Okoko, Lucca, Otatosh, Urupa, Threeboys, Hester and Athlinata but as a universal figure whose attachment to his origins, to his territory and family, encompassed the "others," beyond self-interest, beyond the boundaries of kin, nation and culture. He felt that love of homeland that inspired him to forego Fitz-Roy's invitation to return with him and Darwin to England. He chose to stay home, to remain a "savage," though he never forgot his English friends.

Notes

Introduction

1. I use the term "Tierra del Fuego" in a generic sense, to apply to all the islands south of the Magellan Strait to Cape Horn, including Diego Ramirez. I was not able to give the correct UK spelling of quite a few words so I hope the British readers will not be offended. The many references to chapters in this text are meant as a manner of substitution for the lack of a subject index.

2. For example, Eric R. Wolf: *Europe and the People Without History*, 1982, University of California Press, Berkeley.

3. Barclay spoke of this discrimination in a lecture in 1888, which was published in the preface to the 1987 edition of Thomas Bridges' dictionary. "Those native Yahgans have always been misunderstood and made out worse than they are." The reference to *The Descent of Man* is the 1981 edition: vol. 1: 404–5.

   For the reader of English, two really outstanding books on the Yamana are available: E. Lucas Bridges (1987), son of the missionary Thomas Bridges, which has become a classic, and that of the late British explorer Eric Shipton (1973). Bruce Chatwin's book (1977), though widely read, is quite personal, anecdotal and hardly at all concerned with the contents of my text. The journal of the Anglican missionaries is an essential reference covering as it does the years from 1856 to 1916 (see Bibliography). It is partly available in the Library of Congress and probably in the British Library in London. Father Martin Gusinde's great work on the Yamana is indispensable. His entire publication on the Yamana, Selk'nam and Alakaluf has been translated from German into Spanish in eight volumes. As a reference the main problem with Gusinde's volumes is that they have no indexes. The tables of contents are a help but far from sufficient for the reader who is looking for a specific subject. This lack explains why I make so many page references to his three volumes in Spanish on the Yamana.The latter has been only partly translated into English in five small volumes. Published by Yale University it may possibly be located in university libraries. Johannes Wilbert (1977) in English includes most of the Yamana myths published by Gusinde. Hyades publications are fundamental, although they have not as yet been translated into English from their original French. John Cooper (1917) is an indispensable historical reference to that date. The archaeologist Samuel K. Lothrop (1928) is very useful. At least two articles by Robert Lowie (1938 and 1952) are very pertinent. A large book, *Cap Horn: Rencontre avec les Indiens Yahgan 1882–1883*, that contains over 100 photos, which are among the first (and best) taken of the Yamana, is out of print. A film (now in DVD) entitled *Homage to the Yahgans*, that I produced and directed, may be rented or purchased (see Bibliography). Marshall Sahlins, in his often quoted *Stone Age Economics* (1972), refers to Gusinde's work on the Yamana in English. Dallas Murphy (2004) treats the same people and some of the same places as my text. As a journalist, his style is very vivid. He is also knowledgeable about maritime matters. The numerous books and articles by the Chilean historian Mateo Martinic are also indispensable; a book and several articles have been translated (see Bibliography). A testimony of one of the last grandmothers has been published in English by Patricia Stambuk, a Chilean journalist. The archaeologists Orquera and Piana published (1999, in Spanish) a very useful reference to nearly all the cultural attributes of the Yamana in the historical sources. They also published a few articles in English (see Bibliography) For a beautifully illustrated book in Spanish on Darwin in Chile see the edition prepared by Yudilevich Levy. Diana Alonso's novel *Memoria y Olvido* about the Yamana is very well written and often documented.

4. For a critical analysis of the adaptation paradigm, see, for example, O'Brien and Holland, 1992.

5. Nick Hazelwood is to be congratulated for his book *Savage. The Life and Times of Jemmy Button*. He consulted a number of archives that I did not, as well as secondary sources and writes with a dynamic style. However, I might add here that we can "remember" the Fuegians not only "in the person of Jemmy Button" as Hazelwood proposes in the last paragraph of his book, but also with the lives of at least ten other Fuegians (see my Chapters 9 to 14).

6. Wallerstein, 2000: 34. The reference to the above quote of Deacon is 1997: 366.

7. Mayr, 1997: 240. We are twice "*sapiens*" because our very near Neanderthal cousins, the other *sapiens*, "disappeared" some 100,000 years ago. The biologists and paleoanthropologists may know why. K. B. Tankersly (2000: 32) clarified as follows: "Sites [of hunting–gathering Paleoindians] have been discovered on landscapes previously considered too harsh to support hunter–gatherer bands."

8. CD Descent: vol. I: 34–5, 232.

9. CD Emotions: 276, italics added.

10. Lévi-Strauss in Lee and DeVore, 1968: 351 and Lévi-Strauss and Eribon, 1991: 123–4.

11. Prehistory is written in quotation marks to suggest that it is "pre" only because of the lack of knowledge concerning it, and lack of any form of phonetic writing, not because these people preceded history. However, Lévi-Strauss insisted as these and other "primitives" lacked an awareness of history, that they were "cold," not "hot" like "ours." On the contrary, John and Jean Comaroff (1992) suggest that all "social orders exist in time, that all are inherently unstable and generically dynamic; that there are no prehistoric 'anthropological societies.'"

12. Secondary sources are Lynch, 1999; Borrero and McEwan, 1997: 34; Lavallée, 1995: 75–7, 89; Schobinger, 1994: 13. I also consulted the two special numbers of *Scientific American* ("Discovering Archaeology," vol. I, November–December 1999 and vol. 2, January–February 2000 (by Nemecek). The senior assistant editor of *National Geographic*, Rick Gore (1997), reported that a real crisis occurred among archaeologists working in North America when the "Clovis Paradigm" was shattered. This paradigm was based on the premise that the earliest evidence of man in the Americas was big-game hunters whose sites were dated between 11,500 and 10,500 BP (before the present). This paradigm is ardently defended by such professionalists as Thomas F. Lynch (1999) and a number of archaeologists (mostly from the United States and Canada) who for over five decades based their evidence on sites where a certain type of arrowhead known as "Clovis" was found, together with remains of big game. This paradigm was questioned by Tom Dillehay and his multidisciplinary Chilean–US team (see "Special Report Monte Verde Revisited" (22 pages) in *Scientific American*, vol. 2, 2000 (cited above)). Their evidence convinced some of the Clovis Point archaeologists who inspected the site that a pre-Clovis dates occupation existed in central Chile, at the coastal site called Monte Verde. Dillehay was not the first archaeologist to challenge the Clovis Point paradigm, but he was the first to succeed in gaining the acceptance of some of its most steadfast supporters. An alternative road to the past beyond 12,000 BP had finally been freed of its major obstacle. After examining Dillehay's evidence, the visiting archaeologists acknowledged that the Monte Verde site was correctly dated as 16,000 BPE. Gore (1997: 95–6), proposed that the Monte Verde people had "migrated into the lower reaches of North America even before the ice sheets developed more than 20,000 years ago. Indeed, a second site at Monte Verde has revealed stones that may have been flaked by human hands 33,000 years ago." Perhaps more very early sites will be acknowledged. The debate continues. The Monte Verde road to the future of the past is an alternative: not all the scientists agree and some still prefer the Clovis route, as for instance Lynch mentioned above.

13. Soto-Heim, 1992: 386.

14. CD Beagle, 133. The editor Engle points out in note 12 that "The most modern view, however, is that the West Indies are not sinking, but are an area where new land is slowly being formed."

15. McCulloch et al., fig. 16: 28–30.

16. Lambert, 1985, as well as Thornton (1987: 6–7). His sources (not mine) were Hopkins, 1967, 1979; Bryan, 1969; Fladmark, 1986.

17. Flint, 1947: 530. Virginia Alexandria (1998: 13) describes the ingenuity of these migrants while crossing Beringia.

18. Lavallée, 1995: 163–4. See the pioneer article by Latcham, 1922.

19. Betty Meggers and the late Clifford Evans documented contact from Japan (the Jomon culture on the Island of Kyushu) to Valdivia on the coast of Ecuador as of 3,150 years ago.

20. Hornbolstel, 1936: 365; Lomax in Chapman, 2002b: chapter 6.

21. J. Bird in Hyslop, 1988: 3.

22. Bird, 1938: 252–3. Also according to José Emperaire (1955: 75), the Gulf of Peñas was not particularly difficult to navigate for a canoe people.
23. J. Bird in Hyslop and Bird, 1988: 3.
24. More recently Barth (1947: 196) and Borrero (1997: 64) have offered reasons to favour an inland route for the people who later became maritime fishers.
25. Lothrop, 1932: 198. See also John Cooper (1946a: 88). Ibarra Grasso (1949: 97–8) compared the Fuegian canoe with those of Siberia and North America. Although the Yahgan canoe was made of tree bark, a canoe made of sealskin is mentioned in a myth published by Gusinde (1986, vol. 3), which was typical of the canoes farther north.
26. Greenberg (1987: 382–3) and Ruhlen (1987, vol. I: 371–2) classified it in the Southern Andean stock. However, Pinker (1994: 255), an outstanding linguist of the younger generation, seriously questions Greenberg's methods.
27. Cooper, 1924: 413–16; Lowie, 1952: 3–4.
28. Fuegians were living in a world of hunters for 6,000 years, until the nineteenth century. These facts belie Leacock and Lee's (1982: 5) statement that "For many centuries they [the hunting peoples] have not been hunters living in a world of hunters."
29. Cooper, 1917: 219. For linguistic evidence supporting this hypothesis, see Thomas Bridges, author of the only Yamana–English dictionary (1987: XVI), Gusinde (1982, vol. I: 592) and Orquera and Piana (1984: 70–1), though they did not specify that these early settlers were Yamana. Legoupil (1993–94), in a nearby area, gives approximately the same C14 date as Orquera and Piana.
30. Massone, 2002: 126.
31. J. Bird, 1946a: 18.
32. Orquera and Piana, 1999: 115–16; 2002.
33. The memories of the Fuegians may well last for thousands of years to come. Why so long? Let me quote the first lines of *Man the Hunter*: "Culture Man has been on earth for some 2,000,000 years; for over 99 per cent of this period he has lived as a hunter-gatherer." And on the next page: "... as Marshall Sahlins pointed out, nowhere today do we find hunters living in a world of hunters." True enough: not "today" but "yesterday" we do with the memories of the Fuegians who were living in a "world of hunters." That is, insofar as known, the Tierra del Fuego natives, before the European encounters, never had contact with agriculturalists; they had always lived as hunter–gatherers, forever in the past. Therefore their "ways of living," their cultures, were expressions of that 99 per cent of our "period" of 2,000,000 years on this earth. They are among the few groups in America who can give us examples of how we lived during that 99 per cent of 2,000,000 years.

Chapter 1. 1578 to 1775: Drake Encounters the Fuegians; The First Massacres of Europeans and Fuegians; Captain Cook Inaugurates a New Era

1. Shakespeare, *As You Like It*.
2. The reference to Shakespeare and Drake is from Raban (1992: 6) who added: "*The Tempest* owes a good deal to the reports of the captains and travellers...."

3. Fletcher in Drake, 1854: 82.
4. According to Morison (1974: 637, 645–6) the original fleet of six ships was reduced by 17 August 1578, to five (the three mentioned above and two pinnaces of only 15 and 12 tones). A few days later, Drake renamed the *Pelican*, his flagship, the *Golden Hind*, adding the family crest of his principal backer. It was Drake's largest ship, 100 to 120 tones. Winchester (1997: 85) stated that it was "puny" compared with the Spanish galleons of the same period.
5. Fletcher in Drake, 1854: 83–4, 87; D. Wilson, 1977: 100.
6. Fletcher in Drake, 1854: 83–4, 89; Morison, 1974: 647; Vanney stated (1986: 94) that "Drake was the first to think that that Tierra del Fuego was an island and not the promontory of the [legendary] terre australe." Perhaps I should repeat here, as I wrote in the Introduction, that I use the term Tierra del Fuego to apply to the entire region south of Magellan Strait, even though in Argentina and Chile it usually refers only to the largest island called Isla Grande.
7. Shipton (1973: 44) located the island as "possibly [in] Desolate Bay."
8. Fletcher in Drake, 1854: 87. Mainly the Alakaluf lived in this area during the nineteenth century and possibly before.
9. Morison, 1974: 634. On page 648 he gives the exact latitude of Henderson as 55°32′ to 55°37.5′ and noted that he and Henry B. Wagner identified this island as Henderson. On page 658 he wrote that Wagner's book, published in 1926, "is still the best" on Drake's voyage. Beaglehole (1968b: 61, note 1) also stated that it is likely that Drake was on Henderson Island. Mantellero (2000: 187) disagreed with them.
10. Morison, 1974: 649.
11. Fletcher in Drake, 1854: 92. In 1823, when Weddell was there, this island and others nearby were inhabited by the Yamana (Chapter 2), but as this area was contingent to the Alakaluf territory, it is difficult to know which group occupied it in 1578.
12. Morison, 1974: 684–5; Wilson, 1977: 104–5; Winchester, 1997: 84, 87.
13. Most scholars, such as Cooper (1917: 134 and 1946: 82), Gallez (1975), and Gusinde (1986, vol. 1: 48, 50), have stated that L'Hermite, in 1624, was the first European to encounter the Yamana, This is probably true if the natives Drake encountered were Alakaluf.
14. Morison, 1974: 700–8, 714. On page 714 the number 400 is quoted from Tomé Hernández; see also Vanney, 1986: 97–98.
15. Beaglehole (1968b: 128) identified Jacob as his son, not his brother, as other authors have.
16. Boorstin, 1983: 263.
17. Nowell, 1982: 103–4; Callander, 1766, vol. 2: 233, 269; Vanney, 1986: 106.
18. The quotes are from Callander (1766, vol. 2: 271–2). He mentioned only one of the brothers, although Vanney (1986: 107) and most historians report that there were two brothers: Bartolomé and Gonzalo de Nodal. See also Gallez, 1973: 25–6.
19. See especially L. Bridges, 1987: 443, and Chapman, 1982.

20. Callander, 1766, vol. 2: 288–9.
21. Cooper, 1917: 134. The original sources of this expedition are two members of the fleet: Captain Walbeeck, who wrote in Dutch, and Captain Decker, who wrote in German (which included Walbeeck's text translated into German). My other references for this (L'Hermite's) expedition are mainly two historians: John Callander (1766) and Charles de Brosses (1756). Both are based on Decker's publication. Though their texts differ slightly, they are not contradictory. Less complete but reliable are Burney (1807, vol. 3: 12–17) and Gallez (1975, 1976, vol. 2: 286).
22. Callander, 1766, vol. 2: 306.
23. Ibid. Callander stated that Schapenham departed on 25 February to explore the coast of Nassau Bay, while Burney (1807, vol. 3: 13) and Gallez wrote that Schapenham returned to Nassau Bay on 25 February. Therefore I assume that Schapenham departed just before or shortly after the massacre (which occurred on 22 February) because he was gone for only three days. Neither Walbeek nor Decker, the chroniclers, had gone on this exploratory trip, so they obtained their information concerning it from Schapenham and probably from other members of his crew.
24. Callander, 1766, vol. 2: 288; Gallez, 1975: 6. For the Yamana name of Navarino Island, the source is T. Bridges, 1886a: 206.
25. Gallez (1975: 12) convincingly identified the bay the Dutch called Windhond as Grandi Sound. "Windhond" now designates a large bay on the south coast of Navarino.
26. Brosses, 1756, vol. 1: 443; Callander, 1766, vol. 2: 307–8.
27. All these weapons are frequently mentioned in later accounts but not the stone fish hooks, which were probably made of bone.
28. Callander 1766, vol. 2: 308–9; Brosses, 1756, vol. 1: 444–6. Italics added to the quotation.
29. See A. Chapman, *El fenomeno de la Canoa Yagan*, 2003.
30. Lawrence in SAMM 1891: 133.
31. Piana, 1995: 177–9.
32. See Fletcher, 1854: 77–8. For the Yamana canoe in the late nineteenth and early twentieth centuries, some important sources are Lucas Bridges, 1987: 61, 63; Hyades, 1891: 350–2, also 304–6; Gusinde, 1986, vol. 1: 423–1, 605; Lothrop 1928: 143–4 and 1932: 251–2; Reynolds, 1953; Cooper 1917: 197–8 and 1946a: 88–9. Vairo (1995) published a fascinating study of the canoe that includes his reconstruction of a Yamana canoe and terms concerning the canoe in Thomas Bridges' dictionary.
33. Legoupil (1995: 27) reported that the most ancient dates she and her assistants found were 6,160 BP (Before the Present, with a margin of error of 140 years) from a shell mound and another date, at the same site, of 6,120 BP. She referred to the Grandi Bay sites as important base camps.
34. Orquera and Piana (1984: 70). See Ortiz-Troncoso (1994) for the many publications by Orquera and Piana of their work along the north shore of Beagle Channel.
35. T. Bridges named it Lennox Island. The Dutch called it Terhalten Island in honour of one of their officers. The name Terhalten was subsequently given to a tiny island south of Lennox.

36. Callander, 1766, vol. 2: 288–9.
37. FR, 1839: 183.
38. Brosses, 1756, vol. 2: 285–89, 298–301; also FR, 1839: 183; Martinic, 2002: 232.
39. For Brouwer see Cooper 1917: 75. This is the same route the Beauchesne expedition took in 1701; see Duplessis, 2003: 288–89 and Brosses, 1756, vol. 2: 124. Vanney (1986: 116–17) pointed out that the French authorities opposed the publication of the logs of the Bauchesne expedition, to prevent their data from being known to their competitors (mainly Dutch and English).
40. Brosses, 1756, vol. 2: 434–5.
41. Callander, 1766, vol. 3: 386–7, 437. The report on the Villemarin expedition was published by Amédée François Frézier, a military engineer and member of a French scientific expedition (1712–15). Cooper (1917: 88) referred to Frézier's account as "not important."
42. Frézier, as quoted by Callander, 1766, vol. 3: 416.
43. When Dr Hyades, a member of the French expedition, arrived in the same locality (in 1882), he commented that the natives were much the same as those D'Arquisade had met, except that the men hid their women, children and their fur skins when they first sighted him (Hyades). D'Arquisade named the bay "Orange" in memory of the Count of Orange. His document and maps of Tierra del Fuego are reproduced in Martial, 1888: 266–71. Before reaching Orange Bay, along the east coast of Hoste Island, in the bays later named Rice and Lort, D'Arquisade found evidence of the natives, who were probably also Yamana. He thought the inhabitants had fled when they saw his ship. This area of Nassau Bay was populated by the Yamana during the seventeenth and eighteenth centuries and probably long before.
44. Callander, 1766, vol. 3: 670–1.
45. See Byron's *Narrative of Great Distresses on the shores of Patagonia,* also entitled *The narrative of the Honourable John Byron*... first published in London in 1768 and often afterwards. Emperaire (1955: 32) highly praises Byron's work on the Alakaluf and the neighbouring Chonos.
46. Rydell, 1952: 18–20; Vanney, 1986: 153–5.
47. Anson, 1748: 32.
48. Boorstin, 1983: 280.
49. Boorstin, 1983: 286–7; Beaglehole, 1968b: 272. Recall Captain Cook's first voyage, 1768–71; his second, 1772–75; and his third, 1776–79, when he was killed in Hawaii. Most of my references to his second voyage are from Beaglehole's amazing body of research.
50. Boorstin, 1983: 285.
51. Beaglehole, 1968b: 9.
52. Wilson, 1977: 104; Boorstin, 1983: 20, 99, 153, 279–80.
53. Mickleburgh, 1987: 13–14.
54. Beaglehole, 1961: 583.
55. Moorehead, 1987: 244.
56. Beaglehole, 1961: 585–9, 590.
57. Ibid., p. 598. Pecherais (spelt in a variety of ways) is a term for the Alakaluf. It was first published by the French explorer Louis Antoine de Bougainville in 1768, when he met them in Port Gallant, Magellan Strait. Oscar Aguilera

(personal communication), is an authority on the Alakaluf (called Kaweshkar) language, which is still spoken today in Puerto Eden (Chile). He clarified that *pecherais* is the word *paelsc'éwe,* which signifies stranger. For a history of the word *pechera* see Gusinde, 1926: 72, 59–61.

58. Beaglehole, 1961: 598. John Cooper (1917: 200) affirmed that they and the Yamana sometimes used such sails.
59. Beaglehole, 1961: 600.
60. Ibid., p. 598.
61. Lowie, 1952: 3.
62. Beaglehole, 1961: 600, note 2.
63. Boorstin, 1983: 285.
64. Beaglehole, 1974: 302.
65. J. R. Forster, 1966: 191–216, the quotation is on 204–5.
66. G. Forster, 1777, vol. 2: 498–505.
67. Ibid., 614.
68. Gusinde, 1986, vol. 1: 323.
69. For excellent studies of the Alakaluf, see Emperaire, 1955 (translated from French into Spanish); Bird, 1946b; Gusinde, 1991; and many articles by Mateo Martinic. Fortunately the archaeology of the Alakaluf area is being studied in detail by Dominique Legoupil and other archaeologists.
70. Beaglehole, 1974: 139, 298.
71. Clerke in Beaglehole, 1961: 764–5.
72. G. Forster, 1777, vol. 2: 508–10; Beaglehole, 1961: 603.
73. Beaglehole, 1961: 605.
74. Ibid., 614.
75. A. Chapman, 1987.
76. Beaglehole, 1961: 622, 625.
77. Busch, 1985: 21. Pyne (1986: 161) may also be quoted here: "Accounts of Cook's voyages – and a travel literature of all sorts – were widely read by intellectuals and excited a generation much intrigued by nature and the sublime."
78. Moorehead, 1987: 224: italics added.
79. Beaglehole, 1974.
80. Beaglehole, 1968b: 284. According to *The Columbia Encyclopaedia* (1956: 1749), Earl John Montagu Sandwich was the first Lord of the Admiralty in 1748–51 and then again in 1771–82. Note also the following comments "His mismanagement contributed largely to the British failure in the war of the American Revolution." Be that as it may, "his name is repeated endlessly as we ask for a mid-day snack, because he was given to eating them [sandwiches] informally at the gaming table."
81. Beaglehole, 1961: 643.
82. Beaglehole, 1974: 367, 431, 433.
83. Beaglehole, 1974: 107: see Boorstin, 1983: 286–7.
84. Cook in Beaglehole, 1961: 653. The reader is referred to Anne Salmond's fascinating hypothesis (2004). Her first chapter explains the trial of the "cannibal dog," which took place during the third voyage (1776–79), on the ship *Discovery* in Queen Charlotte Sound, New Zealand. This turning point goes

far in explaining the "cross-cultural combination of forces that killed him [in Hawaii] during his third voyage...." A quite similar event occurred, as related above during his second voyage, without a trial of a "cannibal dog," but also with the New Zealand Maories.

85. Beaglehole (1968b), Moorehead (1987: 225), and Boorstin (1983: 288) point out that, in his day, Cook's public recognition came not from his great discoveries but because he did more than any other explorer to cure scurvy.

Chapter 2. 1780 to 1825: Moby Dicks in Tierra del Fuego; The Whalers and Sealers Arrive

1. Stambuk, 1986: 17.
2. Chapman Journal, 1987: 24.
3. Bridges in V. for S.A., 1866: 208, 213: Gusinde, 1986, vol. 1: 500–3.
4. Chapman typescripts, 1987. All the recordings with my four Yahgan informants (Rosa Clemente, Ursula and Cristina Calderón and Hermelinda Acuña) have been transcribed as typescripts in 1987 and 1988 as noted in the Bibliography. My "journal" refers to my typed diary.
5. According to Fogg (1990: 101) and Hyades (1991: 339, 353–7) one of the "zooplanktone" that is most abundant south of the Convergence is krill, *Euphausia superba*, the staple diet of baleen whales. This is a shrimp-like animal up to 2 inches in length. When not actively feeding, it collects in swarms, with several thousand to the cubic metre, which, if near the surface, colour the water red.
6. This myth and the following, quoted from Gusinde's original volume in German (1937), are in Wilbert, 1977. The importance of these mammals for the Yamana is evident in their mythology. The one referred to above, "The Acquisition of Whale Oil" is number 15 in Wilbert. Whales are also featured in numbers 54, 55, 58a, 58b and 66; sea lions in numbers 12, 14, 19 and 34; the elephant seal in number 39; the orca (called Grampus) in number 42; the dolphin in number 40; and the otter in number 25.
7. L. Bridges, 1987: 77, note 1. See Gusinde (vol. 3: 1365–6) for how the shamans (*yékamush*) knew just where to locate seals and whales, from their dreams.
8. Goodall, 1976: 45.
9. Chapman typescript [Rosa Clemente], 1988: 105–8.
10. Chapman Journal [Rosa Clemente], 1987: 24, 34.
11. Chapman typescript [Cristina and Ursula], 1987: 16–17.
12. Chapman Journal [Hermelinda], 1987: 22–3, 101–4 recited Julia's words in Yahgan. See also Gusinde, 1986, vol. 3: 1365–6.
13. Chapman transcript [Ursula], 1988: 85–7, 190 also 1987: 10. Gusinde, 1986 vol. 3: 990 and 1351 for the "game of the whale," which was performed in the Kina ceremony.
14. Billinghurst, 2000: 79–80. For the Twofold Bay whalers the author quoted by Billinghurst is Jacqueline Nayman in *Whales, Dolphins, and Man* published in 1973.
15. L. Bridges, 1987: 62, 97–100; also Gusinde, 1986, vol. 1: 496–500.

16. Horsman (1985) was consulted for the world distribution of the whales and seals.

17. Morison (1974: 714) quoted from Cavendish's log.

18. For detailed information on whales in Tierra del Fuego, contact Natalie Goodall. She and other scientists there have been studying maritine fauna in the area. They are affiliated with a research centre in Ushuaia (the Argentine capital of Tierra del Fuego), known as CADIC.

19. Moorehead, 1987: 232. This author (226–43) offers an exceptionally informative text on whales and other marine life in this area and their extinction by the commercial hunters.

20. According to Roger Payne (1995: 185), the breeding grounds for the blue and fin whales have never been found because they do not exist anywhere.

21. *Reader's Digest* (1985: 116), special issue on the "frozen continent."

22. Payne, 1995: 254.

23. Moorehead, 1987: 236.

24. Weddell, 1970: 164.

25. Moorehead, 1987: 231.

26. Stackpole, 1953: 145; Boyson, 1924: 219; Rydell, 1952: 61; Stein, 1982: 20; *Reader's Digest*, 1985: 92.

27. Melville, chapter 101. I cite Melville by the chapter numbers of his book because thus the reader can easily locate the reference in any of the many editions of his book.

28. Stackpole, 1972: 120, 123, 126, and Stein, 1982: 19.

29. Sutcliffe, 1961: 541.

30. Whipple (1979: 80) and Stein (1982: 26) mentioned two other less famous sperm whales, named New Zealand Tom and Timor Jack. Melville (chapter 45) cited them, another called Don Miguel and many other stories of sperm whales. Pyne (1986: 163–4) also mentioned a white whale known as Mocha Dick, which Josiah Reynolds published in an article, of 1839, and was reworked by Melville.

31. Philbrick, 2001: XIII, 79, 81, 86–7, 91.

32. Whipple, 1979: 84. Francis Drake (1854: Appendix: 286) in 1577 was the first European to visit Mocha Island, although he was not interested in whales. He was wounded in the face by the Indians there and two of his men were killed.

33. Billinghurst, 2000: 75.

34. According to Whipple (1979: 85), this event took place "1,200 miles northeast of the Marquesas Island." Billinghurst (2000: 72) also places it in "the mid-Pacific."

35. Melville, chapter 45. Italics added. For more accounts of this event, see Billinghurst, 2000: 72–4 and Whipple, 1978: 84–8.

36. Moorehead, 1987: 235.

37. Melville, chapter 77.

38. Whipple, 1979: 62.

39. Ibid.

40. Busch, 1985: 11.

41. Vanney, 1986: 171.

42. Ibid., 207. Stackpole, 1972: 123.

43. Stackpole, 1972: 123.

44. Colnett, 1968: VIII. His book was first published in 1798.

45. Ibid., 20, 28; Whipple, 1979: 6.

46. Bonner, 1982: 59.

47. Busch, 1985: 16.

48. Albion, 1972: 112.

49. Fanning, 1833: 355, 422; Busch, 1985: 22. See Pyne (1986: 162–8) for a lucid account of the romantic literature about this epoch: besides Poe (*The Narrative of A. Gordon Pym*) in 1838, also Samuel Coleridge (*The Rime of the Ancient Mariner*) in 1798, Melville (*Moby Dick or, the Whale*) in 1851, James Fenimore Cooper (*The Sea Lions*) in 1849 and finally Jack London (*The Sea Wolf*) in 1907.

50. Bonner, 1982: 59.

51. Boyson, 1924: 219.

52. Busch, 1985: 9. He (p. 22) quoted Weddell for the South Georgia number.

53. In 1792, the Spanish corvette *San Pio* stopped two British sealing sloops (single-mast sailboats) off the north coast of Staten Island, New Year's Islands, where Cook had been that day in 1775. For Staten Island, see Busch, 1985: 6, 9; Stackpole, 1953: 222–2 and 1972: 114; Rydell, 1952: 33–5, 61; Bonner, 1982.

54. Chapman, 1987.

55. Weddell, 1970: 141–2.

56. Fogg, 1990: 25, 28.

57. In 1820 the British sealers Smith and Bransfield claimed to have discovered the Shetland Islands and took possession of them in the name of King George IV. Another contender for the discovery (or first sight of) these outer islands was (or is) Nathaniel Palmer, commander of an American sealing vessel *Hero*, whom Fanning defended. A third candidate was (or is) the Russian explorer Admiral Thaddeus von Bellingshausen. See Busch, 1985: 23; Mickleburgh, 1987: 29–30; Rydell, 1952: 35; Vanney, 1986: 238; Weddell, 1970: 141–2; Whipple, 1979: 134.

58. Orquera and Piana, 1990: 26–7.

59. Martial, 1888: 215.

60. L. Bridges, 1987: 62; Gusinde, 1986, vol. 1: 344–5, 500.

61. Payne, 1995: 255–6.

62. Freese, 2003: 147.

63. Busch, 1985: 164.

64. Billinghurst, 2000: 90.

65. Darling, 1988: 872.

66. *International Herald Tribune*, June 4, 2004.

67. Fuchs V–X in Weddell, 1970: W. Chapman, 1965.

68. Weddell, 1970: 141–2; Busch, 1985: 9; Bonner, 1982: 63. Darwin (CD Diary, 1988: 84) mentioned that the Isla de Lobos, on July 25, 1832, was covered with seals.

69. Weddell, 1970: 142.

70. Boyson, 1924: 89–91.

71. Weddell, 1970: 188, 6–7.
72. All the above references are Weddell, 1970: 149–57.
73. Gusinde, 1986, vol. 2: 733, 1068; L. Bridges, 1987: 101.
74. Weddell, 1970: 158–9.
75. T. Bridges, 1893: 233; *Derrotero* as cited: 245.
76. Weddell, 1970: 161–2.
77. See A. Chapman, 1980 on barter.
78. Weddell 1970: 164–5. Brisbane's ability with the sling contradicts Gusinde's assumption (1986, vol. 1: 494) that the Europeans who tried to show off their ability with a native implement had gone about it "so awkwardly that they became the laughing stock of the Indians."
79. Ibid., 162–5, 187.
80. Ibid., 166.
81. Weddell, 1970: 167–82.
82. Verne, 1879: 246.
83. Weddell, 1970: 181–6.
84. Ibid., 318–25.
85. Herbert, 1974: 250–4.
86. Webster, 1970, vol. 1: 172–83; Hyades, 1985b.
87. Webster, 1970, vol. 1: 181.
88. Ibid., 111–14.
89. Ibid., 199–201.
90. Ibid., 200–1. Tompkins (1938: 104) made a similar observation about the weather in Cape Horn.
91. Webster, 1970, vol. 1: 193–4.
92. Vanney, 1986: 247.
93. Webster, 1970, vol. 1: 190, 196–7.
94. Martial, 1888: 202.
95. Gusinde, 1986, vol. 1: 605.
96. Webster, 1970, vol. 1: 205.
97. Ibid., 199.
98. PK, 1839: 577.
99. CD Beagle, 273, 244–5.
100. PK, 1839: 205–7.

Chapter 3. 1826 to 1830: The First Voyage of His Majesty's Ships to Tierra del Fuego; Four Fuegians Taken to England

1. Thomson, 1998: 40.
2. PK, 1839: XV–XVII; Shipton, 1973: 61.
3. PK, 1839: 16–20; Martinic, 1984: 16. The French naturalist Alcide D'Orbigny (1841: 277–80) during his tour of the continent, arrived only as far south as Port St Julian along the Patagonian coast (49° south latitude). He never visited Tierra del Fuego. He was in Patagonia the middle of 1829, shortly after King and Stokes. As D'Orbigny was unable to describe first-hand the meeting at Gregory Bay with Maria, he quoted King's account (published in 1839) adding his own "pittoresque" version of King's data. On

p. 279, he made an error when he stated that "Maria" was discovered to be a woman. The confusion of sexes was not about Maria but about her son.

4. PK, 1839: 20–1; Thomson, 1998: 80–1.

5. PK, ibid.

6. Stokes in PK, 1839: 73–4.

7. Ibid., 74–7.

8. Thomson, 1998: 83.

9. Stokes in PK, 1839: 68, 77–9; Laming, 1954: chapter 2.

10. Stokes, ibid. According to Horsman (1985: 119) the southern right whale is very similar to the northern species.

11. Stokes in PK, 1839: 66–7.

12. Ibid., 67, 80; Shipton, 1973: 65–7.

13. PK, 1839: 142–3.

14. Ibid., 123–4. The word "peña" meaning cliff, crag or rock was originally misspelled in English as "pena" which signifies sorrow. However, Stokes and King use the correct spelling: "The Gulf of Peñas." Nevertheless, the mistake of calling it "El Golfo de Penas" (The Gulf of Sorrow) is quite common, as for instance Mantellero, 2000: 190.

15. Stokes for the quote (in PK, 1839: 163); see also 169–73, 180–1; Thomson 1998: 89.

16. Stokes in PK, 1839: 179.

17. Ibid., 181 (end of Stokes' text).

18. PK, 1839: 182.

19. Ibid., 153, 182, 188.

20. Ibid., 182–8; Thomson, 1998: 92.

21. Barlow (1958: 71) is probably the most reliable source.

22. Shipton, 1973: 75.

23. Thomson, 1998: 94.

24. FR in PK, 1839: 216.

25. PK, 1839: 196–7.

26. Ibid., 220–1. There is a second exit to the Pacific, north of the Magellan Strait, at a place called Tamar, via Channel Smyth, where Stokes had been delayed by violent squalls. Skyring discovered this passage in July 1829. See Mantellero (2000: 179, 225) for this alternative route.

27. FR in PK, 1839: 222.

28. Emperaire, 1955: 78.

29. Legoupil (2003), published in Spanish and French for her archaeological work on a site on Riesco Island, along Fitz-Roy Channel. Fitz-Roy named other localities in memory of Stokes: Bahia Stokes, south coast of the Santa Inés Island and Ensenada Stokes, on Captain Aracena Island and two for King along Cockburn Channel.

30. FR in PK, 1839: 226–7, 570–3.

31. Ibid., 227.

32. Ibid., 233–4. This sketch was not published by Fitz-Roy but may exist in his archive. Legoupil and her teams (2000, 2003 and many other publications) carried out intensive archaeology along the shores of the Otway and Skyring lakes, called "waters" because they are salty. In the 2000 article she included

a photograph and mention of Fresia Alessandri Baker (pp. 89–90) one of the last of the Alakaluf people. Fresia passed away in 2003.

33. FR in PK, 1839: 238–40.
34. Ibid., 241–50, 300–1, 21; Skyring in PK, 1839: 323–59.
35. Derrotero (Sailing Instructions published by the Hydrographic Institute of the Chilean Navy), 1973: 69, 79.
36. FR in PK, 1839: 368–72.
37. Ibid., 371, 374, 379.
38. Ibid., 376–7. The map is number 56 of the Instituto Hidrográfico de la Armada de Chile. The name Carlos is used for at least three islands in the area, which leads to confusion.
39. The Alakaluf may have learned to make them from the Chono Indians of Chiloé once they had acquired iron tools from the Europeans. Cooper (1917: 199) referred to them as plank canoes and stated that one was first seen in the Magellan Strait by Byron in 1765, during his second voyage.
40. FR in PK, 1839: 377.
41. Ibid., 379, 382; Derrotero, 1973: 89. See Cooper, 1917: 55, 191–2.
42. Derrotero (1973: 90) states that sealers came to Bahia Furia (Fury Bay) to hunt seals but that it is not a good anchorage for ships.
43. FR in PK, 1839: 381.
44. Hammerley, 1952: map on p. 137. The region between Brecknock Peninsula and the western end of Beagle Channel (Point Divide) was not Yamana territory at this time, as many authors have stated: for instance Stirling in SAMM, 1876: 199; Hyades, 1891: 15; Gusinde, 1986: 196; Furlong, 1917a: 423–4 and 1917b: 174. John Cooper (1917: 7), with his historical perspective, stated that, "in Admiral Fitz-Roy's time the Alakaluf extended as far east as the western end of Beagle Channel [Point Divide]." This statement is confirmed by Fitz-Roy and later by T. Bridges in SAMM, 1879: 235–6.

There can be no doubt that there were "homelands" of these two groups, where each had exclusive territorial rights. The Yamana "home" during the nineteenth century and part of the twentieth century (if not before) included the zone of Beagle Channel, Navarino Island, and the three rather large islands beyond (Picton, Lennox and New), south to Cape Horn, and Hoste Island to its southwestern extremity at Black Cape (Punta Negra). The Alakaluf during the nineteenth century and part of the twentieth century (also if not before) apparently occupied the area north of the Magellan Strait to the Gulf of Peñas, the shores the Magellan Strait from the Pacific exit to the vicinity of the Second Narrows, and south of the Magellan Strait to Brecknock Peninsula, from where they were a majority, although the Yamana mingled with them to Point Divide. Recall that Fuegia Basket's mother was Yamana and she was from Hoste Island, along the Southwest Arm.

45. FR in PK, 1839: 384. See also T. Bridges in SAMM, 1887: 395. For a review of the shortcuts, see Emperaire, 1955: 193–4; Cooper, 1917: 200; Prieto et al., 1997 in McEwan and Gusinde, 1986, vol. 3: 1431–3.
46. FR in PK, 1839: 384. This is the moment to mention a great novel (*Jemmy Button*, in Spanish) by Benjamin Subercaseaux, a highly esteemed Chilean

author. It is the moment because his novel begins here, on Fury Island, in late January 1830, and follows through to March 1834, when Fitz-Roy and Darwin bade farewell to Jemmy.

47. Fitz-Roy's account of the whaleboat chase (FR in PK, 1839: 391–407) is not consistently clear. I have traced it as best I could. I mention localities that had no European name at the time he wrote, such as Basket, Leadline, Burnt, and Smoke islands and Escape Bay. These were officially registered, in English, later on the Chilean Navy maps (as numbers 1201 and 1203) in memory of this expedition. Exceptionally for this episode, I have taken the liberty of not conditioning my identification of the localities visited with the usual terms, such as "apparently" and "possibly," but rather followed his itinerary, interpreting his account as it proceeded.

48. FR in PK, 1839: 391–3.

49. Ibid., 394; Derrotero, 1973: 140, 144.

50. FR in PK, 1839: 394–5. Another island is named Burnt, off Orange Bay on the east coast of Hoste Island.

51. Ibid., 395–6.

52. Ibid., 396–7; Derrotero, 1973: 140.

53. FR in PK, 1839: 398–9. Martial (1888: 129) also identified Burnt Island as the place where Fuegia Basket and the other ten were captured.

54. FR in PK, 1839: 400.

55. Barlow, 1958: 74.

56. FR in PK, 1839: 400–2.

57. CD Beagle: 201.

58. FR in PK, 1839: 402–3. On Burnt Island, Murray had noticed the one-eyed man whom he had seen there before and now thought that he exactly answered the description of the Fuegian who had ill-treated some of Brisbane's crew when they were wrecked in Fury Harbour, three years earlier. This is the only reference I found to a Fuegian ill-treating Brisbane's crew.

59. Ibid., 404–5.

60. The actual pursuit of the thieves ends here on 25 February; FR in PK, 1839: 407.

61. It is spelled Alijulip in the Derrotero, p. 239.

62. FR in PK, 1839: 409–10. For Fuegia's real name, see Appendix to FR, 1839: 148; SAMM, 1900: 112 (the article is signed R.M.M.); also CD Diary, 1988: 448.

63. FR in PK, 1839: 409. For York's real name, see Appendix to FR, 1839: 149; T. Bridges in SAMM, 1874: 24–5.

64. T. Bridges, 1987: 84; T. Bridges in SAMM, 1874: 24–5. Fuegia and York spoke Alakaluf, though T. Bridges wrote that Fuegia's native language was Yahgan (Yamana) because her mother was from Lushoof, on the shore of Hoste Island, near Beagle Channel in Yahgan territory. Thus the confusion arises because she was probably bilingual. Fitz-Roy clearly implied that she was Alakaluf, which refers to her having been born and raised in her father's territory.

65. FR in PK, 1839: 409–41 and Martinic, 1973: 116.

66. FR in PK, 1839: 412–14.
67. Ibid., 414–17, 408.
68. Ibid., 418. The Yamana were very reluctant to attempt navigating Cape Black, but they had access to Brecknock Peninsula through the Northwest and Southwest "Arms." In 1988 the few living Yahgans told me that Black Cape was dangerous, even with their motorised rowboat equipped with a sail.
69. FR in PK, 1839: 420–3.
70. T. Bridges, 1893: 233.
71. FR in PK, 1839: 426–30.
72. L. Bridges, 1987: 36. T. Bridges (1987: 7) defines the word *aiapux* as referring to the common otter.
73. FR in PK, 1839: 427–8. The term tribe is not well defined here, see note 89 below. Sometimes Fitz-Roy uses it to refer to an entire linguistic group and other times to a lineage of sorts. Their languages were mutually incomprehensible and each occupied a more or less defined territory (see above notes 43 and 44) but the "groups" were not cohesive entities. Some families or lineages of the Yamana, Alakaluf and Selk'nam were hostile while others intermarried and got along peacefully. Nevertheless, stereotypes did exist. York and Boat called the Yamana otters while the latter sometimes referred to the Alakaluf as cannibals. There is little data on Alakaluf mythology. For Yamana myths concerning the Alakaluf as cannibals see Wilbert, 1977: 172–6. According to Gusinde, the Yamana word for cannibals was *asásan*. T. Bridges (1987: 29) defined *asasin-a* (it may be English in origin). The Yamana often feared the Alakaluf because of their greater combative capacities and their large canoes (which could be paddled faster than theirs).
74. FR in PK, 1839: 428.
75. Ibid., 429. Derrotero, 1973: 120.
76. Barros, 1997; also Martinic, 1999.
77. *Columbia Encyclopedia*, 1950: 1981. The currently best-known island south of the Magellan Strait is the Isla Grande (often called Tierra del Fuego in Chile). It is the largest one of all, and covers 140 miles (259 kilometres) from north (the Atlantic coast) to its southern limit (Beagle Channel).
78. FR in PK, 1839: 429–30.
79. Fitz-Roy stated (in PK, 1839: 431) that they anchored off San Joachim Cove using Arquisade's place name that, according to Martial (1888: 266), refers to Lort Bay on the east coast of Hoste Island. The bay Fitz-Roy erroneously mentioned as San Joachim lies on Hermite Island between Cape Seal and Cape Spencer but has no name on map number 1301.
80. FR in PK, 1839: 432.
81. The original in Spanish: "*La Armada de Chile decidió que este testimonio sea conservado en el Museo Naval de Valparaíso, por lo que se le entregó al Almirante don José Toribio Merino Castro en su última visita oficial al Distrito Naval Beagle, dentro de un hermoso cofre de coihue regional.*" What happened since to this historical treasure is not clear.
82. Again Fitz-Roy employed Arquistade's terminology, referring to it as "St Bernard Cove," which Martial (1888: 266) mistakenly identified as Orange Bay.

83. FR in PK, 1839: 434–7. Schapenham, in 1624, had dubbed this island Terhalten for one of his shipmates. For the place names see Goodall, 1975; Belza, 1978: 142; and Mantellero, 2000.
84. FR in PK, 1839: 438–9.
85. Ibid., 439–40. Recall that the inhabitants of Murray Narrows and the nearby coast of Navarino Island along Beagle Channel were called Yahgan (Yagán in Spanish); the few descendants I knew still preferred this designation for the entire group, instead of Yamana (see Glossary).
86. FR in PK, 1839: 440.
87. Ibid., 440; FR, 1839: 177.
88. FR in PK, 1839: 440–1.
89. Ibid., 441–2. See above note 75. Fried (1975) clearly explains the confusion created by the term "tribe." The configuration of the Yamana and Alakaluf communities was not that of a tribe but rather lineages, each composed of a number of related families that inhabited more or less well-defined territories, certain campsites that comprised the radius of their seasonal migrations. All the members of an ethnic "group" never met, simply because the lineages were too dispersed, nor was there a "chief" of the entire group. Curiously the "natural limit," on the north shore of the Magellan Strait, between the Alakaluf and the Teheulche territories, is also named Black Cape (Punta Negra or Cabo Negro).
90. Derrotero, 1973: 47. Fitz-Roy noted three hazards of navigating in the Northwest Arm: the places to land were difficult to locate, the low islets in midchannel were dangerous and the squalls were "strong enough to capsize a vessel."
91. FR in PK, 1839: 443–4. Note that this first mention he is called "Jemmy" though in later sources he is often referred to as "Jimmy."
92. FR (1839: 4) for Jemmy's age; for his name, V. of P., 1859: 78; and CD Diary, 1988: 448.
93. FR in PK, 1839: 444, and FR, 1839: 6; Sullivan (V. of P., 1856: 176), who was present, also expressed doubts that he had been sold for one or more buttons; see Chapman, 2002c.
94. L. Bridges, 1987: 30.
95. Hyades, 1891: 360. Fitz-Roy thought he saw footprints of a puma, but they must have been those of a large dog. Pumas never swam across the Magellan Strait.
96. Gusinde (1986, vol. 1: 77–87) mistakenly identified all four Fuegians taken by Fitz-Roy as Yamana.
97. FR in PK, 1839: 445–9.
98. For Staten Island, see Chapman, 1987, and for the region of Valentine Bay, see my 2002b, last chapter.
99. FR in PK, 1839: 449.
100. Ibid., 450–2, 459.
101. FR, 1848: 160.
102. FR in PK, 1839: 456–9 (for the above quotation also). See also the article by Gillian Beer in McEwan et al., 1997.
103. Engle in CD Beagle, XIV; Thomson, 1998: 81, 11.

Chapter 4. 1830 to 1832: Fuegians in England; Fitz-Roy
and Darwin Meet; The *Beagle* Returns to Tierra del Fuego
with Darwin and Three Fuegians

1. CD Beagle, 223.
2. All the above quotes are from FR, 1839: 1–10; FR in PK, 1839: 462. This was said to be the fourth vaccination, though no mention was found of where the third took place.
3. FR, 1839: 10. Further research may afford data on Boat Memory's funeral and where he was buried.
4. FR, 1839: 10–13; Browne, 1995: 234, 238. The artist Augustus Earle drew a portrait of Fuegia wearing the queen's bonnet during the voyage back to Tierra del Fuego, which I have not found.
5. Browne, 1995: 235.
6. *Encyclopedia Britannica*, 1992 edition; Darwin (CCD, 1988, vol. 3: 345) was sympathetic to Fitz-Roy for the trouble, vexation and sacrifices his support of the Maori had caused him.
7. Fitz-Roy (1839: 13) mentioned a "kind uncle" though not by name. According to CCD (1985, vol. 1: 127, 130) and Browne (1995: 148), the uncle (on his father's side) was the Duke of Grafton. However, Desmond and Moore stated (1992: 103) that Fitz-Roy was a grandson of this third Duke of Grafton. Recall in Chapter 3 that Fitz-Roy named several islands in honour of this uncle (or grandfather).
8. Browne, 1995: 151.
9. Ibid., 148. According to Desmond and Moore (1992: 105–6), Fitz-Roy later briefed Darwin in this same sense.
10. FR, 1839: 17–18; Bowlby, 1991: 121; Thompson, 1975: 671; Browne, 1995: 179–80.
11. FR, 1839: 16.
12. Gould, 1976.
13. Browne, 1995: 3–161; Desmond and Moore, 1992: 5–97. The term "Whig" for a progressive political party may seem strange to non-British readers. According to the *Columbia Encyclopedia*: "It seems to have been a shorten form of *whiggamor* [cattle driver] and was used in the 17th century for Scottish dissenters."
14. Browne, 1995: 272; Keynes in CD Diary, 1988: XXI–XXII. The latter, the second and complete edition of Darwin's diary, published in 1988, was edited by Richard Darwin Keynes, Darwin's great grandson. This edition is more complete than the 1933 diary, edited by Nora Barlow, Darwin's granddaughter. The latter remains an important source because of her preface. For a comparison of the two, see Keynes in CD Diary, 1988: XIII.
15. See Browne, 1994, and Moorehead, 1969.
16. CCD, 1985, vol. 1: 142.
17. CD Autobio, 72; Moorehead, 1987: 12, 25; Browne, 1995: 160.
18. Quoted from Clark (1984: 76), who did not name the son.
19. Clark, 1984; 76; Browne, 1995: 216–17; Degler (1991: 327) made this connection: "The growth of an animal rights movement has no obvious or direct connection with the revival of biology...but are not its intellectual springs

to be found in the fateful continuity that Darwin discerned between animals and us?"

20. Browne, 2002: 418–23, 486. Desmond and Moore observed (1992: 615): "Darwin was typically British, an animal lover who loved his colleagues' autonomy more."

21. CD Beagle, 497–8.

22. CD Autobio, 74; a letter to his sister Catherine in CCD, 1985, vol. 1: 312–13. Though he does not mention the dispute with Fitz-Roy in his diary (1988: 45), it apparently took place on 12 March 1832. For Darwin on slavery, see Desmond and Moore, 1992: 120–4; Browne, 1995: 196–9, and 2002: 214–16, 255–6.

23. It is perhaps time to mention the main sources I consulted for Darwin in Tierra del Fuego. The first published form of Darwin's voyage appeared in 1839 as volume 3 of the *Narration of the Surveying Voyages of H.M.S. Adventure and Beagle*. In 1845 a revised version was published as the *Journal of Researches into the Natural History*. This 1845 version has since appeared in many editions with the title *The Voyage of the Beagle*. Sandra Herbert, an authority on Darwin's notebooks, stated (1974: 226): "It would be taking a misleadingly narrow view of what constitutes a scientific account to denigrate the Diary or the *Journal of Researches* on the grounds that they are popular works." Her comments obviously apply also to the edition entitled *The Voyage of the Beagle*, which I have used, and justify treating this source, as well as his diary as authentic testimonies of his impressions of the Fuegians. I refer to them as CD Beagle and CD Diary, 1988. Darwin frequently mentioned Tierra del Fuego and the Fuegians in his correspondence (CCD, especially vol. I), in his *Autobiography*, written mainly 1876 (CD Autobio); in *The Descent of Man and Selection in Relation to* Sex, first published in 1871 (CD Descent); and occasionally in *The Expression of the Emotions in Man and Animals*, first published in 1872 (CD Emotions). The questionnaire he sent to the missionary Thomas Bridges, for the last-named book, in 1860, and Bridges' answers, are reproduced in my Appendix of Chapter 10. I rely also mainly on Browne, 1994, 1995 and 2002; Desmond and Moore, 1992; Keynes 1980, 2002; and Herbert, 1974, 1977 and 2005, for their decisive comments and analyses and because of their knowledge of the sources and the Darwin epoch. Also they had access to documents which I did not.

24. Browne, 1995: 246.

25. CD Descent, vol. 1: 181; Desmond and Moore, 1992: 231–2 (italics added).

26. For Fitz-Roy's descriptions of the Fuegians and Patagonians (1839, chapters VII to IX), he relied mainly on one informant, the sealer William Low, and often cited a book written by the Jesuit missionary Father Thomas Falkner which Cooper (1917: 86) considered an unreliable source.

27. CD Beagle, 231.

28. Marvin Harris (1968: 122); Sagan, 1977: 6, 191–2. James Boon, another anthropologist (1983: 41), contested Sagan's "evolutions opinions." Richard Lee Marks (1991: 14), though he did not cite Darwin, announced that "The culture of the Yahgan Indians was so simple that it antedated the cultures that we conceive for the noble and ignoble savage."

29. Burrow, 1968: 276: Henrika Kuklick (1991: 116–17) should also be quoted here: "evolutionist reasoning proved remarkably durable because it was incorporated in conventional wisdom."

30. Students of Darwin have clarified the manner in which he utilised the notion of biological progress. Although agreement is not unanimous, it may be stated for the moment that he recognised superiority in specific areas of human beings as well as that of "other animals" (for instance bees). In *The Descent of Man*, while he recognised that human beings dominate the biological world, they do not do so because they are innately superior in terms of natural selection. For his appraisal of the two Fuegians, see also *The Descent of Man*, vol. 1: 34, 232.

31. Greene, 1977: 3; Browne, 1995: 248–53.

32. Gould, 1977: 37–8. In Gould's recent voluminous work (2002), published shortly before he died, he dedicated almost fifty pages (952–99) to his approach to culture changes rather than cultural evolution and to punctuated equilibrium rather than gradual evolution.

33. FR, 1839: 11, 16; Desmond and Moore, 1992: 111.

34. Diary, 1988: 133; Huxley and Kettlewell, 1965: 30.

35. Diamond, 1999: 246.

36. CD Diary, 1988: 3–7; Bowlby, 1991: 124.

37. CD Beagle, 442; CCD, 1991, vol. 7: 491, note 6; Thompson, 1995: 151.

38. FR, 1839: 78; CD Beagle, XXIII; Browne, 1995: 279; Desmond and Moore, 1992: 130.

39. Fitz-Roy (1839: 18–22) gave the names of many more.

40. CCD, 1985, vol. 1: 472 in a letter to his sister Caroline; also Browne, 1995: 312.

41. CCD, 1985, vol. 1: 315, note 1, 393, 472, 549–51; the editors of CCD, 611–61. Also FR, 1839: 19–21; Browne, 1995, passim: see her index; Desmond and Moore, 1992, passim; Moorehead, 1969: 26; Thompson 1995: 92, 156; Barlow, 1933: XXI–XXIII. See Keynes (1980 and 2002) for reproductions of Martens' unpublished drawings.

42. Herbert, 1974: 225.

43. Browne, 2002: 6, 7, 54.

44. Desmond and Moore, 1992: 575.

45. Herbert, 2005; Browne, 1995: 186. Keynes (2002: 59) pointed out that Darwin inscribed in Lyell's volume one, "Given me by Capt. F.R. [signed] C. Darwin." Henslow sent him Lyell's second volume, which he received in Montevideo in November 1832. Browne (1995: 338) explained how Darwin improved upon and supplemented Lyell's tenets. According to Desmond and Moore (p. 131), Lyell's second volume [*Elements of Geology*] was "curiously different from the first." Whereas in the first he had dealt with gradual geological changes, in the second he "asked whether animals and plants had been modified to match. Was there a natural mechanism for slowly transforming them to keep pace? "No," was Lyell's short answer. Darwin disagreed. His answer was long and was "yes."

46. Besides CD Beagle, for accounts of these trips in the social and political contexts of the countries where they took place, see Browne, 1995; Desmond and Moore, 1992; and Keynes, 1980 and 2002.

47. Herbert, 1974: 227.
48. CD Beagle, 207–8.
49. FR, 1839: 119. The main source for the Selk'nam is Gusinde, 1982 (translated into Spanish from the German original of 1931). There is no English translation of this work. The outstanding primary source in English for the Selk'nam is Lucas Bridges, 1987, which is fascinating reading. John Cooper's article "The Ona" (HSAI, 1946b) is very useful. Also in English, Chapman, 1982, 1997, 2002a, b, and c.
50. These days in Good Success Bay, 17–20 December 1832, are reported in CD Beagle, 204–11; CD Diary, 1988: 121–8; and FR, 1839: 120–2. Apparently most of the "interaction" took place on 18 December.
51. In CD Beagle, December 18 and 19 are not clearly distinguished, though they are in his diary.
52. Fitz-Roy wrote that five or six men greeted them, while Darwin said there were four.
53. For some rather recent publications on the Haush, see Chapman and Hester, 1975; Chapman, 1982: chapter 2, and 2002b, chapter 8. The Haush undoubtedly arrived (from Patagonia) on the Isla Grande long before the Selk'nam. Lucas Bridges (1987: 443) convincingly presented the basis for this hypothesis. The archaeologists working in the area do not necessarily agree with this hypotheses, partly because the archaeological evidence is composed mainly of instruments, habitats and residues, which are very similar for the two groups, given their common technology and mode of living.
54. Fitz-Roy added that he had the same feeling (as Hamond) and that it had led to his decision to take the four Fuegians to England in 1830, that his decision to take them was "not the effect of individual caprice or erroneous enthusiasm."
55. Taussig (1997: 153–72), in an original and inspired essay, cited this Darwinian scene, on the theme of the mimetic faculty, that he placed in a broad panorama that included Adorno, Artaud, Bataille, Benjamin, Durkheim. I mention only a few that Taussig cited (here in alphabetical order).
56. Even though the Haush language is not well documented, it is known to be entirely different from Yamana and Alakaluf languages, but as the speakers of the three languages (York, Jemmy and the old Haush man) shared many customs, such as repugnance of face hair, the slightest gesture would be sufficient to convey such a meaning.
57. CD Beagle, 501. See Street (1975: 10, 68) for his comments on these concepts in his analyses of the "savage" in English fiction.
58. CCD, 1985, vol. 1: 306–7.
59. Ibid., 303.
60. Ibid., 316.
61. Ibid., 397 (a letter to Charles Thomas Whitley).
62. CD Autobio, 126.
63. It may be of interest to the reader to compare Darwin's comments about the Haush with Captain Cook's (in Beaglehole, 1968a: 44–5) of the thirty or forty Haush he encountered on 16 January 1769. Cook concluded his remarks, as Darwin might have: "In a Word they are perhaps as miserable a set of People as are this day upon Earth."

64. See Chapman, 2002b: chapter 8, for an account of my hike through this area in 1970.
65. CD Beagle, 211.
66. CD Diary, 1988: 127.
67. Ibid., 128.
68. FR, 1839: 123–4; CD Beagle, 212–17; CD Diary, 1988: 128–30; Keynes, 1980: 100–1; Keynes, 2002: 125–6.
69. He also included here later information he obtained from the Scottish sealer William Low, who had spent many years in the area and whom he first met on the Falkland Islands in March 1833.
70. Weddell (1970: 147) also called Saint Martin's Cove, Wigwam Cove. As I noted in Chapter 1, the French archaeologist Dominique Legoupil (1995) and her team located and dated over thirty sites in the area of Cape Horn. It is of course likely more will be found there in the future but hers was the first major effort to survey the area.
71. CD Beagle, 213, italics added; see also CD Diary, 1988: 222–4, for 25 February 1834.
72. Stocking's text (1987: 106) is followed by his analyses of Darwin's concept of race and culture.
73. CD Beagle, 21.
74. Spegazzini, 1882: 163. See my Chapters 3 and 5 and note 37 in the latter for information about the more solid hut called a wigwam.
75. CD Descent, vol. 1: 137.
76. Hyades (1891: 345) wrote the "Fuegians" (Yamana) carry fire everywhere they go and try not to let it extinguish "although they can ignite easily by sparks of iron pyrite, which are produced by the shock (impact) of one piece of mineral against another." Gusinde (1986, vol. 1: 377–8) confused *pedernal* (flint or silex) with pyrite when he stated that "In various places in the extensive Yamana territory grains of pyrite are found, while fragments of *pedernal* are more scarce and constitute a highly esteemed object of trade." Lothrop (1928: 65, 130) mentioned Merton Island as a site for pyrite. He probably misspelled the name and intended to write Morton Island, where Weddell had his second encounter with the Yahgans (Chapter 2). Some of the principal references to fire are Gusinde, 1982, vol. 1: 188–9; 1986, vol. 1: 377–84; Hyades, 1891: 10; Martial, 1888: 202.
77. Webster (1970: 184) pointed out that they "procure fire by friction of two pieces of iron pyrites.... a fire-stone with which their country abounds." However, according to other reports, fire was usually made by using just one piece of pyrite against another of flint or later a nail or other such fragments of hard materials.
78. Cooper, 1917, 191–2: "The pyrites-and-flint method is the only one ever reported for any of the Fuegian tribes.... The iron pyrites is apparently found only in the north of Tierra del Fuego Island and in large quantities near Mercury Sound, Clarence Island." Mercury Sound is not located on Clarence Island, as Cooper and most authors contend, but rather, according to the *Derrotero* (p. 112), on the nearby large island of Capitan Aracena, along Cockburn Channel.

79. I am grateful to Dominque Legoupil for referring me to the book by Jacques Collina-Girard (*Le feu avant les allumettes: experimentation et myths techniques*. Paris. Edition de la Maison des Sciences de l'Homme, 1998, p. 20), from which I have translated the following: "The Greek etymology of this mineral (*pyros*, fire) is proof of the past utilization of this mineral.... The impact of flint (or of quartz) produces enough energy to detach and ignite small particles of pyrite. This combustion is exothermic and it frees the sulfuric gases." According to the *Encyclopedia Britannica* (15th ed., 1983, vol. 8), pyrite contains 46.7% iron and 53.33% sulfur. The pyrite must be struck against a very hard metal (or stone containing one) in order that the tiny particles of pyrite (that result from this strike) liberate their sulfuric gas, which thus produces "white heat," a spark.

80. Gusinde, 1986, vol. 1: 378.

81. L. Bridges, 1987: 64.

82. The Fuegians may also have used the pyrite Fitz-Roy found on the eastern Gilbert Island, also in Alakaluf territory, as well as Skyring and Fury islands, which are closer to the Yamana territory, near Brecknock Peninsula (Chapter 3). Hyades (1891: 406) noticed pyrite on an islet near Packsaddle Island, although on p. 10 he wrote that all the pyrite the Fuegians used was from Mercury Sound, Clarence Island. The Fuegians probably knew about the former sites, although I found no published evidence that they did. There is considerable confusion in the sources concerning the relative importance of these different minerals or stones used to obtain a spark. For instance, Gusinde writes that flint (pedernal) was found along Canal Cockburn (Mercury Sound), when in reality this was the source of pyrite, as noted by Lucas Bridges.

83. CD Beagle, 212; CD Diary, 1988: 130.

84. CD Beagle, 213.

85. FR, 1848: 153; CD Beagle, 212.

86. L. Bridges, 1987: 81, note 1. For the use of nets, see p. 127.

87. CD Beagle, 214–15. Italics added.

88. FR in PK, 1839: 462.

89. FR, 1839: 2; CD Beagle, 208, 215, 228. Fitz-Roy (1839: 183, 189) clarified that Low's informant, the "native boy" Bob, was a "Chono," from the region north of the Alakaluf territory. He told the same story as Jemmy, imitating "the piercing cries of the miserable victims whom he had seen sacrificed." Fitz-Roy added that Bob recited his horrible story as a great secret and "seemed to be much ashamed of his countrymen, and said, he never would do so – he would rather eat his own hands. He added: "York told me that they [the Alakaluf] always ate enemies whom they killed in battle; and I have no doubt that he told me the truth." Fitz-Roy recalled that this statement had been told to him by Jemmy and York on the *Beagle* and by "many different persons" as proof "that they eat human flesh ... namely when excited by revenge or extremely pressed by hunger." The brother of the catechist Garland Phillips who arrived at the Falklands with Despard in 1856, wrote, in the biography of G. Phillips, published in 1861 on p. 190 " ... in the extremity of their hunger they lay violent hands on the oldest woman of their party, hold

her head over a thick smoke made by burning green wood, and pinching her throat, choke her. They then devour every particle of the flech!" The author doesn't cite any source, not even his brother's (who was killed in 1859, see Chapter 9) as he almost invariably did, because the book is a compilation of his brother's writings. He may have read Darwin and Fitz-Roy although he doesn't cite them either. I didn't find any mention of cannibalism in the writings of the catechist Garland Phillips.

90. CCD, vol. 1: 304. See also his comments (CCD, vol. 1: 526, note 1) when he was having tea with Henslow and Joseph Romilly, a "fellow at Trinity College," a few months after he arrived home. Desmond and Moore (1992: 569–70) contrast Darwin's attitude with Wallace's (who also discovered natural selection), who said that, while living with the native Dyaks in Borneo, "The more I see of uncivilized people, the better I think of human nature." Also in Browne, 2002: 127, 352.

91. *On the Origin of the Species*, 1995: 36.

92. L. Bridges, 1987: 33–6, also 166–7. Barclay, in his Preface XIV to Bridges' Dictionary, quoted Bridges as follows: "They have been called cannibals and the sketches of them have been caricatures rather than the truth.... There have been times of extreme famine when on account of the bad weather it has been impossible for them to obtain provisions from the ships, from the coasts, or from the sea. At such times I have known them to eat their foot gear and their rawhide thongs, without a suggestion that they should eat human flesh." Most of the other authorities on the Fuegians also refuted Fitz-Roy's and Darwin's statements concerning cannibalism as for example: T. Bridges in V. for SA, 1866; Hyades, BAS-P, 1887: 340–1, 1888: 502–3, 1891: 257–9; Gusinde, 1986, vol. 1: 240–9; Lothrop, 1928: 18; Cooper, 1917: 194–5.

93. Engel in CD Beagle, 214, note 4.

94. The phrase refers to Napoleon Chagnon's book *Yanomamo: The Fierce People* (New York 1968), concerning the Yanomamo Indians of Venezuela, which became an anthropological best seller. The journalist Patrick Tierney (see bibliography) challenged him for having stimulated their interethnic tensions in order to "document" his book (and films) on them as a "fierce people." This allusion to Chagnon's book is justified because of the references to Edward O. Wilson, who supported Chagnon's work and cited Darwin in this context, as I quoted below.

95. CD Beagle, 216.

96. FR, 1839: 179, 183.

97. Lumsden and Wilson, 1983: 160, 163.

98. Hyades, 1991: 374.

99. L. Bridges, 1987: 34.

100. Mainly Gusinde, 1986, vol. 3: 1074–111.

101. CD Beagle, 215, 216. On the latter page he cited York again in an obscure story about his brother, who killed a "wild man," and a storm that raged as if to avenge the man's murder.

102. CD Descent, vol. 1: 182, 184, and vol. 2: 395.

103. Gusinde, 1986, vol. 3: 1065–9.

104. CD Beagle, 216; Gusinde 1986, vol. 1: 187–8; vol. 3: 1234–49, 1359–412.
105. CD Descent, vol. 1: 181.
106. CD Diary, 1988: 141.
107. CD Beagle, 217.
108. Hyades, 1884b: 558–9.
109. CD Beagle, 217.
110. Street, 1975: 6.
111. CD Descent, vol. 1: 34.
112. Ibid., 232: italics added.
113. Mayr, 1995: IX.
114. CD Diary, 1988: 3.

Chapter 5. 1833 to 1834: The Three Fuegians with Darwin and Fitz-Roy in Tierra del Fuego; Darwin and Fitz-Roy Visit the Falkland Islands; Adios Fuegians

1. FR, 1839: 124.
2. CD Beagle, 218; CD Diary, 1988: 133; CCD, 1985, vol. 1: 303, a letter to his sister Caroline.
3. CD Beagle, 218; FR, 1839: 125–6.
4. CD Diary, 1988: 132.
5. CD Beagle, 218.
6. CCD, 1985, vol. 1: 316.
7. FR, 1839, 126–7; FR in Keynes, 1980: 163.
8. FR, 1839, 127. According to Darwin (CD Diary, 133) they numbered twenty-eight, though he did not name the officers.
9. FR, 1839: 202–3.
10. CD Beagle, 218.
11. Ibid., 219.
12. CD Diary, 134; FR, 1839: 203.
13. CD Beagle, 219.
14. FR, 1839: 203; Sulivan in SAMM, 1881: 131. Sulivan quotes T. Bridges though this expression, spelt in a variety of ways, is not in Bridges' dictionary (1987, 638–44).
15. CD Diary, 1988: 134; CD Beagle, 220–1.
16. FR, 1839: 203–4.
17. CD Beagle, 221; CD Diary, 1988: 135.
18. CD Beagle, 221.
19. The reader of Darwin should recall that he invariably called Murray Narrows "Ponsonby Sound," even though Fitz-Roy had already used the name Murray Narrows, as it appears on all the maps. Murray Narrows (8 miles long) flows into Ponsonby Sound at its southern extremity. It was named for Lord Ponsonby, the British minister in Buenos Aires from 1826 to 1828, whom Fitz-Roy had probably met in Buenos Aires in 1828.
20. FR, 1839: 204. Recall that neither Fitz-Roy nor Darwin used the terms "Yahgan" or "Yamana" and referred to them as Fuegians or Tekeenica.
21. FR, 1839: 181, 204: CD Diary, 1988: 137.

22. FR, 1839: 205.

23. CD Beagle, 221.

24. The outstanding source book for the Selk'nam is Gusinde, originally published in German in 1931 and translated into Spanish in 1982, though not into English. Easily available and one of the best in English is L. Bridges, 2008 (reprinted in English); as well as Lothrop, 1928; Cooper, 1917; and Chapman, 1982 (out of print in English but reedited in 2007 in Spanish); and Chapman in English and Spanish, 2008a and 2008b.

25. Fitz-Roy's explanations (1839: 205–6) proved to be accurate, although Gusinde (1986, vol. 2: 231–2, note 315) thought that Jemmy's accounts were false. Cooper (1917: 196) confirmed "that the Onas occasionally ventured and venture on the water is well enough attested."

26. FR, 1839: 206.

27. CD Beagle, 222

28. FR, 1839: 207.

29. CD Beagle, 222. Wulaia, Lewaia, and Ushuaia are among the few localities whose original Yamana names have been respected. A favourite pastime of the explorers, the missionaries and some later visitors was bestowing names on topographical features that caught their attention, usually names of the members of their expeditions, faraway friends, localities in their homelands or a faithful vessel, such as that given to the great channel. Today many of the ancient Yahgan names have been forgotten; however, a dictionary could be composed of the Yahgan place names that have been published.

30. FR, 1839: 208–9.

31. CD Beagle, 222–3; CD Diary, 1988: 137.

32. FR (1839: 209) dated the reunion of Jemmy with his family as the day of their arrival in Wulaia, on 23 January, while Darwin (CD Beagle, 223) stated that it occurred the following day, which is more likely.

33. CD Diary, 1988: 137.

34. FR, 1839: 209; CD Beagle, 223.

35. FR, 1839: 210; CD Beagle, 223; CD Diary, 1988: 137.

36. CD Beagle, 223. Not mentioned in his diary nor in Fitz-Roy.

37. Lothrop (1928: 128–9) referred to another type of Yamana "wigwam" used in the winter. It was covered with pieces of sealskin sewn together, and as these structures were heavy and cumbersome, they were transported in separate canoes. Each hut sheltered two or three families. The tops of these dwellings were kept low and the floor was scooped to a depth of 2, 3 or even 5 feet to conserve the heat of the fire, which was sometimes placed at the bottom of the pit. Lothrop added that the smoke was a constant annoyance.

38. FR, 1839: 210–11.

39. L. Bridges, 1987: 36.

40. CD Beagle, 223; CD Diary, 138; FR, 1839: 213.

41. CD Beagle, 223; CD Diary, 138; FR, 1839: 210–11.

42. FR, 1839: 212–13. It seems obvious to me that the practice-shooting took place in the evening of the twenty-sixth, while it was still light, before the serious incident of the old men trying to assault a tent (referred to in the text), even though Fitz-Roy stated that he organized the shooting demonstration as

a "consequence" of this incident. This is not possible because this incident (about the old men) occurred "after dark," well after midnight; therefore Fitz-Roy was either mistaken or the incident with the old men happened the night before.

43. CD Diary, 1988: 138; CD Beagle, 224; FR, 1839: 212.
44. CD Beagle, 224; CD Diary, 138; FR, 1839: 212–14.
45. CD Beagle, 224; FR, 1839: 214.
46. CD Beagle, 224.
47. FR, 1839, 215; CD Diary, 1988: 139.
48. CD Beagle, 224–5; CD Diary, 1988: 139.
49. FR, 1839: 215; FR in PK, 1839: 441.
50. CD Beagle, 225. See Herbert (1999) for the importance of Darwin's comments on these glaciers, especially for the Swiss scientists.
51. FR, 1839: 216; *Derrotero*, 1973: 144, 167.
52. FR, 1839: 216.
53. CD Beagle, 225.
54. FR, 1839: 217–19; CD Beagle, 226; CD Diary, 1988: 140–1; *Derrotero*, 1973: 394. FR in PK, 1839: 441.
55. FR, 1839: 219–20.
56. Ibid., 138–9.
57. Ibid., 220.
58. CD Beagle, 223–7; FR, 1839: 221–2.
59. FR, 1839: 222.
60. CD Diary, 141, 143.
61. CD Beagle, 227, is compared with CD Diary, 143.
62. FR, 1839: 222–3.
63. FR, 1839: 224–5; also Shipton, 1973: 103. Not in Darwin because he had left Wulaia on 6 February (1833).
64. CD Diary, 1988: 143–4.
65. FR II, 225–6, 272–3; CD Diary, 1933: 138–9.
66. FR II, 226–7, 269; CD Diary, 1933: 139.
67. FR II, 332–5. Fitz-Roy published only extracts from Brisbane's log. For more details, the latter source would have to be found.
68. Ibid., 239, 254.
69. Crow, 1980: 678.
70. Desmond and Moore, 1992: 136.
71. Ibid., 239–40.
72. Ibid., 227, 271.
73. CD Diary, 1933: 138–9. In CD Beagle, 189, Darwin also referred to this trip only very briefly.
74. CCD, 1985, vol. 1: 304; see also his letter to Henslow, ibid., p. 307.
75. CD Diary, 1933: 141.
76. CD Diary, 1933: 141; FR II: 273–4.
77. CD in Keynes, 1980: 190.
78. CD Diary, 1933: 209–10.
79. CCD, 1985, vol. 1: 380.
80. CCD, 1985, vol. 1: 350.

81. FR II, 328–32.
82. His *Voyage* (CD Beagle, 57, 189–203, 399–400) includes many more notes made during this visit on the fauna and geology of the Falklands.
83. For this period of his voyage, see CD Beagle, chapters 3–9: CD Diary, 1988: 144–217; CCD, 1985, I: 311–59; FR II, chapters XIII–XV; Browne, 1995: 254–68; Desmond and Moore, 1992: 139–45; Moorehead, 1987; chapters 6–8; Keynes, 2002: chapters 10–14.
84. Duviols (1997: 127–39) concluded his article on the Patagonian "giants" with this phrase: "Thus by the end of the eighteenth century, this durable myth of giants had finally been laid to rest."
85. FR, 1839: 322; CD Beagle, 233: CD Diary, 1988: 217–18.
86. CD Beagle, 234. J. B. Hatcher, in an excellent article on his expedition in Patagonia in 1896–97, wrote: "Not only was the advent of the horse the determining factor in supplanting the bow and arrow by the bola among these Indians, but the introduction of that useful animal produced other most decided changes in the life and habits of the Tehuelches."
87. CD Diary, 1988: 218–20; FR, 1839: 322; Moorehead, 1987: 217.
88. CD Diary, 1988: 221: Fitz-Roy (1839: 323) does not mention this incident.
89. CD Diary, 1988 221.
90. CD Diary, 1988: 222.
91. CD Beagle, 213, 227–8; CD Diary, 1988: 222–24; FR, 1839: 323.
92. CD Beagle, 228; CD Diary, 1988: 226.
93. See A. Chapman, 1980.
94. CD Beagle, 228–31, 233–4; CD Diary, 1988: 217–27: FR, 1839: 322–32; Moorehead, 1987: 217. See beginning of Chapter 3 and Vanney (1986: 214) for the French woman, who came with her husband, Captain Louis de Freycinet, through or around Tierra del Fuego in 1820.
95. FR, 1839: 323.
96. CD Beagle, 229.
97. FR, 1839: 323–4; CD Beagle, 229; CD Diary, 1988: 226.
98. CCD, 1985: 380.
99. FR, 1839: 325.
100. CD Beagle, 229–30; CD Diary, 1988; 227; Fitz-Roy, 1839: 325–26.
101. FR, 1839: 327.
102. CD Beagle, 230; less in CD Diary, 227.
103. Eiseley, 1961: 265.
104. CD Diary, 1988: 240; CD Beagle, 234–5.
105. CD Beagle, 235.
106. CD Diary, 241. These incidents are not mentioned in Fitz-Roy (1839: 358–9).
107. FR, 1839: 358–9.
108. Personal communication from the linguist Oscar Aguilera (2003), who has been working among the Kaweskars for many years. Other important references for the Alakaluf are Emperaire, 1955; Gusinde, 1991; Laming, 1957; and H. Wegmann, 1976.
109. For instance Browne, 1995; Herbert, 1974; Desmond and Moore, 1992; Keynes, 2002.
110. CD Beagle, 498.

111. Keynes, 2002: 374.
112. Browne, 1995: 340.
113. Browne, 1995: 348; Herbert, 1974: 245–58; 1977: 178; Desmond and Moore, 1992: chapters 14 and 15.
114. CD Autobio, 76–80.
115. Nora Barlow, 1933: XVI. See the biographies of Fitz-Roy: especially H. E. L. Mellersh, 1968; and the recent one by Peter Nichols, 2003.
116. Thomson, 1975 and 1998: 269.

Chapter 6. 1838 to 1843: United States and Great Britain Antarctic Expeditions Encounter the Yamana

1. Viola, 1985: 9–10; Wilkes, 1978: 322.
2. Vanney, 1986: 281–2; Viola, 1985: 10; Wilkes, 1978: 381–2.
3. Vanney, 1986: 297–8.
4. Erskine, 1985: 120.
5. Vanney, 1986: 281; Viola, 1985: 16; Wilkes, 1978: XIX, 411.
6. Wilkes, 1845: 27; ibid., 1849: 56.
7. Vanney, 1986: 281–2; Viola, 1985: 10.
8. Viola, 1985: 9; Rydell, 1952: 36.
9. Viola, 1985: 20–1.
10. Ibid., 21; Wilkes, 1978: 524, note 1.
11. Wilkes, 1978: 584.
12. Wilkes's claim is supported by Viola, 1985: 18–20: 146–53; W. Chapman, 1965: 107; Fogg, 1990: 34; David, B. Tyler, 1968; and probably many others. Yves Jacob, author of a recent biography of Urville, affirmed (1995: 360) that Urville offered "the first tangible proof of the existence of a southern continent." However I rely more on the French historian Vanney (1986: 297–8) who vividly described the essentials of this controversy and leaves the question open of who was the first to prove that the Antarctic is the seventh continent, earth.
13. Moorehead, 1987: 104.
14. Stanton, 1975: 308; The Columbia Encyclopedia, second edition, 1950; W. Chapman, 1965: 107. Wilkes' reputation as a "thorny public figure" was partly due to an incident, the famous Trent Affair, which occurred at the beginning of the Civil War. As commander of the U.S.S. *San Jacinto*, Wilkes forcibly stopped a British mail steamer, the *Trent*, in international waters, and contrary to all regulations, took two Confederate commissioners "into custody" and nearly involved the Union in a war with England, although he thereby became a "Union hero," according to Viola, 1985: 23.
15. Colvocoresses, 1852: 34–6, 38; Wilkes, 1845: 2122; 1849: 45–7.
16. Colvocoresses, 1852: 38–40.
17. Wilkes (1845: 21) mistakenly wrote that Capital King had reported on Orange Harbour.
18. Cooper, 1917: 197–8.
19. Colvocoresses, 1852: 41–2. Lothrop (1928: 128–9) noted the deepest floor I have read about. He noted that "the pitted house floors reach as much as five feet below the surface." He commented that the Yahgans were "snugly

logged against winter gales," though "the smoke from the hearth made their eyes red and inflamed."

20. Stanton, 1975: 104–6.
21. Wilkes, 1845: 23–4; 1849: 49–51; Erskine, 1985: 44–5, 47; Tyler, 1968: 53.
22. Viola, 1985: 15; also Wilkes, 1845: 23; 1849: 49; Colvocoresses, 1852: 42.
23. Tyler, 1968: 53.
24. Wilkes, 1845: 24; 1849: 52–3. Erich von Hornbostel, published two articles on the Yahgan and Selk'nam chants in 1936 and 1948.
25. All the below are also from Wilkes, 1845: 25; 1849: 52–4.
26. CD Beagle, 213.
27. Wilkes, 1849: 59–60; italics added.
28. Erskine, 1985: 19.
29. Wilkes, 1845: 28–9, 32–3; Ibid., 1849: 60–1, 66–7.
30. W. Chapman, 1965: 116–17.
31. Pyne, 1986: 120.
32. W. Chapman, 1965: 117. The South Magnetic Pole was finally located between 1907 and 1909 by Ernest Shackleton during his second expedition to the Antarctic. See an article published in *Scientific American*, April 2005, on what flips the magnetic poles to different localities in the vicinity of the poles.
33. Boorstin, 1983: 444.
34. Ross, 1847: vol. 2: 289–94.
35. Taken from Gusinde, 1986, vol. I: 122–4.
36. Ross, 1847, vol. 2: 303–5; Also FR, 1839: 185; Gusinde, 1986, vol. 1: 121, note 140.
37. Ross, 1847, vol. 2: 305–8.
38. M'Cormick in Gusinde, 1986, vol. 1: 124.

Chapter 7. 1848 to 1851: Allen F. Gardiner Searches for Heathens and Finds the Yamana

1. Despard, 1854: 14–15, 106–21; Marsh and Stirling, 1878: 8; see Canclini, 1959a for a biography of Gardiner; Canclini (1979: 15–84) also for details on many of these trips.
2. Braun, 1945: 63–4; Canclini, 1979: 41–2; Despard, 1854: 16–17; Ross, 1847 vol. 2: 201.
3. Braun, 1945: 66–7; Marsh and Stirling, 1878: 30.
4. Marsh and Stirling, 1878: 31–2 (italics added); ibid., 39.
5. V. of P., 1859: 170: italics in the original.
6. V of P., 1855, 220. See also Shipton, 1973: 109–10 and Gardiner's brother-in-law Reverend John W. Marsh, who explained (1857: 321) why he chose the Fuegians.
7. Braun, 1945: 67–8; Despard, 1854: 11; Marsh, 1857: 322–3.
8. L. Bridges, 1987: 37.
9. AG-D, 111–3; King James' version of the Bible is cited.
10. AG-D, 114–5, 117; Marsh, 1857: 325–7.
11. Shipton, 1973: 109.

12. AG-D, 117–20, 123.
13. Despard, 1854: 121–2.
14. AG-D, 122–3.
15. Despard, 1854: 123; Marsh, 1857: 331–4.
16. Shipton, 1973: 110.
17. Braun, 1945: 69; Shipton, 1973: 110–11. According to a website, £1,000 in 1850 was equivalent, in 2001, to £62,689 or $90,727.
18. Braun, 1945: 70; Canclini, 1959a: 11; Hamilton, 1854: 156.
19. AG-D, 139, 158; Braun, 1945: 71–2; Marsh, 1857: 345–6.
20. Shipton, 1973: 111.
21. Marsh, 1857: 346–7.
22. RW-D, 315–17, italics added.
23. AG-D, 162, 203; JM-D, 174; RW-D, 315; Derrotero, 1973: 221.
24. AG-D, 163; RW-D, 321–2.
25. AG-D, 204; RW-D, 323–4.
26. AG-D, 163.Williams (RW-D, 324) had undoubtedly also read Fitz-Roy.
27. RW-D, 324, italics added.
28. Ibid., 320, 325.
29. AG-D, 204; RW-D, 326; JM-D, 174–5.
30. RW-D, 344–7.
31. AG-D, 164–5.
32. RW-D, 330–1; AG-D, 167.
33. RW-D, 332; Canclini, 1959a: 22.
34. AG-D, 169–71.
35. RW-D, 332; letter by Capt. Cooper in Despard, 1854: 176–7.
36. RW-D, 332; AG-D, 167.
37. Despard, 1854: 177; Shipton, 1973: 112.
38. Canclini, 1959a: 22.
39. RW-D, 343; Braun, 1945: 81.
40. RW-D, 333; AG-D, 204; RW-D, 333–7.
41. AG-D, 205; Braun, 1945: 80–1.
42. AG-D, 205–9; RW-D, 338–9; Canclini, 1959a: 22.
43. AG-D, 209–10; RW-D, 339–40.
44. No entry for Gardiner in Despard (1854: 208–11) from 23 December to 4 January 1851. The citations in Canclini (1959a: 23) from Gardiner's journal are very brief for these days.
45. RW-D, 340–2, 344; Canclini, 1959a, 23.
46. RW-D, 342. For Gardiner's diary in Canclini (1959a: 23) and A-GD, there are no annotations at all from 28 to 31 December; Williams' journal (RW-D) also omits the days from 27 to 30 December as well as 1 to 3, and 5 to 7 January; that is, Williams' diary refers only to 31 December and 4 January.
47. Canclini, 1959a: 23. In Despard, none for Dec. 23 to Jan. 3; Gardiner begins again on 4 Jan. Williams, none for 27 to 30 Dec., nor 5 to 7 Jan.; only for 31 Dec. and Jan. 4.
48. RW-D, 347–8: italics added.
49. AG-D, 213.

50. Ibid., 211–13.
51. RW-D, 344, 348.
52. Ibid., 348.
53. However, Canclini (1979: 99) mistakenly wrote that the escape occurred two days later, on 6 January, when they were already in Lennox Harbour. He probably made this error because Gardiner was not clear that on 6 January (when he was already in Lennox Cove) he wrote concerning events that took place on 4 January, as I quote here (AG-D, 211): "Banner Cove, Monday, January 6, 1851. After a lapse of 9 days, the longest period during which the natives had been away from us, they returned about seven o'clock on Saturday morning, January 4."
54. Hyades and Deniker, 1891: 380–2. Bridges' original in English is part of his *Mémoire inédit* (often quoted with this title by Hyades), which apparently has not as yet been published. Thomas Bridges did not refer to this text, nor to his brief visit to Paris, in his publications that I consulted. The text quoted above was published in French by Hyades (see Hyades and Deniker, 1891: 20, 405) as part of Bridges' *Mémoire inédit*, dated October 1886, which "he very obligingly put at our disposal." Bridges probably gave Hyades a copy of this and other material during his brief visit to Paris (from England) some time late 1886. Hyades copied a good deal of Bridges *Mémoire inédit* in his 1891 volume. Cooper (1917: 73) was aware of its importance.
55. Beauvoir (1902: 215) wrote in Spanish, quoting part of the same text by Thomas Bridges, published by Hyades in French. As he probably had not read Hyades and Deniker, 1901, I don't know where he obtained Bridges' text.
56. The killing(s) by Gardiner is (are) not mentioned where the Gardiner tragedy is described, in the following: Braun Menéndez (1945: 80–1); L. Bridges (1987: 38); Canclini (1959a, 1959b); Despard (1854); Gusinde (1986, vol. 1: 135, 281); Hamilton (1854: 160–2).
57. Shipton (1973: 114) doubted that the Yahgans were so threatening and pointed out that they did not attack the missionaries then nor in March, when they returned to Banner Cove (see below).
58. RW-D, 349; AG-D, 212–14; Canclini, 1959a: 23–4.
59. RW-D, 350–1, 355; AG-D, 214–15. Gardiner referred to Lennox Cove as Lennox Road and Lennox Harbour.
60. RW-D, 352, 354, 358–9, 355; AG-D, 215.
61. Later named Caleta Cutter on the Chilean maps.
62. RW-D, 359–61; AG-D, 216; Canclini, 1959a: 24.
63. RW-D, 361, 383.
64. RW-D, 362, 383; AG-D, 217; Canclini, 1959a: 24.
65. RW-D, 364.
66. AG-D, 217; Canclini, 1959a: 24; RW-D, 365.
67. Shipton, 1973: 114.
68. L. Bridges, 1987: 39.
69. RW-D, 365–9; AG-D, 218; Canclini, 1959a: 25.
70. RW-D, 370, 372.
71. AG-D, 218–20; RW-D, 372–9; Canclini, 1959a: 25; AG-D, 219–20; RW-D, 374–9, 376–9.

72. RW-D, 377. This paragraph was not reproduced by Williams' biographer Hamilton (1854: 191) or in the Spanish version of his journal published by Canclini (1959b: 69–70).

73. RW-D, 380–1: italics added; also quoted in Canclini, 1959b: 70–1 and Hamilton, 1854: 193–4.

74. RW-D, 381–2, 385. Italics added.

75. AG-D, 220–1; Braun, 1945: 85; Canclini, 1959a: 25; Canclini (1979: 94, note 1) clarified that Gardiner entitled the notes he rewrote "Reminiscences of the Lost Journal" going back to 1 February 1851. He continued writing in it, though only a few lines daily, until 2 September. This journal was in addition to his diary, which was saved, and is dated from 14 June to 6 September, the day he died. Both were published by Despard in 1854 as one continuous document.

76. AG-D, 221–6; Canclini, 1959a: 24–5; RW-D, 385–7.

77. Canclini (1959a: figure 1) erroneously situated Reliance Cove on the extreme south shore of Picton.

78. AG-D, 226–8; RW-D, 389–95.

79. RW-D, 396.

80. AG-D, 229–30; Canclini, 1959a: 26; RW-D, 396–400.

81. AG-D, 231; Williams (RW-D, 400–1) gives a slightly different version of the message left in the bottles.

82. RW-D, 400.

83. L. Bridges, 1987: 39.

84. AG-D, 231.

85. RW-D, 401–2.

86. AG-D, 232.

87. RW-D, 404–5; also in AG-D, 232–3; Canclini, 1959a: 26.

88. RW-D, 405, 402.

89. Braun, 1945: 87–8.

90. Hamilton (Dr Williams' biographer), 1854: 220–2.

91. Canclini, 1959a: 27; Hamilton, 1854: 224.

92. Hamilton, 226–30; Braun, 1945: 87; Canclini, 1959a: 27.

93. Hamilton, 1854: 231–2; Canclini, 1959a: 27.

94. Hamilton, 1854: 236, 237–8.

95. Marsh and Stirling, 1878: 66.

96. RW-D, 426–7; Hamilton, 1854: 239–40.

97. RW-D, 425, 427; Smyley in Despard, 1854: 188–9; Hamilton, 1854: 242.

98. Smyley in Despard, 1854: 188–9; also Braun, 1945: 88–9; Canclini, 1959a: 27; Hamilton, 1854: 241–2; Marsh and Stirling, 1878: 370.

99. Marsh and Stirling, 1878: 373.

100. AG-D, 264–5; Canclini, 1959a: 27 and 1959b: 96; Hamilton, 1854: 242; Marsh and Stirling, 1878: 74–7.

101. AG-D, 265–6.

102. Braun, 1945: 89–91; Canclini, 1959b: 96 and 1979: 111; Despard, 1854: 440; Hamilton, 1854: 242; Marsh and Stirling, 1878: 81. Maidment's notebook included some rough sketches and poetry; also fragments of Erwin's journal were found, but I did not locate them.

103. AG-D, 266–7; Despard, 1854: 440–1. The last quotation is complete, as published, including the intervening dots. Gardiner's and Williams' original journals should be consulted.
104. Boyson, 1924: 120; also Braun, 1945: 73; Canclini, 1959a: 12.
105. Smyley in Despard, 1854: 188–90. Italics added in the quotation; also Marsh and Stirling, 1878: 82.
106. Piedra Buena in Destéfani, 1983: 65–6.
107. See Despard (1854: 197–202) for the letter by Captain Morshead dated 21–22 January 1852. Note also that Hamilton (Dr Williams' biographer) added: "The Indians, whose naked footprints were observed on the sand, had no doubt found him [Pearce] still alive and had murdered him." But had there been such footprints, they certainly would have been mentioned by Smyley or Morshead. See also Despard, 1854: 442; Hamilton, 1854: 244; Martial, 1888: 218. An editorial in the mission journal the *Voice of Pity for South America* (1859: 171–2) explained that Sulivan, who was then a captain in the Navy and stationed in the Falklands at the time, had not been informed by Gardiner of his intention to establish a mission station in Tierra del Fuego. Therefore, the assumption is that no one in the Falklands knew he was there during the period 1850–51. See also McHaffie, 2001 Web site.
108. Braun, 1945: 93; V. of P., 1855: 34.
109. Sulivan in SAMM, 1 June 1881: 130–1, from his speech at the 13th annual meeting of the South American Missionary Society held in London on 26 April 1881.
110. Braun, 1945: 91.

Chapter 8. 1852 to 1858: The Missionaries Carry On; Jemmy Button Is Located

1. Editorial in SAMM, 1884: 53; M. Braun, 1945: 93.
2. Braun, 1945: 94.
3. Barbance, 1969: 89, 95; P. Marks, 1994: 23.
4. Martinic (1973: 32) points out that in the year 1890 alone a total of 1,122 sailing boats (English, French, German and US among others) rounded Cape Horn.
5. Snow, 1857, vol. 1: 17, vol. 2: 72–3. Cooper wrote in 1917 (p. 128) that Captain Snow's "account is sympathetic and seems to be careful and exact as far as it goes." Gusinde (1986, vol. 1: 134) also had a high opinion of Snow as the first navigator who considered the Yamana human beings. Last quote from Snow: 1857, vol. 1: 21–2.
6. Snow, 1857, vol. 1: 19.
7. Braun, 1945: 97–9; Shipton, 1973: 117–18.
8. McHaffie, 2000 Web site (ref. to the purchase of Keppel Island): Snow, 1857: vol. 1: 71, 98, 196, 200; V. of P., 1855: 147 and 1857: 109.
9. Shipton, 1973: 117–18.
10. Ibid.; V. of P., 1856: 74.
11. Snow (1857, vol. 1: 288–308) wrote in great detail about his, and particularly his wife's, feelings during their two days in Spaniard Harbour,

where they recovered remains of clothing and a few other items that had belonged to "those who had suffered there." Phillips in V. of P., 1856: 74.

12. Snow, 1857, vol. I: 315–18.
13. Ibid., 17.
14. Ibid., 321–3.
15. Ibid., 324–5.
16. Phillips in V. of P., 1856: 73–4.
17. Snow, 1857, vol. I: 325–6.
18. Phillips in V. of P., 1856: 73–4; Snow, 1857, vol. I: 325–8.
19. Snow, 1857, vol. I: 327; Phillips in V. of P., 1856: 75.
20. Snow, 1857, vol. I: 328.
21. Phillips in V. of P., 1856: 75–6.
22. Snow, 1857, vol. I: 336–8.
23. Ibid.; Phillips in V. of P., 1856: 76–7.
24. Snow, 1857, vol. I: 349.
25. Phillips in V. of P., 1856: 77–8; Snow 1857, vol. I: 340.
26. Snow, 1857, vol. I: 340–1.
27. Phillips in V. of P., 1856: 78–9.
28. Phillips in V. of P., 1856: 82; Snow, 1857, vol. I: 341–6.
29. Snow, 1857: 347–55.
30. Phillips in V. of P., 1856: 79–82.
31. Snow, 1857, vol. I: 357–75.
32. Snow, 1857, vol. II: 1–3, 9–11.
33. Ibid., 12–26.
34. Ibid., 27–30.
35. Ibid., 30–4. Marsh and Stirling (1878: 96–7) mentioned the same incident. The rather long quotes from Snow's two-volume work are justified insofar as they were published only once, in 1857, and have not been translated into Spanish. Obviously his work is a primary source and should be published again.
36. Ibid., 34–5.
37. Ibid., 32, 51–2.
38. Ibid., 35. Lucas Bridges (1987: 42) gave a slightly different version: "The offer was firmly refused, possibly because of Jimmy's wives and family, though they would probably all have been welcome, for fish, penguin and seal were superabundant in the Falklands and there would have been no difficulty about provisions. Jimmy did his utmost, however, to prevail on some of his countrymen to make the venture, but all in vain, and the vessel [under the command of Captain Snow] returned, after this feeble effort, to Keppel Island."
39. G. W. Phillips, 1861: 68. Garland W. Phillips, brother of the missionary, published a biography of his brother following his death in 1859.
40. Snow, 1857, vol. II: 35–6.
41. Ibid., 37–8: the phrase in parenthesis is in the original text.
42. Ibid., 39, 41, 44.
43. Ibid., 48–9.
44. Ibid., 50.

45. Mellersh, 1968: 247–8.
46. Snow, 1857, vol. II: 51–6.
47. Ibid., 69–70, 84–9, 96. The recent surveys of French archaeologist Dominique Legoupil (1993–94) and evidence seen by Ortiz-Troncoso (1972) prove that the Yamana camped on islands very near Horn Island and could easily have gone over to Horn Island.
48. Snow, 1857, vol. II: 42, 272–3; Mellersh, 1968: 248. For the mission's reply to Snow's accusations (which I didn't find), see the publications of the mission journal.
49. Mellersh, 1968: 249.
50. Ibid., 254; V. of P., 1860: 2.
51. Snow, 1867, vol. II: 50.
52. Braun, 1945: 106–7.
53. Despard in V. of P., 1856: 168.
54. V. of P., 1856: 148–9. Italics added.
55. Browne, 1995: 235.
56. V. of P., 1857: 21; Braun (1945: 107) also mentions Teófilo Schmith, a linguist, but no mention was found of him in the other sources consulted.
57. V. of P., 1858: 215; Braun, 1945: 106–7; L. Bridges, 1987: 42; Marsh and Stirling, 1878: 90; Phillips in V. of P., 1857: 134.
58. Braun, 1945: 109.
59. V. of P., 1858: 54. An editorial (in V. of P., 1857: 185) commented as follows on Gardiner's omission of remarks concerning his visit to his father's grave in Spaniard Harbour in April 1857: "He does not attempt any account of his own feelings, on visiting his devoted father's grave, and the graves of those who with him sacrificed their all.... The feelings of a son under such circumstances could not be described, and he therefore wisely refrains from any attempt. We can, however, imagine what they must have been.... He is the son of the Christian warrior who fell nobly in the battle of the Lord, and to him his father's sword descended. He is his father's heir...." My comment: Despite such a heavily symbolic heritage, Gardiner's son, though a devoted missionary, appears to have been remarkably different from his father.
60. Gardiner in SAMM, 1878: 136. Curiously, in the issue of the *Voice of Pity*, which deals with this trip (1857: 182–8, 223–8) no mention was made of any homage to the martyrs in Spaniard Harbour, which surely was rendered. However, Gardiner's son did describe it twenty-one years later, as cited in this text.
61. Ellis in V. of P., 1857: 182–3; also Gardiner in ibid., 185–8.
62. Ellis and Gardiner in V. of P., 1857: 182–7.
63. V. of P., 1858: 219–28.
64. Gardiner in SAMM, 1878: 135–7.
65. Gardiner in V. of P., 1858: 220: italics added.
66. Gardiner in SAMM, 1878: 135–7.
67. SAMM, 1878: 135; italics added.
68. Gardiner in V. of P., 1858: 221–2.
69. Gardiner in V. of P., 1858: 223–4.
70. Gardiner in SAMM, 1878: 135–6.

71. Ibid., 225–6.

72. Ibid., 227–8; italics added. Despard, 1854: 228–32.

73. Gardiner in SAMM, 1878: 136; italics added.

74. Gardiner in V. of P., 1858: 227–8; Despard (1854: 228) referred very briefly to the trip and he did not mention why Jemmy consented to come with Gardiner. Nor did Marsh and Stirling, 1878: 96.

75. Gardiner in SAMM, 1878: 136.

Chapter 9. 1858 to 1860: The Yamanas Visit the Keppel Mission; Massacre in Wulaia

1. Mrs Despard, V. of P., 1858: 251.

2. Despard, V. of P., 1858: 230–1; 1859: 80–1. Italics added.

3. Despard, V. of P., 1858: 229.

4. Ibid., 78; Mrs Despard, 1858, 252–3.

5. Despard, V. of P., 1858: 230–2; Mrs Despard, ibid., 254.

6. Despard (V. of P., 1859: 81–2) found no difficulty writing every sound in Yahgan employing the Ellis Phonetic Characters, subsequently used by Thomas Bridges.

7. For these five concepts, in the order in the text, see T. Bridges, 1987: 632 (for God), 13 (for spirit), 18 (for soul), 175 (for mind), 629 (for heaven).

8. Despard, V. of P., 1859: 85; Mrs Despard, V. of P., 1858: 253–4.

9. Despard, V. of P., 1858: 231–2.

10. Despard, V. of P., 1859: 78, 87–90.

11. Despard, ibid., 87, 89; Turpin, ibid., 92–3.

12. Despard, ibid., 78–81, 85–6; Turpin, ibid., 92.

13. Despard, ibid., 80–1.

14. Despard, ibid., 79–81, 85, 88; Mrs Despard on the same subject, 1859, 165–8.

15. Despard, ibid., 79, 88.

16. Despard, ibid., 99–100.

17. Despard, ibid., 80.

18. Despard, ibid., 109.

19. Mrs Despard, ibid., 166–8.

20. Despard, ibid., 104–7; Fell, ibid., 156.

21. Despard, ibid., 108–19, italics in the original.

22. According to T. Bridges (1987: 371) *Pallill-awa* seemed "to represent the jargon of the English language when they first heard it."

23. Despard, ibid., still 1859: 117–20, 126; Fell, ibid.,175–177.

24. Despard, ibid., 120; Fell, ibid., 178.

25. Despard, ibid., 121; Fell (ibid., 179–81), identified Dr Button as Jemmy's brother, but he was undoubtedly his uncle (father's brother) because he was too old and experienced to be Tommy, Jemmy's oldest brother.

26. A clan may be defined as a unilateral (either patrilineal or matrilineal) kinship unit that traced back to a "founder," usually a famous person, a mythological hero or a "totemic ancestor." The clan eliminates many ancestors in order to trace the kinship back to the one prestigious personage, real or imagined. A lineage is also unilateral and may simply trace back four or five generations of

ancestors known to have existed. With these definitions in mind, the Yahgan "clan" should be called a lineage.

27. Despard, V. of P., 1859: 121. His spelling of the names gives only a vague idea of the real word, but I quote most of them here in order not to confuse the reader. However Despard is not clear about Tellon, who later in this chapter was correctly identified as Jemmy's brother-in-law. Jemmy's mother had died long before: she was mentioned for the last time in 1833 (Chapter 5). Among the other "important people" absent was another of Jemmy's daughters, his youngest sister, who lived with him and his family and was erroneously thought to be his third wife. Also absent were his youngest brother (Billy) and three of his nephews, Pinoense (Tom's son), Lucca (Tellon's son), and the child later called Jack (Harry's son). Squire Muggins was also probably Harry's son. All who were alive have already appeared or will appear later on.

28. Despard, ibid., 1859: 120–2; Fell, in ibid., 181–2.

29. Despard, ibid., 122–3; Fell, ibid., 182.

30. Despard, ibid., 124–7. Fitz-Roy had also noticed a good-looking Yahgan woman near Beagle Channel who also reminded him of a gypsy (Chapter 5).

31. For the definition of "districts" see Gusinde, 1986, vol. 1: 196–204.

32. Sahlins, 1972.

33. See above, note 27. Despard, ibid., 128–9; Fell, ibid., 184–6.

34. Despard, ibid., 130.

35. Fell, ibid., 183–4; Despard, ibid., 123–6; G. W. Phillips, 1861: 144–5. Note on page 146, Phillips, the brother of the missionary, stated that there was a tribe of nine natives of Oens-men living chiefly on Lennox Island and "about Good Success Bay." There is an obvious confusion here of those in the six canoes who were very probably from the Isla Grande.

36. Fell, ibid., 186–8; Despard, ibid., 132, 135, 147.

37. Despard, ibid., 133–7.

38. Despard, ibid., 138–41, 145–6.

39. Despard, ibid., 142–3, 146.

40. Despard (ibid., 141–7) also presented this group of nine "Keppel Fuegians" in a letter to friends dated 22 May 1859, nearly five months after their arrival at Keppel. Also L. Bridges, 1987: 43; G. W. Phillips, 1861: 177.

41. Despard, ibid., 148–50; see G. W. Phillips (1861: 151–91) for details of this second visit.

42. Mrs Despard, ibid., 1859: 265–9.

43. Garland Phillips, V. of P., 1860: 26–7.

44. Despard, 1860, 6–13; G. W. Phillips, 1861.

45. Garland Phillips, V. of P., 1860: 28.

46. Fell, in G. W. Phillips, 1861: 250–1; Garland Phillips in V. of P., 1860: 28.

47. Garland Phillips, 1860, 125; Despard, 1860, 51.

48. Despard, ibid., 50–2. Italics added.

49. Mellersh, 1968: 251–2.

50. L. Bridges, 1987: 43.

51. Cole (SAMM, 1912: 109) undoubtedly identified them correctly in 1912. After he returned to England, he probably discovered their true identities and notified their families.

52. Despard, V. of P., 1860: 12–13; G. W. Phillips, 1861: 96; Braun, 1945: 111.
53. Despard, V. of P., 1860: 123–9.
54. Mrs Winn, SAMM, 1912: 178. Italics added.
55. Garland Phillips, V. of P., 1860: 29–31; G. W. Phillips, 1861: 186–7. The missionary's brother, quoted from his brother's unpublished letters as well as Fell's diary. He quoted Fell's diary (p. 252) that while in Stanley, on 11 October: "Took the natives on shore (the young ones) to have their likenesses taken." If so this is the only reference I found of photographs being taken at this time (1859) and place (Falklands).
56. Fell's diary, in G. W. Phillips, 1861: 254.
57. Cole's deposition, V. of P., 1860: 136–9.
58. Fell's diary, in G. W. Phillips, 1861: 254.
59. Ibid.; Cole, in V. of P., 1860: 136.
60. G. W. Phillips (the missionary's brother) added that the schooner had been in Wulaia "five times." In reality the *Allen Gardiner* schooner had been there only twice (since Fitz-Roy and Darwin left Wulaia in March 1834) with Gardiner Jr. in June 1858, and with Despard, Phillips and Fell in December 1858. In November 1855, here G. W. Phillips (1861: 194–5) apparently quoted a "Missionary Journal" for the number of natives (300) who arrived. Fifty-three years later, Mrs Christian, the Fells' sister (SAMM, 1912: 108), gave the same figure.
61. Fell's diary, in G. W. Phillips, 1861: 255; Cole's deposition, V. of P., 1860: 136; Cole, SAMM, 1912: 109.
62. Fell's diary, in G. W. Phillips, 1861: 255. Fell's diary ended on 5 November, while Garland Phillips' diary ended on 11 October, the day before the departure from Port Stanley. Cole, SAMM, 1912: 109.
63. Cole's official deposition, copied from the Colonial Secretary's Office, Port Stanley, East Falkland Island, 10 March 1860, as published in V. of P., 1860: 136–9.
64. Cole, in SAMM, 1912: 109.
65. Christian, SAMM, 1912, vol. 46: 108. Italics added.
66. G. W. Phillips, 1861: 196.
67. Winn, SAMM, 1912, vol. 47: 179. Italics added.
68. Cole's deposition is paraphrased and cited here as it was published in V. of P., 1860: 136–9, with additional data from Cole's description of the events as told to Despard and as published in V. of P., 1860: 129–31; fifty years later his comments were published in a very brief article in SAMM, 1912: 109–10.
69. Winn in SAMM, 1912: 178–9.
70. Editorial, V. of P., 1860: 173–4; Despard, V. for S.M., 1863: 185.
71. Editorial, V. of P., 1860: 170; Smyley report to Despard, ibid., 173; Despard, V. of P., 1861:12–13.
72. The other references for this section are: Editorial, V. of P., 1860: 170; Smyley report to Despard, ibid., 173–4; Despard, V. of P., 1861: 12–13.
73. L. Bridges, 1987: 45.
74. Marsh and Stirling, 1878: 101.
75. Cole's deposition in V. of P., 1860: 136–9. Cole repeated this accusation twice in 1912 (109 and 110): "I was pretty much in touch with Jimmy Button, and

soon found that plunder had been the reason for the massacre. . . . I am sure that Jimmy Button was the ringleader."

76. The *Times* of 8 December 1859, as quoted in Toumey 1987: 206; also Toumey with other sources: 205–6. Toumey added: "Despard used a legal technicality to avoid testifying at the hearing."

77. G. W. Phillips (1861: 212–13) quoted from the record of 9 May 1860, of the Colonial Office at Port Stanley.

78. Okoko, in Marsh and Stirling, 1878: 103.

79. Stirling, V. for S.A., 1863: 195.

80. L. Bridges, 1987: 46.

81. T. Bridges, SAMM, 1879: 78–9.

82. Gusinde, 1986, vol. 1: 276; Hyades, 1891: 385; Shipton, 1973: 124–5. The latter two did not name a guilty party, although Shipton implied that Jemmy was aware of the plot.

83. Lewis Burgess, 1998: personal communication.

84. Editorial, V. of P., 1860: 121–2, italics added; 146–7.

85. Editorial, V. of P., 1860: 125–7.

86. Despard, V. of P., 1861: 12–14.

87. Sulivan, V. of P., 1862: 147.

88. Marsh and Stirling, 1878: 102; Stirling, V. for S.A., 1864: 200.

89. FR, 1839: 326; CD Beagle, 229; CD Diary, 227.

90. John Cooper states (1917: 49): "The fact that they [the Onas-Selk'nam] do not use canoes now is not conclusive proof that they never either made use of or borrowed them." And again on p. 195, Cooper states: "That the Onas occasionally ventured and venture on the water is well enough attested" (see Chapter 5).

91. See the informative essay on Selk'nam war and peace by Alfredo Prieto, 1994.

92. Editorial, V. of P., 1860: 147–8.

93. Ibid., 149–50. Identical text in G. W. Phillips (1861: 210–12) except that Owen is spelt Oen's.

Chapter 10. 1860 to 1869: The First Devastating Epidemic; The Missionaries Seek a Location; Four Other Yamanas Visit England

1. Marsh and Stirling, 1878: 103; Despard, in V. of P., 1860: 173–5.

2. Despard, in V. of P., 1861: 9.15.

3. Lucas Bridges, 1987: 47; SAMM, 1894: 53.

4. Despard, in V. of P., 1861: 175.

5. Shipton, 1973: 126.

6. T. Bridges, in V. of P., 1862: 35.

7. Lucas Bridges, 1987: 47.

8. Bartlett, in V. for S.A., 1863: 43.

9. Marsh and Stirling, 1878: 105–6.

10. Braun, 1945: 125; Marsh and Stirling, 1878: 105; Macdonald, 1929; Shipton, 1973: 127.

11. Marsh and Stirling, 1878: 110; Canclini, 1980: 17.

12. Stirling, in V. for S.A., 1863: 190–3, 211–20.

13. Marsh and Stirling, 1878: 111.
14. Stirling, in V. for S.A., 1863: 195–6.
15. L. Bridges, 1987: 47.
16. Stirling, in V. for S.A., 1863: 196, 216–17.
17. T. Bridges, 1886a: 205.
18. Ibid., 217–19.
19. Ibid., 197.
20. Marsh and Stirling, 1878: 117.
21. Ibid., 114; Canclini, 1980: 21.
22. Marsh and Stirling, 1878: 115–18.
23. Ibid., 114–16.
24. See Gusinde, 1986, vol. 3: 1015, 1142. For English translation of the myths, see Wilbert.
25. Marsh and Stirling, 1878: 115–18. G. H. Luquet in 1927 published an interesting essay on this subject. He related the Yahgans' morality as expressed in their mythology to Kant's, as expressed in his *Critique of Practical Reason*.
26. Stirling, in V. for S.A., 1864: 188–92.
27. Ibid., 192–5, 232. For this visit, see Stirling, ibid., 187–204. Perhaps the 1863 epidemic was not the first. When Despard (V. of P., 1859: 121) arrived in Wulaia (4 December 1858), he commented on the number of "great mounds of shells...where Wigwams stood," and asked Jemmy about them. Jemmy replied "Much people die here – when me little, very little, piccianinny [baby]." If he was about 13 years old in 1830, when Fitz-Roy picked him up, an epidemic may have occurred about 1818.
28. See Gusinde (1986, vol. 1: 218–19) for a summary of Bridges' data. Here I refer to only four of Bridges' estimates. Until a more precise estimate is made, I accept his estimates that the 1863–64 epidemic reduced the Yahgan population from 3,000 to 2,500. The first two are not quoted here because of the difficulty of interpreting them, but references to them are as follows:

> First: In SAMM, 1869: 113.
> Second: In the *Journal of the Anthropological Institute of Great Britain and Ireland*, 1885, vol. 14: 289.
> Third: T. Bridges (1886a: 205) wrote: "I am sorry to say that thirty-six years ago [1860] this Yahgan tribe had [a population] of at least 3,000 individuals and that now [1886] they are not more than 400 souls.
> Fourth: In an article (1892: 316–17), T. Bridges wrote: "The Yahgans...their number now to be about 320, whilst 30 years ago [in 1862] they were 3000, as fully proved by lists of families then taken by me. This decrease is chiefly owing to imported diseases as measles, smallpox &c."

29. Stirling (SAMM, 1867: 154) refers to an "accurate census" of more than 400 male heads of family who represented only two-thirds of the "Tekeenica" (Yahgan) population, that is, 2,000 "souls and probably many more." Therefore his number corresponds to Bridges' 3,000 as the population before the 1863–64 epidemic. Although Stirling does not date his "accurate census," it was obviously prior to 1867.

30. There are reports of much sickness in Keppel in 1864 and "many deaths" on Button Island in 1867. But I found no mention of any other devastating illness until 1881, when the new series of epidemics began.
31. Stirling, in V. for S.A., 1864: 196–8.
32. Ibid., 200; Mrs Stirling, in SAMM, 1867: 54.
33. Stirling, in V. for S.A., 1864: 229–31.
34. Ibid., 204.
35. Ibid., 228–9.
36. Editorial in V. for S.A., 1866: 81–2.
37. Ibid., 231–2, 235–6, 202–3.
38. Turpin, Jemmy's tutor, in 1858 during the first visit to Keppel, was an exception. In Keppel, Turpin had worried that the two (civilise and Christianise) might not go together. While praising Jemmy for his cleanliness, his neat house, his neatly arranged knives and forks, etc., Turpin had observed that (V. of P., 1859: 93) "Jemmy is as civilised as we might wish; but the main point is, the salvation of his own and his countrymen's souls."
39. Stirling in V. for S.A., 1864: 232–5, 257.
40. Ibid., 202–3.
41. Stirling in V. for S.A., 1864: 228–9, 237. A canoe eighteen feet (5.48 m.) long was exceptional, the average being about twelve feet (3.65 m.). Rau annotated a vocabulary in Yahgan, while he and Stirling were in Wulaia, which was published by Felix Outes in 1926 (see Bibliography). Canclini (1980: 25) explained that Rau separated from the mission in Keppel in 1865, because the methods employed by the English missionaries were not to his liking (somewhat like Captain Parker Snow).
42. Stirling, in V. for S.A., 1864: 238, 257.
43. Mrs Stirling, in SAMM, 1867: 24–6.
44. Mrs Stirling, in Macdonald, 1929: 53, 59.
45. Stirling, in V. for S.A., 1864: 256–8; Bridges, in V. for S.A., 1864: 256–61; ibid., 1865: 6–9; Jacob Rau, in V. for S.A., 1864: 290–1; Macdonald, 1929: 52–4.
46. Bridges, in V. for S.A., 1865: 49–50.
47. Ibid., 51–3.
48. In Keppel sometime in June 1865, Lucca confided the above quote to Bridges (V. for S.A., 1865: 276) concerning Okoko's troubles, which no doubt Okoko confided in Lucca in Wulaia during the week he was there in October 1864.
49. Bridges, in V. for S.A., 1865: 49–54, 151–2.
50. Stirling, in V. for S.A., 1865: 169; Marsh and Stirling, 1878: 130.
51. Stirling, in V. for S.A., 1865: 170–1; Bridges in ibid., 277; Marsh and Stirling, 1878: 130; Macdonald, 1929: 61.
52. Macdonald, 1929: 60. Note 1, quoted from SAMM, June 1927: 71–4; Bridges in V. for S.A., 1865: 271–8, and in V. for S.A., 1866: 176.
53. Bridges, in V. for S.A., 1866: 82–3.
54. Ibid., 176–7.
55. Ibid., 177–9.
56. Stirling, in V. for S.A., 1865: 218–19.
57. Canclini, 1980: 29.

58. Macdonald, 1929: 65–6.
59. Beddof, in V. for S.A., 1865: 222–3.
60. Macdonald, 1929: 63.
61. Canclini, 1980: 30–1.
62. Marsh and Stirling, 1878: 131.
63. See comments by Stringer and Mckie (1996: 188) on the Fuegians.
64. SAMM, 1867: 19.
65. Stirling, in V. for S.A., 1866: 126.
66. Bridges, in V. for S.A., 1866: 179–80.
67. Canclini, 1980: 30.
68. Stirling, in SAMM, 1867: 153. The Gardiner referred to is usually written Allen F. Gardiner (Chapter 7).
69. Macdonald, 1929: 73; Stirling, in SAMM, 1867: 66–7, 126.
70. Editorial comment, SAMM, 1867: 125.
71. Stirling in Macdonald, 1929: 77; Bridges in SAMM, 1867: 165.
72. Bridges in SAMM, 1867: 165.
73. Stirling in SAMM, 1867: 157–8.
74. Bridges in SAMM, 1867: 162–3.
75. Stirling in SAMM, 1867: 158–9.
76. Bridges in SAMM, 1867: 164–5.
77. Perhaps the burial places of Urupa and Threeboys have already been located in the Port Stanley cemetery.
78. Canclini, 1980: 34. Follows the original: "Pero el hijo de Jemmy Button murió el día antes de llegar. Allí ocupó un lugar vecino a su amigo Urupa. El episodio era muy doloroso, pero sin embargo, mirando hacía atrás, a los empeños de Fitz Roy por su padre tres décadas y media antes, a la traición y la muerte sin arrepentimiento de éste, aquello tenía una aureola de triunfo."
79. Stirling in SAMM, 1867: 159.
80. Bridges in SAMM, 1867: 162–6.
81. Bridges in SAMM, 1867: 163; and Stirling (SAMM, 1867: 155) made a "very rough guess" that the Oens-men numbered 3,000.
82. Bridges in SAMM, 1867: 163–4; Stirling in SAMM, 1867: 155–6. Stirling calculated that the population in Wulaia was between 150 and 180. If these figures are exact, they are about half the number there (300–400) in March 1863, as Bridges thought, which would account for the deaths during the 1863–64 epidemic.
83. Bridges in SAMM, 1867: 164, 165; Stirling in SAMM, 1867: 159; ibid., 1868: 33–4.
84. Stirling in SAMM, 1868: 33–5. Stirling wrote many details about an accident of the *Allen Gardiner*. There were no casualties, but he was delayed there for three or more weeks while the ship was being repaired.
85. Stirling in SAMM, 1868: 116–21, 146–50; Bridges in SAMM, 1869: 10–14.
86. Bridges in SAMM, 1869: 10–12.
87. Stirling in SAMM, 1868: 117–18.
88. Ibid., 119. This last phrase may be an allusion to the frightful underwater creatures, the Lakúma, who were said to seriously harm anyone who came close to them. See Gusinde in Wilbert, 1977: 177. However, there is no

published myth about beings who dropped down from some other world, although the missionaries did suddenly appear from "some other world."

89. Stirling in SAMM, 1868: 148–50.

90. Canclini, 1999: 59–61.

91. Stirling, SAMM, 1869: 10. On ibid., p. 15 Stirling wrote that he was "about to try a residence ashore at Le-wy-a."

92. Bridges in SAMM, 1869: 14.

93. L. Bridges, 1987: 53–4.

94. Stirling in SAMM, 1869: 106.

95. Bridges in SAMM, 1869: 119. The above declaration expresses the Anglican conviction that to become a Christian one must be "converted" to civilisation. See also Bridges' article "Manners and Customs of the Fire-landers" in V. for S.A., 1866: 181–4, 201–14.

96. Stirling in SAMM, 1869: 15.

97. Editorial in SAMM, 1869: 37–8.

98. Shipton, 1973: 128.

99. SAMM, 1869: 140–1; Braun, 1948: 143.

100. CCD, 1993, vol. 8: 19–20. See Hyades, 1991, chapter 5, entitled "Caracteres Psychologiques," which treats the same subjects as Darwin's questionnaire but with far more themes and comments, some by Hyades himself, and many quoted from Bridges.

101. For Bridges' answers, see also CCD, 1993, vol. 8: 400–1, and CD Emotions, 278, 327.

102. CCD, 1993, vol. 8: 401, note 8.

103. CD Emotions, see my Chapters 11 and 13, for Bridges' comments on his answers, to Darwin.

Chapter 11. 1869 to 1880: The Missionaries Settle in Tierra del Fuego; The Yamanas Attempt to Adjust

1. Stirling in SAMM, 1868: 151; ibid., 1869: 106. The main sources for Stirling, when he installed the mission in Ushuaia Bay, are the letters to his two daughters in SAMM, 1869: 105–12; 1870: 9–11, 32–6, 147–52.

2. Canclini (1980: 38) noted that only part of this letter to his daughters was published in the society's journal (SAMM) and that the original had been lost. Perhaps Stirling wrote about this first visit to Ushuaia in the lost portions of this letter. See Canclini (1980: 37–51) for an account of Stirling's six months in Ushuaia.

3. Apropos of the Five Brothers (Cinco Hermanos): though I didn't find the Yamana name of these mountains, if it is the same it may refer to myths featuring five brothers translated from German into English by Wilbert, 1977: 70–3, 32–40 and in Spanish in Gusinde, 1986, vol. 3: 1166–8 and 1216–23. The quotation of the myth is from T. Bridges (1987: 265). The word for the moon in Yahgan is *hannu-ka*. For other versions of the deluge myth, see Bridges, V. of P., 1866: 211; Wilbert, 1977: 186–95: Gusinde, 1986, vol. 3: 1124–30.

4. Gusinde, 1986, vol. 3: 1117–31; in Wilbert, 1977: 17–30. We might consider that "human" time began with the origin of the patriarchy for the Yamana and the Selk'nam. I refer to Salomon and Schwartz (1999) for the distinction between "History of Indians" and "Indian history." Another example (besides the origin of the patriarchy) of the latter follows. The Yamana tradition relates that the first humans were born when the younger Yoalox who was much more clever than his elder brother, seduced Mákuxipa. The human epoch (my term), "Indian History," may have begun for the Yamana when Makuxipa gave birth to the first human beings. The Selk'nam "mythology," "Indian History," tells us (Gusinde, 1982, vol. 2: 563–5 and Wilbert, 1975: 37–8) that the younger Kwanyip was also much more clever than his elder brother, but instead of "creating" the first humans, he introduced death in the *hoowin* world. The Selk'nam tradition of the *hoowin* epoch terminated when death was installed and the *hoowin beings* were transformed into celestial "beings" (especially certain stars), mountains, lakes, rivers, trees in Selk'nam territory. Thus "History of the Selk'nam" would begin with death, that is the "transformation" of the *hoowin beings* and the beginning of real people, "Human history" that is "Indian History."

5. Bridges, in SAMM, 1870: 160.

6. Stirling, in SAMM, 1869: 15, 35–6; Canclini, 1980: 37. Stirling (SAMM, 1869: 106) preferred Gable Island as the site for the mission. But there the natives were "not so trustworthy" (as those in the Ushuaia area).

7. Bridges, in SAMM, 1880: 75; Lewis, in SAMM, 1873: 32; Bridges, in SAMM, 1877: 107.

8. Stirling in SAMM, 1870: 32.

9. Stirling (SAMM, 1869: 107) referring to the Bay of Ushuaia wrote: "The Falkland Island sealers clean sweep the rocks of seal, and the natives, without suitable boats, cannot compete."

10. Stirling, in SAMM, 1869: 105–12; Lewis, in SAMM, 1871: 87.

11. Stirling, in SAMM, 1870: 150.

12. Stirling, in SAMM, 1869: 105–9.

13. Ibid., 110–12.

14. Stirling in SAMM, 1870: 33, 75.

15. Ibid., 34–5.

16. Ibid., 9–11.

17. Ibid., 33. Italics added.

18. Canclini, 1980: 80.

19. L. Bridges, 1987: 51; Braun, 1945: 143; Bridges in SAMM, 1869: 15.

20. Bridges in SAMM, 1870: 39–43.

21. L. Bridges, 1987: 52; Bridges, in SAMM, 1870: 39, 43, 95.

22. L. Bridges, 1987: 52–3; Bridges, in SAMM, 1872: 153.

23. Ibid., 1870: 132–3.

24. Bridges, in SAMM, 1870: 127–31; L. Bridges, 1987: 53.

25. Bridges, in SAMM, 1870: 131–2, 136; L. Bridges, 1987: 64.

26. L. Bridges, 1987: 53–4; Bridges, in SAMM, 1870: 131–2.

27. L. Bridges, 1987: 54; Bridges in SAMM, 1870: 131, 136.

28. Ibid., 1870: 133. Italics added.

29. Bridges, in SAMM, 1872: 153.
30. The historian Anthony Pagden (1995: 82) commented on this quote as follows: "Most European jurists would have expressed themselves in much the same way." Not only did Diderot and Melville express aversion to this sort of take-over of the natives' lands, Beaglehole (1968a: 514–19) cited an extraordinary text, written in 1764 by James Douglas (then president of the Royal Society), that reads like a United Nations declaration of human rights today, as does Diderot's.
31. Moorehead, 1987: 114.
32. L. Bridges, 1987: 541; Bridges, in SAMM, 1870: 136.
33. Ibid., 1870: 129.
34. Ibid., 1872: 154–9.
35. Ibid., 1871: 22, 40–3; ibid., 1872: 154–5.
36. Lewis, in SAMM, 1871: 88–9.
37. Bridges, in SAMM, 1871: 137–8.
38. Ibid., 1872: 155.
39. Ibid., 1871: 140–1; L. Bridges, 1987: 56–7.
40. Lewis in SAMM, 1872: 32.
41. Ibid., 34–5.
42. Bridges, in SAMM, 1872: 29.
43. Shipton, 1973: 129; Bridges, in SAMM, 1872: 29–30.
44. L. Bridges, 1987: 59–61.
45. Bridges, in SAMM, 1872: 30–1, 156.
46. Shipton, 1973: 134–5.
47. Bridges, in SAMM, 1872: 156.
48. Stirling, in SAMM, 1872: 88–9, 94.
49. Ibid., 89–90; Bridges, in SAMM, 1872: 96, 99. Even nineteen years later, at the height of the devastating mortality, Bridges' (1892: 23) conviction in the validity of the "double-C" policy remained undisturbed.
50. Stirling, in SAMM, 1872: 88–9, 90–8.
51. Bridges, in SAMM, 1873: 32, 100, 118.
52. Lewis, in SAMM, 1873: 91–2.
53. Bridges, in SAMM, 1873: 28, 30–1.
54. Ibid., 1873: 30, 88; 1875: 38.
55. Bridges in SAMM, 1873: 86–7, 120–2.
56. Ibid., 1874: 23–4.
57. Bridges, 1874: 23. Italics in the original.
58. Lewis, in SAMM, 1875: 45–6.
59. Lawrence, in SAMM, 1873: 155.
60. Bridges, in SAMM, 1874: 26–7; Snow, 1857, vol. 2: 28. Burnt Island, where she was captured by Fitz-Roy, was undoubtedly considered Atisimoon, even though it is not located on the far outer coast.
61. Bridges, in SAMM, 1874: 23–4.
62. Ibid., 27, 24.
63. Lawrence, in SAMM, 1874: 92.
64. Bridges, in SAMM, 1874: 22–3.

65. L. Bridges, 1987: 82.
66. Gusinde, 1986, vol. 3: 1070.
67. Lawrence, in SAMM, 1874: 92–3. See pp. 94–6 for the Christian names of the fifty natives baptised from March 1867 to March 1873, including the names in Yahgan of their parents.
68. Bridges, in SAMM, 1875: 41–2.
69. Ibid., 1874: 189–90. See also L. Bridges, 1987: 80–1.
70. Bridges in SAMM, 1875: 5.
71. Ibid., 1874: 190–1; ibid., 1875: 5.
72. Ibid., 1875: 6, 12, 14.
73. Gusinde, 1986, vol. 3: 1370.
74. Bridges, in SAMM, 1875: 12–15, 37–8, 41–2.
75. Lewis, in SAMM, 1875: 43–6.
76. See, for example, Bridges, 1886a, 1892, 1893.
77. Bridges, in SAMM, 1875: 215–19. Italics in the original except in the last paragraph.
78. Bridges, in SAMM, 1876: 56–61; italics added to the quote; ibid., 1878: 33–5.
79. L. Bridges, 1987: 70–3.
80. Bridges, in SAMM, 1876: 199. Neither the name of the American vessel nor the number of natives killed was given but some record could probably be found in Punta Arenas, as there were not many US ships sailing in this area in March 1876.
81. Whaits, in SAMM, 1876: 270–1.
82. Bridges, in SAMM, 1877: 33.
83. Lucas Bridges (1987: 86) quoted from a report dated 22 May 1876, written by his father while he was still in Punta Arenas. His father sent the report to the governor of the Falkland Islands. It was later published in London.
84. L. Bridges, 1987: 86–8.
85. Willis, in SAMM, 1876: 222–3.
86. Twenty pounds in 1877 are equivalent today to 919 pounds and 1,350 dollars US. Bridges (SAMM, 1877: 155) refers to them as the Adoovians and Oofyaroogans, probably referring to place names in the area of New Year's Sound.
87. Bridges, in SAMM, 1877: 275–6. Note that on average each canoe from New Year's Sound carried ten passengers. Stirling in L. Bridges, 1987: 88.
88. Bridges, in SAMM, 1877: 106–10.
89. Ibid., 1877: 109, 274; 1878: 32–5, 78–9.
90. Stirling, in SAMM, 1878: 106–7.
91. Bridges, in SAMM, 1878: 103–7, 125. In 1889 a Salesian mission was established on Dawson Island. Alakaluf and Selk'nam were rounded up and taken there, where through the years the great majority died mainly because the mission became a focus of contagious diseases, against which the Indians had no natural defences and very little medical aid. Almost a hundred years later Dawson would become even more famous as a prison camp for political dissenters, following Pinochet's coup in September 1973.
92. Bridges, in SAMM, 1878: 127–8.

93. Bridges, in SAMM, 1878: 247, 271.

94. L. Bridges, 1987: 76. Thomas Bridges' accounts should be studied by a linguist, in the light of the words defined in his dictionary and the names of people and places he often cited in Yahgan, which include almost the entire area of Beagle Channel, Navarino and islands as far as Cape Horn.

95. Bridges, in SAMM, 1879: 35, 156–8; L. Bridges, 1987: 98–9.

96. Gusinde (1986, vol. 1: 327) described the event, though he gave the name of the sealing vessel as *La Chilota*. He related that when the captain (Stroll) asked the Yahgans to leave the ship, they refused and adopted a threatening attitude, so the captain had them killed and their cadavers thrown into the water.

97. The historian Mateo Martinic (1973: 50) pointed out that often the cargos of abandoned, wrecked ships were stolen by *raqueros*, sealers in the area, and "known and honourable people of Punta Arenas," who made fortunes by selling the contents of cargos of ships that had been wrecked.

98. Bridges, in SAMM, 1879: 35.

99. Bridges, in SAMM, 1879: 79, 35–7, 55–7. See Canclini (1981: 75) for details of the version told to Bridges.

100. Martial, 1888: 107.

101. Aspinal, in SAMM, 1889: 245.

102. Bridges, in SAMM, 1879: 55.

103. Shipton, 1973: 135.

104. Burleigh, in SAMM, 1879: 107; ibid., 1882: 59–60, 103.

105. Bridges, in SAMM, 1879: 79–80, 103; italics added.

106. Ibid., 1870: 128–9. Bridges' main informants were not acknowledged in his dictionary, perhaps because it was published after his death. They were Jemmy Button (in 1858) and his brother Tom (in 1859), Okoko (1859, then 1860 to 1864), Jack and Urupa (in 1864), later Lucca, and probably others. Sisoi became his favourite and apparently last informant.

107. Bridges, in SAMM, 1870: 159; ibid., 1874: 23.

108. Bridges, in SAMM, 1879: 222. Even though his dictionary comprised 32,432 words, he agreed with Stirling (SAMM, 1880: 75), that the Yahgan language was a "very inadequate medium to convey clearly our instruction to them, and the sooner they learn English the better." In his dictionary he concentrated on the declinations of verbs and synonyms. He failed to achieve an understanding of the grammar, so it must have been difficult for him to translate the gospels of St Luke and St John and the Acts of the Apostles.

109. Bridges in SAMM, 1882: 11–12.

110. Ibid., 1879: 236–7; Whaits, in SAMM, 1880: 218–19.

111. Bridges, in SAMM, 1881: 92. Italics added.

112. Ibid., 1880: 74–6.

113. Ibid., 1881: 227.

114. Whaits, in SAMM, 1880: 218–19; article signed by E. P. in SAMM, 1880: 265; Lawrence and Willis, in SAMM, 1880: 123–4.

115. Bridges, in SAMM, 1881: 227. Another example of good treatment, also noted by Bridges (SAMM, 1879: 221), was that of the *Golden West*, a sealing vessel, which came from New London and stopped over in the

Bay of Ushuaia in May 1879. The captain of the *Wanderer*, another sealing vessel, was also known for hiring the Yahgans and not cheating them.

116. Lawrence, in SAMM, 1880: 222.

Chapter 12. 1881 to 1882: First Signs of Epidemics; Alakaluf Kidnapped to Europe; Last News of Fuegia Basket

1. Bridges, long letter in SAMM, 1881: 225–31, 249–55, dated 25 May 1881, covers most of the ten days since his arrival in Ushuaia.
2. Bridges, in SAMM, 1882: 14–15, made a list of the twenty-six orphans, indicating their Yamana and Christian names, their parents, place of origin, and "supporters" of each child.
3. Bridges, in SAMM, 1881: 230–1.
4. Lawrence, in SAMM, 1882: 31–2, dated 17 August 1881.
5. Bridges, in SAMM, 1882: 10–13, 16: letter dated 12–22 August 1881.
6. Lawrence, in SAMM, 1885: 128.
7. Bridges, in SAMM, 1882: 103–4; letter of 1 November 1881.
8. Bridges, in SAMM, 1882: 53–7; ibid. letter; Braun, 1945: 157.
9. Ibid., and Bridges, in SAMM, 1882: 104; letter dated 5 January 1882. Eventually one of the model houses was inhabited by the Whaits family, another by Otatosh, for which he paid a half-year's rent with ox hide and beef, valued at 13 shillings. The third was rented to Henry Lory, a Yahgan trained as a pilot, who reappears in Chapter 13.
10. Ibid., 102–3.
11. Lawrence, in SAMM, 1881: 61. More could probably be found about Otatosh, the first Yamana of Ushuaia to contact the missionaries.
12. Bridges, in SAMM, 1882: 141–3; letter dated 14 February 1882.
13. Stirling, in SAMM, 1882: 149.
14. Bove and his companions were commissioned by the Italian and Argentine governments to carry on scientific research. The geologist Lovisato and the botanist Spegazzini, who accompanied Bove, published a chapter in Bove's work (1883).
15. L. Bridges, 1987: 104–10, 173; on p. 212 he published five Haush words. This language was never documented.
16. Bridges, in SAMM, 1882: 224–6; letter dated 16 June 1882. Gusinde (1986, vol. 1: 145) had no use for Bove's writings on the Fuegians, while Cooper (1917: 71–2) considered them "among our most important sources for Yahgan culture."
17. Bridges, in SAMM, 1882: 271; letter dated June 28.
18. Bridges, in SAMM, 1882: 226, also 270; letters of 16 and 28 June 1882.
19. Bridges, in SAMM, 1882: 222–3; letter of 16 June 1882.
20. Ibid., note 17 above.
21. Bridges, in SAMM, 1882: 143, 221, 252–5, 270–3; letters of 14 February, 16 June and 28 June 1882; ibid., 1884: 157.
22. Barclay, 1926: 144–50.
23. Bridges, in SAMM, 1882: 104–5; letter of 1 November 1881.

24. L. Bridges, 1987: 85.
25. FR, 1839: 399.
26. Bridges, in SAMM, 1882: 252, referred to the Alakaluf family as comprising the four mentioned in my text.
27. Hyades, 1891: 13; Revol, 1995a: 29. Deniker (B.S. de Paris, 1881: 183) was informed (erroneously) by the anthropologist Topinard that they were Yamana, taken from Hermite Island or Horn Island (see Manouvrier, 1881: 785). Nicolas, in *Discussion sur les Fuegiens*, 1881: 847, also quoted Topinard to the effect that they were from Saint Martin's Cove (Hermite Island), Yamana territory. Topinard's source was probably the "guide" (Waalen), who may have given this false information on purpose to make them appear even more exotic.
28. Hyades, 1891: 6; Jullierat, 1881: 298; Martial, 1888: 115; Nicolas, in Manouvrier, 1881a: 782.
29. Mason, 2001: 24.
30. Juillerat, 1881: 295.
31. One of the French anthropologists, Lucy-Fossarieu (1884: 165), contended that the Fuegians continued their practice of cannibalism, stating (as proof) that one of the Fuegian women had been found chewing on a human humerus. This is absolute slander. He made it up to nourish his researches on cannibalism. See Revol, 1995a: 36.
32. Topinard in Manouvrier, 1881a: 776.
33. Le Bon, 1883: 271.
34. Manouvrier, 1881a: 777–8.
35. Mason, 2001: 25. Revol (1995a: 31–2) points out that only one of the French anthropologists, Lucy-Fossarieu (1884: 174), reported on the child's death, and that it was not mentioned during the meetings of the Société d'Anthropologie or reported in the newspapers.
36. Virchov (1881: 373–94) measured Antonio, Henri, Lise, El Capitán and a woman Virchov identified as "Trine" who was undoubtedly Catherine. For a Spanish translation of this text, see *Impactos*, No. 65. Año 6. 1995 (a journal published in Punta Arenas).
37. Deniker, 1884: 182.
38. Hyades (1891: 235) described the illnesses but stated that nine Alakaluf were kidnapped from Clarence Island. The place may be exact but the number is an error, as they were eleven in all. I did not include Leipzig, Stuttgart and Nuremberg, mentioned by Mason (2001: 25), because I found no information on visits to these cities. But my research is incomplete. Further study will certainly reveal more details and cast more light on the mentality of that epoch, including that of the anthropologists, and honour those who tried to alleviate the Fuegians' suffering, such as Manouvrier.
39. Bridges (SAMM, 1882: 252) referred to the Alakaluf family as comprising the four mentioned in my text.
40. Hyades, 1891: 13, 391.
41. Bridges, in SAMM, 1882: 252, 254; ibid., 1883: 56, 59–60, 104, 139.
42. Corbey, 1993: 356.

43. Personal communication of a French friend who recalled going there as a child.
44. Manouvrier, 1894a: 597.
45. Topinard in Manouvrier, 1881b: 785.
46. Nicolas, in *Discussion*..., 1881b: 861–2.
47. Ibid., 1881b: 862. Also see Darwin's *Voyage*..., chapter 10.
48. Nicolas, in *Discussion*..., 1881b: 852.
49. Ibid.; see also Manouvrier, "Les Aptitudes et les Acts" in B.S.A. de Paris, 1890, and the *Revue Sicentifique*, 1891.
50. Hecht, 2003: 304–5, 212, 214, 100.
51. Bridges, in SAMM, 1883:138–9.

Chapter 13. 1882 to 1886: The French Arrive; Then the Argentines; The Epidemics Become Uncontrollable

1. More of her story was published (in a French translation) in Chapman, 1995a.
2. Gusinde, 1986, vol. 1: 175; Cristina Calderón in Chapman Journal, 1965–88.
3. Chapman, 1995b.
4. Martial, 1888: 48. Martial's volume (1888) is the first of eight volumes detailing the results of the research by members of this French expedition. Cooper (1917: 110) considered the ethnographic contribution in Martial's volume as: "A very important source on Yahgan culture in all its phases."
5. The French expedition was financed by the ministries of the Navy and of Public Instruction and was supervised by the French Academy of Science.
6. L. Bridges, 1987: 114.
7. Hyades, 1885a: 388.
8. Ibid., 1882.
9. Martial, 1888: 30–1.
10. Ibid., 31, 44, 95; Hyades, 1885a: 399–400.
11. T. Bridges, in SAMM, 1883: 59; Captain Willis, ibid., 62.
12. Martial, 1888: 31, 44, 95.
13. Ibid., 33, 36, 45–9, 110.
14. L. Bridges, 1987: 115.
15. The identification by these two French photographers of the individuals they photographed by their Yahgan names marks an epoch in the history of photography. Usually, even today, "indigenous" people of the world appear as illustrations of their ethnicity, rarely with their names.
16. Hyades (1891) published thirty photographs at the end this volume (No. 7). A great many of these photographs have been published in *Cap Horn. Rencontre avec les Indiens Yahgan*, Paris 1995.
17. The capes made of guanaco skin were worn by only the Yamana on Navarino Island and along the north shore of Beagle Channel (Isla Grande), in guanaco territory. The Yamana capes were not as large as those used by the Selk'nam, which reached to the knees or feet, because such a cumbersome garment would be a hindrance for canoe travel. The Selk'nam hunters threw them off when they were pursuing a guanaco.

18. Hyades, 1885a: 413; 1891: 253, 383–6.
19. Recall that Gusinde's work on the Yamana was first published in German in 1937 as one volume and translated into Spanish in 1986 as three volumes.
20. Hyades is coauthor of volume 7 (1891) of the Cape Horn Mission series. See pp. 386–8 for his comments on the Anglican mission. His coauthor, Joseph Deniker, a scientist working in the Museum of Natural History (Paris), was a great help to Hyades, although all the data were collected by Hyades. Cooper (1917: 99–100) referred to the Hyades–Deniker volume as "The most important extant study of Yahgan anthropology . . . almost everything else that had been published previously by the Rev. Mr. T. Bridges . . . may be safely neglected." Cooper was justifiably enthusiastic about Hyades' work, but it would be a great mistake to ignore or underestimate the publications by Thomas Bridges. See Revol (1995b) for an excellent essay on Hyades.
21. Bridges, in SAMM, 1883: 54; Hyades, 1885a: 390–1.
22. Hyades, 1885a: 391–2.
23. Hyades, 1891: 228; Martial, 1888: 225–6.
24. Bridges, in SAMM, 1883: 54.
25. Lucas Bridges, 1987: 114.
26. Bridges, in SAMM, 1883: 53–5.
27. Hyades, 1891: 230, 233–4; he referred to Bridges in SAMM, 1882: 104.
28. Hyades again referred to Bridges in SAMM, 1883: 56.
29. Hyades, 1891: 391.
30. Hyades, 1891: 222–3. Here he also described the pathology of two cadavers (of a man and a young woman), preserved in alcohol, which were examined in Paris by Professor Corneal in 1884. Hyades had treated the man in Orange Bay who was affected by gangrene in his leg and foot but he refused to continue the treatment with Hyades. He died soon afterwards and his skeleton was taken to Paris along with that of the young woman, mentioned in the text. Payen took a photograph of the man with his two Alakaluf wives and a daughter (MSCH 2669). His skeleton and that of a young woman are illustrated in Hyades, 1891. Garson (1886) described the osteological material made available by Fitz-Roy, and the Alakaluf who died in Europe in 1881–82 mentioned in Chapter 12.

In an article that same year, Hyades (1884b: 580–1) gave details of the sicknesses he treated in Orange Bay: an eye infection, which did not result in blindness, headaches, tonsillitis among some women, which lasted only two or three days. Bronchitis and troubles in the lungs happened rarely and were found not to be tuberculosis. There was some diarrhoea following too copious meals, also skin irritations and frequent rheumatism, though rarely severe. For curing by the Yahgan shamans and medicines used by them see Gusinde, 1986, vol. 3: 1435–40.
31. Bridges, in SAMM, 1883: 55–60.
32. Hyades, 1885a: 394–5.
33. Lawrence, in SAMM, 1883: 104–5.
34. Bridges, in SAMM, 1883: 57–8.
35. Hyades, 1885a: 410.
36. Hyades, 1891: 242, 243.

37. Hyades, 1885a: 410; also 1891: 22, 257–9.
38. See note 30 above and Hyades, 1883: 617–21 for a description of the two skeletons taken to Paris and Deniker's chapter in Hyades, 1891: 25–104 for analyses of all the osteological material (the two skeletons and the skulls) acquired by Hyades.

   Gusinde (1986, vol. 1: 325–6) quoted his informant Calderón (in 1922), who related that the sick Yahgans who went from the mission in Ushuaia to Orange Bay for treatment by the French (in 1882–83) always died and that the French had killed them, because "we saw there, near their houses, human bones that surely came from those who were sick." So far as I know, this is not true. Calderón may have simply invented this story or if he went to the French base in Orange Bay, he confused animal bones with human bones.
39. Hyades, 1885a: 406, 416; 1891: 223, 405–6. See 1891: 354–5 for details of Athlinata making a harpoon. Furlong also thought Athlinata was the most intelligent (Chapter 15).
40. Hyades, 1891: 234, 409.
41. Martial, 1888: 238. There is no account of Martial meeting Pinoense. He is identified as "Allen or Boumaouientsis." "Allen" undoubtedly refers to Allen Gardiner, his baptismal name. "Boumaouientsis" is another spelling of Pinouayentsis (written Pinoense), his real name.
42. This is the same visit to Paris referred to in Hyades, 1891: 405.
43. Bridges quoted (and translated) in Hyades, 1891: 407–8. I translated again, into English, as I didn't see Bridges' original text.
44. Martial, 1888: 82–93.
45. Martial, 1888: 222, 224.
46. Ibid., 61, 94–5, 226. During this first visit, Bridges agreed to keep a meteorological record for the entire year of the expedition's stay, using the instrument that Martial had given him.
47. Bridges, in SAMM, 1883: 61–2.
48. Martial, 1888: 113.
49. Bridges, in SAMM, 1883: 61; Martial, 1888: 115.
50. Martial, 1888: 117–19.
51. Martial (1888: 169–70) calculates that about 200 Yahgan camped in New Year's Sound, but six years later a missionary (Aspinal in SAMM, 1889: 244) heard that there were between 300 and 400 natives living there. If there were from 200 to 400 Yahgan living there, it is strange that Martial encountered so few. They may have hidden from the ship, fearful of being kidnapped. The first stop in New Year's Sound was Indian Cove, where Weddell had been in 1823 and Fitz-Roy in 1830. Fifty years later, there was no trace of anyone there.
52. Martial, 1888: 170–1.
53. Dominguez, 1883.
54. Martial, 1888: 12.
55. Bridges in SAMM, 1883: 273–4; Martial, 1888: 470.
56. Martial, 1888: 15–22, 180–1, 232, note 1. Chapter six of Martial's volume appears to have been mostly written by Hyades because no informants are

cited, sources very rarely, and because Hyades reiterated in his own volume (published in 1891) much of the contents of Martial's sixth chapter.

57. Bridges (SAMM, 1884: 154–61) made a chart of the names of 153 baptised in Ushuaia Yahgan (all but a few with their English names) to 1883. The dates of death of only fifty-four are indicated, among whom all but one died between 1881 and 1883, probably mostly from tuberculosis. The dates of death are not given for the other ninety-nine. This chart is followed by one of the thirty-eight orphans. This source should be studied in detail, as it may be possible to identify the Yahgans and thus to complete it.

58. Bridges (SAMM, 1884: 30–3, 223–4) subdivided the thousand as 273 men (whose clan names he registered, though they are not given in this letter), 314 adult females, 358 children, in addition to 55 orphans and very young children, making the total of 1,000. On the next page he gave, apparently based on the same inquiry, a total of 949 living in eight localities of Yahgan and Alakaluf territories to Brecknock Peninsula but did not include those living in Ushuaia. This is not clear. He probably calculated these numbers by estimates given to him by the natives as well as his own impressions while boating in the zone.

For the "Ona," both western (the Selk'nam) and eastern (the Haush), he gave the approximate number as 500, and for the Alakaluf 1,500. With the 1,000 Yahgans he calculated that at this time there were a total of 3,000 Fuegians in all. He certainly underestimated the population of the "Onas" at that time (1884). His total is based on 85 Ona men, whose names were given to him by a young Ona (Selk'nam) who was in Ushuaia in June 1884. This was just before the onslaught of the genocide had intensified, so they were many more than 500 still living in their own territory in Isla Grande. Gusinde (1982, vol. 1: 135) calculated the original "Ona" (Selk'nam and Haush) population as between 3,500 and 4,000. All these figures need to be restudied but for the time being I use Gusinde's figures.

59. Lawrence, in SAMM, 1884: 226–7. The reader of Italian should consult Giacomo Bove's second trip (February–April 1884) to Tierra del Fuego; see also Cooper, 1917: 72.

60. Bridges, in SAMM, 1884: 185.

61. Stirling, in SAMM, 1884: 269–70.

62. Chile (by 1881) was granted both coasts of the Strait of Magellan. The eastern entrance touches the Atlantic coast, thus giving Chile a thin line of territory to the Atlantic, cutting Argentina in two. This line is rarely seen on the maps of these two nations. Chile was also granted all the islands along the Pacific to Cape Horn, all the southern islands including Navarino Island (the southern coast of Beagle Channel) and somewhat more than half of the Isla Grande, which included some of the best pasture land for sheep and was found to be a source of oil later on. Argentina possessed the remaining half of the Isla Grande, which also included excellent land for grazing, and Staten Island.

63. Bridges, in SAMM, 1885: 8–10 (letter of 4 October 1884).

64. Bridges, in SAMM, 1885: 11–12.

65. L. Bridges, 1987: 124–7.

66. Whaits, in SAMM, 1885: 80–1; Gusinde (1986, vol. 3: 1276) is mistaken, as foxes were not reported on Navarino Island, but wild dogs were common by the nineteenth century.
67. Lawrence, in SAMM, 1885: 52, repeated on pp. 81–2. Italics in the original.
68. L. Bridges, 1987: 126.
69. Bridges, 1892: 317.
70. Bridges, in SAMM, 1886: 169–70, 217.
71. Hyades, 1891: 390.
72. Bridges, 1886a: 205.
73. Bridges, 1992: 317. J.C.T. Willis (SAMM, 1885: 127), noted that a visiting captain stated in February that "There are many places where the disease has not spread to, such as Wollaston Island and New Year's Sound." Three months later (1 June) Bridges (SAMM, 1885: 205–6) wrote that in the orphanage one boy was "rapidly wasting away. Two others we fear will not rally and the state of health of others is decidedly bad." He reported that four had died of measles during the past twelve months, that there were still some sick natives "but on the whole their health has greatly improved."
74. Chapman Journal, 1967: 10–12.
75. Lawrence, in SAMM, 1885: 127–8.
76. Hyades, 1885a: 395, note 1 (letter from Bridges dated March 1885) and Hyades in B.S.A. de Paris, 1886: 204. Measles was erroneously reported as pneumonia in October, after the Argentine ships had arrived in late September 1884.
77. CD Beagle, 435; also Payró (1898: 232–40, 244) refers to an epidemic about which he had heard that struck there or thereabouts, on Staten Island, in 1860, brought by crew members who were apparently perfectly healthy.
78. Bridges, in SAMM, 1885: 149–50.
79. Bridges, in SAMM, 1886: 34–5; Hemmings (SAMM, 1886: 172–3) also mentions ironing and baking bread as work the orphan girls performed.
80. Willis, in SAMM, 1886: 78; also Payró, 377.
81. Martinic, 2002: 255.
82. L. Bridges, 1987: chapter 18.
83. Gusinde, 1982, vol. 1: 140–52; Martinic, 1982: 45–118; 1989–90: 23–8; 2002: 255–8. See Lista (1887), Entraigas (1945: 233–47), and Padre Lorenzo Massa (1945: 305) for Lista's campaign of two and a half months beginning in November 1886, when he was accompanied by Monseñor Fagnano, the future director of the Salesian mission in Tierra del Fuego. For Popper's incursion (December 1886), see Odone and Palma, 2002, with numerous photographs taken by Popper.
84. I use the Gusinde (1982, vol. 1: 135) estimate of the original Selk'nam–Haush population as 3,500 to 4,000 until a more thorough analysis can be made.
85. For the occupation of the Isla Grande by the Punta Arenas and Buenos Aires businessmen and the genocide see especially Mateo Martinic, 1982; 1989–90; 1997: 110–26; also Chapman, 2002b: chapter 2.
86. Bridges, in SAMM, 1886: 33, 54–7. On p. 55, Bridges wrote about the families waiting to be helped across the river: "We found about twenty natives in them [in three native huts], with some eight dogs. That day they had killed a

guanaco. The general appearance of these people was pitiable." See Bridges' description of the contents of two of their bags, made of guanaco skin, because none of the objects were European.

87. Bridges, in SAMM, 1884: 181–5.
88. The suffix *waia* (or *uaia*) signifies a bay, as in Ushuaia.
89. L. Bridges, 1987: 137–8; Shipton, 1973: 139.
90. Bridges, in SAMM, 1886: 34.
91. Ibid., 101.
92. Lawrence, in SAMM, 1886: 172.
93. Deniker, in B.S.A. de Paris, 1892: 599; Ten-Kate, 1905: 33–41.
94. T. Bridges, in SAMM, 1886: 103, 217–18.
95. Whaits, in SAMM, 1890: 78; Stirling, in SAMM, 1895: 143; Lawrence, ibid., 159. Tenenesk became known mainly because Gusinde vividly described one of the last performances of the Selk'nam ceremony, known as Hain, in his volume on the Selk'nam, first published in German in 1931. Tenenesk was then, in 1923, the director of the Hain ceremony.
96. Bridges, in SAMM, 1884: 160; 1886: 219; Lawrence, ibid., 260–1.
97. Lawrence, in SAMM, 1887: 173–4; T. Bridges, ibid., 176.
98. L. Bridges, 1987: 136.
99. Bridges, in SAMM, 1885: 150, 206.
100. Lawrence, quoted in SAMM, 1890: 150.
101. Aspinal, SAMM, 1887: 219–20.
102. Anonymous author, SAMM, 1890: 150–1; Lawrence, SAMM, 1888: 216.
103. Utley, 1986: 179. "Sitting Bull, the Hunkpapa Sioux chieftain, held great power among the hunting bands that refused to settle on the reservation and fashioned the mighty coalition of tribes that overwhelmed Custer at the Little Big Horn [battle] in 1875. Forced to surrender in 1881, he remained resolutely opposed to all features of the government's civilization program. Indian policemen shot and killed him during the Ghost Dance troubles in 1890."

Chapter 14. 1887 to 1900: Other Fuegians Kidnapped; The Unending Epidemics; "Is God Very Far Away?"

1. Bridges, in SAMM, 1887: 175; Lucas Bridges, 1987: 141, 527; Captain Willis, in SAMM, 1887: 9; Aspinal, in SAMM, 1887: 222–4; ibid., 1888: 29–30, 76–7, 100.
2. Spears, 1895: 20.
3. Martinic, 1973: chapter 2; Bridges, in SAMM, 1888: 217.
4. Ince, in SAMM, 1890: 33.
5. Spears, 1895: 19, 23.
6. Martinic, 1973: chapter 2; Bridges, 1892: 320; L. Bridges, 1987: 175.
7. Mrs Hemmings, in SAMM, 1889: 31–3, 247.
8. Gusinde (1982: 152–3) clarified that although eleven were kidnapped, only nine appear in the photograph showing Maître with a cane beside them, because two had died by then.

9. The quotations of Dr Webster are from an unsigned article in the *Pall Mall Gazette*, 23 January 1890, reproduced in SAMM, 1890: 29–30.

10. See Báez and Mason, 2006; Mason, his chapter in Mason and Ordone; 2002a, for their stay in Brussels; also Mason, 2001 (26–8) and 2002b. Estraigas (1945: 345–6) for the Paris episode, though he does not mention the woman who died in London: Manouvrier (1894: 596) reported that one of the children died in Paris; also SAMM, 1890: 53, 76; though no author is cited. Again Gusinde, 1982: 152–3; and Beauvoir, 1901: 71–2; 1915: 15.

11. See Mason (2001: 19–54) also for artists, who have been inspired by such exhibits.

12. Mr Robins, in SAMM, 1891: 135; also a report on Keppel by Dean Brandon, in SAMM, 1894: 44–6.

13. Gusinde, 1986, vol. 1: 293.

14. Bridges, SAMM, 1886: 219, 260.

15. Aspinal, SAMM, 1888: 191.

16. Toomeecoo is not defined in Bridges' dictionary; *uchr* simply means dwelling.

17. Aspinal, in SAMM, 1888: 191–2, 239–41; Lewis, in SAMM, 1888: 218.

18. SAMM, 1888: 240–1. The concession was given for Grevy Island, three small adjacent islands and Hermite Island, at Cape West, where the mission was to maintain a lighthouse erected by the government and a lifeboat for service about Cape Horn. The governor of Magellan Straits (Chile) was instructed "to see that his decree is complied with."

19. This sentence was written by Nelly in the past narrative tense, beginning as follows: "we were their friends and that we had left our land...."

20. Martinic, 1980: 52; Burleigh, in SAMM, 1889: 267.

21. Mrs and Mr Burleigh, in SAMM, 1889: 33–6; L. Burleigh, in SAMM, 1889: 98–9.

22. L. Burleigh, in SAMM, 1889: 171.

23. Mrs Burleigh, in SAMM, 1889: 173.

24. Aspinal, in SAMM, 1889: 244.

25. L. Burleigh, in SAMM, 1889: 267–9.

26. Nelly Burleigh, in SAMM, 1890: 107.

27. L. Burleigh, in SAMM, 1889: 268–9.

28. Ibid., 269–70.

29. Stirling, 1890: 103.

30. Nelly Burleigh, in SAMM, 1890: 107–8.

31. Stirling, in SAMM, 1890: 102–4.

32. L. Burleigh, in SAMM, 1890: 176–7; Stirling, in SAMM, 1890: 103–4.

33. L. Burleigh, in SAMM, 1890: 198; Lawrence, in SAMM, 1891: 148.

34. L. Burleigh, SAMM, 1890: 199–202.

35. Aspinal, in SAMM, 1891: 7–10.

36. Lawrence, in SAMM, 1891: 133.

37. L. Burleigh, in SAMM, 1891: 95.

38. Stirling (SAMM, 1892: 523) described as an "overland passage." Actually it was a portage trail used by the Yahgans to go to and from New Year's Sound to the large bay called Allen Gardiner in Hoste Island, and the smaller Takenika Bay. See also the *Derrotero*, 271.

39. Mrs Burleigh, in SAMM, 1892: 156.
40. Biddle, 1995: 152; Lawrence, in SAMM, 1890: 82. On p. 105, Lawrence wrote: "Soon after the arrival of the Argentine relief steamer from Buenos Ayres some of the natives were taken ill with typhoid fever (some of the ship's crew being ill at the same time)."
41. Lawrence, in SAMM, 1890: 105–6.
42. Stirling, in SAMM, 1890: 102–5.
43. Bridges, in SAMM, 1890: 106; L. Bridges, 1987: 146.
44. Biddle, 1995: 127.
45. Aspinal, in SAMM, 1890: 271.
46. Ibid., 1891: 7–8.
47. Ibid., 1891: 7–10; Lawrence, in SAMM, 1892: 28.
48. Biddle, 1995: 25.
49. Godoy, 1893: 395. Godoy's term as governor lasted to 1899.
50. Lawrence, in SAMM, 1891: 131–2.
51. Ibid., 1892: 27–8.
52. Ibid., 1893: 166; 1895: 193.
53. Biddle, 1995: 81.
54. Lawrence, in SAMM, 1893: 39–41.
55. Ibid., 132–4.
56. L. Bridges, 1987: 459; Canclini, 1983: 72, 80–1.
57. L. Burleigh, in SAMM, 1892: 152–4; 1893: 22.
58. Ibid., SAMM, 1893: 38–9.
59. Nelly Burleigh, in SAMM, 1893: 23, 114.
60. Ibid., in SAMM, 1894: 26–7.
61. Nelly Burleigh (SAMM, 1896: 129) wrote this account more than three years after she had left the Tekeenica Mission.
62. L. Burleigh, in SAMM, 1894: 56.
63. Pringle, in SAMM, 1894: 59.
64. Mrs Burleigh, in SAMM, 1894: 55–6.
65. Stirling, in SAMM, 1894: 68–9.
66. Pringle, in SAMM, 1895: 59–60.
67. Stirling, in SAMM, 1894: 68–9.
68. Pringle, in SAMM, 1895: 59–60.
69. L. Bridges, 1987: 527. There is an Ipswich in England as well as Australia.
70. Lawrence, in SAMM, 1895: 160.
71. Perich, 1985: 66–7. *El Magallanes* (11 August 1895, año 2, no. 86), a newspaper of Punta Arenas, published a long article repeating the version given by Lawrence, adding that the guilty sealers claimed that the Indians had intended to attack them. The author of the article insisted that all who navigated in these channels knew very well that the Indians were inoffensive. He urged the governors of Magallanes and of Tierra del Fuego to prosecute the guilty pair so as to avoid such events in the future.
72. Lawrence, in SAMM, 1895: 62–3.
73. Spears, 1895: 73–8.
74. Pringle, in SAMM, 1899: 96–8. A photograph, on exhibit in Puerto Williams at the museum named in honour of Father Gusinde, shows a group of fifty people in the "Tekineeca Mission." It was probably taken about this date.

Among them the following may be easily identified: thirty-nine Yahgans in addition to five white men. Among the babies is Rosa Yagan and among the women Grete, later called Abuela Chacona. The latter became one of Gusinde's informants; the former, Rosa Yagan, became the subject of a very appealing biography edited by Patricia Stambuk.

75. Pringle, in SAMM, 1899: 190.
76. Martinic, 1973: 101–12; Aylwin, 1995: 38–9.
77. Lawrence, in SAMM, 1901: 318.
78. Article (author not noted) in SAMM, 1900: 55–6; 1911: 129, 158. Mr Whaits continued working as manager of the farm until 1911, when the farm was sold.
79. Lawrence, in SAMM, 1899: 150, 216.
80. Scrofula, also called tuberculosis *cutis colliquativa*, is diagnosed as suppurating abscesses and fistulous passages opening on the skin and as tuberculosis of lymph nodes most common on the neck (scrofula). It is known to be a disease of early life. Gusinde, 1986, vol. 3: 1044.
81. Lawrence, in SAMM, 1900: 54–5; 1901: 169.

Chapter 15. The Twentieth Century: Ushuaia, the Ancient Yamana Campsite, Becomes a City

1. Pringle, in SAMM, 1902: 49.
2. Ibid., 1901: 221, 283.
3. Dabbene, 1902: 30–2; 1911: 206.
4. Anonymous, SAMM 1901: 169; 1902: 50, 178, 277.
5. Furlong, 1909b: 130–6.
6. Ibid. The rest of Furlong's story, of the wrestling matches, the mourning scene and the vengeance of the two widows against the murderer is too long to include here.
7. Avery, in Barclay, 1926: 146.
8. Furlong, 1917a: 430 (see also p. 26).
9. Cristina Calderón, Chapman's recording, 1987: 2, 4–6, 160–2; 1988: 27–31.
10. Hermelinda Acuña, in Chapman Journal, 1987: 16–17.
11. Ursula Calderón, in Chapman Journal, 1987: 11, 24–5; 1988: 64–70.
12. Lawrence, in SAMM, 1901: 318.
13. It was usual to locate national penitentiaries far beyond the mother country and in any case as far as possible from the more populated areas, ideally where escape would be worse than confinement. Chile's national penitentiary was located in faraway Punta Arenas until 1868. France had her *bagnes* in French Guyana, New Caledonia and Algeria and England had hers in Australia.
14. Furlong, 1909a: 338–9.
15. Vairo, 1997: 103, 125. This rather recent work is a very informative account of the former prison before it was converted into a museum.
16. Martinic, 1973: chapter 4.
17. Lipschutz and Mostny (1946: 306–7) counted thirty-nine Yahgans in the Mejillones Reserve in 1945 and thirty-four more who considered themselves or were considered by others as Yahgan, Alakaluf or Ona or crosses between these three groups. Once, while Lipschutz was taking photographs of them,

a lad of sixteen rode by him on horseback, and shouted: "I don't want to have my picture in the papers... I don't want to be an aborigine." See also Ortiz-Troncoso, 1973.

18. Lawrence, in SAMM, 1913: 145; also Bridges, in SAMM, 1912: 78. Barclay (T. Bridges, 1987: XIII) wrote: "In 1908 the tribe numbered only 170." Cooper (1946: 83) stated that the population in 1899 was 200, but by 1902 it had dwindled to 130 and in 1913 to less than 100. Furlong (1917c: 181) estimated the total population in 1907–8 at 175 and that ten years later "possibly not more than 100 remain."

19. SAMM, 1915: 39; SAMM, 1916: 129; Canclini, 1983: 98; Furlong, 1917a; Gusinde, 1986, vol. 1: 221, 296; Martinic, 1973: 114, 119–20; also 1980: 20; SAMM, 1902: 50.

20. Aylwin, 1995: 36.

21. For Gusinde's volumes translated from German into Spanish and English see the Bibliography. Unfortunately none of these volumes include an analytical index. The German historian–archivist Anton Quack recently published comments on Gusinde's work, which have been translated into English (also in the Bibliography).

22. Gusinde, 1986, vol. 1: 175, and vol. 3: 1114.

23. Canclini, 1983: 92.

24. Besides Canclini, ibid., for references to Nelly see Gusinde, 1986, vol. 1: XXII, 167–9, 172–3, 189; vol. 2: 778–9; vol. 3: 1365, 1376; and Koppers, 1997: 175–8. L. Bridges (1987: 520) mentions a measles epidemic in 1924 in "Ona Land," which is probably the same one that spread to Ushuaia.

25. Rosa Clemente, in Chapman Journal, 1987: 42.

26. Chapman Journal, 1988: 15, 185; 1987: 41.

27. Rosa Clemente, in ibid., 1987: 73–86; 1988: 117–23.

28. Though the Kina was influenced by the Hain ceremony of the Selk'nam, it had many scenes and personages that were exclusively its own. Also the women were treated more equally than the Selk'nam women during the Hain. For the Hain, besides Gusinde and Koppers, see Lowie, 1938; Chapman, 1982: chapters 3 to 10 and 2002a.

29. The Kina again: Gusinde was told that the Kina had been presented the last time some twenty years before, at the beginning of the twentieth century. I suggest that it had been performed in the interlude because Gusinde gathered most of his data from informants who had participated in a Kina, obviously in more recent times. He wrote seventy-three pages on the subject (1986, vol. 3: 1286–339), and Koppers wrote twenty-three pages (1997: 98–120).

30. The Chexaus: Lowie (1952) thought that formerly it was only for young male initiates. The first presentation for Gusinde, in 1920, lasted ten days and the second, with Koppers in 1922, only six days. Gusinde's "Chiexaus" photographs are the only illustrations known. Even though he stated (1986, vol. 1: 348) that the Chexaus had not been presented since 1890, three of his informants told him (1986, vol. 2: 836, 844) that they had been initiated in the Chexaus fifteen years afterwards, which meant in 1905. Rosa Yagan (Stambuk, 1986: 43–5, 80, 83–4) was initiated in a Chexaus about 1910, and she participated in many others. Gusinde wrote about 170 pages on the

ceremony (1986, vol. 1: 175–83; vol. 2: 771–929; vol. 3: 1288–92); and Koppers over fifty (1997: 47–98). Thomas Bridges (1987: 203) spelt Chexaus as "ja-kaus" and defined it as "rites and ceremonies (being superstitious, lying, obscure, dramatic and semi-religious plays)." He often (ibid., 203, 262, 276, 659) referred to it as the Murana drama (another name for the "sacred wigwam"). For a comparison of the Chexaus and the Hain ceremonies, see Chapman, 1997.

31. Ursula, in Chapman Journal, 1987: 1; Gusinde, 1986, vol. 2: 805–7.

32. Ibid., 840–52.

33. Gusinde published many of the myths recited during the Chexaus in his Yamana volumes, most of which Wilbert (1975) translated into English.

34. Hermelinda, in Chapman Journal, 1987: 17; Cristina in ibid., 1988: 189; Ursula in ibid., 1987: 37–8.

35. Gusinde, 1986, vol. 2: 889–90; also Ursula in Chapman Journal, 1987: 76, 203; 1988: 194–5.

36. Koppers, 1997: 87.

37. Ursula, in Chapman Journal, 1987: 41; 1988: 2.

38. Gusinde, 1986, vol. 2: 817–18. The Yetaite scene resembles that of the Shoort spirit of the Selk'nam Hain ceremony and the initiation rite resembles that to which the Selk'nam youth, the *kloketen*, were submitted, though the Yahgan rite was less violent and less dramatic.

39. Ursula, in Chapman Journal, 1987: 45–6; Hermelinda, ibid., 1988: 91.

40. Ursula and Cristina, in Chapman Journal, 1987: 10, 24–5, 37; 1988: 86, 190–2; Hermelinda, in ibid., 1988: 68–9. Also Gusinde, 1986, vol. 2: 771–928.

41. Hermelinda, in Chapman Journal, 1987: 9–11, 15, 38–41; Ursula in ibid., 1988: 187–8. See also Stambuk (1986: 43–5, 80, 84) for the initiation of Rosa Yagan (Abuela Rosa) in a Chexaus (spelt chiajóus) when she was young, about 1910, in the Douglas mission station and later in Mejillones Bay.

42. Cristina, in Chapman Journal, 1988: 191–3.

43. Cristina, in ibid., 1987: 35–6; 1988: 193–8.

44. In *Current Biography*, 1942, on Rockwell Kent.

45. Kent, 1968: 447–9.

46. Rosa Yagan (Stambuk, 1986: 18) had also heard a similar story: Burleigh was having "an affair" with a pretty Yahgan woman in the shed when her daughter surprised them. He felt so ashamed that he took a boat and went into the turbulent waters of the bay, where he drowned.

47. Kent, 1968: 132–4, 154, 163–76, 183–4.

48. See Spencer's Tierra del Fuego journal, edited by R. R. Marett and T. K. Penniman in 1931.

49. Abuela Julia told Ursula (Chapman Journal, 1988: 108) that she had heard about a grandmother who lived long ago who understood all that the gulls talked about when they shouted *ka ka*. While she would be sitting in her hut, a gull would come by and give her the news. This was how she knew what was going on in other places. Only the gulls spoke to her, no other birds.

50. For the myth of Hanush, see Gusinde, 1986, vol. 3: 1262–8.
51. Miss Hamilton wrote the last seventy-nine pages (44 to 123) following Spencer's journal as edited by Marett and Penniman (1931). Alfredo Prieto, an archaeologist of Punta Arenas, recently informed me that he had visited Spencer's grave in the cemetery of Punta Arenas, where he was buried in 1929.
52. See Vairo (1997: 130) for the political prisoners who had arrived with Professor Rojas on 13 January 1934, who had opposed the military coup.
53. For instance, after he had returned to Buenos Aires, he published an article entitled "Problema Indigena" in 1948.
54. Rojas, 1942: 10.
55. Ibid., 17.
56. Augustín Clemente, was one of the last Fuegians to work on the Bridges' Harberton farm. The municipal government in Ushuaia took care of him during his final years and paid for his treatment for cancer in Cordoba, where he died in 1969.
57. Rojas, 1942, passim.
58. Aylwin, 1995: 41.
59. Cristina Zárraga, 2005. *Hai kur mamashu shis*, editorial *El Kultün*, Puerto Williams, Chile. The title is in Yahgan. The book presents myths and legends told to Zárraga by her grandmother Cristina Calderón and is published in Spanish and English with beautiful drawings.

Bibliography

Abbreviations

AG-D	"Journal of Allen F. Gardiner," in Despard, 1854.
A.I.P.	Anales del Instituto de la Patagonia, Punta Arenas, Chile.
B.S.A. de Paris	Bulletin de la Société d'Anthropologie de Paris.
C.A.	Current Anthropology.
CCD	Burkhardt, Frederick, and Sydney Smith (eds.). *The Correspondence of Charles Darwin* (13 volumes from 1985 to 2002), Cambridge University Press.
CD Autobio	Barlow, Nora. *Autobiography of Charles Darwin.* 1958.
CD Beagle	Darwin, Charles. *The Voyage of the Beagle.* L. Engle (ed. and introduction). 1962.
CD Descent	Darwin, Charles. *The Descent of Man, and Selection in Relation to Sex.* 1981 (from his revised edition).
CD Diary 1933	Barlow, Nora (ed.). *Charles Darwin's Diary of the Voyage of H.M.S., "Beagle."* Cambridge University Press, 1933.
CD Diary 1988	Keynes, Richard Darwin (ed.). *Charles Darwin's Beagle Diary.* Cambridge University Press, 1988.
CD Emotions	Darwin, Charles. *The Expression of the Emotions in Man and Animals,* with introduction by Konrad Lorenz. University of Chicago Press, 1965.
FR, 1839	Fitz-Roy, Robert (editor and author of most of the text). Title below.
HSAI	*Handbook of South American Indians,* Smithsonian Institution, Bureau of American Ethnology. Bulletin 143, 1946: Reprint by Cooper Square Publishers Inc., New York, 1963.
Hyades, 1891	Hyades and Deniker, 1891, Title below.
J.S.A.	*Journal de la Société des Américanistes.*
JM-D	"Journal of John Maidment," in Despard, 1854.
PK, 1839	Parker King (Robert Fitz-Roy was the editor of the volume and author of much of this text, even though Parker King appears as the author). Title below.
RW-D.	"Journal of Richard Williams," in Despard, 1854.

SAMM   *South American Missionary Magazine.* The Patagonian Missionary Society changed its name in 1867 to the South American Missionary Society and the name of its journal, also in 1867. It continued to be published until the 1920s in London. See below, V. of P. and V. for S.A.

V. of P.   *Voice of Pity for South America* – the first journal of the Patagonian Missionary Society, London, 1854–1862.

V. for S.A.   *Voice for South America*: continuation of the above from 1863 to 1866.

Notes For the Reader

1. None of the titles of the articles in the Anglican mission magazine (see directly above) are mentioned below. Such a listing would overload this Bibliography and is not necessary. The articles are indicated by the author, volume and pages in the notes at the end of the book.

2. All translations from Spanish, French and German to English have been done by me unless otherwise indicated.

3. The locations of the university presses are not always mentioned. When the publisher of a "work" has more than one locality (usually a city), that is, when the publisher is located in a number of localities; then only the first is noted.

4. The date of the original or first publication of a book is in brackets next to date of the edition consulted.

5. The bibliography which follows includes some titles that are not cited as references but which were important to me to understand certain subjects, as for instance Darwin.

Aguilera F., Oscar E. 2001 *Gramática de la Lengua Kawésqar.* LOM Ediciones Ltda, Santiago, Chile.

2003 Personal communication.

Albion, Robert, et al. 1972 *New England and the Sea.* Mystic Seaport Museum.

Alexandria, Virginia 1998 *The First Americans.* Silver Burdett, Morristown, NJ.

Alland, Alexander, Jr. 1985 *Human Nature: Darwin's View.* Columbia University Press.

Alonso, Diana 1991 *Memoria y Olvido* (novel about the Yamana), Buenos Aires.

Anson, George 1748 *A Voyage Round the World in the Years 1740, 1, 2, 3, 4...* London.

Armstrong, Eduardo, see Barros, Alvaro.

Aylwin Oyarzún, José 1995 *Comunidades Indígenas de los Canales Australes: Antecedentes Históricos y Situación Actual.* Arena Impresores, Santiago, Chile.

Báez, Christian, and Peter Mason 2006 *Zoológicos humanos. Fotografías de fueguinos y mapuche en el Jardin d'Acclimatation en Paris, siglo XIX.* Pehuén Editores, Santiago, Chile.

Bancel, Nicolas, et al. 2002 *Zoos Humains XIX et XX siècles.* Editions la Découverte, Paris.

Barbance, Marthe 1969 *Vie Commerciale de la Route du Cap Horn au XIXe Siècle.* A. A. Bordes et Fils. Paris.

Barclay, William S. 1926 *The Land of Magellan*. London.

1987 "Preface," in Thomas Bridges, 1987.

Barlow, Nora 1933 *Charles Darwin's Diary of the Voyage of H.M.S. "Beagle."* Cambridge University Press, Cambridge, UK. (This is the first publication of his diary: see Keynes for the complete text.)

1958 *The Autobiography of Charles Darwin 1809–1882* (With the original omission restored.). W.W. Norton, New York.

Barrett, Paul H., Peter J. Gautrey, Sandra Herbert, David Kohn, and Sydney Smith 1987 *Charles Darwin's Notebooks 1836–1844*. Cornell University Press.

Barros, Alvaro, and Eduardo Armstrong 1975 *Aborígenes Australes de América*. Editorial Lord Cochrane, Santiago, Chile.

Barros, José Miguel 1999 "El Canal Beagle: Un Descubrimiento del Siglo XVI." *Boletín de la Academia Chilena de la Historia*, no. 107: 197–211, Santiago, Chile.

Barth, Fredrik 1947 "Cultural Development in Southern South America: Yahgan and Alakaluf vs. Ona and Tehuelche." *Acta Americana*, vol. 6: 192–9.

Beaglehole, John C. 1961 *The Journals of Captain James Cook on His Voyages of Discovery. The Voyage of the Resolution & the Adventure 1772–1775*. Cambridge University Press, Cambridge, UK.

1968a *The Journals of Captain James Cook on His Voyages of Discovery. The Voyage of the Endeavour 1768–1771*. Cambridge University Press, Cambridge, UK.

1968b *The Exploration of the Pacific*. Stanford University Press.

1974 *The Life of Captain James Cook*. Stanford University Press.

Beauvoir, José María 1901 "Memorias del R. B. Beauvoir. Misionero Salesiano." *Boletín Salesiano*, año XXII: 71–2.

1902 Ibid., año XXIII: 215–17.

1915 *Diccionario. Los Shelknam. Indigenas de la Tierra del Fuego: Sus tradiciones, costumbres y lengua*. (A facsimile edition has been published by the Editorial Ateli, Punta Arenas, Chile, 1997.)

Belza, Juan E. 1974 *En la isla del Fuego, Encuentros*. Instituto de Investigaciones Históricas de Tierra del Fuego, Buenos Aires.

1978 Ibid. *Romancero del Toponimo Fueguino*.

Bender, Barbara, and Brian Morris 1988 "Twenty years of history, evolution and social change in gatherer-hunter societies," in Ingold et al., 4–14.

Beauchesne (see Duplessis)

Biddle, Wayne 1995 *A Field Guide to Germs*. Doubleday, New York.

Billinghurst, Jean 2000 *The Spirit of the Whale: Legend, History, Conservation*. Grantown on Spey, Scotland.

Bird, Junius 1938 "Antiquity and Migrations of the Early Inhabitants of Patagonia." *Geographical Review*, vol. 28, no. 2: 250–75.

1946a "The Archaeology Patagonia," in HSAI, vol. I: 17–24.

1946b "The Alacaluf," in HSAI, vol. I: 55–79.

1988 (see Hyslop).

Bonner, John Tyler 1988 *The Evolution of Culture in Animals*. Princeton University Press.

Bonner, John Tyler, and Robert M. May 1981 "Introduction," in Charles Darwin, *The Descent of Man, and Selection in Relation to Sex*.

Boon, James A. 1983 *Other Tribes, Other Scribes. Symbolic Anthropology in the Comparative Study of Cultures, Histories, Religions, and Texts.* Cambridge University Press, Cambridge, UK.

Boorstin, Daniel J. 1983 *The Discoverers: A History of Man's Search to Know His World and Himself.* Random House, New York.

Borrero, Luis Alberto 1997 "The Origins of ethnographic subsistence patterns in Fuego-Patagonia," in McEwan et al., 60–81.

Borrero, Luis Alberto, and Colin McEwan 1997 "The Peopling of Patagonia," in McEwan et al., 32–45.

Bove, Giacomo 1883 *Expedición austral argentina. Informes preliminares presentados a S.S.E.E. los ministros del Interior y de Guerra y Marina de la República Argentina.* Instituto Geográfico Argentino, Buenos Aires.

Bowlby, John 1991 *Charles Darwin: A New Life.* W.W. Norton, New York.

Bowler, Peter J. 1984 *Evolution: The History of an Idea.* University of California Press.

1993 *Darwinism.* Twayne Publishers, New York.

1996 [1990] *Charles Darwin: The Man and His Influence.* Cambridge University Press, Cambridge, UK.

Boyson, V. 1924 *The Falkland Islands.* Clarendon Press, Oxford, UK.

Braun Menéndez, Armand 1945 *Pequeña Historia Fueguina.* EMECE editores, Buenos Aires.

Bridges, E. Lucas 1987 [1948] *Uttermost Part of the Earth.* Century Hutchinson Ltd., London.

2008 (New edition in English of the above.)

Bridges, Thomas 1885 An extract from a letter by Bridges to Prof. Flower, dated August 24, 1884. *Journal of the Anthropological Institute of Great Britain and Ireland*, vol. 14: 288–9.

1886a "El Confín sur de la República: La Tierra del Fuego y sus habitantes." *Boletín de la Sociedad de Geografía* (Buenos Aires), tomo VII, 200–12.

1886b in Hyades, *B.S.A. de Paris*, vol. IX: 202–4.

1892 "Datos sobre Tierra del Fuego." *Revista del Museo de la Plata*, vol. III: 19–32, 313–20.

1893 "La Tierra del Fuego y sus Habitantes." *Boletín del Instituto Geográfico Argentino*, vol. XIV: 221–41.

1894 "A few notes on the structure of Yagan." *Journal of the Anthropological Institute* (London), tome 23: 53–80.

1987 [1933] *Yamana–English: A Dictionary of the Speech of Tierra del Fuego.* Dr Ferdinand Hestermann and Dr Martin Gusinde (eds.), with a new preface by Natalie Goodall. Zagier y Urruty Publicaciones, Buenos Aires.

Briones, Claudia, and José Luis Lanata (eds.) 2002 *Archaeological and Anthropological Perspectives on the Native Peoples of Pampa, Patagonia, and Tierra del Fuego to the Nineteenth Century.* Bergin & Garvey, Westport, CT.

Brosses, Charles de 1756, *Histoire des navigations aux terres australes.* 2 vols. Chez Durand, Paris.

Browne, Janet 1994 "Missonaries and the Human Mind: Charles Darwin and Robert FitzRoy," in MacLeod and Rehbock (eds.), 263–79.

1995 *Charles Darwin Voyaging.* Pimlico, Random House, London.

2002 *Charles Darwin: The Power of Place.* Alfred A. Knopf, New York.

Brüggemann, Anne von 1989 "Der Trauernde Blick: Martin Gusindes Fotos der Letzten Feuerland-Indianer." *Interim* 7. Museum für Volkerkunde, Frankfort am Main.

Bry, Theodor de 1590–1634 *Americae.* Frankfurt am Main.

Burgess, Lewis 1998 Personal communication.

Burkhardt, Frederick, and Sydney Smith (eds.) 1985–2008 *The Correspondence of Charles Darwin.* 16 vols. (covering the years 1821–68). Cambridge University Press, Cambridge, UK.

Burney, James 1807 *A Chronological History of the Discoveries in the South Seas and Pacific Ocean.* 5 vols., London.

Burrow, J. W. 1968 *Evolution and Society: A Study in Victorian Social Theory.* Cambridge University Press, Cambridge, UK.

Busch, Briton Cooper 1985 *A History of the North American Seal Fishery.* McGill–Queen's University Press.

Callander, John 1766 *Terra Australis Cognita or Voyages to the Terra Australis.* 3 vols. Da Capo Press, New York.

Cañas Pinochet, Alejandro 1911 "La Geografía de la Tierra del Fuego y noticias de la antropología y etnografía de sus habitantes." *Trabajos de la III Sección Ciencias naturales, Antropológicas y Etnológicas,* vol. XI, tomo I, Santiago, Chile.

Canclini, Arnoldo 1959a *Últimos Documentos del Capitán Allen F. Gardiner.* Editorial y Libería "La Aurora." Buenos Aires.

1959b *Diario de Ricardo Williams.* Ibid.

1979 *Allen F. Gardiner: marino, misionero, mártir.* Marymar, Buenos Aires.

1980 *Waite H. Stirling. El centinela de Dios en Ushuaia.* Marymar, Buenos Aires.

1981 "La Misión cristiana más austral del mundo." *Karukinka,* no. 27: 72–83.

1983 *Juan Lawrence. Primer maestro de Tierra del Fuego.* Marymar, Buenos Aires.

1984 *Ushuaia 1884–1984 Cien años de una ciudad Argentina.* Arnoldo Canclini (ed.). Municipality of Ushuaia, Tierra del Fuego, Argentina.

1986 *Tierra del Fuego: su historia y sus historias.* Galerna, Buenos Aires.

1992 *Así nació Ushuaia. Orígenes de la ciudad más austral del mundo.* Plus Ultra, Buenos Aires.

1998 *El Fueguino: Jemmy Button y los Suyos.* Editorial Sudamericana, Buenos Aires.

1999 *Navegantes, presos y pioneros en la Tierra del Fuego.* Planeta, Buenos Aires.

2007 *Darwin y los Fueguinos.* Zagier & Urruty Publicaciones, Buenos Aires.

Cap Horn, 1882–1883: Rencontre avec les Indiens Yahgan. Collection de la Photothèque du Musée de l'Homme. Editions de la Martinière, Muséum National d'Histoire Naturelle, et la Photothèque du Musée de l'Homme, Paris. 1995.

Centre National de la Recherche Scientifique 1982 *L'importance de l'Exploration Maritime du siecle des Lumières (A propos du voyage de Bougainville).* Editions du C.N.R.S., Paris.

Chagnon, Napoleon A. 1968 *Yanomani. The Fierce People*. Holt, Reinhart and Winston, New York.

Chagnon, Napoleon A., and William Irons (eds.) 1979 *Evolutionary Biology and Human Social Behavior: An Anthropological Perspective*. Duxbury Press, North Scituate, MA.

Chapman, Anne 1965–88 *Journals of Field Work among the Selk'nam and Yamana*. Typescript.

    1972 *Selk'nam Chants of Tierra del Fuego, Argentina*, vol. I: two records sung by Lola Kiepja: 34 shamanistic chants, 10 laments, 1 lullaby and 2 chants learned in the mission: in collaboration with the Department of Music, Musée de l'Homme, Paris: originally produced by Folkways Inc., # FE 4176. Reissued in two cassettes by the Smithsonian Institution in 1993, Folkways Cassette Series: 04176.

    1978 *Selk'nam Chants of Tierra del Fuego, Argentina*, vol. II: two records also sung by Lola Kiepja: 40 chants of the "Hain" ceremony and 1 chant of the guanaco: in collaboration with the Department of Music, the Musée de l'Homme, Paris: also originally produced by Folkways Inc., # 4179. Reissued in two cassettes by the Smithsonian Institution in 1993. Folkways Cassette Series: 04179.

    1980–81 "Barter as a Universal Mode of Exchange." *L'Homme*, vol. XXI: 33–83.

    1982 *Drama and Power in a Hunting Society. The Selk'nam of Tierra del Fuego*. Cambridge University Press, Cambridge, UK (out of print).

    1987 *Isla de los Estados en la Prehistoria. Primeros datos arqueológicos*. EUDEBA, Buenos Aires.

    1987 Journal; see first entry.

    1988 Ibid.

    1993 *Selk'nam. La Vida de los Onas*. EMECE editores, Buenos Aires (translation of 1982 and reedited in Spanish in 2007).

    1995a "Carrupale kipa parle," in *Cap Horn, 1882–1883: Rencontre avec les Indiens Yahgan. Collection de la Photothèque du Musée de l'Homme*, 17–24.

    1995b "Première année polaire internationale," in *Cap Horn, 1882–1883: Rencontre avec les Indiens Yahgan. Collection de la Photothèque du Musée de l'Homme*, 41–6.

    1995c "Les sept voyages du Commandant Martial," in *Cap Horn, 1882–1883: Rencontre avec les Indiens Yahgan. Collection de la Photothèque du Musée de l'Homme*, 49–86.

    1995d "Compte rendu du livre 'Three Men of the Beagle' de Richard Lee Marks." J.S.A., tome 81: 367–70.

    1997 "The Great Ceremonies of the Selk'nam and the Yamana. A Comparative Analysis," in McEwan et al. (eds.), 82–109.

    2002a *Hain. Initiation Ceremony of the Selk'nam*. Taller Experimental Cuerpos Pintados, Santiago, Chile.

    2002b *End of a World: The Selk'nam of Tierra del Fuego*. Taller Experimental Cuerpos Pintados, Santiago, Chile.

    2002c "Brief History of the Yamana from the Late Sixteenth Century to the Present," in Mason and Odone (eds.), 193–230.

2003 *El fenómeno de la canoa yagán.* Universidad Marítima de Chile, Viña del Mar, Chile.

2004 *La genealogía de mis profesores e informantes.* Universidad de Buenos Aires.

2006 *Darwin in Tierra del Fuego.* Imago Mundi, Buenos Aires.

2007 [1993] *Los Selk'nam. La vida de los Onas.* EMECE-Planeta, Buenos Aires (second edition of the translation of the 1982 edition).

2008a New edition of 2002a in English. Zagier & Urruty Publications, Buenos Aires.

2008b New edition of 2002b in English. Ibid.

2008c *Quand le Soleil voulait tuer la lune: rituals et théâtre chez les Selk'nam de Terre de Feu.* Métailié, Paris.

Chapman, Anne, and Thomas R. Hester 1975 "New Data on the Archaeology of the Haush: Tierra del Fuego." J.S.A., tome 62: 185–208.

Chapman, Walter (ed.) 1965 *Antarctic Conquest: the Great Explorers in Their Own Words.* Selected and introduction by Walter Chapman. The Bobbs-Merrill, Indianapolis.

Chatwin, Bruce 1977 *In Patagonia.* Summit Books, New York.

Chevallay, Denis 1999 "Historia de la Casa Stirling 1868–1998. La edificación más antigua de la Tierra del Fuego." *Actas IV Congreso de Historia de Magallanes,* 185–98. Punta Arenas, Chile.

Clark, Ronald W. 1984 *The Survival of Charles Darwin. A Biography of a Man and an Idea.* Random House, New York.

Cohen, I. Bernard 1985 *Revolution in Science.* Harvard University Press.

Colnett, James 1968 [1798] "A Voyage to the South Atlantic and Round Cape Horn into the Pacific Ocean." *Bibliotheca Australiana,* no. 36. Amsterdam and Da Capo Press, New York.

Coloane, Francisco 2000 *Los Pasos del Hombre, Memorias.* Mondadori, Barcelona.

Columbia Encyclopedia 1950 2nd ed., Columbia University Press, New York.

Colvocoresses, George M. 1852 *Four Years in a Government Exploring Expedition.* Cornish, Lamport, New York.

Comaroff, John, and Jean Comaroff 1992 *Ethnography and the Historical Imagination.* Westview Press, Boulder, CO.

Cook, Captain James (see Beaglehole).

Coon, Carleton S. 1971 *The Hunting Peoples.* Little, Brown & Co., Boston.

Cooper, John M. 1917 Analytical and critical bibliography of the tribes of Tierra del Fuego and adjacent Territory. *Smithsonian Institution, Bureau of American Ethnology,* Bulletin 63, Washington, DC.

1924 "Culture Diffusion and Culture Areas in Southern South America." *International Congress of Americanists, Proceedings:* 406–21, Goteborg.

1946a "The Yahgan." HSAI, vol. I, 81–106.

1946b "The Ona." Ibid., 107–25.

Corbey, Raymond 1993 "Ethnographic show cases: 1870–1930." *Cultural Anthropology,* vol. 8, no. 3: 338–65.

Crow, John A. 1980 *The Epic of Latin America.* University of California Press.

Dabbene, Roberto 1904 "Viaje a la Tierra del Fuego y a la Isla de los Estados." *Boletín del Instituto Geográfico Argentino*, tomo 21: 3–78.

    1911 "Los indígenas de la Tierra del Fuego." Ibid., tomo 25: 162–226, 246–300.

Dampier, William 1906 [1723] *Dampier's Voyages*. John Masefield (ed.), 2 vols., Grant Richards, London.

Darling, James D. 1988 "Whales: An Era of Discovery." *National Geographic*, vol. 174: 872–909.

Darwin, Charles (for more of his original writings see Barrett et al.; Burkhardt and Smith, 1986–2008; Francis Darwin, 1887; Nora Barlow, 1933; Sandra Herbert, 2005; and Richard Darwin Keynes, 1988).

    1962 [1845] *The Voyage of the Beagle*. Edited with an introduction by Leonard Engel. A Doubleday Anchor Book. The American Museum of Natural History, New York.

    1965 [1872] *The Expression of the Emotions in Man and Animals*. Preface by Konrad Lorenz. University of Chicago Press.

    1981 [1871] *The Descent of Man, and Selection in Relation to Sex*. Introduction by John Tyler Bonner and Robert M. May. Princeton University Press.

    1995 [1859] *On the Origin of Species by Means of Natural Selection*. A facsimile of the first edition with an introduction by Ernest Mayr. Harvard University Press.

Darwin, Francis (editor and author) 1887 *The Life and Letters of Charles Darwin, Including an Autobiographical Chapter*. 2 vols. D. Appleton & Company, New York.

    1958 *The Autobiography of Charles Darwin and Selected Letters*. Dover Publications, New York.

    1995 [1902] *The Life of Charles Darwin*. Studio Editions Ltd, London.

Dawkins, Richard 1986 *The Blind Watchmaker. Why the Evidence of Evolution Reveals a Universe without Design*. W.W. Norton, New York.

Deacon, Terrence W. 1997 *The Symbolic Species. The Co-evolution of Language and the Brain*. W.W. Norton, New York.

Degler, Carl N. 1991 *In Search of Human Nature*. Oxford University Press, Oxford, UK.

Deniker, Joseph 1884 Review of Virchow 1881. *Revue d'Anthropologie*, VII: 181–3.

    1991 see Hyades and Deniker.

Dennett, Daniel C. 1995 *Darwin's Dangerous Idea. Evolution and the Meaning of Life*. Simon and Schuster, New York.

Denton, Michael 1996 *Evolution: A Theory in Crisis*. Adler and Adler Publishers, Bethesda, MD.

"Derrotero de la Costa de Chile." Vol. V. *Tierra del Fuego y Canales e Islas Adyacentes*. 1973, 6th ed. Instituto Hidrográfico de la Armada, Valparaíso, Chile.

Desmond, Adrian, and James Moore 1992 *Darwin. The Life of a Tormented Evolutionist*. W. W. Norton, New York.

Despard, Reverend George Pakenham 1854 *Hope Deferred, Not Lost. A Narrative of Missionary Effort in South America*. J. Nisbet, Brighton, UK.

Destéfani, Laurio H. 1983 "El Consul Smiley y su discípulo Luis Piedra Buena," in *Piedra Buena en el Centenario de su Muerte 1883–1983*, 57–69. Buenos Aires.

Diamond, Jared 1999 *Guns, Germs, and Steel. The Fates of Human Societies.* W.W. Norton, New York.

Dillehay, Tom 2000 "Monte Verde Revisited." Special Report. *Scientific American*, vol. 2.

Dominguez, Luis L. 1883 "Los Fueguinos del Cabo de Hornos y los náufragos de la fragata Oracle," *Boletín de la Sociedad de Geografía* (Buenos Aires), tomo IV: 141–3.

D'Orbigny, Alcide 1841 *Voyage Pittoresque dans les deux Amériques. Resumé Générale de tous les Voyages.* Furne et Cie, Libraires-Editeurs, Paris.

Drake, Sir Francis (also see Wilson, Derer) 1854 *The World Encompassed by Sir Francis Drake, Being His Next Voyage to That of Nombre de Dios. Collated with an unpublished manuscript of Francis Fletcher, chaplain to the expedition; with appendices illustrative of the same voyage, and introduction.* Printed for the Hakluyt Society, London.

Duplessis (first name unknown) 2003 *Périple de Beauchesne a la Terre de Feu (1698–1701) Une expeditión mandatée par Lous XIV.* Transboréal, Paris.

Duviols, Jean-Paul 1997 "The Patagonian 'Giants,'" in McEwan et al., 127–39.

Eiseley, Loren 1961 *Darwin's Century: Evolution and the Man Who Discovered It.* Doubleday, Garden City, New York.

Eldredge, Niles, and Ivan Tattersall 1982 *The Myths of Human Evolution.* Columbia University Press.

Emperaire, José 1955 *Les nomades de la mer.* Gallimard, Paris.

Encylopedia Britannica 1992 15th edition. Encylopedia Britannica, Inc.

Engel, Leonard 1962 "Introduction," in Charles Darwin, *The Voyage of the Beagle.*

Entraigas, Raul A. 1945 *Monseñor Fagnano. El Hombre, el Misionero, el Pioneer.* Editorial S.E.I., Buenos Aires.

Erskine, Charles 1985 *Twenty Years Before the Mast.* Smithsonian Institution Press, Washington, DC.

Fanning, Edmund 1833 *Voyages Round the World with Selected Sketches of Voyages to the South Seas, Northern South Pacific Oceans, China, etc.* Collins & Hannay, New York.

Farrington, Benjamin 1966 *What Darwin Really Said: An Introduction to His Life And Theory of Evolution.* Foreword by Stephen Jay Gould. Schocken Books, New York.

Fitz-Roy, Robert 1839 "Narrative of the Surveying Voyages of His Majesty's Ships 'Adventure' and 'Beagle' between the Years 1826 and 1836, Describing Their Examination of the Southern Shores of South America and the 'Beagle' Circumnavigation of the Globe." Vol. 2. *Proceedings of the Second Expedition, 1831–1836, under the Command of Captain Robert Fitz-Roy*, London (see King for vol. 1).

   1848 *Sailing Directions for South America.* Part II. *La Plata, Patagonia, Falkland and Staten Islands, Chile, Bolivia and Peru.* Hydrographic Office, Admiralty, London.

Fletcher, Francis (see Drake)

Flint, Richard Foster 1947 *Glacial Geology and the Pleistocene Epoch*. John Wiley & Sons, New York.

Fogg, G. E., and David Smith (the artist) 1990 *The Explorations of Antarctica. The Last Unpolluted Continent*. Cassell, London.

Forster, Georg 1777 *A Voyage Round the World in His Britannic Majesty's Sloop Resolution, commanded by Capt. James Cook, during the years 1772, -3, -4, and -5*. 2 vols. Robson, James, London.

Forster, John Reinold 1966 [1778] *Observations Made during a Voyage round the World on Physical Geography, Natural History and Ethic Philosophy*. G. Robinson, University of Hawaii Press.

Foster, Captain Henry (see Webster).

Freeman, Derek 1974 "The Evolutionary Theories of Charles Darwin and Herbert Spencer." C.A., vol. 15, no. 2: 211–37.

Freese, Barbara 2003 *Coal. A Human History*. Penguin Books, US.

Frézier, Amadeé François 1716 *Relation du Voyage de la Mer du Sud aux Côtes du Chile, du Pérou et du Brésil, fait pendant les années 1712, 1713, 1714*. Paris (excerpt in Brosses, vol. II: 204–19).

Fried, Morton H. 1975 "The myth of tribe." *Natural History*, vol. 84, no. 4: 12–20.

Furlong, Colonel Charles Wellington 1909a "Amid the Islands of the Land of Fire." *Harpers Monthly Magazine*, vol. 108, February: 335–47.

1909b "The Southernmost People of the World." Ibid., vol. 108, June: 120–34.

1911 "Cruising with the Yahgans." *The Outing Magazine*, vol. 58: no. I: 3–17.

1917a "The Alaculoofs and Yahgans, the World's Southernmost Inhabitants." *Proceedings of the Nineteenth International Congress of Americanists*: 320–431, Washington, DC.

1917b "The Haush and Ona, primitive tribes of Tierra del Fuego." Ibid., 432–44.

1917c "Tribal distribution and settlements of the Fuegians." *The Geographical Review*, vol. III: 169–87, New York.

Gallardo, Carlos 1910 *Tierra del Fuego: Los Onas*. Cabault y Cia Editores, Buenos Aires.

Gallez, Pablo J. 1973 "Valentín y sus dos Bahías Fueguinas." *Karukinka*, no. 6: 17–31, Buenos Aires.

1975 "El Descubrimiento de la Bahia Nassau (aguas fueginas), 1624." Ibid., no. 11: 2–21.

1976 "La Más Antigua Descripción de los Yámana." Ibid., no. 15: 17–31.

Garanger, José 1992 *La Préhistoire dans le Monde*. Presses Universitaires de France, Paris.

Gardiner, Allen F. 1854 "Journal of Allen F. Gardiner," in Despard, 1854.

Garson, J. G. 1886 "On the Inhabitants of Tierra del Fuego." *Anthropological Institute of Great Britain and Ireland*, vol. XV: 141–57.

Geertz, Clifford 1973 *The Interpretation of Cultures*. Basic Books, Publishers, New York.

Godoy, Pedro 1893 "Tierra del Fuego. Informe de su Gobernador Teniente Coronel Pedro Godoy al Señor Ministro del Interior." *Boletín del Instituto Geográfico Argentino*, tomo XIV: 386–96.

Golbert de Goodbar, Perla 1977 "Yagan I. Las partes de la oracion." *VICUS cuadernos. Linguistica*, vol. I: 5–60, Amsterdam.

Goodall, Rae Natalie Prosser de 1976 *Tierra del Fuego: Argentina*. Ediciones Shanamiim, Buenos Aires.

   1987 "Preface" in Thomas Bridges, *Yamana–English. A Dictionary of the Speech of Tierra del Fuego.*

Goody, Jack 1978 *The Domestication of the Savage Mind*. Cambridge University Press, Cambridge, UK.

Gore, Rick 1997 "The most ancient Americans." *National Geographic*, October: 90–8.

Gould, Stephen Jay 1976 "Darwin and the Captain." *Natural History*, vol. 85, no. 1: 32–4.

   1977 *Ever Since Darwin, Reflections in Natural History*. W.W. Norton, New York.

   1996 *Full House. The Spread of Excellence from Plato to Darwin*. Harmony Books, New York.

   2002 *The Structure of Evolutionary Theory*. The Belknap Press of Harvard University Press, Cambridge, MA.

Greenberg, Joseph H. 1987 *Languages in the Americas*. Stanford University Press.

Greene, John C. 1977 "Darwin as a Social Evolutionist." *Journal of the History of Biology*, vol. 10: 1–27.

   1999 *Debating Darwin. Adventures of a Scholar*. Regina Books, Claremont, CA.

Gusinde, Martin 1926 "Der Ausdruck 'Pescherah,' ein Erklarungsversuch." *Petermanns Geografische Mitteilungen*, vol. 72: 59–61.

   1931 *Die Feuerland-Indianer. Band I. Die Selk'nam* (in one volume). Mödling, bei Wien. Translated into Spanish in 1982.

   1937 *Die Feuerland-Indianer. Band II. Die Yamana* (in one volume). Mödling bei Wien. Translated into Spanish in 1986. (See Wilbert for an English translation of the Yamana myths.)

   1961 [1937] *The Yamana: The Life and Thought of the Water Nomads of Cape Horn*. 5 vols. (Off-print.) Human Relations Area Files, New Haven, CT. (Not included in this publication are Gusinde's 1937: Part one "Heimat und Geschichte" (Homeland and History), pp. 1–364 and "Mythen und Sagen" (Myths and Legends), pp. 1185–277. I did not use this edition because of these omissions. I use the Spanish 1986 edition because it is a complete translation and is more available.)

   1974 *Die Feuerland-Indianer. Band III. Die Halakwulup*. Mödling bei Wien. Translated into Spanish in 1991.

   1982 [1931] *Los Indios de Tierra del Fuego, Los Selk'nam*. 2 vols. Centro Argentino de Etnología Americana, Buenos Aires (no English translation).

   1986 [1937] *Los Indios de Tierra del Fuego. Los Yámana*. 3 vols. Ibid. (for a partial English translation, see 1961, above).

   1989 (see Brüggemann).

   1991 [1974] *Los Indios de Tierra del Fuego. Los Halakwulup*. 2 vols. Ibid. (no English translation).

Guyot, Mireille 1968 *Les Mythes chez les Selk'nam et les Yamana de la Terre de Feu*. Institute d'Ethnologie, Paris.

Hahn, Philippe 1883 "La mère et l'enfant chez les Fuégiens du sud (Yaghan)." B.S.A. de Paris: 804–7.

1884 "Les Fuégiens de l'Archipel." *Science et Nature*, no. 1: 337–41, Paris.

Hammerley Dupuy, Daniel 1952 "Los pueblos canoeros de Tierra del Fuego, Patagonia." *RUNA*, vol. 5: 134–70, Buenos Aires.

Hamilton, James 1854 *Memoir of Richard Williams, Surgeon and Catechist to the Patagonian Missionary Society in Tierra del Fuego*. James Nisbet & Co., London.

Harris, Marvin 1968 *The Rise of Anthropological Theory: A History of Theories of Culture*. Thomas Y. Crowell, New York.

Hatcher, J. B. 1901 "The Indian Tribes of Southern Patagonia, Tierra del Fuego, and the Adjoining Islands." *The National Geographic Magazine*, vol. 12, no. 1: 12–22.

Hazelwood, Nick 2001 *Savage: The Life and Times of Jemmy Button*. St. Martin's Press, New York.

Headland, R. K. 1992 *Chronological List of Antarctic Expeditions and Related Historical Events*. Cambridge University Press, Cambridge, UK.

Hecht, Jennifer Michael 2003 *The End of the Soul. Scientific Modernity, Atheism and Anthropology in France*. Columbia University Press, New York.

Hellman, Hall 1998 *Great Feuds in Science. Ten of the Liveliest Disputes Ever*. John Wiley & Sons, New York.

Herbert, Sandra 1974 "The Place of Man in the Development of Darwin's Theory of Transmutation. Part I." *Journal of the History of Biology*, vol. 7, no. 2: 217–58.

1977 "The Place of Man in the Development of Darwin's Theory of Transmutation. Part II." Ibid., vol. 10, no. 2: 155–227.

1987 "Introduction" and "The Red Notebooks" in Barrett et al., 7–16, 21–81.

1999 *An 1830s View from Outside Switzerland: Charles Darwin on the 'Beryl Blue.'* Birkhauser Verlag, Sael, Switzerland.

2005 *Charles Darwin, Geologist*. Cornell University Press.

Holy Bible 1962 Revised standard version containing the Old and New Testaments. The Oxford Annotated Bible, Oxford University Press, Oxford, UK.

Hopkins, Robert S. 1969, *Darwin's South America*. John Day Co., New York.

Horgan, John 1999 *The Undiscovered Mind*. Simon and Schuster, New York.

Hornbolstel, Erich M. von 1936 "Fuegian Songs." *American Anthropologist*, vol. 38, no. 3: 357–67.

1948 "The Music of the Fuegians." *Ethnos*, vol. 13, nos. 3–4: 69–97.

Horsman, Paul V. 1985 *Seawatch: The Seafarer's Guide to Marine Life*. Facts on File, New York.

Hough, Richard 1995 *Captain James Cook*. W.W. Norton, New York.

Hovelacque, M., et al. 1881 "Discussion sur les Fuégiens," B.S.A. de Paris, tome IV: 841–68.

Hull, David L. 1973 *The Reception of Darwin's Theory of Evolution by the Scientific Community*. University of Chicago Press.

Huxley, Julian, and H. B. D. Kettlewell 1965 *Charles Darwin and His World*. Viking Press, New York.

Hyades, Paul Daniel Jules 1882 (no title; only comments), *Review d'Ethnographie*, tome I: 542.

1883 "Observations sur les Fuégiens," B.S.A. de Paris, tome VI: 617–21.

1884a "Sur les Fuégiens," ibid., tome VII: 616–20, 716–25.

1884b "Notes hygiéniques et médicales sur les Fuégiens de l'archipel du Cap Horn." *Revue d'Hygiène et de Police Sanitaire*, vol. VI: 550–9.

1885a "Une Année au Cap Horn." *Le Tour du Monde*, 385–416.

1885b "La Chasse et la pêche chez les Fuégiens de l'Archipel du Cap Horn." *Revue d'Ethnographie*, tome IV: 514–53.

1886 "Les Epidémies chez les Fuégiens," B.S.A. de Paris, tome IX: 202–5 (includes a letter from Thomas Bridges).

1887 and 1888 notes in B.S. A. de Paris.

1887 "Ethnographie des Fuégiens," ibid., tome X: 327–41.

Hyades, P., and J. Deniker 1891 "Anthropologie, ethnographie," tome VII of the series of the *Mission scientifique du Cap Horn 1882–1883*, Ministères de la Marine et de l'Instruction Publique. Gauthier-Villars et Fils, Paris.

Hyslop, John, and Margaret Bird (eds.) 1988 *Travels and Archaeology in South Chile by Junius Bird*. University of Iowa Press, Iowa City.

Ibarra Grasso, Dick E. 1949 *Historia de la Navegación Primitiva*. Francisco Livelari Editor, Buenos Aires.

Ingold, Tim (ed.) 1987 *What Is an Animal?* Routledge, London.

Ingold, Tim, David Riches and James Woodburn (eds.) 1988a *Hunters and Gatherers 1: History, Evolution and Social Change*. St. Martin's Press, Oxford, UK.

1988b *Hunters and Gatherers 2: Property, Power and Ideology*. Ibid.

Jacob, Yves 1995 *Dumont d'Urville. Le Dernier grand marin de Découvertes*. Editions Glénat, Grenoble, France.

Juillerat, Paul 1881 "Fuégiens du Jardin d'Acclimatation." *La Nature*, no. 418: 295–8, Paris.

Kate, Hermanten 1903 "Materiaux pour servir a l'anthropologie des Indiens en la République Argentine." *Revista del Museo de la Plata*, tomo XII: 3–4, 35–41.

Kent, Rockwell 1968 [1924] *Voyaging Southward from the Strait of Magellan, with Illustrations by the Author*. Grosset and Dunlap Publisher, New York (revised edition).

Keynes, Richard Darwin (author and editor) 1980 *The Beagle Record. Selections from the Original Pictorial Records and Written Accounts of the Voyage of H.M.S. Beagle*. Cambridge University Press, Cambridge, UK.

1988 *Charles Darwin's Beagle Diary*. Cambridge University Press, Cambridge, UK.

2002 *Fossils, Finches and Fuegians. Charles Darwin's Adventures and Discoveries on the Beagle, 1832–1836*. Harper Collins, London.

King, Phillip Parker 1839 "Narrative of the Surveying Voyages of His Majesty's Ships 'Adventure' and 'Beagle' between the Years 1826 and 1836, Describing Their Examination of the Southern Shores of South America and the 'Beagle' Circumnavigation of the Globe." Vol. I. *Proceedings of the First Expedition, 1826–1830, under the Command of Captain P. Parker King*. London (see Fitz-Roy for vol. 2).

Koppers, Wilhelm 1997 [1924] *Entre los Fueguinos*. Universidad de Magallanes, Punta Arenas (translated from *Unter Feuerland-Indianern*, Stuttgart, 1924).

Kuklick, Henrika 1991 *The Savage Within. The Social History of British Anthropology, 1885–1945.* Cambridge University Press, Cambridge, UK.

Latcham, Ricardo E. 1922 "Los animales domésticos de la América precolombina." *Museo de Etnología y Antropología de Chile,* tomo III, número 1: 1–200.

Lambert, David 1985 *The Cambridge Field Guide to Prehistoric Life.* Cambridge University Press, Cambridge, UK.

Laming, Annette 1954 *Tout au bout du monde, avec les hommes et les bêtes en Patagonie.* Amiot-Dumont, Paris.

La Pérouse, Jean-François de Galaup 1964 *Voyage de Lapérouse autour du monde pendant les années 1785, 1786, 1787 et 1788.* Cercle du Bibliophile, Paris.

Laughlin, William S. 1968 "Hunting: An Integrating Biobehavior System and Its Evolutionary Importance," in Lee and DeVore (eds.), 304–20.

Lavallée, Danièle 1995 *Promesse d'Amérique. la Préhistoire de l'Amérique du Sud.* Hachette, Paris.

Leacock, Eleanor, and Richard Lee 1982 *Politics and History in Band Societies.* Cambridge University Press, Cambridge, UK.

Le Bon, Gustave 1883 "Les Fuégiens." *Bulletin de la Société de Geographie,* tome IV: 266–78, Paris.

Lee, Richard B., and Irven DeVore (eds.) 1968 *Man the Hunter.* Aldine Publishing Company, Chicago.

Legoupil, Dominique 1993–94 "El Archipiélago del Cabo de Hornos y la Costa sur de la Isla Navarino: Poblamiento y Modelos Económicos," A.I.P., vol. 22: 101–21.

  1995 "Les indigènes au Cap Horn: conquête d'un territoire et modèle de peuplement aux confins du continent Sud-Américain," J.S.A., tome 81: 9–45.

  2006 "El sistema socioeconomico de los nomades del Mar Skyring (Archipelago de Patagonia)," A.I.P., vol. 28: 81–119.

Lévi-Strauss, Claude 1966 *The Savage Mind.* University of Chicago Press.

  1984 *Paroles données.* Libraire Plon, Paris.

Lévi-Strauss, Claude, and Didier Eribon 1991 *Conversations with Claude Lévi-Strauss.* University of Chicago Press.

Lipschutz, Alexander, Grete Mostny and Louis Robin 1946 "The Bearing of Ethnic and Genetic Conditions of the Blood Groups of Three Fuegian Tribes." *American Journal of Physical Anthropology,* vol. 4, no. 3: 301–21.

Lista, Ramon 1887 *Viaje al Pais de los Onas.* Buenos Aires.

Lomax, Alan 1973 "Cantometrics on Ona Song Style," in Anne Chapman, 2002b, chapter 8.

Lothrop, Samuel K. 1928 *The Indians of Tierra del Fuego.* Museum of the American Indian, Heye Foundation, New York.

  1932 "Aboriginal Navigation off the West Coast of South America." *Journal of the Royal Anthropological Institute,* vol. 62: 229–56.

Lowie, Robert H. 1939 "[Review of] *Die Feuerland-Indianer. Band ll: Die Yamana,* by Martin Gusinde." *American Anthropologist,* vol. 40, no. 3: 495–503.

1952 "The Heterogeneity of Marginal Cultures," in *Indian Tribes of Aboriginal America, Selected Papers of the XXIX International Congress of Americanists*, 1–7. Sol Tax (ed.), University of Chicago Press.

Lucy-Fossarieu and Pierre Henry Richard 1884 *Ethnographie de l'Amérique Antarctique. Patagons, Araucaiens, Fuégiens*. Paris.

Lumsden, Charles J., and Edward O. Wilson 1983 *Promethean Fire, Reflections on the Origin of Mind*. Harvard University Press.

Luquet, G. H. 1927 "La critique de la raison pratique chez les Yagan de la Terre de Feu." *Journal de Psychologie normal et pathologique*, 15 mars 1927.

Lynch, Thomas F. 1999 "The Earliest South American Lifeways," in Frank Salomon and Stuart B. Schwartz (eds.). *The Cambridge History of the Native Peoples of the Americas*. Vol. III *South America*, Part I: 188–263.

Macdonald, Frederick C. 1929 *Bishop Stirling of the Falklands. The Adventurous Life of a Soldier of the Cross Whose Humility Hid the Daring Spirit of a Hero & an Inflexible Will to Face Great Risks*. Seeley, Serven, London.

MacLeod, Roy, and Philip E. Rehbock (eds.) 1994 *Evolutionary Theory and Natural History in the Pacific Darwin's Laboratory*. University of Hawaii Press, Honolulu.

Maidment, John 1854 "Journal of John Maidment," in Despard, 1854.

Manouvrier, Léonce 1881a "Sur les Fuégiens du Jardin d'Aclimatation," B.S.A. de Paris, tome IV: 760–82.

1881b "Discussion sur les Fuégiens," ibid., 841–68.

1894a "Le Cerveau d'un Fuégien," B.S.A de Paris, 596–609.

1894b (Comments during the Séance du 22 Novembre, ibid., 610–14.)

Mantellero Ognio, Carlos Alberto 2000 *Diccionario geográfico náutico de la toponimia Austral de Chile*. Valparaíso.

Maps of the Instituto Hidrográfico de la Armada de Chile, numbers 1201, 1203, 1301, 1307. Scale 1:200,000. Instituto Hidrográfico de la Armada de Chile.

Marcel, M. G. 1892 "Les Fuégiens à la fin du XVIII siècle." *Congrès International des Américanistes*: 485–96, Paris.

Marett, R. R., and T. K. Penniman (eds.) 1931 *Spencer's Last Journey. Being the Journal of an Expedition to Tierra del Fuego by the Late Sir Baldwin Spencer*. Oxford at the Clarendon Press, Oxford, UK.

Marks, Paula Mitchell 1994 *Precious Dust. The American Gold Rush Era: 1848–1900*. William Morrow, New York.

Marks, Richard Lee 1991 *Three Men of the Beagle*. Alfred A. Knopf, New York.

Marsh, John W. 1857 *A Memoir of Allen F. Gardiner, Commander, R.N.* James Nisbet & Co., London.

Marsh, John W., and Waite H. Stirling 1878 *The Story of Commander Allen Gardiner, R.N., with Sketches of Missionary Work in South America*. 5th edition, London.

Martial, Louis Ferdinand 1888 "Histoire du voyage," vol. I of the series of the *Mission Scientifique du Cap Horn 1882–83*. Ministères de la Marine et de l'Instruction Publique. Gauthier-Villars et Fils, Paris.

Martin, M. Kay 1969 "South American Foragers: A Case Study in Cultural Devolution." *American Anthropologist*, vol. 71: 243–60.

Martinic B., Mateo 1973 *Crónica de las Tierras del Sur del Canal Beagle*. Editorial Francisco de Aguirre S.A., Santiago, Chile.

1980 "La Misión de Bayly (Archipielago del Cabo de Hornos)," A.I.P., vol. 11: 47–61.

1982 *La Tierra de los Fuegos: Historia Geografía Sociedad Economia*. Municipalidad de Porvenir, Tierra del Fuego, Chile.

1986 [1971] *Nogueira el pionero*. Universidad de Magallanes, Punta Arenas, Chile.

1989 "Los canoeros de la Patagonia Meridional. Población histórica y distribucíon geográfica (siglos XIX y XX). El fin de una etnia," J.S.A., vol. 75: 35–61.

1989–90 "El genocidio Selknam: Nuevos antecedentes," A.I.P., vol. 19: 23–8.

1997 "The Meeting of Two Cultures. Indians and Colonists in the Magellan Region," in McEwan et al., 110–26.

2002 "Brief History of the Selk'nam from the Late Sixteenth Century to the Present," in Mason and Odone, 231–59.

2002 *Brief History of the Land of Magellan*. Universidad de Magallanes, Punta Arenas, Chile.

Mason, Peter 1998 *Infelicities. Representations of the Exotic*. Johns Hopkins University Press.

2001 *The Lives of Images*. Reaktion Books Ltd., London.

2002a "In Transit: Fuegians and Their Images in Europe, and the Few That Returned," in Mason and Odone, 315–71.

2002b (no title), in Bancel et al., 245–52.

Mason, Peter, and Carolina Odone (eds.) 2002 *12 Perspectives. Essays on the Selknam, Yahgan and Kawesqar*. Taller Experimental Cuerpos Pintados, Santiago, Chile.

Massa, Padre Lorenzo 1945 *Monografia de Magallanes. Sesenta años de accion Salesiana en el sur 1886–1946*. Escuela Tipográfica del Instituto Don Bosco, Punta Arenas, Chile.

Massone, Mauricio 2002 "The Ancient Hunters of Fire," in Mason and Odone, 123–48.

Mayr, Ernst 1988 *Towards a New Philosophy of Biology. Observations of an Evolutionist*. Harvard University Press.

1995 "Introduction" to *On the Origin of Species*, by Charles Darwin. A facsimile of the first edition (1859), Harvard University Press.

1997 *This Is Biology. The Science of the Living World*. Harvard University Press.

Maybury-Lewis, David (ed.) 1979 *Dialectical Societies. The Gê and Bororo of Central Brazil*. Harvard University Press.

McClung, Robert M. 1978 *Hunted Mammals of the Sea*. William Morrow, New York.

McCulloch, Robert D., et al. 1997 "The Glacial and Post-Glacial Environmental History of Fuego-Patagonia," in McEwan et al., 12–31.

McEwan, Colin, Luis A. Borrero, and Alfredo Prieto (eds.) 1997 *Patagonia. Natural History, Prehistory and Ethography at the Uttermost End of the Earth*. British Museum Press, London.

McHaffie 2000 *The History of Christ Church Cathedral, Falkland Islands*, at http://www.horizon.co.fk/cathedral/history.htm.

Mellersh, H. E. L. 1968 *Fitz-Roy and the Beagle.* Rupert Hart-Davis Publishers, London.

Melville, Herman 1992 *Moby Dick or, the Whale.* Illustrations by Rockwell Kent, The Modern Library, New York.

Mickleburg, Edwin 1987 *Beyond the Frozen Sea. Visions of Antarctica.* St. Martin's Press, New York.

Moorehead, Alan 1969 *Darwin and the Beagle.* Harper & Row, New York (reprinted in 1988 as a Penguin Book).

   1987 *The Fatal Impact. The Invasion of the South Pacific 1797–1840.* 2nd edition. Mead & Beckett Publishing, Sydney, Australia.

Morison, Samuel Eliot 1974 *The European Discovery of America. The Southern Voyages 1492–1616.* Oxford University Press, New York.

Murphy, Dallas 2004 *Rounding the Horn.* Basic Books, New York.

Murray, Cristian, et al. 2008 *Tras la estela del Horn. Arqueología de un naufragio holandés en la Patagonia.* Editores Vazquez Mazzini, Argentina.

Nemecek, Sasha 2000 "Who Were the First Americans?" *Scientific American*, September: 80–7.

Nichols, Peter 2003 *Evolution's Captain. The Tragic Fate of Robert FitzRoy, the Man Who Sailed Charles Darwin around the World.* Harper Collins Publishers, New York.

Nowell, Charles 1982 *The Great Discoveries and the First Colonial Empires.* Cornell University Press.

O'Brien, Michael J., and Thomas D. Holland 1992 "The Role of Adaptation in Archaeological Explanation." *American Antiquity*, 57: 36–59.

Odone, Carolina, and Marisol Palma 2002 "Death on Display: Photographs of Julius Popper in Tierra del Fuego (1886–1887)," in Mason and Odone (eds.), 264–313.

Orbigny (see D'Orbigny)

Orquera, Luis Abel 1999 "El consumo de moluscos por los canoneros del extremo sur." *Relaciones de la Sociedad Argentina de Antropología*, vol. 29: 307–26.

   2002 "The Late-Nineteenth-Century Crisis in the Survival of the Magellan–Fueguian Littoral Natives," in Claudia, Briones, and José Luis Lanata (eds.), 145–58.

Orquera, Luis Abel, and Ernesto Luis Piana 1984 "Los asentamientos indígenas," in Canclini (ed.), 69–74.

   1995 "La imagen de los canoeros Magallánico-Fueguinos: Conceptos y tendencies." *Runa*, vol. XXII: 187–245.

   1999 *La vida material y social de los Yámana.* EUDEBA, Buenos Aires.

   2002 "The Canoe People of the Far South: Archaeology of the Magallanes Region of Tierra del Fuego," in Mason and Odone (eds.), 169–92.

Orquera, Luis Abel et al. 1979 "8000 años de historia en el Canal Beagle." *Revista de Antropología y Ciencias Naturales*, Año I, no. 1: 10–23, Buenos Aires.

Ortiz-Troncoso, Omar R. 1972 "Nota sobre un yacimiento arquológico en el archipiélago del Cabo de Hornos," A.I.P., vol. III, nos. 1–4: 83–6.

1973 "Los Yámana, vienticinco años después de la Misión Lipschutz," A.I.P., vol. IV, nos. 1–3: 77–107.

1994 *Bibliographical Guide for the Archaeology of Southern Patagonia and Tierra del Fuego.* Ultramarine, Amsterdam.

Outes, Félix F. 1926 "Sobre el idioma de los Yámana de Wulaia (Isla Navarino) Materiales reunidos por el misionero Rau con anterioridad a 1866." *Revista del Museo de La Plata,* tomo XXX: 1–77.

Pagden, Anthony 1982 *The Fall of Natural Man. The American Indian and the Origins of Comparative Ethnology.* Cambridge University Press, Cambridge, UK.

1995 *Lords of All the World. Ideologies of Empire in Spain, Britain and France, c. 1500–c. 1800.* Yale University Press.

Payne, Roger 1995 *Among Whales.* Scribner, New York.

Payró, Roberto J. 1898 *La Australia Argentina. Excursión periodstica a las Costas Patagónicas, Tierra del Fueto é Isla de los Estados. Buenos Aires* (no editorial cited).

Perich S., José 1985 *Extinción Indigéna en la Patagonia.* Punta Arenas, Chile.

Pessagno Espora, Mario A. 1971 *Los Fueguinos.* Buenos Aires.

Philbrick, Nathaniel 2001 *In the Heart of the Sea. The Tragedy of the Whaleship Essex.* Penguin Books.

Philippi Izquiero, Julio 1979 (?) *La estructura social del pueblo Yámana.* Instituto de Chile, Santiago.

Phillips, G. W. 1861 *The Missionary Martyr of Tierra del Fuego: Being the Memoir of Mr. J. Garland Phillips, Late Catechist of the Patagonian, or South American Missionary Society* (the author, the missionary's brother, often quoted from his brother's unpublished diary). London.

Piana, Ernesto Luis (see Orquera and Piana) 1995 [1990] "Antiguedad de la navigación en Tierra del Fuego," reprinted in Vairo, 172–83.

Pinker, Steven 1994 *The Language Instinct.* William Morrow and Company, New York.

Pinochet (see Canas Pinochet Popper, Julius) 1887 "Exploración de la Tierra del Fuego." *Boletín del Instituto Geográfico Argentino,* vol. 8: 74–115.

1891 "Apuntes geográficos, etológicos, estadísticos e industriales sobre la Tierra del Fuego." Ibid., vol. 12: 130–70.

Prichard, James Cowles 1836–47 *Researches into the Physical History of Mankind: Containing Researches into the History of the Oceanic and the American Nations.* 5 vols., 3rd edition, Houlston and Stoneman, London.

Prieto Iglesias, Alfredo 1994 *Arquería Selk'nam: la Guerra y la Paz en la Tierra del Fuego.* Ediciones Colegio Punta Arenas, Puenta Arenas, Chile.

Pyne, Stephen J. 1986 *The Ice, A Journey to Antarctica.* University of Iowa Press, Iowa City.

Quack, Anton 2002 "Mank'acen: The Shadow-Snatcher: Martin Gusinde as Ethnographer and Photographer of the Last Indians of Tierra del Fuego," in Mason and Odone (eds.), 15–37.

Raban, Jonathan 1992 *The Oxford Book of the Sea.* Oxford University Press, New York.

Reader's Digest 1985 "Antarctica: Great Stories from the Frozen Continent." Special number.

Revol, Philippe 1995a "1881 Des Fuégiens en Europe," in *Cap Horn, 1882–1883: Rencontre avec les Indiens Yahgan. Collection de la Photothèque du Musée de l'Homme*, 28–38.

1995b "Hyades anthropologue physique et ethnographe," ibid., 89–114.

Reynolds Bridges, Robert T. 1953 "Las Canoas de los Yahganes y un pequeño recuerdo al Artesano indígena." *Anales del Museo Nahuel Huapí*, tomo 3: 33–5.

Rojas, Ricardo 1942 *Archipiélago. Tierra del Fuego*. Editorial Losada, S.A. Buenos Aires.

1948 "El pensamiento en acción. El problema indígena." *Revista Sustancia*, no. 14, Buenos Aires.

Ross, Captain Sir James Clark 1847 *Voyage of Discovery and Research in the Southern and Antarctic Regions during the Years 1839–43*. 2 vols. J. Murray, London.

Roth, Hal 1989 *Two Against Cape Horn*. W.W. Norton, New York.

Ruhlen, Merritt 1987 *A Guide to the World's Languages*. Vol. I. Stanford University Press.

Rydell, Raymond A. 1952 *Cape Horn to the Pacific: The Rise and Decline of an Ocean Highway*. University of California Press.

Sagan, Carl 1977 *The Dragons of Eden. Speculations on the Evolution of Human Intelligence*. Random House, New York.

Sahlins, Marshall 1972 *Stone Age Economies*. Aldine, Chicago.

Sahlins, Marshall, and Elman R. Service 1973 *Evolution and Culture*. University of Michigan Press.

Salmond, Anne 2004 *The Trial of the Cannibal Dog. Captain Cook in the South Seas*. Penguin Books.

Salomon, Frank, and Stuart B. Schwartz (eds.) 1999 *The Cambridge History of the Native Peoples of the Americas*. Vol. III *South America*, Part I. Cambridge University Press.

Salomon, Frank, and Stuart B. Schwartz 1999 Ibid. Introduction, 1-95.

Samitier, Llaras 1967 "El Grupo Chono o Wayteka y los demás Pueblos fuego-patagona." *Runa*, vol. X (1960–65): 123–94, Buenos Aires.

Sanderson, Stephen K. 1990 *Social Evolution. A Critical History*. Basil Blackwell, London.

2001 *The Evolution of Human Sociality. A Darwinian Conflict Perspective*. Rowman & Littlefield Publishers, Lanham, UK.

Schobinger, Juan 1994 *The First Americans*. William B. Eerdmans, Grand Rapids, MI.

Scientific American: Discovering Archaeology 1999 "Special report: Monte Verde Revisted," vol. 1, Nov.–Dec.

2000 "The Changing Face of the First Americans," vol. 2, Jan.–Feb.

Seelstrang, Arturo 1885 "Apuntes históricos sobre la Patagonia y la Tierra del Fuego." *Boletin del Instituto Geográfico Argentino*, tomo V: 1–6, 78–81.

Shipton, Eric 1973 *Tierra del Fuego: the Fatal Lodestone*. Charles Knight, London.

Slocum, Sally 1975 "Woman the Gatherer: Male Bias in Anthropology," in Reiter, R. R. *Toward an Anthropology of Women*. New York, 36–50.

Snow, W. Parker 1857 *A Two Years Cruise off Tierra del Fuego, the Falkland Islands, Patagonia and in the River Plate: A Narrative of Life in the Southern Seas*. 2 vols. Longman, Brown, Green, Longmans & Roberts, London.

Soto-Heim, Patricia 1992 "Le peuplement Paléo-Indien et Archaique d'Amérique du Sud." Doctoral thesis, Muséum National d'Histoire Naturelle, Tome I, Paris.

Spears, John R. 1895 *The Gold Diggings of Cape Horn. A Study of Life in Tierra del Fuego and Patagonia*. G.P. Putnam's Sons, New York.

Spegazzini, Carlos 1882 "Costumbres de los habitantes de la Tierra del Fuego." *Anales de la Sociedad Científica Argentina*, tomo 14: 159–81.

Spencer, Sir Baldwin (see Marett and Penniman)

Stackpole, Edouard A. 1953 *The Sea-Hunters. The New England Whalemen during Two Centuries, 1635–1835*. J.B. Lippincott, Philadelphia.

    1972 *Whales and Destiny. The Rivalry between America, France and Britain for the Control of the Southern Whale Fishery, 1785–1825*. University of Massachusetts Press.

Stambuk M., Patricia 1986 *Rosa Yagán. El ultimo eslabón*. Editorial Andrés Bello, Santiago, Chile (published in English as *Rosa Yagan. The Last Link*, 1998).

Stanton, William 1975 *The Great United States Exploring Expedition of 1838–1842*. University of California Press.

Stein, R. Conrad 1982 *The Story of the New England Whalers*. Children's Press, Chicago.

Stocking, George W., Jr. 1968 *Race, Culture, and Evolution. Essays in the History of Anthropology*. The Free Press, New York.

    1987 *Victorian Anthropology*. The Free Press, New York.

Street, Brian V. 1975 *The Savage in Literature. Representations of "Primitive" Society in English Fiction 1858–1920*. Routledge and Kegan Paul, London.

Stringer, Christopher and Robin McKie 1997 *African Exodus: the Origins of Modern Humanity*. Hevrholt Co., New York.

Subercaseaux, Benjamin 1962 [1949] *Jemmy Button*. Ercilla, S.A., Santiago, Chile.

Sutcliff, Danham 1961 "Afterword," in *Moby Dick or the White Whale*, by Herman Melville, 537–43. New York.

Tankersly, K. P. 2000 "Comments..." *Scientific American: Discovering Archaeology*, vol. 2.

Tasch, Paul 1985 "Darwin's Beagle Voyage and Galapagos Experience." *Journal of Geological Education*, vol. 33: 4–10.

Taussig, Michael 1997 "Tierra del Fuego – Land of Fire, Land of Mimicry," in McEwan et al., 153–72.

Tax, Sol, and Charles Callender (eds.) 1960 "Evolution after Darwin." *Issues in Evolution*. Vol. III. University of Chicago Press.

Tello, Mariano 1896 *Viaje alrededor de la Tierra del Fuego*. Salta, Argentina.

Ten-Kate, Herman 1905 "Matériaux pour servir à l'anthropologie des Indiens de la République Argentine." *Revue del Museo de La Plata*, vol. 12: 33–59.

Thomson, Keith Stewart 1975 "H.M.S. Beagle 1820–1870." *American Scientist*, 63: 664–72.

1995 *H.M.S. Beagle. The Story of Darwin's Ship*. W.W. Norton, New York.

Thornton, Russel 1987 *American Indian Holocaust and Survival. A Population History Since 1492*. University of Oklahoma Press.

Tierney, Patrick 2000 *Darkness in El Dorado. How Scientist and Journalist Devastated the Amazon*. W.W. Norton, New York.

Tompkins, Warwick M. 1938 *To Fifty South. The Story of a Voyage West around Cape Horn in the Schooner Wander Bird*. W.W. Norton, New York.

Toumey, Christopher P. 1987 "Jemmy Button." *The Americas: A Quarterly Review of Inter-American Cultural History*, vol. 44: 195–207.

Tyler, David B. 1968 *The Wilkes Expedition. The First United States Exploring Expedition (1838–1842)*. The American Philosophical Society, Philadelphia.

Utley, Robert 1986 *The Indian Frontier of the American West 1846–1890*. University of New Mexico Press.

Vairo, Carlos Pedro 1995 *Los Yámana. Nuestra única tradición martíma autóctona*. Zagier y Urruty Publications, Buenos Aires.

1997 *The Prison of Ushuaia – A Photo Collection*. Ibid.

Vanney, Jean-René 1986 *Histoire des Mers Australes*. Librairie Arthème Fayard, Paris.

Verne, Jules 1879 *Grands voyages et des grands voyageurs. Les voyageurs du xix siècle*. Vol. VI, dieuxième partie. J. Hetzel et Cie., Paris.

Viola, Herman J. 1985 "The Story of the U.S. Exploring Expedition," in Herman J. Viola and Carolyn Margolis, 9–23.

Viola, Herman J., and Carolyn Margolis (eds.) 1985 *Magnificent Voyagers. The U.S. Exploring Expedition 1838–1842*. Smithsonian Institution Press, Washington, DC.

Virchow, Herr 1881 "Ausserordentliche Zusammenkunft: die Feuerländer." *Zeitschrift für Ethnologie*, vol. 13: 373–94.

Wallerstein, Immanuel 1975 *World Inequality. Origen and Perspective on the World System*. Black Rose Books, Montreal.

2000 "From Sociology to Historical Social Science: Prospects and Obstacle." *British Journal of Sociology*, vol. 51, no. 1: 25–35.

Webster, W. H. B. 1970 [1834] *Narrative of a Voyage to the Southern Atlantic Ocean, in the Years 1828, 29, 30, Performed in H.M.S. Sloop Chanticleer, under the Command of the Late Captain Henry Foster*. 2 vols. Dawsons of Pall Mall, London.

Weddell, James 1970 [1827] *A Voyage towards the South Pole, Performed in the Years 1822–24*. (The 1970 edition is a reprint of the second edition of 1827 with a new introduction by Sir Vivian Fuchs.) London.

Weiner, Jonathan 1993 *The Beak of the Finch*. Vintage Books, Random House, New York. (This is the story of two scientists, Peter and Rosemary Grant, who spent twenty years working on the Galapagos Islands and analyzing their finds, "proving that Darwin did not know the strength of his own theory.")

Wegmann H., Osvaldo 1976 *La ultima canoa*. 2 vols. Hersprint, Punta Arenas, Chile.

Welche, John R. 2001 "The End of Prehistory?" *Anthropology News*, vol. 42, no. 5: 9–10.

Whipple, A. B. C. 1979 *The Whalers*. Time–Life Books, Alexandria, VA.

White, Michael, and John Gribbin 1995 *Darwin. A Life in Science*. Dutton, New York.

Wilbert, Johannes 1975 *Folk Literature of the Selknam Indians. Martin Gusinde's Collection of Selknam Narratives*. University of California at Los Angeles Press.

1977 *Folk Literature of the Yamana Indians. Martin Gusinde's Collection of Yamana Narratives*. Ibid.

Wilkes, Charles 1845 *Narrative of the United States Exploring Expedition during the Years 1838–1842*. Condensed and abridged in one volume. Whittaker, London.

1849 *Voyage around the World, Embracing the Principal Events of the Narration of the United States Exploring Expedition in One Volume*. G.W. Gorton, Philadelphia.

1978 *Autobiography of Rear Admiral Charles Wilkes, U.S. Navy 1798–1877*. William James Morgan, David B. Tyler, J. L. Leonhart, Mary F. Loughlin (eds.). Naval History Division, Department of the Navy, Washington, DC.

Williams, Richard 1854 "Journal of Richard Williams," in Despard, 1854.

Wilson, Derer 1977 *The World Encompassed, Francis Drake and His Great Voyage*. Harper & Row Publishers.

Wilson, Edward O. (see Lumsden and Wilson) 1975 *Sociobiology. The New Synthesis*. Harvard University Press.

1978 *On Human Nature*. Harvard University Press.

Winchester, Simon 1997 "Sir Francis Drake Is Still Capable of Kicking up a Fuss." *The Smithsonian*, vol. 27, no. 10: 83–91.

Yester, David R. 1980 "Maritime Hunter-Gatherers: Ecology and Prehistory." C.A., vol. 21, no. 6: 724–50.

Yudilevich Levy, David and Eduardo Castro Le-Fort 1995 *Darwin in Chile (1832–1835) Viaje de un naturalista alrededor del mundo*. Editorial Universitaria, Santiago, Chile.

Zárraga, Cristina 2005 *Hai kur mamashu shis*. Editorial El Kultün, Puerto Williams, Chile. (The title is in Yahgan; myths and legends told to the author by her grandmother Cristina Calderón; published in Spanish and English.)

Index of Proper Names

Index of Place Names